FINANCIAL ACCOUNTING

Fourth Edition

Practical Tools for Analyzing Financial Statements

Bruce R. Neumann, Ph.D.
University of Colorado at Denver and Health Sciences Center

Elizabeth C. Conner, M.S., C.P.A.
University of Colorado at Denver and Health Sciences Center

KENDALL/HUNT PUBLISHING COMPANY
4050 Westmark Drive Dubuque, Iowa 52002
www.kendallhunt.com

Book Team

Chairman and Chief Executive Officer *Mark C. Falb*
President and Chief Operating Office *Chad M. Chandlee*
Vice President, Higher Education *David L. Tart*
Director of National Book Program *Paul B. Carty*
Editorial Development Manager *Georgia Botsford*
Senior Developmental Editor *Angela Willenbring*
Vice President, Operations *Timothy J. Beitzel*
Assistant Vice President, Production Services *Christine E. O'Brien*
Senior Production Editor *Charmayne McMurray*
Permissions Editor *Renae Horstman*
Cover Designer *Janelle Edwards*
Senior Managing Editor, Higher Education *John V. Coniglio*

Cover image credits:

Chapter opener image credits:

ISBN 978-0-7575-4242-8

Library of Congress Control Number: applied for

Printed in the United States of America
10 9 8 7 6 5 4 3 2 1

BRIEF CONTENTS

CONTENTS

PREFACE

This is an exciting time in accounting education; accounting scandals have been in the news every week, if not every day! Accountants and their critics emphasize the need for change and accounting educators have responded. New course materials have been tested and incorporated into this exciting new text!

Bruce Neumann and Elizabeth Conner have revised a previous version of their innovative and easy-to-read introductory accounting text. This book offers a particularly unique approach to introductory financial accounting. It provides a "blended approach" between cash and accrual accounting. In fact, one of the book's sub-texts is **"Where's the Cash?"** as the authors believe that many of the recent accounting scandals and crises could have been avoided, or noticed earlier, if analysts had followed the cash. This new book will help students and business professionals "find the cash" and understand how cash is impacted by a variety of common and complex transactions.

Many introductory texts have offered new and various pedagogical features that proclaim to follow a "user-oriented" approach. Neumann and Conner have advanced this trend as *Financial Accounting* is truly written from the user's perspective. The book emphasizes (1) the interpretation of financial statement information, (2) the interrelationships among the financial statements, and (3) the effects of transactions on financial statements.

Perhaps one reason why the book is so popular is that the mechanical aspects of the accounting process, such as journals, ledgers, debits/credits, trial balances, etc., are eliminated from the core chapters of the text and moved to a supplementary chapter. Beginning students too frequently become immersed in detailed bookkeeping procedures and lose sight of the underlying objective of accounting: to assist in making business and economic decisions.

By taking an analytical and interpretative approach, students are able to understand and use financial statements. They retain this ability longer than the knowledge of detailed accounting procedures. This approach "adds value" to students' future contributions as business professionals.

Features

This text's distinctive combination of features appeals to students and business leaders. These features include:

- the use of transaction analysis, rather than journal entries, to describe business events

- incorporation of "Reality Checks" that personalize the text material and apply it to current real-world companies
- attention to international issues and accounting conventions for non-U.S. firms
- discussions and problem materials dealing with ethical issues facing managers and accountants
- evaluations of the **cash consequences** associated with many accounting transactions
- diverse and flexible assignment material
- an Application Suite in workbook format
- a Technology Suite on CD-ROM media
- Internet-based problems in each chapter

Organization

This book is arranged into three major components that make it readily adaptable for use in quarter, semester, or executive programs.

Chapters 1 through 5 introduce financial accounting and three primary financial statements: the balance sheet, the income statement, and statement of cash flows. This section provides the foundation for the entire book; indeed for the entire study of financial accounting!

Chapters 6 through 10 examine in more detail current and noncurrent assets, current and noncurrent liabilities, and shareholders' equity. This section should be read in consecutive order as it matches a traditional examination of the balance sheet.

Chapter 11 is a synthesis of financial statement analysis. Although all chapters focus on the analysis and interpretation of financial statements, Chapter 11 provides an overall framework for financial statement analysis. Most instructors will use this chapter to unify the topics covered earlier in the text. Chapter 11 may serve as the "final" chapter in either a quarter or semester-based course.

Mini-chapters, called **TOPICMODS,** provide self-contained sections that explore relatively complex topics such as leases, pensions, consolidated reporting, international reporting, time value of money, accounting careers, and accounting procedures (debits and credits!). These TOPICMODS can be used in a variety of ways, either in conjunction with earlier chapters or as selected topics to be explored after completing the first eleven chapters. The following table shows how these TOPICMODS might be best used:

TOPICMODS can be used in flexible and innovative ways. They can be sequenced according to your objectives and course design. See the following table for recommendations regarding particular chapters, which should be covered *before reading* each TOPICMOD.

TOPICMOD	RECOMMENDED BACKGROUND CHAPTERS	
TOPICMOD-I	The Time Value of Money	Chapter 8
TOPICMOD-II	Leases	Chapter 9
TOPICMOD-III	Pensions and Other Postretirement Benefits	Chapter 9
TOPICMOD-IV	International Aspects of Financial Accounting	Chapter 11
TOPICMOD-V	Reporting Issues for Affiliated Companies	Chapter 11
TOPICMOD-VI	Earnings Management	Chapter 4
TOPICMOD-VII	Accounting Changes	Chapter 4
TOPICMOD-VIII	Financial Reporting Issues (SEC)	Chapter 11
TOPICMOD-IX	Accounting Research and the Efficient Market Hypothesis	Chapter 11
TOPICMOD-X	Careers in Accounting	Chapter 5
TOPICMOD-XI	Accounting Procedures	Chapter 5

To provide more real-world linkages, three appendices contain excerpts from the annual reports of Wal-Mart, eBay, and Target. These reports serve as the basis for a number of problems.

We have changed many of the questions and problems in this edition in order to remove ambiguities and make them more accessible and easy to read. A team of students reviewed all of these materials, from a student's perspective, in order to emphasize material that they felt was most important and to clarify terms that might have confused earlier readers. Each chapter contains questions that can be used for class discussions or short-answer quizzes. Each chapter also contains a rich assortment of problems, ranging from short problems to those that are quite comprehensive. We include internet-based problems throughout the text, the Application Suite and the Technology Suite. These real-world problems permit the reader to search for relevant information about real issues and real problems!

Application Suite

The Application Suite to each chapter contains additional questions, some of which are more conceptual and less concrete. The problems in the Application Suite are generally longer than those in the text, and many are more suited for class discussion. Some might be viewed as "mini-cases". The Application Suite also contains a rich variety of short problems we have labeled "Worksheets". Worksheets comprise fill-in-the-blank definitions, matching definitions, and fill-in-the-blank computational grids. Some grids are like spreadsheets where transactions can be analyzed using the accounting equation. Some grids are in a financial statement format, where students are asked to fill in the blanks.

You will notice that the Application Suite is printed on perforated pages, so that they can be removed and used in class in a variety of ways. Our intent is that the worksheets can be used as quizzes or short exams or as the basis for in-class group discussions. Of course, they can be used as "regular" assignments that students prepare before class. Note that the Application Suite also includes answers to selected problems. Answers are NOT provided for any worksheet-based problems.

Technology Suite

The Technology Suite on a CD-ROM contains additional problems, often the most complex and most conceptual of any of the problem materials. It also contains additional "worksheet" problems that can be completed and submitted electronically. These materials will be particularly useful in online courses.

ACKNOWLEDGMENTS

We could not have completed this revision without the tremendous assistance and enthusiasm of an entire cadre of colleagues and research assistants. Ann Martin, a colleague at the University of Colorado at Denver, helped revise the material on international reporting, now contained in TOPICMOD-IV. Matthew Blackburn, a graduate student now working at Comcast, Inc., helped revise the material on consolidations and affiliated companies. This material is now contained in TOPICMOD-V. Cristina Sagray was particularly helpful in developing the worksheet material contained in the Application Suite and Technology Suite. Kelly Wells and Sadie Flint were instrumental in revising and updating the problems and solutions in the text, Application Suite, and Technology Suite. Without this dedicated team, we could not have met our deadlines, and the results would not have been as creative and innovative! Of course, any remaining errors or inconsistencies remain our responsibility. Please let us know how we might improve the next edition.

ABOUT THE AUTHORS

Bruce R. Neumann, Ph.D., is Professor of Accounting and Health Management at the University of Colorado at Denver and Health Sciences Center. He received his doctoral degree from the University of Illinois and his undergraduate and master's degrees from the University of Minnesota. Dr. Neumann's primary research interests focus on analyses of costs in public and private organizations and on behavioral issues related to the interpretation and use of financial reports. His work has appeared in the *Journal of Accounting Research, Journal of Accountancy, Strategic Management,* and *Healthcare Financial Management.* He has held visiting professorships at EDHEC Business School, Nice (France), Bond University (Australia), Murdoch University (Australia), and the University of Auckland. He has also served as a research fellow at the National Center for Health Services Research (Washington, D.C.) and at the Health Services Management Unit at the University of Manchester (UK). He continues to provide litigation support in cases involving costs, activity measures, government payments for health care services, and statistical studies.

Elizabeth C. Conner, M.S., C.P.A., is a Senior Instructor of Accounting at the University of Colorado at Denver and Health Sciences Center. She received her Master of Science degree in financial accounting from Colorado State University and her undergraduate degree from Vanderbilt University. Elizabeth won the 2003 outstanding teacher of the year award for the entire campus (University of Colorado at Denver and Health Sciences Center)! Elizabeth primarily teaches introductory and intermediate financial accounting courses. She has also been teaching an MBA introductory accounting course and an intermediate accounting course, *both online,* and has assisted other Business School faculty in developing their online courses. She is a certified public accountant (CPA) and provides accounting and tax consulting services to her clients. Her primary research interests focus on developing cases pertaining to revenue recognition issues and (individual) income tax issues. Some of her published cases are currently being used in accounting courses at other colleges and universities.

Both authors teach at the University of Colorado at Denver and Health Sciences Center. Both are pleased with the outcome of the revision process. We are excited to continue the innovative approaches to accounting education that began during the first three editions. Please contact either of us with your suggestions regarding the new edition.

Bruce R. Neumann, Ph.D.
Professor of Accounting and Health Management
Bruce.Neumann@cudenver.edu

Elizabeth C. Conner, C.P.A.
Senior Instructor, Accounting
Elizabeth.Conner@cudenver.edu

CHAPTER 1

FINANCIAL ACCOUNTING AND ITS ENVIRONMENT

Learning Objectives

1. *Define accounting and identify its objectives.*
2. *Understand the clear and dominant objectives of "Where's the Cash?"*
3. *Differentiate the three major types of accounting.*
4. *Identify three primary financial statements and briefly summarize the information contained in each.*
5. *Identify financial statement users and the decisions they make.*
6. *Describe the role of generally accepted accounting principles and how they are determined.*
7. *Describe the role of auditing.*
8. *List the economic consequences of choosing accounting principles.*
9. *Assess the importance of ethics in accounting.*

INTRODUCTION

Jane Johnson is considering selling T-shirts in the parking lot during her university's football season. Jane, of course, will do this only if she expects to make a profit. To estimate her profits, Jane needs certain pieces of information, such as the cost of a shirt, the university's charge for the right to conduct business on its property, the expected selling price, and the expected sales volume. Suppose Jane has developed the following estimates:

Sales price per shirt	$12
Cost per shirt	$7
Number of shirts sold each game day	50
University fee each game day	$100

Although developing estimates is tricky, let's take these estimates as given. Based on the estimates, Jane would earn a profit of $150 each game day.

Sales Revenue ($12 × 50)		$600
Less expenses:		
Cost of merchandise ($7 × 50)	$350	
University fee	100	
Total expenses		450
Net income		$150

Since this looks like a reasonable profit, Jane puts her plan into action. After her first game day, Jane needs to assess her success (or failure). Based on her actual results, Jane prepares the following information:

Sales Revenue ($12 × 40)		$480
Less expenses:		
Cost of merchandise ($7 × 40)	$280	
University fee	100	
Total expenses		380
Net income		$100

Jane's business was profitable, but not as profitable as she planned. This is because Jane sold fewer shirts than she hoped, but Jane is confident that she can sell any remaining shirts on the next game day.

The preceding illustration shows two ways to use accounting. First, Jane used accounting to ***help plan her business.*** That is, she used accounting to project her expected profit. Second, after Jane operated her business for a day, she *used accounting to determine if, in fact, she had made a profit.* In general, accounting is used during all phases of planning and operating a business.

ACCOUNTING

Accounting is the systematic process of measuring the economic activity of a business to provide useful information to those who make economic decisions. Accounting information is used in many different situations. The illustration in the introductory section shows how a business owner (Jane) can use accounting information. Bankers use accounting information when deciding whether or not to make a loan. Stockbrokers and other financial advisers base investment recommendations on accounting information, while government regulators use accounting information to determine if firms are complying with various laws and regulations.

Where's the Cash?

The accounting industry has been subjected to tremendous pressures and changes in public opinion. Corporate governance and the relationship of auditors to corporate boards have changed markedly, especially under the **Sarbanes-Oxley Act of 2002.** Rules for membership on Boards of Directors have been tightened. Board members are no longer members of a "cozy club" who meet solely to ratify management's decisions. Board members must be active and must have proper financial management and auditing experience. The Sarbanes-Oxley Act imposes strict disclosure and corporate governance mandates for all U.S. and non-U.S. public companies filing periodic reports with the Securities and Exchange Commission (SEC).

We have seen many corporate frauds involving accountants, auditors, and corrupt managers. The term "**Enron-accounting**" has entered our lexicon, being used by politicians, comedians, and regulators to indicate any kind of "funny-business" in the financial statements. We have seen the demise of huge companies, and the loss of billions of dollars in companies ranging from WorldCom, to Adelphia, to Arthur Andersen. Every one of these frauds or related bankruptcies involved some significant "players" who ignored the danger signs in the financial statements. Every one involved someone who was gullible; who accepted too quickly much of what the accountants, auditors, or managers wanted the public to believe. Every one could have been avoided or the effects could have been mitigated by a more critical examination of the financial statements. This book will help you perform the critical examinations necessary to at least ask the important questions.

Each of these corporate scandals, with resulting losses of billions of dollars, was impacted by a failure to determine "Where's the Cash?" If a regulator or a Board member had asked this question, and pursued the answer to a logical conclusion, many of the losses could have been avoided. We have seen instances where revenues and profits were inflated by exchanges of property rights that would never result in increased cash flows! We have seen profits increased by charging expenses that were too low, or that did not reflect prior or future cash outflows. In each case, finding the cash would have identified the inherent subjectivity and potential biases created by the perpetrators.

In this book, we will show you how to interpret generally accepted accounting principles (GAAP) in a way that is more cautious and more conservative than is typical. We will show you how to adjust revenues to reflect cash flows. Conceptually, we will show you how to modify GAAP-based financial statements to reflect more objectivity and more certainty, as they pertain to cash flows. While financial statements are based on GAAP, we see evidence that GAAP is changing to adopt a more conservative perspective. We hear the Chairperson of the Financial Accounting Standards Board (FASB) calling for modifications to the traditional rules of accrual accounting. All of these pressures will lead to more useful and more objective financial statements, such that the skills developed in this book will be even more important!

TYPES OF ACCOUNTING

Jane Johnson's T-shirt business (in the first section) showed how accounting information is helpful in a number of situations. In fact, the field of accounting consists of several specialty areas that are based on typical business decisions. The following sections describe the three major types of accounting, which are summarized in Exhibit 1-1.

Financial Accounting

Financial accounting provides information to decision makers who are *external to the business.* To understand the role of financial accounting, consider a large corporation such as IBM. The owners of corporations are called shareholders, and IBM has more than *1.7 billion shareholders.* Obviously, each shareholder cannot participate directly in the running of IBM, and because IBM needs to maintain various trade secrets, its many thousands of shareholders are not permitted access to IBM's accounting system. Because of this, shareholders delegate most

EXHIBIT 1-1 THE THREE MAJOR TYPES OF ACCOUNTING

ACCOUNTING SPECIALITY	DECISION MAKER	EXAMPLES OF DECISIONS
Financial accounting	Shareholders	Buy shares Hold shares Sell shares
	Creditors	Lend money Determine interest rates
Managerial accounting	Managers	Set product prices Buy or lease equipment
Tax	Managers	Comply with tax laws Minimize tax payments Assess the tax effects of future transactions

of their decision-making power to the corporation's Board of Directors and officers. Exhibit 1-2 contains an organizational chart for a typical corporation. Shareholders, however, need information to *evaluate (1) the performance of the business, and (2) the advisability of retaining their investment in the business.* Financial accounting provides some of the information for this purpose; potential shareholders use this information to determine whether to buy more shares in the business.

Creditors and potential creditors also use financial accounting information. Firms seek loans from banks, insurance companies, and other lenders. Although creditors are not internal parties of those firms, they need detailed information from the firm's accounting system so that creditors make loans only to creditworthy organizations. Financial accounting will usually provide at least some of the information needed by these decision makers.

Managerial Accounting

Managers make numerous decisions. These include (1) whether to build a new plant, (2) how much to spend for advertising, research, and development, (3) whether to lease or buy equipment and facilities, (4) whether to manufacture or buy component parts for inventory production, or (5) whether to sell a certain product. **Managerial accounting** provides information for these decisions. This information is usually more detailed and more tailor-made to internal decision making than financial accounting information. It is also proprietary; that is, the

EXHIBIT 1-2 ORGANIZATION CHART OF A TYPICAL CORPORATION

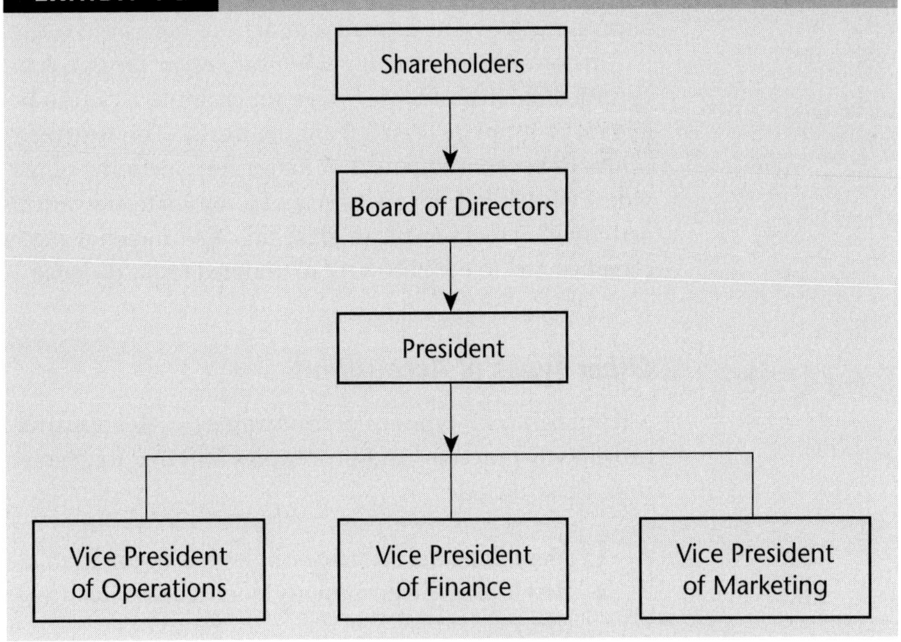

information is not disclosed to parties outside the firm. **Cost accounting** is a subset of managerial accounting that relates to the determination and accumulation of product, process, or service costs.

Sterling Collision Centers, Inc. provides a good illustration of managerial accounting at work. Although Sterling only has 18 shops, it hopes to put a major dent in the automotive body shop business through aggressive expansion and the introduction of innovative management techniques. One of its strategies is to use computers to better track repair times, which will provide both standards for different types of repair jobs as well as measures of how individual workers perform relative to the standards. By tying pay to performance, Sterling hopes to improve worker productivity. Knowledge of repair times will also help Sterling to determine estimated bids for its repair jobs. Managerial accountants play a major role in all these activities.

Although distinguishing between financial and managerial accounting is convenient, the distinction is somewhat blurred. For example, financial accounting provides information about the performance of a firm to outsiders. Because this information is essentially a performance report on management, managers are appropriately interested in and influenced by financial accounting information. Accordingly, the distinction between financial and managerial accounting depends on who is the primary user of the information.

Tax Accounting

Tax accounting encompasses two related functions: tax compliance and tax planning. *Tax compliance refers to the calculation of a firm's tax liability.* This process entails the completion of sometimes lengthy and complex tax forms. Tax compliance takes place after a year's transactions have been completed.

In contrast, *tax planning takes place before the fact.* A business transaction can be structured in a variety of ways; for example, a car can be purchased by securing a loan, or it can be leased from the dealer. The structure of a transaction determines its tax consequences. A major responsibility of tax accountants is to provide advice about the tax effects of a transaction's various forms. Although this activity may seem to be an element of managerial accounting, it is separately classified due to the necessary specialized tax knowledge.

Other Types of Accounting

A few additional types of accounting exist. **Accounting information systems** provide the processes and procedures required to generate accounting information. These include:

1. identifying the information desired by the ultimate user,
2. developing the documents (such as sales invoices) to record the necessary data,

3. assigning responsibilities to specific positions in the firm, and
4. applying computer technology to summarize the recorded data.

Another type of accounting deals with **nonbusiness organizations.** These organizations do not attempt to earn a profit and have no owners. They exist to fulfill the needs of certain groups of individuals. Nonbusiness organizations include:

1. hospitals,
2. colleges and universities,
3. churches,
4. Federal, state, and local governments, and
5. many other organizations such as museums, volunteer fire departments, and disaster relief agencies.

Nonbusiness organizations have a need for some types of accounting we have just reviewed. For example, a volunteer fire department might need to borrow money to purchase a new fire truck. Its banker would then require financial accounting information to make the lending decision.

Nonbusiness organizations are fundamentally different from profit-oriented firms: They have no owners and they do not attempt to earn a profit. Because of this, the analysis of the financial performance of business and nonbusiness organizations is considerably different. This text addresses only business organizations. Most colleges and universities offer an entire course devoted to the accounting requirements and performance evaluation of nonbusiness organizations.

A CLOSER LOOK AT FINANCIAL ACCOUNTING

This text is primarily concerned with financial accounting, which summarizes the firm's past performance and its current financial status. An overview of financial accounting is presented in Exhibit 1-3. Each element of the exhibit is discussed in the following sections.

Past Transactions and Other Economic Events

Past transactions and events are the raw materials (inputs) for financial accounting. **Transactions** typically involve an *exchange of resources* between the firm and other parties. For example, purchasing equipment with cash is a transaction that would be incorporated in the firm's financial accounting records. Purchasing equipment on credit is also a transaction; equipment is obtained in exchange for a promise to pay for it in the future.

Financial accounting also incorporates significant economic events that do not involve exchanges with other parties. For example, assume that a firm owns an uninsured automobile that is completely destroyed in a fire. Financial accounting would reflect the effect of this event.

EXHIBIT 1-3 OVERVIEW OF FINANCIAL ACCOUNTING

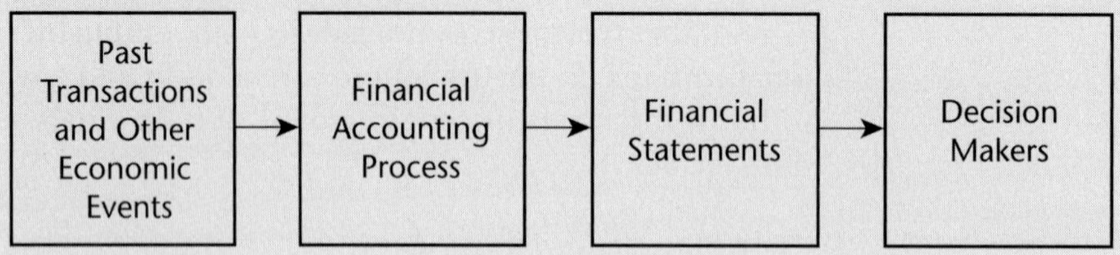

In most cases, financial accounting deals with past transactions and events. It provides information about the firm's *past performance and current financial standing*. Financial accounting does not usually include predictions about the future. Although financial statement users need to assess a firm's future prospects, financial accounting does not make these predictions; but it does provide information about the past and present that is useful in making predictions about the future.

The Financial Accounting Process

The **financial accounting** process consists of:

1. categorizing past transactions and events,
2. measuring selected attributes of those transactions and events, and
3. recording and summarizing those measurements.

The first step places transactions and events into **categories** that reflect their type or nature. Some of the categories used in financial accounting include (1) purchases of inventory (merchandise acquired for resale), (2) sales of inventory, and (3) wage payments to workers.

The next step *assigns values* to the transactions and events. The attribute measured is the fair value of the transaction on the exchange date. This is usually indicated by the amount of cash that changes hands. If equipment is purchased for a $1,000 cash payment, for example, the equipment is valued at $1,000. The initial valuation is not subsequently changed. (Some exceptions are discussed in later chapters.) This original measurement is called **historical cost.**

The final step in the process is to *record and meaningfully summarize* these measurements. Summarizing is necessary because, otherwise, decision makers would be overwhelmed with an extremely large array of information. Imagine, for example, that an analyst is interested in Ford Motor Company's sales for 2007. Providing a list of every sales transaction (and amounts) would yield a huge volume of detailed information. Instead, the financial accounting process summarizes the dollar value of all sales during a given time period and this single sales revenue number is included in the financial statements.

Financial Statements

Financial statements are the end result of the financial accounting process. Firms prepare three major financial statements: the balance sheet, the income statement, and the statement of cash flows. The following sections briefly describe these statements.

THE BALANCE SHEET. The **balance sheet** shows a firm's assets, liabilities, and owners' equity. ***Assets** are valuable resources that a firm owns or controls.* The simplified balance sheet shown in Exhibit 1-4 includes four assets. **Cash** obviously has value. **Accounts receivable** are amounts owed to Newton Company by its customers; these have value because they *represent future cash inflows.* **Inventory** is merchandise acquired that is to be sold to customers. Newton expects its inventory to be converted into accounts receivable and ultimately into cash. Finally, **equipment** (perhaps delivery vehicles or showroom furniture) enables Newton to operate its business. Newton could have used cash to purchase its equipment.

Liabilities are obligations of the business to convey something of value in the future. Newton's balance sheet shows two liabilities. Accounts payable are unwritten promises that arise in the ordinary course of business. An example of this would be Newton purchasing inventory on credit, promising to make payment within a short period of time. Cash will be used to pay these accounts in the near future. Notes payable are more formal, written obligations. Notes payable often arise from borrowing money.

The final item on the balance sheet is **owners' equity,** which refers to the owners' interest in the business. It is a *residual amount that equals assets minus liabilities.* The owners have a positive financial interest in the business only if the firm's assets exceed its obligations.

EXHIBIT 1-4 A BALANCE SHEET

The Newton Company
Balance Sheet
December 31, 2007

ASSETS		**LIABILITIES AND OWNERS' EQUITY**	
Cash	$ 5,000	Liabilities	
Accounts receivable	7,000	Accounts payable	$ 8,000
Inventory	10,000	Notes payable	2,000
Equipment	7,000	Total liabilities	10,000
Total assets	$29,000	Owners' equity	19,000
		Total liabilities and owners' equity	$29,000

THE INCOME STATEMENT. Just as each of us is concerned about our salary, investors and creditors are interested in the ability of an organization to produce income (sometimes called earnings or profits). The **income statement** summarizes the earnings generated by a firm during a specified period of time. Exhibit 1-5 contains Newton Company's income statement for 2007.

Income statements contain at least two major sections: revenues and expenses. **Revenues** are inflows of assets from providing goods and services to customers. Newton's income statement contains one type of revenue: sales to customers. This includes sales made for cash and sales made on credit. Credit sales will eventually be collected in cash.

Expenses are the costs incurred to generate revenues. Newton's income statement includes three types of expenses. **Cost of goods sold** is Newton's cost of merchandise sold to its customers. **General and administrative expenses** include salaries, rent, and other items, also known as **overhead. Tax expense** reflects the payments that Newton must make to the Internal Revenue Service and other taxing authorities. Most expenses will be paid in cash, at some point. The difference between revenues and expenses is **net income** (or **net loss** if expenses are greater than revenues).

THE STATEMENT OF CASH FLOWS. From a financial accounting perspective, *net income is not the same as cash.* For example, suppose that a sale is made on credit. Will this sale be recorded on the income statement? Yes. It meets the definition of a revenue transaction: an inflow of assets (the right to receive cash in the future) in exchange for goods or services. Moreover, including this transaction in the income statement provides financial statement readers with useful information about the firm's accomplishments. However, no cash has been received. Thus, *the income statement does not provide information about cash flows.*

EXHIBIT 1-5 AN INCOME STATEMENT

The Newton Company
Income Statement
For the Year Ended December 31, 2007

Revenues		
Sales		$63,000
Expenses		
Cost of goods sold	$35,000	
General and administrative	20,000	
Tax	3,000	
Total expenses		58,000
Net Income		$ 5,000

Financial statement users, though, are also interested in a firm's ability to generate cash. After all, cash is necessary to buy inventory, pay workers, purchase equipment, and so on. The **statement of cash flows** summarizes a firm's inflows and outflows of cash. Exhibit 1-6 illustrates Newton Company's statement of cash flows, which has three sections. One section deals with cash flows from **operating activities,** such as the buying and selling of inventory. The second section contains information about **investing activities,** such as the acquisition and disposal of equipment. The final section reflects cash flows from **financing activities.** These activities include obtaining and repaying loans, as well as obtaining financing from owners.

NOTES TO FINANCIAL STATEMENTS. A full set of financial statements includes a number of notes that clarify and expand the material presented in the body of the financial statements. The **notes to financial statements** indicate the accounting principles (rules) that were used to prepare the statements, provide detailed information about some items in the financial statements, and, in some cases, provide alternative measures of the firm's assets and liabilities.

Notes to financial statements are not illustrated in this chapter because they are highly technical and apply to specific accounting topics covered in subsequent chapters. Notes are, however, emphasized throughout much of this book.

ANNUAL REPORTS. All large firms, and many smaller ones, issue their financial statements as part of a larger document referred to as an **annual report.** In addition to the financial statements and their accompanying notes, the annual report includes descriptions of significant events that occurred during the year,

EXHIBIT 1-6 A STATEMENT OF CASH FLOWS

The Newton Company
Statement of Cash Flows
For the Year Ended December 31, 2007

Cash flows from operating activities:		
Cash received from customers	$61,000	
Cash paid to suppliers	(37,000)	
Cash paid for general and administrative functions	(19,900)	
Taxes paid	(3,000)	
Net cash provided by operating activities		1,100
Cash flows from investing activities:		
Purchase of equipment		(2,000)
Cash flows from financing activities:		
Net borrowings		1,000
Net increase in cash		100
Cash at beginning of year		4,900
Cash at end of year		$5,000

commentary on future plans and strategies, and a discussion and analysis by management of the year's results. Appendices A–C of this text contain substantial portions of three companies' annual reports (Wal-Mart, eBay, and Target).

Decision Makers

Recall that the primary goal of financial accounting is to provide decision makers with useful information. This section identifies the *major* ***users of financial statements*** *and describes the decisions they make.*

OWNERS. Present and potential **owners (investors)** are prime users of financial statements. They continually assess and compare the prospects of alternative investments. The assessment of each investment is often based on two variables: expected return and risk.

Expected return refers to the investor's expected increased wealth over the investment's time horizon. This wealth increase is comprised of two parts: (1) increases in the market value of the investment and (2) dividends (periodic cash distributions from the firm to its owners). Both sources of wealth depend on the firm's ability to generate cash. Accordingly, *financial statements can improve decision-making by providing information that helps current and potential investors estimate a firm's future cash flows.* In many cases, the expected return is also known as opportunity cost. **Opportunity cost** is the economist's favorite term for the value of the next best alternative!

Risk refers to uncertainty surrounding estimates of expected return. The term "expected" implies that the return is not guaranteed. For most investments, numerous alternative future returns are possible. For example, an investor may project that a firm's most likely return for the upcoming year is $100,000. However, the investor recognizes that this is not the only possibility. There is some chance that the firm might generate returns of $90,000 or $110,000. Still other possibilities might be $80,000 and $120,000. The greater the difference among these estimates, the greater is the risk. *Financial statements help investors assess risk by providing information about the historical pattern of past income and cash flows.*

Investment selection involves a trade-off between expected return and risk. Investments with high (expected) returns generally have a high risk. Each investor must assess whether investments with greater risk offer sufficiently higher expected returns.

To illustrate the *trade-off between risk and expected return,* assume that an investor has two choices: Investment A and Investment B. Each investment costs $100. The return on each investment during the next year might depend on whether the economy expands or suffers a recession. The following chart summarizes the possibilities:

EXPECTED RETURN

	Investment A	*Investment B*
Expansion	$10	$4
Recession	$ 0	$2

Assuming that expansion and recession are equally likely, the **expected return** of the two investments can be calculated as follows:

Investment A ($10 × .5) + ($0 × .5) = $5

Investment B ($4 × .5) + ($2 × .5) = $3

Although Investment A has the higher expected return, it also has the higher risk. Its return next year can vary by $10, while Investment B's return can vary by only $2. Investors must decide whether Investment A's higher expected return is worth its greater risk.

CREDITORS. The lending decision involves two issues: whether or not credit should be extended, and specification of a loan's terms. For example, consider a bank loan officer evaluating a loan application. The officer must make decisions about the amount of the loan (if any), interest rate, payment schedule, and collateral. Because repayment of the loan and interest depends on the applicant's ability to generate cash, *lenders need to estimate a firm's future cash flows and the uncertainty surrounding those flows.* Although investors generally take a long-term view of a firm's cash generating ability, creditors are most concerned about the firm's ability to repay the loan at maturity.

Lenders are not the only creditors who find financial statements useful. Suppliers often sell on credit, and they must decide which customers will or will not honor their obligations.

OTHER USERS. A variety of other decision makers find financial statements helpful. Some of these decision makers and their decisions include the following:

1. *Financial analysts and advisors.* Many investors and creditors seek expert advice when making their investment and lending decisions. These experts use financial statements as a basis for their recommendations.
2. *Customers.* The customers of a business are interested in a stable source of supply. They can use financial statements to identify suppliers that are financially sound.
3. *Employees and labor unions.* These groups have an interest in the viability and profitability of firms that employ them or their members. As described in Reality Check 1-1, unions in the airline industry have recently made several important decisions based, in part, on financial statements.

REALITY CHECK 1-1

United Airlines: Employees of United Airlines gained controlling ownership of United's parent, UAL Corporation, by agreeing to billions of dollars in wage and benefit concessions. The employees needed to estimate the value of UAL so that they could determine the extent of the wages and benefits to sacrifice. Financial statements are frequently used in valuing businesses.

Delta Airlines: After declaring bankruptcy in September 2005, Delta's pilots agreed to wage concessions totaling $280 million a year savings. In April 2006, Delta reported its first profit of $22 million since filing for bankruptcy. As part of the pilot's labor agreement, pilots are entitled to annual raises of up to 6% when Delta's profit margins reach a certain level. You can be certain that the pilots will be using financial statements to ensure Delta's profit margins as Delta continues to emerge from bankruptcy.

4. *Regulatory authorities.* Federal and state governments regulate a large array of business activities. The Securities and Exchange Commission (SEC) is a prominent example. Its responsibility is to ensure that capital markets, such as the New York Stock Exchange, operate smoothly. To help achieve this, corporations are required to make full and fair financial disclosures. The SEC regularly reviews firms' financial statements to evaluate the adequacy of their disclosures. Reality Check 1-2 describes another regulatory use of accounting information.

The accounting profession views financial statements as being **general purpose.** They are intended to meet the *common information needs of a wide variety of users,* such as those in the preceding list.

REALITY CHECK 1-2

California has perhaps the country's toughest standards for vehicle emissions. One aspect of its program requires the major automakers to generate 10% of their California sales from electric vehicles during the period 2003–2008. Compliance with this regulation will be assessed from financial accounting information.

GENERALLY ACCEPTED ACCOUNTING PRINCIPLES

Decision makers often wish to compare the financial statements of several firms. To permit valid comparisons, the firms' statements need to be based on the same set of accounting principles, which are the rules and procedures used to produce the financial statements.

To illustrate how one event might be accounted for in more than one way, consider a movie production company that has just produced a new film costing $25,000,000. Assume that a balance sheet is to be prepared before the film is marketed. Does the firm have a $25,000,000 asset? The real value of the film rests on its capability to generate future revenues. A successful film will generate revenue that is many times greater than its cost; an unsuccessful film may not even cover its cost. At the balance sheet date, the future revenue is unknown.

As a potential investor or creditor, how would you prefer that this film be reflected on the balance sheet? Two obvious alternatives are $25,000,000 and $0. The latter is clearly more conservative; it results in a lower asset value. Some financial statement readers would prefer this conservative approach. Others would maintain that management expects to reap at least $25,000,000 in revenue; otherwise, they would not have undertaken the project. Thus, they feel that $25,000,000 is the most reasonable figure. There is no obvious answer to this issue. However, to permit valid comparisons of various firms' balance sheets, the same accounting principle should be used. Current accounting practice, in general, is to record assets at historical cost; in this case, the movie would be recorded at $25,000,000.

THE FINANCIAL ACCOUNTING STANDARDS BOARD

The most widely used set of accounting principles is referred to as **generally accepted accounting principles (GAAP).** The **Financial Accounting Standards Board (FASB)** currently sets GAAP.

The FASB is a private organization located in Norwalk, Connecticut. The board is comprised of seven voting members who are supported by a large staff. As of March, 2006, the FASB issued 156 **Statements of Financial Accounting Standards (SFAS),** and 47 interpretations. These standards and interpretations are the primary source of GAAP.

The FASB's predecessor was the **Accounting Principles Board (APB).** The APB issued 31 Opinions, which are still part of GAAP, unless they have been superseded by an SFAS. The FASB faces a difficult task in setting GAAP. Financial accounting is not a natural science; no fundamental accounting laws have been proven to be correct. Accounting exists to provide information useful for decision making. The FASB's responsibility is to specify the accounting principles that will result in highly useful information. However, given that financial statement users are rather diverse, this is not a simple task.

The FASB employs an elaborate **due process** procedure prior to the issuance of an SFAS. Exhibit 1-7 summarizes the FASB's procedures. This process is designed to ensure that all those who wish to participate in the setting of accounting standards have an opportunity to do so.

The FASB publishes several preliminary documents during its deliberations on each SFAS. The documents include an Invitation to Comment or a Discussion Memorandum that identifies the fundamental accounting issues to be addressed. An Exposure Draft is the FASB's initial attempt at resolving such issues. These documents are widely disseminated, and interested parties are invited to communicate with the board, both in writing and by making presentations at public hearings. An affirmative vote of five of the seven FASB members is needed to issue a new SFAS.

An interesting aspect of GAAP is that more than one accounting method (or principle) is acceptable for some transactions. For example, there are several acceptable inventory accounting methods. This provides managers with considerable discretion in preparing their financial statements.

EXHIBIT 1-7 FASB'S DUE PROCESS PROCEDURES

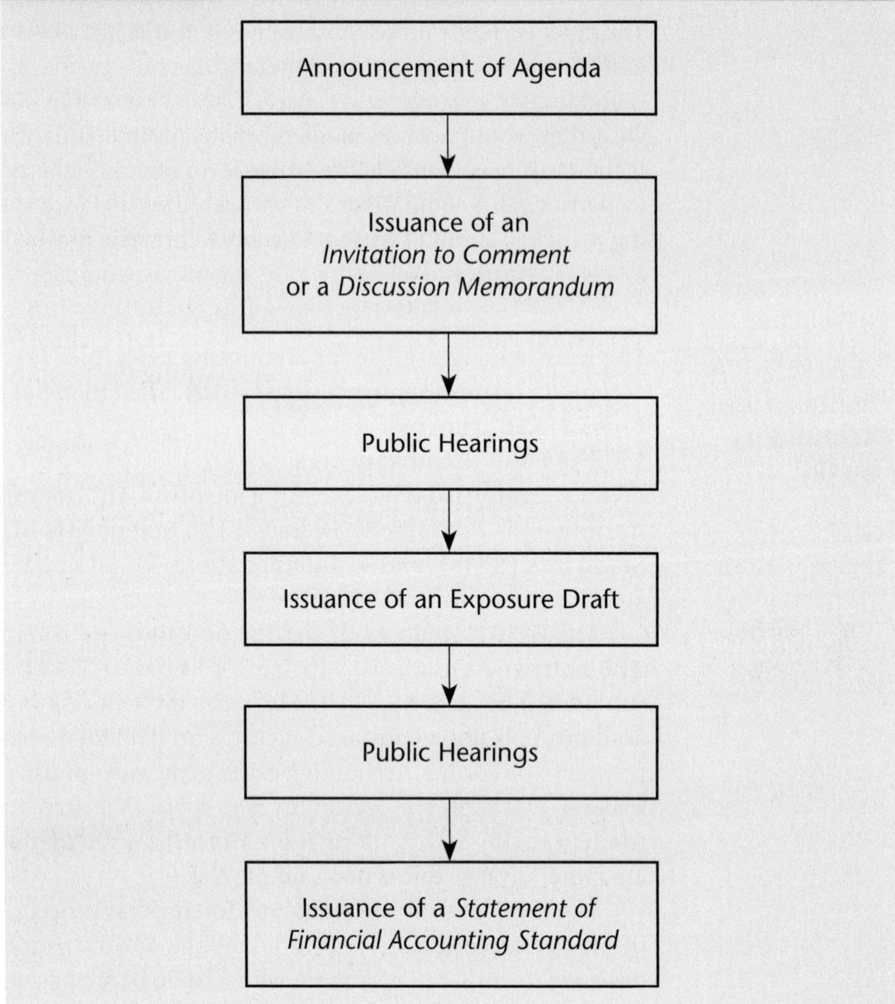

Numerous commentators, accountants, judges, and legislators have criticized this situation. They believe that only a single method should be allowed for a given transaction. In general, the FASB is attempting to narrow the availability of multiple acceptable accounting procedures.

THE SECURITIES AND EXCHANGE COMMISSION

The **Securities and Exchange Commission (SEC)** was created by the **Securities Exchange Act of 1934.** The act empowered the SEC to set accounting principles and financial disclosure requirements for the corporations that it regulates. These corporations are quite large and have ownership interests that are widely dispersed among the public. Such corporations are referred to as "**publicly held**". Thus, for at least publicly held corporations, the SEC has legislative authority to set GAAP. This raises a question about the relationship between the SEC and the FASB.

The FASB is a private (nongovernmental) organization whose authority to set GAAP derives from two sources. First, the business community and the accounting profession, by accepting FASB rulings, provide one source of support. In the United States, accounting principles have traditionally been set in the private sector, and the FASB's standards have received a reasonable amount of support. At the same time, not everyone is entirely happy with the FASB's pronouncements. Some people criticize the FASB for issuing standards that are too complex and too costly to implement. Part of the FASB's responsibility is to balance financial statement users' demands for better information with the costs incurred by those who provide that information.

The second source of the FASB's standard-setting authority is the SEC. Although the SEC has legislative authority to set GAAP for publicly held corporations, it prefers to rely on the accounting profession's private rule-making bodies to do this. In fact, the SEC has formally indicated that it will recognize GAAP as prescribed by the FASB. The SEC does, however, retain the right to overrule FASB pronouncements, and it occasionally exercises this right. Exhibit 1-8 shows the relationships among the different organizations involved in setting accounting standards.

THE ROLE OF AUDITING

A firm's management is primarily responsible for preparing its financial statements. Yet the financial statements can be viewed as a report on the performance of management. The **conflict of interest** in this situation is apparent. As a result, *the financial statements of all corporations reporting to the SEC must be audited.*

EXHIBIT 1-8 GROUPS INVOLVED IN SETTING ACCOUNTING STANDARDS

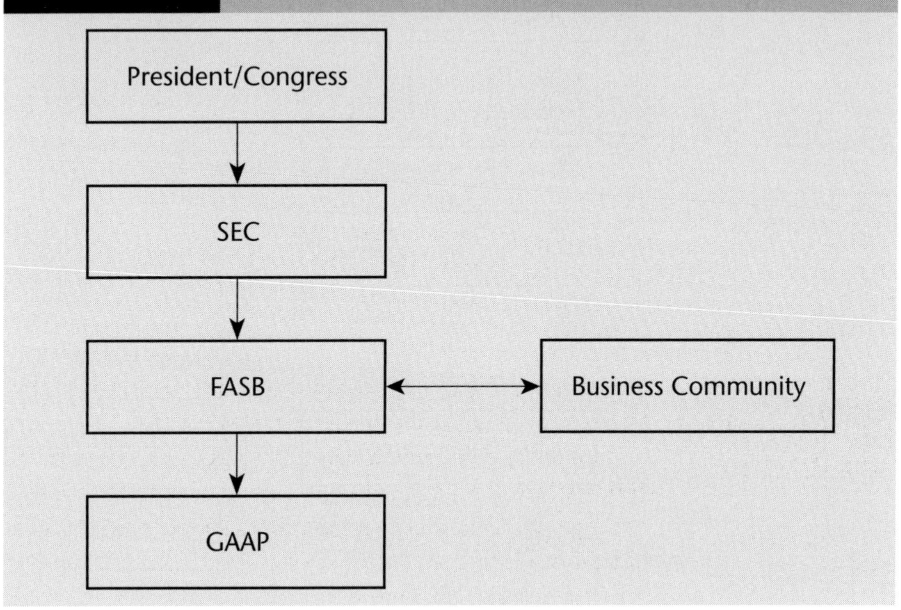

Audits are required because they *enhance the credibility* of the financial statements. The financial statements of many privately held businesses are also subject to an audit. Banks, for example, require many loan applicants to submit audited financial statements so that lending decisions can be based on credible financial information.

One of the most important auditing relationships, which are depicted in Exhibit 1-9, is the role of the independent **certified public accountant (CPA)** who conducts the audit. CPAs are licensed by the individual states by meeting specified educational and experience requirements and passing the uniform CPA exam, which takes 14 hours to complete. CPAs are also required to attend continuing professional education classes and participate in a peer review process, whereby one **CPA firm** reviews and critiques the work of another firm. More detailed descriptions of the accounting profession are shown in TOPICMOD-X.

Exhibit 1-10 contains an auditor's report. The wording has been carefully chosen by the accounting profession to communicate precisely what an audit does and does not do. The first paragraph identifies the company, the specific financial statements that were audited, and the years of the audit. Management's responsibility for the financial statements is also acknowledged.

The second paragraph states that the audit has been conducted in accordance with **the standards of the Public Company Accounting Oversight Board.** These standards have been developed by the accounting profession to provide guidance in the performance of an audit, which consists of an examination of evidence supporting the financial statements. Because audits are costly, auditors cannot

EXHIBIT 1-9 AUDITING RELATIONSHIPS

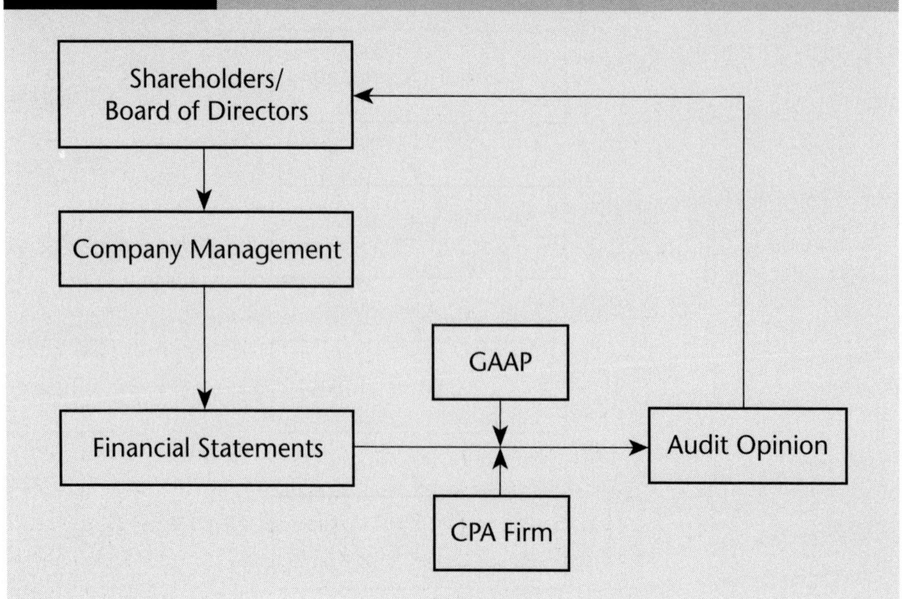

EXHIBIT 1-10 AN AUDITOR'S REPORT

REPORT OF INDEPENDENT REGISTERED PUBLIC ACCOUNTING FIRM **WAL-MART**

The Board of Directors and Shareholders,
Wal-Mart Stores, Inc.

We have audited the accompanying consolidated balance sheets of Wal-Mart Stores, Inc. as of January 31, 2006 and 2005, and the related consolidated statements of income, shareholders' equity and cash flows for each of the three years in the period ended January 31, 2006. These financial statements are the responsibility of the Company's management. Our responsibility is to express an opinion on these financial statements based on our audits.

We conducted our audits in accordance with the standards of the Public Company Accounting Oversight Board (United States). Those standards require that we plan and perform the audit to obtain reasonable assurance about whether the financial statements are free of material misstatement. An audit includes examining, on a test basis, evidence supporting the amounts and disclosures in the financial statements. An audit also includes assessing the accounting principles used and significant estimates made by management, as well as evaluating the overall financial statement presentation. We believe that our audits provide a reasonable basis for our opinion.

In our opinion, the financial statements referred to above present fairly, in all material respects, the consolidated financial position of Wal-Mart Stores, Inc. at January 31, 2006 and 2005, and the consolidated results of its operations and its cash flows for each of the three years in the period ended January 31, 2006, in conformity with U.S. generally accepted accounting principles.

We also have audited, in accordance with the standards of the Public Company Accounting Oversight Board (United States), the effectiveness of Wal-Mart Stores, Inc.'s internal control over financial reporting as of January 31, 2006, based on criteria established in *Internal Control—Integrated Framework* issued by the Committee of Sponsoring Organizations of the Treadway Commission and our report dated March 27, 2006 expressed an unqualified opinion thereon.

Ernst + Young LLP

Rogers, Arkansas
March 27, 2006

retrace the accounting for every transaction. Accordingly, only a sample of a corporation's many transactions are reviewed. Based on the results of these tests, the auditor draws an inference about the fairness of the financial statements.

The second paragraph also notes that audits provide reasonable (not absolute) assurance that financial statements are free of material error. The lesser standard of reasonable assurance is employed for two reasons. First, auditors do not examine every transaction and thus they are unable to state conclusions in too strong a fashion. Second, even if auditors were to examine every transaction, collusion between two parties could make the detection of an error virtually impossible. Therefore, *auditors do not guarantee that the financial statements are error free.*

The third paragraph contains the **auditor's opinion.** The opinion reflects the auditor's professional judgment regarding whether the financial statements are **fairly presented in accordance with GAAP.** Some readers mistakenly assume that auditors "certify" the financial statements. Auditors do not provide financial statement readers with that level of assurance. *Auditors do not guarantee the* *correctness of the financial statements.* Auditors merely express an educated professional judgment based on audit tests conducted according to acceptable professional standards. The fourth paragraph, a recent addition to the audit report, contains the auditor's opinion on the company's system of internal control.

An analogy can be drawn to a medical doctor diagnosing a patient. Based on a series of appropriate tests, the doctor develops a diagnosis. In many cases, the doctor cannot be absolutely certain of the diagnosis. This is why, for example, exploratory surgery is sometimes necessary. Doctors do not issue guarantees, and neither do auditors!

The report that appears in Exhibit 1-10 is an **unqualified opinion,** indicating that Ernst and Young has no reservations about the reasonableness of Wal-Mart's financial statements. However, a variety of concerns may arise that would cause the auditor to issue a **qualified opinion** or to include additional explanatory material. We know, for example, that there are several acceptable methods of accounting for inventory. If a company were to change its inventory method from one year to the next, the comparability of the financial statements for those years would be impaired, and financial statement readers would certainly want to be aware of such a situation. Because of this, changes in accounting methods are noted in the auditor's report.

ECONOMIC CONSEQUENCES AND MANAGERIAL PREFERENCES FOR ACCOUNTING PRINCIPLES

The selection of accounting principles occurs at two levels. First, the FASB determines which principles constitute GAAP. In a number of instances, however, the FASB allows the use of more than one method. Thus, corporate managers also make accounting policy decisions. Which criteria do the FASB and corporate managers use to select accounting principles?

The FASB's primary objective is to select accounting principles that provide useful information to financial statement readers. However, businesses incur costs to generate FASB's required information. Thus, the FASB *attempts to balance the costs and benefits* of its rulings.

Some commentators suggest that corporate managers act in the same way. For example, in choosing an inventory method, managers balance the costs of implementing each method with the quality of the information that each method yields. A more sophisticated view recognizes that *accounting principles have economic consequences* to managers and their firms. Managers consider these consequences when choosing accounting principles. Beyond implementation costs, accounting principles can affect the wealth of managers and firms via (1) **compensation plans,** (2) **debt contracts,** and (3) **political costs.**

Compensation Plans

Many corporations pay their top managers a fixed salary plus an annual bonus, which is often a percentage of reported net income. A number of bonus agreements include a floor and a ceiling on the bonus. The floor requires that net income must exceed a predetermined amount before the bonus is activated. The ceiling places a limit on the size of the bonus; once the annual bonus reaches the ceiling, additional increases in net income no longer increase the bonus.

Bonus plans are intended to *align the interests of managers and shareholders.* Managers frequently face alternative courses of action, where one course is in their best interest, and another course is in the shareholders' best interest. For example, a manager's career might be aided by expanding the business ("empire building"), even when such expansion is not particularly profitable and is not in the shareholders' best interest. Expansion may result in more prestige and visibility for the firm and its managers, thus enhancing a manager's employment opportunities. Because (1) bonus plans motivate managers to make decisions that increase net income, and (2) increased net income is usually in the shareholders' best interest, the goals of these two groups come more in line when a manager's compensation depends on reported net income.

Given that managers' compensation is tied to net income, how would we expect managers to select accounting principles? Most managers probably consider the effect that different accounting principles have on net income, and consequently on their compensation. In particular, *bonuses often motivate managers to select accounting methods that increase reported net income.*

Debt Contracts

Lenders are concerned about limiting their risk and maximizing the probability that principal and interest will be paid. **Debt contracts** between borrowers and lenders can help accomplish this. Many of these contracts impose constraints on the behavior of borrowers. For example, some contracts limit the total amount of debt a borrower can incur. In such cases, measurement of the borrower's debt is based on the liabilities reported in the balance sheet. As another example, some contracts limit the cash dividends a borrower can distribute. This limitation is defined in terms of retained earnings, a component of owners' equity that appears on the balance sheet. *Penalties exist for violating debt contracts.* These include:

1. an interest rate increase,
2. an increase in collateral (assets pledged to secure the debt),
3. a one-time renegotiation fee, and
4. an acceleration in the maturity date.

Because these contracts are defined in terms of financial statement numbers, the use of accounting principles that increase reported net income can reduce the chances of contract violation. Accordingly, the *likelihood of violating debt contracts is another influence on managers' accounting policy choices.*

Political Costs

Federal and state governments have the power to regulate many operations of a business. Pollutant emissions and employment practices are just two illustrations. Governments also have the power to tax corporations. Because regulation and taxation are costly to firms, managers can be expected to take actions that minimize these costs. Because these costs are imposed via the political process, they are referred to as **political costs.**

Some accountants suggest that highly profitable firms are more exposed to political costs than less profitable ones. Relatively profitable firms are more likely to be the target of antitrust investigations or special tax assessments. For example, in the mid-1970s, firms in the oil industry earned unusually high profits due to a steep rise in oil prices. As a result, Congress enacted the Windfall Profits Tax, which subjected these companies to an additional tax on their earnings. More recently, Microsoft, Inc. has been the target of intense scrutiny by Federal regulators because of its dominance in the computer operating system market and its resultant profitability.

On the other hand, large firms may be somewhat insulated from some political costs. Wal-Mart is one of the largest "economic engines" in the world. It has the ability to dictate terms to most of its suppliers. Its effect on the national economy is certainly pronounced and material. Wal-Mart certainly enjoys political risks that are different than those experienced by your "corner grocery".

Some accountants also argue that larger firms are more susceptible to regulation and taxation because their size attracts more attention. Accordingly, the managers of larger firms are particularly motivated to undertake actions that minimize political costs. One of these actions is the selection of accounting principles that reduce reported net income. *Note that compensation plans and debt contracts motivate managers to select accounting principles that increase reported income, whereas political costs have the opposite effect.*

The Two Roles of Financial Accounting

At the beginning of this chapter, the **informational role** of financial accounting was emphasized. From this perspective, both the FASB and corporate managers select accounting principles that yield the most useful information. However, as shown above, accounting principles also have economic consequences. These consequences arise in several ways. First, *accounting serves as a basis for contracting.* That is, some contracts (compensation plans and debt contracts) are based on accounting numbers. Because different accounting principles result in different accounting numbers, the choice of accounting principles can modify the terms of these contracts. Second, *accounting principles affect a firm's exposure to political costs,* such as taxes and regulation. Finally, the costs to implement different accounting principles vary. Some accounting principles are quite complex and costly, whereas others are rather simple.

For all these reasons, *accounting principles can affect a firm's wealth and its managers' wealth!* Managers have an obvious incentive to select the principles that increase their wealth. Such an incentive may conflict with the notion that managers select accounting principles to provide useful information. This implies that *financial statement readers must carefully evaluate the accounting principles used by a firm.* The firm's choice of accounting principles may not result in the most useful financial statement information. In subsequent chapters, managers' selections of accounting principles will be examined from both informational and economic incentive perspectives.

The Political Nature of Accounting Standard Setting

Economic incentives associated with accounting principles might motivate an additional element of managerial behavior. As mentioned in an earlier section, the FASB conducts an elaborate due process procedure prior to issuing an accounting standard. This process provides corporate managers an opportunity to lobby the FASB. What underlies their comments to the Board? Again, two possibilities exist. The comments may reflect managers' assessments of which principles generate the most useful financial statement information. Alternatively, their comments may also reflect, perhaps in a disguised way, how the various accounting principles will affect their wealth.

Some observers believe that the FASB has been overly responsive to the latter arguments. Of course, others believe that the FASB is not sufficiently sensitive to the effects its pronouncements have on individual managers or firms. Thus, *accounting standards setting is now widely recognized as a political process* in which various parties argue for the selection of the accounting principles that further their own self-interest. Some accountants believe that self-interest arguments have had a negative effect on the usefulness of the information required by some FASB rulings.

ETHICS AND ACCOUNTING

Accountants have a significant responsibility to the public. This responsibility exists because outside shareholders, creditors, employees, and others rely on financial statements in making various business decisions. Business organizations employ internal accountants to prepare financial statements. A firm of independent CPAs then audits these statements. Both the internal accountants and the external auditors have a responsibility to perform their tasks with integrity and due care.

Various accounting organizations promote high standards of ethical behavior. One example is the **American Institute of Certified Public Accountants (AICPA)**, which is a professional organization that serves CPAs who work for public accounting firms or other organizations (such as corporations). Its Code of Professional Conduct emphasizes the obligation of CPAs to serve the public interest, and their responsibility to act with integrity, objectivity, independence, and due professional care.

In a given situation, formalized **codes of ethics** can often help in deciding the proper course of action. However, some situations are sufficiently complex that the codes do not provide clear guidance. Fortunately, ethicists can help develop frameworks for examining ambiguous ethical situations. Each of us can develop our own moral and ethical framework based on beliefs and value systems.

Some ethicists judge the moral correctness of an act based solely on its consequences. According to this perspective, the act that should be taken is the one that maximizes overall favorable consequences (net of unfavorable ones). Consequences not only to the actor, but also to all parties should be considered.

Another view is that the consequences of an act do not exclusively dictate moral correctness. This view suggests that the underlying nature of the act itself influences its correctness. The nature of an act is the only thing to be considered in assessing its moral correctness. For example, killing and lying may be considered as morally wrong under any circumstances. Others assert that the nature of the act and its consequences in a particular situation should both be considered.

To illustrate these alternative views of **ethics,** imagine you are in the process of filling out an expense report after having just completed a business trip. Your employer does not reimburse childcare costs while away from home, yet most of your colleagues (including your immediate supervisor) feel that childcare is a legitimate expense. They recoup this expenditure by overstating the cost of meals (most restaurants provide you with a blank receipt). Is it ethically correct for you to overstate your meal cost?

A strict view would assert that the act of lying is ethically wrong, and that falsifying an expense report is the equivalent of lying. On the other hand, some would examine the consequences of the action, and it is not clear that their analysis would reach the same conclusion. They might say "no harm, no foul" on the rationale that childcare costs balance out with the traveling expenses. An assessment would need to be made of how the manager's interests versus the shareholders' interests are affected by the falsification.

Consider another example in Reality Check 1-3 where a private foundation has now learned that its CEO has settled an SEC inquiry involving his former position at Xerox.

What Would You Do?

Lifetime Products, Inc., sold part of its business to its chief executive and to the wife of its board of directors' chairman. Some of Lifetime's shareholders subsequently filed a lawsuit seeking to rescind the sale.

Why might Lifetime's shareholders be upset? Would you have authorized the sale?

REALITY CHECK 1-3

An interesting ethical dilemma was recently considered by the board of the Ford Foundation, one of the country's largest private charitable foundations, who decided to keep its chairman, despite accusations by federal regulators that he participated in accounting fraud when he was chairman and chief executive of the Xerox Corporation. The decision came after the chairman, Paul A. Allaire, agreed to pay a $1 million penalty and forfeit $7.6 million in bonus pay and the proceeds from stock sales at Xerox and interest on those sums. He and five other Xerox executives were accused of allowing the company to overstate its profits by $1.4 billion over four years. Under the settlement agreement with the SEC, the officials neither admitted nor denied wrongdoing.

The Ford Foundation's executive committee concluded that no changes were necessary as "We were committed to doing what we consider the right thing, and that is what is best for the foundation, which is to stay with a man who has been an exemplary leader," said Kathryn S. Fuller, a member of the executive committee (Stephanie Strom, "Foundation to Keep Leader Accused of Fraud at Xerox," *The New York Times,* July 8, 2003, p. A16).

The ethical question here concerns whether the Ford Foundation should have followed the spirit of the SEC settlement, which prohibited the five former Xerox executives from serving as board members of public companies. While private, should the Ford Foundation consider whether its leaders should have the same level of confidence and credibility as leaders of public companies?

The Ford Foundation responded: "As the terms of that settlement do not relate to Mr. Allaire's service with private organizations and having considered the matter carefully, the board strongly reaffirms his role as its chairman," the board said in a statement read by Alex Wilde, Ford's spokesman (*Ibid.*)

Another view was expressed by Evelyn Brody, professor at Chicago-Kent College of Law who said: "This is not a good time for the nonprofit sector to be attracting attention in this kind of way." "Foundations especially are vulnerable at a federal level." Professor Brody said that appearances sometimes mattered more than legal conditions. "It's probably not legally required that he step down," she said, "but one of the things a charity has to decide is not just what's legal, but also what's prudent and good practice." (*Ibid.*)

Note that the Sarbanes-Oxley Act of 2002, which requires greater disclosure and executive and board accountability at corporations, does not apply directly to nonprofit institutions, but many might question whether it has implications for tax-exempt organizations. Betsy Buchalter Adler, chairwoman of the exempt organizations committee of the tax section of the American Bar Association, suggested that: "People in the nonprofit and the for-profit sectors have been discussing whether that law is going to evolve into a de facto standard of good corporate practice in sectors where it does not directly apply." (*Ibid.*)

In this case, the executive is barred from taking a leadership role in a public company. Should he continue to shoulder many of the same responsibilities for a private organization? Here the CEO is following the letter of the settlement agreement, but perhaps not the spirit in which it was intended?

To develop a strong personal code of ethics, each of us must develop our own responses to ethical situations. We suggest that you consider how different ethical solutions can be used to analyze ethical situations, and that you assess which ethical framework is consistent with your own moral framework.

Summary of Learning Objectives

1. **Define accounting and identify its objectives.**
   Accounting is the systematic process of measuring the economic activity of an entity. The primary objective of accounting is to provide useful information to those who make business and economic decisions. Users of accounting information include present and potential investors and creditors, investment advisers, corporate managers, employees, unions, and government regulators. A secondary objective of accounting is to help develop and enforce contracts. In various business circumstances, people and organizations find the use of accounting numbers in contracts to be quite helpful.

2. **Understand the clear and dominant objectives of "Where's the Cash?"**
   Recent corporate frauds or related bankruptcies involved some significant "players" who ignored the danger signs in the financial statements. Every one involved someone who accepted too quickly much of what the accountants, auditors, or managers wanted the public to believe. Every one could have been avoided or the effects could have been mitigated by a more critical examination of the financial statements, with an emphasis on cash flows.

   Each of these corporate scandals, with resulting losses of billions of dollars, was impacted by a failure to determine **"Where's the Cash?"** Try to identify instances where revenues and profits were inflated by exchanges of property rights that will not result in increased cash flows! Similarly, try to identify profits that increase by charging expenses that were too low, or that did not reflect prior or future cash outflows. In each case, **"find the cash"** in order to identify the inherent subjectivity and potential bias that may cause confusion or distortion. Be aware that a fundamental skill will be how to adjust revenues to reflect cash flows or how to modify GAAP-based financial statements to reflect more objectivity and more certainty, as they pertain to cash flows.

3. **Differentiate the three major types of accounting.**
   The three major types of accounting are based on identifying the user of financial statements. Financial accounting provides information to outsiders who do not have access to the firm's confidential records. This includes shareholders, creditors, employees, unions, and government regulators. Managerial

accounting provides information to corporate managers to help them with their decisions. Tax accounting has two elements: (1) Tax compliance involves the periodic preparation of tax forms as required by various taxing authorities. The purpose of this is to calculate a firm's tax liability. It takes place after transactions have been completed. (2) Tax planning takes place before transactions have been undertaken. Its purpose is to structure transactions so as to minimize their tax effect.

4. **Identify three primary financial statements and briefly summarize the information contained in each.**
   The balance sheet, income statement, and statement of cash flows are the three primary financial statements. The balance sheet shows a firm's assets, liabilities, and owners' equity at a point in time. The income statement summarizes a firm's revenues and expenses for a period of time. The difference between revenues and expenses is net income (or loss). The statement of cash flows shows a firm's inflows and outflows of cash for a period of time. The three categories on this statement are cash flows from (1) operating activities, (2) investing activities, and (3) financing activities. This statement will help us find out **"Where's the Cash?"**

5. **Identify financial statement users and the decisions they make.**
   The main users of financial statements are shareholders, creditors, managers, and government regulators. Shareholders decide whether to buy, hold, or sell shares in the firm. Creditors must determine whether to extend credit and on what terms. Because financial statements are a performance report on corporate management, managers are concerned about the effect of their decisions on the financial statements. Government regulators use financial statements to determine if firms are complying with various laws and regulations.

6. **Describe the role of generally accepted accounting principles and how they are determined.**
   Generally accepted accounting principles (GAAP) are the most widely used set of accounting rules. Currently, the FASB sets GAAP. The FASB's authority rests on (1) the acceptance of its rulings by the financial community, and (2) the delegation by the SEC of its legislative authority to determine GAAP for large, publicly held corporations. Prior to issuing a new ruling, the FASB conducts an elaborate process that permits participation by all interested parties.

7. **Describe the role of auditing.**
   A firm's management is responsible for preparing financial statements. Yet those same statements are a performance report on management. Because of this conflict of interest, independent CPAs audit the financial statements of many firms. Auditors examine a sample of an organization's transactions to provide a reasonable basis for expressing an opinion on the fairness of the financial statements. CPAs do not certify financial statements; they merely express a professional opinion regarding their fairness in conformity with GAAP.

8. **List the economic consequences of choosing accounting principles.**
Accounting principles not only affect the quality of the information contained in financial statements, they also affect the wealth of various parties. Accounting principles have economic consequences because of implementation costs, compensation plans, debt contracts, and political costs. Managers therefore have certain preferences for accounting principles that are not necessarily related to the inherent quality of the resulting information. Accordingly, care must be taken in interpreting both financial statements and managers' recommendations about accounting standards.

9. **Assess the importance of ethics in accounting.**
Accountants have an important responsibility to the public that arises because financial statements are used by large numbers of people for a variety of purposes. It is essential that accountants adhere to the highest levels of ethical conduct.

KEY TERMS

Accounting
Accounting information systems
Accounting Principles Board (APB)
Accounts receivable
American Institute of Certified Public Accountants (AICPA)
Annual report
Assets
Audit
Auditor's opinion
Balance sheet
Cash
Categories
Certified public accountant (CPA)
Codes of ethics
Compensation plans
Conflict of interest
Cost accounting
Cost of goods sold
CPA firm
Debt contracts
Due process
Enron accounting
Equipment
Ethics
Expected return
Expenses
Fairly presented in accordance with GAAP
Financial accounting
Financial Accounting Standards Board (FASB)
Financing activities
General and administrative expenses
General purpose
Generally accepted accounting principles (GAAP)
Generally accepted auditing standards (GAAS)
Historical cost
Income statement
Informational role
Inventory
Investing activities
Liabilities
Managerial accounting
Net income
Net loss
Nonbusiness organizations
Notes to financial statements
Operating activities
Opportunity cost
Overhead
Owners (investors)
Owners' equity
Political costs
Publicly held
Qualified opinion
Revenues
Risk
Sarbanes-Oxley Act of 2002
Securities Exchange Act of 1934
Securities and Exchange Commission (SEC)
Statement of cash flows
Statements of Financial Accounting Standards (SFASs)
Tax accounting
Tax expense
Transactions
Unqualified opinion
Users of financial statements

Exercises and Problems

1-1 The chapter discussed two general functions of financial accounting. Briefly describe them.

1-2 List the three types (specialty areas) of accounting. Who are the users of each type of accounting? How do the needs of these users differ?

1-3 Compare the cash flows of a business to its profits. How do cash flows differ from income or profits?

1-4 Describe the financial accounting process. Discuss its relationship to decision makers.

1-5 List the three major financial statements. What information do they contain? How are they different?

Company Perquisites and Cash Transactions

1-6 Assume that you are employed by a law firm as a staff accountant. The firm has purchased four season tickets for the Colorado Rockies (a baseball franchise). Your boss, one of the partners in the firm, has offered individual tickets to you, but also asked you to pay $10 for each ticket. Since they are $14 tickets, you are happy to get a bargain. You are even happier to get a chance to go to the game because tickets are in short supply.

Next month, while reviewing the financial statements for your department, you are unable to find the $40 of cash receipts for these tickets. Since you know that the firm has purchased these tickets, you wonder what happened to your $40 payment. After discussing this matter with several other junior staff members who had also paid the partner for tickets to Rockies' games, you guess that the partner has pocketed the money and not reported the revenue to the other partners.

Required

a. What should or would you do? Why?

b. Would it make any difference if the firm were a single proprietorship and not a partnership? Why?

c. Would it make any difference if all the partners followed the same procedure and pocketed the ticket money? Why?

d. Is this an issue that should be reported to any other parties such as the Internal Revenue Service, the State Auditor, or the Attorney General? Why?

Essay (or Discussion): Identifying Useful Information

1-7 The auditor's report, shown in Exhibit 1-10, contains much useful information. Write a short essay, or form small groups in your class, discussing the kinds of information you think auditors should provide. You may identify specific kinds of information that you think would be helpful to an investor or creditor. Indicate why you think such information would be helpful.

Compare and Contrast Two Audit Reports

1-8 Compare and contrast the auditor's report for Wal-Mart by Ernst & Young in Exhibit 1-10 with the report (below) for Merck & Co. by Arthur Andersen. (Note that Arthur Andersen, who ceased operations after the Enron scandals, issued this report!)

To the Stockholders and
Board of Directors of Merck & Co., Inc.:

We have audited the accompanying consolidated balance sheet of Merck & Co., Inc. (a New Jersey corporation) and subsidiaries as of December 31, 2001 and 2000, and the related consolidated statements of income, retained earnings, comprehensive income and cash flows for each of the three years in the period ended December 31, 2001. These financial statements are the responsibility of the Company's management. Our responsibility is to express an opinion on these financial statements based on our audits.

We conducted our audits in accordance with auditing standards generally accepted in the United States. Those standards require that we plan and perform the audit to obtain reasonable assurance about whether the financial statements are free of material misstatement. An audit includes examining, on a test basis, evidence supporting the amounts and disclosures in the financial statements. An audit also includes assessing the accounting principles used and significant estimates made by management, as well as evaluating the overall financial statement presentation. We believe that our audits provide a reasonable basis for our opinion.

In our opinion, the financial statements referred to above present fairly, in all material respects, the financial position of Merck & Co., Inc. and subsidiaries as of December 31, 2001 and 2000, and the results of their operations and their cash flows for each of the three years in the period ended December 31, 2001, in conformity with accounting principles generally accepted in the United States.

New York, New York
January 22, 2002

ARTHUR ANDERSEN LLP

Essay: Changes in Accounting Disclosure Requirements

1-9 The accounting profession considered increasing its required disclosures and the type of information that is required from public companies. The following paragraphs appeared in *The Wall Street Journal* (August 26, 1993, p. A4):

A key accounting group calls for a sharp increase in the amount of information companies must disclose in their annual reports. The prospect alarms corporate financial officers.

If adopted, the recommendations could force companies to change the way they figure profits. It could make them disclose more data about the competitive pressures they face. They could transform the auditor's report from the current boilerplate message to a longer and much more revealing statement about the company's health. Information about changes in the firm's product prices in response to competitive price shifts would be required.

The new requirements would favor more segmenting of data so that sales and profits for each company unit would be shown. More meaningful breakdowns of company data would be required. Much more data would be required from larger companies than from small companies.

Required

Write a short memo to the key accounting group noted in the article from the perspective of a company president, responding to the proposed changes in accounting disclosures.

Compare and Contrast Two Audit Reports

1-10 Compare and contrast the audit reports for e-Bay and Target. How do they differ? How are they similar? Are there any significant issues raised by the auditors that should be studied further?

Sarbanes-Oxley Act of 2002

1-11 Conduct a web-search on **Sarbanes-Oxley Act,** or just Sarbanes-Oxley, or in popular terms, known as Sar-box or SOX for short. Identify recent instances of how this legislation is affecting corporate reporting. Identify, if possible, any corporations or audit firms that have been significantly affected by this legislation. Describe your findings.

Enron Accounting

1-12 Conduct a web-search on "Enron accounting" or any variation on this term. Identify recent instances of how this phenomenon is affecting corporate reporting. Identify, if possible, any corporations or audit firms that have been significantly affected by accusations of "Enron accounting". Describe your findings.

CHAPTER 2

BASIC CONCEPTS OF FINANICAL ACCOUNTING

Learning Objectives

1. *Define the terms assets, liabilities, and owners' equity.*
2. *Explain why the balance sheet must balance.*
3. *Describe revenues and expenses.*
4. *Understand the basic issue underlying revenue recognition.*
5. *Use the basic accounting equation to analyze transactions.*
6. *Prepare simple balance sheets and income statements.*
7. *Describe the relationship between the balance sheet and the income statement.*
8. *Distinguish between the accrual basis and the cash basis of accounting.*
9. *Explain the differences between the balance sheets of sole proprietorships and those of corporations.*

INTRODUCTION

This chapter describes the financial accounting process. It shows how information about transactions and events is accumulated to produce the balance sheet and the income statement. This early presentation is quite basic; subsequent chapters will present more complex issues. Also, although the cash flow effects of various transactions are addressed in this chapter, the statement of cash flows is actually covered in detail in Chapter 5, "Statement of Cash Flows".

THE BASIC ACCOUNTING EQUATION

A balance sheet, also called the statement of financial position, illustrated in Exhibit 2-1, contains three sections: assets, liabilities, and owners' equity. The total of the left side (assets) equals the total of the right side (liabilities and owners' equity).

Financial accounting is based on one simple, three-element equation, referred to as the **basic accounting equation:**

ASSETS = LIABILITIES + OWNERS' EQUITY

The basic accounting equation is simply an algebraic form of the balance sheet. The following sections elaborate on the definitions of the equation's elements.

Assets

Assets are valuable resources that are owned or controlled by a firm. They represent probable future economic benefits and arise as the result of past transactions or events. Examples of assets include cash, accounts receivable (the right to receive cash in the future), inventory (merchandise manufactured or acquired for resale to customers), equipment, land, and investments.

EXHIBIT 2-1 A BALANCE SHEET

Newton Company
Balance Sheet
December 31, 2007

ASSETS		**LIABILITIES AND OWNERS' EQUITY**	
Cash	$ 5,000	Liabilities	
Accounts receivable	7,000	Accounts payable	$ 8,000
Inventory	10,000	Notes payable	2,000
Equipment	7,000	Total liabilities	10,000
Total assets	$29,000	Owners' equity	19,000
		Total liabilities and owners' equity	$29,000

Two aspects of the definition deserve emphasis. First, the term probable suggests that in some situations future economic benefits may not exist. Many business owners, for example, feel that a loyal customer base and a highly skilled workforce enhance a firm's competitive advantage. Although few would argue with this, the link in any particular situation between customer loyalty or workforce skill and future benefits is sufficiently uncertain that these factors are not recognized as assets.

Second, assets must be owned or controlled by the firm. This component of the definition is designed to exclude public goods from balance sheets. Although many firms benefit from roadways, sewers, national defense, and the public education system, firms do not own the roads or schools in their communities. Because of this, they do not appear on balance sheets of individual firms. In addition, a firm may "control" an asset but not actually hold the ownership title to it.

Liabilities

Liabilities *are present obligations of the firm. They are probable future sacrifices of economic benefits (usually cash) that arise as the result of past transactions or events.* Common examples of liabilities are notes payable (written obligations), accounts payable (verbal obligations to suppliers arising in the normal course of business), and taxes payable.

Two aspects of the definition of liabilities need elaboration. First, as with assets, the term probable is used. This is an important part of the definition. Although in some instances, the existence of a liability is virtually certain (as when one arises from obtaining a bank loan), other situations are less clear. For example, consider a firm that has been sued. At the inception of the suit, the outcome may be highly uncertain, but as the litigation proceeds, it may seem more likely (but not certain) that the firm will be forced to pay some amount. Accountants need to exercise judgment in determining the existence of a liability. They do so by assessing whether a potential future sacrifice is probable.

Second, the definition requires that liabilities arise from past transactions or events. Consider a definition that did not include this criterion. Most firms expect to be in existence for a considerable period of time. They anticipate employing workers, buying inventory, and so on. These planned activities may well result in probable future sacrifices of economic benefits, yet the organization is not obliged to make those payments until a transaction has occurred.

Because of the "past transaction" criterion, financial accounting does not reflect **executory contracts,** which are contracts that initially involve merely an exchange of promises. For example, on December 4, 2006 CBS announced that David Letterman signed a new contract to host the Late Show with David Letterman through the fall of 2010 worth over $120 million. At the time of contract signing, a substantive exchange had not taken place. Neither side had actually done anything. Letterman had not yet hosted the shows, and CBS had not provided payment. This type of contract is not incorporated in the financial accounting process. Subsequently, when one or both parties have performed, a substantive exchange has occurred, and then it is appropriate to reflect the transaction in the financial statements.

Owners' Equity

***Owners' equity** represents the owners' interest in the assets of the business. Owners can obtain an interest in their business either by making direct investments or by operating the business at a profit and retaining the profits in the firm.*

Owners' equity is also referred to as **residual interest,** a term that implies the owners' interest is what remains after creditors' claims have been honored. Residual interest can be calculated by rearranging the basic accounting equation:

ASSETS − LIABILITIES = OWNERS' EQUITY

This version of the equation shows that at a given point in time, if assets exceed liabilities, the excess (residual) amount is attributed to the owners. Other terms used to refer to assets minus liabilities are **net assets** and **net worth.**

The right and left sides of the balance sheet and the original form of the basic accounting equation can both be interpreted as providing two views of the business. The left side details the composition of the firm's assets: cash, inventory, and the like. It shows "what the firm has." The right side indicates the amount of financing supplied by the creditors and the amount supplied by the owners. It shows how assets were acquired. It also shows the extent to which the creditors and the owners have a claim against the assets.

TRANSACTION ANALYSIS

Transaction analysis is the central component of the financial accounting process. A firm may engage in many business transactions during the period. *Business transactions are defined as quantifiable, economic events that affect the firm's financial position or, as discussed earlier, its basic accounting equation.* The accountant identifies the transactions and records the effects of the transactions on the three elements of the basic accounting equation. The remainder of this section analyzes a number of transactions.

Owners' Original Investment

Harry Jacobs has decided to open a golf and tennis store. The business is organized as a sole proprietorship. Sole proprietorships are businesses owned and operated by one individual. Keep in mind that we are concerned about the records of Harry's business; we are not interested in Harry's personal affairs. The **entity assumption** indicates that accounting records are kept for business units (entities) distinct from their owners.

Harry opens a bank account in the name of the business, Jacobs Golf and Tennis (JG&T), and deposits $50,000 of his own money. From the firm's perspective, the $50,000 deposit is a transaction (an exchange between the business and its owner), and it would be analyzed by increasing cash and owners' equity by $50,000 each. Note: even though there is one owner in this example, we will use the plural of owners' equity throughout our discussion. Increasing owners' equity indicates that the owner has invested $50,000 and that he has an interest in, or claim, against the assets to the extent of $50,000. The word **capital** is conventional terminology in sole proprietorships. It simply denotes the owners' interest in (or claim on) the assets of the business.

ASSETS	=	LIABILITIES	+	OWNERS' EQUITY	
Cash + $50,000				H. Jacobs, capital + $50,000	(1)

Notice that the equation balances for this transaction, as it does for all transactions.

Exhibit 2-2, shown later, contains a summary of all the transactions to be reviewed in this section. For simplicity, assume that all transactions occur on January 1, 2007.

Bank Loan

Harry realizes that his new business needs more cash than the $50,000 he invested. The firm applies for, and is granted, a $20,000 bank loan. The loan carries an interest rate of 8%, and both principal and interest are due on January 1, 2008.

This transaction increases cash and liabilities by $20,000. Liabilities increase because a past transaction has occurred obligating JG&T to repay the loan in the future. This constitutes a virtually certain sacrifice of future economic benefits. The liability item that increases is notes payable. Banks usually require borrowers to sign written promises to repay loans, and the word notes indicates that JG&T has a written obligation to repay the loan.

ASSETS	=	LIABILITIES	+	OWNERS' EQUITY	
Cash + $20,000		Notes payable + $20,000			(2)

The equation balances for this transaction, too. Summing up the first two transactions, JG&T has cash of $70,000, which equals liabilities of $20,000 plus owners' equity of $50,000.

You might be wondering about the interest on the loan. Interest is a charge for borrowing money during a specified period of time. Because this time period has just begun, no interest is immediately recorded. As you will see later, interest is recorded periodically throughout the life of the loan.

Rent

JG&T enters into an agreement to lease retail space from another company. The lease is for one year, and the entire $12,000 rent is paid on January 1, 2007, the date the lease is signed. Cash declines by $12,000 but what other equation item is affected? JG&T has acquired another asset: the right to occupy the retail space for a year. This enables JG&T to carry on its normal business operations. The asset is referred to as **prepaid rent** and is assigned a value equal to its **historical cost** (exchange price on the date of acquisition). Assets are usually recorded at their historical cost. Note: the basic accounting equation shows that one asset is simply exchanged for another. There is no effect on the JG&T's liabilities or owners' equity.

ASSETS		=	LIABILITIES	+	OWNERS' EQUITY	
Cash	Prepaid rent					(3)
– $12,000	+ $12,000					

Inventory

Inventory is merchandise manufactured or acquired for resale to customers. It is an asset because firms expect to receive cash from selling inventory to customers.

JG&T is in the business of buying and selling sporting goods. Assume JG&T purchases goods for $30,000, **on account** (on credit). This transaction increases inventory, and because payment is not made immediately, liabilities increase. Because notes are not used for ongoing purchases from suppliers, another liability item, **accounts payable,** is increased. Accounts payable are unwritten obligations, verbal promises that arise in the normal course of business.

ASSETS	=	LIABILITIES	+	OWNERS' EQUITY	
Inventory		Accounts payable			(4)
+ $30,000		+ $30,000			

Equipment

Because the retail space that JG&T leased contains no equipment (cash registers, display cases, and so on), equipment must be purchased. JG&T makes a purchase for $25,000 and pays cash. Cash decreases, equipment increases, and total assets are unchanged.

ASSETS		=	LIABILITIES	+	OWNERS' EQUITY	
Cash	Equipment					(5)
– $25,000	+ $25,000					

Preparation of the Balance Sheet

The last two lines in Exhibit 2-2 reflect the cumulative effect of JG&T's transactions. This summary is equivalent to the balance sheet. To prepare a balance sheet, simply summarize the various equation elements into the appropriate balance sheet format. The balance sheet for JG&T as of January 1, 2007, is shown in Exhibit 2-3 and is based directly on the last two lines of Exhibit 2-2. Remember that the left side of the balance sheet details the composition of JG&T's assets and the right side indicates the amount of financing supplied by the creditors and the amount supplied by the owner, Harry Jacobs.

Evaluation of Historical Cost

An asset's historical cost is a very good indication of its economic value to the firm at the time of acquisition. As times goes on, however, the historical cost becomes outdated. That is, it no longer reflects the asset's economic value.

Instead of valuing assets at historical cost, accountants could use other measures. For example, current replacement cost could be used. This value is **relevant,** meaning that it *depicts what a firm would have to pay to replace the asset on the*

EXHIBIT 2-2 TRANSACTION ANALYSIS

	ASSETS				=	LIABILITIES		+	OWNERS' EQUITY
	Cash	Prepaid Rent	Inventory	Equipment		Accounts Payable	Notes Payable		H. Jacobs, Capital
(1)	+ 50,000								+ 50,000
(2)	+ 20,000						+ 20,000		
(3)	– 12,000	+ 12,000							
(4)			+ 30,000			+ 30,000			
(5)	– 25,000			+ 25,000					
Totals	33,000	12,000	30,000	25,000		30,000	20,000		50,000
	100,000					100,000			

EXHIBIT 2-3 JG&T BALANCE SHEET

Jacobs Golf and Tennis
Balance Sheet
January 1, 2007

ASSETS		**LIABILITIES AND OWNERS' EQUITY**	
Cash	$ 33,000	Liabilities	
Prepaid rent	12,000	Accounts payable	$ 30,000
Inventory	30,000	Notes payable	20,000
Equipment	25,000	Total liabilities	50,000
Total assets	$100,000	Owners' equity	
		H. Jacobs, capital	50,000
		Total liabilities and owners' equity	$100,000

balance sheet date as opposed to the value that a firm paid when the asset was acquired. Many analysts feel that this amount better reflects the value (the future economic benefit) of an asset to the firm. Historical cost is usually determined by an **arms-length transaction** between two independent parties.

Why then does financial accounting use historical cost? Primarily because it is **reliable,** *meaning that it is objective, free of bias.* Historical cost is the result of an actual bargained transaction between two independent parties. Moreover, supporting documents, such as canceled checks, contracts, or invoices, exist to verify the amount. In contrast, current replacement cost is based on appraisals and estimates, which accountants view as "soft" numbers. In general, the accounting profession believes that the use of historical cost provides the best trade-off between relevance and reliability.

REVENUES AND EXPENSES

The transactions examined thus far are related to start-up activities. Businesses are organized to earn a profit, and this section discusses revenue and expense transactions. All transactions reviewed in this section are summarized in Exhibit 2-4.

Revenues

Revenues are inflows of assets (or reductions in liabilities) in exchange for providing goods and services to customers. *The point of delivery (point of sale) of the goods and services in the exchange signals that the earnings process is complete. In addition, if the assets received and/or liabilities reduced are reasonably assured, revenue can be recorded.*

Suppose that during January JG&T provides services (golf lessons) to customers and charges them $600. The customers pay $200 immediately and agree

EXHIBIT 2-4 TRANSACTION ANALYSIS

	ASSETS					=	LIABILITIES				+ OWNERS' EQUITY	
	Cash	Accts. Receivable	Prepaid Rent	Inventory	Equipment		Accounts Payable	Notes Payable	Unearned Revenue	Util. Payable	H. Jacobs, Capital	
Bal.	33,000	0	12,000	30,000	25,000		30,000	20,000	0	0	50,000	
(6)	+ 200	+ 400									+ 600	(service revenue)
(7)	+ 100								+ 100			
(8)	– 700										– 700	(salary expense)
(9)										+ 120	– 120	(utility expense)
(10)		+ 4,000									+ 4,000	(sales revenue)
				– 2,200							– 2,200	(cost of goods sold)
Totals	32,600	4,400	12,000	27,800	25,000		30,000	20,000	100	120	51,580	
			101,800						101,800			

to pay the remaining $400 in February. First, JG&T has received assets of $600. The receipt of the $200 is obviously an asset inflow. The $400 to be received next month is also an asset because it provides probable future benefits and is called an **account receivable.** Second, the services were provided by the end of January. That is, they have been earned; JG&T has done everything it has promised to do. In essence, the transaction meets both aspects of the definition of revenue: the earnings process is complete and collection is reasonably assured. Accordingly, revenue of $600 is recorded in January.

This transaction increases cash by $200, accounts receivable by $400, and owners' equity by $600. Why has owners' equity increased by $600? The assets of the business have expanded, and it must be decided who has a claim against (or an interest in) those assets. Because this transaction has not increased the creditors' claims, the owners' interest, Harry Jacobs, must have increased. This conclusion makes sense. Owners are the primary risk takers. They take risks with the hope of expanding their wealth. If the firm enters into a profitable transaction, the owners' wealth (their interest in the business) should expand. For a sole proprietorship, we record all owners' equity transactions to one account called the capital account.

ASSETS		=	LIABILITIES	+	OWNERS' EQUITY	
Cash	Accounts receivable				H. Jacobs, capital	
+ $200	+ $400				+ $600 (service revenue)	(6)

Of course, we cannot be absolutely certain that the customers will eventually pay the additional $400. This concern will be addressed in a subsequent chapter. For now, assume we are quite confident about this future receipt.

This transaction holds an important lesson. Although revenue equals $600, only $200 of cash has been received. Thus, from an accounting perspective, revenue does not necessarily equal cash inflow. *Although revenue is recorded when assets are received in exchange for goods and services, the asset received need not be cash. This underscores the need for both an income statement to summarize earnings and a statement of cash flows to identify the sources and uses of cash.*

As another illustration, assume that on January 10 a customer pays $100, in advance, for golf lessons. The lessons are to be rendered during the last week in January and the first week in February. Has a revenue transaction occurred on January 10? No. A requirement for revenue recognition is that the services must be rendered. As of January 10, this has not yet occurred. The transaction increases cash, but the owners' claim on assets has not increased. Instead, the customer now has a claim on the assets. If JG&T does not provide the lessons, the customer has the right to expect a refund; JG&T has a liability. It is obligated to either provide the lessons, which have a $100 value, or return the $100 payment. In either case, a $100 liability exists on January 10. **Unearned revenue** is the liability that has increased. Another appropriate name is **advances from customers.**

Reality Check 2-1 illustrates a revenue situation in the franchising industry.

ASSETS	=	LIABILITIES	+	OWNERS' EQUITY	
Cash + $100		Unearned revenue + $100			(7)

As you are probably aware the business environment, the stock market, and ultimately investor confidence have been shaken by accounting scandals. At the heart of many of these scandals is the issue of revenue recognition. It was evident from our example above that JG&T had to perform golf lessons before it could record revenue. However, in many firms it is not so obvious when revenue is earned. Remember that revenues create very positive effects on the basic accounting equation because they are an inflow of assets and/or a reduction in liabilities. Some firms have abused revenue recognition in order to enhance both the earnings on their income statement and the assets on their balance sheets by either prematurely recording revenue or fraudulently recording revenue that will never be **realized** in cash. *Many analysts, investors and creditors now are beginning to focus on the question of "Where's the cash?" when it comes to revenue recognition. In addition, they ask "Is the earnings process complete?"* We will further explore revenue recognition in Chapter 4.

REALITY CHECK 2-1

Franchisors are firms that sell the right to market their products. McDonald's Corporation, for example, sells the right to operate its restaurants to other businesses and individuals. These franchisees usually pay a fee at the time of signing the contract, plus ongoing fees based on the amount of their sales.

In exchange for the initial fee at the time of contract signing, a franchisor is required to help the franchisee select an appropriate site, supervise construction, train employees, and install the franchisee's accounting system.

Required

When should the franchisor recognize the revenue associated with the initial fee?

SOLUTION

Many franchisors prefer to recognize the revenue when the cash is received at the time of contract signing. This enables them to show improved performance. However, are the revenue recognition rules met at that point in time? In particular, has the franchisor performed the promised services? No, it has not. Because of this, the FASB has ruled that revenue from the initial franchise fee cannot be recognized as revenue until all the initial services have been performed. In general, this occurs when the franchisee opens for business.

Expenses

Expenses occur when resources are consumed in order to generate revenue. For example, during January, JG&T employed salespersons and golf instructors. Assume these employees earned total wages of $700, which were paid in cash by JG&T. Because JG&T used the employees' services during January, this is an expense transaction for that month.

The transaction decreases cash and owners' equity by $700. The decrease in cash is obvious. Why does owners' equity decrease? An analogy can be drawn to revenue. When assets increase because of profitable operations, the owners' interest in the firm's assets expands. With expenses, when assets decrease in order to generate revenue, the owners' interest in the firm's assets declines.

ASSETS	=	LIABILITIES	+	OWNERS' EQUITY	
Cash				H. Jacobs, capital	(8)
– $700				– $700 (salary expense)	

Exhibit 2-5 graphically depicts this analysis. The first rectangle reflects JG&T's assets, liabilities, and owners' equity before the salary expense transaction. The second rectangle reflects the situation after the expense transaction. Assets and the owners' claim have both decreased.

Consider another example. Assume that JG&T receives its utility bill on January 31 for electricity used during January. The bill is for $120. JG&T elects not to pay immediately. Even though cash has not been paid, an expense transaction has occurred in January. JG&T has consumed resources (electricity) in order to generate revenue.

EXHIBIT 2-5 EXPENSE TRANSACTION ANALYSIS

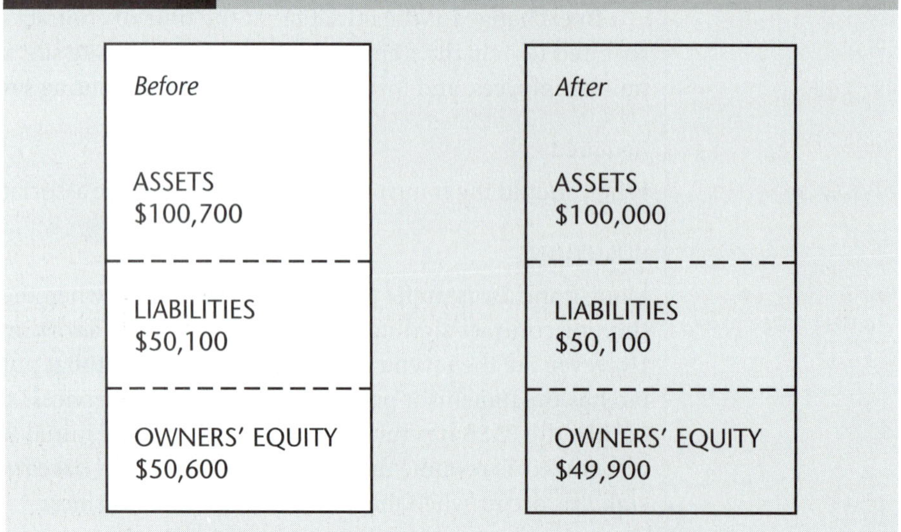

Because JG&T is now obligated to the utility company, liabilities increase by $120, and owners' equity decreases by $120. Owners' equity decreases because assets have not changed; yet the creditors' claims have increased by $120. There is no alternative but to recognize that owners' equity has decreased by $120.

ASSETS	=	LIABILITIES	+	OWNERS' EQUITY	
		Utilities payable + $120		H. Jacobs, capital – $120 (utility expense)	(9)

Exhibit 2-6 displays the analysis graphically. It shows the assets remaining fixed while (1) the creditors' claims increase and (2) the owners' claims decrease. Also note that expenses do not necessarily equal cash outflows. Goods and services can be consumed to generate revenue without a cash outflow.

Sales of Inventory

Sales of inventory contain both revenue and expense components. Assume that JG&T makes sales on account (credit) during the month totaling $4,000. The cost of the inventory to JG&T was $2,200.

A revenue transaction exists because an asset (accounts receivable) has been obtained, and the goods have been provided to customers. An expense transaction exists because the asset inventory has been consumed to generate the revenue. That is, JG&T has fewer assets because the inventory has been transferred to its customers. This expense is called **cost of goods sold** (COGS). The net increase in assets and owners' equity is $1,800.

EXHIBIT 2-6 EXPENSE TRANSACTION ANALYSIS

Before	*After*
ASSETS $100,000	ASSETS $100,000
LIABILITIES $50,100	LIABILITIES $50,220
OWNERS' EQUITY $49,900	OWNERS' EQUITY $49,780

ASSETS		= LIABILITIES +	OWNERS' EQUITY	
Accounts Receivable	Inventory		H. Jacobs, capital	
+ $4,000			+ $4,000 (sales revenue)	(10)
	– $2,200		– $2,200 (cost of goods sold)	

Adjustments

At the end of January, Harry Jacobs wishes to prepare a balance sheet and an income statement. Before doing so, several **adjustments** must be made to the accounting records. *These adjustments are necessary because certain events do not have normally occurring source documents, such as sales tickets or checks, to trigger their accounting recognition.* At the end of each period (usually each month or year), the accountant undertakes a deliberate search to identify and record these items. These items are recorded as adjusting entries. All adjustments reviewed in this section are summarized in Exhibit 2-7.

Interest

As previously mentioned, on January 1, 2007, JG&T borrowed $20,000 at 8% interest (on an annual basis). Although the interest payment is not required until January 1, 2008, JG&T has incurred interest expense during January 2007. During that month, JG&T has consumed a resource: the use of the money. The utilization of that resource has enabled JG&T to operate and to generate revenues. Accordingly, an expense has been incurred, and it must be reflected in the accounting records before the financial statements are prepared. The interest charge for January is calculated as:

$$\begin{aligned}\text{Interest expense} &= \text{Principal} \times \text{Rate} \times \text{Time}\\ &= \$20{,}000 \times .08 \times 1/12\\ &= \$133 \text{ (rounded)}\end{aligned}$$

The principal is the amount borrowed, in this case, $20,000. The annual interest rate is 8%. Stated in decimal form, it is .08. Because the interest rate is stated on an annual basis, the time period must be expressed similarly. Given that one month has elapsed, the time period is 1/12 of a year.

The general form of the analysis is similar to the earlier utility bill situation. Because the bank's services (use of the bank's money) have been consumed, JG&T has an additional obligation (interest payable) in the amount of $133. Further, because assets have remained constant and liabilities have increased, owners' equity must decrease.

EXHIBIT 2-7 ADJUSTMENTS AND OWNER WITHDRAWAL

	ASSETS					= LIABILITIES					+ OWNERS' EQUITY	
	Cash	Accts. Rec.	Prepaid Rent	Inventory	Equip.	Accts. Pay.	Notes Pay.	Unearned Revenue	Util. Pay.	Interest Pay.	H. Jacobs, Capital	
Bal.	32,600	4,400	12,000	27,800	25,000	30,000	20,000	100	120		51,580	
(11)										+ 133	– 133	(interest expense)
(12)			– 1,000								– 1,000	(rent expense)
(13)					– 208						– 208	(depreciation expense)
(14)								– 50			+ 50	(service revenue)
(15)	– 100										– 100	(withdrawal)
Totals	32,500	4,400	11,000	27,800	24,792	30,000	20,000	50	120	133	50,189	
	100,492					100,492						

ASSETS	=	LIABILITIES	+	OWNERS' EQUITY	
		Interest payable + $133		H. Jacobs, capital − $133 (interest expense)	(11)

Rent

On January 1, JG&T paid one year's rent in advance. The amount was $12,000, and an asset (prepaid rent) was appropriately recorded. By January 31, one month of the payment had been consumed and thus, an expense should be reflected in the accounting records. Remember that expenses are incurred to generate revenue. The analysis is:

ASSETS	=	LIABILITIES	+	OWNERS' EQUITY	
Prepaid rent − $1,000				H. Jacobs, capital − $1,000 (rent expense)	(12)

Depreciation

On January 1, JG&T purchased equipment for $25,000. As you recall, this transaction increased the asset equipment. Assume that the estimated life of the equipment is 10 years, at which time it will be worthless. Since the equipment is used during its 10-year useful life to generate revenue, the cost of the equipment should be charged as an expense over that period. This expense is referred to as **depreciation**. Monthly depreciation expense is calculated as:

$$\text{Depreciation expense} = \frac{\text{Historical cost (less anticipated salvage value)}}{\text{Number of months in the useful life}}$$

$$= \frac{\$25{,}000}{120}$$

$$= \$208 \text{ (rounded)}$$

Because the equipment's service potential has declined by one month, the asset's recorded value is decreased, and because an expense has been incurred, owners' equity declines.

ASSETS	=	LIABILITIES	+	OWNERS' EQUITY	
Equipment − $208				H. Jacobs, capital − $208 (depreciation expense)	(13)

Note: We showed the $208 as reduction of the equipment's value. In reality, the $208 is recorded to another asset called accumulated depreciation. It has a negative balance, which is contrary to the normal balance for assets. Therefore, it is called a contra asset. The historical cost of the equipment of $25,000 remains intact and the accumulated depreciation has a balance of –$208. The equipment, net of the accumulated depreciation, is $24,792. This amount (cost minus accumulated depreciation) is referred to as the equipment's net book value and represents the equipment's remaining cost to be allocated to future periods. Bear in mind that the net book value does not represent the current market value of the equipment. We will discuss the concept of accumulated depreciation and net book value in depth in Chapter 3.

Unearned Revenue

On January 10, JG&T received a $100 advance payment from a customer for golf lessons to be delivered during the last week of January and the first week in February. At that time, cash increased, as did a liability, unearned revenue. Assume that half of the lessons were given in January. An adjustment to the accounting records is now required because (1) JG&T's obligation to its customer has declined by $50, and (2) $50 of revenue has been earned. Revenue is now recognized because assets have already increased and the services have now been provided. Because $50 of revenue has been earned, owners' equity increases.

ASSETS	=	LIABILITIES	+	OWNERS' EQUITY	
		Unearned revenue – $50		H. Jacobs, capital + $50 (service revenue)	(14)

WITHDRAWAL BY OWNER

Assume that Harry withdraws $100 from JG&T's bank account on January 31 so that he can pay some personal living expenses. Because Harry worked in the shop during the month, the withdrawal could be viewed as an expense to the business (Harry's salary). Because the owner of a sole proprietorship cannot really establish an independent relationship with the business, however, the "salary" amount does not have a great deal of reliability. For example, Harry could simply withdraw amounts based on his personal needs, rather than on the value of the services he contributed to the business. Because of this, owner withdrawals are not viewed as salary expenses. Instead, they are considered to be capital transactions, which involve investments or disinvestments by the owner. Thus, the analysis is exactly the opposite of a contribution by the owner.

ASSETS	=	LIABILITIES	+	OWNERS' EQUITY	
Cash – $100				H. Jacobs, capital – $100 (withdrawal)	(15)

WHAT WOULD YOU DO?

In the late 1990s, Microstrategy, a computer software company specializing in computer modeling, found itself under extreme pressure to show consistent earnings growth to support its rising stock price and to meet analysts' expectations. Microstrategy reported quarterly figures that subsequently needed to be restated. An investigation into this matter determined that senior management created an environment that prompted inaccurate reporting. Senior management placed great emphasis on reporting quarterly profits.

One way to report consistent earnings is by manipulating revenue recognition. For example, a corporation might sell services under a multi-year licensing agreement, but instead of reporting revenue ratably over the licensing period, a larger portion of revenue is recorded in a quarter to boost that quarter's profits.

Imagine that you work for a large corporation whose senior managers are quite intent on bunching the recording of revenues in the current quarter. Assume that you supervise the quarterly adjustment process. What would you do if the chief executive officer and the chief financial officer instructed you to record more revenues from the licensing agreement for the most recent quarter?

TRANSACTIONS THAT AFFECT OWNERS' EQUITY

Note that four types of transactions affect owners' equity:

1. owner contributions,
2. owner withdrawals,
3. revenues, and
4. expenses.

FINANCIAL STATEMENTS

All transactions and events for JG&T have now been properly recorded. The accounting records are correct and up to date, so they can be used to prepare the financial statements.

The Balance Sheet

The cumulative effect of all transactions and events on the various equation items is shown in the last two lines of Exhibit 2-7. The **balance sheet** is prepared by simply rearranging the numbers so that they appear in the proper format. The balance sheet as of January 31 appears in Exhibit 2-8. Each item on the balance sheet is often referred to as an **account.**

Note the date on the balance sheet: *January 31, 2007. The balance sheet is often portrayed as a "snapshot" of a firm because it summarizes the firm's assets, liabilities, and owners' equity on a particular date.*

EXHIBIT 2-8 JG&T BALANCE SHEET

Jacobs Golf and Tennis
Balance Sheet
January 31, 2007

ASSETS		**LIABILITIES AND OWNERS' EQUITY**	
Cash	$ 32,500	Liabilities	
Accounts receivable	4,400	Accounts payable	$ 30,000
Prepaid rent	11,000	Unearned revenue	50
Inventory	27,800	Utilities payable	120
Equipment	24,792	Interest payable	133
Total assets	$100,492	Notes payable	20,000
		Total liabilities	50,303
		Owners' equity	
		H. Jacobs, capital	50,189
		Total liabilities and owners' equity	$100,492

The Income Statement

*The **income statement** summarizes a firm's revenues and expenses for a period of time. Net income is computed by subtracting expenses from revenues* (also known as **net profit**). JG&T's income statement for the month of January appears in Exhibit 2-9.

Note that income statements are prepared for periods of time, usually a month, quarter, or year. Income must be related to a specific period of time to be interpretable. For example, assume that you apply for a job and are told the job pays $5,000. An evaluation of the job's desirability would be impossible without knowing if you would earn $5,000 per week, month, year, or some other time period. For this reason, the income statement in Exhibit 2-9 contains the caption "For the Month Ended January 31, 2007."

Many firms prepare income statements for calendar years, that is, for the period January 1 through December 31. Other firms use 12-month periods that do not end on December 31. These firms usually select an ending date that corresponds to a low point in their activity. For example, many clothing stores, such as Wal-Mart, have **fiscal years** that run from February 1 through January 31. January 31 is selected as the end of the fiscal year because it closely follows the busy holiday period and provides time for refunds and exchanges to take place.

The income statement is prepared by compiling information from the owners' equity account. Recall that all revenue transactions increase owners' equity and that all expense transactions reduce owners' equity. This makes owners' equity a convenient place to look for information about revenues and expenses. To help you see that JG&T's income statement summarizes its revenue and expense transactions for the month of January, Exhibit 2-10 summarizes all of JG&T's transactions for that month.

EXHIBIT 2-9 JG&T INCOME STATEMENT

Jacobs Golf and Tennis
Income Statement
For the Month Ended January 31, 2007

Revenue		
Sales	$4,000	
Service	650	
Total revenue		$4,650
Expenses		
Cost of goods sold	2,200	
Rent	1,000	
Salary	700	
Depreciation	208	
Interest	133	
Utilities	120	
Total expenses		4,361
Net income		$ 289

An alternative method that can be used to prepare the income statement is to examine asset and liability accounts. However, such an approach would be much more cumbersome. For example, some revenue transactions affect cash, other revenue transactions affect accounts receivable, and still others affect unearned revenue. Thus, the information about revenue transactions appears in a variety of asset and liability accounts. Moreover, many nonrevenue transactions affect assets and liabilities, complicating the identification of revenue transactions. An easier approach is simply to examine owners' equity. A similar argument can be made for expenses.

Care must be taken, however, not to include in the income statement all transactions that affect owners' equity. Direct contributions by owners increase owners' equity, but they do not constitute revenue. Similarly, withdrawals by owners reduce owners' equity, but they are not viewed as expenses.

The income statement provides financial statement readers with information about the profitability of the organization for a past period of time. It indicates how successful the organization was in generating revenues and controlling costs. During January, JG&T earned net income of $289. Although this amount might not seem very impressive in light of total revenues of $4,650 and an investment of $50,000 by Harry, January was JG&T's first month of operation. Simply operating above break-even (a zero profit or loss) is an accomplishment.

Within the context of a large corporation, an income statement can also be thought of as a report on management's performance. One of management's major responsibilities is to enhance shareholder wealth. Managers serve as agents of the shareholders, and they must be held accountable for their performance.

EXHIBIT 2-10 TRANSACTION ANALYSIS SUMMARY

	ASSETS					= LIABILITIES					+ OWNERS' EQUITY	
	Cash	Accts. Rec.	Prepaid Rent	Inventory	Equip.	Accts. Pay.	Notes Pay.	Unearned Revenue	Util. Pay.	Interest Pay.	H. Jacobs, Capital	
(1)	+ 50,000										+ 50,000	
(2)	+ 20,000						+ 20,000					
(3)	– 12,000		+ 12,000									
(4)				+ 30,000		+ 30,000						
(5)	– 25,000				+ 25,000							
(6)	+ 200	+ 400									+ 600	(service revenue)
(7)	+ 100							+ 100				
(8)	– 700										– 700	(salary expense)
(9)									+ 120		– 120	(utility expense)
(10)		+ 4000									+ 4,000	(sales revenue)
				– 2,200							– 2,200	(cost of goods sold)
(11)										+ 133	– 133	(interest expense)
(12)			– 1,000								– 1,000	(rent expense)
(13)					– 208						– 208	(depreciation expense)
(14)								– 50			+ 50	(service revenue)
(15)	– 100										– 100	(withdrawal)
Totals	32,500	4,400	11,000	27,800	24,792	30,000	20,000	50	120	133	50,189	
			100,492					100,492				

Because profitable operations are essential to adding value to the firm, the income statement can be used to assess how well managers have performed.

Reported net income is an extremely useful figure to investors and plays a major role in their decisions. To illustrate, when Nordstrom Inc. reported healthy second-quarter earnings, the value of the company's stock surged $4.34 per share (14%). On the other hand, Adobe Systems' stock fell $3.44 per share (11%) on the day it warned of a possible small loss for its third quarter.

In recent years we have witnessed the demise of some very large prominent corporations due to fraudulent accounting practices. At the heart of these accounting scandals was management's need and desire to report profits to enhance their own wealth even if it meant creating fictitious transactions. As we discussed in Chapter 1, Congress has taken action to make firms accountable for their actions with the creation of the Sarbanes-Oxley Act which imposes strict disclosure and corporate governance mandates for all U.S. and non-U.S. public companies filing periodic reports with the Securities and Exchange Commission (SEC). The SEC now requires the chief executive officer and the chief financial officer to assume personal risk for the financial reports of their company by submitting a sworn statement asserting that the financial statements are free from any materially misleading items and that they present fairly the financial position of the company. Exhibit 2-11 contains a statement submitted by one of the corporate officers of Sears, Roebuck, and Company.

Statement of Owners' Equity

In addition to the balance sheet and the income statement, firms also prepare a **statement of owners' equity.** This statement summarizes the changes that took place in owners' equity during the period under review. Because investments and withdrawals by the owners affect owners' equity, they appear on this statement, sometimes referred to as the **statement of shareholders' equity.** Revenue and expense transactions also affect owners' equity. Instead of listing each revenue and expense transaction separately, their difference (net income) is included in the statement of owners' equity.

Exhibit 2-12 contains JG&T's statement of owners' equity for the month of January. Now refer back to Exhibit 2-10. As you can see, the statement of owners' equity reflects all of JG&T's transactions that affected owners' equity.

Relationship Between the Balance Sheet and the Income Statement

As you know, the balance sheet reports assets, liabilities, and owners' equity at a moment in time. The income statement summarizes revenue and expense transactions that occur during a period of time. Since revenue and expense transactions affect owners' equity, net income explains most of the change that takes place in owners' equity during a period. Contributions and withdrawals by owners also affect owners' equity. *Thus, the change in owners' equity is explained by net income,*

EXHIBIT 2-11 CERTIFICATION STATEMENT

I, Aylwin B. Lewis certify that:

1. I have reviewed this annual report on Form 10-K of Sears Holdings Corporation;
2. Based on my knowledge, this report does not contain any untrue statement of a material fact or omit to state a material fact necessary to make the statements made, in light of the circumstances under which such statements were made, not misleading with respect to the period covered by this report;
3. Based on my knowledge, the financial statements, and other financial information included in this report, fairly present in all material respects the financial condition, results of operations and cash flows of the registrant as of, and for, the periods presented in this report;
4. The registrant's other certifying officer(s) and I are responsible for establishing and maintaining disclosure controls and procedures (as defined in Exchange Act Rules 13a-15(e) and 15d-15(e)) and internal control over financial reporting (as defined in Exchange Act Rules 13a-15(f) and 15d-15(f)) for the registrant and have:
   (a) Designed such disclosure controls and procedures, or caused such disclosure controls and procedures to be designed under our supervision, to ensure that material information relating to the registrant, including its consolidated subsidiaries, is made known to us by others within those entities, particularly during the period in which this report is being prepared;
   (b) Designed such internal control over financial reporting, or caused such internal control over financial reporting to be designed under our supervision, to provide reasonable assurance regarding the reliability of financial reporting and the preparation of financial statements for external purposes in accordance with generally accepted accounting principles;
   (c) Evaluated the effectiveness of the registrant's disclosure controls and procedures and presented in this report our conclusions about the effectiveness of the disclosure controls and procedures, as of the end of the period covered by this report based on such evaluation; and
   (d) Disclosed in this report any change in the registrant's internal control over financial reporting that occurred during the registrant's most recent fiscal quarter (the registrant's fourth fiscal quarter in the case of an annual report) that has materially affected, or is reasonably likely to materially affect, the registrant's internal control over financial reporting, and;
5. The registrant's other certifying officer(s) and I have disclosed, based on our most recent evaluation of internal control over financial reporting, to the registrant's auditors and the audit committee of registrant's board of directors (or persons performing the equivalent functions):
   (a) All significant deficiencies and material weaknesses in the design or operation of internal control over financial reporting which are reasonably likely to adversely affect the registrant's ability to record, process, summarize and report financial information; and
   (b) Any fraud, whether or not material, that involves management or other employees who have a significant role in the registrant's internal control over financial reporting.

Date: March 14, 2006

By: /s/ AYLWIN B. LEWIS

Aylwin B. Lewis
Chief Executive Officer and President
Sears Holding Corporation

owner contributions, and owner withdrawals. Because owners' equity must equal assets minus liabilities (net assets), the changes in one side of the equation must equal the changes in the other side. Therefore, changes in net income, owner contributions, and owner withdrawals also explain changes in net assets.

EXHIBIT 2-12 STATEMENT OF OWNERS' EQUITY

Jacobs Golf and Tennis
Statement of Owners' Equity
For the Month Ended January 31, 2007

Balance, January 1	$ 0
Investment by owner	50,000
Net income	289
Withdrawal by owner	(100)
Balance, January 31	$50,189

THE ACCRUAL BASIS OF ACCOUNTING

An important aspect of a financial accounting system is the decision about when to record revenue and expense transactions. Recording a transaction in the accounting records is referred to as **recognition.** Consider JG&T's first revenue transaction in January. Customers were given golf lessons and charged $600. The customers paid $200 in January and promised to pay the remainder in February. (Keep in mind our assumption that the customers will honor this pledge.) There is little argument that at least $200 of revenue should be recorded in January. But when should the other $400 be recorded? In January when the services were provided, or in February when the cash is ultimately collected?

The **accrual basis of accounting** records revenues when goods or services have been delivered or provided, regardless of when cash is received. At the time of rendering the service, JG&T has earned the revenue; the entire $600 is recognized as revenue at that time under the accrual basis. All of JG&T's previous transactions have used the accrual basis.

The **cash basis of accounting** records revenue when cash is received. Under that approach, JG&T recognizes $200 of revenue in January and $400 of revenue in February.

Let's evaluate these two approaches. Which provides the most useful information to financial statement readers? If the income statement is viewed as providing information about increases in a firm's wealth, the accrual basis seems to be the preferable approach. In January, JG&T received not only $200 in cash, but also the right to receive $400 in the future. Recording $600 of revenue in January is appropriate.

Income statements can also be viewed as reports on a firm's performance. Which number, $600 or $200, is a better indicator of JG&T's accomplishments in January? Because $600 of golf lessons were provided in January, $600 seems a better measure of accomplishment (or performance).

Now consider one of JG&T's expense transactions. During January, $120 of utility services were consumed. This amount will be paid in February. Should a $120 expense be recorded in January or February? The accrual basis records expenses when resources are consumed (regardless of when payment is made), while the cash basis records expenses when the cash is actually paid. The utility's services were used in January, and the accrual basis would record the $120 as an expense in that month. The cash basis would defer recognition until JG&T pays the utility company in the following month.

Again, let's evaluate the usefulness of the information produced by the two approaches. Consumption of the utility services took place in January. At that time, the firm's liabilities increased, and its net worth decreased. This reduction in the firm's value should be reflected in January's income statement; the accrual basis would do this. Moreover, in measuring a firm's performance, all resources consumed in generating revenue should be shown on the same income statement as that revenue. Accountants refer to this as the **matching principle.** The utility services were consumed in January to help generate the revenue reported on January's income statement. Accordingly, the accrual basis provides a better portrayal of a firm's performance because some believe that it is less likely to be manipulated. We believe that the cash basis offers complementary perspectives that will be further described throughout this text.

GAAP requires the use of the accrual basis, yet as previously discussed, cash flow information is also important to financial statement readers. Accordingly, GAAP also requires the statement of cash flows, which is discussed in Chapter 5, "Statement of Cash Flows." Also note that some small businesses, which do not need audited financial statements, use the cash basis.

As a result of highly publicized accounting scandals the question is being raised, "Should revenue continue to be recognized on an accrual basis or should there be some form of cash basis recognition of revenue required to ensure that revenues actually earned and realized in cash are recorded?" We are likely to see changes to the long-standing accrual basis method of accounting.

Note also that GAAP assumes that firms are likely to continue in business in similar fashion as in the current year. This is known as the **going-concern concept.** If JG&T's assets were not valued as a going-concern, the golf balls would likely be almost worthless!

FORMS OF BUSINESS ORGANIZATION

Financial accounting is used by a wide variety of organizations, including businesses organized to earn a profit, nonprofit organizations, and governmental entities. This book focuses on profit-oriented enterprises, which can be organized in one of the four ways described next.

Sole Proprietorships

Sole proprietorships are businesses that are owned by one individual and usually operated by that individual. They are not separate legal entities apart from the owner, and no special legal steps are required to launch or operate this form of business. Jane's T-shirt business, discussed in Chapter 1, would probably be organized as a sole proprietorship. As another example, if you decided to earn money by mowing lawns during the summer, your business would probably be organized as a sole proprietorship.

Because no legal procedures are needed to begin operating sole proprietorships, their primary advantage is ease of formation. The major disadvantage is unlimited legal liability. Because owners are not legally distinct from their businesses, any claims against sole proprietorships are also claims against the owners' personal assets.

Although sole proprietorships are not separate legal entities, they are separate accounting (or economic) entities. The entity assumption indicates that the actions of the owner, serving as an agent of the business, can be (and should be) separated from the personal affairs of the owner. Based on this distinction, information about the transactions of the business can be accumulated via the financial accounting process. This enables the owner to assess the status and performance of the business on a stand-alone basis.

Partnerships

Partnerships are very similar to sole proprietorships, except that partnerships have more than one owner. Partnerships are not separate legal entities apart from their owners, but they are separate accounting entities. They are almost as easy to form as sole proprietorships, yet because there are multiple owners, care must be taken to specify the rights and responsibilities of each owner. This is usually done in a partnership agreement, which is a legal contract among the partners.

Corporations

Corporations differ substantially from sole proprietorships and partnerships because they are separate legal entities. They are granted their right to exist by the individual states. A corporation must develop bylaws governing its operation, issue stock to its owners (shareholders or stockholders) to represent their ownership interests, elect a board of directors who are responsible for the management of the corporation, pay taxes, and adhere to a variety of laws and regulations. Most large and many smaller businesses are organized as corporations.

As might be expected, forming a corporation is a relatively cumbersome and expensive process. Costs include filing fees paid to the state of incorporation, legal fees, and amounts paid for corporate records, such as stock certificates, bylaws, and so on. Corporations, unlike sole proprietorships and partnerships, must pay income taxes. Moreover, shareholders are also taxed on any dividends paid to them. Thus, corporations are subject to **double taxation.** Because sole proprietorships and partnerships are not separate legal entities, they do not pay income taxes; sole proprietors and partners include the income of their businesses on their individual income tax returns.

The corporate form of organization has certain advantages that can outweigh the costs. Perhaps the primary benefit is the limited liability offered to shareholders. Because the corporation is a legal entity, the corporation itself is responsible for its actions.

Although shareholders risk losing their investment, their personal assets are protected from claims against the corporation. Such is not the case for sole proprietorships and partnerships.

Hybrid Forms of Organization

Many states are now offering forms of organization that combine certain characteristics of partnerships and corporations. These forms include professional corporations, limited liability companies, and limited liability partnerships. Although an evaluation of the advantages and disadvantages of these forms of organization is beyond our scope, keep in mind that careful consideration must be given to this issue when starting a new business.

Accounting Implications

The accounting differences among these three organizational forms lie mainly in the owners' equity section of the balance sheet. The accounting for partnerships is very similar to that for sole proprietorships. Because each partner is an owner, each partner has a capital account where his or her interest in the firm is shown. The accounting for corporations is slightly more complex.

ACCOUNTING FOR CORPORATIONS

Two differences exist in the accounting for owners' equity in corporations. First, because shareholders are the owners of the corporation, this section is called shareholders' equity. Second, the shareholders' equity section is divided into two subcategories. *One category is **invested capital.** It reflects the shareholders' interest in the firm that arises from direct contributions by the shareholders.* If Harry Jacobs had formed a corporation when he started his golf and tennis shop, for example, his initial investment would be recorded by increasing both cash and the invested capital part of shareholders' equity.

ASSETS	=	LIABILITIES	+	SHAREHOLDERS' EQUITY
Cash + $50,000				Invested capital + $50,000

*The other category of shareholders' equity is **retained earnings.** This section contains the effect of revenue and expense transactions on shareholders' equity. That is, it reflects the increase (or decrease) in the shareholders' interest in the firm that arose from operations since the firm's inception.*

Consider again transaction (10) from earlier in this chapter. Inventory that was previously purchased for $2,200 was sold, on account, for $4,000. The only change in the analysis for a corporation is that the retained earnings component of shareholders' equity reflects the effect of this transaction on the shareholders' interest in the firm.

ASSETS		=	LIABILITIES	+	SHAREHOLDERS' EQUITY
Accounts receivable	Inventory				Retained earnings
+ $4,000					+ $4,000 (revenue)
	– $2,200				– $2,200 (cost of goods sold)

In Chapter 10, we will discuss, in depth, the various types of transactions that affect shareholders' equity.

Summary of Learning Objectives

1. **Define the terms assets, liabilities, and owners' equity.**
   Assets are valuable resources owned by a firm. They represent probable future economic benefits. Liabilities are present obligations of a firm. They represent probable future sacrifices of economic benefits. Owners' equity reflects the owners' interest in the firm.

2. **Explain why the balance sheet must balance.**
   The balance sheet shows two views of the same thing: the resources of the firm. The left side of the balance sheet shows the composition of a firm's resources (cash, inventory, and so on). The right side shows the amount of resources supplied by creditors and the amount supplied by owners. Because resources must be supplied by creditors or owners, the total of the left side of the balance sheet must equal the total of the right side.

3. **Describe revenues and expenses.**
   Revenues are inflows of assets (or reductions in liabilities) in exchange for providing goods and services to customers. Expenses occur when resources are consumed in order to generate revenue.

4. **Understand the basic issue underlying revenue recognition.**
   Revenue is generally recorded when the earnings process is complete and the firm has rights to assets such as accounts receivable. Since cash may not have been realized yet some firms may be tempted to prematurely record revenue in order to enhance their financial position.

5. **Use the basic accounting equation to analyze transactions.**
The basic accounting equation is

ASSETS	=	LIABILITIES	+	OWNERS' EQUITY

The financial accounting process consists of analyzing a transaction's effect on the elements of this equation. The equation balances for each transaction and for the summation of all transactions.

6. **Prepare simple balance sheets and income statements.**
Balance sheets are prepared by cumulating the effect of all transactions on the elements of the basic accounting equation. Income statements summarize all revenue and expense transactions that took place during a period of time. The difference between revenues and expenses is net income.

7. **Describe the relationship between the balance sheet and the income statement.**
Revenue and expense transactions affect owners' equity. Therefore, the income statement summarizes the impact these transactions have on the balance sheet item owners' equity.

8. **Distinguish between the accrual basis and the cash basis of accounting.**
The accrual basis recognizes revenues when they are earned, that is, when the goods are delivered or the service is rendered. The cash basis recognizes revenues when cash is received from the customer. The accrual basis recognizes expenses when resources are consumed. The cash basis recognizes expenses when cash is paid. The accrual basis provides an objective measure of performance. GAAP requires use of the accrual basis. We suggest that the cash basis also offers a useful perspective.

9. **Explain the differences between the balance sheets of sole proprietorships and those of corporations.**
The primary difference involves owners' equity. In sole proprietorships, only one component of owners' equity is used; it is referred to as capital, and it reflects the owners' interests that arise from both direct contributions and profitable operations. Corporations use two components: invested capital, which reflects shareholders' direct contributions, and retained earnings, which show the shareholders' interest that arose from profits.

KEY TERMS

Account
Accounts payable
Accounts receivable
Accrual basis of accounting
Adjustments
Advances from customers
Arms-length transaction
Assets
Balance sheet
Basic accounting equation
Capital
Cash basis of accounting
Corporation
Cost of goods sold (COGS)
Depreciation
Double taxation
Entity assumption
Executory contracts
Expenses
Fiscal year
Going-concern concept
Historical cost
Income statement
Inventory
Invested capital
Liabilities
Matching principle
Net assets
Net profit
Net worth
On account
Owners' equity
Partnership
Prepaid rent
Realized
Recognition
Relevant
Reliable
Retained earnings
Residual interest
Revenues
Sole proprietorship
Statement of owners' equity
Statement of shareholders' equity
Unearned revenue

Exercises and Problems

2-1 Describe each part of the basic accounting equation. Identify one example of each item or term in this equation and describe why it fits in that particular category.

2-2 Indicate whether each of the following statements concerning possible organization structures is true or false. If a statement is false, indicate why.

a. A sole proprietorship and its owner are legally the same entity.
b. The partners in a partnership are not liable for the debts of the partnership.
c. All partners in a partnership must agree on all decisions.
d. A sole proprietorship and its owner are the same entity for financial reporting.
e. A partnership is less risky (for the partners) than a sole proprietorship.
f. Two people can form a sole proprietorship.
g. Twenty people cannot form a partnership.
h. It is more expensive to form a partnership than a sole proprietorship.
i. Any group of people can form a partnership by oral agreement.
j. A corporation and its investors are legally the same entity.
k. The shareholders of a corporation are not liable for the debts of the corporation.
l. A publicly held corporation usually sends its financial statements to all of its owners (investors).
m. A corporation is less risky (for its owners) than a partnership or sole proprietorship.
n. It is more expensive to form a corporation than a sole proprietorship.
o. Shareholders are taxed on the corporation's net income.

2-3 Define accrual accounting. Contrast accrual accounting with cash basis accounting.

2-4 Define an asset. Define a liability. How can one firm's asset be another firm's liability?

2-5 Define owners' equity. How does this differ from retained earnings? How can one firm's asset be another firm's equity?

2-6 Indicate the effects [(1) increase, (2) decrease, (0) no effect] on the accounting equation from the following transactions:

a. Owner invested cash in the business.
b. Performed services for cash.
c. Purchased equipment by signing a note payable.
d. Customers paid in advance for services to be performed.
e. Purchased a two-year insurance policy.
f. Paid employees for the period's work.
g. Purchased supplies on account.

h. Performed services referred to in part d.
i. Paid note from part c in full, plus interest.
j. Recorded depreciation adjustment.

Transaction Analysis

2-7 The Western Fittings Corporation began business on July 1, 2007. The following transactions occurred during its first six months:

1. Three individuals each invested $30,000 in exchange for capital stock.
2. One year's rent was paid for $12,000 on July 1.
3. On August 1, several pieces of property, plant, and equipment were purchased for $75,000 on account.
4. During the six months, clothing, boots, and accessories were purchased for $60,000 cash.
5. The corporation had sales revenue of $85,000, of which $35,000 has not yet been collected in cash.
6. The cost of the clothing, boots, and accessories sold in item 5 was $55,250.
7. Employees were paid $24,000 in wages.
8. The corporation paid utilities and telephone expenses of $5,000.

Required

a. Analyze and record these transactions using the basic accounting equation.
b. Record the following adjustments for the six months ended December 31, 2007: rent expense and depreciation expense. Assume a 10-year life and zero residual value.
c. What is the net income (loss) for the six months ended December 31, 2007?

Fill in the Blanks

2-8 Find the missing elements in the following (independent) cases:

ASSETS	=	LIABILITIES	+	SHAREHOLDERS' EQUITY
a. $100,000		$ 30,000		?
b. ?		$450,000		$200,000
c. $350,000		$450,000		?
d. $675,000		?		$310,000

Transaction Analysis: Preparing Financial Statements

2-9 The following account balances are shown on November 30, 2007, for the Clever Bookstore:

Cash	$ 8,000	Accounts payable	$ 4,000
Accounts receivable	9,000	Salaries payable	2,000
Inventory	60,000	Notes payable	35,000
Supplies	3,000	J. Clever, capital	39,000
Total	$80,000	Total	$80,000

The following transactions occurred during December:

1. Paid workers the $2,000 owed them on November 30.
2. Made sales totaling $40,000. Half of the sales were for cash. The other half was on account. The cost of goods sold was $25,000.
3. Purchased inventory on account, $15,000.
4. Collected in cash $22,000 of receivables.
5. Used supplies totaling $800.
6. Paid accounts payable of $12,000.
7. Paid all December's interest on the note payable in the amount of $300.

Required

a. Analyze all transactions using the basic accounting equation. Begin your analysis by entering the November 30 account balances into a worksheet. Then enter each of the transactions above into your worksheet.

b. Prepare a balance sheet as of December 31, 2007.

c. Prepare an income statement for the month ended December 31, 2007.

Fill in the Blanks

2-10 Ascertain the missing items (A–L) in the following independent situations. (**Note:** You do not have to find the answers in any particular sequence.)

	1	*2*	*3*
Assets, January 1	$ 5,000	E	I
Assets, December 31	$ 8,000	F	$ 9,000
Liabilities, January 1	A	$ 2,000	$ 9,000
Liabilities, December 31	$ 3,000	$ 2,200	J
Owners' equity, January 1	$ 3,000	$ 4,000	K
Owners' equity, December 31	B	$ 4,800	$ 7,000
Revenues	$20,000	$15,000	L
Expenses	$18,500	G	$20,000
Contributions by owners	$ 1,000	H	$ 1,000
Withdrawals by owners	C	$ 1,200	$ 3,000
Net income	D	$ 2,000	$ 5,000

Note: The solutions for Situation 1 are shown below:

January 1:	Assets	=	Liabilities	+	Owners' equity
	$5,000	=	(A)	+	$3,000
	$5,000	=	$2,000	+	$3,000
December 31:	Assets	=	Liabilities	+	Owners' equity
	$8,000	=	$3,000	+	(B)
	$8,000	=	$3,000	+	$5,000
	Revenues	−	Expenses	=	Net income
	$20,000	−	$18,500	=	(D)
	$20,000	−	$18,500	=	$1,500

Beginning owners' equity + Contributions by owners − Withdrawals by owners + Net Income = Ending owners' equity

$3,000 + $1,000 − (C) + $1,500 = $5,000

$3,000 + $1,000 − $500 + $1,500 = $5,000

Analyzing Investment Alternatives

2-11 Assume that you inherit $10,000, which according to the terms of the bequest must be invested in a single company. After much research, you find two attractive alternatives: The Salt Company and The Pepper Company.

Required

a. On the basis of the following limited information, which of the following would you prefer (M = millions of dollars)?

	Salt Co.	Pepper Co.
Total assets	$40M	$25M
Net income	$ 4M	$ 4M

b. If you then find the following additional information about each company's liabilities, which company would you prefer? Why?

	Salt Co.	Pepper Co.
Total liabilities	$20M	$23M

c. If you then read a newspaper article predicting each firm's future income prospects, which firm is now preferable? Why?

	Salt Co.	Pepper Co.
Next year's predicted net income	$ 1M	$10M

d. What additional information might you find helpful in making the decision to invest in either of these two companies?

Transaction Analysis: Describing Underlying Events

2-12 Shown below are several transactions recorded by Beth's coffee shop, The Bitter Bean (TBB):

	ASSETS	=	LIABILITIES	+	OWNERS' EQUITY
a.	Cash, + $30,000				Capital, + $30,000
b.	Inventory, + $12,000		Accounts payable, + $12,000		
c.	Cash, – $3,000		Loans, – $3,000		
d.			Loans, – $27,000		Capital, + $27,000
e.	Accounts receivable, + $10,000				Revenue, + $10,000
f.	Inventory, – $3,000				Costs of goods sold, – $3,000
g.	Cash, + $8,000 Accounts receivable, – $8,000				
h.			Accounts payable, + $30,000		Operating expenses, – $30,000

Required

For each transaction, describe the event or activity that occurred. For example:

Answer: The firm borrowed $20,000.

Analyzing Effects of Cash and Accrual Accounting

2-13 Assume that you are auditing a small bank that uses the cash basis of accounting to record interest on its customers' accounts and uses the accrual basis of accounting for interest earned on its investments.

a. If most of the bank's investments were earning daily interest, while most of the bank's customers had their money invested in five-year certificates of deposit, do you think that the income reported by the bank represents a fair or useful measure of accomplishment? Why?

b. Reconsider your prior answer. What if you find out that most of the five-year certificates of deposit had just been issued? What if you find out that the bank issued and redeemed the same number of five-year certificates every month? How do the issues of timing or renewal cycles affect your view of this situation?

CHAPTER 3

THE BALANCE SHEET

Learning Objectives

1. *Identify basic balance sheet terms.*
2. *Recognize typical assets, liabilities, and owners' equity found on most balance sheets.*
3. *Understand how balance sheet items are ordered and classified.*
4. *Appreciate why balance sheets differ for firms in different industries.*
5. *Use balance sheet relationships to obtain information useful to investors and lenders.*
6. *Be alert to the limitations as well as the usefulness of balance sheet information.*
7. *Identify which balance sheet items typically affect cash flows.*

INTRODUCTION

This chapter focuses on the **balance sheet,** which is often called the **statement of financial position.** Beginning with formal definitions of the basic elements of the balance sheet, the following discussion describes the types of assets, liabilities, and owners' equity that are found on the balance sheets of most business firms. A variety of balance sheet ratios are presented to show how managers and investors use balance sheet information in making decisions.

ELEMENTS OF THE BALANCE SHEET

The previous two chapters introduced you to the three basic financial statements. They showed how transactions and accruals cause changes in basic financial statements. This chapter focuses solely on the balance sheet, which reflects the firm's resources and its sources of financing. At any given date, the balance sheet shows the sources from which the firm has obtained its resources and the ways in which those resources are currently employed. Recall the basic accounting equation:

ASSETS = LIABILITIES + OWNERS' EQUITY

Another way to state this relationship is:

Uses of resources = Sources of resources

In other words, liabilities and owners' equity are the sources of the firm's funds, and the listing of assets shows the way in which the firm's managers have used those funds. The balance sheet for Sample Company at the end of 2007 (Exhibit 3-1) illustrates these relationships.

Uses of resources	=	Sources of resources
Assets	=	Liabilities + Owners' equity
$2,057,000	=	$1,199,000 + $858,000
$2,057,000	=	$2,057,000

Viewed in this manner, there is no mystery as to why both sides of the balance sheet have the same total; they are merely two sides of a coin, or two ways of describing the total wealth of the firm. The firm's wealth can be viewed in terms of **sources of financing** (from creditors and owners) and in terms of **uses of resources** (owning or controlling assets).

The balance sheet can also be viewed as the cumulative result of the firm's past activities. Liabilities represent the total amount the firm has borrowed during its existence, minus the amounts that have been repaid to date. *The owners' equity items show the total amount invested by owners, plus the total profits earned by the firm during previous periods, minus any amounts that have been distributed to owners.* Similarly, the assets of the firm represent the total resources obtained by the

EXHIBIT 3-1 A BALANCE SHEET

Sample Company
Balance Sheet
at December 31, 2007

ASSETS			**LIABILITIES AND OWNERS' EQUITY**		
Current assets			Current liabilities		
Cash	$110,000		Accounts payable	$260,000	
Accounts receivable	466,000		Notes payable	225,000	
Inventories	812,000		Warranty obligations	112,000	
Prepaid expenses	32,000		Accrued expenses	75,000	
Total current assets		$1,420,000	Taxes payable	27,000	
Noncurrent assets			Total current liabilities		$ 699,000
Land	$85,000		Noncurrent liabilities		
Buildings and equipment			Bonds payable	$350,000	
(net of accumulated			Mortgage payable	150,000	
depreciation of $313,000)	552,000		Total noncurrent liabilities		500,000
Total noncurrent assets		637,000	Total liabilities		$1,199,000
Total assets		$2,057,000	Shareholders' equity		
			Invested capital	$600,000	
			Retained earnings	258,000	
			Total shareholders' equity		858,000
			Total liabilities and shareholders' equity		$2,057,000

firm from lenders and owners, minus those that have been consumed in the firm's operations, repaid to lenders, or distributed to owners.

Definitions of Assets, Liabilities, and Owners' Equity

The Financial Accounting Standards Board (FASB) has identified the essential characteristics of assets, liabilities, and owners' equity. The FASB definitions, which were introduced in Chapter 2, and are summarized in Exhibit 3-2, provide a frame of reference that helps accountants identify the items to be included in the balance sheet. They will be referred to frequently during the remaining discussions in this chapter. For now, note that according to the FASB's definitions, *assets represent probable future benefits, liabilities represent probable future sacrifices, and owners' equity is the residual amount, or difference, between assets and liabilities.*

The following pages introduce you to the types of individual assets, liabilities, and owners' equity to be found on the balance sheets of most business firms. In studying these individual balance sheet items, keep in mind the FASB's definitions shown in Exhibit 3-2.

EXHIBIT 3-2 FASB DEFINITIONS OF ASSETS, LIABILITIES, AND OWNERS' EQUITY

Assets are probable future economic benefits obtained or controlled by a particular entity as a result of past transactions or events.

Liabilities are probable future sacrifices of economic benefits arising from present obligations of a particular entity to transfer assets or provide services to other entities in the future as a result of past transactions or events.

Equity is the residual interest in the assets of an entity that remains after deducting liabilities. In a business enterprise, the equity is the ownership interest.

SOURCE: *Statement of Financial Accounting Concepts No. 6,* "Elements of Financial Statements" (Stamford, CT: FASB, 1980).

Assets

As noted in Exhibit 3-2, assets represent "probable future economic benefits obtained or controlled by a particular entity as a result of past transactions or events." Future economic benefits come in many forms. For example, cash is an asset because it represents purchasing power; the firm can use cash to acquire goods and services, to repay debts, or to make distributions to owners. Inventories are assets because they are merchandise intended for sale to customers for cash and other assets. The firm's buildings and equipment are assets because they enable the firm to perform its operations and to earn profits in the future.

Assets typically represent tangible economic resources, such as cash, buildings, and trucks. On the other hand, some economic resources are intangible, such as patent rights and copyrights to a text or musical score. Assets may also be represented by promises of future payments from customers who bought goods or services on credit. Assets can be created by contract or acquisition of property rights, and yet they may not be visible to the human eye. All assets, however, have a common characteristic in that they represent probable future economic benefits to the firm.

Asset Classifications

Assets are classified into two overall categories: **current assets** and **noncurrent assets.** This distinction is based on the *expected length of time* before the asset is consumed or converted to cash. Current assets include cash and other assets that will typically become cash or be consumed in one year or one operating cycle, whichever is longer. Current assets are used quickly and repeatedly during a firm's normal operations. This notion of using assets on a cyclical basis corresponds to a concept called **turnover.** Current assets turn over quickly, anywhere from daily to annually, and are usually generated in the normal course of business operations. The notion of turnover is used to differentiate current assets from other asset categories that are used (turned over) much more slowly over a number of years.

To illustrate, Sample Company's balance sheet in Exhibit 3-1 shows that the firm's total assets of $2,057,000 are comprised of $1,420,000 in current assets and $637,000 in noncurrent assets. The balance sheet equation is easily expanded to show this additional detail:

ASSETS		=	LIABILITIES	+	OWNERS' EQUITY
Current	Noncurrent				
$1,420,000	+ 637,000	=	$1,199,000	+	$858,000
$2,057,000		=	$2,057,000		

This classification of assets is used when analyzing the firm's liquidity. **Liquidity** reflects the firm's ability to generate sufficient cash to meet its operating cash needs and to pay its obligations as they become due. This focus on liquidity will become clear as we discuss the ordering and valuation of individual current assets in the next section.

Current Assets

Current assets are listed in the order in which they will be consumed or converted to cash. For example, Sample Company's current assets are listed (in Exhibit 3-1) in the following typical order of maturity or **collectibility:**

- cash and cash equivalents,
- accounts receivable,
- inventories, and
- prepaid expenses.

Cash and **cash equivalents** include currency, bank deposits, and various marketable securities that can be turned into cash on short notice merely by contacting a bank or broker. These amounts are presently available to meet the firm's cash payment requirements. Note that only securities that are purchased within 90 days of their maturity dates, may be classified as cash equivalents.

Accounts receivable represent credit sales that have not been collected yet. They are converted into cash as soon as the customers or clients pay their bills (their accounts). Accounts receivable should turn over, or be collected, within the firm's normal collection period, which is usually 30 or 60 days. A slower accounts receivable turnover embodies more risk to the organization because the probability of nonpayment usually increases as turnover decreases. Overdue accounts may imply that the customer is either unable to pay or is unwilling to pay because of disagreement over the amounts billed. Both cases imply that the amount of cash that will ultimately be collected is less than the amount originally billed to the customer.

Managers are interested less in the total amount of accounts receivable than in the estimated cash to be generated from collections of the accounts. For this reason, accounts receivable are listed on the balance sheet as the amounts estimated to be actually collectible. This amount is termed the **net realizable value** of the receivables. For example, if management estimates that some portion of the amounts billed to customers will ultimately be **uncollectible,** and then the estimated uncollectible portion will be deducted in valuing the accounts receivable on the balance sheet. The uncollectible portion of the receivables is termed an allowance account and is discussed in Chapter 6.

Inventory represents items that have been purchased or manufactured for sale to customers. That is, inventory can either be created through the manufacturing and assembly efforts of the organization or be acquired from others and held for resale. Inventory is the "stuff of commerce" dating back to merchants on camels and pirates raiding the high seas looking for bounty. Inventory can be as prosaic as black tea or salt, or it can be as glamorous as gold bullion or silver coins. Today, inventory is often "high tech," such as silicon wafers, memory chips, or disk drives. Should the company discover that some of its inventory is not salable, or marketable only at a greatly reduced price, the reported value of the inventory should be reduced accordingly.

Prepaid expenses, the final category of current assets shown in Exhibit 3-1, represent unexpired assets such as insurance premiums. Insurance policies, for example, are frequently paid ahead on an annual basis. The unexpired portion, the portion of the policy paid for but not yet used, is shown as part of prepaid expenses, which are interpreted as current assets. Prepaids are usually minor elements of the balance sheet, and, in the usual course of events, prepaids will not be converted or turned into cash. Instead, the rights to future benefits will be used up in future periods.

The Operating Cycle and Liquidity

Manufacturing and merchandising firms' operating cycles include turning inventory into cash. Using three of the current assets discussed earlier, the **operating cycle** evolves from the purchase of inventory, to the exchange of inventory for a promised payment by a customer (an account receivable), and finally to the conversion of the receivable into cash. Operating cycles may vary in length from just a few days (in the case of food retailers) to months (consumer appliance sellers) or even years (defense contractors). Exhibit 3-3 illustrates the operating cycle.

The more quickly this cycle is completed, the more quickly the inventory is turned into cash, and liquidity is higher. When the operating cycle becomes longer, the firm's liquidity usually is lower. Should the operating cycle become too long, the firm will be forced to incur debt in order to pay its suppliers of inventory. To some extent, the length of the operating cycle is outside management's control. The length of time permitted customers to pay their accounts, for example, may be governed by industry practice. To attract and retain customers,

EXHIBIT 3-3 THE OPERATING CYCLE

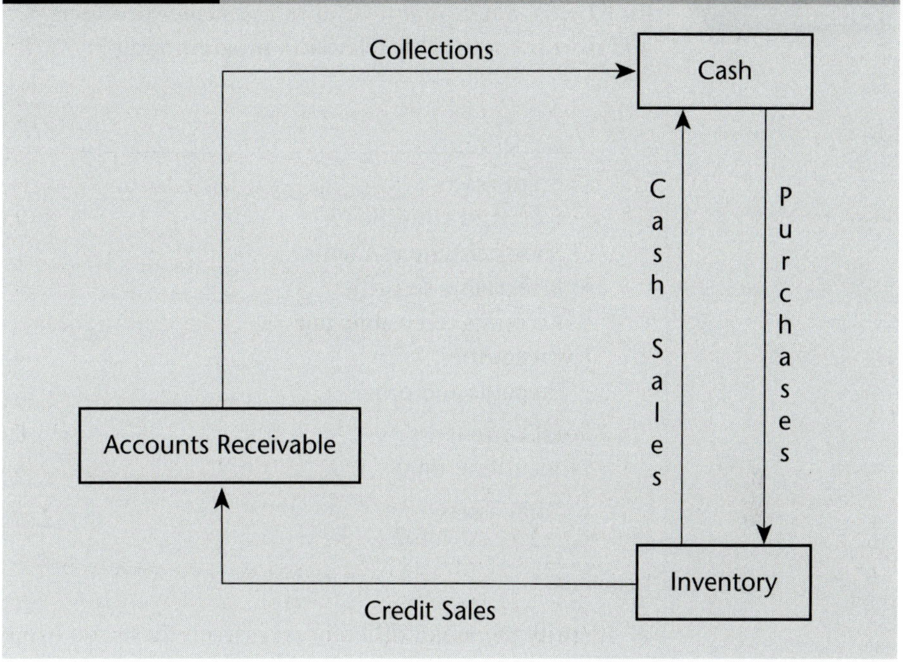

the firm may need to offer credit terms as liberal as those offered by its competitors. Likewise, the amount of inventory that the firm keeps on hand may be related to the length of its "production pipeline." Some products require a lengthy production process that entails a substantial investment in inventory at various stages of completion.

On the other hand, managers have significant influence on accounts receivable turnover and on inventory turnover. For instance, managers may have considerable leeway in offering credit terms to customers or in deciding how much inventory to keep on hand. The analyst, in attempting to assess the firm's liquidity, needs to understand these underlying factors that cause differences in the amounts of accounts receivable and inventories across firms and industries. Reality Check 3-1 illustrates how the composition of current assets differs for two firms engaged in different industries.

Noncurrent Assets

Noncurrent assets are long-term assets that are used in the conduct of the business. Whereas current assets are liquid and turn over in relatively short time periods, noncurrent assets usually turn over very slowly, on the order of once in several years. In other words, while the operating cycle for current assets is usually less than a year, the replacement cycle for noncurrent assets is longer than a

REALITY CHECK 3-1

The following schedule summarizes the current assets from recent balance sheets for Costco, a national retailer of consumer products, and Monster, a producer and distributor of cable television programming:

	Costco	*Monster*
	(Dollars in millions)	
Current assets		
Cash and equivalents	$ 2,063	$ 197
Short-term investments	1,397	—
Marketable securities	—	124
Accounts receivable, net	400	393
Inventories	4,015	—
Prepaids and other	212	60
Total current assets	8,087	774
Noncurrent, total	8,427	906
Total assets	$16,514	$1,680

Required

a. Identify the major differences between these two firms in the composition of current assets. Try to explain these differences in terms of the types of goods and services that each company produces.

b. Based solely on the information provided here, which company appears to be more liquid?

SOLUTION

a. The major differences in the composition of current assets are the amounts invested in inventories and accounts receivable.

- **Inventories:** Costco is a retailer of consumer products and maintains inventories of merchandise in regional warehouses and retail stores. Monster is a service firm and, hence, does not require inventories.
- **Accounts receivable:** Monster invests about 23.4% of its total assets in customer accounts receivable ($393/$1,680 = 23.4%), whereas Costco's accounts receivable represent a much smaller portion of total assets. Providers of an online service, such as recruiting, sell primarily on credit and have relatively large accounts receivable balances, while retailing firms such as Costco derive much of their revenues from cash and credit card sales and require smaller accounts receivable balances.

b. Costco's current assets include a substantial proportion in inventories, while Monster's current assets consist primarily of cash and accounts receivable. As a result, most analysts would consider Monster to be more liquid, based solely on the information provided.

year. In a high-tech organization, however, some noncurrent assets may be replaced more frequently.

All noncurrent assets are recorded on the balance sheet at their historical acquisition costs. The disadvantage of this is that as time passes the historical costs of many noncurrent assets become out of date relative to their current market values. Consequently, they indicate little about the market value of the organization and about the future resources necessary to replace the assets. However, the historical costs listed on the balance sheet do represent the costs of these assets that will eventually be consumed by future operations.

Property, Plant, and Equipment

For most firms, noncurrent assets consist mainly of **property, plant, and equipment.** These assets are widely referred to as **fixed assets. Property** usually represents the land on which the firm's offices, factories, and other facilities are located. In most cases, property is a relatively minor portion of the total noncurrent assets, yet in some cases, such as firms engaged in mining, logging, or oil and gas exploration, property constitutes a major operating asset. Property is also valued on the balance sheet at its historical acquisition cost, and because property is usually one of the oldest assets held by an organization, its recorded historical cost is often the most out of date in terms of current market values.

Buildings and equipment represent the largest category of noncurrent assets, as shown in Exhibit 3-1. **Buildings** or **plant** may be office, retail, or factory buildings; warehouses or supply depots; or hospitals or health clinics. **Equipment** includes office desks and chairs, tools, drill presses, robots, computers, x-ray and other scanners, podiums, and so on. In other words, buildings and equipment are the primary productive assets of many organizations. Whether widgets or rings are produced, whether knowledge or health is improved, buildings and equipment are necessary to produce most goods and services.

Because buildings and equipment are long-lived assets, it would not make sense to treat their entire cost as expenses in the year they are acquired. On the other hand, because buildings and equipment gradually lose their economic value over time, it does not make sense to wait until the end of their service lives to recognize their declining usefulness to the firm. As a consequence, accountants *gradually and systematically reduce the reported values of buildings and equipment* on successive balance sheets in order to allocate expenses to individual years of asset use. The reduction in the reported value of buildings and equipment during a period is called **depreciation expense.**

On the balance sheet, the total amount of depreciation expense recognized to that date is called **accumulated depreciation.** It is subtracted from the initial cost of the asset. The resulting carrying value is referred to as the **net book value** of the asset. In Exhibit 3-1, the net book value of $552,000 for buildings and equipment is calculated by subtracting the $313,000 of accumulated depreciation from the original cost of $865,000:

Buildings and equipment	$865,000
Less: Accumulated depreciation	– 313,000
Net book value	$552,000

In other words, of the original cost of $865,000, a total of $313,000 has been expensed, or written off, in previous periods. The net book value of these assets is *unlikely to reflect their current resale value because of changes in technology, price inflation, and many other factors.* Accumulated depreciation is not an attempt to adjust carrying values to current resale values. It also does not represent any cash or other investments that the company has set aside for replacing the buildings and equipment. Rather, depreciating an asset is an attempt to apportion or allocate its original cost as an expense to the periods that benefit from the asset's use.

The net book value of buildings and equipment can be used to *estimate the remaining productive capacity* of the organization. For example, Sample Company's buildings and equipment are about 36% depreciated ($313,000 accumulated depreciation divided by $865,000 initial cost). If Sample Company does not purchase additional buildings and equipment, then each successive balance sheet will show a lower net book value for these assets. Such a declining net book value will signal to analysts that Sample Company is not replenishing its **productive capacity** on a regular basis.

As a practical matter, most firms regularly invest in new plant and equipment and, as a result, the net book value of these assets usually increases over time. The percentage relationships between the initial cost and the accumulated depreciation of these assets may give analysts a rough gauge of the overall age of the firm's productive capacity. However, the analyst must usually refer to other disclosures in the financial statements to evaluate the firm's productive capacity.

Other Noncurrent Assets

In addition to property, plant, and equipment, many firms possess other noncurrent assets such as intangibles. **Intangibles** are noncurrent assets that lack physical substance and yet are important resources in the regular operations of a business. Intangibles often consist of legal rights, such as patents or copyrights. Such legal rights are vital to the operations of many firms and, in some cases, may be the most valuable resources owned by the organization.

Consider, for example, the importance of copyrights to computer software developers or book publishers. The value of such firms depends almost entirely on the value of the copyrights that protect their legal rights to the products they have developed. Accounting for intangible assets with finite lives is similar to that of buildings and equipment because the initial costs are systematically recognized as expenses over the years that benefit from the use of the assets. These intangible assets are valued on the balance sheet at their historical costs, minus any amounts subsequently recognized as expenses. The term **amortization** is used in place of depreciation when referring to the consumption of finite life intangible assets.

Another important type of intangible asset is goodwill. **Goodwill** is a general label used by accountants to denote the economic value of an acquired firm in excess of the value of its identifiable net assets (assets minus liabilities). Goodwill reflects the adage that "the value of the whole differs from the sum of its parts." This economic value is largely due to factors such as customer loyalty, employee competence and morale, management expertise, and so on. In other words, the value of a successful business firm is usually much greater than the total values of its individual assets.

The balance sheet recognition of goodwill depends on whether the firm's goodwill is internally generated or externally acquired. **Internally generated goodwill** evolves gradually as the firm develops a good reputation and customer base. It also evolves as the firm cultivates successful relationships with its suppliers, trains and retains a skilled labor force, and conducts other value-enhancing activities. The costs incurred in generating this goodwill are generally not recorded as assets by the firm and instead are recognized as expenses when incurred. The argument used to support the immediate expensing of these costs is the uncertainty and subjectivity involved in identifying future benefits. **Externally acquired goodwill,** on the other hand, usually arises when one business firm acquires another. In this case, appraisers can more objectively determine the amount that the purchaser is paying for the goodwill of the seller. Externally acquired goodwill is deemed to have an infinite life, meaning that it is not amortized. Instead, management is required to regularly evaluate the goodwill's carrying value to determine if it must be written down due to impairment. Goodwill is discussed more extensively in Chapter 7 and TOPICMOD-V, which deals with reporting business combinations.

The composition of noncurrent assets, and the relative amounts of current to noncurrent assets, varies across industries. Reality Check 3-2 shows how noncurrent assets differ between two firms in different industries.

Assets: Summary and Evaluation

Before leaving the asset side of the balance sheet, it is helpful to summarize the conventions used by accountants to define and value the firm's assets. We also identify here some of the limitations faced by analysts who must use asset values shown in the balance sheet to evaluate the firm's liquidity and productive capacity.

As we have seen, accountants classify assets into two broad groups: current and noncurrent. In reporting current assets, the focus is on liquidity. For this reason, current assets are generally valued at the lower of their acquisition costs or present resale values. An exception to this rule is made for investments in the securities of other firms, as we discuss in Chapter 6. These practices are useful to the analyst concerned with the firm's ability to meet its short-term cash needs.

Noncurrent assets, on the other hand, are generally valued at their acquisition costs minus amounts that have been recognized as expenses in previous periods. These previously recognized expenses will have been shown as depreciation

REALITY CHECK 3-2

The following schedule summarizes the noncurrent assets reported in recent balance sheets of Hewlett-Packard, a company that designs, manufactures, and services electronic data and communications systems, and ConocoPhillips, an international, integrated energy company.

	Hewlett-Packard	*Conoco-Phillips*
	(Dollars in millions)	
Current assets (total)	$43,334	$19,612
Noncurrent assets		
Property, plant, and equipment (at cost)	13,880	76,332
Less: Accumulated depreciation	(7,429)	(21,663)
Net	6,451	54,669
Long-term receivables and other	27,532	32,718
Total noncurrent assets	33,983	87,387
Total assets	$77,317	$106,999

Required

a. Identify the major differences between these two firms in the composition of noncurrent assets. Try to explain these differences based on the types of products that each company produces.

b. Based solely on the information provided here, which company appears to have the older assets?

SOLUTION

a. ConocoPhillips invests 81.7% of its resources in noncurrent assets ($87,387/$106,999 = 81.7%), and the corresponding amount for Hewlett-Packard is just 44% ($33,983/$77,317 = 44%). ConocoPhillips is a highly capital-intensive firm because the technology related to energy research and exploration requires large investments in plant and equipment. Energy firms also usually invest in properties containing natural resources (such as crude oil) used in refining procedures. In comparison, Hewlett-Packard is moderately capital intensive because of the property, plant, and equipment required by its product development and manufacturing activities.

b. Hewlett-Packard appears to have the older assets, which are about 53.5% depreciated ($7,429/$13,880 = 53.5%), while ConocoPhillips' are about 28.4% depreciated ($21,663/$76,332 = 28.4%). These percentages are only approximations, however, because these amounts include property (land) that is not being depreciated.

of buildings and equipment or as amortization of intangibles such as patents or copyrights. In reporting noncurrent assets, the focus is on the **operating capacity** of the firm; that is, the firm must focus on its long-lived assets, both tangible and intangible, which are necessary in order for the firm to produce goods or services. The carrying values of these noncurrent assets represent the portion of their original acquisition costs that will be recognized as expenses in future periods. The carrying values of noncurrent assets rarely reflect their market values because inflation has usually caused asset replacement costs to increase beyond their reported values.

The experienced financial statement analyst is alert to two central issues in examining a firm's asset structure as reported on the balance sheet:

1. *Different valuation methods are used* for various types of assets (cost, market values, lower of cost or market value).
2. Many assets that are critical to the firm's successful operations are *not shown* on the balance sheet.

With respect to these "missing" assets, chief executive officers (CEOs) are fond of proclaiming:

"Our employees are our most important resource."
"Research today provides profits tomorrow."
"Our reputation for quality ensures our success."

Regardless of these lofty statements, resources such as employee morale, productivity, research and development expertise, and a loyal and satisfied network of customers and suppliers are absent from the balance sheet. Accountants justify these omissions either because these valuable resources do not meet the conditions stated in the FASB's definition of assets (refer to Exhibit 3-2) or because there is no reliable method for measuring or valuing such resources.

Consider Target's assets shown on its balance sheet:

CONSOLIDATED STATEMENTS OF FINANCIAL POSITION (Target, excerpts)

(millions, except footnotes)	*January 28, 2006*	*January 29, 2005*
Assets		
Cash and cash equivalents	**$ 1,648**	$ 2,245
Accounts receivable, net	**5,666**	5,069
Inventory	**5,838**	5,384
Other current assets	**1,253**	1,224
Total current assets	**14,405**	13,922
Property and equipment		
Land	**4,449**	3,804
Buildings and improvements	**14,174**	12,518
Fixtures and equipment	**3,219**	2,990

CONSOLIDATED STATEMENTS OF FINANCIAL POSITION (cont.)

(millions, except footnotes)	*January 28, 2006*	*January 29, 2005*
Computer hardware and software	**2,214**	1,998
Construction-in-progress	**1,158**	962
Accumulated depreciation	**(6,176)**	(5,412)
Property and equipment, net	**19,038**	16,860
Other non-current assets	**1,552**	1,511
Total assets	**$34,995**	$32,293

All of these assets are relatively easy to understand and interpret. Note that accumulated depreciation is shown as a negative number, deducted from all of the "Property and equipment" assets. Note also the "Other" assets included in both current and non-current assets. Neither of these other asset categories is very large, relative to all of the remaining assets.

Liabilities

As noted in Exhibit 3-2, **liabilities** represent "probable future sacrifices of economic benefits" that are the result of past transactions or events. Many times they entail cash payments to other entities, such as repayment to lenders of amounts that have been previously borrowed. The concept of a liability is somewhat broader than this. Liabilities include any probable obligation that the firm has incurred as a consequence of its past activities. For example, many firms warranty their products and consequently are obliged to perform repairs or pay refunds when defects are later uncovered, so, as you can see, not all liabilities require that the firm repay specific dollar amounts on specified dates. Moreover, some liabilities require estimation and judgment in order to determine their amounts. All liabilities, however, have a common characteristic: they represent probable future economic sacrifices by the firm arising from past transactions or events.

Liability Classifications

Just as with assets, liabilities are classified into two overall categories: current liabilities and noncurrent liabilities. The distinction is based on the length of time before the liability will be repaid or otherwise satisfied by the firm and on whether payment will require the use of assets that are classified as current. **Current liabilities** are short-term obligations that are expected to utilize cash or other current assets within a year or an operating cycle (whichever is longer). **Noncurrent liabilities** represent obligations that generally require payment over periods longer than a year.

To illustrate, Sample Company's balance sheet in Exhibit 3-1 shows that the firm's total liabilities of $1,199,000 are comprised of $699,000 in current liabilities and $500,000 in noncurrent liabilities. The following balance sheet equation shows this additional detail:

ASSETS		=	LIABILITIES		+	OWNERS' EQUITY
Current	Noncurrent		Current	Noncurrent		
$1,420,000 +	637,000	=	$699,000 +	$500,000	+	$858,000
$2,057,000		=			$2,057,000	

CURRENT LIABILITIES. The current liabilities of Sample Company, shown in Exhibit 3-1, consist of accounts payable, notes payable, warranty obligations, accrued expenses, and taxes payable. These liabilities represent various claims against the firm's economic resources.

Accounts payable usually represent debts that the firm incurs in purchasing inventories and supplies for manufacturing or resale purposes. Accounts payable also includes amounts that the firm owes for other services used in its operations, such as rentals, insurance, utilities, and so on. Accounts payable are often called trade debt because they represent liabilities that occur in the normal course of any trade or business.

Notes payable, the next current liability shown in Exhibit 3-1, is a more formal current liability than the accounts payable. A note may be signed when cash is borrowed from a bank (or from your father!). The note represents a legal document that a court can enforce.

Warranty obligations represent the firm's estimated future costs to fulfill its obligations for repair or refund guarantees. These obligations refer to any products sold or services provided prior to the balance sheet date. Unlike accounts and notes payable, the exact amount of the firm's obligations for warranties cannot be determined by referring to purchase documents, formal contracts, or similar evidence. Instead, the amount reported for the warranty obligation is based on management's judgment about future claims for repairs and refunds that may arise from past sales. The amount reported is an estimate, based in part on the past experience of the firm and its competitors. Recall that the FASB defines liabilities in terms of "probable future economic sacrifices" (refer to Exhibit 3-2). If Sample Company's products have required warranty repairs in the past, then it is probable that items sold recently will also require warranty repairs in the future. Because the sales have already occurred, the obligation exists at the balance sheet date, and these estimated amounts must be reported as liabilities.

The next item listed among Sample Company's current liabilities is **accrued expenses,** which represent liabilities for services already consumed but not yet paid for or included elsewhere in liabilities. These accrued liabilities usually constitute only a minor part of current liabilities. Examples of accrued expenses are wages that have been earned but not paid, or revenues that have been received already, but the services have not yet been performed.

Taxes payable comprise the final account listed among the current liabilities of Sample Company. Taxes payable represents unpaid taxes that are owed to the government and will be paid within a year. Taxes payable may include employee withholding taxes, unemployment taxes, employer income taxes, or any number of other taxes that are incurred in the normal course of operations. Taxes payable are typically a relatively minor portion of current liabilities because governmental units require that taxes be paid on a timely basis.

The current liabilities of Sample Company are a representative sample of many short-term liabilities. Businesses engage in many credit-based transactions; most sales to businesses involve accounts receivable, and most purchases by businesses correspondingly involve accounts payable. As a result, the largest of the current liabilities usually consists of **trade accounts payable.** The other liability items, although less significant in dollar amount, also represent common business transactions and circumstances.

NONCURRENT LIABILITIES. **Noncurrent liabilities** generally have longer maturities than the current liabilities discussed in the preceding section. Their maturity date is more than one year. Most noncurrent liabilities represent contracts to repay debts at specified future dates. In addition, these borrowing agreements often place some restrictions on the activities of the firm until the debt is fully repaid. In Chapter 9, we discuss a variety of different borrowing arrangements that are widely used.

Exhibit 3-1 shows that Sample Company has two types of noncurrent liabilities: bonds payable and mortgage payable. These liabilities are similar because they require Sample Company to make future payments of interest and principal. Yet they differ in terms of the **collateral** that Sample Company used to obtain the loan.

Bonds payable are a major source of funds for larger business firms. They represent liabilities that the firm incurs by selling a contract called a bond. A **bond** contains the firm's promise to pay interest periodically (usually every six months) and to repay the money originally borrowed **(principal)** when the bond matures. The amount of money that the firm receives from investors for its bonds depends on investors' views about the riskiness of the firm and the prevailing rate of interest. Investors rely on the ability of the firm to generate sufficient cash flows from its operations to meet the payments as they become due.

Mortgage payable is similar to bonds payable because firms must also make **principal** and **interest payments,** as they are due. Unlike most bonds, a mortgage represents a pledge of certain assets that will revert to the lender if the debt is not paid. The simplest example of a mortgage is that of a bank holding title to your house until your loan is fully paid. If the loan is not paid, the bank can sell the house and use the proceeds to pay off the debt. Mortgages on factories and hospitals are very similar. The problem in such cases is that there are often very few buyers of specialized assets such as factory buildings and equipment. In such cases, possible mortgage default represents more risk and higher costs to lenders. It also indicates that most lenders will cooperate with borrowers to find alternative solutions to avoid defaults. From an analytical perspective, the analyst or manager must make sure that mortgage terms are being satisfied and that payments have been promptly remitted. For both bonds and mortgages, analysts will try to discern whether cash flows from operations are sufficient to pay the interest and principal.

Liabilities: Summary and Evaluation

Before leaving the liabilities or "borrowed resources" part of the balance sheet, it is useful to summarize various liabilities and to point out some limitations faced by analysts in assessing the firm's liabilities.

Liabilities are classified as either current or noncurrent, based on their maturity dates. The current liabilities of the firm are closely related to its operations. As examples, trade accounts payable arise as a direct consequence of purchasing inventory; accrued expenses and taxes payable result from the firm's operating and tax expenses; and product warranty obligations occur because the firm has sold products covered by warranties. For this reason, analysts often refer to these types of obligations as **spontaneous or operating liabilities.**

In contrast, noncurrent liabilities consist mainly of long-term borrowing contracts that managers have negotiated with investors, banks, and other parties. This type of borrowing reflects a deliberate decision by managers to obtain funds from lenders, rather than to obtain additional investments from owners. All firms face a fundamental decision about how resources will be financed through long-term borrowing or how much should be invested by owners.

Financial statement users are concerned with the firm's ability to pay both its short-term and long-term obligations as they mature. Later in this chapter, we discuss some ratios that are useful for making these assessments. The analyst is aware of two important features of liability reporting. First, not all liabilities result from promises by the firm to repay specific amounts at determinable future dates. Instead, many liabilities require estimates of future events, such as the warranty obligations reported in Sample Company's balance sheet. Many other obligations reported by business firms entail similar liability estimates, as we discuss later in Chapters 8 and 9.

Second, the analyst is aware that some potential obligations of business firms either are not reported on the balance sheet or are reported at amounts that do not adequately reflect their potential future claims against the assets of the firm. Consider, for example, lawsuits against the firm. At present, tobacco firms are disputing a lengthy list of ailments allegedly associated with cigarette smoking. Similarly, large chemical and nuclear industry firms are being sued over toxic wastes. In these cases, the potential damages awarded to plaintiffs could result in awards of billions of dollars. Although these potentially ruinous lawsuits are based on business activities prior to the current balance sheet date, none of these firms reports significant contingent liabilities because the loss cannot be reliably estimated at this time. Contingent liabilities are discussed further in Chapter 8.

Consider Target's liabilities shown on its balance sheet:

CONSOLIDATED STATEMENTS OF FINANCIAL POSITION (Target, excerpts)

(millions)	*February 1, 2006*	*February 2, 2005*
Liabilities and shareholders' investment		
Accounts payable	**$6,268**	$5,779
Accrued liabilities	**2,193**	1,633
Income taxes payable	**374**	304
Current portion of long-term debt and notes payable	**753**	504
Total current liabilities	**$9,588**	$8,220
Long-term debt	**9,119**	9,034
Deferred income taxes	**851**	973
Other non-current liabilities	**1,232**	1,037

Again, these liabilities are fairly self-explanatory, all except "Deferred income taxes and other" which will be discussed later in Chapter 9. Note that Target only shows a total for current liabilities, but not for all of its liabilities. This is common on many balance sheets. The analyst must calculate the total liabilities, as needed for any further ratio calculations.

Owners' Equity

This final element of the balance sheet represents the equity of the firm's owners. As shown in Exhibit 3-2, the FASB defines **owners' equity** simply as the "residual interest in the assets of an entity that remains after deducting liabilities." This definition makes it clear that the balance sheet's *valuation of owners' equity is determined by the firm's valuation of assets and liabilities.* This view of owners' equity as a "residual amount" is apparent when we rearrange the balance sheet equation in the following way:

OWNERS' EQUITY = ASSETS − LIABILITIES

Sample Company's balance sheet in Exhibit 3-1 shows a firm that has been organized as a **corporation,** which is an entity that is owned by a group of shareholders. A corporation's owners' equity is usually called **shareholders' equity** or stockholders' equity. In a corporation, shareholders' equity often includes a variety of different accounts. In most cases, these are relatively minor sub-divisions of the overall owners' equity. For the purposes of this chapter, *focus mostly on the total owners' or shareholders' equity.*

In Sample Company, shareholders' equity comprises both **invested capital** (some companies may use the term **paid-in-capital**), which represents direct investments by the owners of the firm, and **retained earnings**, which represent the earnings of the firm that have been reinvested in the business. Sample Company's balance sheet in Exhibit 3-1 shows that owners have paid $600,000 for shares of stock of the company. Sample Company has received this invested capital (probably cash from investors) in exchange for shares of stock. In addition, the firm has been profitable in the past, and Sample Company has reinvested $258,000 of those profits in the business. This $258,000 represents Sample's retained earnings.

If in the next year, Sample Company reports profits of $200,000 and pays dividends to shareholders of $75,000, then retained earnings will increase by $125,000 ($200,000 – $75,000). Bear in mind, however, that *retained earnings do not represent cash available for the payment of dividends.* Rather, *retained earnings reflect resources that a firm has obtained as a result of operations.* The firm has retained this increase for use in its operations, rather than returning it immediately to the investors as dividends. Those resources are presently invested as shown on the asset side of the balance sheet. For this reason, it is possible that a firm may have a large retained earnings balance, but have insufficient cash available for dividends.

Consider Target's shareholders' equity (shareholders' investment) shown on its balance sheet:

CONSOLIDATED STATEMENTS OF FINANCIAL POSITION (Target, excerpts)

(millions)	*January 28, 2006*	*January 29, 2005*
Shareholders' investment		
Common stock*	**73**	74
Additional paid-in-capital	**2,121**	1,810
Retained earnings	**12,013**	11,148
Accumulated other comprehensive income	**(2)**	(3)
Total shareholders' investment	**14,205**	13,029
Total liabilities and shareholders' investment	**$34,995**	$32,293

Target's balance sheet disclosures of "Shareholders' investment" are, again, fairly straightforward. One new set of terms includes "common stock" and "additional paid-in-capital". Together, these two items comprise Target's invested capital. We will defer detailed discussion on these terms until Chapter 10, at which time we will also examine the asterisk on the term "common stock". The item shown as "Accumulated other comprehensive income" will be discussed in Chapter 4. For now, note the separate sub-total for "Total shareholders' investment" and the important balance sheet total at the bottom of this section, labeled "Total liabilities and shareholders' investment". This total must match Target's total assets shown earlier. How would you quickly compute Target's total liabilities, given the last two sub-totals on its balance sheet?

Reality Check 3-3 illustrates the reporting of shareholders' equity for two other firms, one of which reports a **negative (deficit) balance** in retained earnings.

This discussion of the equity section completes our tour of the balance sheet. At this point, you are aware of the typical terms and sections on most balance sheets. In future chapters, you will encounter a variety of terms describing the owners' interests in the firm, ranging from shareholders' equity, to shareholders' investment, or the more generic term owners' equity. The following section illustrates a variety of balance sheet ratio relationships that are of interest to analysts.

BALANCE SHEET ANALYSIS

Various ratios are used to help interpret and understand financial statements. These **ratios** are guides to understanding changes in financial performance for one company from year to year. They are also useful for analyzing differences in financial performance between two or more companies. Ratios are most useful when comparisons are made, either between time periods or between different companies. *Ratios are useful shortcuts* that permit the analyst to collapse the myriad details in financial statements into a few simple numbers. But remember that the ratio calculations are not the answers; they just show relationships. The analyst or manager must understand those relationships and make decisions on the basis of diverse information.

Ratios are just one input to those decisions. In other words, ratios are one indicator of financial health and viability, but they do not tell the whole story. Users of financial statements must be careful not to become too enamored of the ratios themselves and should not forget to look for other indicators that will permit better decision-making. Also, *ratios are historical.* Judgment is needed to use them for decision making because future conditions may change. Remember that *ratios are only as good as the data used to compute them!* Discussions in later chapters will help you be aware of differences in accounting policies that can cause differences in ratios. One of the main points in this text is that ratio results can be biased, if the underlying accounting numbers are biased or manipulated in a way that is favorable to the firm's interests.

Balance sheet ratios aid the analyst in assessing a firm's liquidity, asset management, and debt management policies, each of which is discussed in this section.

Vertical Analysis

Analysts usually begin with a review of the firm's assets, as well as its liabilities and owners' equity. This review begins with the preparation of a **common-size balance sheet,** which shows the percentage component of each major section to the grand totals on each side of the balance sheet. This analysis is called **vertical analysis, or vertical percentage analysis,** because it is based on the percentage relationship of each line in the balance sheet to the total. Exhibit 3-1 has been revised as Exhibit 3-4, showing the vertical percentages for each account on the balance sheet. *These percentages are calculated by dividing each line by the total assets* ($2,057,000). Note that either total assets or total liabilities plus owners' equity can be used as the denominator for this calculation because the number is the same ($2,057,000).

REALITY CHECK 3-3

The following schedule summarizes the components of shareholders' equity reported on recent balance sheets of Amgen and Lear Corporation:

	Amgen	*Lear Corporation*
	(Dollars in millions)	
Shareholders' equity:		
Invested capital	$23,561.00	$ 883.80
Retained earnings (deficit)	(3,132.00)	361.80
Other	22.00	(134.60)
Total shareholders' equity	$20,451.00	$1,111.00

Required

a. Which firm has obtained the larger amount of capital through sale of stock to investors?

b. Which firm has obtained the larger amount of capital through reinvestment of earnings?

c. Explain why Amgen reports a negative (deficit) balance in retained earnings at the end of the year.

d. Suppose that Lear earns $150 and pays dividends of $90 during next year. What would be the firm's ending balance in retained earnings? (All dollars are in millions.)

SOLUTION

a. Invested capital represents the amount that each firm has received through the sale of stock to investors. Amgen has obtained the larger amount, $23,561 million, as opposed to Lear who obtained $884 million from this source.

b. Lear has obtained $362 million of its investment in net assets through retention of earnings. Amgen, on the other hand, has a negative balance in its retained earnings. For this reason, Amgen has not obtained any of its capital through reinvestment of earnings.

c. Retained earnings are increased when a firm is profitable and decreased when a firm pays dividends to shareholders or incurs losses. The negative (deficit) balance in Amgen 's retained earnings indicates that since the firm began operations, its total dividends and losses have exceeded its total income.

d. Lear would report a balance in retained earnings at the end of the next year of $421.8 (in millions), computed as follows:

Retained earnings, beginning of year	$361.8
Add: Net income for year	150
Less: Dividends in year	(90)
Retained earnings, end of year	$421.8

EXHIBIT 3-4 VERTICAL ANALYSIS

Sample Company
Balance Sheet
Vertical Analysis at December 31, 2007

ASSETS		
Current assets		
Cash	5.3%	
Accounts receivable	22.6	
Inventories	39.5	
Prepaid expenses	1.6	
Total current assets		69.0%
Noncurrent assets		
Land	4.1%	
Buildings and equipment (net of accumulated depreciation of $313,000)	26.9	
Total noncurrent assets		31.0
Total assets		100.0%

LIABILITIES AND OWNERS' EQUITY		
Current liabilities		
Accounts payable	12.6%	
Notes payable	10.9	
Warranty obligations	5.4	
Accrued expenses	3.6	
Taxes payable	1.3	
Total current liabilities		33.8%
Noncurrent liabilities		
Bonds payable	17.1%	
Mortgage payable	7.3	
Total noncurrent liabilities		24.4
Total liabilities		58.2%
Shareholders' equity		
Invested capital	29.3%	
Retained earnings	12.5	
Total shareholders' equity		41.8
Total liabilities and shareholders' equity		100.0%

Liquidity Ratios

Liquidity represents the ability of a company to convert its assets to cash, and **liquidity ratios** are often calculated from balance sheet data. Although there are many types of liquidity ratios, we focus here on a few of the more basic ones.

Current Ratio

The most popular liquidity ratio is the current ratio. The **current ratio** is calculated by dividing all current assets by all current liabilities:

$$\text{Current ratio} = \frac{\text{Current assets}}{\text{Current liabilities}}$$

For the data in Exhibit 3-1,

$$\text{Current ratio} = \frac{\$1{,}420{,}000}{\$699{,}000} = 2.03$$

Current ratios that represent good liquidity and strong financial health vary widely across firms and industries. Currently, many companies have a current ratio between 1.3 and 1.5. Many companies have short-term lines of credit and other borrowing capacities that permit them to operate with a nearly balanced amount of current assets and current liabilities. In any event, the analyst would be worried to find current liabilities substantially in excess of current assets (in other words, when the current ratio is considerably less than 1.0). Declining trends in the current ratio would also cause concern, especially in conjunction with declining trends in other liquidity ratios.

Quick Ratio

Another major liquidity ratio is the **quick ratio,** which is often called the **acid test.** In this context, "quick" means close to cash. To calculate this ratio, cash and receivables are added and then divided by all current liabilities. In computing the current and quick ratio, the net accounts receivable should be used. All cash equivalents should be included in the quick ratio.

The purpose of the quick ratio is to indicate the resources that may be available quickly, in the short term, for repaying the current liabilities. For this reason, inventory and prepaid expenses are left out. In other words, the quick ratio is a type of "disaster" ratio that is used to indicate a "worst case scenario" that might apply if no other resources are available to pay the current liabilities that are due within the next year.

$$\text{Quick ratio} = \frac{(\text{Cash} + \text{Receivables})}{\text{Current liabilities}}$$

For the data in Exhibit 3-1,

$$\text{Quick ratio} = \frac{(\$110{,}000 + \$466{,}000)}{\$699{,}000}$$

$$= .82$$

Values for the quick ratio are often less than 1.0, and a rule of thumb used by some analysts is that the quick ratio should not be less than .30. Again, declining trends should cause the most concern. When comparing two companies, a lower quick ratio and a lower current ratio do not, in and of themselves, indicate that the company with the lower values is in worse financial condition. Lower liquidity may be offset by a variety of other financial indicators, such that the company with lower liquidity ratios could still rank higher on its overall financial stability and financial health.

Information useful for calculating the current and quick ratios for a firm at two successive dates is shown in Reality Check 3-4.

REALITY CHECK 3-4

The following schedule summarizes the composition of current assets and current liabilities reported in Apple Computer's year-end balance sheets:

	Year 2	*Year 1*
	(Dollars in millions)	
Total current assets	$10,300	$7,055
Inventories included in current assets	165	101
Prepayment and supplies included in current assets	648	485
Total current liabilities	3,484	2,651

Required

a. Based on the information given here, determine the firm's current ratio and quick ratio at the end of each year.
b. In which year do you consider the firm to be in better financial condition? Explain.

SOLUTION

a. Calculation of current ratio and quick ratio:

	Year 2	*Year 1*
Current ratio $= \dfrac{\text{Current assets}}{\text{Current liabilities}}$	$\dfrac{\$10{,}300}{\$3{,}484}$	$\dfrac{\$7{,}055}{\$2{,}651}$
	= 2.96	= 2.66
Quick ratio $= \dfrac{\text{Quick assets*}}{\text{Current liabilities}}$	$\dfrac{\$9{,}487}{\$3{,}484}$	$\dfrac{\$6{,}469}{\$2{,}651}$
	= 2.72	= 2.44

b. Apple Computer has about the same current ratio in each year. Apple's quick ratio, however, has increased from 2.44 to 2.72. Although Apple appears to be more liquid at the end of Year 2, the analyst would seek additional information from the financial statements and elsewhere before making a final judgment.

*Quick assets are estimated as current assets, minus the amounts in inventories, prepayments, and supplies.

Asset Management Ratios

Asset management ratios focus on the composition of the firm's assets and on changes in the composition of assets over time (changes between successive balance sheets). A vertical analysis of the left side of the balance sheet allows the analyst to examine the percentages of the total assets devoted to each category.

This examination gives some indication of the resources used for current assets relative to those used to provide operating capacity.

In reviewing the **percentage composition** of a firm's assets, the analyst keeps several factors in mind. First, to a large extent, the composition of assets depends on the industry in which the firm operates. In some cases, comparisons between industries may be meaningless. "Smokestack" industries, for example, such as metal fabrication, require large investments in factory buildings and heavy equipment, such that many manufacturing firms have many noncurrent assets. On the other hand, merchandising industries, such as department stores, require large amounts of accounts receivable and also substantial investments in inventories available for resale, but relatively minor investment in buildings and equipment. Financial firms such as banks and insurance companies have relatively little in the way of inventories, factory buildings, and equipment. Instead, the assets of financial firms consist mainly of loans receivable and investments in securities (stocks and bonds) of other firms. A first step for the analyst in assessing a firm's asset composition is to be aware of any peculiar industry norms or special circumstances.

In addition to industry characteristics, the analyst knows that managers may have sound business reasons for structuring a firm's assets differently than those of its competitors. For example, some managers may extend liberal credit terms to customers as a way of improving sales and, as a result, may have a large accounts receivable balance. Other managers may carry large inventories for customer convenience or may stockpile inventories in anticipation of rising price or supply bottlenecks. On the other hand, large amounts of accounts receivable may indicate that a firm has difficulty collecting its accounts. Similarly, large inventories may reflect obsolete items or declining product sales. In short, increases or decreases in specific components of a firm's total assets may be either good news or bad news. Any ratio computations are only the first step for the analyst. The creative art in ratio analysis is to understand the reasons for ratio differences among firms and over time.

Debt Management Ratios

The most inclusive and most useful **debt management ratios** are the composition ratios drawn from a vertical analysis of the right side of the balance sheet. Note the liability and equity composition ratios in the right-hand column of Exhibit 3-4. These percentage composition ratios indicate the relative proportions of various forms of debt and owners' equity used to finance the organization.

The vertical analysis of Sample Company's sources of funds shows that 33.8% of all financing came from current liabilities. A smaller amount (24.4%) came from long-term liabilities, and the largest portion (41.8%) came from owners. Of the 41.8% portion that came from owners, 29.3% was in the form of direct investment, and 12.5% was in the form of profits reinvested in the business.

The ratio of total debt to total assets, also called the **debt-to-assets ratio or financial leverage ratio,** is often used as a primary indicator of the firm's debt management. Exhibit 3-4 shows that Sample Company's total liabilities are equal to 58.2% of total assets. As this key ratio increases or decreases, it indicates the firm's changing reliance on borrowed resources. The lower the ratio, the lower the firm's risk because the organization will usually be better able to meet its obligations for interest and debt payments. A lower debt-to-assets ratio also suggests a lower risk of default. Default on a firm's liabilities is a costly event from both a lender's and a borrower's perspective and should be avoided if at all possible.

The fact that Sample Company's owners' equity provides 41.8% of the firm's resources suggests that the owners' equity of this firm offers substantial protection to lenders. Suppose, for example, Sample Company was unable to continue its operations and had to **liquidate** its assets, or, in other words, convert its assets to cash. In such a situation, Sample Company could incur losses of 41.8% of the assets' carrying value, and the cash received would still be sufficient to pay off all the firm's debts. Of course, nothing would then be left for the owners!

Limitations of Balance Sheet Analysis

Although the ratios reviewed in this section provide a useful starting point for assessing a firm's financial management policies, several limitations must be considered. First, *ratio calculations are only the initial step in analyzing a firm's condition.* They merely provide the analyst with a point of departure for asking further questions. Second, individual financial statements such as the balance sheet are seldom analyzed separately from other statements described in the next two chapters. In fact, many of the most useful ratios used by analysts measure relationships between balance sheet and income statement data. For this reason, we will expand and enrich our study of ratio analysis after first describing the other primary financial statements. Third, information useful for analyzing and clarifying financial statements is contained in other parts of a company's financial reports.

An important limitation in comparing financial ratios across firms is the fact that their accounting methods may differ. Later chapters discuss the varieties of different methods that firms may use in measuring assets, liabilities, shareholders' equity, revenues, and expenses. For now, be aware that *financial ratios may be significantly affected by alternative accounting methods.* The analyst attempts to adjust for differences caused by accounting methods in order to make valid ratio comparisons among different firms. The **notes to the financial statements** alert the analyst to the principal methods being used.

Some balance sheet items may not affect cash flows. While most balance sheet items are created by spending cash, or will ultimately require cash to be spent, there are some items that do not have a future cash flow effect (except for possible tax saving consequences). For example, goodwill represents cash that has been paid to someone else, but it probably cannot be sold or used to recover cash from a third party. Accumulated depreciation, of course, will not represent any future cash flows.

On the other hand, most current assets and current liabilities will represent immediate cash flows (within the year). Accrued taxes, especially long-term tax accruals, will probably not be paid in cash at any time in the foreseeable future (tax deferrals are covered in Chapter 8). Most of the items in shareholders' equity represent cash flows in the distant past, but will not have any immediate near-term impact on cash flows. The point is that when an analyst looks at a balance sheet, some items will not affect future cash flows to any appreciable extent.

Summary of Learning Objectives

1. **Identify basic balance sheet terms.**
   The basic elements of the balance sheet are assets, liabilities, and owners' equity. Liabilities and owners' equity are the sources from which a firm has obtained its funds, and assets show the way that the firm's managers have invested those funds.

2. **Recognize typical assets, liabilities, and owners' equity found on most balance sheets.**
   Assets are resources that are expected to benefit the firm in future periods, including cash, accounts receivable, inventories held for production and sale, prepayments of expenses, and property, plant, and equipment. Liabilities are obligations to provide future services or to make future payments, and include trade accounts payable, short- and long-term borrowings, and other debts. Owners' equity is the difference between assets and liabilities. For a corporation, owners' equity consists of invested capital, which has been paid by investors to obtain ownership shares, and retained earnings, which represent earnings that have been reinvested in the business.

3. **Understand how balance sheet items are ordered and classified.**
   Both assets and liabilities are listed in order of liquidity or maturity on the balance sheet. They are further classified into current and noncurrent portions. Current assets will become cash or be consumed in a year or an operating cycle, whichever is longer; current liabilities require payment from current assets.

4. **Appreciate why balance sheets differ for firms in different industries.**
   "Smokestack" industries require large investments in factory buildings and heavy equipment; major portions of assets in such industries are non-current. Merchandising industries, however, require large investments in accounts receivable and inventories and relatively minor investments in buildings and equipment. Financial firms such as banks have relatively little investment in inventories, factory buildings, and equipment. Instead, their assets consist mainly of loans receivable and investments in securities (stocks and bonds) of other firms.

5. **Use balance sheet relationships to obtain information useful to investors and lenders.**
   Various ratios help assess a firm's liquidity, asset management, and debt management policies. Liquidity ratios aid in assessing how the firm may pay its debts and meet its other short-term cash requirements. Asset management

ratios show how the funds invested in the firm are being used. Debt management ratios show the firm's reliance on borrowed capital and the buffer or "safety zone" provided by owners' equity.

6. **Be alert to the limitations as well as the usefulness of balance sheet information.**
   Balance sheet relationships do not provide direct answers to the analyst in assessing the firm's potential risks and returns; they merely provide a base for further questions. The balance sheet is also rarely analyzed separately from the other financial statements, which will be discussed in subsequent chapters. Moreover, an important limitation in comparing financial relationships across firms is the fact that their accounting methods may differ.

7. **Identify which balance sheet items typically affect cash flows.**
   Some balance sheet items do not have a future cash flow effect (except for possible tax saving consequences). When an analyst examines a balance sheet, some items will not affect future cash flows to any appreciable extent. On the other hand, most current assets and current liabilities will represent immediate cash flows (within the year).

KEY TERMS

Accounts payable
Accounts receivable
Accrued expenses
Accumulated depreciation
Acid test
Amortization
Asset management ratios
Balance sheet
Bond
Bonds payable
Buildings
Cash
Cash and cash equivalents
Cash equivalents
Collateral
Collectibility
Common-size balance sheet
Corporation
Current assets
Current liabilities
Current ratio
Debt management ratios
Debt-to-assets ratio
Depreciation expense
Equipment
Externally generated goodwill
Financial leverage
Fixed assets
Goodwill
Intangibles
Interest payments
Internally generated goodwill
Inventory
Invested capital
Liabilities
Liquidate
Liquidity
Liquidity ratio
Mortgage payable
Negative (deficit) balance
Net book value
Net realizable value
Noncurrent assets
Noncurrent liabilities
Notes payable
Notes to the financial statements
Operating capacity
Operating cycles
Owners' equity
Paid-in-capital
Percentage composition
Plant
Prepaid expenses
Principal
Productive capacity
Property
Property, plant, and equipment
Quick ratio
Ratios
Retained earnings
Shareholders' equity
Sources of financing
Spontaneous or operating liabilities
Statement of financial position
Taxes payable
Trade accounts payable
Turnover
Uncollectible
Uses of resources
Vertical analysis
Vertical percentage analysis
Warranty obligations

Exercises and Problems

3-1 Rearrange the balance sheet equation into several variations. Why are these differences helpful? How might each version be used? Should an analyst always use the simplest version possible? Why or why not?

3-2 Explain why both sides of the balance sheet must have the same total dollar amount. Does this equality imply that the balance sheet is "correct" as a measure of financial position? Discuss.

3-3 All assets represent probable future economic benefits to the firm. Identify the probable future benefit associated with each of the following: (a) inventories, (b) accounts receivable, and (c) buildings and equipment.

3-4 Analysts often attempt to estimate the values of assets that are "missing" from the balance sheet. Identify at least two kinds of missing assets and discuss reasons for this omission from the balance sheet.

3-5 Identify several examples of liabilities that do not require payments of specific dollar amounts to lenders.

3-6 Discuss the concept of owners' equity on the balance sheet. In what ways does owners' equity represent a residual interest? Why is owners' equity called a residual amount?

3-7 How much flexibility should the analyst or manager accept in constructing ratio definitions for use within the same company or organization? For example, why might the analyst be more flexible in defining the quick ratio but not the current ratio? On the other hand, would the same flexibility be associated with a vertical analysis? Why or why not?

Preparing a Balance Sheet with Missing or Inconsistent Information

3-8 The following information is provided for Tom's Track Shoe Store at the end of 2007:

Accounts receivable	$ 6,500
Accounts payable	106,500
Bonds payable	180,000
Invested capital	300,000
Cash	14,500
Equipment	88,000
Income taxes payable	11,500
Inventory	497,500
Other long-term assets	110,000
Notes payable	50,000
Prepaid rent	54,000
Retained earnings, 12-31-06	94,500
Retained earnings, 12-31-07	?

Required

a. Prepare a balance sheet, and make it balance. Discuss the steps necessary to balance it along with any necessary assumptions.
b. What conclusions can be drawn regarding this business? Why?

Effects of Transactions on Balance Sheet

3-9 The following transactions are given:

a. A corporation issued common stock for cash.
b. The firm bought land with part of the cash.
c. The firm issued common stock in exchange for a building and equipment.
d. The firm purchased inventory on account.
e. The firm collected cash from a customer for merchandise sold several months previously.
f. The firm issued some of its common stock in exchange for a parcel of land.
g. The firm paid cash to its creditors.
h. The firm sells obsolete equipment at its net book value.

Required

Indicate the effects of the transactions on the balance sheet equation:

ASSETS	=	LIABILITIES	+	SHAREHOLDERS' EQUITY

Using Ratios to Evaluate Performance

3-10 The following balance sheet data are given:

	2007	*2006*
Cash	$ 45,000	$ 35,000
Fixed assets	330,000	270,000
Current liabilities	95,000	45,000
Long-term liabilities	300,000	320,000
Accounts receivable	115,000	95,000
Invested capital	100,000	100,000
Inventories	100,000	80,000
Retained earnings	95,000	15,000

Required

a. Prepare a balance sheet for each year.
b. Compute the liquidity ratios described in this chapter, along with the asset management and debt management ratios. Evaluate the company's liquidity. Evaluate its asset management and debt management.

c. What strategies does the company seem to be following in managing its finances?

Transaction Analysis: Expanded Accounting Equation

3-11 Given these transactions:

1. An engineering firm was formed when three engineers each invested $50,000 (cash).
2. Each founder also invested an assortment of utility trucks, inclinometers, and other specialty equipment, valued at $10,000 (each).
3. Borrowed $50,000 from an owner on accounts payable to provide additional operating funds.
4. Rented office space at $1,000 per month.
5. Paid the first month's rent.
6. Paid a security deposit of $2,000.
7. A wealthy individual also wanted to invest in the firm, but not as an owner, so the firm borrowed $500,000 from this individual at 18% per year.
8. Two additional staff members were hired at $6,000 per month.
9. The staff earned their first month's salary of $6,000 but was not yet paid.
10. Supplies costing $45,000 were purchased.
11. Recorded depreciation for the first month. Assume that the equipment (in transaction 2) has useful lives of five years.
12. Accrued interest on the loan for one month.

Required

a. Arrange five columns in a worksheet or spreadsheet, corresponding to the following expanded balance sheet equation (assume zero beginning balances):

CURRENT ASSETS + FIXED ASSETS = CURRENT LIABILITIES + LONG-TERM LIABILITIES + OWNERS' EQUITY

Enter transactions 1 through 12 in the five columns. Total each column and verify that the balance sheet does indeed balance. Prepare a classified balance sheet, using the column totals from your spreadsheet.

b. Evaluate the firm's liquidity, using the ratios described in this chapter.

c. Evaluate the firm's asset management and debt management.

d. On an overall basis, evaluate the firm's performance. What important information is missing? Even though the firm's performance seems somewhat questionable, could the missing information change your opinion? Why?

Composition of Current Assets

3-12 The following schedule summarizes the current assets reported in the 2005 balance sheets of Target and eBay (as shown also in Appendices B & C):

	Target	*eBay*
	(Dollars in millions)	
Current Assets		
Cash and cash equivalents	$ 1,648	$ 1,314
Short-term investments	—	775
Accounts receivable, net	5,666	323
Funds receivable	—	255
Inventory	5,838	—
Other	1,253	516
Total current assets	14,405	3,183
Noncurrent, total	20,590	8,606
Total assets	$34,995	$11,789

Required

a. Identify the major differences between these two firms in their composition of current assets. Try to explain these differences in terms of the types of goods and services each company produces.

b. On the basis of the liquidity ratios, which company appears to be more liquid?

c. Conduct a vertical analysis for each company. Do these results support your earlier conclusions in part b? Why or why not?

Sorting Balance Sheet Information

3-13 The account balances given below are shown on the balance sheet of a corporation.

Marketable securities	$ 20,000
Invested capital	200,000
Buildings and equipment	400,000
Accounts receivable	80,000
Prepaid rent	17,000
Bonds payable	230,000
Inventories	85,000
Taxes payable	30,000
Accounts payable	16,000
Advance payments from customers	3,000
Interest payable	9,000
Land	19,000
Retained earnings	133,000

Required

a. Arrange three columns corresponding to the balance sheet equation:

ASSETS	=	LIABILITIES	+	SHAREHOLDERS' EQUITY

b. Calculate the balance sheet totals and show that they balance.

CHAPTER 4

THE INCOME STATEMENT

Learning Objectives

1. *When are revenues recognized?*
2. *When are expenses recognized?*
3. *Interpret more complex income statements.*
4. *Use ratios to analyze income statement information.*
5. *Describe how reported earnings may affect managers' performance evaluations and, consequently, their accounting policy decisions.*
6. *Understand and interpret comprehensive income.*
7. *Identify which income statement items will not usually be reflected in cash flows.*

INTRODUCTION

The income statement summarizes the results of a firm's operations for a period of time. Four major types of items appear on income statements: revenues, expenses, gains, and losses.

Revenues are inflows of assets (or reductions in liabilities) that result from providing goods and services to customers; they arise from a firm's ongoing operations. Sales of inventory to customers, for example, will usually increase cash or accounts receivable (assets). Sales to customers are called revenues. Sales revenues will generally increase assets and shareholders' equity.

Expenses occur when resources are consumed in the process of generating revenues. The cost of inventory sold to customers (cost of goods sold) illustrates an expense. Expenses necessary to satisfy customers will generally decrease assets and shareholders' equity.

Gains are similar to revenues, yet they are more complicated because they arise from activities that are not central to a firm's major operations. Gains will increase assets or decrease liabilities, and correspondingly increase shareholders' equity. For example, a gain would be recognized when land is sold for more than its carrying (book) value. **Losses** are the opposite of gains, and they are also not central to a firm's major activities. Losses will decrease assets or increase liabilities and correspondingly decrease shareholders' equity. Sale of land at an amount less than its carrying value would result in a loss.

INCOME STATEMENT EXAMPLE

Exhibit 4-1 contains the fiscal 2007 income statement for Techtron Incorporated, a manufacturer of component parts used in advanced electronics equipment. The income statement is for the year ended January 3, 2007. Although most firms use a **calendar year-end** of December 31, Techtron uses a **52-week year** and prepares its financial statements as of the Saturday or Sunday closest to December 31 (e.g., Johnson & Johnson Company uses Sunday). A 52-week year enhances comparisons across quarterly reports because each quarter will have 13 weeks. Some firms use a **natural year-end** instead of a calendar year-end. That is, the financial statements are prepared shortly after the firm's busy season. Wal-Mart, for example, prepares its annual financial statements on January 31, which is a good fiscal year-end for them because December is their busiest time of year. By the end of January, Wal-Mart has completed its busy season; it has made any exchanges or refunds, and its inventory levels are probably rather low. This is a good time to tally results.

Techtron's income statement, similar to the income statements of many corporations, is highly condensed. It contains two revenue items, four expense items, and no gains or losses. However, Techtron almost certainly did experience gains and losses, but their relative sizes were probably so small that they were combined with other items on the income statement. This is an application of the **materiality principle**, which states that separate disclosure is not required if an item is so small that knowledge of it would not affect the decision of a reasonable financial statement reader. This principle can actually improve the usefulness of financial statements by eliminating the disclosure of inconsequential items, which helps analysts concentrate on items of importance.

The major revenue line on Techtron's income statement is labeled **Net sales.** Note the terms sales and revenue are used interchangeably by many firms, while the term **"net"** implies that certain items have been deducted from the gross (or full) sales price. For example, most firms allow their customers to return merchandise within a specified period, and customers are usually offered a full refund upon returning the merchandise. The original sales amount is included in gross sales. The refund amount is termed a **sales return**, and it is subtracted from gross sales in calculating net sales. Even if the term net is omitted, reported sales on the income statement are usually net sales. When only a single sales revenue term is shown on the income statement, it can be interpreted as "net sales".

Cost of sales is often referred to as cost of goods sold. It reflects the cost to Techtron of the goods sold to its customers. The difference between sales and **cost of goods sold** (COGS) is called gross profit or gross margin.

Techtron has elected to combine selling, general, and administrative expenses, although some companies report separate figures. **Selling expenses** include advertising costs, commissions to salespersons, depreciation of equipment used in the selling function, and a number of other items. **General and administrative expenses** consist of senior managers' salaries, accounting and auditing costs, insurance, depreciation of administrative offices, and so on.

Operating income equals sales revenue minus all costs and expenses incurred during normal operations. Operating income is a primary indicator of how well a firm has managed its operations and, as you will see, serves as a basis for comparing firms within the same industry. Operating income is often used to make predictions about the firm's potential future success. Operating income is usually a better predictor of cash flows than most other items on the income statement.

Techtron's income statement contains several other items. Other income can arise from a variety of sources, such as interest on investments. **Interest expense** reflects the firm's cost of borrowing money from creditors. **Income taxes** are imposed by Federal, state, and local governments, and by foreign jurisdictions. Interest and income taxes do not directly relate to a firm's operations. For example, interest expense is largely a function of how much the firm has borrowed to finance its operations. Differences in interest expense between firms are determined primarily by financing decisions made by each firm. Some firms elect to borrow heavily, which results in large interest charges. Other firms rely on investments by owners, which do not accrue any interest charges. Interest expense is not included in operating income and is deducted after operating income on the income statement.

The **bottom line** of the income statement is called **net income, earnings,** or **profit.** Interest and income tax expenses and all gains and losses are used to calculate the firm's overall profitability. Because net income reflects the increase in net assets from all profit-oriented activities, it is the focus of much scrutiny by analysts, investors, and other financial statement readers. It is often too prominent as a focal point on the income statement. Our goal is to suggest that various items on the income statement must be more carefully reviewed, and that analysts not focus only on the bottom line.

Keep in mind that revenues and profits are not the same. One is the top line on the income statement; the other is the bottom line! **Revenue** refers to the total inflow of assets (or reduction in liabilities) from customers. **Profit** is the net increase in a firm's recorded wealth after deducting expenses from revenue.

Techtron's income statement presented in Exhibit 4-1 is in the **multiple-step format.** Multiple-step income statements calculate certain subtotals for the reader. Techtron's statement contains subtotals for gross profit and operating income. In contrast, income statements using the **single-step format** summarize all revenues in one section and all expenses in another. Exhibit 4-2 illustrates a single-step income statement. Whereas the single-step approach is simpler, the multiple-step approach provides more information. The analyst must often construct important subtotals using the available information on the income statement.

USES OF THE INCOME STATEMENT

A major purpose of the income statement is to show a firm's profitability, yet it also provides a number of additional performance measures. Revenue, for example, is a key measure of **growth** that reflects a firm's success in expanding its market. Additionally, comparisons of expense numbers from year to year indicate a firm's success in controlling costs. As previously mentioned, operating income measures managers' performance in conducting a firm's operations.

Income statement information is used for a variety of decisions. Because earnings underlie a firm's ability to generate cash flows for dividends and future investments, equity investors are interested in the income statement. Lenders are also interested in the income statement because a firm's ability to pay principal and interest in a timely manner ultimately depends on its profitability.

EXHIBIT 4-1 MULTIPLE STEP INCOME STATEMENT

Techtron Incorporated
Income Statement
For the Year Ended January 3, 2007
(Dollars in thousands)

Net sales	$172,428
Cost of sales	134,373
Gross profit	38,055
Selling, general, and administrative expenses	14,844
Income from operations	23,211
Other income	1,503
Interest expense	31
Income before provision for income taxes	24,683
Provision for income taxes	10,016
Net income	$ 14,667

EXHIBIT 4-2 SINGLE-STEP INCOME STATEMENT

Techtron Incorporated
Income Statement
For the Year Ended January 3, 2007
(Dollars in thousands)

REVENUES		
Net sales	$172,428	
Other income	1,503	
		$173,931
EXPENSES		
Cost of sales	134,373	
Selling, general, and administrative expenses	14,844	
Interest expense	31	
Provision for income taxes	10,016	
		159,264
Net income		$ 14,667

A firm's management can use income statement information to make a variety of decisions. For example, managers must constantly evaluate the prices they set for the firm's products and services. Pricing affects both profitability and growth. The income statement tells managers and investors how well the firm's pricing strategy has accomplished stated objectives.

Corporations always strive to reduce the costs of their operations, and the income statement can also measure the success of cost-cutting initiatives. However, cost-cutting, such as employee layoffs, do not ensure increased profitability. Apple Computer Inc. cut thousands of jobs in the late 1990s, yet continued to post losses. Continued competition from industry rivals and the loss of human talent are issues that must also be addressed.

As a final illustration, managers often use the income statement when setting dividends. Net income is a primary measure of a firm's ability to pay dividends. In fact, some firms set a dividend target equal to a certain percentage of net income.

REVENUE RECOGNITION

A firm's earnings process often takes place over an extended period of time. A manufacturer's typical earnings process, which is depicted in Exhibit 4-3, entails purchasing raw materials, manufacturing, storing and selling the finished product, and collecting cash from the customer. The manufacturer creates value

EXHIBIT 4-3 TIME LINE OF A MANUFACTURER'S EARNINGS PROCESS

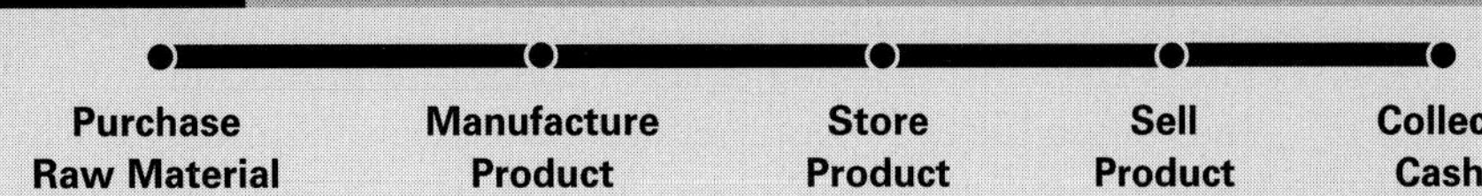

through all these steps, but for accounting purposes, firms usually select a discrete point in time to recognize (record) revenue.

General Rule

The **revenue recognition principle** states that revenue should be recognized in the accounting records when:

1. the earnings process is *substantially complete,* and
2. the amount to be collected is *reasonably determinable.*

The first criterion prevents the recognition of revenue before a firm has fulfilled its obligation to the customer. The second criterion indicates that the sales price has been set and that the customer will probably pay the amount due. Both criteria ensure that revenue is not recognized prematurely. If revenue is recognized too soon, the income statement will indicate that the firm has accomplished activities that it has not, which would mislead financial statement users.

In most situations, these criteria are met at the point of sale, that is, when a product is delivered or a service is rendered to a customer. Even if payment is not immediately received, an expected future cash inflow (an account receivable) has been obtained, and revenue recognition is proper.

Two additional comments need to be made about revenue recognition at the point of sale. First, many sellers guarantee their products' performance for a period of time. If a product malfunctions, the seller is obligated to incur the cost of correcting the problem. Does the existence of such a warranty indicate that the earnings process is not substantially complete at the time of sale? No, it does not. For most sellers, the warranty cost is relatively minor. Thus, the earnings process is substantially complete at the time of sale. Chapter 8 discusses warranty costs in more depth.

Second, when accounts receivable are obtained at the point of sale, can we be certain that cash will ultimately be collected? In most cases, absolute assurance cannot be obtained, but if the seller has done a good job of checking customers' credit histories, a reasonable estimate of worthless accounts receivable can be made. This estimate is used to adjust both the income statement and the balance sheet. Chapter 6 discusses this issue in more detail.

Most companies will describe their revenue recognition policies in the Notes to the financial statements. Consider the following excerpt from Wal-Mart's notes describing its revenue recognition policies:

Revenue Recognition

The Company recognizes sales revenue at the time it sells merchandise to the customer, except for layaway transactions. The Company recognizes layaway transactions when the customer satisfies all payment obligations and takes possession of the merchandise. The Company recognizes SAM'S CLUB membership fee revenue over the twelve-month term of the membership. Customer purchases of Wal-Mart/SAM'S CLUB shopping cards are not recognized until the card is redeemed and the customer purchases merchandise by using the shopping card.

Wal-Mart clearly recognizes most revenue when items are sold to customers. Some revenue is deferred for "layaway" transactions. SAM'S CLUB membership fees are recognized as revenues over the membership year. Shopping card revenues are not recognized until the card is redeemed (used). What do you suppose happens to revenue recogniton when shopping cards are lost or damaged?

Exceptions

A number of exceptions exist to the general rule of thumb that revenue is recognized at the point of sale. One exception deals with the collectibility of receivables. *If the seller is highly uncertain about the collectibility of a receivable, revenue recognition should be delayed beyond the point of sale to the point when cash is actually collected.* This approach is sometimes used in the real estate industry. Many firms defer revenue recognition because of the uncertainties associated with the collection of receivables. In cases where collectibility is highly uncertain at the point of sale, the associated revenue must be deferred. Other firms are more aggressive and record all sales as revenues immediately, which could overstate revenues and profits. In order to better estimate future cash flows when there are revenues that may not be collected, the analyst must adjust future estimates of cash collections from accounts receivable.

Another exception deals with long-term construction contracts (for bridges, highways, and so on). These projects can take several years to complete. If revenue recognition is delayed until the earnings process is substantially complete, no revenue is recognized in any contract year except the final one, at which point all the revenue is recognized. Such an uneven pattern of revenue recognition would contrast with the actual earnings process, which takes place throughout the life of the contract. Accordingly, if (1) a binding contract exists between the buyer and the seller, and (2) the seller can reasonably estimate the costs to complete the project, then revenue, the related costs, and the resultant profit should be estimated and recognized each year by the **percentage of completion method.** This method recognizes a portion of the revenue, cost, and profit each year according to the percentage of the job completed.

A similar situation exists with some service contracts. For example, consider a health club that sells one-year memberships for an immediate payment of $600. Revenue recognition at the point of sale is inappropriate because the earnings process has barely begun. However, delaying revenue recognition until the twelfth month, when the earnings process is substantially complete, is also inadvisable. GAAP permits **proportional revenue recognition** each month over the contract's life. Note that Wal-Mart's revenue policies (described above) indicate that membership fees from Sam's Club are deferred, and recognized as revenue proportionately over the membership period.

Most firms describe their revenue recognition policies in a note to the financial statements. Reality Check 4-1 contains an excerpt from the financial statements of *Reader's Digest,* which frequently receives payments for subscriptions at the inception of a contract. Because the earnings process has just begun at that point, the magazine records a liability instead of revenue. Recording a liability recognizes that *Reader's Digest* has an obligation to provide its customers something of value: either the magazine or a refund. Revenue is recognized as the magazines are mailed to the customers.

REALITY CHECK 4-1

Reader's Digest records sales of magazine subscriptions as unearned revenue at the gross subscription price at the time the orders are received. Proportionate shares of the gross subscription price are recognized as revenue when each monthly issue is mailed.

Required

a. Assume that *Reader's Digest* receives $48 from a customer for a two-year subscription. Analyze this transaction in terms of the basic accounting equation.

b. Assume that the subscription is for 24 monthly issues. In terms of the basic accounting equation, what analysis would *Reader's Digest* undertake when each issue is mailed?

SOLUTION

a.

ASSETS	=	LIABILITIES	+	SHAREHOLDERS' EQUITY
Cash + $48		Unearned revenue + $48		

b.

ASSETS	=	LIABILITIES	+	SHAREHOLDERS' EQUITY
		Unearned revenue – $2		Retained earnings + $2 (subsciption revenue)

EXPENSE RECOGNITION

The **matching principle** governs expense recognition. It states that all costs that were incurred to generate the revenue appearing on a given period's income statement should appear as an expense on the same income statement. In other words, we should match expenses against revenues. Revenues are first recognized and expenses are then matched with those revenues. By doing this, the income statement contains measures of both accomplishment (revenue) and effort (expenses), thereby enabling an assessment of firm performance. The matching principle is implemented in one of three ways, explained below.

Associating Cause and Effect

One method of implementing the matching principle is known as **associating cause and effect.** This implies that a clear and direct relationship exists between the expense and the associated revenue. Cost of goods sold is a good example. A retail store certainly cannot generate sales revenue without consuming inventory. Salespersons' commissions are another example. Because commissions are usually paid as a percentage of sales revenue, commission expense is tied directly to revenue.

Systematic and Rational Allocation

Another method used to implement the matching principle is **systematic and rational allocation**. Many costs cannot be directly linked to specific revenue transactions. They can, however, be tied to a span of years and allocated as an expense to each of those years. Sales equipment, as an example, is essential to generate revenue. However, linking the cost of each display case, piece of furniture, and the like to specific sales transactions is difficult. Instead, the equipment's cost is systematically allocated as depreciation expense to the years during which the equipment helps generate revenue.

Immediate Recognition

The final method of applying the matching principle is **immediate recognition.** Some expenditures have no discernible future benefit. In these cases, the expenditure is expensed immediately. Officers' salaries, utilities, and interest are treated in this manner.

Reality Check 4-2 addresses revenue and expense issues for Cendant Corporation.

A CLOSER LOOK AT THE INCOME STATEMENT

As indicated earlier, **income statements** summarize past transactions and events. Many users of income statements are interested in the past only to the extent that it can help predict the future. Financial statement users are concerned about **sustainable earnings,** which refer to the likelihood that earnings will persist in the future. Operating income is often used to estimate sustainable earnings.

Note that Wal-Mart provides a sub-total on its income statement showing "operating profit". In this case, operating profit is synonymous with operating income and sustainable earnings. Note also that Wal-Mart shows income from two sources, "net sales" and "other income". Which is more important to Wal-Mart's future success? We suggest that **sustainability** is most important.

REALITY CHECK 4-2

Cendant Corporation markets memberships in discount purchasing clubs. Typical subscriptions last one year. The first month is a trial membership; members pay no fee. After the first month, members are billed monthly. However, at any time during the year-long subscription period, a member can terminate the agreement and receive a refund for all amounts paid. Cendant also incurs marketing costs in attracting new members (such as mailings and phone solicitations).

Required

a. Describe two methods that Cendant could use to recognize revenue. Which method is the most conservative?

b. For each of the two revenue recognition methods described above, suggest a method of expense recognition that adheres to the matching principle.

c. Because Cendant has experienced significant accounting irregularities, the SEC has forced Cendant to use certain revenue and expense methods. Which methods do you suspect these are?

SOLUTION

a. Cendant could recognize revenue ratably over the 11-month period following the trial membership. This method is supported by the fact that Cendant provides the services over this period. However, Cendant would also need to establish an allowance for its estimate of the number of memberships that will be canceled. Alternatively, Cendant could recognize revenue at the end of the twelfth month, when cancellation is no longer possible. This method defers revenue recognition as long as possible, requires no estimates, and is the most conservative.

b. The first method of revenue recognition would be accompanied by deferring the marketing costs and expensing them over months 2 through 12. The second method would be accompanied by deferring the marketing costs and expensing them at the end of the twelfth month. In both cases, a portion of the marketing costs should be expensed more quickly to reflect the canceled subscriptions.

c. The SEC has required Cendant to use the most conservative methods possible. Accordingly, revenue is recognized at the end of the twelfth month. Expenses are recognized when incurred because they cannot be recovered in the event of cancellation.

CONSOLIDATED STATEMENTS OF INCOME (WAL-MART)
(AMOUNTS IN MILLIONS EXCEPT PER SHARE DATA)

Fiscal years ended January 31,	*2006*	*2005*	*2004*
Revenues:			
Net sales	$312,427	$285,222	$256,329
Other income, net	3,227	2,910	2,352
	315,654	288,132	258,681
Costs and expenses:			
Cost of sales	240,391	219,793	198,747
Operating, selling, general and administrative expenses	56,733	51,248	44,909
Operating income	18,530	17,091	15,025

Historical income statements will be less useful for predicting the future if the results of ongoing operations are combined with the effects of events that are unusual or are not expected to recur in the future. Consequently, GAAP requires that income statements separately report certain items. This section describes these items and shows how they are displayed on the income statement.

Discontinued Operations

If a firm ceases to operate (or plans to cease operating) a **"distinguishable operating component"** of its business, separate income statement disclosure is required of its (1) continuing operations, and (2) **discontinued operations.** Note that an "operating component" must have operations and cash flows that are clearly distinguishable from the rest of the firm. Exhibit 4-4 contains the income statement of American Greetings Corp., which designs and sells greeting cards. In July 2004, American Greetings made the decision to sell its Magnivision line of nonprescription reading glasses in order to focus on business more related to the core business.

The first 10 lines of American Greetings' income statement reflect the results of continuing operations. The discontinued operations section contains the results of operating this component and the income on disposal of the Magnivision division. In making predictions about future earnings, most analysts would ignore the effects of these items by focusing on income from continuing operations.

For example, a *Wall Street Journal* article stated: "HCA-Hospital Corporation of America, bowing to weakness in the psychiatric hospital industry, said it will sell 22 hospitals and take an after-tax charge of as much as $300 million in the third quarter." The charge reflects operating losses and anticipated losses on the sale. Because HCA retained ownership of 26 psychiatric hospitals and 73 general hospitals and the hospitals that were sold did not constitute a separate operating component; treatment as a discontinued operation was not required (assuming

What Would You Do?

Software Programs International (SPI) designs and markets several software packages. SPI's word processing program has not generated as many sales as management had forecast. Because of this, SPI is evaluating two alternative strategies. One strategy is to discontinue the product. The other strategy involves a renewed effort to improve the product and make it more attractive to potential customers. SPI's consideration of these strategies began in October of 2006. A final decision will be made around July 2007.

SPI is a calendar year-end firm. SPI realizes that its financial statement readers would find information about these plans useful. On the other hand, disclosing that the word processing product might be discontinued would probably make customers hesitant to purchase the product. They would also be reluctant to buy and learn a system that will never be upgraded or improved. The decline in sales would, of course, negatively affect SPI's shareholders.

Should SPI disclose its strategy evaluation in its 2006 financial statements?

EXHIBIT 4-4 INCOME STATEMENT WITH DISCONTINUED OPERATIONS

American Greetings Corp.
Consolidated Statement of Income
For the Year Ended February 28, 2005
(Dollars in thousands except share and per share amounts)

Net sales	$1,883,367
Cost and expenses:	
Material, labor, and other production costs	895,110
Selling, distribution, and marketing	648,120
Administrative and general	249,984
Goodwill impairment	—
Interest expense	79,397
Other income—net	(96,069)
	1,776,542
Income from continuing operations before income tax expense	106,825
Income tax expense	37,328
Income from continuing operations	69,497
Loss from discontinued operations, net of tax	25,782
Net income	$ 43,715

HCA no longer had a "major involvement" in the 22 hospitals that were sold). The $300 million charge would be included in continuing operations. Thus, financial statement readers must be aware that continuing operations might contain revenues, expenses, gains, and losses that will not persist in the future. Some analysts would prefer to remove the $300 million charge from the current quarter's earnings when making projections about the future. On the other hand, some analysts might view HCA's sale of hospitals as a normally recurring modification of the firm's strategy. If these charges were expected to occur periodically, the $300 million would not be used to adjust reported earnings.

A similar example concerning losses, labeled "special charges" by Sears, Roebuck, and Company, is shown in Reality Check 4-3. Again, this did not qualify as a separate operating component and yet analysts might want to make an adjustment when estimating sustainable earnings (adjusted net earnings).

REALITY CHECK 4-3

Sears, Roebuck, and Company reported an annual profit of $3,397 million for fiscal year 2003. However, that profit included a $140 million special charge related to closing facilities and reducing its workforce. Even though this action did not constitute a discontinued operation, some analysts might prefer to exclude the disposal loss from Sear's earnings when making projections about future earnings.

Required

Eliminate the special charge from Sear's reported net income.

SOLUTION

Reported net income	$3,397,000,000
Plus special charge	140,000,000
Adjusted net income	$3,537,000,000

Extraordinary Items

Extraordinary items are events and transactions that are unusual in nature and infrequent in occurrence. Unusual in nature implies that the event or transaction is, at most, incidentally related to a firm's typical operations. Infrequent in occurrence suggests that the item is not expected to recur in the foreseeable future. Extraordinary items usually include natural disasters and actions by foreign governments, such as expropriation of assets. Separate disclosure of extraordinary items enables analysts to make better projections of a firm's future operations.

Exhibit 4-5 shows a partial income statement for a California-based company, American Enterprises, Inc. (AE) and an accompanying note. It shows that

EXHIBIT 4-5 PARTIAL INCOME STATEMENT

American Enterprises, Inc.
Partial Income Statement
For the Year Ended October 31, 2007
(Dollars in thousands)

Income before extraordinary gain	$ 9,846
Extraordinary gain (net of income taxes of $1,047)	1,387
Net income	$11,233

Note: The Companys' former headquarters building in San Francisco was severely damaged by an earthquake. After the settlement with the insurers, the Company retired the building and recognized an extraordinary gain of $1,387,000, net of income taxes of $1,047,000.

AE lost a building in an earthquake, which meets the criterion of being unusual in nature. A question arises as to whether they are expected to recur in the foreseeable future. In California, earthquakes continue to occur with some regularity. This is another accounting situation that requires judgment. Evidently, AE and its auditors feel that earthquakes in their area occur with sufficient irregularity that they are not expected to recur in the foreseeable future. Based on the footnote disclosures, analysts can exercise their own judgment about reported extraordinary items.

Note also that AE recognized a gain. A gain arose because the proceeds from the insurance settlement exceeded the carrying value of the building. Recall that buildings are carried in the accounting records at depreciated historical cost, which does not reflect current market values.

When making predictions about AE's future income levels, most analysts would remove the extraordinary gain from AE's reported net income:

Reported net income	$11,233,000
Less extraordinary gain	1,387,000
Adjusted net income	$ 9,846,000

Income Taxes

Given that many income statements have several major sections (continuing operations, discontinued operations, and extraordinary items), a decision must be made about where to report income tax expense. GAAP takes the reasonable position that taxes should be allocated to each major section. Consider again Exhibit 4-4; one item listed is income tax expense. However, this is not American Greetings' total income tax expense. It is the income tax associated with continuing operations. The tax effects associated with discontinued operations are included in the calculation of those reported losses. This format shows discontinued operations **net of tax**.

Note that discontinued operations generated a loss and that the tax effect is considered a **tax benefit.** Losses yield tax benefits because they lower a firm's taxes.

Consider a simple example. In 2007, Crimp Corporation earned, before taxes, a profit of $10,000 on continuing operations. It also incurred a $2,000 loss on discontinued operations. Assume a tax rate of 30%. Had the $2,000 loss not been incurred, Crimp's total tax expense would have been $3,000:

$$\text{Total tax expense} = \$10{,}000 \times .3 = \$3{,}000$$

However, given that Crimp did incur the $2,000 loss, its total tax expense is $2,400:

$$\text{Total tax expense} = (\$10{,}000 - \$2{,}000) \times .3 = \$2{,}400$$

Thus, the loss from discontinued operations reduced income tax expense by $600. The tax expense allocated to continuing operations is $3,000, and the tax benefit allocated to discontinued operations is $600. A partial income statement would appear as follows:

CRIMP CORPORATION
PARTIAL INCOME STATEMENT
FOR THE YEAR ENDED DECEMBER 31, 2007

Earnings before taxes	$10,000
Income tax expense	3,000
Net earnings from continuing operations	7,000
Loss from discontinued operations (less income tax benefit of $600)	1,400
Net income	$ 5,600

Earnings per Share

Many financial numbers are stated on a per-share basis. Price per share and dividends per share are widely quoted in the financial press. Because a share of stock is the basic ownership unit in corporations, this mode of expression is quite useful. Consequently, GAAP requires that publicly held companies state net income on a per-share basis. In general terms, this requires dividing net income by the average number of shares of stock outstanding. The result is earnings per share (EPS):

$$\text{EPS} = \frac{\text{Net income}}{\text{Shares outstanding}}$$

Per-share amounts make it easier to relate the dividends, prices, and earnings of a given firm.

Analyzing the Income Statement

As you've seen by now, the income statement contains a great deal of useful information about a firm. This section shows how to extract and interpret that information. The income statements of Cisco Systems, Inc. (CSCO) for the years 2002 and 1996, which are summarized in Exhibit 4-6, serve as the basis for this section.

One item on Cisco's income statement deserves special mention. In 2001, Cisco incurred a $1170 million special charge. The charge includes costs to close facilities, write down assets, and lay off employees (see the note in Exhibit 4-6). Because Cisco did not discontinue a clearly distinguishable operating component of its business, these changes do not qualify as a discontinued operation, yet this charge might not recur in the near future. Consequently, some analysts would delete this $1170 million loss in calculating ratios and evaluating trends. Such adjustments are demonstrated later in the chapter.

Vertical Analysis

Vertical analysis examines relationships within a given year. To do this with the income statement, divide each line by the first item, net sales. Net sales are a

EXHIBIT 4-6 INCOME STATEMENTS FOR 2002 AND 2001

Cisco Systems, Inc.
Income Statements
(Dollars in millions)

	YEAR ENDED JULY 27, 2002 AND JULY 28, 2001,	
	2002	**2001**
Total net sales	$18,915	$22,293
Total cost of sales	6,902	11,221
Gross margin	12,013	11,072
Selling, general, and administrative expenses	8,330	9,996
Restructuring costs and special charges	—	1,170
Amortization of intangible assets and goodwill	699	1,055
In-process R&D	65	855
Total operating expenses	9,094	13,076
Operating income (loss)	2,919	(2,004)
Interest and other income (loss)	(209)	1,130
Income (loss) before taxes	2,710	(874)
Income taxes	817	140
Net income (loss)	$ 1,893	$ (1,014)

Note: On April 16, 2001, due to macroeconomic and capital spending issues affecting the networking industry, the Company announced a restructuring program to prioritize its initiatives around a focus on profit contribution, high-growth areas of its business, reduction of expenses, and improved efficiency. This restructuring program included a worldwide workforce reduction, consolidation of excess facilities, and restructuring of certain business functions.

summary measure of a firm's total activities, so evaluating each income statement item relative to net sales makes sense. The result yields **common-size income statements** in percentage terms. Cisco 's common-size statements appear in Exhibit 4-7.

The first line of a common-size income statement is always 100% because the net sales figure is divided by itself. The second line of the common-size income statement, cost of products sold divided by net sales, is referred to as the **cost of goods sold percentage.** For a firm that is a **merchandiser,** one that simply buys and resells goods without changing their shape or form, this percentage reflects the relationship between the price the firm pays for the goods and the price it charges customers. For a **manufacturer,** a firm that buys raw materials and component parts and reshapes them into a finished product, the cost of goods sold percentage can also indicate the efficiency of the manufacturing process.

In assessing a firm's ability to generate cash flows, low costs and consequently low cost of goods sold percentages are desirable. This provides a larger profit per item sold. For every dollar of revenue in 2002, Cisco paid about $0.36 to manufacture the associated clothing.

The third line, **gross profit** (or **gross margin**) **percentage,** is calculated either by dividing gross profit by net sales or by subtracting the cost of goods sold percentage from 100%. It reflects the percentage of the sales price that exceeds the cost of goods sold. It measures the percentage of revenue that is available to cover expenses other than cost of goods sold and to contribute toward profits. In 2002, about $0.64 of every Cisco sales dollar was available for these purposes. Given that a lower cost of goods sold percentage is desirable, most managers will also appreciate the resulting increases in the gross profit percentage.

EXHIBIT 4-7 COMMON-SIZE INCOME STATEMENTS

Cisco Systems, Inc.
Common-Size Income Statements

	2002	2001
Total net sales	100.00%	100.00%
Total cost of sales	36.49	50.33
Gross margin	63.51	49.67
Selling, general, and administrative expenses	44.04	44.84
Restructuring costs and special charges	—	5.25
Amortization of intangible assets and goodwill	3.70	4.73
In-process R&D	0.34	3.84
Total operating expenses	48.08	58.66
Operating income (loss)	15.43	(8.99)
Interest and other income (loss)	(1.10)	5.07
Income (loss) before taxes	14.33	(3.92)
Income taxes	4.32	0.63
Net income (loss)	10.01%	(4.55)%

Two basic strategies exist to increase the gross profit percentage (or, in other words, to decrease the cost of goods sold percentage). First, selling prices could be increased. This option is limited because of competition from other companies in the firm's industry. Second, efforts can be made to reduce the cost of goods sold. This can be done, for example, through more astute purchasing (such as buying in bulk to obtain a discount) or a more efficient manufacturing process. These strategies all assume that quality is held constant, that is, that quality is not increased at the same time as selling prices, nor that quality is decreased in order to decrease the cost of goods sold percentage.

The fourth line of Cisco's common-size income statement reflects the relationship between selling, general, and administrative expenses and net sales. Managers have substantial control over these costs, and percentages that increase over time are usually viewed with disfavor.

Of the remaining items in Exhibit 4-7, the two most important are the **operating income percentage** and the **net income percentage.** The operating income percentage is an indicator of management's success in operating the firm. The numerator, *operating income (or loss), excludes both interest expense and taxes*. Because these expenses are not directly affected by operating (buying and selling) decisions, the operating income percentage is a better reflection of how management handles the day-to-day affairs of the firm. The net income percentage reflects the firm's overall profitability, after interest and taxes, relative to its level of activity (net sales). Both ratios are indicators of a firm's financial success.

Exhibit 4-8 graphically depicts the information contained in Exhibit 4-7.

Trend Analysis

Trend analysis involves comparing financial statement numbers over time. One way to implement this is to compare the common-size income statement items over time. The trends in Cisco's cost of goods sold percentage and its gross profit percentage are favorable. For example, the cost of goods sold percentage decreased from 50.3% in 2001 to 36.5% in 2002. This decrease could reflect decreases in the prices of raw materials, increased demand for its products (allowing an increase in selling prices), or efficiencies in the manufacturing process.

The trend in selling, general, and administrative expenses as a percentage of net sales is favorable, however, management should continue efforts to decrease these expenses going forward. They have remained virtually unchanged in both 2001/2002. However, as Exhibit 4-6 shows, the total dollar amount of these costs has declined.

Both operating income and net income show very desirable trends. However, if Cisco's special charge is not expected to recur, the operating income percentage and net income percentage should be adjusted for purposes of assessing performance and forecasting future results. To adjust the 2001 operating income percentage, the special charge should be added to operating income because it has already been subtracted in arriving at that number.

EXHIBIT 4-8 CISCO GRAPHIC DEPICTION OF COMMON-SIZE

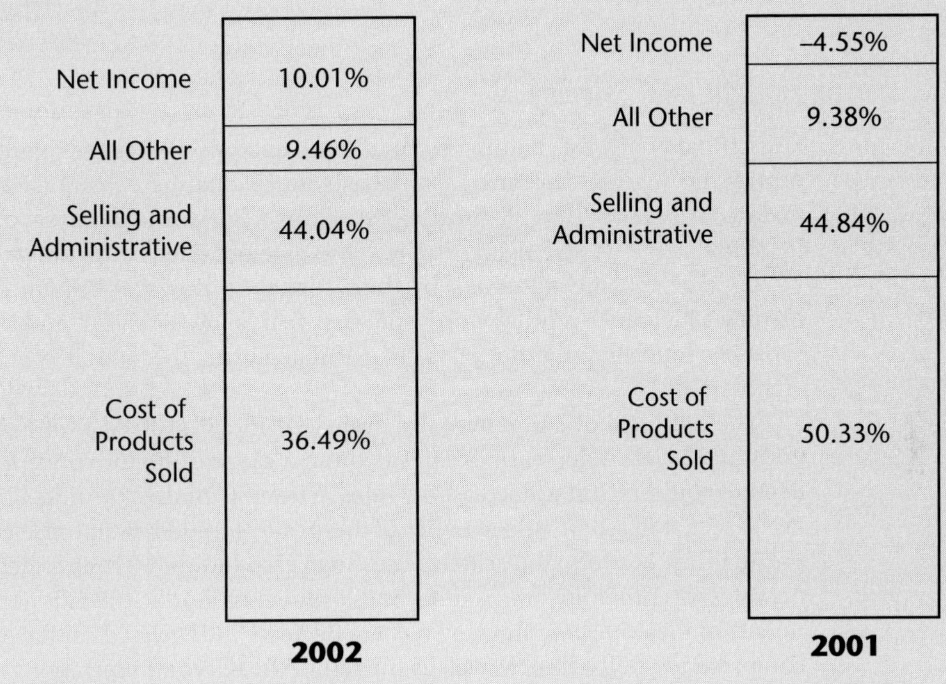

$$\text{Adjusted operating income percentage} = \frac{\text{Operating income (loss)} + \text{Special charge}}{\text{Net sales}}$$

$$= \frac{(\$2{,}004) + \$1{,}170}{\$22{,}293} = -0.04\%$$

Because net income is an after-tax figure, the adjusted net income percentage must be modified on an after-tax basis. Assume that Cisco's tax rate is 40%. The after-tax effect on the special charge would be $702,000,000. The after-tax cost is smaller than the pre-tax cost of $1,170 million because it reflects the benefit of a reduction in taxes due to the loss. The adjustment is accomplished by adding the $702,000,000 after-tax loss to net income.

$$\text{Adjusted net income percentage} = \frac{\text{Net income (loss)} + \text{After-tax special charge}}{\text{Net sales}}$$

$$= \frac{(\$1{,}014) + \$702}{\$22{,}293} = -0.014\%$$

Using these adjusted percentages for 2001 as a benchmark, Cisco's performance in 2002 has still improved, but not to the same degree as the unadjusted percentages indicated.

Horizontal Analysis

Horizontal analysis is another form of trend analysis. It uses the figures from a prior year's income statement as the basis for calculating percentage increases and decreases over time. Exhibit 4-9 contains a horizontal analysis of Cisco's income statements. The figures in the exhibit are obtained by dividing the items in the 2002 income statement by their corresponding amounts in the 2001 income statement. In other words, the first year is the base year, and the corresponding ratios for all other years are calculated using the "oldest" year as a reference point.

The exhibit shows that net sales decreased 15.2% (100%–84.8%) between 2001 and 2002. A decrease in sales is often a cause of major concern. A sales decline could reflect a decrease in sales activity (number of units sold) or a decrease in unit selling prices. Either of these causes could have adverse effects on profitability. Additional research regarding Cisco indicates that the decrease in net sales was primarily due to unfavorable global economic conditions. A major impact of the economic slowdown was a decrease in IT related capital spending compared to 2001. Cisco, as well as the rest of the telecommunications industry, were greatly impacted by the economic slowdown between 2001 and 2002.

EXHIBIT 4-9 HORIZONTAL ANALYSIS OF INCOME STATEMENTS

Cisco Systems, Inc.
Income Statements—Horizontal Analysis

	2002	**2001**
Total net sales	84.8%	100%
Total cost of sales	61.5	100
Gross margin	108.5	100
Selling, general, and administrative expenses	83.3	100
Restructuring costs and special charges	—	100
Amortization of intangible assets and goodwill	66.3	100
In-process R&D	7.6	100
Total operating expenses	69.5	100
Operating income (loss)	NA	100
Interest and other income (loss)	NA	100
Income (loss) before taxes	NA	100
Income taxes	583.6	100
Net income (loss)	NA	100%

NA = Not available

A positive note for Cisco is that net service revenue increased in 2002 primarily from technical support services on its products. Revenue from consulting services increased, as well as service contract renewals. Fortunately for Cisco the increase in service revenue helped to offset the decrease in product sales.

Cisco's reduced product sales, as described above, should also impact its expenses. Cost of products sold is the largest single expense item. Exhibit 4-9 shows that this item declined 38.5% (100%–61.5%) from 2001 to 2002. The decrease in cost of products sold is larger than the decrease in sales (15.2%). This suggests that the actions taken by Cisco will have a positive effect on profitability. The decline in cost of products sold is also attributable to two other reasons; Cisco was able to find less expensive sources of raw materials, and Cisco improved the efficiency of its manufacturing operations. The latter was accomplished, in part, by plant closings, the costs of which were contained in the 2001 income statement. Also note that the decline in cost of products sold relative to sales is consistent with the results of the common-size income statements (refer to Exhibit 4-7) that showed that the cost of products sold had decreased as a percentage of sales.

Exhibit 4-9 indicates that the percentage change in operating income for 2002 is not available. This is due to the fact that an operating loss was generated in 2001 and operating income was generated in 2002. Although the 2002 figure can be calculated (2,919 / −2,004) = −146%), care must be exercised when dealing with negative numbers. We prefer to show the resulting calculation as NA (not available) or as undefined. The negative denominator yields a negative percentage, yet the income in 2002 is much more positive than the 2001 loss. Even if absolute values are used, knowing that the 2002 operating income is over two times as large as the 2001 operating loss is not particularly insightful. Regardless of the difficulties with this calculation, the trend in operating income is extremely favorable. The trend in net income is also undefined for the same reason as above. Although not depicted in Cisco's horizontal analysis, another pitfall in calculating ratios is the small denominator problem. A large percentage increase may not be primarily due to a year being so favorable. Rather, a small amount generated in the prior year has the effect of inflating the calculated value. Although one year's data may have improved substantially, a significant percentage increase over the prior year probably overstates the improvement.

Other Ratios

Several ratios link the income statement and the balance sheet. **Return on shareholders' equity (ROE)** is of utmost importance to shareholders. To calculate ROE, divide net income by average shareholders' equity:

$$\text{ROE} = \frac{\text{Net income}}{\text{Average shareholders' equity}}$$

ROE relates the earnings generated by a firm to the assets invested by its shareholders. It is obviously in the shareholders' best interest to have larger earnings generated on their investments. A potential investor, faced with competing investment choices, will use ROE to help identify the preferred investment.

The denominator of ROE is average shareholders' equity. Because net income is earned over the course of a year, it makes sense to use the firm's average shareholders' equity during the year. The results of any return ratio are probably more meaningful when an average is used in the denominator. As a practical matter, average shareholders' equity is usually calculated by averaging beginning and end-of-year shareholders' equity amounts, which are found on the balance sheet. Exhibit 4-10 summarizes certain items from Cisco's balance sheet. Cisco's 2002 ROE was:

$$\text{ROE} = \frac{\$1{,}893}{(\$28{,}656 + \$27{,}120)/2} = 6.79\%$$

A ROE of 6.8% is close to Cisco's industry average of 9.2%. The 2002 ROE compares extremely favorably to the 2001 ROE of –3.68%.

Another important ratio is **return on assets (ROA).** This ratio relates a firm's earnings to all the assets the firm has available to generate those earnings. ROA differs from ROE in that ROE utilizes only the assets that the shareholders supplied. ROE measures management's success in using the assets invested by shareholders, whereas ROA measures how successfully management utilized all the assets entrusted to it. To calculate a basic ROA, divide net income by average total assets (or if you prefer, by the year-end asset amount):

$$\text{ROA} = \frac{\text{Net income}}{\text{Average total assets}}$$

A more accurate ROA will include an adjustment for interest expense. To calculate interest adjusted ROA, divide net income, adjusted for interest expense, by average total assets:

$$\text{ROA} = \frac{\text{Net income} + \text{interest expense } (1 - \text{tax rate})}{\text{Average total assets}}$$

EXHIBIT 4-10 SUMMARY OF SELECTED INFORMATION

Cisco Systems, Inc.
Selected Balance Sheet Information
(Dollars in millions)

	2002	2001
Total shareholders' equity	$28,656	$27,120
Total assets	$37,795	$35,238
Number of shares used to calculate eps	7,301	7,196

Why is interest expense added to net income in the numerator? Recall that a firm can acquire assets from two sources: owners and creditors. Interest expense is a cost incurred to acquire assets from creditors (e.g., interest expense on bank borrowings). It arises from a financing decision (obtaining funds from creditors rather than owners), not an operating decision (utilizing assets). Because ROA is designed to measure managers' success in utilizing assets, interest expense is irrelevant. The effect of interest expense on net income is often eliminated when calculating ROA. We will generally use the basic ROA calculation.

Interest expense has direct and indirect effects on net income, and both effects should be eliminated. Regarding the direct effect, because interest expense has already been subtracted in calculating net income, it is now added back. The indirect effect relates to taxes. Because interest expense is a deduction for tax purposes, tax expense is lower and net income is higher by an amount equal to interest expense multiplied by the tax rate. Therefore, to adjust fully for the elimination of interest expense, net income must be increased by interest expense and decreased by interest expense multiplied by the tax rate. The difference between these two amounts is interest expense multiplied by (1 minus the tax rate):

$$\begin{array}{l} + \text{ Interest expense} \\ - \text{ Interest expense} \times \text{tax rate} \\ \hline \text{Interest expense} \times (1 - \text{tax rate}) \end{array}$$

Eliminating the effects of interest expense facilitates the comparison of asset utilization across firms that have different amounts of debt. Unless specified otherwise, this text *usually does not adjust for interest expense* in the basic ROA calculation. Cisco's basic ROA for 2002 was:

$$\text{ROA} = \frac{\$1{,}893}{\$36{,}517} = 5.18\%$$

$$\text{Average total assets} = (\$37{,}795 + \$35{,}238) / 2 = 36{,}517$$

The more complicated ROA requires use of the firm's tax rate. Cisco's effective rate in 2002 was 30% and its interest-adjusted ROA for 2002 was:

$$\text{Interest adjusted ROA} = \frac{\$1{,}893 + \$209^{*}\ (1 - .310)}{(\$37{,}795 + \$35{,}238/2)} = 5.58\%$$

Cisco's 2002 ROA greatly exceeded its performance in 2001. The dramatic improvements in Cisco's ROE and ROA reflect the success of its operational changes mentioned above.

The final ratio discussed in this section is **times interest earned.** Because profits ultimately are a source of cash, and because cash is necessary for the

*Since Cisco reported interest expense and other income (loss) together the analyst should review Cisco's footnotes to determine actual interest expenses.

payment of interest charges, creditors are concerned about the relationship between profits and interest expense. The times interest earned ratio shows how many times interest expense is covered by resources generated from operations, and creditors prefer higher times interest earned ratios. It is calculated by dividing earnings before interest and taxes by interest expense:

$$\text{Times interest earned} = \frac{\text{Earnings before interest and taxes}}{\text{Interest expense}}$$

Earnings before interest and taxes (EBIT), rather than net income, is used in the numerator. Because interest expense is already deducted in calculating net income, net income understates the resources available to cover interest expense. Tax expense should not reduce the numerator because, in a worst-case scenario, as income declines, taxes would be eliminated.

Cisco's income statement, presented in Exhibit 4-6, does not contain a line item for income before interest and taxes. The easiest way to calculate this figure, given Cisco's income statement format, is to add interest expense to income before taxes. In 2002, Cisco's income before interest and taxes would be determined as follows (dollars in millions):

Income before taxes	$2,710
Interest expense	209*
Income before interest and taxes	$2,919

Cisco's 2002 times interest earned ratio was 13.97:

$$\text{Times interest earned} = \frac{\$2{,}919}{\$209} = 13.97$$

This ratio indicates that interest expense is covered 13.97 times at present income levels. This is a positive result and reflects that Cisco has relatively little outstanding debt. Given that potential creditors would look favorably on this ratio, Cisco would likely have little problem securing additional financing, if it so desires.

LIMITATIONS OF ACCOUNTING INCOME

Although financial statement readers find reported accounting income very useful, it does have several limitations. Conceptually, we often think of income as an increase in wealth. If our bank account grows by $100 because of interest, we feel as though our income is $100. For many assets, however, accounting does not recognize an increase in value when it occurs. Instead, the value increase and the associated income are recognized at the time of the asset's disposal.

*Since Cisco reported interest expense and other income (loss) together the analyst should review Cisco's footnotes to determine actual interest expenses.

Sometimes the difference between historical cost and current value can be quite large. Consider Hiroshi Fujishige, who owns a 58-acre farm across the street from Disneyland. The farm was purchased in 1953 for $2,500. Southern California real estate experts estimate its value to be $55,000,000. In spite of this estimate, the Fujishige Farm balance sheet reflects the land at $2,500, and the increase in value has not appeared on any of Fujishige's income statements. In general, to recognize a value increase, accounting rules require the occurrence of a transaction for verification purposes.

Financial statements do not reflect still other accomplishments of a firm. For example, the *Wall Street Journal* reported that the Food and Drug Administration planned to approve an anticlotting drug developed by COR Therapeutics, Inc. This was extremely good news for COR; in fact, its stock soared 79% on the news. However, this event was not included in its accounting records when the announcement was made. At that time, COR had not engaged in any transaction; no sales had been made. The financial statement effects of the drug sales will be recognized in the accounting records as they occur.

Accounting's **conservatism principle** can also limit the extent to which accounting income reflects changes in wealth. This principle states that when doubt exists about the accounting treatment for a given transaction, a conservative alternative should be selected. In other words, select the alternative that reports lower asset values and lower net income. For example, expenditures for research and development are immediately expensed, even when they result in valuable products or patents. Spending on employee training is expensed immediately, even though its objective is to create a more highly skilled workforce. These examples suggest that the balance sheets of some companies may have undervalued or unrecorded assets; this, of course, implies that the net income figure on the income statement does not necessarily reflect changes in wealth. On the other hand, most accountants support the conservatism principle because it helps avoid overly optimistic financial statements.

In summary, to ensure that reliable and verifiable financial statements emerge from the accounting process, GAAP precludes the recognition of certain potential value changes. Because of this, accounting income does not strictly measure changes in wealth. However, it is a very useful performance measure on which the business community relies heavily.

ACCOUNTING INCOME AND ECONOMIC CONSEQUENCES

Recall from Chapter 2 that the managers of many publicly-held corporations receive bonuses that are based on reported accounting net income. These bonus plans typically include a floor and a ceiling. The floor requires that net income must reach a certain level before the bonus is activated, while the ceiling places a limit on the size of the bonus. That is, the bonus is not increased as net income increases above the ceiling. Thus, managers prefer that net income fall at the high end of the range between the floor and the ceiling.

Bonuses can motivate managers to undertake actions that will improve the operations of the firm, thereby increasing profits. Unfortunately, bonuses can also motivate managers to make accounting-related decisions that do not affect the underlying profitability of the firm, but that do affect reported accounting income.

For example, firms occasionally engage in "big baths." These are accounting decisions that result in large losses in a single year in order to avoid a series of small losses in succeeding years. If reported earnings would otherwise have been below a bonus plan's floor, such losses have no effect on the current year's bonus. Moreover, by taking the losses all at one time, subsequent periods are relieved of those charges, and the chances of higher reported profits and bonuses in the future are maximized. Reality Check 4-4 describes a **big bath** taken by Waste Management, Inc.

The actions taken by Waste Management are within the bounds of allowable managerial discretion. Other corporations, however, have been accused of much more questionable actions. For example, Miniscribe, a bankrupt disk-drive manufacturer, is alleged to have recognized revenue prematurely on shipments that customers had not ordered, improperly estimated uncollectible accounts receivable, and falsified inventory.

The application of GAAP requires the exercise of judgment. At the same time, manager's self-interest is affected by reported accounting income. Accordingly, financial statement users should not be surprised that managers' self-interests influence their accounting policy judgments. As a result, financial statements may not be unbiased reflections about the underlying economic activities of firms.

REALITY CHECK 4-4

Waste Management, Inc. recently took several large charges totaling $1.6 billion. These charges included asset write-downs, the cost of severance packages, costs to discontinue serving several large customers because of lost contracts, and other items. These charges contributed to Waste Management's loss of $1.2 billion. Perhaps more than coincidentally, Waste Management had recently selected a new chairman. Some analysts suggest that new corporate administrations are inclined to take big baths.

Required

List two reasons why recently installed corporate managers might want to take a big bath.

SOLUTION

First, these charges can easily be blamed on the former management. Second, they help the company report favorable earnings in the future, which reflects well on the new management team. Moreover, the higher reported net income might increase the bonuses paid to the new managers.

COMPREHENSIVE INCOME

Net income is always a major focus of interest in every income statement. As of the beginning of 1998, firms were required to disclose another important income measure: **comprehensive income**. The motivation for requiring disclosure of this new measure is that generally accepted accounting principles (GAAP) require that all changes in equity (except investments by owners or distributions by owners) be shown in a single number "comprehensive income", and that net income continue to be reported as the major focus of income statements. Therefore, comprehensive income includes all revenues and expenses, all gains and losses normally shown on the income statement, *plus all gains and losses that affect shareholders' equity.* Hence, the name "comprehensive income" because it includes all changes in shareholder wealth other than those due to investments or "withdrawals" by owners.

Many financial statement readers believe that the normal definition of net income excludes too many important changes in shareholders' equity and, thus, reduces the usefulness of the net income figure. Because of this, the FASB requires firms to report comprehensive income, which is defined as net income plus revenues, expenses, gains, and losses that are excluded from net income. Some examples of such items include unrealized gains and losses on certain marketable securities, foreign currency items, and changes in the market value of certain futures contracts. Some of these will be illustrated in future chapters; e.g., Chapter 6 will show how unrealized gains and losses on marketable securities are included in comprehensive income.

Financial Statement Presentation

In displaying comprehensive income, firms can choose among three alternative disclosures: the one-statement approach or the two-statement approach or to show these changes on the Statement of Shareholders' Equity. While the third method can be more confusing and less useful, it has become the preferred method. Unfortunately, this treatment de-emphasizes the importance of comprehensive income and relegates it to a section of the financial statements with low visibility. The two-statement approach leaves the conventional income statement intact and a new statement, the **Statement of Comprehensive Income**, is included. This statement starts with net income and the other items of comprehensive income are then added to (or subtracted from) net income. The final figure is comprehensive income. Exhibit 4-11 illustrates the two-statement approach. Note that eBay uses this method to disclose comprehensive income.

The one-statement approach extends the conventional income statement. Compared to the conventional format ending with net income, the extended statement includes the other items of comprehensive income and ends with comprehensive income. Exhibit 4-12 illustrates the one-statement approach.

EXHIBIT 4-11 **COMPREHENSIVE INCOME: TWO-STATEMENT APPROACH**

Bosch, Inc.
Statement of Income
Year Ended December 31, 2007
(Dollars in thousands)

Net sales	$250,000
Cost of products sold	(150,000)
Gross profit	100,000
Marketing and administrative expenses	(40,000)
Operating profit	60,000
Income taxes	(25,000)
Net income	$35,000

Bosch, Inc.
Statement of Comprehensive Income
Year Ended December 31, 2007
(Dollars in thousands)

Net income	$35,000
Other comprehensive income, net of tax:	
+ Foreign currency translation adjustment	4,000
– Unrealized loss on securities	(5,000)
Comprehensive income	$34,000

EXHIBIT 4-12 **COMPREHENSIVE INCOME: ONE-STATEMENT APPROACH**

Bosch, Inc.
Statement of Income and Comprehensive Income
Year Ended December 31, 2007
(Dollars in thousands)

Net sales	$250,000
Cost of products sold	(150,000)
Gross profit	100,000
Marketing and administrative expenses	(40,000)
Operating profit	60,000
Income taxes	(25,000)
Net income	35,000
Other comprehensive income, net of tax:	
+Foreign currency translation adjustment	4,000
– Unrealized loss on securities	(5,000)
Comprehensive income	$ 34,000

Assessment of Comprehensive Income Reporting

Differences between net income and comprehensive income arise solely because GAAP requires that the recorded value changes in certain assets and liabilities be excluded from net income. Many FASB critics argue that these exclusions are the result of undesirable political compromises by the FASB and reduce the usefulness of net income. The required disclosure of comprehensive income has the effect of reporting a figure that would equal net income if the FASB had not made those compromises. Thus, many financial statement readers view comprehensive income as a more useful number than net income. This suggests that *analyses and ratio calculations that include net income should also be conducted a second time using comprehensive income.*

Target's 2005 financial statements did not include much detailed information on comprehensive income. There was no mention of comprehensive income on the income statement; nor was there any separate statement describing comprehensive income. Target's disclosure of comprehensive income is described in the following note:

Other Comprehensive Income/(Loss)

Other comprehensive income/(loss) includes revenues, expenses, gains and losses that are excluded from net earnings under GAAP and are recorded directly to shareholders' investment. In 2005, 2004 and 2003, other comprehensive income/(loss) primarily included gains and losses on certain hedge transactions and the change in our minimum pension liability, net of related taxes.

This note is not very descriptive, as the analyst must look at the Consolidated Statement of Shareholders' Investment to find any details on comprehensive income. The note provides no evidence of the relative importance of each component of comprehenive income. Target's comprehensive income was relatively minor and was primarily derived from hedge transactions that are beyond the scope of this chapter.

In contrast, consider Wal-Mart's extensive balance sheet disclosure of comprehensive income:

Accumulated Other Comprehensive Income

Comprehensive income is net income plus certain other items that are recorded directly to shareholders' equity. Amounts included in accumulated other comprehensive income for the Company's derivative instruments and minimum pension liability are recorded net of the related income tax effects. The following table gives further detail regarding the changes in the composition of accumulated other comprehensive income during fiscal 2006, 2005 and 2004 (in millions):

(continues)

	Foreign Currency Translation	Derivative Instruments	Minimum Pension Liability	Total
Balance at January 31, 2003	$(1,125)	$822	$(206)	$(509)
Foreign currency translation adjustment	1,685	—	—	1,685
Change in fair value of hedge instruments	—	(444)	—	(444)
Reclassification to earnings	—	103	—	103
Subsidiary minimum pension liability	—	—	16	16
Balance at January 31, 2004	$ 560	$481	$(190)	$ 851
Foreign currency translation adjustment	2,130	—	—	2,130
Change in fair value of hedge instruments	—	(235)	—	(235)
Reclassification to earnings	—	41	—	41
Subsidiary minimum pension liability	—	—	(93)	(93)
Balance at January 31, 2005	$2,690	$287	$(283)	$2,694
Foreign currency translation adjustment	(1,920)	—	—	(1,920)
Change in fair value of hedge instruments	—	157	—	157
Reclassification to earnings	—	71	—	71
Subsidiary minimum pension liability	—	—	51	51
Balance at January 31, 2006	$ 770	$515	$(232)	$1,053

Wal-Mart's comprehensive income (aside from net income) was derived from three sources: foreign currency translations, derivative transactions, and minimum pension liability. Several of these topics will be discussed in later sections of the book. The table above shows the effects of Wal-Mart's comprehensive income (as disclosed in the notes) for each of the three years. Wal-Mart's other comprehensive income increased by $1,562 million [ending balance of $1,053 million – beginning balance ($509)]. The main item that contributed to this increase was foriegn currency adjustment gains in 2003 and 2004 that outweighed the foreign currency adjustment losses in 2005. Note that the table in the notes expands the disclosures on comprehensive income that were shown in the Consolidated Statements of Shareholders' Equity.

Income Statement Items with Little Impact on Cash

In this section we identify several income statements that do not usually have a large impact on cash flows. In general, the analyst can assume that most items comprising operating income also will have similar effects on cash flow. In Cisco's case, the special charge associated with plant closings may not have the same impact on cash flow as on income. Some of these charges may represent accruals and write-offs of assets that will never affect cash flow (except for any associated tax benefits). The analyst must read the notes to determine how much of these special charges are likely to also represent cash flows. Depreciation, if it were separately identified, would not directly affect cash flows. In Cisco's case, other income may not directly affect cash flow. Interest expense will almost always have a large effect on cash flows. Income taxes will similarly have a large effect on cash flows, although there may be deferrals shifting the cash flows in later years. The relationship between tax accruals and tax payments will be discussed further in Chapter 8.

The conclusions to be drawn about the impact of Cisco's income statement on its cash flows are similar to our earlier discussions regarding sustainable income. At this point, the analyst would expect future cash flows from Cisco's operations to closely parallel its sustainable income, after adjusting for the effects of the special charges for plant closings. Other more complicated examples of income statement items that do not affect cash flows will be discussed in later chapters. In summary, analysts must exercise significant judgment and subjective evaluation in identifying non-cash items on the income statement. However, the gains in understanding a firm's future prospects will be well worth the effort.

Summary of Learning Objectives

1. **When are revenues recognized?**
   Revenue should be recognized when the earnings process is substantially complete and the amount to be collected is reasonably determinable. These criteria ensure that revenue is not recognized before the firm has honored its obligation to the customer and is reasonably assured of collecting cash from the customer. Revenue is usually recognized at the point of sale.

2. **When are expenses recognized?**
   The matching principle states that expenses should be recognized when resources have been consumed to help generate revenue. Showing revenues and the related expenses on the same income statement results in a net income figure that best reflects a firm's performance for the period. The matching principle is implemented in one of three ways: associating cause and effect, systematic allocation, and immediate recognition.

3. **Interpret more complex income statements.**
   Income statements may contain several major sections: income from continuing operations, income from discontinued operations, and extraordinary items. This format helps financial statement users assess the past performance of a firm and predict the results of future operations. We recommend that operating income be used to estimate **sustainable earnings.** When making forecasts based on historical information, the effect of transactions and events that are not expected to recur in the future should be eliminated from net income. Because of the way accounting definitions have been developed, even income from continuing operations may include nonrecurring items.

4. **Use ratios to analyze income statement information.**
   The income statement contains a number of measures related to a firm's ability to generate earnings. This helps analysts assess a firm's expected return. Vertical analysis examines relationships within the income statement of one period; each line of the income statement is expressed as a percentage of sales. Horizontal analysis shows the trend over time in income statement numbers. Return on shareholders' equity and return on assets are good summary measures of a firm's performance. Finally, the times interest earned ratio provides creditors with an indication of the firm's ability to pay interest charges.

5. **Describe how reported earnings may affect managers' performance evaluations and, consequently, their accounting policy decisions.**
   Many corporations tie the compensation of their top officers to reported accounting earnings. These bonus plans often contain a floor and a ceiling. The floor is the level of net income that must be exceeded before the bonus is activated, while the ceiling limits the amount of the bonus, regardless of how large net income is. This situation motivates managers to report a net income figure that is at the high end of the floor-ceiling range. Managers are also motivated to undertake "big baths". Taking large charges in one year relieves future years' income of those expenses and paves the way for higher reported earnings and higher bonuses for management.

6. **Understand and interpret comprehensive income.**
   Changes in the value of several assets and liabilities (e.g., marketable securities) are normally excluded from net income. Because of this, some financial statement readers believe that the usefulness of net income is compromised. Consequently, GAAP now requires firms to report **comprehensive income,** which includes net income and any changes in shareholders' equity except investments or withdrawals by owners.

7. **Identify which income statement items will not usually be reflected in cash flows.**
   Most operating income items on the income statement will also affect cash flow. The analyst must watch carefully for special charges, gains, and losses on disposal, and any other category of non-operating gains and losses that may not have a similar effect on cash flows. Depreciation will only affect cash flow through its effect on reducing taxes. Taxes and interest will generally affect cash flows, though perhaps not in the same fiscal year as shown on the income statement.

KEY TERMS

Administrative expenses
Associating cause and effect
Big bath
Bottom line
Calendar year-end
Common-size income statements
Comprehensive income
Conservatism principle
Cost of goods sold (COGS)
Cost of goods sold percentage
Cost of sales
Discontinued operations
Distinguishable operating component
Earnings
Earnings before interest and taxes (EBIT)
Earnings per share (EPS)
Expenses
Extraordinary items
Gains
General and administrative expenses
Gross margin
Gross margin percentage
Gross profit
Gross profit percentage
Growth
Horizontal analysis
Immediate recognition
Income statement
Income taxes
Interest expense
Losses
Matching principle
Materiality principle
Manufacturer
Merchandiser
Multiple-step format
Natural year-end
Net
Net income
Net income percentage
Net of tax
Net sales
Operating income
Operating income percentage
Percentage of completion method
Profit
Proportional revenue recognition
Return on assets (ROA)
Return on shareholders' equity (ROE)
Revenue recognition principle
Revenues
Sales
Sales return
Selling expenses
Single-step format
Statement of comprehensive income
Statement of earnings
Sustainable earnings
Sustainability
Systematic and rational allocation
Tax benefit
Times interest earned
Trend analysis
Vertical analysis
Vertical percentage analysis
52-week year

Exercises and Problems

4-1 Describe the differences between revenues and gains. Also distinguish between expenses and losses. Explain why these items are usually disclosed separately on income statements.

4-2 Why do most companies disclose the cost of goods sold as a separate item on the income statement? How might this item differ for merchandising firms versus manufacturing firms? Why might some firms not want to disclose this item?

4-3 Distinguish between a single-step and a multiple-step income statement. Why is a multiple-step format usually more informative to the reader?

4-4 Explain the two criteria that must be met for a firm to recognize revenue in its income statement. Discuss how these criteria might be applied to revenue recognition by (a) a fast-food restaurant and (b) a home appliance merchandiser.

4-5 Discuss the purpose of the matching principle, and explain the three ways in which this principle is implemented.

4-6 Why are extraordinary items reported separately in the income statement? Identify an event that would be classified by one firm as an ordinary item and by another firm as an extraordinary item? Discuss.

4-7 Discuss the differences between revenues and profits. Where do each appear on the income statement? Why is it important to keep these two separate?

4-8 Discuss the meaning of a "restructuring charge" and explain why you believe that such charges should (or should not) be reported as extraordinary items in the income statement. How does the concept of sustainability affect how extraordinary items are reported on the income statement?

4-9 Provide two examples of ratios that link the income statement and the balance sheet. In each case, explain why it is useful to relate the items that appear in the numerator and the denominator of the ratio.

4-10 The ratios discussed in this chapter include return on assets, return on shareholders' equity, and times interest earned. In each case, a different measure of income is used. Identify and discuss those differences. Explain why income is measured differently in each of these ratio calculations.

Matching Income Statement Items

4-11 For each numbered item, indicate (by letter) where in the income statement it belongs.

a. Revenues
b. Cost of goods sold
c. Selling expenses
d. General and administrative
e. Other income and expenses
f. Separate line item, net of tax after income from continuing operations
g. Not on the income statement

____ 1. Commissions expense

____ 2. Gain on sale of land

____ 3. Dividends declared and paid

____ 4. Prepaid rent

____ 5. Depreciation expense for office equipment

____ 6. Interest expense

____ 7. Tornado loss (business located in Kansas)

____ 8. Merchandise inventory

____ 9. Income tax payable

____ 10. Loss on discontinued operations

Financial Ratios

4-12 Answer each of the following independent questions:

a. The return on equity for the Harmond Corporation for the year ended December 31, 2007, is 9%. The owners' equity balances on December 31, 2006 and 2007 were $180,000 and $200,000, respectively. What is the net income for 2007?

b. The Beachfront Resort Company had the following income statement information:

Sales revenue	$500,000
Gross profit percentage	30%
Net income percentage	5%

What is the cost of goods sold? What are the total operating and other expenses?

c. The return on assets for the Wicker Chair Company is 12%. The average total assets is $230,000 and net income is $20,100. What is interest expense, net of tax? What is gross interest expense if the income tax rate is 25%?

Income Statement

4-13 The following data were provided by Bluebird Company for calendar year 2007:

Sales	$350,000
Gross margin percentage	45%
Net income percentage	8%
Income tax percentage	25%

Required

a. Based on the previous data, determine the following:
(1) Cost of goods sold
(2) Net income
(3) Income taxes
(4) Operating expenses (assume no "other expenses and revenues")

b. Prepare a multiple-step income statement for the year ended December 31, 2007.

Recording Transactions and Preparing an Income Statement

4-14 Spinner Sewing Corporation was incorporated on January 1, 2007. Three investors each invested $150,000 in exchange for $150,000 of common stock of the corporation. The following transactions took place during 2007:

1. Purchased merchandise inventory on account, $200,000.
2. Rent paid on January 2 for a two-year period, $48,000.
3. Borrowed $100,000 on March 31 at a 10% annual interest rate for one year.
4. Sold goods at retail, $300,000; half for cash, half on account. The cost of goods sold was $135,000.
5. Paid $120,000 on outstanding bills owed to inventory suppliers.
6. Received $80,000 from receivables customers.
7. Incurred operating expenses of $36,000, of which $14,000 was paid in cash and the balance on account.

Required

a. Record the above transactions, including the initial investment, in the accounting equation. Set up separate account columns for assets, liabilities, and shareholders' equity.

b. Record the following year-end accruals (adjust the figures from part a):
(1) Expired portion of prepaid rent
(2) Accrued interest expense
(3) Accrued income tax. Assume 20% tax rate.

c. Prepare a multiple-step income statement for the year ended December 31, 2007.

d. Calculate:
(1) Gross profit percentage
(2) Operating income percentage
(3) Net income percentage

e. Calculate:
(1) Return on assets
(2) Return on equity

f. Evaluate the performance of the corporation. What other transactions would you typically expect to see?

g. What if the corporation discontinued part of its operations during the year and incurred a loss of $45,000 on the disposal? What impact would this have on the income statement?

Interpreting Income Statements: Ratio Analysis

4-15 Use the following comparative income statements to evaluate Clarkson Brewery's performance for the year ended December 31, 2007 and 2006.

	2007	*2006*
Net sales	$405,000	$378,000
Operating expenses:		
Cost of goods sold	163,250	154,400
Selling expense	81,000	48,360
General and administrative expense	121,500	102,650
Total operating expenses	365,750	305,410
Operating income	39,250	72,590
Other income:		
Gain on sale of property	34,000	—
Income before tax	73,250	72,590
Income tax expense	21,975	21,777
Income before extraordinary item	51,275	50,813
Extraordinary loss net of tax	—	(25,000)
Net income	$ 51,275	$ 25,813

Required

a. Calculate a horizontal and vertical analysis, using the data from Clarkson Brewery.

b. In which year was the company more successful?

c. What underlying business reasons might have resulted in differences in the company's gains and losses each year?

Transaction Analysis: Preparing an Income Statement, Cash versus Accrual

4-16 Jill Zimmer wants to evaluate the success of her restaurant, Planet Broadway. She has assembled the following 2007 data:

1. Wages were $270,000, paid in cash.
2. Collections from customers were $675,000. (The other half of the customers had not paid their bills by year-end).
3. A $5,000 deposit for a future wedding reception is included in these collections.
4. Insurance expense was $3,500, paid in cash.
5. Rental expense was $120,000, paid half in cash and half in promissory notes due in 2008.

6. Food costs were $85,000, paid in cash.
7. Advertising bills of $13,000 were paid; however, Jill had only agreed to pay $1,000 each month under her contract with the advertising firm. The extra $1,000 payment pertained to 2006.
8. Interest revenues were $350, collected in cash.
9. Cab fares (for inebriated customers) were $875.
10. Jill's salary was $10,000 per month, but due to concerns about cash flow, she was only paid $5,000 each month.
11. The income tax rate is 28% of income before taxes.

Required

a. Prepare a single-step income statement, using the accrual basis of accounting.
b. Prepare a similar income statement, using the cash basis of accounting.
c. Discuss the differences between these two statements.
d. What managerial concerns might Jill have upon seeing your income statement?
e. What additional items usually appear in such an income statement for a small business?
f. Which costs do you feel are high, relative to Jill's volume of business?
g. On which costs should she concentrate most in order to improve her profitability?
h. What else could she do to improve her net income?

Transaction Analysis

4-17 The Bichette Company had the following transactions during the year ended December 31, 2007:

1. Sales on account were $155,000. Cash sales were $38,000.
2. Cost of goods sold during the year was $42,000.
3. Wages earned by employees were $32,000. Three-quarters of the amount was paid during the year as the wages were incurred. The remainder was accrued at year end.
4. A two-year insurance policy was purchased on January 1, 2007, for $4,800.
5. Equipment with a five-year life was acquired on June 30, 2007, for $10,000, with a note bearing interest at an annual rate of 9%. The interest and principal are not due until June 30, 2008.
6. Rent and other operating expenses paid in cash were $14,500.
7. The company sold a short-term investment and recorded a gain of $800.
8. Dividends declared and paid were $24,015.
9. The income tax rate was 30%.

Required

a. Prepare a multi-step income statement similar to Exhibit 4-1 for the year ended December 31, 2007. Note: Make the necessary adjustments before preparing the income statement.

b. Assume that stockholders' equity at the beginning of the year was $740,000. The only changes recorded in stockholders' equity during 2007 were net income and dividends. Calculate return on equity and evaluate your results.

c. Calculate earnings per share. Assume that 140,000 shares were outstanding.

d. Calculate times interest earned.

Interpreting Financial Statements

4-18 Alpha Designs is a high-tech software development company specializing in imaging and multimedia computer applications. Alpha's balance sheets are reproduced below (dollars in thousands):

	2007	*2006*
Assets		
Cash and equivalents	$ 5,086	$ 9,283
Marketable securities	14,326	19,537
Accounts receivable, net of allowances	6,471	2,987
Inventories	12,275	10,066
Prepaid expenses	435	753
Income taxes receivable	1,582	2,428
Total current assets	40,175	45,054
Equipment, net	1,626	1,607
Other assets	2,466	2,388
Total assets	$44,267	$49,049
Liabilities and Shareholders' Equity		
Current liabilities		
Accounts payable	$ 4,933	$1,826
Accrued salary and benefits	809	594
Other accrued liabilities	737	1,119
Total current liabilities	6,479	3,539
Other long-term liabilities	—	755
Total liabilities	6,479	4,294
Shareholders' Equity		
Common stock	19,287	19,088
Retained earnings	18,501	25,667
Total shareholders' equity	37,788	44,755
Total liabilities and shareholders' equity	$44,267	$49,049

Alpha's 2005–2007 statements of operations are summarized below (dollars in thousands):

	2007	*2006*	*2005*
Net sales	$ 27,058	$ 27,567	$35,968
Costs and expenses:			
Cost of sales	23,045	20,255	23,438
Sales and marketing	7,476	7,261	6,840
Research and development	5,043	5,105	3,323
General and administrative	1,951	1,788	1,722
Total cost and expenses	37,515	34,409	35,323
Income (loss) from operations	(10,457)	(6,842)	645
Interest income, net	1,207	1,742	1,964
Other, net	(67)	(6)	59
Income (loss) before income taxes	(9,317)	(5,106)	2,688
Provision for income taxes	2,151	1,663	(880)
Net income (loss)	$ (7,166)	$ (3,443)	$ 1,788

Required

a. Before making any calculations, state in your own words what each item in the income statement means. In particular, identify which items are positive or negative and why.

b. Using information from both statements, evaluate Alpha's profitability and operating performance. To accomplish this objective, conduct the following analyses:

(1) Conduct horizontal and vertical analyses.

(2) Calculate operating income ratios and net income ratios for each year.

(3) Calculate Alpha's return on assets ratio for 2006 and 2007. Assume that the average total assets for 2006 was $51,000 and assume that the interest expense included in the line item "Interest income, net" for 2007 and 2006 was $35 and $105. All numbers are in the thousands.

(4) Calculate Alpha's return on equity ratio for 2006 and 2007. Assume that the average total equity for 2006 was $46,000. All numbers are in the thousands.

c. Identify any unusual items and information that are typically found in an income statement, but not included in Alpha's. How would access to this information affect your analysis of Alpha's performance?

d. How does the information shown in the categories of "Interest income, net" and "Other, net" affect your conclusions about Alpha's performance? What other information might be helpful?

4-19 Compare and contrast comprehensive income disclosures by Wal-Mart and Target. Refer to their Notes, Statements on Shareholders' Equity, and any other comments by management. How important is the comprehensive income to each firm, relative to its net income? Discuss the differences between comprehensive income and net income for each firm.

4-20 Calculate sustainable income for Wal-Mart and Target. How does sustainable income differ from net income for each firm? What conclusions would you draw about each firm's future income trends?

4-21 Calculate sustainable income for eBay. How does sustainable income differ from net income? What conclusion would you draw about the sustainability of eBay's future income trends?

4-22 Identify eBay's comprehensive income disclosures in its Notes, financial statements, and any commentary by management. Note that eBay provides a separate statement of consolidated income. How important is comprehensive income for eBay, relative to net income? Discuss the differences between comprehensive income and net income.

CHAPTER 5

STATEMENT OF CASH FLOWS

Learning Objectives

1. *Describe the objectives of the statement of cash flows.*
2. *Explain the complementary nature of accrual earnings and cash flows.*
3. *Identify the three types of activities that generate and use cash.*
4. *Explain the difference between the direct and indirect methods of presenting a statement of cash flows.*
5. *Draw inferences about the financial performance of a firm from the statement of cash flows.*
6. *Learn how to identify "Where's the Cash?"*

Appendix: *Calculate cash flow from operating activities by using relationships among income statement and balance sheet items.*

INTRODUCTION

Thus far, our focus has been on the two long-standing, conventional financial statements: the balance sheet and the income statement. In terms of assessing the timing and uncertainty of future cash flows, primary emphasis continues to be placed on these financial statements. Keep in mind, though, that these statements are on the accrual basis. Accrual earnings (net income on the income statement) do not necessarily reflect cash flows. Many revenue and expense transactions have no immediate cash flow effect. Nevertheless, net income can be a very useful performance measure because it reflects accomplishments by the firm (such as credit sales that will subsequently result in cash inflows) as well as resources consumed by the firm in generating revenue (for example, employee salaries that remain unpaid at the end of a period).

If net income is a useful performance measure, why is cash flow information needed? An analogy to baseball can be drawn. Many aspects of a baseball player's performance are measured. For example, home runs measure power hitting, while on-base percentage reflects the ability to reach base safely. Similarly, earnings and cash flows are different performance measures of a business organization. They should be viewed as complements, rather than substitutes. Each measure contains information not necessarily reflected in the other.

It is important to note that firms were not required to prepare a **statement of cash flows** until 1988 when FASB issued SFAS 95. The statement of cash flows is designed to provide information about a firm's inflows and outflows of cash during a period of time. It also explains the change in cash from the beginning of a period to the end of the period. Exhibit 5-1 contains an illustration of a statement of cash flows.

Objectives

According to SFAS No. 95, the statement of cash flows is intended to help financial statement readers assess:

1. a firm's ability to generate positive future net cash flows;
2. a firm's ability to meet its obligations, its ability to pay dividends, and its need for external financing;
3. the reasons for differences between net income and associated cash receipts and payments; and
4. the effects on a firm's financial position of both its cash and its noncash investing and financing transactions.

Ultimately, a firm's cash-generating ability affects its solvency, its capacity to pay dividends and interest, and the price of its securities. Accordingly, a firm's ability to generate cash is important to financial statement users.

One well-known portfolio manager suggested "*Cash flow for a company is the* ***same as air*** *for you and me. Without cash, a company can't live* (emphasis added)." The author goes on to add, "If a company generated excess amounts of greenbacks, it can reinvest in new systems and plants . . . In any case, shareholders

EXHIBIT 5-1 STATEMENT OF CASH FLOWS—DIRECT APPROACH

The Peak Company
Statement of Cash Flows
(Direct Approach)
For the Year Ended December 31, 2007

Cash flows from operating activities:		
Cash received from customers	$68,200	
Interest received	1,300	
Payments to employees	(17,100)	
Payments to suppliers	(40,500)	
Interest paid	(800)	
Taxes paid	(2,000)	
Net cash provided from operating activities		$ 9,100
Cash flows from investing activities:		
Purchase of equipment	(3,500)	
Purchase of IBM stock	(12,000)	
Net cash used in investing activities		(15,500)
Cash flows from financing activities:		
Proceeds from issuing long-term debt	25,000	
Proceeds from issuing common stock	5,000	
Payment of short-term debt	(12,000)	
Net cash provided by financing activities		18,000
Net increase in cash		11,600
Cash at beginning of year		22,000
Cash at end of year		$33,600

stand to benefit. Companies in the S&P500 producing the most cash relative to their share price have trounced the market during the past three years—with an average annualized gain of 20.7% . . . What's more, cash-rich companies have handily beat the broader index since 1986." (David Rynecki, "Cash Power", *Fortune*, April 11, 2003, p. 149.)

OVERVIEW

The statement of cash flows is a relatively new statement and up to this point many analysts, investors, and creditors continue to focus their attention not on this statement but on the income statement, namely, net income and earnings per share (EPS). How many times have you heard in the news that a firm's stock price soared or plummeted because the actual earnings were higher or lower than what was projected?

Recent history shows that cash flows should become a primary focus. From 1997 to July 2002 the SEC investigated 227 firms for alleged financial misstatements. There were 126 cases of improper revenue recognition, 80 cases of outright fictitious revenue recognition, and 21 cases of improperly valued revenue. (Andrew Gillies, "Is that revenue for real?" *Forbes,* April 14, 2003, vol. 171, no. 8, p. 161).

In April 2002, the SEC announced that Xerox Corporation was assessed the largest fine in history for a public corporation. The fine was $10 million and was assessed for improper accounting. Xerox abused the revenue recognition principle by accelerating revenues of approximately $2 billion from 1997–2000 from certain equipment contracts.

In 2001, Qwest overstated its revenues and net earnings by swapping fiber-optic capacity with other telecom companies.

Andrew T. Gillies commented poignantly, "Spend as much time with the cash flow statement as with the profit-and-loss statement that precedes it. If a company is counting dubious transactions in its revenues, in all likelihood the buyers haven't paid yet, and so the cash flow from operations will be anemic in relation to reported profit. Look back at Enron's fiscal 1999 results, for instance, and you'll see growth in sales and net income of 27% but a 25% decrease in net cash from operations. It wasn't a good sign then; keep an eye out for it now." (Andrew Gillies, "Is that revenue for real?" *Forbes,* April 14, 2003, Vol. 171, no. 8, p. 161.)

Another well-known company, WorldCom, reported revenues and net income in 2000 that were up 5% and 4% but the company's cash flows from operations fell 30% from the previous year.

These are just a few examples of corporations abusing revenue recognition and the core concept of accrual basis accounting. It is time to give the statement of cash flows the attention that it deserves. As we emphasize throughout this text, investors should be asking the question, **"Where's the cash?"**

This chapter describes the statement of cash flows, indicates how cash flow information can be used in analyzing the financial performance of a business, and explains the relationships among this statement, the balance sheet, and the income statement.

Cash and Cash Equivalents

Firms can elect to focus their statement of cash flows on either (1) cash or (2) cash and cash equivalents. The term **cash** includes cash on hand and cash in bank accounts that can be withdrawn on demand. **Cash equivalents** are short-term, highly liquid financial instruments with maturities of less than three months from date of purchase; they are quickly convertible into cash. Examples include money market funds, treasury bills, and certificates of deposit (CDs). Because cash equivalents are so similar to cash, many firms prefer to combine them with cash, rather than with other investments.

The statement of cash flows explains the change in a firm's balance sheet cash or cash and cash equivalent asset account from the beginning of the period to the end of the period. Note: a firm must consistently apply a policy of using cash or cash and cash equivalents.

CLASSIFICATION OF ACTIVITIES

As illustrated in Exhibit 5-1, a firm's cash flows are placed in one of three categories: operating, investing, or financing. Examples of each activity are given in Exhibit 5-2.

Operating Activities

Operating activities typically involve transactions related to providing goods and services to customers. They reflect the cash flow effects of the typical and recurring transactions that appear on the income statement. Examples of operating cash inflows are receipts from customers and the receipt of interest and dividends from investments. Operating cash outflows include payments to employees and suppliers and payments for interest and taxes. Both operating cash inflows and outflows make up **cash flows from operating activities.**

Investing Activities

Investing activities usually involve cash flows from the acquisition and disposal of noncurrent assets. Cash inflows result from disposing of property, plant, and equipment; collecting loans (other than the interest); and selling investments.

EXHIBIT 5-2 **SUMMARY OF ACTIVITIES GENERATING CASH FLOWS**

Cash Inflows	Cash Outflows
OPERATING ACTIVITIES	
Cash Inflows	Cash Outflows
From customers	To employees
From interest	To suppliers
From dividends	For interest
All other cash inflows not defined as an investing or financing activity	For taxes
	All other cash outflows not defined as an investing or financing activity
INVESTING ACTIVITIES	
Cash Inflows	Cash Outflows
Sale of property, plant, and equipment	Purchase of property, plant, and equipment
Collections of loans	Making of loans
Sale of investments	Acquisition of investments
FINANCING ACTIVITIES	
Cash Inflows	Cash Outflows
Issuing common stock	Reacquiring common stock
Obtaining loans	Repaying loans
	Paying dividends

Cash outflows arise from purchasing (investing in) property, plant, and equipment, making loans, and acquiring investments in other corporations. Both investing cash inflows and outflows make up **cash flows from investing activities**.

Financing Activities

Financing activities include cash flows from obtaining and repaying financing. Cash inflows result from contributions by owners (issuing stock to shareholders in exchange for cash) and from loans. Cash outflows arise from payments to shareholders (as dividends or payments to repurchase their shares) and the repayment of loans to creditors (but not the associated interest). Both financing cash inflows and outflows make up **cash flows from financing activities.**

Exhibit 5-1 shows that the net cash provided (or used) in each of the three classifications is summarized in the far right column of the statement. The sum of these amounts equals the change in the cash balance that occurred during the period. This change is combined with the cash balance at the beginning of the year to compute the ending cash balance. These beginning and ending cash amounts must, of course, correspond to the cash figures appearing on the balance sheet.

The remainder of this section addresses two additional format issues: (1) the direct versus the indirect approach to preparing the operating activities section, and (2) noncash investing and financing activities.

Direct versus Indirect Approach

Firms have a choice of preparing the cash flows from the operating activities section using the direct approach or the indirect approach. Both approaches will produce the same net figure for cash provided from operating activities. However, the internal components of the statements differ substantially. *These different approaches only apply to the cash flows from operating activities.* The investing and financing activities sections will be exactly the same.

The operating activities section of Peak's statement of cash flows in Exhibit 5-1 is prepared based on the **direct approach**. Under the direct approach, a separate line item is provided for each type of operating cash inflow and outflow. These items usually correspond to categories on the income statement. For example, cash received from customers corresponds to sales revenue on the income statement. Keep in mind, however, that the income statement and the statement of cash flows provide different information. For example, the income statement discloses sales made to customers during the year, regardless of whether cash has been collected during the year. The statement of cash flows indicates the amount of cash collected during the year from customers for the current year's sales, past years' sales, and even future sales if the firm has collected cash prior to the point of sale.

An acceptable alternative in preparing the operating activities section is the **indirect approach**. This method begins with net income and makes adjustments to it in order to arrive at cash generated by operating activities. The indirect approach is illustrated in Exhibit 5-3.

A major advantage of the direct method is that the primary sources and uses of cash are listed. As will be seen in a later section, this is highly useful information. A major advantage of the indirect method is that the reasons for the difference between net income and cash generated by operations is detailed. This can help reduce uncertainties or answer questions raised by financial statement readers.

As Exhibit 5-3 shows, under the indirect approach, depreciation expense is added to net income. *Because of this, some financial statement readers erroneously believe that depreciation expense is a source of cash. It is not.* Depreciation expense is added to net income in arriving at cash provided from operating activities because

EXHIBIT 5-3 **STATEMENT OF CASH FLOWS—INDIRECT APPROACH**

The Peak Company
Statement of Cash Flows
(Indirect Approach)
For the Year Ended December 31, 2007

Cash flows from operating activities:		
Net income	$ 5,300	
Adjustments to net income		
Depreciation expense	2,000	
Increase in accounts receivable	(500)	
Decrease in interest receivable	200	
Increase in inventory	(1,000)	
Increase in accounts payable	3,000	
Decrease in salaries payable	(100)	
Increase in interest payable	200	
Net cash provided from operating activities		$ 9,100
Cash flows from investing activities:		
Purchase of equipment	(3,500)	
Purchase of IBM stock	(12,000)	
Net cash used in investing activities		(15,500)
Cash flows from financing activities:		
Proceeds from issuing long-term debt	25,000	
Proceeds from issuing common stock	5,000	
Payment of short-term debt	(12,000)	
Net cash provided by financing activities		18,000
Net increase in cash		11,600
Cash at beginning of year		22,000
Cash at end of year		$33,600

(1) it has already been subtracted in the computation of net income, and (2) it does not involve any cash outflow. Adding depreciation expense to net income therefore eliminates the effect of this noncash expense.

The FASB has expressed a preference for the direct approach. In spite of that, the indirect approach is used more frequently. This is partly due to historical convention; the indirect approach is similar to the statement that was required prior to SFAS No. 95. Additionally, a firm using the direct approach must provide a schedule that reconciles net income with cash provided by operating activities. This reconciliation essentially consists of the information contained in the indirect approach. Thus, a firm that opts for the direct approach must really provide both methods. Some firms are reluctant to do this, either because additional costs are involved or because they feel that the statement will become too cluttered and, therefore, less informative. (For brevity, the reconciliation has been omitted from Peak's statement of cash flows appearing in Exhibit 5-1.)

Noncash Investing and Financing Activities

A firm may engage in investing and financing activities that do not involve cash. For example, a firm might acquire property by issuing common stock. Although no cash is involved, this transaction is both an investing activity (the acquisition of a noncurrent asset) and a financing activity (the issuance of stock). Because these transactions do not involve cash, they do not appear in the major sections of the statement of cash flows. However, **noncash investing and financing activities** are summarized in a schedule that appears at the end of the statement. This provides readers of the cash flow statement with a complete picture of a firm's investing and financing activities.

Johnson & Johnson Corporation, a prominent pharmaceutical company, disclosed in its 2002 annual report, a supplemental schedule to its statement of cash flows showing that it acquired several businesses during the year and issued debt in addition to cash in consummating these transactions.

USING CASH FLOW INFORMATION: OPERATING, INVESTING, AND FINANCING ACTIVITIES

It might appear that a firm would want to have as much positive cash flows (net cash inflows) from all activities: operating, investing, and financing. However, taking a closer look, a firm, over time, should have the following net cash flows:

Operating activities	+ net cash flows
Investing activities	– net cash flows
Financing activities	– net cash flows

Operating Activities

Operating activities are the lifeblood of a firm. If a firm does not generate positive cash flows from its operations over time it will not be able to survive.

Keep in mind, however, that not all healthy firms have a large positive cash flow from operations every year. Firms that experience growth in sales invariably need to expand their accounts receivable and inventory. These asset acquisitions must be financed, and cash generated by operations is a frequently used source.

For example, Digital Power Corp., which designs, develops, and manufactures component parts for computers and other electronic equipment, increased its sales from $13,835,008 to $18,884,259 in one year. Digital's 36% increase in sales was accompanied by a $1,673,340 increase in accounts receivable and inventory. So even though net income increased 21% to $1,400,790, the increased investment in receivables and inventory resulted in a net cash outflow from operating activities of $80,252 during that year. In Digital's case, the cash outflow does not indicate poor operating performance. Instead, it reflects growth. In general, however, a negative cash flow and even an erratic positive cash flow from operating activities over time should prompt further investigation.

Investing Activities

Generally, healthy firms have consistently negative cash flows from investing activities (net cash outflows) because they are acquiring noncurrent assets (e.g., property and equipment) that will be used in the operations to generate future operating cash flows. Troubled firms, on the other hand, tend to have positive investing cash flows over time because they often sell productive assets to try and generate cash.

Financing Activities

Similar to investing activities it is a good sign to see firms with negative cash flows from financing activities (net cash outflows) because it shows that financing activities such as loans are being reduced. It is important, though, to recognize that young, start-up companies may have positive overall cash flows from financing for a period of years because they are securing funds for growth. Mature firms, on the other hand, generally show negative cash flows from paying loans, buying back stock, and paying dividends. Some firms are labeled "cash cows" because they generate so much cash flow from operations they can pay for all investing and financing activities with these cash flows. Troubled firms, on the other hand, have positive financing cash flows because they are trying to generate cash by issuing debt and/or issuing more company stock.

Comprehensive Example: Techtron

To illustrate the insights that can be drawn from cash flow numbers, consider Exhibit 5-4, which contains Techtron's statement of cash flows. Recall that Techtron's income statement appears in Exhibit 4-1. Additional information that will be helpful in interpreting the cash flow statement is in Exhibit 5-5.

EXHIBIT 5-4 STATEMENT OF CASH FLOWS

Techtron
Statement of Cash Flows
For the Year Ended January 3, 2007
(Dollars in thousands)

Cash flows from operating activities:		
Net income	$14,667	
Adjustments to reconcile net income to net cash		
Depreciation and amortization	6,637	
Deferred taxes	2,345	
Changes in current assets and liabilities:		
Accounts receivable	(941)	
Inventory	(10,072)	
Other current assets	(529)	
Accounts payable	3,490	
Accrued payroll and other employee benefits	(543)	
Other accrued expenses	(626)	
Net cash provided by operating activities		$14,428
Cash flows from investing activities:		
Purchases of investments	(14,920)	
Proceeds from sale of investments	21,577	
Capital expenditures	(25,944)	
Net cash used in investing activities		(19,287)
Cash flows from financing activities:		
Proceeds from issuance of common stock	1,086	
Income tax benefit of stock options	750	
Net cash provided by financing activities		1,836
Net change in cash and cash equivalents		(3,023)
Cash and cash equivalents at beginning of year		14,949
Cash and cash equivalents at end of year		$11,926
Supplemental disclosures:		
Cash paid during the year for:		
Interest		$ 533
Taxes		7,256

Operating Activities

First, note that Techtron chose the indirect format for the operating section of the cash flow statement. Because of this, the specific sources and uses of cash are not detailed. We will soon show how to estimate some of these numbers. The bottom of the operating section shows that a positive cash flow of $14,428,000 was

EXHIBIT 5-5 SELECTED FINANCIAL INFORMATION USED TO ILLUSTRATE CASH FLOW RATIOS

Techtron
Selected Financial Statement Information
(Dollars in thousands)

	2007	2006
Total assets	$155,603	$134,561
Accounts receivable	25,781	24,840
Inventory	28,626	18,554
Investments	17,438	24,095
Property, plant, and equipment	65,311	45,727
Sales revenue	172,428	165,310

generated by operating activities. Keep in mind, however, that this figure does not reflect the cash needed to replace worn-out equipment.

Ratios

Several cash-based ratios can be computed from the statement of cash flows. Because the statement of cash flows is a relatively recent addition to GAAP, the development of cash flow ratios is at an early stage, and there is no general consensus about which ratios are the most informative. Also note that some of these ratios require information disclosed only by the direct approach for preparing the operating activities section. We will illustrate ways to estimate this information from statement of cash flows using the indirect approach.

Cash Return on Assets

The cash return on assets ratio is calculated by dividing the cash flow from operating activities (CFOA) by average total assets:

$$\text{Cash return on assets} = \frac{\text{CFOA}}{\text{Average total assets}}$$

Cash return on assets is similar to return on assets (ROA) discussed in Chapter 4. CROA, however, measures management's success, given the assets entrusted to it, in generating cash from operating activities. Because CFOA is available to pay dividends and to finance investments, a high ratio is desirable. Note that the cash return on assets ratio may be calculated by including interest payments in the numerator, just as ROA may be calculated with interest expense added to the numerator. Again, we will follow the convention of excluding interest from the numerator of both ratios.

A related cash ratio could be calculated by dividing operating cash flows by the number of shares. Michael Markowski, Research Director at StockDiagnostics.com suggested "Cash per share more accurately describes the health of a company than typical earnings-per-share figures." Only 27 companies out of the S&P500 demonstrated increasing **cash flow per share** over 12 consecutive quarters. (David Rynecki, "Cash Power," *Fortune,* April 11, 2003, pp. 149–150.)

Techtron's fiscal year 2006[1] cash return on assets is:

$$\text{Cash return on assets} = \frac{\text{CFOA}}{\text{Average total assets}}$$

$$= \frac{\$14{,}428}{(\$155{,}603 + \$134{,}561)/2}$$

$$= 9.95\%$$

Techtron's cash return on assets appears reasonable, but it does not compare very favorably to the prior year when operating activities generated $22,686,000 and the cash return on assets was 18.7%. What caused the decline in cash flow? Statements of cash flows prepared under the indirect approach show the adjustments needed to convert net income to cash generated by operations. Techtron's largest adjustment is $10,072,000 for inventory. That is, inventory increased by approximately $10 million and that inventory expansion was essentially funded from operations. The advisability of increasing inventory holdings is usually assessed by comparing the percentage increase in sales to the percentage increase in inventory. Sales increased only 4.3% [($172,428/$165,248) − 1], while inventory increased 54.3% [($28,626/$18,554) − 1]. Thus, the decline in Techtron's cash return on assets raises concerns about its inventory management or the salability of its inventory.

Some analysts question the use of CFOA in cash return on assets and other ratios. Their reservation is that CFOA makes no provision for replacing worn-out equipment. These expenditures are necessary to maintain productive capacity and current operating levels. Because CFOA is not reduced for these expenditures, it overstates the amount of discretionary cash flow generated from operations.

Instead of using CFOA in ratio calculations, some analysts use **free cash flow.** One way to calculate free cash flow is to subtract from CFOA the cash payment necessary to replace worn-out equipment. A similar calculation would be to subtract capital expenditures and dividends from operating cash flow. Unfortunately, firms rarely disclose free cash flow figures, so many analysts have their own unique formula. Although the investing activities section of the statement of cash flows shows total payments for the acquisition of productive assets, the amounts spent to (1) replace assets and (2) expand productive capacity are not detailed. Because of this, depreciation expense is sometimes used as an imperfect estimate of the cash expenditure needed to maintain productive capacity. Because depreciation

[1] Even though Techtron's statement of cash flows is dated 2007, it is usually referred to as the 2006 statement of cash flows, since the beginning date of the fiscal year is in 2006.

expense is based on historical cost, it probably understates the cash necessary to replace productive assets.

Quality of Sales

The **quality of sales ratio** is computed by dividing cash received from customers by sales (revenue):

$$\text{Quality of sales} = \frac{\text{Cash received from customers}}{\text{Sales}}$$

All other things being equal, a firm is in a more advantageous position if a large portion of its sales is collected in cash. Not only is final realization of the transaction assured, but also the investment in accounts receivable is minimized.

This ratio is particularly useful for analyzing firms that use liberal revenue recognition policies or firms that, of necessity, employ revenue recognition policies that require the use of judgment. In both of these situations, a deterioration of this ratio over time might indicate that a firm is inflating earnings by the use of questionable accounting judgments. For example, some of Techtron's sales arise from firm contracts with other businesses for the design and manufacture of custom-made products. Although Techtron records revenue at the time goods are shipped, it could argue for using the more liberal percentage-of-completion method. Utilizing this procedure too aggressively would likely result in recognizing significant amounts of revenue before cash is collected and would be reflected in a low quality of sales ratio.

The quality of sales ratio can also reflect a firm's performance in making collections from customers. Suppose that a firm increases sales by the questionable strategy of reducing the credit standards that customers must meet. These customers are likely to be relatively tardy in making payments. This situation will be revealed to financial statement readers by a declining quality of sales ratio.

Techtron's quality of sales ratio cannot be computed from the information shown in Exhibit 5-4. Why not? The numerator, cash received from customers, is available only from the cash flow statement under the direct approach. However, this figure can be approximated by the following relationship:

$$\text{Cash received from customers} = \text{Beginning balance in accounts receivable} + \text{Sales} - \text{Ending balance in accounts receivable}$$

To understand this relationship, recognize that both the beginning balance in accounts receivable and sales for the year might potentially be collected in cash during the current year. In fact, the sum of these two amounts is collected in cash, except for the balance that remains in accounts receivable at the end of the year.

Techtron's estimated cash collections from customers are $171,487 (in thousands).

$$\text{Cash received from customers} = \text{Beginning balance in accounts receivable} + \text{Sales} - \text{Ending balance in accounts receivable}$$

$$\$171{,}487 = \$24{,}840 + \$172{,}428 - \$25{,}781$$

Techtron's quality of sales ratio for 2006 is 99.5%.

$$\text{Quality of sales} = \frac{\text{Cash received from customers}}{\text{Sales}} = \frac{\$171{,}487}{\$172{,}428} = 99.5\%$$

This is a very high quality of sales ratio and reflects good accounts receivable management and conservative revenue recognition policies.

Reality Check 5-1 describes how the quality of sales ratio provides useful insights into the software industry.

Quality of Income

The quality of income ratio is computed by dividing CFOA by net income:

$$\text{Quality of income} = \frac{\text{CFOA}}{\text{Net income}}$$

This ratio indicates the proportion of income that has been realized in cash. As with quality of sales, high levels for this ratio are desirable. The quality of income ratio has a tendency to exceed 100% because (1) depreciation expense has reduced the denominator and (2) cash spent to replace productive assets has not been subtracted in calculating the numerator. Techtron's 2006 quality of income ratio is 98.4%.

$$\text{Quality of income} = \frac{\$14{,}428}{\$14{,}667} = 98.4\%$$

Techtron's 2006 ratio is less than 100% and does not compare favorably to its 2005 ratio of 128%. The decline in this ratio is largely due to the growth in inventories that was mentioned previously.

In the discussion of quality of sales, we indicated that revenue recognition might be judgmental. The same is true with expense recognition. A variety of alternatives for expense allocations are available to firms, and firms have considerable discretion in the selection of these alternatives. The quality of income ratio can provide an overall indication of how liberal a firm's accounting judgments have been. Reality Check 5-2 provides information about quality of income ratios in the software industry.

REALITY CHECK 5-1

Several firms in the software industry have been criticized for their revenue recognition policies. The allegations suggest that these firms have recognized revenue prematurely. Such a practice would not only overstate sales, but net income as well.

Revenue overstatements can be achieved in various ways. Some companies were said to double-bill customers. Other companies booked revenue when they shipped goods to their own warehouses in foreign countries. Ultimately, such practices catch up with companies. For example, Oracle Corporation paid $24,000,000 to settle shareholder lawsuits, and Cambridge Biotech Corporation was forced to file for bankruptcy.

The quality of sales ratio can help investors detect and avoid such situations. Consider the following information for two software companies.

	Cambridge Biotech	*Kendall Square Research*
	(Dollars in thousands)	
Accounts receivable		
Beginning of year	$ 5,951	$ 804
End of year	10,520	2,785
Sales for year	28,981	10,066

Required

a. Estimate the cash collected from customers for each firm.
b. Compute the quality of sales ratio for each firm.
c. What do you conclude from these ratios?

SOLUTION

a.

	Cambridge Biotech	*Kendall Square Research*
Sales	$28,981	$10,066
Plus: Beginning accounts receivable	5,951	804
Less: Ending accounts receivable	(10,520)	(2,785)
Cash collected from customers	$24,412	$ 8,085

b. Quality of sales $= \frac{\$24,412}{\$28,981}$ and $\frac{\$8,085}{\$10,066}$

$=$ 84% and 80%

c. These ratios are considerably below 100%. This should certainly prompt financial statement readers to undertake further investigation.

REALITY CHECK 5-2

As with the quality of sales ratio, the quality of income ratio can help detect situations involving questionable accounting judgments. Reality Check 5-1 showed that the quality of sales ratios for Cambridge Biotech and Kendall Square Research were both below 85%. Consider the following information:

	Cambridge Biotech	*Kendall Square Research*
	(Dollars in thousands)	
Cash provided by operating activities	($5,696)	($27,194)
Net income (loss)	$ 348	($21,619)

Required

a. Compute the quality of income ratio for each firm.
b. What inferences can you draw from these ratios?

SOLUTION

a.

		Cambridge Biotech	*Kendall Square Research*
Quality of income	=	($5,696) / $ 348	($27,194) / ($21,619)
	=	– 1,637%	126%

b. Cambridge's negative quality of income ratio results from a negative numerator and a positive denominator. This indicates that although Cambridge generated a positive net income, its operations resulted in a net cash outflow. The ratio is quite large (in absolute terms), which should be rather alarming to financial statement readers.

Regarding Kendall Square, interpreting ratios generated from negative numbers is often difficult. A ratio of 126% usually indicates that a firm generated more cash than income. However, when a 126% ratio is computed from two negative numbers, it indicates that the firm's cash outflow exceeded its reported loss. Both the loss and the cash outflow from operations should concern financial statement readers.

You should realize that management could manipulate cash flows. For example, customers can be induced to remit payments early if they are provided with a sufficiently large cash discount. Although the short-term consequences of this action may be to increase net cash flow, large discounts might not be in the shareholders' best long-term interest.

Cash Interest Coverage

Creditors use the **cash interest coverage ratio** to assess a firm's ability to pay interest. Calculate this ratio by summing CFOA, interest payments, and tax payments and then dividing by interest payments. Interest and tax payments are added to CFOA because they have been subtracted in the calculation of CFOA and because those payments are available to cover interest. In particular, tax payments are added because in the unfortunate case of zero profitability, those payments would not be made and would provide another measure of relief for the creditors. Interest and taxes paid are summarized at the bottom of the statement of cash flows or in the notes.

$$\text{Cash interest coverage} = \frac{\text{CFOA} + \text{Interest paid} + \text{Taxes paid}}{\text{Interest paid}}$$

The cash interest coverage ratio reflects how many times greater cash provided by operations is than the interest payment itself. Creditors prefer high levels of this ratio.

Techtron's 2006 cash interest coverage ratio is 4,168% or 41.68 to 1:

$$\text{Cash interest coverage} = \frac{\$14{,}428 + \$533 + \$7{,}256}{\$533} = 4{,}168\%$$

This ratio is quite high and should provide creditors with considerable assurance that Techtron is currently generating more than enough cash to meet its interest payments.

OPERATING ACTIVITIES EXAMPLE: TARGET CORPORATION

Recall that Target's annual report is contained in Appendix C. Please refer to their primary financial statements as you read the following analysis.

Similar to Techtron, Target chose the indirect format for the operating section of the cash flow statement. Because of this, the specific sources and uses of cash are not detailed. The bottom of the operating section shows that a positive cash flow of $4,451,000,000 was generated by operating activities in 2005. However, looking at the previous two years, cash flows from operating activities in 2004 and 2003 were $3,808,000,000 and $3,188,000,000. In addition, if we calculate Target's cash return on assets ratio we see a large increase as well.

Target's 2005 cash return on assets is:

$$\text{Cash return on assets} = \frac{\text{CFOA}}{\text{Average total assets}}$$

$$= \frac{\$4{,}451}{(\$34{,}995 + \$32{,}293)/2}$$

$$= 13.23\%$$

What Would You Do?

As a successful college student, you feel that you can make money by sharing your secrets of success with others. Specifically, you decide to offer Scholastic Aptitude Test (SAT) review courses. You and several of your friends will teach the courses. Classroom space can be rented at a local community college.

Because of the costs you will incur, a minimum of 20 students is necessary to generate a positive cash flow from operations. If fewer than 20 students enroll, you intend to cancel the course.

Marketing is, of course, a key to the success of any new business. Attracting new students is essential. This presents you with a dilemma. On the one hand, you cannot afford to run the course with less than 20 students. On the other hand, potential students always ask if you are certain that the course will be offered. Understandably, they prefer to enroll in a course that will not be canceled. You have many competitors; students can choose from several review courses.

How would you respond to the students' questions about course cancellation? Keep in mind that being perfectly honest may result in the failure of your business.

Target's cash return on assets appears strong when compared to the company's return a few years prior (2002). In 2002, Target's cash return on assets was 6.03%, which does not compare very favorably to the current trend. A decline in operating cash flows is not a trend that investors want to see. What caused the decline in cash flow from 2001 to 2002? Recall that statements of cash flows prepared under the indirect approach show the adjustments needed to convert net income to cash generated by operations. Target's largest adjustment was $2,194,000,000 for accounts receivable. That is, accounts receivable increased by approximately $2 billion and this receivable increase was not the result of a tremendous increase in sales but, according to the footnotes, was due to a change in the way Target accounted for its receivables.

Each year Target would transfer substantially all of its accounts receivable to another company, Target Receivable Corporation (TRC), in exchange for an interest in TRC's assets. TRC was set up as a **special purpose entity (SPE)**, a separate independent company, whose purpose was to obtain loan financing for Target by collateralizing the receivables. It is important to note that SPEs were very popular vehicles for firms to obtain funds through "off-balance sheet financing". Prior to 2002, Target accounted for the transaction by removing the accounts receivable and recording cash. No liability was recorded on Target's books. The receivables and debt were recorded on TRC's books.

In light of the accounting scandals and abuse in this area, the FASB issued more stringent accounting guidelines. Target's SPE was determined not to be a qualifying SPE. Therefore, Target had to change the way it accounted for the transfer of its receivables. It had to essentially put back on its books the accounts receivable and record the loan balances as long-term liabilities. This action resulted in a 100 percent increase in accounts receivable in 2002, which caused the decline in the cash flows from operating activities.

As another example, the demise of Enron Corporation was partly due to its abuse of SPEs. Enron set up SPEs that were supposed to be independent but it was later discovered that they were actually owned and operated by certain key executive officers of Enron. These SPEs engaged in various transactions that were not independent at all and were designed to enhance Enron's operating cash flows.

It is important to remember that firms will continue to find ways to improve their operating cash flows even if it's only for the short-term through such actions as delaying the payment of their accounts payable, encouraging receivable customers to pay early by offering incentive discounts, and engaging in transactions with other "special purpose entities".

INVESTING AND FINANCING ACTIVITIES: TECHTRON

As we described earlier, the investing activities section of the statement of cash flows summarizes the cash inflows from disposing of investments, and the cash outflows from purchasing investments. Techtron's investments (both short-term and long-term) consist primarily of government and municipal bonds. The short-term investments, in particular, are highly liquid and readily available to satisfy pending cash needs. In 2006, Techtron purchased investments for $14,920,000 and liquidated investments of $21,577,000, resulting in a net decline in investments of $6,657,000.

The investing activities section also shows that Techtron spent $25,944,000 on capital expenditures. Most of this amount was for a new 100,000 square foot manufacturing plant. The prior year-end balance sheet shows a property, plant, and equipment (PPE) figure of $45,727,000. Thus, Techtron made a considerable investment in PPE during 2006. Techtron is in an industry that requires firms to stay up-to-date in terms of technology. However, Techtron should not increase its investment in high technology facilities to such an extent that its profitability and/or cash flows are ultimately compromised. Cause for concern is further heightened if we assume the 2005 cash flow statement shows capital expenditures of $21,175,000. Summing over 2005 and 2006, Techtron has spent about $47 million on capital improvements. This amount is approximately equal to 70% of the PPE figure on the 2006 balance sheet! Questions certainly arise regarding the necessity for Techtron to continue such expenditures, as well as its ability to do so.

So far, we have learned the following about Techtron's 2006 cash flows:

Cash provided by operating activities	$14,428,000
Net cash generated by liquidating investments	6,657,000
Cash paid for capital improvements	(25,944,000)
Net cash outflow (excluding financing activities)	$ (4,859,000)

The financing activities section shows two items. Techtron issued common stock in exchange for approximately $1,086,000. Techtron also received an income tax benefit related to its stock option plans. These two financing activities were not sufficient to fund the $4,859,000 outflow. Consequently, the cash balance declined:

Net cash outflow (excluding financing activities)	$(4,859,000)
Net cash provided by financing activities	1,836,000
Net change in cash and cash equivalents	$(3,023,000)

A $3 million decline in cash and cash equivalents is not an extremely large drop. Moreover, Techtron has a considerable investment in government securities that can be liquidated. Also, Techtron does not have much debt outstanding, and therefore would likely have little trouble in securing additional borrowings. Nevertheless, management's plans for funding future capital expenditures should be examined.

A CLOSER EXAMINATION OF A FIRM'S STATEMENT OF CASH FLOWS

As we discussed earlier, firms may accelerate the recording of revenues and delay the recognition of expenses in an attempt to improve earnings. These activities, though, do not affect cash flows. Therefore, the statement of cash flows may reveal problems in a firm's operations long before they show up on the income statement.

A Case in Point: Xerox Corporation

In 1998, Xerox reported positive net income but negative cash flows from operating activities. A closer look at the cash flows from operating activities revealed that the cash flows took a tremendous hit because the company's receivables and inventories rose considerably during that year. Keep in mind that an increase in receivables generally results from accruing revenues not yet collected in cash. Likewise, an increase in inventories does not affect net income but can decrease cash flows.

In 1999, the company's operating cash flows showed a similar trend in receivables and inventories. A prudent financial statement user would have questioned this trend. Why were receivables and inventories increasing? Was it due to legitimate growth in operations or was it an indication of slow moving inventory and the granting of looser credit terms?

In 2000, it became apparent that the company was having problems. Looking at the company's statement of cash flows, operating cash was again weak indicating that cash was not being realized from its operations. Apparently, to compensate for the drain in operating cash the company borrowed a large amount of cash as shown by the tremendous increase in the cash flows provided by financing activities.

In 2002, the news broke that Xerox was charged with overstating revenues during 1997–2000 and was fined heavily for this accounting impropriety. Was this really surprising? Not really because the statement of cash flows painted a vivid picture of Xerox's operating problems long before they became public information.

Several prominent companies have gone into bankruptcy, and their failure can be directly linked to declines in cash flows from operating activities. In order to "follow the cash", always examine trends in operating cash flows!

Summary of Learning Objectives

1. **Describe the objectives of the statement of cash flows.**
   The statement of cash flows explains the change in cash from the beginning to the end of a period. It provides financial statement users with information to assess a firm's ability to generate positive future net cash flows, to meet its obligations, to pay dividends, and to generate financing internally.

2. **Explain the complementary nature of accrual earnings and cash flows.**
   Accrual earnings reflect a firm's success in providing goods and services to customers. Cash flow figures show a firm's solvency and its capacity to pay dividends and interest.

3. **Identify the three types of activities that generate and use cash.**
   Operating activities include providing goods and services to customers (for example, collecting cash from customers and paying cash to suppliers). Investing activities involve acquiring or disposing of noncurrent assets (such as property, plant, and equipment and investments in other corporations). Financing activities include obtaining funds from shareholders and returning funds to shareholders; financing activities also include obtaining and repaying loans.

4. **Explain the difference between the direct and indirect methods of presenting a statement of cash flows.**
   This distinction lies in the operating section. Under the direct method, a separate line item is provided for each major operating inflow and outflow of cash. In contrast, the indirect approach starts with net income and makes various adjustments to arrive at cash generated by operating activities. Although the direct method provides the most useful information, most firms use the indirect method.

5. **Draw inferences about the financial performance of a firm from the statement of cash flows.**
   Studying the trends in a firm's operating cash flows can point out weaknesses before any indication is revealed in the firm's net income. Additionally, much of the information included in the statement of cash flows can be extracted by the use of ratios. These ratios provide insights into a firm's ability to generate cash in light of the assets it has, the quality of the firm's sales and net income, and the ability of the firm to generate cash to meet its interest payments.

6. **Learn how to identify "Where's the Cash?"**
   We examined several prominent companies whose failure can be directly linked to declines in cash flows from operating activities. In order to follow the cash, always examine trends in operating cash flows!

KEY TERMS

Cash
Cash flow from financing activities
Cash flow from investing activities
Cash flow from operating activities
Cash flow per share
Cash equivalents
Cash interest coverage ratio
Cash return on assets ratio
Direct approach
Financing activities
Free cash flow
Indirect approach
Investing activities
Noncash investing and financing activities
Operating activities
Quality of income ratio
Quality of sales ratio
Statement of cash flows
Special purpose entities (SPE)

APPENDIX 5

PREPARING A STATEMENT OF CASH FLOWS

INTRODUCTION

Conceptually, you could analyze the cash flow effects of each transaction and then prepare the statement of cash flows by accumulating that information. Most accounting systems, however, are not designed to implement such an approach. Instead, cash flows are inferred from items on the balance sheet and income statement.

Operating Activities under the Direct Method

This section examines the income statement and balance sheet relationships that are relevant to determining cash flows from operating activities under the direct approach. The income statement and comparative balance sheets for the Peak Company that appear in Exhibits 5A-1 and 5A-2, respectively, are used to illustrate these relationships and to generate the statement of cash flows that appears in Exhibit 5-1.

Collections from Customers

Peak began 2007 with an accounts receivable balance of $4,000. Let us assume that Peak collected these receivables in 2007. (This is a reasonable assumption, but our result would not be affected by changing it.) The $4,000 is a cash inflow in 2007. Peak then made sales of $68,700 in 2007. What portion of these sales was collected in cash in 2007? Because we assumed that the beginning balance in accounts receivable has already been collected, the ending balance must have

EXHIBIT 5A-1 INCOME STATEMENT

The Peak Company
Income Statement
For the Year Ended December 31, 2007

REVENUES:		
Sales	$68,700	
Interest revenue	1,100	
		$69,800
EXPENSES:		
Cost of goods sold	42,500	
Salary expense	17,000	
Depreciation expense	2,000	
Interest expense	1,000	
Tax expense	2,000	
		64,500
Net income		$ 5,300

EXHIBIT 5A-2 BALANCE SHEET

The Peak Company
Balance Sheet

	DECEMBER 31	
	2007	**2006**
Cash	$33,600	$22,000
Accounts receivable	4,500	4,000
Interest receivable	100	300
Inventory	11,000	10,000
Property, plant, and equipment (net)	31,500	30,000
Investments	12,000	0
Total assets	$92,700	$66,300
Accounts payable	$ 6,000	$ 3,000
Salaries payable	300	400
Interest payable	200	0
Short-term debt	0	12,000
Long-term debt	30,000	5,000
Common stock	35,000	30,000
Retained earnings	21,200	15,900
Total liabilities and shareholders' equity	$92,700	$66,300

been part of 2007 sales. Therefore, all of 2007 sales have been collected in cash, except for the ending balance in accounts receivable. Accordingly, cash collected from customers can be computed as the beginning balance in accounts receivable plus the portion of 2007 sales that has been collected in 2007.

Cash received from customers	=	Beginning balance in accounts receivable	+	Sales	−	Ending balance in accounts receivable
\$68,200	=	\$4,000	+	\$68,700	−	\$4,500

Interest Received

A similar relationship can be used for cash collected in the form of interest on the firm's investments.

Interest received from customers	=	Beginning balance in interest receivable	+	Interest revenue	−	Ending balance in interest receivable
\$1,300	=	\$300	+	\$1,100	−	\$100

Payments to Employees

During 2007, Peak incurred a salary expense of \$17,000. But how much cash did it actually pay to its employees in 2007? At the beginning of 2007, Peak had a liability to its employees of \$400. Let us make the reasonable assumption that this amount was paid to employees in the early part of 2007, and thus constitutes a cash outflow in that year. This implies that the ending balance in salaries payable must have arisen from 2007's expense and reflects that part of the expense that has not been paid at the end of 2007. Accordingly, cash payments to employees can be computed as the beginning balance in salaries payable plus the amount paid in 2007 for 2007's salary expense (salary expense minus the ending balance in salaries payable).

Payments to employees	=	Beginning balance in salaries payable	+	Salary expense	−	Ending balance in salaries payable
\$17,100	=	\$400	+	\$17,000	−	\$300

Payments to Suppliers

Calculating cash paid to suppliers (for merchandise) is a bit more complex than the preceding illustrations. First, note that cost of goods sold is the income statement item related to cash paid to suppliers. However, the purchases for a period are more closely related to cash outflows than is cost of goods sold. How can purchases be computed based on the information contained in the financial statements? The following equation can help:

Cost of goods sold = Beginning inventory + Purchases − Ending inventory

The sum of beginning inventory plus purchases reflects the cost of goods available for sale. That is, this sum equals the cost of goods on hand during the year that could have been sold. All of these goods will have been sold by year-end, except for those that remain on hand at the end of the year (ending inventory). Thus, subtracting ending inventory from the sum of beginning inventory plus purchases yields the cost of goods that have been sold during the year.

The equation can be rearranged to solve for purchases:

$$\text{Purchases} = \text{Cost of goods sold} + \text{Ending inventory} - \text{Beginning inventory}$$

$$\$43{,}500 = \$42{,}500 + \$11{,}000 - \$10{,}000$$

Because purchases can be made on credit, they do not necessarily reflect cash outflows. Assume that accounts payable relate solely to the acquisition of merchandise and that the beginning balance is paid in early 2007. This represents a cash outflow in 2007. Moreover, the ending balance in accounts payable must have arisen from 2007 purchases. Thus, all the purchases made in 2007 have been paid for in that year, except for the ending balance in accounts payable. Therefore, cash paid to suppliers equals the beginning balance in accounts payable plus the portion of 2007's purchases that was paid in 2007 (purchases minus the ending balance in accounts payable).

$$\text{Payments to suppliers} = \text{Beginning balance in accounts payable} + \text{Purchases} - \text{Ending balance in accounts payable}$$

$$\$40{,}500 = \$3{,}000 + \$43{,}500 - \$6{,}000$$

Payments for Interest

The previous discussions can be used to justify the following relationship regarding cash paid for interest:

$$\text{Interest paid} = \text{Beginning balance in interest payable} + \text{Interest expense} - \text{Ending balance in interest payable}$$

$$\$800 = \$0 + \$1{,}000 - \$200$$

Depreciation

Although Peak's income statement contains a \$2,000 depreciation charge, depreciation expense does not appear on the statement of cash flows prepared under the direct approach. This is because depreciation expense does not involve a cash outflow. Recall the analysis of depreciation:

ASSETS	=	LIABILITIES	+	SHAREHOLDERS' EQUITY
Equipment – $2,000				Retained earnings – $2,000 (depreciation expense)

Because cash is not affected, depreciation expense has no place in the direct approach to the statement of cash flows.

Taxes

Peak's 2007 tax expense of $2,000 happens to equal the amount of taxes paid on the statement of cash flows. Because no tax liability appears on either the beginning or the ending balance sheet, this makes sense. More generally, if the related balance sheet item has the same balance at the beginning and the end of the year, the cash flow statement amount will equal the expense reported on the income statement.

Other Items

Peak's income statement and balance sheets contain only a sampling of the accounts that could possibly appear. For example, the income statement could include selling expenses and the balance sheet could include prepaid expenses and accrued liabilities. Accordingly, Peak's situation is only an illustration of the steps needed to adjust income statement numbers to cash flow figures.

As a general guide to preparing the operating activities section of the statement of cash flows under the direct approach, the following steps should be taken:

1. Ignore income statement items that are unrelated to cash flows (such as depreciation expense).
2. Ignore gains and losses associated with nonoperating activities (such as extraordinary gains and losses or gains and losses on disposals of noncurrent assets).
3. Adjust all the remaining income statement items by the changes in related balance sheet accounts. Be sure to include in the adjustments all balance sheet accounts related to operating activities.

OPERATING ACTIVITIES USING THE INDIRECT METHOD

As you know, the operating activities section can also be prepared under the indirect approach. This approach starts with net income and makes adjustments to convert net income to cash flow from operating activities. Exhibit 5-3 contains Peak's cash flow statement using the indirect approach. The first adjustment is depreciation expense, which has been subtracted in calculating net income. Yet it does not result in a cash outflow. Accordingly, net income understates the cash flow generated from operating activities. Therefore, to modify net income so that it reflects cash flow, depreciation expense must be added back.

The next adjustment relates to accounts receivable. Recall how Peak's sales were converted to a cash flow figure under the direct method:

$$\text{Cash received from customers} = \text{Beginning balance in accounts receivable} + \text{Sales} - \text{Ending balance in accounts receivable}$$

$$\$68{,}200 = \$4{,}000 + \$68{,}700 - \$4{,}500$$

Rearranging the equation slightly yields:

$$\text{Cash received from customers} = \text{Sales} + \text{Beginning balance in accounts receivable} - \text{Ending balance in accounts receivable}$$

$$= \$68{,}700 + \underbrace{\$4{,}000 - \$4{,}500}_{-\$500}$$

$$\$68{,}200 = \$68{,}700 - \$500$$

If the ending balance in accounts receivable is greater than the beginning balance, combining these components results in a negative number. Thus, to convert sales to a cash flow figure, sales must be reduced by the increase in accounts receivable. Because sales are included in net income, net income must be reduced by the increase in accounts receivable to compute a cash flow figure. More intuitively, an increase in accounts receivable suggests that not all the current year's sales have been collected in cash. Therefore, sales (or net income) must be reduced by an increase in accounts receivable.

The other adjustments in Exhibit 5-3 are handled in a similar fashion.

INVESTING AND FINANCING ACTIVITIES

Although the information for preparing the operating activities section can often be obtained from the income statement and balance sheets, this is not usually the case for investing activities and financing activities. A detailed analysis of the relevant accounts is needed to identify the inflows and outflows of cash. This information is usually readily available to a firm's accountants, because relatively few transactions are involved and documentation (such as bank notes) is easily accessible. Also note that the investing and financing activities sections are the same under both the direct and indirect approaches.

Summary of Learning Objective

Calculate cash flow from operating activities by using relationships among income statement and balance sheet items.

Under the direct approach, individual income statement line items are adjusted by their related balance sheet accounts. For example, sales are adjusted by the change in accounts receivable. Under the indirect approach, net income is adjusted for the change in these same balance sheet accounts. Additionally, nonoperating items and items with no cash flow consequence must also be eliminated from net income.

Exercises and Problems

5-1 The income statement and the cash flow statement focus on various aspects of profitability and liquidity. Distinguish between these concepts and discuss their importance to users of financial statements.

5-2 Contrast cash and cash equivalents. Why would managers want to include both when preparing a statement of cash flows?

5-3 What information is provided in a statement of cash flows that is not disclosed in a balance sheet or an income statement?

5-4 Identify three types of operating, financing, and investing activities. Contrast these with several noncash investing or financing activities.

5-5 How could a firm report positive amounts of net income and negative cash flows from operating activities? Identify specific instances where this might occur.

5-6 Define the following cash flow concepts in your own words, as you would describe them to the owner of a small business:

a. Cash flow from operating activities
b. Cash used to purchase investments
c. Cash obtained from bank loans
d. Cash collected from clients
e. Cash paid to vendors
f. Taxes paid to federal, state, and local governments
g. Loan repayments to bank (including principal and interest)

5-7 Describe two investing and financing activities that do not involve cash receipts or payments. Why might a financial analyst want to know about such noncash transactions?

5-8 Compare and contrast the two methods of preparing cash flow statements: the direct vs. the indirect method. What are the essential differences between these two methods? What are the similarities?

5-9 In each of the following cases, indicate whether the amount of cash inflow (or outflow) is greater or less than the related revenue (or expense):

a. A firm's accounts receivable balance has increased during the period.
b. A firm's salaries payable balance has increased during the period.
c. A firm's accumulated depreciation balance has increased during the period.
d. A firm's inventory balance has increased during the period and the supplier accounts payable balance has also increased by a greater amount.

Effects of Transactions: Cash versus Accrual

5-10 Consider the following transactions or events:

1. Sold merchandise on account.
2. Sold a used computer for cash.
3. Paid a supplier's overdue account.
4. Recorded depreciation expense on a building.

5. Signed a mortgage and received cash.
6. Purchased inventory on account.
7. Gave a refund after hearing a customer's complaint.
8. Received payment from a customer.
9. Sold shares of IBM stock for cash and recorded a gain.
10. Recorded a loss after discarding obsolete inventory.
11. Received a personal cash gift from a friend.
12. Made an "even" swap of a used truck for another truck.
13. Paid quarterly unemployment taxes.
14. Received a tax refund after sending duplicate checks to the IRS.

Required

a. Show the effects on cash of each transaction or event, using the format below:

Effects on Cash		
Increase	**Decrease**	**No Change**

b. Show the effects of each transaction or event on net income, using a similar format:

Effects on Net Income		
Increase	**Decrease**	**No Change**

Converting from Cash Flows to Revenues and Expenses

5-11 Determine the amounts of revenue or expense associated with each of the following cash flows:

1. Cash received from customers was $8.5 million; accounts receivable increased by $1.6 million.
2. Paid salaries of $3 million; salaries payable decreased by $.6 million.
3. Paid cash of $4.5 million to suppliers; supplier accounts payable increased by $.5 million. Inventories decreased by $1 million.

Interpreting Cash Flow Statements

5-12 The following cash flow statement was prepared by the Brainard Music Company for the year ended December 31, 2007:

Cash flow from operating activities		$(346,000)
Cash flow from investing activities:		
Purchase of Musicbox, Ltd.	$(280,000)	
Purchase of property and equipment	(120,000)	
Total from investing activities		(400,000)
Cash flow from financing activities:		
Proceeds from issuance of stock	130,000	
Proceeds from short-term bank loans	540,000	
Payment of dividends	(110,000)	
Total from financing activities		560,000
Net decrease in cash		$(186,000)

Required

a. Give three reasons why Brainard engaged in these investing and financing activities.

b. Assume that Brainard received dividends from Musicbox, Ltd. Why aren't they reported as part of investing activities?

c. Discuss the concept of depreciation as it affects cash flows and as it affects Brainard Music Co.

d. Do you think the future outlook for this company is optimistic? Why or why not?

Interpreting Financial Statements: Cash Flow Effects

5-13 A condensed version of Microbyte Corporation's consolidated statements of cash flows for 2006 and 2007 are shown below (dollars in thousands):

	2007	*2006*
Cash flows from operating activities:		
Cash received from customers	$164,177	$82,152
Cash paid to suppliers and employees	(142,336)	(69,507)
Interest received	2,622	722
Interest paid	(87)	(224)
Income taxes paid	(16,121)	(5,187)
Net cash provided by operating activities	8,255	7,956
Cash flows from investing activities:		
Sale (purchase) of short-term investments	600	(16,200)
Capital expenditures	(9,740)	(1,932)
Net cash used for investing activities	(9,140)	(18,132)
Cash flows from financing activities:		
Proceeds from issuing common stock	496	22,114
Payments under capital leases	(472)	(347)
Other	(9)	31
Net cash provided by financing activities	15	21,798
Net increase (decrease) in cash	(870)	11,622
Cash balances at beginning of year	14,808	3,186
Cash balances at end of year	$ 13,938	$14,808

Required

a. Is Microbyte's statement of cash flows based on the direct or indirect method? What evidence supports this view?

b. By how much did Microbyte's cash flow from operations increase?

c. During these two years, how much did Microbyte spend to purchase marketable securities and other short-term investments? Did Microbyte buy or sell securities in either year?

d. How much did Microbyte spend on capital expenditures during the two years? Did Microbyte purchase or sell capital assets each year? How do you know?

e. During these two years, how much money did Microbyte receive by issuing common stock? Given these proceeds, what do you suppose Microbyte did with it? Why would Microbyte take these actions?

f. By how much did Microbyte's collections from customers increase between 2006 and 2007? Does this increase represent modest or significant growth? Is the increase in cash paid to suppliers and employees consistent with this growth? Why?

g. By how much did Microbyte's cash balances increase between the beginning of 2006 and the end of 2007? Is this increase significant? Does it represent a significant increase in Microbyte's liquidity? Why?

h. Why do you think the amounts shown for interest payments are so low? Why is interest received so much larger than interest payments? Under what circumstances is this a favorable relationship?

i. During 2006, Microbyte's cash increased by $11,622,000. On the other hand, during 2007 its cash decreased by $870,000. Is this trend alarming? Does it indicate any problems for Microbyte?

j. How would an analyst evaluate the relationship between Microbyte's cash provided by operations of $8,255,000 and its cash used for investing activities of $9,140,000? How is this relationship affected by Microbyte's financing activities? Has Microbyte been a prudent manager of its cash during 2004? Why?

k. Compute the following ratios or amounts for Microbyte Corporation for 2007. Discuss each ratio in the context of Microbyte's statement of cash flows.

(1) Cash flow from operating activities
(2) Cash return on assets, assuming average total assets are $81,613,000
(3) Cash return on stockholders' equity, assuming average stockholders' equity is $60,386,000
(4) Quality of sales, assuming sales revenues are $170,290,000
(5) Quality of income, assuming net income is $40,513,000
(6) Cash interest coverage

l. Compute the following ratios or amounts for Microbyte Corporation for 2006 and discuss each ratio in the context of Microbyte's statement of cash flows.

(1) Cash flow from operating activities
(2) Quality of sales, assuming sales revenues are $88,655,000
(3) Quality of income, assuming net income is $17,848,000
(4) Cash interest coverage

m. Evaluate the trends in these ratios over the two years.

n. Evaluate Microbyte's future prospects.

Preparing an Income Statement and a Statement of Cash Flows

5-14 Beth's Espresso Cart finished its second year of operations.

1. Cash collections from clients	$35,505
2. Payments to suppliers (beans, etc.)	17,347
3. Replacement of cups, pots, etc.	1,000
4. Depreciation of coffee cart	1,300
5. Withdrawals for personal use	6,000
6. Purchases of propane, electricity, etc.	510
7. Amortization of insurance (final year)	400
8. Repaid start-up loan (to her father)	4,000
9. Paid interest on loan, two years at 10% simple interest (for last year and this year)	

Required

a. Prepare an income statement and a statement of cash flows on the basis of the data (assuming that all sales and purchases are for cash). Assume there have been no significant inventory changes (supplies, fuel, coffee beans, etc.) during the past year.

b. Write a short memo evaluating the year's operating performance of Beth's Espresso Cart. Provide suggestions for next year.

Effects of Timing on Revenue Recognition

5-15 Key, Inc., manufactures key rings and "dummy" keys for football fans to shake and rattle at opportune times during football games. These items are sold to sports specialty shops and sidewalk vendors during the football season. The company's fiscal year ends December 31 each year. In 2006, just before the "bowl" season, the company received orders and payment for $23,000 worth of keys and key rings. The goods will be manufactured and shipped on January 1, 2007, just in time for the major bowl games later that day. The effects these orders have in December 2006 on key's balance sheet equation is as follows:

ASSETS	=	LIABILITIES	+	SHAREHOLDERS' EQUITY
Cash + $23,000				Sales revenue + $23,000

The company's overall financial results, summarized under the accounting equation, were:

ASSETS	=	LIABILITIES	+	SHAREHOLDERS' EQUITY
$275,000		$266,000		$9,000

Key's summarized income statement for 2006 is as follows:

Revenues	$115,000
Expenses	109,000
Net income	$ 6,000

Required

a. Show how the $23,000 in December 2006 orders should have been recorded.

b. Reconstruct the income statement, showing how it might have appeared without the inclusion of the $23,000 in December orders. For this purpose, assume that the expenses associated with the orders were $11,000.

c. Show how the balance sheet would have changed if the $23,000 in orders had been recorded correctly. Why might Key management be unhappy with these results?

d. Discuss the ethical problems inherent in this situation for the company, for its financial managers, and for its auditors.

CHAPTER 5 APPENDIX

Using Direct Method to Calculate Cash Flow from Operating Activities

5A-1 The following financial statements for Lucy Enterprises are provided:

Income Statement for Year Ending December 31, 2006

Sales revenues	$550,000	
Cost of goods sold	210,000	
Gross margin		$340,000
Salary expenses	115,000	
Interest expense	15,000	
Interest revenue	(20,000)	110,000
Net income before taxes		230,000
Tax expense		92,000
Net income		$138,000

BALANCE SHEET AT YEAR-END

	2006	*2005*		*2006*	*2005*
Cash	$225,000	$100,000	Accounts payable	$ 30,000	$ 20,000
Accounts receivable	124,000	135,000	Salaries payable	5,000	4,000
Inventory	35,000	21,000	Interest payable	3,000	12,000
			Taxes payable	2,500	3,500
Current assets	384,000	256,000	Current liabilities	40,500	39,500
Property, plant, and equipment	101,000	134,000	Shareholders' equity	444,500	350,500
	$485,000	$390,000		$485,000	$390,000

Required

Prepare the cash flow from operating activities section of the statement of cash flows, using the direct method and the indirect method. The following amounts must first be calculated when using the direct method:

- Cash collections from customers
- Cash payments to suppliers
- Cash payments to employees
- Taxes paid
- Interest paid
- Interest collected
- Purchases

Using Direct Method to Calculate Cash Flow from Operating Activities

5A-2 The following condensed information (dollars in thousands) is available from Mary's Muffins. Assume that all sales are credit sales (accounts receivable) and all purchases are also on credit (accounts payable).

	December 31	
	Year 1	*Year 2*
Balance Sheet Data:		
Accounts receivable	$55	$ 53
Prepaid expenses	13	15
Salaries payable	22	25
Taxes payable	17	13
Inventory	32	26
Accounts payable	27	21
Income Statement Data:		
Sales revenues		$550
Cost of goods sold		210
Salaries expense		112
Tax expense		57
Depreciation expense		29
Other expense		$ 21

Required

Prepare the operating activities section of Year 2's statement of cash flows, using the direct method.

Preparing a Statement of Cash Flows

5A-3 The following are comparative balance sheets for the Paulino Corporation for 2007 and 2006 and the income statement for the year ended December 31, 2007:

PAULINO CORPORATION
COMPARATIVE BALANCE SHEETS
DECEMBER 31

	2007	*2006*
Assets		
Cash	$ 89,000	$ 60,000
Accounts receivable	65,000	50,000
Inventory	200,000	90,000
Land	100,000	225,000
Equipment, net	371,000	380,000
	$825,000	$805,000
Liabilities and Shareholders' Equity		
Accounts payable	$ 54,000	$ 32,000
Dividends payable	15,000	0
Interest payable	6,000	8,000
Mortgage payable	130,000	305,000
Invested capital	280,000	280,000
Retained earnings	340,000	180,000
	$825,000	$805,000

PAULINO CORPORATION
INCOME STATEMENT
FOR THE YEAR ENDED DECEMBER 31, 2007

Sales		$1,200,000
Cost of goods sold		(720,000)
Gross profit		480,000
Operating and other expenses		
Depreciation	(9,000)	
Other operating expenses	(275,000)	
Gain on sale of land	15,000	
Interest expense	(10,000)	(279,000)
Net income		$ 201,000

Additional information:

1. Dividends declared during the year were $41,000.
2. Land at a cost of $125,000 was sold for $140,000.
3. The only change in equipment was the depreciation expense.
4. All other balance sheet account changes are from normal transactions.

Required

Use the direct method to prepare a statement of cash flows for Paulino Corporation.

Preparing a Statement of Cash Flows

5A-4 The following financial statements for Swale, LTD are provided:

SWALE LIMITED
INCOME STATEMENT
FOR THE YEAR ENDED DECEMBER 31, 2007

Revenues:		
Sales	$97,800	
Interest revenue	1,300	
		$99,100
Expenses:		
Cost of goods sold	56,500	
Salary expense	19,000	
Depreciation expense	3,000	
Interest expense	1,500	
Tax expense	2,500	82,500
Net Income		$16,600

SWALE LIMITED
BALANCE SHEET
DECEMBER 31

	2007	*2006*
Cash	$35,600	$24,000
Accounts receivable	5,500	3,000
Inventory	21,000	11,000
Property, plant, and equipment (net)	21,500	20,000
Investments	12,000	0
Total assets	$95,600	$58,000
Accounts payable	$5,000	$ 2,000
Salaries payable	600	500
Short-term debt	0	12,000
Long-term debt	25,000	6,000
Common stock	36,000	25,100
Retained earnings	29,000	12,400
Total liabilities and shareholders' equity	$95,600	$58,000

Required
Prepare a statement of cash flows.

Working from Operating Cash Flows to Net Income

5-A5 The Blunt Instrument Company reports cash flow from operations of $65 million for 2007. You are provided the following additional information for the year:

1. Customer accounts receivable increased by $6 million.
2. Dividends paid to common shareholders were $20 million.
3. Depreciation expense was $24 million.
4. Noncurrent debt was increased by $35 million.
5. Supplier accounts payable decreased by $8 million.
6. Inventory balances increased by $18 million.
7. Income tax payable increased by $9 million.

Required
Based on the above information, determine the amount of net income reported by Blunt for 2007.

Preparing a Cash Flow Statement Using Comparative Balance Sheets

5-A6 The Limpid Pool Company reports net income of $25 million for 2007. Balance sheets at the beginning and end of the year are shown below.

	December 31	
	2006	*2007*
	(Dollars in millions)	
Cash	$ 50	$ 70
Other current assets	80	145
Property, plant, and equipment (net)	170	135
Total assets	$300	$350
Current liabilities	$ 20	$ 15
Noncurrent liabilities	180	195
Common stock	80	110
Retained earnings	20	30
Total liabilities and shareholders' equity	$300	$350

The firm did not acquire any noncurrent assets during 2007.

Required
Determine the following amounts for 2007:

a. Dividends paid
b. Cash flow from operating activities
c. Cash flow from investing activities
d. Cash flow from financing activities

CHAPTER 6

CURRENT ASSETS

Learning Objectives

1. *Identify cash and cash equivalents.*
2. *Understand the need for cash planning and how firms exercise control over cash.*
3. *Comprehend the basic valuation principles for marketable securities.*
4. *Evaluate accounts receivable management.*
5. *Assess adequacy of the allowance for uncollectible accounts.*
6. *Understand various inventory cost flow assumptions and the related effects on taxes, management compensation, loan covenants, stock prices, and the quality of financial statement information.*
7. *Analyze inventory management practices.*
8. *Understand the nature of prepaid expenses.*
9. *Identify relationships between cash and other current assets.*

Appendix 6A: *Prepare a bank reconciliation.*

Appendix 6B: *Compare LIFO and FIFO firms.*

INTRODUCTION

This chapter examines five prominent current assets:

1. cash and cash equivalents,
2. marketable securities,
3. accounts receivable,
4. inventories, and
5. prepaid expenses.

For each asset, we examine accounting issues and information contained in the financial statements.

CASH AND CASH EQUIVALENTS

Cash is the most liquid asset a business can own! Most firms devote considerable effort to the management and control of cash. Because a firm's creditors expect payment in cash, sufficient amounts of cash must always be available to meet obligations when they are due. This necessitates careful scheduling of cash outflows, and establishing some correspondence between cash outflows and inflows.

Although an adequate cash balance is essential, excessive holdings of cash should be avoided. Cash deposited in checking accounts (or even savings accounts) usually does not earn very much, if any, interest. Cash amounts over and above those needed to meet scheduled payment dates in the near future should be invested in assets earning higher returns.

The liquidity of cash also makes it easily pilfered. Firms must institute internal control procedures so that cash is properly accounted for and safeguarded. Failure to do so may tempt employees to misappropriate the firm's cash and may also result in various accounting errors.

Composition of Cash

Cash is composed of funds that are *readily available*. This includes cash on hand and cash on deposit in bank accounts that do not restrict the withdrawal of cash. Deposits in checking accounts would qualify because those balances can be withdrawn on demand. Because banks rarely enforce restrictions on withdrawals from savings accounts, they are usually classified as cash. Cash also includes money market funds with check-writing privileges, checks from customers awaiting deposit, and foreign currency (converted to dollars). Items *not* classified as cash include rare coins, stamps, and postdated checks.

Large corporations may have hundreds of checking accounts. Multiple accounts are needed because firms have numerous physical locations and each location makes expenditures. Firms also find it convenient to use separate accounts for specific purposes. For example, many firms use one or more checking accounts solely for payroll purposes. All bank accounts are condensed into the one cash item on the balance sheet.

Many firms keep **petty cash funds** on hand to pay for small, incidental expenditures, such as cab fare or delivery charges. These funds are included as cash on the balance sheet. Many retailers also keep *change funds.* These funds enable cashiers to make change for their customers. **Change funds** are also included as cash on the balance sheet.

As a part of borrowing agreements with banks, firms sometimes agree to maintain **compensating balances.** These are minimum amounts the firm agrees to keep on deposit at the lending bank in accounts that pay little or no interest. As a result, the bank is able to use these funds interest free. This provides the bank with additional compensation for lending funds to the firm. Compensating balances are usually included in the balance sheet cash amount and are disclosed in the notes to the financial statements.

Instead of showing a cash item on their balance sheets, some firms use the term **cash and cash equivalents.** Recall from previous chapters that **cash equivalents** are short-term, highly liquid investments that will mature within three months of their purchase date. Examples include certificates of deposit, treasury bills, and commercial paper (short-term obligations of corporations). Because cash equivalents can readily be converted into known amounts of cash, reporting a combined cash and cash equivalents figure is probably as informative as reporting each figure separately. Dayton, Inc. follows the practice of reporting a combined figure for cash and cash equivalents. Exhibit 6-1 contains an excerpt from its financial statement note describing this policy.

EXHIBIT 6-1 DISCLOSURE OF CASH REPORTING POLICY

Dayton, Inc.
2007 Annual Report
Note 1 (Partial)

Cash equivalents consist of highly liquid debt instruments such as money market accounts and commercial paper with original maturities of three months or less from date of purchase. The Company's policy is to invest cash in conservative instruments as part of its cash management program and to evaluate the credit exposure of any investment. Cash and cash equivalents are stated at cost, which approximates market value.

Control of Cash

As previously mentioned, because cash is so liquid and so easily transported, special care must be exercised to ensure that it is properly recorded and safeguarded. Most corporations design sound management practices that enhance their control over cash. Employees who are permitted access to cash, for example, should not also have access to the accounting records for cash. Access to both cash and the accounting records might enable an employee to misappropriate cash and to conceal the theft by altering the records.

As an illustration, retail clerks (who have ready access to cash) should not "read" the cash register. That is, they should not have the responsibility of ascertaining the daily sales total from the register's internal record and recording this amount in the accounting records. As shown in Exhibit 6-2, clerks with such dual access could take some cash and hide the theft by reducing the firm's recorded cash collections.

Checking accounts with banks provide firms with several cash control advantages. First, cash receipts should be deposited daily. Limiting the amount of time that cash is on the firm's premises reduces the possibility that it will be misappropriated.

Second, checks provide a written record of a firm's disbursements. Such records would not exist if disbursements were made in currency. Moreover, most firms require that checks be supported by underlying documentation such as purchase orders, invoices, and receiving reports. This helps ensure that only valid expenditures are made and provides a basis for analyzing costs and expenses.

Third, by limiting the number of people authorized to sign checks, firms restrict access to cash; thus reducing the temptation that cash will be used for unintended purposes.

Finally, bank statements provide a monthly listing of deposits and withdrawals. So not only does the firm keep track of its cash flows, but so does the bank! Thus, the bank statement can be used to verify or reconcile the firm's cash records.

This verification process is accomplished by preparing the **bank reconciliation,** which is a detailed comparison of the firm's records and the bank statement. Because the bank reconciliation may uncover errors related to cash, an employee who has no other cash-related responsibilities should prepare it. Bank reconciliations are illustrated in Appendix 6A.

EXHIBIT 6-2 POOR CONTROLS OVER CASH

Analysis of Cash

The most informative analysis of cash pertains to cash flows. As you recall from Chapter 5, the statement of cash flows summarizes and explains cash inflows and outflows. A firm's ability to generate cash enables it to pay obligations as they become due, replace and expand productive assets, and provide a return to investors. Chapter 5 described analyses that provide insights into this ability.

The balance sheet does not contain information about a firm's cash flows. It simply indicates the amount of cash a firm holds on a given date. Nevertheless, some useful information about cash can be obtained from the balance sheet. The amount of cash on hand and the trend in the cash balance over time can be ascertained. Also, because most current liabilities are paid in cash, many analysts relate the cash balance to current liabilities. This is done via the **cash to current liabilities ratio:**

$$\text{Cash to current liabilities ratio} = \frac{\text{Cash}}{\text{Current liabilities}}$$

Exhibit 6-3 contains cash-related information for Dayton, Inc. Dayton's cash position decreased substantially from 2006 to 2007. The cash balance declined from \$31,201,000 to \$13,779,000. The cash to current liabilities ratio also decreased significantly, from 70.4% in 2006 to 28.5% in 2007.

	2007	2006
Cash to current liabilities ratio	$\frac{\$13{,}779}{\$48{,}286} = 28.5\%$	$\frac{\$31{,}201}{\$44{,}293} = 70.4\%$

The decline in the cash balance and the cash to current liabilities ratio is potentially worrisome. What caused this decline? Dayton, Inc. has attempted to operate more efficiently by utilizing a smaller cash balance. Recall that although firms need to maintain a cash balance sufficient to meet their obligations, excessive cash balances are undesirable because idle cash earns, at best, a modest return. Given that Dayton, Inc. has virtually no debt, has unused lines of credit available, and has strong cash flow from operations, the decline in the cash balance should not cause alarm.

EXHIBIT 6-3 FINANCIAL STATEMENT INFORMATION

Dayton, Inc.
Selected Cash-Related Information
(Dollars in thousands)

	2007	2006
Cash and cash equivalents	\$ 13,779	\$ 31,201
Current assets	\$131,048	\$148,934
Current liabilities	\$ 48,286	\$ 44,293

Note that the cash to current liabilities ratio is a severe test of liquidity. To see this, compare Dayton's 2007 cash to current liabilities ratio of 28.5% to its current ratio:

$$\text{Current ratio} = \frac{\text{Current assets}}{\text{Current liabilities}} = \frac{\$131{,}048}{\$48{,}286} = 2.71$$

Both ratios contain current liabilities in the denominator. However, because the cash to current liabilities ratio has a much smaller numerator, a lower ratio results.

Implications for Managers

Financial statements provide managers and others with historical information about cash. Managers must ensure that sufficient cash is available on an ongoing basis to enable the firm to meet its commitments. As in many cases, managers must be proactive, not reactive, and the historical information can help with decision making.

Cash management begins with *projecting the amount and timing of future cash flows.* This enables firms to forecast their cash balances over the course of a specified time period. If positive net cash flows are expected, managers must identify profitable uses of that cash. Alternatively, if negative net cash flows are projected, managers must identify additional sources of cash. Possibilities include short-term debt, long-term debt, additional investments by owners, and the liquidation of assets. Other strategies include attempting to speed up cash collections from customers and delaying payments to suppliers.

MARKETABLE SECURITIES

Many firms experience uneven cash flows during a year. Department stores, for example, make a large portion of their sales during November and December, resulting in significant cash inflows. In many instances, such large amounts of cash are not immediately needed to fund operations. Many firms elect to put excess cash balances into short-term investments. These investments, known as **marketable securities,** typically produce higher earnings than those available from bank accounts, thus enabling firms to increase their earnings.

Types of Investments

Firms can choose from two general types of securities. **Equity securities** represent ownership interests in other corporations. For example, General Motors (GM) can purchase shares of IBM stock, which would be reflected on GM's balance sheet as an asset.

Firms can also invest in **debt securities,** which result from lending transactions. For example, if GM were to lend funds to IBM, IBM would probably issue a debt security as written evidence of the indebtedness. The security might be commercial paper (indicating short-term borrowing) or a bond (indicating long-term borrowing). In either case, the security would appear on GM's balance sheet as an asset.

This chapter deals primarily with investments in equity securities that are classified as current assets. As you know, current assets are either consumed or converted into cash within one year. Thus, we cover only investments that will be held a relatively short period of time. Long-term investments are covered in TOPICMOD-V dealing with reporting issues for affiliated companies

Marketability

This chapter is also restricted to securities that are **marketable**. A **security** is marketable if it is traded on a securities exchange registered with the Securities and Exchange Commission (SEC) or if its price is available through the National Association of Securities Dealers Automated Quotations (NASDAQ) systems or the National Quotation Bureau. Securities traded on foreign exchanges may also qualify.

Securities that are not readily marketable are unlikely candidates for short-term investments of excess cash. Nonmarketable securities cannot necessarily be liquidated when the investor desires to do so. Investments in nonmarketable securities are usually classified as long-term investments.

Basic Accounting

SFAS No. 115, Accounting for Certain Investments in Debt and Equity Securities, governs the accounting for short-term investments in marketable securities. This standard requires that a firm classify such investments as either **trading securities** or **available-for-sale securities.** Firms intend to hold trading securities for brief periods of time to generate profits from short-term price increases. For example, investment banks will often buy an entire stock issue from a corporation with the intent of almost immediately selling the stock to the public. The investment bank would classify the stock as a trading security.

Marketable equity securities not classified as trading securities are classified as available-for-sale. Nonfinancial organizations classify most of their investments in marketable equity securities as available-for-sale. Proper classification is important because the accounting treatment differs for the two categories. Because most corporations classify their securities as available-for-sale, this chapter emphasizes the accounting procedures for that classification.

Available-for-Sale Securities

Marketable equity securities classified as available-for-sale should be accounted for at market value on the balance sheet date. The difference between a security's historical cost and its market value is an **unrealized gain or loss**. The term unrealized indicates that the gain or loss has not been confirmed by an actual sale.

However, because the securities are highly marketable, the value change is virtually certain, and, accordingly, the gain or loss is a valid and useful measure of a change in wealth.

Unrealized gains and losses on available-for-sale securities are not shown as part of net income! They are shown as part of "other comprehensive income" as part of shareholders' equity (but not part of invested capital or retained earnings). Note that the marketable securities account reflects both the securities' historical cost and its fair market value. The adjustment to market value is made to a valuation account, often labeled "Securities fair value adjustment".

To illustrate, assume that on December 1, 2006, Mega Company purchased marketable securities for $1,000. This analysis is straightforward.

	ASSETS		=	LIABILITIES	+	SHAREHOLDERS' EQUITY
	Cash	Marketable securities				
Dec. 1	– $1,000	+ $1,000				

On December 31, the securities are still on hand and have a market value of $980. To record the value change, reduce marketable securities by $20 by reducing the "Securities fair value adjustment" account and reduce shareholders' equity by $20 (Unrealized holding gain (loss)).

	ASSETS		=	LIABILITIES	+	SHAREHOLDERS' EQUITY
	Marketable securities	Securities fair value adjustment				Unrealized holding gain (loss) on marketable securities
Dec. 31 Balance	$1,000					
		– $20				– $20

In the asset section of the balance sheet, the $20 balance in "Securities fair value adjustment" is subtracted from marketable securities to show a net asset of $980. The "Unrealized holding gain (loss)" on marketable securities (account) is a separate component of shareholders' equity. Keep in mind that this loss is *not* part of net income, but it is part of "other comprehensive income".

Assume further that the securities are sold on January 10, 2007, for $990. Looking at the purchase and sale together, a $10 loss has been incurred. Because no loss was realized in 2006, when the securities were revalued, a $10 loss must now be reflected in net income.

The analysis is most easily completed in two steps. First, because the $20 loss is no longer unrealized, *the entry to record that loss should be reversed.* Second, cash is increased by $990, marketable securities are reduced by $1,000, and a $10 loss is recognized. This loss is termed realized because it has been confirmed by a cash transaction. This loss appears on the 2007 income statement.

	ASSETS			=	LIABILITIES	+	SHAREHOLDERS' EQUITY	
	Cash	Marketable securities	Securities fair value adjustment				Unrealized holding gain (loss) on marketable securities	Retained earnings
Balance		$1,000	– $20				– $20	(realized loss)
Jan. 10			+ $20				+ $20	
Jan. 10	+ $990	– $1,000						– $10

Trading Securities

Trading securities are also accounted for at market value. One major difference exists between the accounting for trading securities and that for securities classified as available-for-sale. *Unrealized gains and losses on trading securities are included in net income,* as opposed to being reflected in a special section of shareholders' equity. The FASB believes that, because trading securities are purchased to generate profits on short-term price changes, all unrealized gains and losses on trading securities should be immediately reflected on the income statement.

Debt Securities

The accounting for debt securities is a bit more complex. If a firm intends to hold a debt security until its maturity date, the security is valued at historical cost. Debt securities not intended to be held until maturity are shown on the balance sheet at market value. However, because debt securities classified as current assets will be liquidated within the next year, a large discrepancy between cost and market value is unlikely. Thus, in most cases, financial statement readers can view the marketable debt securities figure in the current asset section as a very close approximation to market value.

Analysis of Marketable Securities

Marketable securities are reflected on the balance sheet at market value. Because these securities can be readily converted into known amounts of cash, such a valuation rule seems quite reasonable. Analysts evaluate the liquidity of a firm, in part, by examining current assets. The potential cash that could be generated by selling a marketable security is much more relevant for assessing liquidity than is a security's historical cost. *It is truly an indicator of "where's the cash"!*

Your accounting common sense probably suggests that all unrealized gains and losses on marketable securities should appear on the income statement; however this is only true for trading securities, whereas available-for-sale securities are shown as part of comprehensive income under SFAS No. 115.

These valuation rules can be challenged on at least three grounds. First, some argue that changes in the value of marketable securities are valid gains and losses and should always be included in net income. Not doing so reduces the usefulness of net income as a measure of wealth changes and as an indicator of managerial performance.

Second, these rules provide an *opportunity for profit manipulation by management.* By electing to sell certain securities that have either risen or fallen in value, managers can dictate whether gains or losses will be reported.

Third, the FASB created a new element of shareholders' equity (unrealized holding gain (or loss) on marketable securities) in order to exclude changes in the value of marketable securities from net income. This element is a new (and somewhat unusual) addition to the conventional balance sheet. Its existence compromises the basic notion that the change in shareholders' equity for a period equals net income plus the effects of direct contributions/withdrawals by the shareholders. It creates confusion among investors, creditors, and other financial statement users.

This reporting treatment for holding gains and losses will probably continue to change, such that income statements may someday reflect all market value changes in marketable securities. As you interpret net income and make the "adjustment for special charges," include significant holding gains or losses, as shown in comprehensive income, as part of adjusted net income.

ACCOUNTS RECEIVABLE

Revenue transactions are usually undertaken for cash or credit terms. Firms obviously prefer to make sales for cash because funds are immediately available to meet obligations, invest in productive endeavors, pay dividends, and so on. Moreover, cash sales entail no uncertainty about collectibility.

Credit Sales

Many firms, however, make a significant portion of their sales on credit. They do so because customers prefer deferring their payments. Credit transactions enable purchasers to use their cash for a longer period of time before paying the seller. Moreover, credit transactions permit the purchaser to inspect and actually use the goods prior to payment. Industry practices and competitive pressures force many firms to sell on credit, and credit sales to customers in the ordinary course of business give rise to **accounts receivable (trade receivables).**

Before making a credit sale, the credit standing of the customer should be assessed. Credit-worthiness is an important consideration in making a credit sale because it bears directly on a potential customer's ability and willingness to ultimately make payment. Various credit bureaus (such as Dun & Bradstreet and Equifax) provide **credit ratings** and other information for this purpose.

Selling only to customers with high credit ratings, however, will not necessarily maximize profits. Although such a policy would minimize receivables that prove to be **uncollectible,** a number of potentially profitable sales might be eliminated and the profit on these sales may well overshadow the expense of uncollectible accounts. Thus, a firm must decide how much credit to grant and to whom credit should be offered. Selecting a "mid-range" credit-rating cutoff is probably optimal.

Accounting for Credit Sales

The analysis of credit sales is quite straightforward. The credit sale of merchandise for $100 would increase accounts receivable and shareholders' equity (sales revenue).

ASSETS	=	LIABILITIES	+	SHAREHOLDERS' EQUITY
Accounts receivable + $100				Retained earnings + $100 (sales revenue)

When the cash is ultimately collected, the balance in cash is increased, and the accounts receivable balance is decreased.

ASSETS		=	LIABILITIES	+	SHAREHOLDERS' EQUITY
Cash	Accounts receivable				
+ $100	− $100				

Notice that *revenue is recognized when the sale is made.* The *collection of cash does not result in the recognition of revenue*. Rather, cash collection merely transforms one asset (accounts receivable) into another (cash).

Discounts

When selling on credit, many firms offer **discounts** for early payment. Such discounts are offered primarily for two reasons. First, early payment by the customer enables the seller to have access to cash sooner. Second, the sooner an account is paid, the less opportunity there is for nonpayment.

Typical discount terms are 2/10, net 30. This indicates that a 2% discount will be granted if payment is made within 10 days of sale; otherwise, full payment is due within 30 days of sale.

These particular terms offer a significant inducement for early payment. To see this, consider the 2% to be a finance charge assessed for extending credit from the 10th to the 30th day after sale. That is, the customer must pay 2% more than otherwise required if payment is delayed for those 20 days. Because there are about 18 20-day periods in a year (365/20), the quoted discount implies an approximate annual interest rate of 36% (2% × 18), which is quite high relative to other sources of financing.

Factoring Accounts Receivable

In some industries, sellers extend very generous credit terms to their customers. For example, furniture retailers sometimes do not require any payment until six months or a year after sale. To obtain cash more quickly, these firms **factor** (sell) their receivables (**factor receivables**). In most cases, the receivables are factored to a financial institution that charges a fee as compensation for the cost of collection, the delayed receipt of the cash, and potential uncollectible accounts.

To illustrate, assume that a furniture store has previously made a credit sale for $1,500. If the receivable is subsequently factored for $1,300, cash would increase by $1,300, accounts receivable would decrease by $1,500, and a $200 financing loss would be incurred.

ASSETS		=	LIABILITIES	+	SHAREHOLDERS' EQUITY
Cash	Accounts receivable				Retained earnings
+ $1,300	– $1,500				– $200 (financing loss)

Sales or factoring accounts receivable at year-end can be a "red-flag" warning. "Selling receivables is common, but it could signal that company is facing a cash crunch . . . It could be a sign that the company's customers, who could be dying dot-com companies, for example, are having trouble paying their bills." (Ken Brown, "How to Spot the Dirt in Rosy Annual Reports, *The Wall Street Journal*, February 14, 2003, p. C3.)

Uncollectible Accounts

As noted earlier, revenue is recognized at the time a credit sale is made. Recognizing revenue increases a firm's assets and net income. However, given that some of the receivables may ultimately prove to be uncollectible, assets and net income might be overstated.

Year-End Adjustment

To avoid this possibility, firms make **year-end adjustments** to recognize that some of their accounts receivable will probably not be collected. Because firms are unlikely to know which particular accounts will prove to be uncollectible, the amount of the adjustment is an estimate.

To illustrate, assume that on December 31, 2006, at the end of its first year of operation, the Box Company estimates that $2,400 of its year-end accounts receivable balance of $100,000 will be uncollectible. Keep in mind that this is an overall estimate and that Box is currently unable to identify which particular customers will not fulfill their obligations. Accordingly, the adjustment does not directly reduce accounts receivable. Instead, a negative (contra) asset, allowance for uncollectible accounts, is used.

An expense is also recorded, which is consistent with the matching principle. One cost of generating sales is the receivables that will ultimately prove to be uncollectible. This cost (even though it must be estimated) should be deducted from the sales revenue that gave rise to those receivables. The analysis follows.

	ASSETS		=	LIABILITIES	+	SHAREHOLDERS' EQUITY
	Accounts receivable	Allowance for uncollectible accounts (contra asset)				Retained earnings
Balance	$100,000					
Dec. 31		– $2,400				– $2,400 (uncollectible accounts expense)

The net difference between the balances in accounts receivable and the **allowance for uncollectible accounts** is **net accounts receivable,** which is included in total assets on the balance sheet.

Accounts receivable (gross)	$100,000
Less allowance for uncollectible accounts	(2,400)
Accounts receivable, net	$ 97,600

Note that Wal-Mart does not report any **allowance for uncollectible accounts** on its balance sheet, nor in its notes. Wal-Mart does not even suggest that there is any consideration of bad debts, which is highly unusual. Wal-Mart's experience with bad debts must be such that they are not material. On the other hand, Target reports its receivables as "net" on its balance sheet. Target discusses receivables in a long note called "Accounts Receivable". In the first paragraph of this note, we find that Target's allowance for uncollectible accounts is $451 million for 2005 and $387 million for the prior year. Those numbers are fairly small compared to the net Accounts Receivable balances of $5,666 million in 2006 and $5,069 million in the prior year. These amounts must be viewed as negative numbers, as the contra account usually carries a negative balance.

Exhibit 6-4 contains Dayton's partial balance sheet. It shows the balance in the allowance account, as well as the net accounts receivable included in total assets.

EXHIBIT 6-4 PARTIAL BALANCE SHEET

Dayton, Inc.
Partial Balance Sheet
(Dollars in thousands)

	DECEMBER 31, 2007	DECEMBER 31, 2006
Accounts receivable, less allowance of $4,225 in 2007 and $5,474 in 2006	$23,278	$20,504

From the information provided, gross accounts receivable on December 31, 2007, can be computed as $27,503,000:

Net receivable	=	Gross receivable	–	Allowance
$23,278,000	=	Gross receivable	–	$4,225,000
$23,278,000	=	$27,503,000	–	4,225,000

Write-Offs

When a firm subsequently ascertains that a particular customer will not pay, that customer's account is **written off.** **Write-offs** are recorded by reducing the balances in accounts receivable and in the allowance for uncollectible accounts. Continuing with the Box Company illustration, assume that on February 11, 2007, Box becomes aware that a customer who owes $450 has just gone out of business and that collection is extremely unlikely. The balances in the accounts receivable and allowance accounts would each be reduced by $450.

	ASSETS		=	LIABILITIES	+	SHAREHOLDERS' EQUITY
	Accounts receivable	Allowance for uncollectible accounts				
Balance	$100,000	– $2,400				
Feb. 11	– $ 450	+ $ 450				
Balance	$ 99,550	– $1,950				

Because the balance in accounts receivable is reduced, as is the accompanying contra asset, the write-off has no effect on total assets or expenses. This is proper, because the asset reduction and expense were previously recorded. Box's net receivable is $97,600, both before and after the write-off.

	Before	After
Accounts receivable, gross	$100,000	$99,550
Less allowance	2,400	1,950
Accounts receivable, net	$ 97,600	$97,600

The effect of the write-off is depicted graphically in Exhibit 6-5.

EXHIBIT 6-5 EFFECT OF WRITE-OFFS ON ACCOUNTS RECEIVABLE

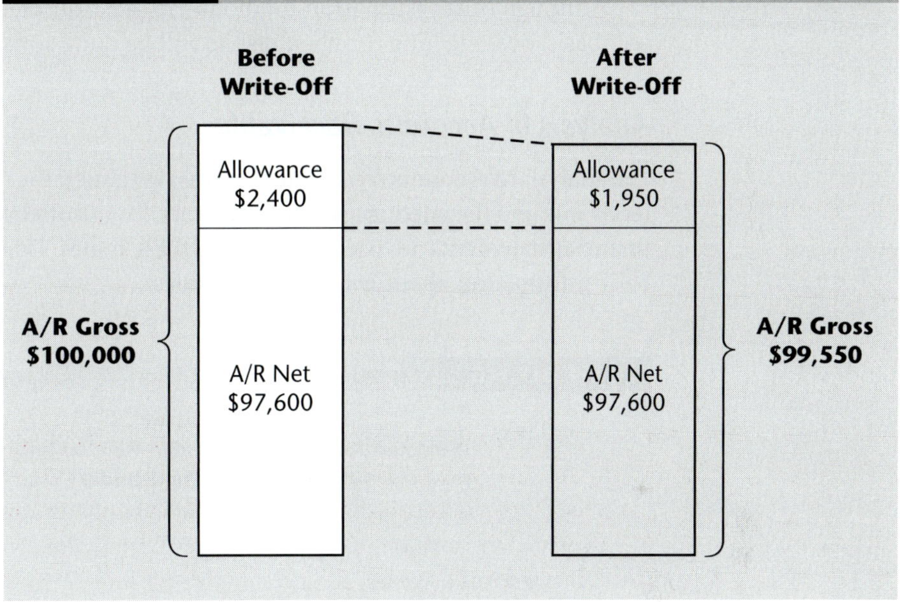

Estimation Methods

Firms can estimate the year-end adjustment for uncollectible accounts in several ways. One approach is the **aging method**. In its simplest form, the aging method classifies the year-end accounts receivable balance into two categories: (1) current and (2) past due. Suppose, for example, that a firm's sales terms are 2/10, net 30. This indicates that all accounts are due within 30 days of sale. On the balance sheet date, accounts that have been outstanding for 30 or fewer days are classified as current. The remainder is classified as past due.

Based on a firm's past experience, industry norms, and current trends, the firm estimates the percentage of each category that will not be collected. This is the step that requires the most judgment. Also, because older accounts are more likely not to be collected, the past-due category has a higher percentage of uncollectibles than the current category. These percentages are multiplied by each category's balance to estimate the allowance for uncollectible accounts.

Recall that Box Company estimated its allowance to be $2,400 at the end of 2006. The aging analysis that resulted in this estimate is as follows:

Age category	Balance	×	Percentage estimate to be uncollectible	=	Estimated amount uncollectible
Current	$ 90,000		2%		$1,800
Past due	10,000		6%		600
Total	$100,000				$2,400

Although other estimation methods can yield different results on a year-to-year basis, over the long run their results will be quite similar.

Analysis of Accounts Receivable

The analysis of accounts receivable involves two issues: the relative size of accounts receivable and the adequacy of the allowance for uncollectible accounts. Dayton's financial statements are used to illustrate these issues. Exhibit 6-6 contains some basic information about Dayton's receivables.

EXHIBIT 6-6 FINANCIAL STATEMENT INFORMATION

Dayton, Inc.
Selected Accounts Receivable-Related Information
(Dollars in thousands)

	2007	2006
Accounts receivable (gross)	$ 27,503	$ 25,978
Allowance for doubtful accounts	$ 4,225	$ 5,474
Sales	$395,196	$444,766
Accounts receivable as a percentage of sales	7.0%	5.8%
Collection period	25 days	21 days
Allowance as a percentage of accounts receivables	15.4%	21.1%

Size of Accounts Receivable

Because accounts receivable earn no return (after the discount period has expired), firms should limit their investment in accounts receivable. Accounts receivable balances are usually evaluated relative to the amount of credit sales, using **accounts receivable as a percentage of sales**. This seems appropriate because credit sales give rise to accounts receivable. Most firms do not separately disclose credit sales; net sales are usually used. A straightforward analysis divides gross accounts receivable by net sales:

$$\text{Accounts receivable as a percentage of sales} = \frac{\text{Accounts receivable (gross)}}{\text{Sales}}$$

Dayton's percentage increased from 5.8% in 2006 to 7.0% in 2007:

		2007	2006
Accounts receivable as a percentge of sales	=	$\frac{\$27,503}{\$395,196} = 7.0\%$	$\frac{\$25,978}{\$444,766} = 5.8\%$

Dayton's trend is not favorable. Notice that although sales declined from 2006 to 2007, the balance in accounts receivable actually increased. Although the unfavorable trend might be due to less effective management of accounts receivable, it could also be due to a changing sales pattern. If, in 2007, Dayton made a relatively larger proportion of its sales near year-end, we would expect to see an increase in year-end accounts receivable.

An alternative analysis involves calculating the average length of time it takes to collect a receivable. This is known as the **collection period.** It is calculated in two steps. First, calculate the average sales per day:

$$\text{Average sales per day} = \frac{\text{Sales}}{365}$$

Next, the collection period is calculated by dividing gross accounts receivable by average sales per day.

$$\text{Collection period} = \frac{\text{Accounts receivable (gross)}}{\text{Average sales per day}}$$

This ratio indicates the **number of day's sales in accounts receivable.**

Dayton's collection period increased from 21 to 25 days. This is consistent with the analysis of accounts receivable as a percentage of sales.

		2007	2006
Average sales per day	=	$\frac{\$395,196}{365} = \$1,083$	$\frac{\$444,766}{365} = \$1,219$
Collection period	=	$\frac{\$27,503}{\$1,083} = 25 \text{ days}$	$\frac{\$25,978}{\$1,219} = 21 \text{ days}$

Exhibit 6-7 contrasts three retail firms' accounts receivable ratios, comparing Carter's (apparel), Hartmarx Corporation (apparel), and, as a point of contrast, Albertson's (food). Carter's accounts receivable, as a percentage of sales, and its collection period are about two-fifths as large as those of Hartmarx. At least four interpretations are possible: (1) Carter's is doing much better than Hartmarx in quickly collecting its receivables and minimizing its investment in this asset; (2) Carter's sales pattern during the year differs markedly from that of Hartmarx (that is, Carter's makes substantially fewer sales at year-end than Hartmarx does); (3) Carter's is inducing its customers to pay quickly either through strong pressure or steep discounts; or (4) Carter's factors more accounts receivable than does Hartmarx.

EXHIBIT 6-7 COMPARISONS OF ACCOUNTS RECEIVABLE RATIOS

Accounts Receivable Ratios
Interfirm Comparisons

	CARTER'S INC.	HARTMARX CORP.	ALBERTSONS
Accounts receivable as a percentage of sales	8.93%	21.45%	1.78%
Collection period	33 days	79 days	7 days
Allowance as a percentage of accounts receivable	3.94%	4.08%	2.5%

Also note that food stores have a much shorter collection period than apparel manufacturers, which is due to the nature of food stores' credit sales. Most credit sales are made via customers' credit cards at major banks and food stores are able to collect these receivables from the banks very quickly. Some credit sales are made to businesses (such as restaurants and caterers), but these customers pay by check within a reasonable period of time.

Reality Check 6-1 summarizes an accounts receivable issue that arose for Topps Co., Inc., the sports card producer.

REALITY CHECK 6-1

Topps Co., Inc., produces sports cards. During two consecutive quarters, Topps' accounts receivable increased by more than 50%, while sales declined. Such a trend might indicate that Topps is experiencing difficulty collecting from its customers.

Topps asserts, however, that receivables have increased because of a change in its shipping schedule. It has begun to ship 50% of its cards in the final few weeks of a quarter. Thus, many of its accounts receivable are outstanding at quarter's end, and at the same time, are not yet past due.

Required

a. Does Topps' explanation make sense?
b. Can Topps' claim be verified with publicly available information?

SOLUTION

a. Topps' explanation may well make sense. Because sales and accounts receivable are recorded when goods are shipped, making shipments closer to a quarter's close increases the accounts receivable balance on the balance sheet date. Topps' explanation, however, raises the question of why its shipping schedule has changed. Some firms who have difficulty meeting sales expectations pressure customers to place orders toward the end of a quarter.

b. Verifying Topps' claim would be difficult. Firms do not publish shipping schedules or any other information that might indicate when shipments occurred during a quarter. Perhaps the best source of information is Topps' customers. They would certainly know if shipping schedules have changed and the reason for any change.

Adequacy of Allowance for Uncollectible Accounts

Recall that writing off a specific account as uncollectible has no effect on total assets or net income. Assets and income are affected by the year-end adjustment in which uncollectible accounts are estimated. Managers must use judgment and discretion in making this estimate. Accordingly, analysts must carefully assess the reasonableness of the allowance for uncollectible accounts.

Few firms disclose their uncollectible accounts expense, yet most firms do disclose the year-end balance in the allowance for uncollectible accounts. The adequacy of this balance is usually assessed relative to the year-end accounts receivable balance. Calculate the **adequacy of the allowance for uncollectible accounts** by dividing the allowance by gross accounts receivable:

$$\text{Allowance for uncollectible accounts as a percentage of accounts receivable} = \frac{\text{Allowance for uncollectible accounts}}{\text{Accounts receivable (gross)}}$$

Dayton's percentage decreased from 21.1% in 2006 to 15.4% in 2007. Note that in this calculation, we *ignore the negative sign* on the allowance account.

	2007	2006
Allowance for uncollectible accounts as a percentage of accounts receivable	$\frac{\$4,225}{\$27,503} = 15.4\%$	$\frac{\$5,474}{\$25,978} = 21.1\%$

The reason for such a decrease is not entirely apparent. Perhaps OAI made a conscious decision to decrease its sales to customers with dubious credit ratings. Such a change in the customer base would allow a decrease in the allowance for uncollectible accounts. In 2007 Dayton ceased its European operations and terminated its relationship with certain domestic distributors. These changes altered the composition of Dayton's customer base and might justify the decline in the allowance for uncollectible accounts.

Refer again to Exhibit 6-7 comparing two apparel firms, Carter's Inc. with a competitor Hartmarx. Hartmarx's uncollectible accounts estimate is slightly more conservative than Carter's. Most analysts view conservative accounting practices with favor and feel that they result in earnings numbers of high quality.

Firms can use the allowance for uncollectible accounts to adjust net income. If a firm is taking a *big bath* in the current year, it can increase the allowance for uncollectible accounts as estimated by management. This will increase expenses on the income statement. In the following year, the firm can show a gain by reducing the allowance.

Alternatively, the firm could lower the allowance as a percentage of receivables during a period of increasing receivables. This would increase revenues. In early 2000, Lucent reduced its allowance to 3.16% of receivables. Then in the fourth quarter, raised it back to 4.98%. In 2001 they announced a $125 million reduction of revenue in the fourth quarter due to a change in revenue recognition policies.

Another revenue recognition abuse occurs when a company recognizes revenue before the revenue is earned (before the work is done!). For example, Qwest recognized revenue in one year on a sale to Global Crossing, instead of apportioning the revenue over the 20-year term of the agreement. Note that Global Crossing since went bankrupt, thus effectively changing Qwest's expected revenue stream.

Implications for Managers

As with any asset, managers should attempt to maximize the return on accounts receivable. One way to do this is to reduce the firm's investment in accounts receivable. Managers can employ several strategies to do this. Sales terms can be set so that the customer is obligated to pay in a relatively short period of time. Managers should closely monitor accounts receivable collections to ensure that customers are paying within the agreed period.

Discounts for early payment can also induce customers to pay quickly. However, discounts large enough to prompt early payment may prove to be quite expensive for the seller. Also keep in mind that sales terms may be constrained by industry practices. That is, a firm must provide terms that are competitive with those offered by its rivals. In general, sales terms are just one product attribute in a firm's overall promotional strategy.

Managers must also decide which customers will be granted credit. As mentioned previously, a trade-off exists between the amount of sales that can be generated and the level of uncollectible accounts expense incurred. Managers should set minimum credit ratings for its customers so that profitability is maximized.

INVENTORY

Inventory consists of products acquired for resale to customers. For many companies, inventory is a major asset and a significant source of revenue.

Accounting for Inventories

Assume that several inventory items are acquired for a total price of $100. This transaction results in an increase in inventory and a decrease in cash.

ASSETS		=	LIABILITIES	+	SHAREHOLDERS' EQUITY
Cash	Inventory				
– $100	+ $100				

Now assume that half the inventory is sold for $75. This transaction is analyzed in two steps. The revenue part increases cash and shareholders' equity by $75. The expense part decreases inventory and shareholders' equity by $50 (half of the $100 historical cost).

ASSETS		=	LIABILITIES	+	SHAREHOLDERS' EQUITY
Cash	Inventory				Retained earnings
+ $75					+ $75 (sales revenue)
	– $50				– $50 (cost of goods sold)

The difference between the sales price of $75 and the $50 **cost of goods sold (COGS)** is the gross profit or gross margin ($25).

Cost Flow Assumptions

Most firms regularly purchase inventory. Usually, these purchases are not made at a uniform price. This poses an accounting problem when inventory is sold: What is the cost of the goods that were sold and what is the cost of the goods that remain on hand?

Some firms find it advantageous to keep a record of the cost of individual inventory items. These situations involve inventory units with a high dollar value and relatively few sales. Car dealerships are good illustrations. When negotiating with a customer over the selling price of a given car, for example, the cost of that particular car is important information for the dealer. Thus, these firms are motivated to keep a record of each car's cost. Moreover, a dealer's inventory consists of perhaps no more than 100–200 cars, and the dealer makes only a few sales per day. Such activity levels do not present a significant record-keeping challenge. The **specific identification method** maintains accounting records showing the cost of each inventory item.

For most businesses, however, the number of inventory units and the volume of purchases and sales are so large that the specific identification method would be very costly to implement. A grocery store, for example, may sell 1,000 cereal boxes in one day. This requires firms to use a **cost flow assumption.** Consider the following summary of inventory acquisitions:

	# of Units	×	Unit Price	=	Total Cost
Beginning inventory	30		$4		$120
Purchase on February 18	10		5		50
Purchase on June 8	20		6		120
Purchase on October 22	20		8		160
Total	80				$450

Assume that 48 units were sold during the year and 32 units remain on hand at year-end. To prepare the financial statements, the cost of the ending inventory and the cost of goods sold must be determined.

Average Cost

The **average-cost method** calculates the weighted-average cost of an inventory item on hand during the period and applies this cost to the units sold and to the ending inventory. The average cost is calculated by dividing the cost of goods available for sale by the number of units available for sale. The **cost of goods available for sale** equals the cost of the beginning inventory plus the cost of all purchases during a period. It reflects the total cost of goods that were on hand at any time during the period and that were available for sale:

$$\text{Average cost} = \frac{\text{Cost of goods available for sale}}{\text{Number of units available for sale}}$$

$$\frac{\$450}{80} = \$5.625$$

To calculate the cost of the 48 units that have been sold, multiply the average cost of $5.625 by 48:

$$\text{Cost of goods sold} = \$5.625 \times 48 = \$270$$

To calculate the cost of the 32 units in ending inventory, multiply the average cost of $5.625 by 32:

$$\text{Ending inventory} = \$5.625 \times 32 = \$180$$

Alternatively, once either cost of goods sold or ending inventory has been calculated, the following equation can be used to compute the other.

$$\text{COGS} = \text{Beginning inventory} + \text{Purchases} - \text{Ending inventory}$$

Adding beginning inventory and purchases yields the cost of goods available for sale. Subtracting the cost of goods that have not been sold (the ending inventory) from the cost of all goods available for sale results in COGS (the cost of the goods that have been sold). If ending inventory is calculated first, the cost of goods sold can be computed as follows:

COGS	=	Beginning inventory	+	Purchases	−	Ending inventory
$270	=	$120	+	$330	−	$180

On the other hand, assuming that cost of goods sold is computed first, the equation can be rearranged and ending inventory can be calculated as follows.

Ending inventory	=	Beginning inventory	+	Purchases	–	COGS
$180	=	$120	+	$330	–	$270

This *general equation can be used with all the inventory methods described* in this section.

First-In, First-Out

Another commonly used inventory method is the **First-in, First-out (or FIFO) method.** This method assumes that inventory costs move on a first-in, first-out basis. This implies that the cost of the beginning inventory and the cost of purchases made early in the period are the first to flow out of the firm and comprise the cost of goods sold. In our illustration, the cost of goods sold under the FIFO method is based on the cost of the 48 units that were acquired first.

	# of Units	×	Unit Price	=	Total Cost
Beginning inventory	30		$4		$120
February 18	10		5		50
June 8	8		6		48
COGS	48				$218

Because the cost of goods sold under the FIFO method is based on the cost of the earliest acquisitions, ending inventory must consist of the costs from the most recent purchases (those made closest to the period's end). Based on the inventory and purchase data given in the last subsection, ending inventory consists of the costs associated with the 32 units acquired closest to the end of the year. This includes the 20 units purchased on October 22 and 12 of the units purchased on June 8. Only 12 of the 20 units purchased on June 8 are included because the ending inventory consists of 32 units.

	# of Units	×	Unit Price	=	Total Cost
June 8	12		$6		$ 72
October 22	20		8		160
Ending inventory	32				$232

Last-In, First-Out

The **Last-in, First-out (LIFO) inventory method** assumes that the costs associated with the purchases made closest to the period's end comprise the cost of goods sold. Therefore, the cost of goods sold is based on the cost of the 48 units acquired most recently.

	# of Units	×	Unit Price	=	Total Cost
October 22	20		$8		$160
June 8	20		6		120
February 18	8		5		40
COGS	48				$320

Ending inventory, therefore, must be composed of the beginning inventory cost and the cost of the period's earliest acquisitions. Based on the preceding illustration, ending inventory is calculated by identifying the cost of the 32 units acquired the earliest.

	# of Units	×	Unit Price	=	Total Cost
Beginning inventory	30		$4		$120
February 18	2		5		10
Ending inventory	32				$130

The difference between FIFO and LIFO can be described by examining the cost of goods available for sale. Recall that the cost of goods available for sale equals the cost of beginning inventory plus the cost of the year's purchases. By year-end, each inventory item either will have been sold or will remain on hand. FIFO assumes that the cost of goods sold consists of the costs of the beginning inventory and the earliest purchases, and that the ending inventory is comprised of the more recent costs. In contrast, LIFO assumes that the cost of goods sold consists of the most recent costs and that the costs of beginning inventory and the earliest purchases are included in ending inventory. These partitions of cost of goods available for sale are depicted in Exhibit 6-8.

Financial Statement Effects of Inventory Method

The choice of inventory method can have significant effects on financial statements. In the Exhibit 6-8 illustration, the effects of inventory method choice can be summarized as follows:

	FIFO	Average Cost	LIFO
Cost of goods sold	$218	$270	$320
Ending inventory	232	180	130
	$450	$450	$450

EXHIBIT 6-8 **PARTITIONING COST OF GOODS AVAILABLE FOR SALE: FIFO vs LIFO**

FIFO

Beginning inventory	Purchase of February 18	Purchase of June 8	Purchase of October 22
30 × $4	10 × $5	20 × $6	20 × $8

Cost of goods sold:
30 × $4 = $120
10 × 5 = 50
8 × 6 = 48
48 $218

Ending inventory:
12 × $6 = $ 72
20 × 8 = 160
32 $232

LIFO

Beginning inventory	Purchase of February 18	Purchase of June 8	Purchase of October 22
30 × $4	10 × $5	20 × $6	20 × $8

Ending Inventory:
30 × $4 = $120
2 × 5 = 10
32 $130

Cost of Goods Sold:
20 × $8 = $160
20 × 6 = 120
8 × 5 = 40
48 $320

Notice that the illustration reflects a period of rising inventory costs, which is the typical situation for many firms. The conclusions drawn in this section are dependent on rising prices. Opposite conclusions would be warranted in periods of price declines.

LIFO results in the highest cost of goods sold because (1) it assumes that the more recent costs are the first ones sold, and (2) these most recently acquired costs are the most expensive ones. FIFO results in the lowest cost of goods sold, and the average-cost method yields results between LIFO and FIFO. *Because LIFO reports the highest cost of goods sold figure, it results in the lowest reported net income.*

LIFO results in the lowest ending inventory value because it assumes that the earliest costs remain on hand at year-end, and these costs are the least expensive. FIFO yields the highest inventory value, and average cost falls between the two.

LIFO liquidation can be used to manage earnings. This happens when a company dips into its inventory quantities, which are older and have a lower cost. Then COGS is overstated because these older, lower costs are matched with current, higher revenues. Dayton, Inc. reported liquidation of certain **LIFO layers** that increased net income. To calculate Dayton's adjusted net income, consider removing these LIFO layer reserve adjustments. Appendix 6B illustrates how reductions in LIFO inventory can increase gross margins.

What Would You Do?

You are the sole owner of a local CPA firm. Your firm has been quite successful, primarily because of your hard work.

It is December 31 and you are working on the audit of The Boot Warehouse. Part of your audit program requires that you test count Boot's inventory. You have decided that counting seven sections of Boot's warehouse would provide sufficient assurance that the inventory is correctly stated.

There's just one problem. Because you have been so successful, and because you are so busy, you arrived at the warehouse late. Because Boot is scheduled to make a number of large shipments soon after midnight, there is not enough time to count the seven sections as you planned. Delaying the shipments would be very costly. In fact, Boot's lost profits would probably be greater than your audit fee. What would you do?

Choosing an Inventory Valuation Method

FIFO, LIFO, specific identification, and average cost are all acceptable inventory methods. Firms are free to choose one of these methods and consistently apply it across periods. Interestingly, GAAP does not require that the assumed flow of costs reflect the actual flow of goods. Supermarkets, for example, put their older products on the front of shelves so that they will be sold before items acquired more recently; this helps preserve the general freshness of the merchandise available to customers. In this case, goods actually flow on a FIFO basis. However, supermarkets are not required to use FIFO in the preparation of their financial statements.

This raises a question about the factors that are considered by managers in selecting an inventory method. Because LIFO and FIFO yield the most dissimilar results, the following discussion focuses on them.

Taxes

The example we used to illustrate the various inventory methods was characterized by a period of rising prices. Many industries have experienced decades of inflation in inventory costs. In such periods, LIFO assigns the higher, recently acquired inventory costs to cost of goods sold. Of course, a higher cost of goods sold results in lower reported income. Thus, *the selection of LIFO in inflationary periods reduces both reported pre-tax income and income taxes*. Because a smaller check will be written to the IRS, the use of *LIFO actually increases a firm's cash flow,* even though reported net income is lower than under FIFO. LIFO firms are expected to have higher operating cash flows than other firms!

In general, firms are not required to select the same accounting principle for financial reporting and for taxes. Because financial statements and tax returns serve different purposes, this makes sense. *LIFO, however, is an exception to this general rule. If LIFO is used for tax purposes, it must be used for financial reporting*. Many firms prepare their tax return using LIFO to obtain the associated tax savings and are thus required to use it for their financial statements.

Implementation Costs

Although we need not be concerned about the details, simply note that *LIFO is more costly to implement than FIFO or average cost*, especially for small firms. This may help explain why large firms tend to adopt LIFO more often than small firms. Managers must balance the tax savings from LIFO with the costs of implementation.

Quality of Financial Statement Information

LIFO and FIFO result in different financial statement numbers for inventory, cost of goods sold, and net income. Which method results in the most useful information? The answer is not clear-cut.

FIFO's ending inventory calculation is based on a firm's most recent acquisition costs. Thus, the inventory amount on the balance sheet is likely to be very close to current value. In contrast, LIFO's ending inventory is based on the costs of beginning inventory and the earliest acquisitions. Keep in mind that this occurs each year and that the beginning inventory may contain components carried forward from many years ago. Thus, *in a period of rising prices, LIFO ending inventory values may be dramatically understated*.

On the other hand, *LIFO provides more informative income statement numbers because it matches current inventory costs with revenues.* Cost of goods sold under LIFO consists of the costs of the most recent acquisitions. These costs approximate amounts necessary to replace inventory as it is depleted. Because of this, *LIFO is more consistent with the matching principle.* Furthermore, gross profit under LIFO is a useful measure of the resources generated from inventory sales that are available to cover other expenses and provide for net income. Managers can then view the gross profit measure as an indicator of "spendable" resources.

LIFO and Loan Agreements

As mentioned in previous chapters, many firms have loan agreements that require them to maintain certain levels of financial ratios. The current ratio is one example. Given that during a period of rising prices, LIFO results in a lower inventory figure, current assets will also be lower. This results in a lower current ratio and a greater likelihood of loan agreement violations. A number of other ratios will be similarly affected. When adopting LIFO, managers must be confident that the use of LIFO will not result in financial ratios that violate loan agreements.

LIFO and Management Compensation

Because LIFO reduces reported net income in a period of rising prices, *LIFO may also reduce the compensation of managers who have bonuses based on reported income.* This could limit management's motivation to adopt LIFO.

LIFO and Stock Prices

LIFO results in lower reported net income during a period of rising prices. Some managers may fear that the stock market will react negatively to lower income. A more sophisticated view, however, recognizes that LIFO results in lower taxes, thereby increasing a firm's cash flow. The increased cash flow benefits the firm and its shareholders, and should result in higher stock prices. Research evidence is ambiguous regarding the stock market reaction to LIFO adoptions.

Actual Usage of Inventory Methods

Accounting Trends and Techniques conducts an annual survey of 600 major U.S. corporations to ascertain their financial reporting practices. Exhibit 6-9 shows the number of firms using various inventory methods. FIFO continues to be most popular. We note that the use of LIFO is slipping as 26 fewer firms in the sample used LIFO in 2005 as compared to 2003 (*AICPA Accounting Trends and Techniques,* New York: AICPA, 2006, Table 2-9).

FIFO is the most frequently used method, followed by LIFO, with the average-cost method a distant third. The total number of firms exceeds the 600 that were surveyed because many firms use multiple inventory methods. Keep in mind that the results are for major corporations; as mentioned, because LIFO is relatively expensive to implement, smaller businesses utilize LIFO less frequently. Also, LIFO is not widely used outside the United States.

Note that Wal-Mart presents both replacement costs of inventory and the associated LIFO cost. Its balance sheet (Appendix A) shows inventory replacement costs less a **"LIFO Reserve"** which adjusts the replacement costs to the appropriate LIFO values. The analyst would focus mostly on the LIFO costs. The analyst would only consider the replacement costs if there was significant disparity between replacement costs and the LIFO costs.

Valuation of Inventories at Lower of Cost or Market

GAAP requires that inventories be valued at **lower of cost or market (LCM).** Inventory cost is determined based on one of the cost flow assumptions discussed earlier. Market is defined as the current replacement cost, which is the amount that would be required to replace the firm's inventory on the balance sheet date.

The LCM rule is based on the rationale that a decline in replacement cost indicates that the inventory's utility to the firm has decreased. Conservatism would

EXHIBIT 6-9 INVENTORY METHOD USAGE

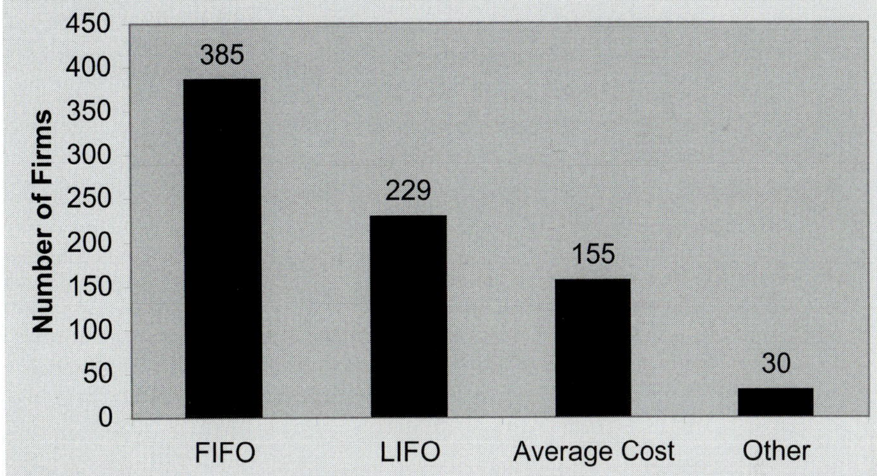

Note: Some firms simultaneously use several inventory methods.
SOURCE: AICPA Accounting Trends and Techniques. New York: AICPA, 2006.

dictate that this loss should be reflected immediately in the financial statements, rather than postponing such recognition until the time of sale. When inventory is written down to market, the loss is sometimes disclosed separately on the income statement, but more frequently, it is included in the cost of goods sold.

Manufacturers

The inventories of manufacturers are comprised of three broad categories. **Raw materials** are the basic components of the inventory items produced by the firm. **Work-in-process** inventory consists of inventory items that are partially completed on the balance sheet date. **Finished goods** are completed inventory items that are awaiting sale.

Firms usually report just one total inventory figure on the balance sheet. The composition of the inventory is found in the notes to the financial statements. Exhibit 6-10 contains Dayton's inventory note. It shows inventory categorized in three basic components (raw materials, work in process, and finished goods).

Looking at these components could reveal useful information. "A rise in inventories could be a warning sign of future trouble, or it could show that business is booming. The trick here is to look for what is in the warehouses. If finished goods are piling up and raw materials are down, that is a sign the company is having trouble selling its product. If raw materials are up and finished goods are down, it could mean that business is good and management is stockpiling inventories in

EXHIBIT 6-10 FINANCIAL STATEMENT INVENTORY NOTE

Dayton, Inc.
Inventory Note
(Dollars in thousands)

	DECEMBER 31,	
	2007	**2006**
Finished goods	$49,400	$51,584
Work in process	14,782	10,698
Raw materials	4,044	4,517
Total	$68,226	$66,799

The replacement cost of inventory exceeds the above LIFO costs by $14,138 and $15,100 at December 31, 2007 and 2006, respectively. Partial liquidation of certain LIFO layers in 2007 and 2006 increased net income by approximately $577 and $610, respectively.

anticipation of rising sales. Such a breakdown can generally be found in a footnote to the company's annual statements." (Ken Brown, "How to Spot the Dirt in Rosy Annual Reports," *The Wall Street Journal,* February 14, 2003, p. C3.)

Analysis of Inventories

The income statement contains information about profitability and the balance sheet contains useful information about inventory levels.

Profitability

The income statement contains information about cost of goods sold and gross profit. Gross profit is often expressed as a percentage of sales revenue:

$$\text{Gross profit \%} = \frac{\text{Gross profit}}{\text{Sales}}$$

A higher gross profit percentage helps cover other expenses and contributes to net income. Exhibit 6-11 contains inventory-related information for Dayton, Inc. The gross profit percentages in Exhibit 6-11 are calculated as follows:

	2007	**2006**
Gross profit % =	$\frac{\$144,381}{\$395,196} = 36.5\%$	$\frac{\$144,271}{\$444,766} = 32.4\%$

Dayton's gross profit percentage showed a reasonable increase between 2006 and 2007. Several factors may have caused this. First, Dayton's inventory costs may have fallen. Second, competitive forces may have enabled Dayton, Inc. to increase its selling prices. Finally, keep in mind that Dayton's different products

EXHIBIT 6-11 FINANCIAL STATEMENT INFORMATION

Dayton, Inc.
Selected Inventory-Related Information
(Dollars in thousands)

	2007	2006
Inventory	$ 68,226	$ 66,799
Sales	$395,196	$444,766
Cost of goods sold	$250,815	$300,495
Gross profit	$144,381	144,271
Gross profit %	36.5%	32.4%
Number of days' sales in ending inventory	99	81

probably have varying gross profit percentages. A change in the mix of products sold can affect the gross profit percentage. Dayton's gross profit percentage compares favorably to other apparel manufacturers.

Industries differ with respect to gross profit percentage. For example, the pharmaceutical industry's average gross profit percentage exceeds 50%. Drug companies incur substantial costs when researching and developing their products. Accordingly, they must sell their goods at relatively high markups so that they can cover these costs and remain profitable.

Reality Check 6-2 examines the effect on gross profit of applying the lower of cost or market (LCM) inventory valuation rule.

Inventory Levels

The balance sheet contains information about the cost of inventories remaining on hand at year-end. This provides insights into whether the level of inventory is adequate to meet customer demands. Inadequate levels may result in lost sales and reduced profitability, while excessive levels increase carrying costs, which also has a negative impact on profitability. Carrying costs include storage, handling, insurance, and the opportunity cost of the funds invested in inventory. An opportunity cost exists because cash invested in inventory that remains on hand for several months cannot be invested in more profitable alternative opportunities.

The **number of days' sales in ending inventory (NDS)** is frequently used to measure inventory levels. It is computed in two steps. First, divide cost of goods sold by 365. This indicates the cost of inventory sold in one day.

$$\text{COGS per day} = \frac{\text{COGS}}{365}$$

Next divide ending inventory by COGS per day to obtain NDS.

$$\text{NDS} = \frac{\text{Ending inventory}}{\text{COGS per day}}$$

REALITY CHECK 6-2

Calloway Mini-Drive Corporation (CMD) manufactures and markets integrated thin-film, silicon-based termination and filtering components and active electronic circuitry. During the year ended March 31, 2007, CMD recorded inventory write-downs of $900,000. The write-downs were due to potential obsolescence and severe price competition by Asian manufacturers. CMD reported the following results (in thousands):

	For the year ended March 31, 2007	2006
Revenue	$33,043	$32,936
Cost of sales	24,701	21,255
Gross profit	$ 8,342	$11,681

Assume that the write-down is reflected in cost of sales.

Required

a. Calculate CMD's gross profit percentages for 2007 and 2006.
b. Recalculate the 2007 gross profit percentage, assuming that the write-down did not occur.
c. What concerns are raised by the trend in gross profit percentages and the effect of the write-down?

SOLUTION

a.

		2007	2006
Gross profit percentage = $\frac{\text{Gross profit}}{\text{Sales}}$	=	$\frac{\$8,342}{\$33,043}$	$\frac{\$11,681}{32,936}$
	=	25.2%	35.5%

b. Had the write-down not occurred, gross profit would have been:

Gross profit, as reported	$8,342,000
Plus: Write-down	900,000
Cost of sales, adjusted	$9,242,000

Based on this, an adjusted gross profit percentage can be calculated.

$$\text{Gross profit percentage} = \frac{\text{Gross profit}}{\text{Sales}} = \frac{\$9,242}{\$33,043} = 28\%$$

As can be seen, the write-down reduced the 2007 gross profit percentage by almost three percentage points (28% prospectively, vs. 25.2% as reported).

c. CMD would have experienced a significant decline in gross profit percentage even in the absence of the inventory write-down. The decline in gross profit percentage, coupled with the causes for the write-down (obsolescence and pricing pressures from Asian manufacturers) suggests that CMD is in a rapidly changing and competitive industry. CMD must develop a plan to increase its profitability.

NDS reflects inventory size relative to the level of sales activity. Dayton's NDS for 2007 and 2006 are calculated as follows:

	2007	2006
COGS per day (in thousands) =	$\frac{\$250{,}815}{365} = \$687$	$\frac{\$300{,}495}{365} = \$823$
NDS =	$\frac{\$68{,}226}{\$687} = 99$ days	$\frac{\$66{,}799}{\$823} = 81$

Dayton's NDS increased from 81 days in 2006 to 99 days in 2007. This occurred because inventory levels increased while sales (and cost of goods sold) declined. Dayton, Inc. ceased dealing with certain wholesalers and curtailed its European operations, which resulted in a smaller scale of operations. Dayton, Inc. does not seem to have fully adjusted its inventory levels to this smaller scale.

It is interesting to contrast apparel manufacturers' NDS with that of food stores, who maintain about 40 days' sales of inventory on hand. This reflects the perishable nature of food stores' inventories, coupled with their high volume of sales.

PREPAID EXPENSES

In many situations, firms pay for goods and services in advance. Insurance is a good example. Quite often, firms make full payment at the inception of a policy's term. The accounting issue involves the proper treatment of assets and expenses. An asset has been acquired at the beginning of a policy's term: the right to be covered by insurance for the next year (or other time period). As the policy's term progresses, the **prepaid expense** (asset) is used up and an expense is incurred.

Prepaid expenses are recorded at their historical cost. Because prepaids usually have a short life, their cost corresponds closely to market value, and few analysts would object to this valuation practice.

Prepaid expenses generally constitute a very small proportion of a firm's assets. For example, in 2007, Dayton's prepaid expenses comprised less than 1% of its assets. Consequently, prepaids are not subjected to extensive analysis. Recall, however, that they are included in the numerator of the current ratio. Because prepaids will be utilized in the near future, most analysts feel that this is proper. Note that *prepaids are not a source of future cash inflows,* but they do reflect the reduced need for future cash outflows.

IDENTIFY RELATIONSHIPS BETWEEN CASH AND OTHER CURRENT ASSETS

We have shown that cash inflows will usually increase with decreases in accounts receivable as customers pay their accounts with cash. Cash outflows may increase when inventories and prepaid expenses increase. As marketable securities increase, cash usually decreases. As marketable securities are sold, cash usually increases. Most analysts will view current assets as a proxy for liquid resources. Much of the analyst's focus on liquidity will focus on cash and on all current assets. We have also shown how LIFO inventories may contribute to cash flows by decreasing taxes. As such, we wonder why more firms don't use LIFO?

Summary of Learning Objectives

1. **Identify cash and cash equivalents.**
   Cash includes funds on hand and cash on deposit in bank accounts that do not restrict withdrawals. Most firms also classify as cash amounts in money market funds on which checks can be drawn.

2. **Understand the need for cash planning and how firms exercise control over cash.**
   Firms must carefully plan their cash inflows and outflows so that sufficient cash is available to meet obligations as they become due. At the same time, because cash earns virtually no return, excessive balances should be avoided. Also, because cash is easily misappropriated, management should take steps to safeguard cash and to ensure that the accounting for cash is proper. This can be accomplished through effective internal control procedures, including the use of checking accounts and bank reconciliations.

3. **Comprehend the basic valuation principles for marketable securities.**
   Marketable securities are shown on a balance sheet at market value. Revaluing marketable securities from their historical cost to market value requires that unrealized gains/losses be recorded. Most industrial firms own securities classified as available-for-sale. The rule for these securities requires that unrealized gains/losses not be shown on the income statement. Instead, they appear on the balance sheet in a separate component of shareholders' equity. This rule's major shortcoming is that the value change is not reflected in net income.

4. **Evaluate accounts receivable management.**
   Collections of accounts receivable should be made in a timely manner. This reduces the firm's investment in a nonproductive asset and reduces the opportunity for nonpayment. A firm's success at doing this is measured by its collection period.

5. **Assess adequacy of the allowance for uncollectible accounts.**
   On the balance sheet date, an adequate allowance for uncollectible accounts should be established. Divide the allowance by the ending accounts receivable balance to assess the adequacy of the allowance account. We note that some firms, e.g., Wal-Mart, do not even report any allowance for uncollectible accounts.

6. **Understand various inventory cost flow assumptions and the related effects on taxes, management compensation, loan covenants, stock prices, and the quality of financial statement information.**
   The most commonly used inventory cost flow assumptions are average cost, FIFO, and LIFO. FIFO (LIFO) assumes that the oldest (newest) costs relate to the first items sold. The choice of inventory method can have a significant effect on the reported financial statement numbers. In a period of rising prices, LIFO results in the highest cost of goods sold and the lowest inventory value.

The reverse is true for FIFO. The average cost method yields results between LIFO and FIFO. Because LIFO has an adverse effect on net income and financial ratios, the adoption of LIFO may reduce managerial compensation and increase the likelihood of loan covenant violations. However, a lower reported net income number also reduces taxes. Regardless of the direction of inventory prices, LIFO results in a cost of goods sold figure that reflects current costs, and FIFO results in an ending inventory value that reflects current costs.

7. **Analyze inventory management practices.**
   To be profitable, a firm must sell inventory for more than its cost. The gross profit percentage measures a firm's success in doing this. A firm should also have an adequate, but not excessive, supply of inventory on hand. The number of days' sales in ending inventory measures the amount of inventory on hand.

8. **Understand the nature of prepaid expenses.**
   Prepaid expenses reflect payments made prior to the time that services are actually used. Prepayments often occur for insurance and rent. Prepayments are usually small in dollar amount and, accordingly, do not require detailed examination by analysts.

9. **Identify relationships between cash and other current assets.**
   Cash inflows usually increase with decreases in accounts receivable. Cash outflows increase when inventories and prepaid expenses increase. As marketable securities increase, cash usually decreases (and vice versa). LIFO inventories may contribute to cash flows by decreasing taxes. Consider why more firms don't use LIFO?

Appendix 6A—Prepare a bank reconcilation.
This section provides the basic steps necessary to prepare a reconciliation of the reported cash balances with cash balances actually held by banks.

Appendix 6B—Compare LIFO and FIFO firms.
Comparing the financial statements of a LIFO firm with a FIFO firm can be troublesome and confusing. This section demonstrates how to recast one firm's inventory accounts to be more comparable with another firm in order to gain better comparability as if each firm used uniform accounting methods.

KEY TERMS

Accounts receivable (trade receivables)
Accounts receivable as a percentage of sales
Adequacy of the allowance for uncollectible accounts
Aging method
Allowance for uncollectible accounts
Available-for-sale securities
Average-cost method
Bank reconciliation
Cash
Cash and cash equivalents
Cash equivalents
Cash to current liabilities ratio
Change funds
Collection period
Compensating balances
Cost flow assumption
Cost of goods available for sale
Cost of goods sold (COGS)
Credit ratings
Deposit-in-transit
Debt securities
Discounts
Equity securities
Factor
Factor receivables
FIFO
Finished Goods
Gross profit (margin)
Inventory
LIFO
LIFO layers
LIFO liquidation
LIFO reserves
Lower of cost or market (LCM)
Marketable
Marketable securities
Net accounts receivable
Number of day's sales in accounts receivable
Number of day's sales in ending inventory (NDS)
Outstanding checks
Petty cash funds
Prepaid expenses
Raw materials
Security
Specific identification method
Trading securities
Trade receivables
Uncollectible
Unrealized gain or loss
Work-in-process
Write-offs
Written off
Year-end adjustments

BANK STATEMENTS AND RECONCILIATIONS

As an earlier part of the chapter noted, bank statements provide an accounting of cash that is independent of the accounting undertaken by the firm. Exhibit 6A-1 contains an illustration of Quick Company's bank statement for the month of April. One column shows withdrawals, one column reflects deposits, and the final column keeps a running total of the account's balance. This particular bank statement contains check numbers, which makes comparing the bank statement and the accounting records much easier. Notice that two withdrawals were not made by check. One withdrawal was preauthorized, which means that Quick has previously instructed the bank to make certain payments. A monthly loan payment is a good example. The other direct withdrawal was the service charge assessed by the bank for processing checks, making preauthorized payments, and so on.

As of any given date (such as April 30), the cash balance reported on the bank statement might not agree with the balance in the firm's accounting records (often called the book balance). This situation can arise for three general reasons. First, some transactions may be reflected in the accounting records, but not on the bank statement. For example, after a check is written and mailed to the payee, several days (or weeks) may elapse before the payee cashes the check and the check clears through the banking system. Until this happens, the bank is unaware of the check. Checks that are included in the accounting records but not shown on the bank statement are called **outstanding checks.**

A **deposit-in-transit** is another reconciling item that is recorded in the accounting records but not yet recorded on the bank statement. Most banks delay, by one business day, processing deposits made after a certain time of day (say, 3 P.M.). These cash receipts, however, are already recorded in the firm's accounting records. Therefore, deposits made after 3 P.M. on the last business day of a month will be included in the month-end book balance, but not the bank balance.

EXHIBIT 6A-1 BANK STATEMENT

Quick Company
Balance Sheet
April 2007

DATE	DESCRIPTION	WITHDRAWALS	DEPOSITS	BALANCE
4-1	Balance			$7,780
4-6	Check # 210	$ 180		7,600
4-10	Check # 212	500		7,100
4-13	Check # 213	1,000		6,100
4-15	Deposit		$2,300	8,400
4-21	Check # 215	200		8,200
4-25	Check # 216	400		7,800
4-30	Preauthorized	140		7,660
4-30	Service charge	10		7,650

The second major reason why the bank balance and the book balance might differ is that the bank statement may reflect items not yet shown in the accounting records. For example, prior to receiving the bank statement, firms usually will not have made entries in the accounting records for bank service charges and preauthorized withdrawals.

Errors, either in the accounting records or on the bank statement, are the third reason why the bank balance and the book balance might differ. If errors are unintentional and occur infrequently, they are not a cause for alarm; they simply need to be corrected. However, frequent or intentional errors involving cash warrant careful investigation.

Exhibit 6A-2 contains Quick Company's April accounting records for cash, and Exhibit 6A-3 illustrates Quick's April 30 bank reconciliation. Several valid approaches exist for preparing a bank reconciliation. The approach in Exhibit 6A-3 modifies both the bank and the book balances to obtain a corrected balance. The goal of the reconciliation is for the two corrected balances to agree. If this is accomplished, all the differences between the two sets of records have been identified, and the firm can have increased confidence that the accounting for cash is proper.

To prepare a bank reconciliation, compare the bank statement and the accounting records to identify those items appearing on one but not the other. These items result in differences between the book and the bank balances and must be included in the reconciliation.

Exhibit 6A-2 shows that Quick received $1,000 on April 30. That amount does not appear on the bank statement. Evidently, it was deposited after the close of business on April 30. This deposit-in-transit must be added to the bank balance.

Exhibit 6A-2 also shows that Quick wrote nine checks during April. However, checks 211, 214, 217, and 218 do not appear on the bank statement. Accordingly, these outstanding checks are subtracted from the bank balance.

EXHIBIT 6A-2 ACCOUNTING RECORDS FOR CASH

Quick Company
Internal Cash Records

DATE	DESCRIPTION	AMOUNT
4-1	Balance	$7,780
4-2	Check # 210	– 180
4-3	Check # 211	– 750
4-5	Check # 212	– 500
4-8	Check # 213	– 1,000
4-12	Check # 214	– 300
4-14	Deposit	2,300
4-17	Check # 215	– 200
4-22	Check # 216	– 400
4-26	Check #217	– 50
4-28	Check # 218	– 250
4-30	Deposit	1,000
4-30	Balance	$7,450

EXHIBIT 6A-3 BANK RECONCILIATION

Quick Company
Bank Reconciliation
April 30, 2007

Bank Balance		$7,650
Plus: Deposit-in-transit		1,000
		$8,650
Less: Outstanding checks		
# 211	$750	
# 214	300	
# 217	50	
# 218	250	
		(1,350)
Corrected balance		$7,300
Book balance		$7,450
Less: Preauthorized withdrawal		(140)
Service charge		(10)
Corrected balance		$7,300

Quick's bank statement (refer to Exhibit 6A-1) contains two entries that do not appear in the accounting records: the preauthorized withdrawal and the service charge. The book balance should be reduced by these amounts. Also note that when Quick receives the bank statement and discovers the preauthorized withdrawal and the service charge, the accounting records should be adjusted accordingly.

At this point in the reconciliation, the book balance and the bank balance have been adjusted and show the same corrected balance. This indicates that the reconciliation is complete.

One final point must be made about the Quick Company illustration. All the reconciling items for the April 30 reconciliation arose during the month of April. This is not always the case. For example, Quick could have written a check in March that did not clear the bank by the end of April. This check would be outstanding at the end of April and would need to appear on the April 30 reconciliation. In general, items from the immediately preceding reconciliation should be reviewed to ascertain if they should be carried forward to the current month's reconciliation.

Summary

Prepare a bank reconciliation.

A bank reconciliation explains why a firm's bank statement balance differs from its book balance. Differences arise for three general reasons: (1) transactions were recorded in the accounting records but not the bank statement; (2) transactions were recorded on the bank statement but not the accounting records; and (3) errors.

APPENDIX 6B

COMPARING LIFO AND FIFO FIRMS

Comparing the financial statements of firms that use different inventory methods is troublesome. In these situations, differences in ratios might be due to the different accounting methods or to the different underlying economic conditions of the firms. When several firms are compared, financial statement numbers should be recast to reflect the use of uniform accounting methods.

Although firms do not usually make disclosures enabling such analyses, companies using LIFO often reveal their FIFO-based inventory values. In all likelihood, these firms are motivated to do this because FIFO usually results in a lower COGS number than LIFO. Regardless of the motivation, the disclosures provide the basis to generate ratios on a FIFO basis for firms that actually use LIFO.

Dayton, Inc., which uses LIFO, elected to disclose the replacement cost of its inventories. Replacement cost approximates the FIFO cost of inventories and allows the analyst to adjust Dayton's financial ratios for purposes of comparisons to FIFO firms. Recall the calculation for cost of goods sold:

$$\text{COGS} = \text{Beginning inventory} + \text{Purchases} - \text{Ending inventory}$$

Under LIFO, the calculation for 2007 was:

COGS	=	Beginning inventory	+	Purchases	–	Ending inventory
$250,815,000	=	$66,799,000	+	$252,242,000	–	$68,226,000

The inventory disclosures indicate that under FIFO (or replacement cost), the beginning inventory would have been higher by $15,100,000 and the ending inventory would have been higher by $14,138,000. The only differences in the cost of goods sold calculations relate to the valuation of beginning and ending inventory. Therefore, FIFO-based cost of goods sold can be computed by adjusting LIFO-based cost of goods sold by these inventory valuation differences.

COGS under LIFO	$250,815,000
Plus the increase in the beginning inventory valuation under FIFO	15,100,000
Less the increase in the ending inventory valuation under FIFO	(14,138,000)
COGS under FIFO	$251,777,000

Notice that in this particular situation COGS under FIFO is higher than under LIFO. This is rather unusual. Firms typically employ LIFO to capture the tax benefit of higher COGS and lower taxable income. Dayton's lower LIFO-based COGS could be due to two factors. First, the unit cost of its inventory items might be declining. Under LIFO, these recently acquired, lower-priced goods are the ones assumed sold. Alternatively, recall that Dayton, Inc. scaled back some operations. In the process, Dayton, Inc. might have liquidated certain lines of apparel. If these lines had been held for a number of years, their recorded LIFO cost was likely based on rather old (and low) prices. In fact, Dayton's inventory note appearing in Exhibit 6-10 references such a situation by using the phrase "liquidation of certain LIFO layers."

Exhibit 6-10 provided sufficient information to recalculate Dayton's ratios on a FIFO basis. Dayton's FIFO-based and LIFO-based ratios are summarized in Exhibit 6B-1. As often happens, little difference exists in the gross profit percentages generated by the two methods. This occurs because the beginning and ending inventories are higher under FIFO by roughly the same amount; the previous calculation of FIFO cost of goods sold showed that these two inventory increases tend to cancel each other.

Inventory method has a more dramatic effect on NDS. The FIFO ratio indicates that Dayton, Inc. has more inventory on hand than suggested by the LIFO ratio. Given that many analysts believe FIFO yields more relevant balance sheet numbers, Dayton's inventory levels may be more problematic than they first appeared.

To further illustrate the impact of liquidating part of a LIFO inventory, consider the data in Exhibit 6B-2. In the subsequent year, 2006, Dayton, Inc. is assumed to cut its inventory by 50% (2,000 units to 1,000 units). Coupled with an increase in selling price due to the increased cost of new purchases, the reduction in the LIFO inventory has contributed to more than a 20% increase in gross margin.

EXHIBIT 6B-1 INVENTORY RATIOS UNDER LIFO AND FIFO

Dayton, Inc.
Inventory Ratios

	2007	
	LIFO	**FIFO**
Gross profit %	36.5%	36.3%
Number of days' sales in ending inventory	99 days	119 days

EXHIBIT 6B-2 LIQUIDATION OF LIFO INVENTORY

Dayton, Inc. prices its products at 150% of the most recent cost. The following information is from 2005:

Sales (4,000 @ $2.25*)		$9,000
Cost of sales:		
Beginning LIFO inventory (2,000 @ $1.25)	$2,500	
Purchases (4,000 @ $1.50)	6,000	
Ending LIFO inventory (2,000 @ $1.25)	(2,500)	6,000
Gross profit		$3,000
Gross profit margin		33%

*$2.25 price = $1.50 cost × 150% markup

Specifically, $400 of the increase in gross margin is due to liquidation of the LIFO layer comprising half the Beginning Inventory balance [$1,000 × ($1.65 – $1.25)]. The remainder of the increase in gross margin is due to the increase in selling price.

In 2006, Dayton's costs increase by 10%. Management determines the ending inventory of 2,000 units is too high and purchases 1,000 fewer units so that ending inventory drops by 1,000 units. In doing so, they sell 1,000 units with a lower cost of $1.25 instead of the most recent cost of $1.65. This inventory reduction generates an extra $.40 per unit in gross margin.

Sales (4,000 @ $2.48*)		$9,920
Cost of sales:		
Beginning LIFO inventory (2,000 @ $1.25)	$2,500	
Purchases (3,000 @ $1.65)	4,950	
Ending LIFO inventory (1,000 @ $1.25)	(1,250)	6,200
Gross profit		$3,720
Gross profit margin		38%

*$2.48 price = $1.65 cost × 150% markup

Exercises and Problems

6-1 What does the term cash, as shown on financial statements, usually include? Discuss cash and cash equivalents separately.

6-2 Describe how market valuations are applied to short-term equity investments.

6-3 Why would a firm extend credit to its customers? Identify some firms that rarely offer credit terms. How have bank credit cards changed some of these credit practices? Identify some industries where credit is an essential part of daily business.

6-4 Discuss the typical relationship between inventory and accounts receivable. How are the dollar amounts reported in inventory related to those reported as accounts receivable? Are the dollar amounts comparable or related to each other in any systematic manner? Under what circumstances could a firm have inventory and not accounts receivable? What types of firms might have neither?

6-5 Under what circumstances can accounts receivable be turned into cash, almost "overnight"?

6-6 What steps can a firm take to protect cash held on its premises?

6-7 Describe how LIFO provides better matching of revenues and expenses than FIFO. Why would such an attribute be desirable for income measurement?

6-8 Describe five general types of current assets. Why do you think managers and analysts might prefer that firms generally use these categories and definitions for current assets?

6-9 Define prepaid expenses and identify examples of two types of prepaid expenses.

6-10 With regard to accounts receivable, explain how the average sales per day ratio and collection period ratio could be used. As a company relaxes its credit policies, how would the values of these ratios usually change? Why?

Describing Inventory Methods

6-11 Compare and contrast each of the following methods used to value inventories:

a. FIFO
b. LIFO
c. Weighted average
d. Specific identification
e. Lower of cost or market

Analysis: Marketable Securities

6-12 The Amber Corporation purchased three different stocks during the year as follows:

- 100 shares of Fancy Corporation, cost $23 per share
- 250 shares of Traylor Corporation, cost $15 per share
- 180 shares of Sensor Corporation, cost $7 per share

Amber Corporation intends to sell these soon when its cash flow gets low. On the balance sheet date, these securities had a market price as follows:

1. Fancy Corporation: $24 per share
2. Traylor Corporation: $12 per share
3. Sensor Corporation: $ 9 per share

Required

a. Assuming that these securities are considered available-for-sale, what would be the effect on the financial statements of holding these securities?

b. Assuming that these securities are considered trading securities, what would be the effect on the financial statements?

c. What if, after the balance sheet date, Amber decides to sell Traylor Corporation stock for a market price of $14 per share? What would be the effect on the financial statements if the security is (1) available-for-sale or (2) trading?

Transactions Related to Accounts Receivable: Effects on Selected Financial Statement Items

6-13 Spit-Spot Cleaners, Inc., recognized the following events related to customer accounts receivable during the firm's first year of operation:

1. Sales on credit totaled $4,000,000 for the year.
2. The firm estimated that 2% of its credit sales would ultimately prove to be uncollectible.
3. Cash collections of accounts receivable totaled $3,480,000 during the year.
4. The firm wrote off uncollectible accounts of $75,000.

Required

a. Determine the effects of each of these events on the following financial statement items:

- Accounts receivable (net of allowance)
- Total assets
- Revenues
- Expenses

b. Determine the firm's balance of accounts receivable (net) at December 31 (year-end).

Ratio Calculations: Accounts Receivable

6-14 Frosty King, Inc., reported the following information in its 2007 financial statements:

	Years Ended November 30	
	2007	2006
Net sales	$228,542,157	$231,845,632
Accounts receivable, net	21,402,613	19,280,407
Allowance for uncollectible accounts	650,811	1,018,416

Required

a. Calculate the adequacy of Frosty King's allowance for uncollectible accounts for each year.

b. Calculate its average sales per day for each year.

c. Calculate its collection period for each year.

d. Calculate its accounts receivable as a percentage of sales for each year.

e. Based on your analyses, discuss Frosty King's management of accounts receivable.

Ratio Calculations: LIFO and FIFO

6-15 Teddie Bower, Inc., reported the following data in its annual financial statements (dollars in thousands):

	2006	2007
Sales	$333,667	$313,456
Cost of goods sold—LIFO	32,587	44,690
Cost of goods sold—FIFO	30,198	45,833
Ending inventory—LIFO	11,189	10,567
Ending inventory—FIFO	15,999	14,234
Net income—LIFO	34,000	33,500
Net income—FIFO	38,980	37,765

Required

a. Calculate the number of days' sales in ending inventory (NDS) under both LIFO and FIFO.

b. Calculate the gross profit percentage under both LIFO and FIFO.

c. Discuss the differences in inventory levels, income, and gross profit under both LIFO and FIFO.

d. Discuss why a firm might prefer LIFO under these circumstances.

Comprehensive Marketable Securities, Accounts Receivable, Inventory

6-16 Pratsky, Inc., had the following account balances:

DECEMBER 31, 2006

Assets		*Liabilities*	
Cash	$12,500	Accounts payable	$10,000
Accounts receivable	22,400		
Allowance for uncollectible accounts	(3,400)	*Stockholders' Equity*	
		Invested capital	20,000
Inventory	17,500	Retained earnings	19,000
	$49,000	Total stockholders' equity	39,000
			$49,000

During 2007, the corporation had the following transactions:

1. Issued common stock for $40,000 cash.
2. Purchased inventory on account; 200 units @ $38, then 150 units @ $39. Note: Beginning inventory was comprised of 500 units @ $35.
3. Purchased 200 shares of IBM for $45/share and purchased 100 shares of Microsoft for $90/share.
4. Sales at retail during 2007 were $75,000 (half received in cash, and the balance on account).
5. Write-offs of uncollectible accounts totaled $2,600.
6. Received $38,000 from receivable customers.
7. Paid creditors on account, $18,000. Paid operating expenses for the current period of $51,000.
8. At year-end, a physical inventory equaled 225 units. The company uses the LIFO inventory costing method.
9. Assume that marketable securities are "available-for-sale", and the market price at December 31, 2007, for IBM is $42/share, and for Microsoft $102/share.
10. Based on the accounts receivable aging, management feels that the allowance for uncollectible accounts should have a balance of $5,700 at year-end.

Required

a. Set up the beginning balances in the balance sheet equation. Leave enough room to add new columns as necessary.
b. Record transactions 1 through 10 using the balance sheet equation.
c. Calculate the following ratios for 2006 and 2007 and evaluate the company's management of its accounts receivable:

- Accounts receivable/sales (assume that sales in 2006 were $125,786)
- Sales/day

- Collection period
- Allowance as a percentage of accounts receivable

Accounts Receivable: Effects on Allowance for Uncollectibles

6-17 Becca's Finance and Collection Company has had a lot of trouble collecting its receivables recently. Discuss how each of the following circumstances might be reflected in the Allowance for Uncollectible Accounts:

1. Dagwood Bumpstead has an "open" account that is always overdue. Dagwood makes regular payments of $500 each month, but the balance in his account is always about $4,000.
2. Blondie purchased a car using $4,000 borrowed from Becca's. Blondie has not made any payments for six months, and her overdue balance exceeds $1,200.
3. Sad Sack has just borrowed $4,000 from Becca's, has excellent credit references, and after borrowing the money has sent Becca's a change-of-address notification showing a new address in Brazil.
4. Blondie paid her overdue balance.
5. Dagwood's son purchased a car using $4,000 borrowed from Becca's. He has no credit references, other than the family connections and circumstances discussed earlier. Becca's is unable to get Dagwood to cosign the note!
6. Blondie's daughter purchased a new sound system for her house and car, using $4,000 borrowed from Becca's. She has an excellent credit history, but after purchasing the sound system, it failed; she informed Becca's that because the seller provided no warranty, she was not going to make any payments on the defective sound system.

Calculating Ending Inventory: FIFO, LIFO, and Average-Cost Method

6-18 S. Claus Company makes toys and gifts. At the beginning of July, it owned 200 gallons of red paint, which were recorded on the balance sheet at $4.00 per gallon. The following events occurred in the next quarter.

1. Purchased 300 gallons on July 1 at $4.25 each.
2. Purchased 500 gallons on August 1 at $4.50 each.
3. Purchased 800 gallons during September at $4.75 each.
4. Used 1,450 gallons during July through September.

Required

a. Calculate the inventory balance at the end of September and the cost of goods sold (given away!) during these three months, using FIFO accounting.

b. Calculate the inventory balance at the end of September and the cost of goods sold (given away!) during these three months, using LIFO accounting.

c. Calculate the inventory balance at the end of September and the cost of goods sold (given away!) during these three months, using the average cost method to determine inventory balances.

d. Explain and discuss the differences shown under each method. Explain why the total costs of goods available for sale (delivery!) must be identical under all methods.

e. Under what circumstances would S. Claus prefer one method to the others? Under what circumstances would S. Claus prefer one result to the others? Discuss how S. Claus might make a choice between inventory costing methods.

CHAPTER 6A APPENDIX

Bank Statement Reconciliation

6A-1 Theraux Corporation received its bank statement for the month ended October 31, 2006. Contained in the bank statement were the following items:

	Check #	$ Amount
Checks cleared:	1140	$100
	1156	400
	1159	250
	1161	500
	1162	183
	1163	175
	1165	194

	Date	$ Amount
Deposits cleared:	10/3/03	$1,250
	10/5/03	480
	10/16/03	1,595
	10/25/03	942
	10/28/03	2,106

Other Items:	
(NSF) from J. Strauss	$ 275
Bank charges	80
Note receivable collected	640
Interest on note receivable	15
Beginning bank balance	5,300
Ending bank balance	$10,171

Theraux's check register showed the following during October:

	Check #	$ Amount
Checks written:	1140	$100
	1155	65
	1156	400
	1157	320
	1158	82
	1159	520
	1160	125
	1161	500
	1162	183
	1163	175
	1164	104
	1165	194
	1166	220

	Date	$ Amount
Deposits:	10/3	1,250
	10/5	480
	10/12	1,190
	10/16	1,595
	10/20	1,800
	10/25	942
	10/28	2,106
	10/31	745

Other Items:
Outstanding check from September's bank reconciliation: #1142 for $195.
Beginning checking balance: $5,105
Ending checking balance: $12,225

Required

a. Prepare a bank reconciliation for October, 2006. (Be aware of transposition errors.)

b. What adjustment to the accounting equation is necessary for October?

Note to students:

There are no exercises or problems associated with Appendix 6B.

CHAPTER 7

NONCURRENT ASSETS

Learning Objectives

1. *Identify three major types of noncurrent assets: (1) property, plant, and equipment; (2) intangible assets; and (3) natural resources.*
2. *Explain how to account for the acquisition of these assets.*
3. *Describe how depreciation, amortization, and depletion are recorded and interpreted.*
4. *List the factors affecting managers' selection of a depreciation method.*
5. *Explain the accounting issues associated with post-acquisition expenditures, asset write-downs, and disposals.*
6. *Explain why intangible assets developed internally are accounted for differently as compared to intangible assets acquired externally. Note, some intangibles may have unlimited useful lives.*
7. *Identify how natural resources are recorded and depleted.*
8. *Interpret financial statement disclosures about noncurrent assets.*
9. *Identify cash flow effects associated with noncurrent assets.*

INTRODUCTION

Recall from the previous chapter that current assets are associated with short time periods, such as a year. Current assets will be converted into cash or used in operations within a year (or the firm's operating cycle, whichever is longer). **Noncurrent assets** will not be fully used within a year; thus, they are long-lived assets.

This chapter examines three noncurrent assets: (1) property, plant, and equipment; (2) intangible assets; and (3) natural resources.

PROPERTY, PLANT, AND EQUIPMENT

Property, plant, and equipment (PPE) are tangible, **long-lived assets** used by a firm. Tangible assets derive value from their physical substance. These assets include land, land improvements (such as parking lots and roads), office buildings, office equipment, manufacturing facilities (factories), and factory equipment. These assets are sometimes referred to as **fixed assets.**

Initial Valuation

Property, plant, and equipment are initially valued at their **historical cost,** which includes *all costs incurred to acquire an asset, place it in its desired location, and make it operational.* Costs include invoice amounts (less any discounts), sales taxes, transportation charges, installation costs, costs of trial runs to adjust equipment, and costs to refurbish equipment purchased in a used condition.

As an example, assume that a machine was purchased at an invoice price of $5,000. The sales tax was 7% and transportation charges were $145. The machine required a concrete base, which cost $80 for materials and $120 for labor. The machine's total cost is calculated as follows:

Invoice cost	$5,000
Sales tax ($5,000 × .07)	350
Transportation	145
Concrete base ($80 + $120)	200
Total cost	$5,695

To record the purchase, increase the asset machine and decrease the asset cash.

ASSETS		=	LIABILITIES	+	SHAREHOLDERS' EQUITY
Cash	Machine				
– $5,695	+ $5,695				

Initially valuing property, plant, and equipment at historical cost is quite reasonable. Because a firm's managers have paid this amount, they certainly expect this level of benefit; otherwise, the asset would not have been acquired. Moreover, historical cost is an objective valuation basis, meaning it can easily be verified by examining invoices and canceled checks.

Sometimes, however, the proper accounting for asset acquisition and development is not obvious. Let's examine Chambers Development, Inc., a business that develops landfill sites for waste disposal. In developing its sites, Chambers incurs public relations and legal costs, as well as costs to pay its executives who work on various projects. Conceptually, two accounting alternatives are possible for these costs. *One option is to expense them immediately.* The analysis involves a decrease in cash and a decrease in shareholders' equity via an expense.

ASSETS	=	LIABILITIES	+	SHAREHOLDERS' EQUITY
Cash – $xxx				Retained earnings – $xxx (various expenses)

Because net income and shareholders' equity are reduced, this approach is quite conservative.

The second option views these expenditures as part of the cost of the asset, "landfill sites". Accordingly, these costs are **capitalized;** that is, the asset, landfill sites, is increased as these costs are incurred. The analysis decreases cash and increases landfill sites. Note that this is much less conservative, perhaps even an aggressive approach.

ASSETS		=	LIABILITIES	+	SHAREHOLDERS' EQUITY
Cash – $xxx	Landfill sites + $xxx				

GAAP requires that costs be capitalized only when they reflect future economic benefits. Thus, one must ask, how closely tied are these expenditures to future economic benefits? At one time, Chambers capitalized these costs. Subsequently, however, the business began expensing those costs and restated prior years' financial statements to reflect the more conservative accounting alternative. Such accounting issues can have serious consequences, and Chambers' accounting practices were the subject of an SEC probe and a criminal investigation by the U.S. Attorney General's Office.

Depreciation

Many fixed assets will last a long time, but not indefinitely. Because these assets help generate revenues throughout their useful lives, their costs must be reflected as expenses during that time. **Depreciation** is the process of allocating the cost of a fixed asset as an expense in the years when the asset helps generate revenue.

What Would You Do?

As chief accountant for the Craig Manufacturing Company (CMC), you oversee all accounting functions. Both you and Mr. Craig are very concerned about this year's financial statements. CMC will probably violate its loan covenant dealing with the debt to assets ratio. CMC's loan agreement specifies that CMC must maintain a ratio of .4 or lower. Failure to do so will result in a renegotiation of the loan's terms. Interest rates have risen since the loan was obtained, and there is every reason to believe that the bank would require a higher interest rate. This additional cash drain could force CMC to lay-off up to 100 workers.

CMC, like most corporations, has an accounting policy regarding the capitalization of fixed assets. All fixed assets costing $100 or more are capitalized and depreciated. Fixed assets costing less than $100 are expensed immediately. The **materiality principle** justifies CMC's policy. This principle states that items that are sufficiently small in dollar value need not be treated in strict accordance with GAAP. Most accountants feel that the clerical costs of capitalizing modest expenditures, developing depreciation schedules, and making annual depreciation adjustments outweigh the benefits of small increases in the precision of the financial statements.

Mr. Craig has just suggested that CMC change its capitalization policy. He wants CMC to capitalize all fixed asset acquisitions. Mr. Craig states that this policy is not forbidden by the materiality principle and that more accurate financial statements would result.

Depreciation is an application of the matching principle. *Because land has an unlimited life, it is not depreciated.*

GAAP permits the use of any depreciation method that is **systematic and rational.** Methods differ in the *timing* of expense recognition during an asset's life, yet over the course of an asset's entire life, *total depreciation expense will be the same under all methods.* Three commonly used methods are illustrated here: straight-line, sum-of-the-years' digits, and declining-balance.

Straight-Line Method

The **straight-line (SL) method** *allocates an equal amount of depreciation expense to each year* in an asset's life. This method is based on the rationale that each year benefits equally from the asset's services.

To illustrate, assume that a machine has a cost of $4,900, an economic life of five years, and an estimated residual value of $400. **Residual value** (or **salvage value**) is the amount the firm expects to receive from selling the asset at the end of its useful economic life.

Useful economic lives and **residual values** are estimates. Both are affected by the physical deterioration an asset is expected to undergo and by technological obsolescence. Computers don't deteriorate very fast, but they are soon obsolete! Computers can physically perform their tasks for extended periods of time (perhaps a decade or more), but due to rapid advances in the computer industry, computers frequently become outdated. This affects both the length of time a firm expects to use a computer (its **economic life**) and the **estimated residual value** when the computer is taken out of service.

Annual **straight-line depreciation expense** is calculated by first subtracting the residual value from the cost. This difference is the **depreciable basis.** Next divide the depreciable basis by the number of years in the asset's estimated useful life:

$$\text{Annual depreciation expense} = \frac{\text{Historical cost} - \text{Residual value}}{\text{Number of years}}$$

$$= \frac{\$4{,}900 - \$400}{5 \text{ years}}$$

$$= \$900 \text{ per year}$$

To record depreciation expense, the asset is decreased and shareholders' equity is decreased by an expense. Although we suggested, earlier in Chapter 2, that the asset account should be decreased, actual practice uses a **contra-asset account** called **accumulated depreciation.**

ASSETS		=	LIABILITIES	+	SHAREHOLDERS' EQUITY
Equipment	Accumulated depreciation				Retained earnings
Bal. $4,900					
	– $900				– $900 (depreciation expense)

On the balance sheet, accumulated depreciation is deducted from the cost of property, plant, and equipment, and the difference, called the **book value** (or property, plant, and equipment, net), is included in total assets. After the preceding analysis, for example, the book value is $4,000:

Historical cost	$4,900
Less accumulated depreciation	– 900
Book value	$4,000

Depreciation expense, accumulated depreciation, and book value over the five years can be summarized as follows:

Date	*Depreciation Expense*	*Accumulated Depreciation*	*Book Value*
At acquisition	$ 0	$ 0	$4,900
End of year 1	900	900	4,000
End of year 2	900	1,800	3,100
End of year 3	900	2,700	2,200
End of year 4	900	3,600	1,300
End of year 5	900	4,500	400

Sum-of-the-Years'-Digits Method

The **sum-of-the-years'-digits (SYD) method** is one of several **accelerated methods.** Such methods result in relatively *large depreciation charges in the early years of an asset's life.* This pattern can be justified by the notion that some assets are more efficient in the earlier years of their life and therefore render greater services. In other words, they help generate more revenue. To properly match costs with revenues, expenses should be larger in those early years.

SYD annual depreciation expense is calculated by multiplying an asset's depreciable basis by a fraction that varies from year to year. The denominator is always the sum of the years' digits in the useful life of the asset. For an asset with a five-year life, the denominator would be $5 + 4 + 3 + 2 + 1 = 15$. The sum of the years' digits can be computed with the following formula:

$$\text{Sum of the years' digits} = \frac{N \times (N + 1)}{2}$$

in which N equals the number of years in the asset's life. For an asset with a five-year life, the computation is

$$\text{Sum of the years' digits} = \frac{5 \times (5 + 1)}{2}$$

$$= 15$$

The fraction's numerator is the number of years remaining in the asset's useful life at the beginning of the year for which depreciation is being calculated. Therefore, depreciation expense for years 1 and 2 would be $1,500 and $1,200, respectively.

	Year 1	**Year 2**
Depreciation expense =	$\$4{,}500 \times \frac{5}{15} = \$1{,}500$	$\$4{,}500 \times \frac{4}{15} = \$1{,}200$

Under the sum-of-the-years' digits method, depreciation expense declines each year. At the end of the fifth year, the entire depreciable basis of $4,500 will be exhausted (fully depreciated).

Date	*Depreciation Expense*	*Accumulated Depreciation*	*Book Value*
At acquisition	$ 0	$ 0	$4,900
End of year 1	1,500	1,500	3,400
End of year 2	1,200	2,700	2,200
End of year 3	900	3,600	1,300
End of year 4	600	4,200	700
End of year 5	300	4,500	400

To make sure you understand this concept, verify the calculation of year 5's depreciation expense of $300.

Declining-Balance Methods

Declining-balance (DBL) methods also result in accelerated depreciation charges. Annual depreciation expense is calculated by multiplying an asset's book value (cost minus accumulated depreciation) at the beginning of the year by a percentage. *The percentage equals a multiple of the straight-line rate.* Frequently used multiples are 200% and 150%. Residual values are not used in the initial determination of declining-balance depreciation rates or depreciation expense.

Because the asset in our illustration has a five-year life, the straight-line rate is 20% (1/5 = 20%). Using a multiple of 200% (200% = 2.0) results in a declining-balance rate of 40% (20% × 2.0). A multiple of 200% is referred to as the **double-declining-balance method (DDB).** Depreciation charges for the first two years are $1,960 and $1,176, respectively:

Depreciation expense year 1 = (Cost − Accumulated depreciation) × .4
= ($4,900 − $0) × .4
= $1,960

Depreciation expense year 2 = (Cost − Accumulated depreciation) × .4
= ($4,900 − $1,960) × .4
= $1,176

A depreciation schedule for the five years is:

Date	*Depreciation Expense*	*Accumulated Depreciation*	*Book Value*
At acquisition	$ 0	$ 0	$4,900
End of year 1	1,960	1,960	2,940
End of year 2	1,176	3,136	1,764
End of year 3	706	3,842	1,058
End of year 4	423	4,265	635
End of year 5	235	4,500	400

To be sure that you understand declining-balance depreciation, verify the calculation of year 3's depreciation expense of $706.

Depreciation expense in the fifth year is not calculated in the typical way. The conventional calculation multiplies the book value at the end of year 4 ($635) by 40%. This yields an expense of $254. However, that expense would result in total accumulated depreciation of $4,519 ($4,265 + $254) and a book value of $381. *Because an asset should not be depreciated to an amount below its residual value,* depreciation in year 5 is limited to $235 (the amount that would leave a book value of $400).

Residual value is not utilized in the original determination of declining-balance depreciation because the computations themselves include an implicit residual value. By setting depreciation expense equal to a percentage of book value, a book value will always remain. Thus, there is no need to consider residual value explicitly until the end of an asset's depreciation schedule; *residual value must then be considered so that an asset's book value is not depreciated below its residual value.*

Exhibit 7-1 summarizes the results of the three depreciation methods discussed in this section.

Tax Depreciation

Tax law requires firms to use the **Modified Accelerated Cost Recovery System (MACRS)**. The **Internal Revenue Service (IRS)** specifies the useful lives to be assigned to different types of assets and also indicates the depreciation method to be used. For example, cars are assigned a five-year life and double-declining-balance depreciation is required. Therefore, cars are depreciated at a 40% declining-balance rate. As another example, land improvements, such as sidewalks and fences, are assigned a 15-year life and a 150% declining-balance rate is used. Sidewalks and fences would then be depreciated at a 10% rate (1/15 × 150% = 10%).

The details of tax depreciation and financial reporting depreciation differ because their objectives differ. *Financial reporting is designed to provide useful information for financial statement readers.* Therefore, utilizing reasonable estimates of useful lives, for example, is desirable. In contrast, *one purpose of our tax laws is to*

EXHIBIT 7-1 SUMMARY OF DEPRECIATION METHODS

ASSUMPTIONS

Cost	$4,900
Residual value	$ 400
Estimated life	5 years

SUMMARY

	SL			SYD			DDBL		
End of Year	**Deprec. Expense**	**Accum. Deprec.**	**Book Value**	**Deprec. Expense**	**Accum. Deprec.**	**Book Value**	**Deprec. Expense**	**Accum. Deprec.**	**Book Value**
0	$ 0	$ 0	$4,900	$ 0	$ 0	$4,900	$ 0	$ 0	$4,900
1	900	900	4,000	1,500	1,500	3,400	1,960	1,960	2,940
2	900	1,800	3,100	1,200	2,700	2,200	1,176	3,136	1,764
3	900	2,700	2,200	900	3,600	1,300	706	3,842	1,058
4	900	3,600	1,300	600	4,200	700	423	4,265	635
5	900	4,500	400	300	4,500	400	235*	4,500	400

*Assets should not be depreciated below their residual value.

Note: Total depreciation expense over the five years combined is the same under all methods. The methods differ only in the timing of depreciation charges. Also note that because total depreciation expense is the same across the five years, total net income over the five years will also be the same.

spur economic growth. Using extremely short estimated lives and highly accelerated methods provides firms with tax benefits more quickly. As a consequence, firms are more inclined to acquire fixed assets, helping to fulfill the objective of economic growth.

Selection of Depreciation Method

Several factors influence managers' selection of a depreciation method for financial reporting. Managers might wish to provide financial statement readers with useful information. This would prompt them to select a depreciation method that best reflects the pattern of benefit usage. For example, if an asset were uniformly productive throughout its life, the straight-line method would be chosen.

Additionally, however, some economic issues may influence their decisions. If managers' compensation is tied to reported earnings, managers are likely to prefer the straight-line method because it initially results in lower depreciation charges and higher reported income.

Lending agreements may also play a role. For example, some agreements require the firm to keep its debt to assets ratio below a specified value. This ratio contains total assets in the denominator. Because recorded asset values decline more quickly under accelerated depreciation methods, managers can reduce the likelihood of violating such agreements by selecting the straight-line method.

Firms do not generally use the same depreciation method for both financial reporting and tax purposes. MACRS is required for tax purposes but is not always acceptable for financial reporting. This is partially due to the permissive nature of MACRS. For example, under MACRS, cars are given a five-year life and a zero residual value. These may not be realistic assumptions for many firms and might yield misleading financial statements. Also, as mentioned earlier, firms frequently wish to report the lower depreciation expense associated with the straight-line method on their financial statements. In fact, as Exhibit 7-2 shows, the vast majority of publicly held companies use the straight-line method for financial reporting.

EXHIBIT 7-2 SELECTION OF DEPRECIATION METHODS

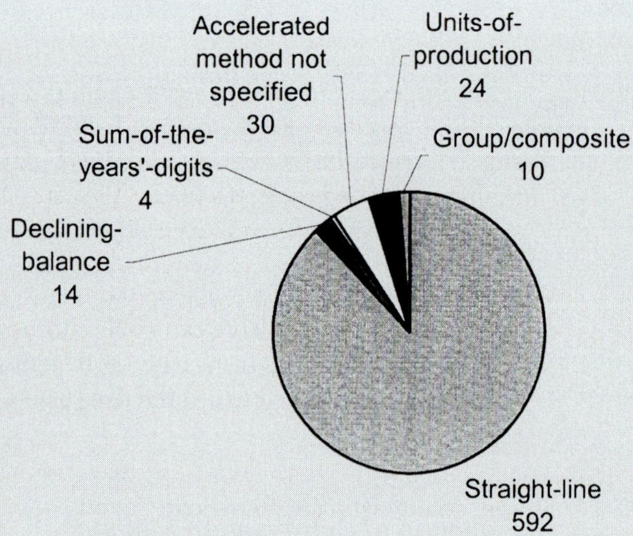

Note: Some companies reported using several different depreciation methods.
SOURCE: AICPA; Accounting Trends and Techniques. New York, 2006.

Some Misconceptions about Depreciation

Two misconceptions frequently arise regarding depreciation. First, some people believe that depreciation is a valuation procedure. That is, they believe the book value that results from depreciation reflects an asset's market value. It does not. Book value results from the application of a rather mechanical depreciation method. No attempt is made to estimate the current market value of an asset by surveying recent transactions. *Book values for noncurrent assets do not often reflect current market values.*

Second, depreciation expense is alleged to be a source of cash. This misconception is due to the format of the statement of cash flows. Recall that under the indirect approach, depreciation expense is added to net income in calculating cash provided by operating activities. Depreciation expense is added, not because it is a source of cash, but because (1) it was previously subtracted in determining net income, and (2) it does not involve a cash outflow. Be especially careful not to fall into this "cash flow trap". *Depreciation, by itself, does not generate cash.*

Expenditures after Acquisition

Firms often make expenditures during a fixed asset's life. Frequently, the expenditures are for routine repairs and maintenance. Because these expenditures merely maintain the economic benefit already contained in the asset, they do not enhance the asset's value. Accordingly, these **post-acquisition expenditures** are immediately expensed. Usually, cash is decreased and shareholders' equity is decreased by an expense.

Some expenditures, however, do enhance an asset's value. For example, Northwest Airlines renovated 40 of its DC-9 twin jets. The renovations included engine modifications to reduce jet noise, new seats, and new carpeting. These changes extended each jet's life by 15 years. Other expenditures can expand an asset or make it more efficient and productive. As another example, a personal computer's hard drive can be replaced with a larger one, and new chips can be installed that enable the computer to perform tasks more quickly. Because all of these expenditures increase an asset's value, they should be capitalized. In other words, *the asset's recorded value should be increased when its economic benefits increase.* Note that a change in an asset's book value or remaining estimated life will necessitate a change in the periodic depreciation charge.

Consider the previous example about an asset that has a book value of $4,000, after accumulating $900 of depreciation:

ASSETS		=	LIABILITIES	+	SHAREHOLDERS' EQUITY
Equipment	Accumulated depreciation				Retained earnings
Bal. $4,900					
	– $900				– $900 (depreciation expense)

Now, assume this asset is upgraded by adding a turbo-charged engine and microprocessor at a cost of $8,000; assets will increase by $8,000 and the next year's depreciation must be recalculated using the new net book value of $12,000.

ASSETS			=	LIABILITIES	+	SHAREHOLDERS' EQUITY
Cash	Equipment	Accumulated depreciation				Retained earnings
Balance	$ 4,900	– $900				
– $8,000	+ $8,000					
Balance	$12,900	– $900				

Disposals

Firms frequently sell fixed assets when needs change or when assets age or become obsolete. To illustrate the accounting for a **disposal**, assume that the machine described in the previous section was depreciated for two years, using the straight-line method. At that point, the machine's book value is $3,100 ($4,900 – $1,800). Also assume that the asset was sold at the beginning of year 3 for $2,500. Because an asset with a book value of $3,100 was sold for $2,500, the firm incurred a $600 loss. The analysis increases cash by $2,500, reduces the asset machine by $4,900, eliminates accumulated depreciation of $1,800, and decreases shareholders' equity via a $600 loss.

ASSETS				=	LIABILITIES	+	SHAREHOLDERS' EQUITY
	Cash	Machine	Accumulated depreciation				Retained earnings
Beginning balance		$4,900	– $1,800				
	+ $2,500	– $4,900	+ $1,800				– $600 (loss on sale)
Ending balance		$ 0	$ 0				

Gains and losses on sales of property, plant, and equipment are included in the income statement. If material, they are separately disclosed; otherwise, they are combined with other items. These gains and losses must be interpreted carefully. *First, note that the loss just illustrated is associated with a cash inflow. Therefore, the firm's overall cash position has improved, even though a loss is reported on the income statement.*

Second, gains and losses on fixed asset disposals do not necessarily reflect good or poor managerial performance in the year of the disposal. They *may be more a function of poorly estimated depreciation charges.* Finally, *managers have considerable discretion over the timing of these transactions.* Therefore, whenever gains or losses appear on the income statement, the reader must *always assess the possible reasons behind such gains or losses.*

Write-Downs

As discussed earlier, most firms value property, plant, and equipment at depreciated historical cost. However, when a fixed asset's utility drops below its book value, an asset **write-down** is recorded. The purpose of this principle is to avoid overstating asset values. A fixed asset's value to a firm can decline for a variety of reasons. Firms in the computer and electronics industry must have state-of-the-art facilities, for instance; the PPE of these firms are particularly susceptible to loss in value due to technological obsolescence. Other facilities can lose value if the firm terminates the production of certain inventory items and the facilities are of little use for other purposes.

To illustrate the accounting for a write-down, consider General Motoring Corporation. General wrote down assets by $6.4 billion in 2003. The analysis of this write-down is:

ASSETS	=	LIABILITIES	+	SHAREHOLDERS' EQUITY
Fixed assets – $6.4 billion				Retained earnings – $6.4 billion (loss on write-down)

Most analysts applaud the conservative nature of write-downs; however, their implementation involves significant ambiguities. For example, GAAP requires a write-down, called **impairment loss,** when the estimated future cash flows (not discounted) from using an asset are less than the asset's book value. Assets should be written-down to their fair value, which can be estimated using the discounted net present value of future cash flows associated with the asset (discounting and net present value techniques are described in TOPICMOD-I).

Estimating cash flows is a difficult task and involves numerous judgments. Because of this, managers enjoy a great deal of discretion and are accordingly able to use write-downs as a tool for earnings manipulation. When it is in their best interests, managers can often successfully argue with their auditors to delay a write-down. Alternatively, managers sometimes engage in a **big bath,** as discussed earlier in Chapter 4. Recall that a big bath involves recording large charges to income in a single year. Managers do this to relieve future years' income of these charges and to pave the way for reporting improved financial performance.

Financial Statement Presentation

Most balance sheets contain only one line item for property, plant, and equipment. This line shows the book value of all fixed assets. Notes to the financial statements contain more detailed information.

Wal-Mart discloses four types of "Property, plant and equipment, at cost" including land, building and improvements, fixtures and equipment, and transportation equipment. Wal-Mart then shows a single number "less accumulated depreciation" which must be viewed as a negative number, because all such **contra accounts** usually are viewed as negative numbers, to be deducted from the main account. Therefore, Wal-Mart shows the gross book value for four categories of fixed assets along with the depreciation accumulated in prior years on all of these assets. It then shows a single number for "net property, plant and equipment" which must be viewed as the net book value of its fixed assets. Wal-Mart also discloses in their first footnote (Appendix A) its use of straight-line depreciation, along with the estimated useful lives for each of the four categories of assets.

Target provides similar disclosures, except that its categories for fixed assets include land, buildings and improvements, furniture and fixtures, and construction-in-progress. Its accumulated depreciation is clearly shown as a negative number in parentheses as it is deducted from the historical cost of the four categories of fixed assets. Target's note on "property and equipment" (Appendix C) shows the estimated lives for its fixed assets, as well as depreciation expense for three years. Note that Target's depreciation expense on its fixed assets is much smaller than the amounts shown as "depreciation and amortization" on its income statement (Consolidated Results of Operations). Why do you suppose there is such a big difference between depreciation expense in the notes and "depreciation and amortization" on the face of the income statement? (The answer to this question will be clearer after you finish reading this chapter, where the term "amortization" is discussed further.) The notes also show that Target uses accelerated depreciation for income tax purposes. Why do you suppose Target does this?

Target also reports a lot of detail on how its retail stores are valued using projected cash flows. Target then considers the asset values to be **impaired** if the book values exceed the value of these projected cash flows. In cases where the expected cash flows do not justify the asset's carrying value, the assets are written down to fair value based on appraisals. This is a case where future cash flows are used to validate the carrying value of Target's assets. Where these values are not justified, market values are used as the basis for the write-downs. Note that this is one of several cases where market values are used to determine the proper balance sheet asset valuations.

Exhibit 7-3 contains a partial balance sheet for Dayton, Inc., which contains the conventional one-line presentation. Exhibit 7-3 also contains excerpts from Dayton's notes. Note 1 indicates that Dayton, Inc. uses straight-line depreciation and also discloses Dayton's estimates of its assets' useful lives. By comparing these estimates to industry norms, analysts can ascertain if a firm is overstating its earnings by selecting useful life estimates that are unduly long. Such estimates understate depreciation expense and overstate net income.

A breakdown of Dayton's property, plant, and equipment is also provided in Exhibit 7-3. It discloses the cost of the major types of fixed assets as well as accumulated depreciation. Notice that the differences between cost and accumulated depreciation agree with the amounts appearing on the balance sheet.

EXHIBIT 7-3 PARTIAL BALANCE SHEET AND RELATED NOTES

Dayton, Inc.
Selected Financial Statement Information
(Dollars in thousands)

	DECEMBER 31	
	2007	**2006**
Property, plant, and equipment, net	$32,955	$41,782

RELATED NOTES

Note 1. Property, plant, and equipment

Property, plant, and equipment are carried at cost or at management's estimate of fair market value if considered impaired under the provisions of Statement of Financial Accounting Standards (SFAS) No. 144. Depreciation and amortization for financial reporting purposes is calculated using the straight line method based on the following useful lives:

	YEARS
Land improvements	10 to 15
Buildings	10 to 40
Leasehold improvements	5 to 10
Machinery and equipment	3 to 10

Note 4. Property, plant, and equipment

A summary of property, plant, and equipment follows:

	DECEMBER 31	
	2007	**2006**
Land and improvements	$ 3,667	$ 3,910
Buildings	15,035	17,999
Leasehold improvements	14,036	15,231
Machinery and equipment	27,640	30,607
Construction in progress	1,814	—
Total	62,192	67,747
Less: Accumulated depreciation and amortization	29,237	25,965
Property, plant, and equipment, net	$32,955	$41,782

Analysis

The analysis of property, plant, and equipment deals with two issues. First, is PPE effectively utilized? Second, what is the age of the assets? That is, *is the firm replacing its productive capacity in a timely manner?*

Utilization

Utilization is measured by fixed asset **turnover.** To calculate **fixed asset turnover,** divide sales by the average book value of property, plant, and equipment. In 2007, Dayton's sales were $395,196,000. Recall that book value equals historical cost less accumulated depreciation; it is also referred to as PPE (net). Calculate the average PPE by adding beginning and ending PPE (net) and dividing by two.

Fixed asset turnover reflects the number of sales dollars generated by a $1 investment in PPE. Dayton's 2007 fixed asset turnover was 10.6:

$$\text{Fixed asset turnover} = \frac{\text{Net Sales}}{\text{Average PPE (net)}}$$

$$= \frac{\text{Net Sales}}{[\text{Beginning PPE (net)} + \text{Ending PPE (net)}]/2}$$

$$= \frac{\$395{,}196}{(\$32{,}955 + \$41{,}782)/2}$$

$$= 10.6$$

Firms generally prefer a higher turnover. A low fixed asset turnover might suggest that property, plant, and equipment are being underutilized and that the firm might have **excess capacity.** On the other hand, a firm might elect the strategy of relying heavily on new, efficient, and costly equipment in the hope of reducing labor and other costs. This would reduce turnover and increase depreciation expense, but other cost savings will be realized. The extent to which a firm relies on **leased assets** can also affect turnover. Because some leased assets might not appear on balance sheets **(off-balance sheet financing),** firms using leased assets might have a smaller denominator and a correspondingly higher turnover.

Some additional factors might also affect fixed asset turnover. *Accelerated depreciation methods reduce PPE (net) more quickly than straight-line depreciation and result in a higher turnover ratio.* Price changes and the maturity of a firm might also affect fixed asset turnover. As an example, let's assume that fixed asset prices are increasing over time. New entrants into an industry will be forced to acquire their productive capacity at higher costs than firms that are already established. New entrants, therefore, would have a higher PPE (net) and a lower turnover. In summary, although fixed asset turnover is intended to measure asset utilization, other factors such as those just described can also affect it.

Exhibit 7-4 summarizes selected ratios for Carter's Inc., which as you recall is in the clothing and apparel industry, Hartmarx (one of Carter's competitors in the apparel industry), and, as a point of contrast, U.S. Steel Corp. Hartmarx's fixed asset turnover is slightly higher than that of its industry rival, Carter's, suggesting that Harmarx is slightly more successful in generating sales dollars from their investment in PPE than Carter's. Also notice from Exhibit 7-4 that U.S. Steel

EXHIBIT 7-4 SELECTED RATIOS

Carter's Inc.
Selected Ratios and Inter-firm Comparisons

	CARTER'S INC.	HARTMARX CORP.	U.S. STEEL CORP.
Fixed asset turnover	16.9	18.44	3.67
Percentage of PPE depreciated	38%	79%	65%

has a relatively low fixed asset turnover. This is because the steel industry is **capital intensive.** Greater amounts of property, plant, and equipment are needed to manufacture steel than to produce clothing.

Percentage of PPE Depreciated (Age)

Financial statements contain information about the original cost of property, plant, and equipment, as well as the depreciation that has been taken since the assets' acquisition. This permits an assessment of the relative age of a firm's assets. The calculation involves dividing accumulated depreciation by PPE (gross). PPE (gross) is simply the assets' historical cost. Older assets have larger proportions of PPE (gross) that have already been depreciated. Dayton's ratio for 2007 is 47%:

$$\text{Percentage of PPE depreciated} = \frac{\text{Accumulated depreciation}}{\text{PPE (gross)}}$$

$$= \frac{\$29,237}{\$62,192}$$

$$= 47\%$$

Notice in Exhibit 7-4 that Carter's age ratio is considerably below Hartmarx's percentage. This suggests that Carter's replaces its equipment more quickly than its competitor (or used a different depreciation method). That is, Carter's might have depreciated a lower percentage of its total property, plant, and equipment because it recently acquired fixed assets that have not yet generated much depreciation. Another interpretation might be that Carter's is a relatively new firm in the apparel industry (an examination of Carter's history, however, indicates that this is not the case).

Evaluation of the Accounting for Property, Plant, and Equipment

GAAP requires the use of **depreciated historical cost.** As previously mentioned, *historical cost does not reflect current market value.* Accordingly, care must be taken when using this information. Lending institutions, for example, sometimes require loan applicants to pledge assets as collateral. In evaluating the adequacy of the pledged assets, historical cost is not particularly relevant; the loan officer is more interested in current market value.

Although the financial statements of U.S. companies do not disclose the market value of fixed assets, a few countries do permit the use of market value. Exhibit 7-5 contains a note from the annual report of an Australian company. The note shows that Boral revalued its land and buildings. Market values can significantly exceed historical cost and therefore should be taken into consideration when comparing financial statements of firms from different countries.

EXHIBIT 7-5 AUSTRALIAN FIRMS WRITE UP FIXED ASSETS

Boral Limited
Property, Plant, and Equipment Note

	2006	2005
Land and buildings:		
At cost	$1,016.7	$ 930.7
At recoverable amount	10.1	10.1
Less: Accumulated depreciation and amortisation	(56.8)	(48.1)
	970.0	892.7
Timber licenses and mineral reserves:		
At cost	75.3	75.1
Less: Accumulated amortisation	(2.4)	(0.7)
	72.9	74.4
Plant and equipment:		
At cost	3,875.5	3,583.0
Less: Accumulated depreciation	(2,012.7)	(1,903.9)
	1,862.8	1,679.1
Leased plant and equipment capitalised	3.5	3.7
Less: Accumulated amortisation	(1.1)	(0.8)
	2.4	2.9
Accumulated amortisation	1,865.2	1,682.0
Total	$2,908.1	$2,649.1

Note: $ in millions

INTANGIBLE ASSETS

Intangible assets are long-lived assets whose values do not depend on their physical substance. Rather, their value is based on the **legal rights** they convey. Various intangible assets are described in this section.

Patents, granted by the Federal government, convey the exclusive right to use a product or process for a period of 20 years. Patents are intended to promote innovation by ensuring that the firm that discovers and applies new knowledge reaps the benefits of its efforts.

Copyrights, also granted by the Federal government, convey the exclusive right to use artistic or literary works for a period of 70 years beyond the author's death. Common examples of works that can be copyrighted include books, songs, and movies. The economic life of a copyright may be considerably shorter than its legal life.

Trademarks are words, symbols, or other distinctive elements used to identify a particular firm's products. You are probably familiar with Kleenex tissue. Kleenex is a registered trademark of the Kimberly-Clark Corporation. McDonald's Golden Arches and MGM's Lion are well-known symbols established and protected by their corporations as trademarks. Trademarks have unlimited legal lives, but their economic lives may be limited.

Franchises and licenses are rights to market a particular product or service or to engage in a particular activity. For example, Pizza Hut sells franchises to various individuals and businesses. A franchise permits the holder to operate a Pizza Hut restaurant at a specified location. This right has economic value to the holder and would be reflected as an asset. As another example, some pharmaceutical companies acquire the right to sell the products of other companies. This right has economic value and would be shown as an asset (see the following discussion on research and development costs).

For accounting purposes, the intangible asset **goodwill** can only arise in one situation: *acquiring an ongoing business.* In many such acquisitions, the purchase price exceeds the total fair value of the separately identifiable assets. The higher purchase price reflects the willingness of the buyer to pay for loyal customers, trained workers, and the like, which many ongoing businesses possess. *Goodwill equals the excess of the purchase price over the total fair value of all specifically identifiable assets acquired.* As an illustration, Storage Technology Corporation (StorageTek) acquired Edata Scandinavia AB for $75,000,000 and recorded $44,700,000 of goodwill. In other words, more than half of the purchase price was recorded as goodwill.

An even more glaring example of how goodwill may dominate an acquisition can be found in eBay's financial statements for the calendar year 2002. eBay acquired PayPal for $1,492,504,000; at the same time it recorded goodwill of $1,135,554,000. PayPal's other tangible and intangible assets were almost negligible. Most of the purchase price represented goodwill!

Acquisition

Intangible assets acquired from others are initially recorded at their historical cost. For example, if a company acquires a patent for $300,000, cash would decrease and patents would increase by $300,000.

ASSETS		=	LIABILITIES	+	SHAREHOLDERS' EQUITY
Cash	Patents				
– $300,000	+ $300,000				

Because the patent has already been developed, future economic benefits seem probable and recording an asset is proper.

As another illustration, StorageTek's purchase of Edata is recorded as follows (in thousands):

ASSETS			=	LIABILITIES	+	SHAREHOLDERS' EQUITY
Cash	Various assets	Goodwill				
– $75,000	+ $30,300	+ $44,700				

Intangible assets can also be developed internally. In most cases, *costs incurred to develop separately identifiable intangible assets are capitalized.* Costs incurred to protect these assets (such as legal costs incurred to protect intangible assets from infringement) can also be capitalized. Nike's trademarks, such as its "swoosh", have a balance sheet value of $376.1 million and Nike considers its trademarks to be its "most valuable assets". However, Nike's 2005 balance sheet shows total assets of $9.8 billion. How can trademarks be Nike's most valuable asset yet represent such a small percentage of its total assets? The answer, of course, is that balance sheets show many assets at their historical cost, which may understate their economic value.

Research and Development Costs

Many firms internally develop new products, as opposed to purchasing patents from others. Because large expenditures can be made without the assurance of ultimate success, this strategy is more risky. Substantial uncertainty exists regarding future economic benefits and, because of this, *GAAP requires that all research and development costs be expensed immediately.* **Research and development costs** are those incurred to generate new knowledge or to translate knowledge into a new product or process. Most countries follow the practice of immediately expensing these costs.

The divergence in the accounting rules for externally acquired versus internally developed patents can reduce the inter-firm comparability of financial statements, particularly in research-intensive industries such as pharmaceuticals. As shown in Exhibit 7-6, King Pharmaceuticals, Inc.'s intangible assets, property rights acquired (from others), increased from (in thousands) $1,370,711 in 2004 to $1,174,028 in 2005. King's strategy is to acquire branded pharmaceutical products and increase their sales through focused marketing and promotion. These rights are obtained in one of two ways: (1) the direct purchase of a patent from the holder, or (2) a licensing agreement with the holder of the patent. The acquisition cost of those rights is capitalized as an asset.

In contrast, Pfizer Inc. internally develops its pharmaceutical products. Accordingly, the nearly $5.2 billion Pfizer spent to develop new products (or collaborate with third-party developers) was expensed immediately, even though some of those products proved successful and resulted in patents. As this situation illustrates, the economic value of patents (and other intangible assets) can be significantly different from the value assigned for accounting purposes.

EXHIBIT 7-6 INTANGIBLE ASSETS

Pfizer Inc.
Excerpts from Financial Statement Notes

Note—Research and Development Expenses (partial)

Research and development (R&D) costs are expensed as incurred. These expenses include the cost of our proprietary R&D efforts as well as costs incurred in connection with our third-party collaboration efforts.

King Pharmaceuticals, Inc.
Excerpts from Financial Statement Notes

Note F-8 Intangible Assets and Goodwill (partial excerpts)

Intangible assets, which include primarily acquired product rights and patents, are stated at cost, net of accumulated amortization. Amortization is computed over the estimated useful lives, ranging from 2 to 40 years, using primarily the straight-line method.

Intangible assets consist of the following:

	2005	2004
Trademarks and product rights	$1,174,028	$1,370,711
Patents	261,277	267,049
Other intangibles	9,459	9,819
Less: Accumulated Amortization	477,570	361,618
	$ 967,194	$1,285,961

Special accounting rules exist for software development costs. For a given project, these costs are expensed until technological feasibility is demonstrated, and costs incurred after that point are capitalized. To some extent, these rules are inconsistent with the general procedures for research and development. Exhibit 7-7 contains a note from OfficeMax's financial statements that describes OfficeMax's accounting for software development costs.

EXHIBIT 7-7 SOFTWARE DEVELOPMENT COSTS

Capitalized Software Costs
Annual Report, Dec. 31, 2005
OfficeMax, Inc.

The Company capitalizes certain costs related to the acquisition and development of internal use software that is expected to benefit future periods in accordance with American Institute of Certified Public Accountants' Statement of Position (SOP) 98-1, "Accounting for the Costs of Computer Software Developed or Obtained for Internal Use." These costs are amortized using the straight-line method over the expected life of the software, which is typically three to five years. Deferred charges in the Consolidated Balance Sheets include unamortized capitalized software costs of $36.7 million and $57.3 million at December 31, 2005 and 2004, respectively. Amortization of capitalized software costs totaled $25.6 million, $25.2 million and $22.7 million in 2005, 2004 and 2003, respectively.

Amortization

Like many fixed assets, many intangible assets have limited useful lives. Accordingly, the cost of these assets must be allocated as an expense to the years when they help generate revenue. With fixed assets, this expense was labeled "depreciation". **Amortization expense** is the term used for intangible assets. Amortizations are usually calculated on a straight-line basis over the shorter of the asset's remaining legal life, or its estimated economic life (as set by management).

Suppose, for example, the patent acquired above for $300,000 was estimated to have a six-year life. Amortization expense in the amount of $50,000 ($300,000/6) would be recorded each year.

Unlike fixed assets, no contra asset account is used and the asset account "patents" is reduced directly. Reality Check 7-1 addresses the issues of capitalization and amortization.

Since there is no longer a fixed amortization period for intangible assets, some intangibles will have an unlimited useful life; for example, some goodwill may exist indefinitely. Trademarks have an infinite life. In these cases, the intangibles must be evaluated annually to determine if (1) the asset's useful life is limited and amortization should begin, and/or (2) the asset's value is impaired meaning that its fair value is less than its book value.

REALITY CHECK 7-1

As described in Exhibit 7-7, StorageTek capitalizes certain software development costs. Because firms outside of the computer industry expense all their research and development costs, StorageTek's financial statements may not be comparable to those of firms in other industries. In 2001, StorageTek reported the following results (dollars in thousands):

Income before taxes	$101,807
Provision for income taxes	34,600
Net Income	$ 67,207

Required

Based on the information contained in Exhibit 7-7, recalculate StorageTek's net income to reflect the immediate expensing of all software development costs.

SOLUTION

	(dollars in thousands)
Income before taxes as reported	$101,807
Less: Costs capitalized	(4,250)
Plus: Amortization of previously capitalized costs	2,033
Income before taxes, adjusted	99,590
Provision for income taxes*	(33,861)
Income, adjusted	$ 65,729

*Using StorageTek's approximate effective tax rate = $34,600/$101,807 = .34
Provision for income taxes = $99,590 × .34 = $33,861

NATURAL RESOURCES

Natural resources are assets such as mines containing gold, silver, copper, or other minerals; wells containing oil or gas; and timberlands. Natural resources (also called **wasting assets**) are important assets of firms in the extractive industries.

Initial Valuation

Natural resources acquired from others are valued at their historical cost, but many firms self-explore and develop natural resource sites. The accounting for this type of situation is somewhat controversial. The issue involves the treatment of exploration costs associated with unsuccessful sites.

One approach, the **full cost method,** *capitalizes the exploration costs of both successful and unsuccessful sites* as an asset. This approach recognizes that a firm cannot expect success every time it attempts to locate valuable resources.

Accordingly, the expenditures associated with both successful and unsuccessful sites are viewed as costs incurred to obtain successful sites.

The **successful efforts method** immediately *expenses the cost of unsuccessful sites.* Only the costs directly associated with locating and developing successful sites are capitalized. Because assets are recorded at lower amounts and expenses are recognized more quickly, successful efforts is the more conservative method. Reality Check 7-2 describes how the Newmont Mining Corporation accounts for its exploration costs.

GAAP permits the use of either method. Large firms such as Exxon Mobil Corporation tend to use successful efforts, while small firms tend to use full cost because higher net income and larger asset values make them appear more profitable in the short term. The higher net income and larger asset values under the full cost method also reduce the likelihood of violating loan covenants based on accounting ratios. Large, established firms are in much less danger of violating

REALITY CHECK 7-2

Newmont Mining Corporation
Excerpt from Financial Statement Notes

Mineral exploration costs are expensed as incurred. When it has been determined that a mineral property can be economically developed, the costs incurred to develop such property are capitalized, including costs to further delineate the ore body and remove overburden to initially expose the ore body. Such costs, and estimated future development costs, are amortized using a units-of-production method over the estimated life of the ore body. Ongoing development expenditures to maintain production are generally charged to operations as incurred.

Significant payments related to the acquisition of exploration interests are also capitalized. If a mineable ore body is discovered, such costs are amortized using a units-of-production method. If no mineable ore body is discovered, such costs are expensed in the period in which it is determined the property has no future economic value.

Required

Does Newmont use the full cost or the successful efforts method? Why?

SOLUTION

Newmont uses the successful efforts method, indicated by two aspects:

1. Exploration costs are expensed as incurred. No costs are capitalized until it is probable that a property has valuable reserves.
2. Costs incurred to acquire exploration interests are capitalized. If no reserves are found, however, the costs are expensed immediately.

loan covenants. They select the conservative successful efforts method because the lower reported net income helps reduce the political costs of the very visible oil industry. That is, lower net income numbers help the oil industry to argue that it is not unduly profiting at the public's expense.

Depletion

Depletion is quite similar to depreciation and amortization. As with all long-lived assets, natural resources help generate revenue over their useful lives. Accordingly, the cost of those resources must be matched as an expense to that revenue.

As an illustration, assume that an oil well was acquired for \$255,000. The analysis increases the asset oil well and decreases cash.

ASSETS		=	LIABILITIES	+	SHAREHOLDERS' EQUITY
Cash	Oil well				
– \$255,000	+ \$255,000				

Further assume that the well is estimated to contain 45,000 barrels of oil, and that the property can probably be sold for \$30,000 after all the oil is extracted. *Depletion is calculated on a per-unit basis.* Subtract the residual value from the historical cost and then divide by the estimated number of barrels in the well:

$$\text{Depletion per barrel} = \frac{\text{Historical cost} - \text{Residual value}}{\text{Estimated number of barrels}}$$

$$= \frac{\$255{,}000 - \$30{,}000}{45{,}000} = \$5$$

The depletion charge per barrel is \$5. If during the first year of operation 8,000 barrels were extracted and sold, the depletion charge would be \$40,000 (\$5 × 8,000). The analysis would decrease the recorded value of the oil well; shareholders' equity would be reduced via depletion expense.

ASSETS	=	LIABILITIES	+	SHAREHOLDERS' EQUITY
Oil well				Retained earnings
– \$40,000				– \$40,000 (depletion expense)

Identify Cash Flow Effects Associated with Noncurrent Assets

We have seen that depreciation is NOT a source of cash. We have also shown how the acquisition of most noncurrent assets requires a cash outflow. These outflows are the primary effect on cash, other than tax savings that can occur as assets are depreciated, depleted, or amortized. In other words, depreciating assets will result in tax savings and actual cash inflows as the taxing authority creates an incentive for the firm to buy more such assets!

Any noncurrent asset acquisitions, affecting the balance sheet, should also be shown in the "investing" section of the Statement of Cash Flows or in a supplemental schedule of noncash investing activities. If you notice a discrepancy here, that is, acquisitions that appear in one statement and not the other, you should investigate whether there have been some asset exchanges. If there is no obvious reason for the increase in assets, shown as acquisitions in the investing section of the cash flow statement, then the firm may be engaging in **"creative accounting"** where assets and revenues are created out of "thin air" with no underlying economic substance.

This is the major source of manipulation that has given rise to "Enron accounting". For example, the infamous WorldCom Corporation arbitrarily increased its assets and revenues at year-end to reflect intended growth in both the balance sheet and income statement. Assets and revenues were recorded when the underlying economic rights were worth nothing! Analysts should have quickly noted that there were no associated cash outflows (or inflows). The astute financial statement reader must always be on the "lookout" for major asset acquisitions (or sales) where there are no related cash flows.

Summary of Learning Objectives

1. **Identify three major types of noncurrent assets: (1) property, plant, and equipment; (2) intangible assets; and (3) natural resources.**
   Property, plant, and equipment (fixed assets) are tangible, long-lived assets. These assets consist of land, land improvements, buildings, factories, furniture, and equipment. Intangible assets have no physical substance. Rather, their value derives from the legal rights they convey to firms. Intangible assets include patents, copyrights, and franchises. Natural resources are important assets to firms in the extractive industries. They include oil and gas wells, timberlands, and mines containing gold, copper, and other minerals.

2. **Explain how to account for the acquisition of these assets.**
   All fixed assets and the intangible assets acquired from others are initially valued at their historical cost.

3. **Describe how depreciation, amortization, and depletion are recorded and interpreted.**
   Many fixed assets have limited useful lives and help generate revenue during only those years. Accordingly, the matching principle requires that these assets (except land) be depreciated. That is, the cost of fixed assets must be allocated

as an expense over their useful lives. Managers are also free to choose from a number of generally accepted depreciation methods. We noted how Target and Wal-Mart have slightly different ways of disclosing their fixed assets and associated accumulated depreciation. We also noted that Target disclosed using accelerated depreciation for tax purposes and that it examines projected cash flows to validate its assets' carrying values. Because many intangible assets have limited lives, they are amortized. This is a procedure very similar to depreciation. Amortization is usually calculated on a straight-line basis over the shorter of the remaining legal life or estimated economic life (as set by management). Natural resources are subject to depletion charges because they are consumed over their useful lives. Depletion charges are calculated on a per-unit (ton, barrel, and so on) basis.

4. **List the factors affecting managers' selection of a depreciation method.**
   Managers might want to provide financial statement users with useful information. If so, they would select the depreciation method that best reflects the expiration of benefits contained in the firm's assets. Because the choice of depreciation method affects reported net income, some managers might be motivated to select the straight-line method, which initially results in the lowest depreciation expense and the highest net income. This tends to increase managers' bonuses and decrease the chances of violating loan covenants.

5. **Explain the accounting issues associated with post-acquisition expenditures, asset write-downs, and disposals.**
   Expenditures that extend an asset's life, enlarge the asset, or make the asset more efficient are capitalized. Expenditures that merely maintain the asset or the asset's productivity are expensed. Asset write-downs are needed when an asset's utility falls below its book value, and the associated impairment loss appears on the income statement. Asset disposals often give rise to gains and losses that do not necessarily reflect the performance of management in the year in which the gain or loss is recorded. Rather, they more frequently reflect faulty estimates used in previous depreciation calculations. Because managers can influence the timing (and perhaps the amount) of gains and losses recognized from write-downs and disposals, these items must be carefully evaluated.

6. **Explain why intangible assets developed internally are accounted for differently as compared to intangible assets acquired externally.**
   The accounting for intangible assets developed internally is more problematic. Given that intangible assets have no physical substance, it is sometimes difficult to verify that expenditures made to develop them really reflect future economic benefits. Because of this, the FASB provides specific guidance in certain situations. For example, all research and development expenditures must be expensed immediately. We also noted that some intangible assets have indefinite or infinite useful lives, but still they must be periodically evaluated.

7. **Identify how natural resources are recorded and depleted.**
   Natural resources acquired from others are recorded at their historical cost and then depleted using unit of production method. Two methods are available to account for oil and gas obtained through self-exploration: the full cost

method and the successful efforts method. The successful efforts method is the more conservative one because assets are valued at lower amounts and expenses are recognized more quickly.

8. **Interpret financial statement disclosures about noncurrent assets.** Analyses of noncurrent assets provide insights into how effectively these assets are being used; firms naturally want to generate as many sales as possible with a given fixed asset base. A firm's success in doing this is measured by fixed asset turnover. Financial statements also provide information about assets' ages. This is measured by the percentage of PPE depreciated. Firms with older assets will find it difficult to compete with firms that have newer, more efficient assets.

9. **Identify cash flow effects associated with noncurrent assets.** Note that *depreciation is NOT a source of cash.* The acquisition of most noncurrent assets requires a cash outflow. Depreciating or depleting assets will only result in tax savings or actual cash inflows from the taxing authority. Be wary of any asset acquisitions, in the notes or shown as increases in PPE (gross) on the balance sheet, that are not shown in the "investing" section of the Statement of Cash Flows or in a supplemental schedule of noncash investing/financing activities. This major source of manipulation arbitrarily increases assets and revenues to reflect intended growth in both the balance sheet and income statement.

KEY TERMS

Accelerated methods
Accumulated depreciation
Amortization expense
Big bath
Book value
Capital intensive
Capitalized
Contra account
Contra-asset account
Copyrights
Creative accounting
Declining-balance (DBL) methods
Depletion
Depreciable basis
Depreciated historical cost
Depreciation
Disposal
Double-declining-balance method (DDB)
Economic life
Estimated residual value
Excess capacity
Fixed assets
Fixed asset turnover
Franchises and licenses
Full cost method
Goodwill
Historical cost
Impaired
Impairment loss
Intangible assets
Internal Revenue Service (IRS)
Leased assets
Legal rights
Long-lived assets
Materiality principle
Modified Accelerated Cost Recovery System (MACRS)
Natural resources
Noncurrent assets
Off-balance sheet financing
Patents
Percentage of PPE depreciated (age)
Post-acquisition expenditures
Property, plant, and equipment (PPE)
Research and development costs
Residual value
Salvage value
Straight-line method (SL)
Systematic and rational
Straight-line depreciation expense
Successful efforts method
Sum-of-the-years'-digits method (SYD)
Trademarks
Turnover
Useful economic lives
Utilization
Wasting assets
Write-down

Exercises and Problems

7-1 Define the following terms related to non-current assets:
- **a.** Depreciation expense
- **b.** Intangibles
- **c.** Amortization
- **d.** Straight-line method versus sum-of-the-years'-digits method
- **e.** Wasting assets
- **f.** Depletion

7-2 Current assets, such as inventory, are not depreciated. Why should non-current assets be depreciated, amortized, or depleted?

7-3 Discuss the differences between the full cost method and the successful efforts methods when accounting for natural resources. Why might large firms prefer one method and small firms the other?

7-4 Discuss two different types of noncurrent assets that may be found on a typical balance sheet.

7-5 Discuss three different types of intangible assets; indicating what types of firms might hold such assets.

7-6 Refute the assertion that "depreciation is a source of cash".

7-7 Refute the assertion that "balance sheets reflect 'true' values (market values) of noncurrent assets".

7-8 How does depletion of natural resources affect cash flows? When does cash change as a result of transactions involving natural resources?

7-9 How does amortization of an intangible asset affect cash flows? When does cash change as a result of transactions involving intangibles?

7-10 Why would a firm choose one depreciation method over another?

Calculating Property, Plant, and Equipment Cost

7-11 A firm purchased machinery on account with an invoice price of $15,000. The terms of payment were 2/10, net 30. In addition, transportation of $250, installation of $420, and sales tax of $1,000 were paid in cash. While installing the machinery, an employee's negligence caused $150 worth of damage to the machine, which was repaired and the repair bill paid in cash.

Required
- **a.** Calculate the total cost of the machinery.
- **b.** How should managers view the damage to the equipment?

Three Methods of Calculating Depreciation Expense

7-12 A firm purchased computer-aided drafting and machining equipment at the beginning of the year for $420,000. The machine has an expected useful life of six years and a $38,000 residual value.

Required

a. Calculate the annual depreciation expense for the first four years of the equipment's life using the straight-line method.

b. Calculate the annual depreciation expense for the first four years of the equipment's life using the double-declining-balance method.

c. Calculate the annual depreciation expense for the first four years of the equipment's life, using the sum-of-the-years'-digits method.

d. Comment on the differences in your results. Which method would managers prefer if they were trying to maximize their net income? Which method is preferred if the objective is to minimize income taxes? Why?

e. Using double-declining-balance depreciation, calculate depreciation expense through the sixth year. What adjustment to depreciation should be made in the sixth year?

Transaction Analysis: Double-Declining-Balance Depreciation

7-13 A firm acquired a $20,000 computer, along with $14,000 of related ancillary equipment that can only be used on this machine. The computer and the related equipment have an estimated life of five years and a residual value of $2,000.

Required

a. Using the balance sheet equation, record the computer's purchase and depreciation using the double-declining-balance method. Show the effects in each year, and be sure to include separate columns for accumulated depreciation and retained earnings in your equation.

b. Show the effects on the balance sheet equation of disposing of the computer and the related equipment under each of the following separate circumstances:

(1) At the end of the fifth year, sold for $2,000.
(2) At the end of the fifth year, sold for $6,000.
(3) At the end of the fourth year, sold for $8,000.

Financial Statement Effects: Recognizing Patents

7-14 A firm acquired a patent for $125,000 and expected its economic useful life to be 15 years.

Required

a. What useful life should be used to amortize the patent?

b. Show the balance sheet effects of holding the patent for three years.

c. What if the firm had to defend its patent in a lawsuit at the beginning of year 4? Assume that the firm spent $5,000 on legal fees and lost the lawsuit.

Financial Statement Effects: Depletion

7-15 A firm acquired a $4.5 million gold mine that is expected to yield 500,000 ounces of gold. During each of the first two years, 100,000 ounces of gold are mined and sold.

Required

a. Show the effects on the balance sheet equation from the mine acquisition and depletion for each of these two years.

b. Discuss the impact on the income statement and balance sheet at acquisition and at the end of each year.

c. What would the depletion be during each of the first two years if the firm estimated it would cost $200,000 to clean up the mine at the end of its productive life? (Note that the mine has a negative residual value.)

d. Assume that the mine is sold for $5 million at the end of the second year. Show the effects on the firm's income statement and the balance sheet.

e. Assume that the mine is fully exhausted and declared worthless at the end of the third year. Show the effects on the firm's income statement and the balance sheet.

Gain or Loss on Disposal of Fixed Assets

7-16 Swen and Jerry are twins who each own an ice cream company. Four years ago, they each purchased an ice cream mixer. Each mixer was identical in all respects, including the cost of $35,000. Each had an estimated useful life of five years and an estimated residual value of $5,000.

The only difference between the two mixers was in the depreciation method chosen. Swen chose the straight-line method, whereas Jerry chose the double-declining-balance method.

Because of the intense competition in the ice cream business and the resulting rapid changes in technology and mixing methods, Swen and Jerry each decided to replace their mixers on the same day at the end of the fourth year. They sold their old mixers to twins Haskin and Dobbins for exactly the same price, $10,000.

Later, at a family reunion, Swen mentioned that he had sold his mixer at a loss of $1,000. Jerry, while smiling under his beard, said that he had done better than that, and that Swen should check with his accountant because Jerry had realized a gain on the sale of his mixer.

Required

Explain how Swen could have had a loss on the sale of the same mixer on which Jerry had a gain. Show the relevant calculations that will convince Swen and Jerry of the accuracy of your analysis.

Property, Plant, and Equipment Ratio Analysis

7-17 The following financial statement information is from WRN, Inc. WRN is a global company specializing in high-tech components for the automotive, space, and computer industries.

PROPERTY, PLANT, AND EQUIPMENT ON THE BASIS OF COST (IN MILLIONS)

	2007	*2006*
Land	$ 104	$ 104
Buildings	1,527	1,461
Machinery and equipment	3,925	3,555
	5,556	5,120
Less: Accumulated depreciation	3,067	2,793
Total property, plant, and equipment	$2,489	$2,327
Other Information		
Sales revenue	$9,087	$7,948

Required

a. Comment on the changes in the property, plant, and equipment accounts.

b. Calculate fixed asset turnover (2007 only) and the percentage of PPE depreciated (both years).

c. Comment on these results. Identify any managerial implications associated with these results.

Comprehensive Analysis: Fixed Assets

7-18 Pfizzel Inc. reported the following information in its property, plant, and equipment note to the 2007 financial statements (dollars in millions):

	2007	*2006*	*2005*
Land	$ 85.2	$ 81.8	$ 71.7
Buildings	1,218.6	1,093.8	953.9
Machinery and equipment	2,108.4	1,897.8	1,706.9
Furniture, fixtures, and other	940.2	812.8	698.3
Construction in progress	640.5	414.5	385.6
Total PPE	4,992.9	4,300.7	3,816.4
Less accumulated depreciation	1,919.7	1,668.2	1,511.3
Book value PPE	$3,073.2	$2,632.5	$2,305.1

Required

Part I

a. Identify and describe each term in this note.

b. During which year(s) did Pfizzel acquire substantial fixed assets? How can you tell?

c. During which year(s) did Pfizzel sell some fixed assets? How can you tell?

d. Did Pfizzel's construction change markedly during these three years? What evidence supports your conclusion?

e. Calculate the percentage of PPE depreciated for each year. Discuss the meaning and implications of your results.

Part II

Given the following additional information from Pfizzel's 2007 annual report (dollars in millions):

	2007	*2006*	*2005*
Net sales	$8,281.3	$7,477.7	$7,230.2
Income from operations	1,972.5	913.3	1,553.9

f. Calculate fixed asset turnover for 2007 and 2006.

g. Evaluate and discuss your results.

Part III

h. If you now learn that the average fixed asset turnover is 1.4 for firms similar to Pfizzel, reevaluate and discuss your earlier results.

Part IV

Pfizzel Inc. reported the following summary of significant accounting policies in its 2007 annual report:

> Property, plant, and equipment are recorded at cost. Significant improvements are capitalized. In general, the straight-line method of depreciation is used for financial reporting purposes and accelerated methods are used for U.S. and certain foreign tax reporting purposes.

i. Discuss each part of this note, indicating how it relates to the concepts described in this chapter.

j. Identify and discuss areas where managers have some discretion to choose between alternative accounting policies or methods.

k. Similarly, identify areas where substantial judgment and subjectivity may be used.

l. What opportunities may Pfizzel use to adjust or to manipulate net income? Are they significant? Why or why not?

CHAPTER 8

CURRENT LIABILITIES (Including Commitments, Contingencies, and Risks)

Learning Objectives

1. *Recognize various current liabilities reported on balance sheets.*
2. *Understand how business transactions and events create current liabilities.*
3. *Appreciate how liability accruals often depend on estimates and judgments.*
4. *Recognize some potential liabilities and risks not usually reported on balance sheets.*
5. *Understand how liabilities affect cash flows.*

INTRODUCTION

Chapters 6 and 7 discussed accounting and reporting for assets. Our focus now shifts to the sources of resources used to acquire those assets. The balance sheet equation indicates that the firm's economic resources or assets are obtained from two sources: creditors and investors.

ASSETS	=	LIABILITIES	+	SHAREHOLDERS' EQUITY

This chapter, and the next, examines liability issues involving creditors. Chapter 10 discusses resources provided by investors (shareholders' equity).

Liabilities arise from a prior transaction or event obligating the firm to use economic resources in the future. Liabilities are generally unavoidable and must be satisfied in the normal course of future business operations, but they are based on transactions or events that have already occurred.

Liabilities are a form of "borrowed capital" that constitutes a major source of funds for business firms. In fact, the average corporation relies on debt for more than half the funds used to acquire its assets. The extent to which firms rely on debt financing depends upon the relative costs of issuing debt or equity securities. These relative costs differ across industries, and consequently the typical percentages of **debt financing** also vary across industries. In some industries (such as public utilities and financial institutions), debt financing can exceed 90% of total assets. Financial statement users pay careful attention to the sources of financing because the success of a firm depends as much on the effective management of its liabilities and shareholders' equity as it does on the efficient utilization of its assets. Management of the firm's liabilities also affects the risks and the returns affecting creditors and shareholders.

TYPES OF CURRENT LIABILITIES

Exhibit 8-1 shows the current liabilities section of a recent balance sheet for Ersatz International Corporation, a firm doing business in the electronics, aerospace, and automotive components industries. The items shown in the exhibit are typical of those reported by many businesses. The next section discusses accounting and reporting issues associated with each major current liability shown on Ersatz International's balance sheet.

Current liabilities are short-term obligations that usually must be paid from current assets within a year. These liabilities are a critical part of the firm's operating cycle. In the course of day-to-day operations, firms incur short-term obligations to suppliers, employees, and other entities. The cash received from sales of goods and services to customers is then used to pay these obligations, as they are due.

Current liabilities can be of several types: (1) obligations to *pay cash* to other entities, such as accounts payable, notes payable, and accrued liabilities; (2) obligations to *provide goods or services* for which payment has already been received, such as revenues received in advance; and (3) obligations to *honor product warranties.* Examples of each are discussed next.

EXHIBIT 8-1 CURRENT LIABILITIES

Ersatz International Corporation
Current Liabilities at October 31, 2007
(Dollars in millions)

Current Liabilities	
Accounts payable-trade	$ 859.8
Short-term debt	166.4
Accrued compensation and benefits	710.1
Current portion of long-term debt	7.4
Advance payments from customers	362.7
Accrued product warranties	165.6
Accrued income taxes	94.1
Accrued costs of exit and disposal activities	62.1
Other	562.7
Total current liabilities	$2,990.9

Accounts Payable

The largest single item listed among Ersatz's current liabilities is **accounts payable-trade. Accounts payable** represent debts that the firm incurs in purchasing inventories and supplies. **"Trade" accounts** also include amounts that the firm owes for other services used in its operations, such as rentals, utilities, insurance, and so on. Most business transactions with suppliers involve short-term credit, for which payments are due within a designated period, such as 30 or 60 days. To illustrate, assume that a firm purchased inventory for $100,000 to be paid within 30 days. The purchase of inventory would increase inventory and accounts payable.

At the date of purchase:

ASSETS	=	LIABILITIES	+	SHAREHOLDERS' EQUITY
Inventory + $100,000		Accounts payable + $100,000		

The $100,000 payment to the supplier would decrease cash and eliminate the accounts payable.

At the date of payment:

ASSETS	=	LIABILITIES	+	SHAREHOLDERS' EQUITY
Cash – $100,000		Accounts payable – $100,000		

Discounts

Suppliers frequently offer **discounts** for early payment and the discount rates are sufficiently high to induce customers to pay promptly. If the buyer intends to pay within the discount period, then the inventory is usually recorded at its (net) cost, net of the discount. In the preceding example, if the supplier offered a 2% discount for early payment and the purchaser intends to pay within the discount period, then the inventory would be recorded initially at a cost of $98,000 ($100,000 invoice price, minus a $2,000 discount).

At the date of purchase:

ASSETS	=	LIABILITIES	+	SHAREHOLDERS' EQUITY
Inventory + $98,000		Accounts payable + $98,000		

If the account subsequently were paid after the discount period has expired, then the purchaser would incur interest expense of $2,000 ($100,000 – $98,000).

At the date of payment:

ASSETS	=	LIABILITIES	+	SHAREHOLDERS' EQUITY
Cash – $100,000		Accounts payable – $98,000		Retained earnings – $2,000 (interest expense)

When the firm's liquidity is low, some managers are tempted to "stretch out" their payments to suppliers by not taking advantage of purchase discounts. Such a tactic represents a very high cost of borrowing and should be avoided. For example, recall from Chapter 6 that discount terms of 2/10, net 30 imply an annual interest rate of more than 36%. Firms can usually borrow elsewhere at rates much lower than this. Consequently, most firms pay their accounts within the discount period and rely instead on other, less costly sources of borrowed capital.

Some firms record purchases at their "gross purchase price" not anticipating any discounts. Then when the discount is taken at the date of payment, the inventory value is decreased. The effects on the balance sheet are the same under either method. For example:

ASSETS		=	LIABILITIES	+	SHAREHOLDERS' EQUITY
Cash	+ Inventory		Accounts payable		Retained earnings
	$100,000		+ $100,000		
– $98,000	– $2,000		– $100,000		

U.S. Foodservice used some "creative accounting" in recording discounts from suppliers as revenue, instead of decreasing the inventory (assets). This overstated both inventory (assets) and revenue (income). Perhaps management was close to the threshold necessary to receive a performance bonus and this aggressive treatment of discounts increased revenues enough to allow them to receive their bonus. Here is a clear case where there was no increase in cash corresponding to the revenues that were shown on the income statement.

Reality Check 8-1 evaluates a computer firm's changes in the amounts of accounts payable between two consecutive balance sheet dates.

REALITY CHECK 8-1

The fiscal 2007 report of Pear Computer, Inc. shows the following current liabilities:

	(Dollars in millions)	
	2007	*2006*
Current liabilities:		
Notes payable to banks	$ 186	$ 461
Accounts payable	791	1,165
Accrued liabilities	675	422
Other current liabilities	351	277
Total current liabilities	$2,003	$2,325

Required

Provide some plausible reasons for the substantial decline in Pear's accounts payable between 2006 and 2007.

SOLUTION

The substantial decline in Pear's accounts payable could be due to several factors. First, Pear's production levels may have declined during 2007. If so, the firm may have reduced its purchases of goods and services from suppliers. Alternatively, Pear may have decided to pay its accounts payable in a shorter time period in order to take better advantage of supplier cash discounts. It is also possible that the firm's suppliers have become more reluctant to extend trade credit to Pear due to changes in the market for Pear's products.

Notes Payable

Ersatz's current liabilities include $166.4 million of short-term debt, which consists mainly of notes payable to financial institutions. Business firms frequently borrow funds from banks or other lenders by signing a formal **note payable** with a fixed repayment date. Notes payable may be either interest-bearing or discounted. To illustrate the accounting for an **interest-bearing note**, assume that a firm borrows $200,000 from a bank to be repaid in six months at an interest rate of 12% per year. Interest rates are usually stated as an annual rate, even if the loan is for a shorter time period. This loan increases cash and notes payable by $200,000.

At the date of borrowing:

ASSETS	=	LIABILITIES	+	SHAREHOLDERS' EQUITY
Cash + $200,000		Notes payable + $200,000		

Recall that the principal amount (P), the interest rate (r), and the time period (t) of the loan are used to determine the interest expense (I) in the following way:

Interest	=	Principal	×	Rate	×	Time
I	=	P	×	r	×	t
I	=	$200,000	×	12%	×	1/2 year = $12,000

When the note is repaid along with accrued interest, cash is reduced by $212,000, the notes payable balance is eliminated, and the firm incurs interest expense of $12,000.

At the date of payment:

ASSETS	=	LIABILITIES	+	SHAREHOLDERS' EQUITY
Cash – $212,000		Notes payable – $200,000		Retained earnings – $12,000 (interest expense)

To illustrate the accounting for a **discounted note**, assume that the firm signs a note promising to pay the bank $200,000 in six months. *The bank discounts the note by deducting the interest charge in advance*. Assuming the interest rate is 12%, the bank deducts interest of $12,000 ($200,000 × 12% × .5 (half year) = $12,000) in advance. The amount paid to the borrower upon signing the note is then $188,000 ($200,000 − $12,000 = $188,000). This transaction increases cash and notes payable by $188,000.

At the date of borrowing:

ASSETS	=	LIABILITIES	+	SHAREHOLDERS' EQUITY
Cash + $188,000		Notes payable + $188,000		

When the note is repaid, cash is reduced by $200,000 (the face amount of the note), the note payable balance is eliminated, and the firm incurs interest expense of $12,000.

At the date of payment:

ASSETS	=	LIABILITIES	+	SHAREHOLDERS' EQUITY
Cash – $200,000		Notes payable – $188,000		Retained earnings – $12,000 (interest expense)

Note in this case that the note was discounted at a **nominal rate** of 12%. The actual rate of interest is greater than 12%, however, because the firm only received $188,000 from the lender and paid $12,000 in interest expense for six months. The interest expense is thus 6.38% ($12,000/$188,000 = 6.38%) for six months, or 12.76% per year (2 × 6.38% = 12.76%).

Accrued Compensation and Benefits

Ersatz International's current liabilities listed in Exhibit 8-1 include $710.1 million in **accrued compensation and benefits**. **Accrued liabilities** represent expenses that have been incurred prior to the balance sheet date, but have not been paid by the balance sheet date. An adjustment must be made to recognize the expense and the related obligation on the balance sheet.

Ersatz's accrued compensation benefits consist primarily of (1) wages and salaries earned, though unpaid, at the balance sheet date, and (2) vacation and holiday pay. To illustrate an adjustment to recognize **accrued wages and salaries**, assume that Ersatz has a weekly payroll of $400 million, and that Ersatz's ending balance sheet date of October 31, 2007, falls on a Wednesday. In such a situation, Ersatz's employees have earned three days' pay, or $240 million (3 days / 5 days = 60%; $400 million weekly payroll × 60% = $240 million) as of the balance sheet date. If so, it is necessary for Ersatz to accrue both the expense and liability as of October 31, 2007:

ASSETS	=	LIABILITIES	+	SHAREHOLDERS' EQUITY
		Accrued compensation + $240 million		Retained earnings – $240 million (2006 compensation expense)

As a result, $240 million of **compensation expense** would be recognized in fiscal 2006. The current liabilities reported at October 31, 2007 would include the accrued liability for $240 million. When the weekly payroll ($400 million) is paid to the employees on FRIDAY, November 2, 2007, the following balance sheet effects occur:

ASSETS	=	LIABILITIES	+	SHAREHOLDERS' EQUITY
Cash – $400 million		Accrued compensation – $240 million		Retained earnings – $160 million (2007 compensation expense)

Note that accruing compensation expense is used to achieve the objective of matching costs and benefits as discussed earlier in several chapters (especially in Chapters 2 and 4). The total compensation expense of $400 million has been appropriately divided between the fiscal years ending on October 31 of 2007 and 2008 in proportion to the benefits obtained each year.

To illustrate vacation benefits accruals, assume that Ersatz's employees earn vacation benefits evenly over the period November 1 through October 31, and the firm incurs total vacation expenses each year of $2 billion. Assume also that employees have fully utilized all of their vacation benefits for the first nine months of the year and that they have used NONE of their vacation benefits for the last three months. In this case, at the balance sheet date of October 31, 2007, Ersatz's employees would have earned three months (August, September, and October) of vacation benefits, or $500 million (3 months / 12 months = 25%; $2 billion annual expense × 25% = $500 million). For this reason, Ersatz's 2006 income statement would include an expense and the balance sheet at October 31, 2007, would include a current liability for accrued employee benefits of $500 million (assume that the remaining $210.1 million in the accrued compensation and benefits account reflects accrued benefits for sickness or illness).

Current Maturities of Long-Term Debt

A variety of long-term borrowing arrangements will be discussed in Chapter 9; bear in mind that, as time goes by, long-term debts become short-term debts. For this reason, the current liabilities of many firms include the **current maturities** portion of long-term debt that matures within the coming year. Note in Exhibit 8-1 that Ersatz International reports $7.4 million among its current liabilities, described as the current portion of long-term debt. On the balance sheets of previous years, this amount was included in Ersatz's long-term debts because it was not due within a year of the balance sheet date. However, this $7.4 million was reclassified from long-term debt to a current liability. This amount is a claim against the company's current assets in the coming year.

Accrued Income Taxes

Ersatz's current liabilities shown in Exhibit 8-1 include **accrued income taxes** in the amount of $94.1 million. Business corporations are **taxable entities** and must file tax returns with the Federal and state governments. In fiscal 2006, Ersatz reported income before taxes of $904.1 million, and was assessed $343.4 million in income taxes. Of this amount, $94.1 million remains unpaid at October 31, 2007. The remaining $249.3 million ($343.4 million tax expense less $94.1 million remaining tax liability) was paid before the balance sheet date.

Accrued Restructuring Costs

Ersatz's current liabilities shown in Exhibit 8-1 include $62.1 million in **accrued costs of exit and disposal activities**. During the difficult economic climate of the early 2000's, many major corporations decided to **restructure,** or to downsize and refocus their operations. Corporate **downsizing** often entails the retraining, layoff, or termination of many employees, and the associated costs to the firms may be substantial. Corporations that refocus their operations may sell or abandon various lines of business, often at considerable losses, and the process of restructuring a firm may take several years.

When a firm decided to restructure prior to December 31, 2002, the total estimated costs of restructuring were estimated and expensed in the current year. However, **Statement on Financial Accounting Standards (SFAS #146)** requires that the costs of exit and disposal activities NOT be recorded until a liability is incurred. Consequently, the costs of restructuring or terminating a portion of the business can no longer be estimated and accrued. Exit and disposal activities require that liabilities be incurred before recording the costs of restructuring. This change eliminated a source of potential abuse involving current charges on the income statement, even though the cash outflows will occur in future years. For example, Ersatz embarked on a restructuring program in fiscal 2006 and in that year reported an expense and an accrual of **costs of exit and disposal activities** of $162.1 million.

During fiscal 2006:

ASSETS	=	LIABILITIES	+	SHAREHOLDERS' EQUITY
		Accrued costs of exit and disposal activities		Retained earnings
		+ $162.1 million		– $162.1 million (2006 expenses)

During fiscal 2006, the firm spent $100 million in satisfying liabilities associated with these exit and disposal activities, leaving an accrued liability of $62.1 at year-end.

During fiscal 2006:

ASSETS	=	LIABILITIES	+	SHAREHOLDERS' EQUITY
Various assets – $100 million		Accrued restructuring costs – $100 million		

As a result, the remaining obligation for restructuring costs is $62.1 million ($162.1 – $100 = $62.1) at year-end (October 31, 2007). Bear in mind that this amount is based on liabilities incurred during the current fiscal year, whereas under prior GAAP, these amounts would have resulted from estimates made in earlier years.

Accounting for restructuring costs has been a controversial issue in financial reporting because the dollar amounts are often material and required difficult estimates of costs to be incurred over several years in the future. Moreover, in many cases, the costs were related to actions to be taken in future periods, rather than being based on completed transactions. Many investors and analysts suggested that the accounting practices in reporting restructuring costs prior to SFAS #146 gave managers too much discretion in shaping the numbers that would appear on the current and future income statements. Now, expenses for exit and disposal activities will more closely parallel the cash flows associated with these activities, rather than being separated by one or more years. SFAS #146 more closely aligns net income and operating cash flows.

Advance Payments from Customers

In many industries, customers pay in advance for goods and services to be provided at future dates. Education, transportation, magazine publishing, advertising, and construction are all examples of industries where advance customer payments are often required. The current liabilities of Ersatz International include an obligation of $362.7 million, described as advance payments from customers.

To illustrate the accounting for such **advance customer payments**, assume that during fiscal 2006 Ersatz received $800 million as advance payments from customers. Assume also that $437.3 million of this amount is earned by fiscal year-end (October 31, 2007), and the remainder is earned in the following fiscal year; a portion of the revenue is recognized each year.

During the year, on receiving customers' deposits, the entire $800 million is unearned and is recorded as advance payments from customers (or "unearned revenue"); the company has an obligation to perform $800 million of future services.

Upon receipt of customer deposits, cash is increased and liabilities are increased:

ASSETS	=	LIABILITIES	+	SHAREHOLDERS' EQUITY
Cash		Advance payment from customers		
+ $800 million		+ $800 million		

By the end of fiscal 2006, $437.3 million of the payments are earned and this amount is recognized as revenue in the 2002 income statement.

ASSETS	=	LIABILITIES	+	SHAREHOLDERS' EQUITY
		Advance payments from customers		Retained earnings
		– $437.3 million		+ $437.3 million (2006 revenue)

Because $800 million was received in advance from customers and $437.3 million has been earned during fiscal 2006, the balance sheet at October 31, 2007, must show the remaining obligation of $362.7 million. When these revenues are earned in the following year, the remaining obligation will be eliminated, and revenues of $362.7 million will be recognized.

As revenues are earned in fiscal 2007:

ASSETS	=	LIABILITIES	+	SHAREHOLDERS' EQUITY
		Advance payments from customers		Retained earnings
		– $362.7 million		+ $362.7 million (2007 revenue)

Although Ersatz's balance sheet at the end of fiscal 2006 reports a $362.7 million obligation for advance payments, this does not represent money that the company must pay to outside entities. Rather, it represents resources that Ersatz has received from customers but has not yet earned. In this case, the cash inflow has already occurred; all that remains is for Ersatz to do the work that it agreed to perform. Ersatz must earn these payments in future periods, and the resulting revenues (together with any related expenses) will be recognized in these future periods. If Ersatz does not fulfill this obligation, the advances would be returnable; this liability would then be payable in cash. Reality Check 8-2 shows how a major airline reports obligations to provide transportation services to its customers, for which payment has been received in advance.

REALITY CHECK 8-2

Tangle Air Lines, a prominent airline, provides scheduled passenger service, airfreight, mail, and other related aviation services. Tangle 's current liabilities at the end of fiscal 2007 include over $1.4 billion in obligations for air traffic liabilities and a frequent flyer program. Accompanying footnotes provide the following explanations:

> FREQUENT FLYER PROGRAM—The Company accrues the estimated incremental cost of providing free travel awards earned under its Fly Miles frequent flyer program when free travel award levels are achieved.
>
> PASSENGER AND CARGO REVENUES—Passenger ticket sales are recorded as air traffic liability in the company's consolidated balance sheets. Passenger and cargo revenues are recognized when the transportation is provided, reducing the air traffic liability.

Required

a. Contrast the ways that Tangle measures its air traffic and frequent flyer liabilities. Attempt to justify the differences in the two measurements.

b. In what way does Tangle's air traffic liability differ from accounts payable included in current liabilities? In what ways are the two items similar?

SOLUTION

a. Tangle measures its air traffic liability based on the value of the unused tickets. In contrast, Tangle's frequent flyer liability is measured at the estimated incremental cost of providing travel. As a result, Tangle reports revenues, costs, and operating profits when the air traffic liability is satisfied.

It is difficult to justify the different methods used in measuring these two obligations. Both represent liabilities to provide future air travel service. Airline company managements prefer measuring frequent flyer obligations at incremental cost because this results in a lower reported obligation than would measurements based on the value of frequent flyer awards.

b. Tangle's air traffic liability obligates the firm to provide passenger services in the future. Assuming that Tangle operates at a profit, the cost of satisfying the liability will be less than the reported amount of the liability. Accounts payable, on the other hand, are recorded at the actual amounts creditors expect to be paid.

The two items are similar in the sense that both items obligate Tangle to disburse current assets or to provide services in the near-term future (in other words, within the longer of a year or operating cycle).

Obligations for Warranties

It is common business practice for companies to stand behind the quality of their products by offering assurances of repairs, replacements, and/or refunds in the event of product failures or customer dissatisfaction. The eventual costs of such **obligations for warranties** cannot be known with certainty at the date of sale, although most companies can make reasonable estimates; these costs are associated with current sales revenues. For revenues and expenses to be properly matched, the future costs of **warranties** and **guarantees** associated with current revenues must be estimated and recorded in the current period. Also, the related obligations must be reported on the balance sheet.

As an example, Ersatz International provides warranties on many of its sales. Exhibit 8-1 shows that Ersatz reports among its current liabilities an obligation for product warranties in the amount of $165.6 million. This implies that Ersatz's managers estimate that the company will eventually make expenditures of about $165.6 million related to merchandise sold prior to the balance sheet date. If we assume that the entire obligation relates to 2006 sales and no costs have yet been incurred for warranties on 2006 sales, the company must have recognized the following event in 2006:

ASSETS	=	LIABILITIES	+	SHAREHOLDERS' EQUITY
		Warranty obligation + $165.6 million		Retained earnings − $165.6 million (2006 warranty expense)

In subsequent years, the firm will spend cash or use other resources to perform warranty repairs. As the warranty repairs occur in subsequent periods, cash is used to satisfy the warranty liability.

In subsequent periods:

ASSETS	=	LIABILITIES	+	SHAREHOLDERS' EQUITY
Cash (or other resources) − $165.6 million		Warranty obligation − $165.6 million		

Note that *no additional expenses are recognized in subsequent years* because the warranty expenses were matched against sales in 2006. Of course, the actual cost of product warranties cannot be known for certain when the product is sold! For this reason, Ersatz must rely on its past experience and on information from other firms engaged in similar activities to make a *reasonable estimate of its obligations for warranties.* If the amounts of warranty expenses and obligations are potentially significant to users of Ersatz's financial statements, the firm's auditors will carefully evaluate the assumptions used to estimate warranty obligations.

COMMITMENTS, CONTINGENCIES, AND RISKS

Most financial statements include a footnote captioned **"commitments and contingencies"**. This note alerts financial statement users to a variety of actual and potential future claims that do not meet the FASB's criteria for recognition as liabilities at the balance sheet date. Yet these claims may be important to users in assessing the firm's risks and debts.

Commitments are agreements with suppliers, customers, employers, or other entities that are not yet completed transactions and consequently have not been recognized in the accounts. If such agreements are significant, they should be disclosed in the notes to the financial statements. **Contingencies** are existing conditions whose resulting gains and losses are currently uncertain, but will be resolved by the occurrence of future events. Loss contingencies that are probable and reasonably estimated must be accrued as a liability. Commitments and contingencies may be referenced in either the current or the non-current liability sections, depending on when they are likely to require payment; or, they may only be disclosed in the notes.

Exhibit 8-2 includes portions of the note discussing commitments and contingencies included in the Itel Corporation's 2007 annual report; the first portion of the exhibit illustrates a commitment. The company has signed a variety of contracts related to its future operations, yet because these contracts are not yet executed, they are not valued in the financial statements.

The second portion of Exhibit 8-2 illustrates Itel Corporation's significant contingent obligations. Many firms in the chemical, petroleum refining, nuclear power, and special metals fabrication industries face similar obligations. Pursuant to environmental laws, firms are required to control potentially hazardous emissions and correct the effects of past disposals of toxic wastes. Although Itel's managers are currently unable to put a "price tag" on the ultimate amount of the liability, the dollar magnitude is potentially substantial.

Exhibit 8-3 shows a portion of eBay's 2005 Notes to consolidated financial statements. These notes discuss eBay's possible losses due to Rolex trademark issues and the sale of counterfeit watches.

OTHER OFF-BALANCE SHEET RISKS

Most business entities are exposed to a wide variety of market risks. These can include changes in the future costs of acquiring materials and supplies, changes in the market values of financial assets and liabilities, effects on future revenues and expenses of swings in foreign exchange rates, potential effects of defaults on accounts receivable from major customers, and many other risks. In some cases, managers insulate themselves from some of these risks by using risk management strategies. Detailed footnote disclosures are required in order to alert readers to various risks that a firm might have, and the actions (if any) that management is taking to insulate the firm from potential losses. Many such transactions do not

EXHIBIT 8-2 COMMITMENTS AND CONTINGENCIES

Itel Corporation
Selected Portions of Footnotes to 2007 Financial Statements

COMMITMENTS

In October 2007, the Company and Digital Management Corporation announced that they have agreed to establish a broad-based business relationship. The agreement includes sale of Digital's semiconductor manufacturing operations to Itel for approximately $700 million, a 10-year patent cross-license, supply of both Itel and Alpha microprocessors by Itel to Digital, development by Digital of future systems based on Intel's 64-bit microprocessors, and termination of litigation between the companies as described below (see "Contingencies"). This agreement is also subject to U.S. government review. The transactions in the agreement are not expected to have a material adverse effect on the Company's financial condition or ongoing results of operations in any reporting period.

CONTINGENCIES

Itel has been named to the California and U.S. Superfund lists for three of its sites and has completed, along with two other companies, a Remedial Investigation/Feasibility study with the U.S. Environmental Protection Agency (EPA) to evaluate the groundwater in areas adjacent to one of its former sites. The EPA has issued a Record of Decision with respect to a groundwater cleanup plan at that site, including expected costs to complete. Under the California and U.S. Superfund statutes, liability for cleanup of this site and the adjacent area is joint and several. The Company, however, has reached agreement with those same two companies that significantly limit the Company's liabilities under the proposed cleanup plan. Also, the Company has completed extensive studies at its other sites and is engaged in cleanup at several of these sites. In the opinion of management, including internal counsel, the potential losses to the Company in excess of amounts already accrued arising out of these matters will not have a material adverse effect on the Company's financial position or overall trends in results of operations, even if joint and several liability were to be assessed.

EXHIBIT 8-3 LITIGATION

eBay Inc.
Notes to Consolidated Financial Statement (Partial)

Note 8—Commitments and Contingencies:

LITIGATION

In April 2001, two of our European subsidiaries, eBay GmbH and eBay International AG, were sued by Montres Rolex S.A. and certain of its affiliates in the regional court of Cologne, Germany. The suit subsequently was transferred to the regional court in Düsseldorf, Germany. Rolex alleged that our subsidiaries were infringing Rolex's trademarks as a result of users selling counterfeit Rolex watches through our German website. The suit also alleged unfair competition. Rolex sought an order enjoining the sale of Rolex-branded watches on the website as well as damages. In December 2002, a trial was held in the matter and the court ruled in favor of eBay on all causes of action. Rolex appealed the ruling to the Higher Regional Court of Düsseldorf, and the appeal was heard in October 2003. In February 2004, the court rejected Rolex's appeal and ruled in our favor. Rolex has appealed the ruling to the German Federal Supreme Court and a hearing is expected in December 2006. In September 2004, the German Federal Supreme Court issued its written opinion in favor of Rolex in a case involving an unrelated company, ricardo.de AG, but somewhat comparable legal theories. Although it is not yet clear what the ultimate effect of the reasoning of the German Federal Supreme Court's ricardo.de decision will have when applied to eBay, we believe the Court's decision has resulted in an increase in similar litigation against us in Germany, although we do not currently believe that it will require a significant change in our business practices.

qualify as liabilities and, therefore, are not shown on the balance sheet. Hence, the label **"off-balance sheet"** refers to risk management strategies that are not reported on the balance sheet.

Exhibit 8-4 shows portions of such disclosures included in Tangle Air Lines' financial report. Many of the terms in the exhibit are probably not familiar to you, and detailed discussions of these items are beyond the scope of this book. Yet it is instructive to review the exhibit as a reminder that each firm faces a somewhat unique set of *exposures that are not measured and reported in the body of the financial statements.* Nonetheless, these risks can be quite important to analysts in assessing the credit-worthiness of the firm.

Exhibit 8-5 shows part of Holloway's Management's Discussion and Analysis, which discusses how they account for off-balance sheet operating leases.

Reality Check 8-3 illustrates how a fund manager evaluates risk. This quote suggests that off-balance sheet transactions can increase investor's risks and may cause enough concern to sell the investor's interest in the firm.

EXHIBIT 8-4 OTHER OFF-BALANCE SHEET RISKS

Tangle Air Lines
Selected Portions of Notes to 2007 Financial Statements

OFF-BALANCE SHEET FINANCIAL INSTRUMENTS: RISKS AND FAIR VALUES—FUEL PRICE RISK MANAGEMENT—Under its fuel hedging program, the Company can enter into certain contracts with counterparties, not to exceed one year in duration, to manage the Company's exposure to jet fuel price volatility. Gains and losses from fuel hedging transactions are recognized as a component of fuel expense when the underlying fuel being hedged is used. Any premiums paid for entering hedging contracts are recorded as a prepaid expense and amortized to fuel expense over the respective contract periods. On June 30, 2007, Tangle had contracted for approximately 441 million gallons of its projected fiscal 2008 fuel requirements. At June 30, 2007, the fair value of option contracts used for purchases of jet fuel at fixed average prices was immaterial. The Company may experience fuel hedging transaction losses in the event of non-performance by counterparties, but management does not expect any counterparty to fail to meet its obligations.

FOREIGN EXCHANGE RISK MANAGEMENT—The Company has entered into certain foreign exchange forward contracts, all with maturities of less than two months, in order to manage risks associated with foreign currency exchange rate and interest rate volatility. The aggregate face amount of such contracts was approximately $29 million at June 30, 2007. Gains and losses resulting from foreign exchange forward contracts are recognized as a component of miscellaneous income (expense), offsetting the foreign currency gains and losses resulting from translation of the Company's assets and liabilities denominated in foreign currencies.

CREDIT RISKS—To manage credit risk associated with its fuel price risk and foreign exchange risk management programs, the Company selects counterparties based on their credit ratings. It also limits its exposure to any one counterparty under defined guidelines and monitors the market position of the program and its relative market position with each counterparty.

CONCENTRATION OF CREDIT RISK—Tangle's accounts receivable are generated primarily from airline ticket and cargo services sales to individuals and various commercial enterprises that are economically and geographically dispersed, and the accounts receivable are generally short-term in duration. Accordingly, Tangle does not believe it is subject to any significant concentration of credit risk.

EXHIBIT 8-5 HOLLOWAY CORPORATION: OFF-BALANCE SHEET OPERATING LEASES

Interest Coverage and Debt Ratio

	2007	2006	2005
Interest coverage	**5.1x**	4.7x	4.4x
Debt ratio	**52%**	52%	52%

Interest coverage and **debt ratio** include the impact of any publicly held receivable-backed securities and **off-balance sheet** operating leases as if they were debt. Interest coverage represents the ratio of pre-tax earnings before unusual items and fixed charges to fixed charges (interest expense excluding loss on debt repurchase, interest equivalent and the interest portion of rent expense). Debt ratio represents the ratio of debt (debt and debt equivalents less cash equivalents) to total capitalization, including debt, deferred income taxes and other, and shareholders' investment.

REALITY CHECK 8-3

INVESCO Portfolio Manager's Advice

"Q: What do you do to keep the risk level of the fund to a minimum?

A: We're not buying highfliers. We keep the turnover of the fund to just 25% to 30% per year. Valuation is really a big part of that. I'm pretty careful and conservative about off-balance sheet assets. Finally, since we hold companies for the long-term, we're vigilant about watching for change in the dynamics of a company—that they're not executing well or they're just not bringing in new customers. Those concerns can be reasons to sell."

SOURCE: Greenberg, Mark, "All the Fun Stuff," *Of Mutual Interest,* INVESCO Funds Group, Inc., Summer 2003, p. 9.

Identify why the fund manager is concerned about off-balance sheet assets.

SOLUTION

Off-balance sheet transactions increase risk for investors and creditors because the assets and liabilities associated with such transactions are not subject to the same audit scrutiny as are more typical transactions affecting the balance sheet. Off-balance sheet assets could be easily misused or lost. Off-balance sheet liabilities distort key ratios used by creditors to monitor potential risks or losses; e.g., the debt/asset ratio is distorted when liabilities are understated. Recognize that off-balance sheet transactions can be used to "hide" assets and/or liabilities. In the case of off-balance sheet leases, neither the liability nor the asset appears on the firm's balance sheet. Also, under most off-balance sheet transactions, there is almost no effect on cash in the year of the initial transaction. Most cash flows associated with off-balance sheet transactions will occur in the future.

HOW DO LIABILITIES AFFECT CASH FLOWS?

We have shown that many liabilities have an immediate or future effect on cash flow. Advance payments from customers should normally be the result of cash inflows in the current period. Similarly, short-term loans and notes should result in cash inflows. If a loan has been incurred, but there is no corresponding cash receipt, the diligent analyst must consider why there was no cash inflow.

Most current liabilities will result in cash outflows in the next year. For example, cash outflows associated with warranties, restructuring, taxes, and vacation benefits will all occur fairly soon. Cash outflows for loan repayments will occur within the next year, or the loans may be refinanced. Of course, a loan that is refinanced does not result in a cash inflow! Some current liabilities such as commitments and contingencies or off-balance sheet financing have an uncertain effect on cash flows. However, even though these cash flows are uncertain, they are potentially large enough and likely enough to occur that their eventual effect on cash outflows is likely to be significant.

Summary of Learning Objectives

1. **Recognize various current liabilities reported on the balance sheets.** Current liabilities belong to one of three broad categories: (1) obligations to pay cash to other entities at specific dates, such as accounts payable, notes payable, and accrued liabilities; (2) obligations to provide goods or services for which payment has already been received in advance; and (3) estimated future cash payments associated with revenues recorded in earlier periods, such as warranty obligations. Each of these three categories of current liabilities shows a common characteristic: Each obligates the firm to use current assets within the coming year or operating cycle.

2. **Understand how business transactions and events create current liabilities.** Most businesses purchase inventories, supplies, and services using short-term credit or accounts payable. Firms also frequently borrow money through short-term loans or notes payable. At the end of each accounting period, most firms accrue current obligations for expenses, such as wages and salaries, income taxes, and other operating expenses that have been used but not yet paid. In addition, firms may guarantee their products and services and must report a liability for the estimated costs of warranties for this year's sales.

3. **Appreciate how liability accruals often depend on estimates and judgments.** The matching concept underlying income measurement requires that all costs associated with current revenues be recognized in the current period. In some cases (such as product warranties), the actual expenditures will be made in future years, and the dollar amounts to be incurred are not known with certainty. For this reason, currently reported expenses and liabilities are the results of estimates, based on past experience, industry norms, and professional judgments.

4. **Recognize some potential liabilities and risks not usually reported on balance sheets.**
   A variety of actual and potential future claims against the firm's assets do not meet the FASB's requirements for recognition in the body of the financial statements, yet they may be important in assessing the firm's risks and debt position. Information about such commitments, contingencies, and risks is contained in the notes to the financial statements. Off-balance sheet transactions can also be a huge risk to the firm and its investors and creditors.

5. **Understand how liabilities affect cash flows.**
   Most current liabilities have an immediate or future effect on cash flows. Advance payments from customers are the result of cash inflows in the current period. Cash inflows are usually associated with short-term loans or notes payable. Most current liabilities require cash outflows within the next year. Some current liabilities such as commitments and contingencies or off-balance sheet financing have an uncertain effect on cash flows. They are so risky, that their eventual effect on cash outflows is likely to be significant.

KEY TERMS

Accounts payable
Accounts payable-trade
Accrued compensation and benefits
Accrued costs of exit and disposal activities
Accrued income taxes
Accrued restructuring charges
Accrued wages and salaries
Accrued liabilities
Advance customer payments
Commitments
Commitments and contingencies
Compensation expense
Contingencies
Current liabilities
Current maturities
Debt financing
Debt ratio
Discounts
Discounted note
Downsizing
Guarantees
Interest-bearing note
Interest coverage
Nominal rate
Note payable
Obligations for warranties
Off-balance sheet
Restructuring
Statement on Financial Accounting Standards (SFAS)
Taxable entities
Trade accounts
Warranties

Exercises and Problems

8-1 **a.** Identify three different types of liabilities.

b. Indicate how they are created, and how they are then reduced or eliminated. What does it mean to reduce a liability?

c. How else might you describe a reduction of a liability?

d. What generally happens when a liability "matures" or reaches its maturity date?

8-2 Why do firms want to have liabilities? Could a firm operate without liabilities? Who would be advantaged or disadvantaged if there were no opportunities for a firm to incur liabilities? Under what circumstances is a firm unable to obtain credit and incur a liability?

8-3 **a.** Describe how three different types of current liabilities might be established.

b. What, or who, restricts the growth of current liabilities?

c. How might current liabilities be abused or misused?

d. Why are current maturities of long-term debt shown as part of current liabilities?

8-4 Explain why most business firms pay their accounts payable within the discount period. As a manager, in what circumstance might you decide to pay after the discount period has expired?

8-5 Indicate which, if any, of the following items would be reported as a current liability:

a. Advance payments from customers for services to be performed at future dates.

b. Agreements signed with suppliers to purchase inventory at future dates.

c. Agreements signed with customers to deliver completed products at future dates.

d. Advanced payment to suppliers for inventory to be shipped at future dates.

e. Accrued wages for work already performed by employees.

f. Accrued vacation and holiday benefits earned by employees.

8-6 Explain why each of the following items should (or should not) be reported as liabilities in the financial statements:

a. Estimated future repair and maintenance costs for equipment owned by the firm at the balance sheet date.

b. Estimated employee retraining costs related to a plant closing that management has planned to implement subsequent to the balance sheet date.

c. Potential effects of defaults on accounts receivable owed by the firm's largest customer.

d. An airline's obligations to redeem $5 billion of unused frequent flyer miles, for which the passengers can claim free or discounted tickets.

8-7 A firm has sold one million units of a product that has a one-year warranty. Management estimates that about 5% of the units will require repairs, and the costs per repair will average about $12. What dollar amount of liability would you recognize in this case?

8-8 To reduce insurance costs, a firm insures its sales automobile fleet with a $1,000 deductible per vehicle (in other words, the insurance company only reimburses losses in excess of $1,000 per accident). The firm insures 800 vehicles and estimates that about 50 of these will incur substantial collision damages in the coming year. What liability dollar amount (if any) would you recognize in the firm's current balance sheet?

8-9 Manuel's Transmission Shoppe, Inc., is comparing prices from two potential suppliers for a similar component part. The first supplier quotes a price of $100, with payment in cash on delivery. The second supplier quotes a price of $105, with full payment due in 60 days. The second supplier also offers a 4% discount for payment within 30 days. Discuss how Manuel should evaluate these competing price quotations. Determine the amount of the liability that would be recorded if the purchase were made from the second supplier.

Transaction Analysis: Inventory and Accounts Payable

8-10 Use the accounting equation to record the effects of each of the following transactions on the firm's balance sheet (create separate columns for cash, inventory, and accounts payable):

1. Purchased $350,000 of inventory on account, terms 2/10, net 30. The firm records the inventory net of the discount.
2. Paid the creditors in transaction 1 within the discount period.
3. Purchased $300,000 of inventory on account, terms 3/15, net 45. The firm records the inventory net of the discount.
4. Purchased $400,000 of inventory, no terms, half for cash and half on account.
5. Paid creditors the amount due from transaction 4.
6. Paid the creditors in transaction 3 after the discount period.

Transaction Analysis: Warranties and Interest

8-11 Set up column headings as necessary (including a Warranty Payable column) and use the accounting equation to record the effects of each of the following transactions on the firm's balance sheet:

1. Accrued warranties estimated at $1,200,000 on December 31, 2006. (Set up a Warranty Payable column.)
2. Paid warranty claims costing $1,300,000 in cash during 2007.
3. Borrowed $10,000,000 at 9% annual interest for 240 days on September 30, 2007. Assume 360 days in a year.
4. Sold goods costing $12,000,000 for $25,000,000 cash during 2007.
5. Accrued interest on the loan on December 31, 2007. (Set up an interest payable column in your worksheet.)

6. Management estimated that the warranties obligation at December 31, 2007 (based on past sales and warranty claims) should be $1,500,000. Why was there a negative balance in the Warranty Payable column before your adjustment?
7. Repaid the loan, plus interest at the maturity date.

Contingencies

8-12 How should the following contingencies be treated in the annual report of Akronite Corporation on December 31, 2006?

1. The corporation is presently being sued for patent infringement. The damages are estimated to be $12 million and Akronite's attorneys feel this will probably be the amount required to be paid. However, the court date is set for June of the following year.
2. The corporation is being sued by the federal government for environmental pollution. The damages alleged by the federal government will probably be assessed against the corporation, yet no estimate has been determined at this point.
3. The corporation is suing another corporation for various patent infringements. The court date is scheduled for March 2007. The lawsuit total is $15 million, and it is almost a sure thing that Akronite will prevail and collect $15 million.

Transaction Analysis: Comprehensive Problem

8-13 In its first year, Sam's Subway Emporium engaged in the following transactions. Indicate the effects of each transaction on Sam's balance sheet by using the balance sheet equation. Total your worksheet at the end of the first year and prepare a simple balance sheet.

1. Sam's was formed with a cash investment of $50,000 in exchange for common stock.
2. Sam's purchased a lunch cart for $10,000 cash.
3. Sam's ordered food and other supplies at a cost of $13,500, not yet received.
4. Sam's received the food and supplies, but intended to pay later.
5. Sam's felt quite generous and gave its employees an advance on their first week's wages of $2,500.
6. Sam's then got a bit nervous about whether it could pay its employees and suppliers in subsequent months, so a bank loan of $100,000 was acquired at an annual interest rate of 10%.
7. Sam's failed to pay for its first month's food and other supplies; the supplier billed Sam's a 20% late fee (record late fee as interest payable).
8. Sam's paid the employees salaries of $67,500 during the year and also recognized the wages that were paid in advance as expenses.

9. Assume that an entire year has passed and Sam's has made no payments on the loan or the supplier's bill. The late fee is assessed quarterly (four times each year) if the account is not paid. Accrue interest on the loan and use an interest payable account for both the late fees and the interest on the loan.
10. On the first day of the next year, will Sam's be able to repay the loan? If so, show the effects of the loan repayment.

Changes in Various Current Liabilities

8-14 The Distraught Novelty Co. reports the following current liabilities in its balance sheet on December 31, 2006:

Accounts payable to suppliers	$2,500,000
Revenues received in advance	920,000
Income taxes payable	480,000
Warranty obligations	650,000
Total current liabilities	$4,550,000

The firm's current liabilities changed during 2007 for the following reasons:

1. Additional credit purchases from suppliers totaled $10,300,000, and cash payments to suppliers totaled $9,800,000.
2. Revenues received in advance were fully earned during 2007. The associated expenses, paid in cash, were $570,000.
3. The firm recognized $1,500,000 in income tax expense during 2007 and made total tax payments of $1,350,000.
4. For merchandise sold prior to 2007, warranty services costing a total of $575,000 were performed during 2007 that fully satisfied all the outstanding warranties. The company estimates that its warranty obligations liability balance for this year's sales is approximately $700,000 at December 31, 2007.

Required

a. Determine how each of the described events affects the firm's balance sheet in 2007.
b. Determine the composition of Distraught's current liabilities on December 31, 2007.

Identifying Transactions from Worksheet Entries

8-15 The following worksheet entries were retrieved from a waterlogged worksheet stored in a flooded basement. Identify the transaction to which the worksheet entry refers. Discuss the underlying business reason supporting each transaction.

	Assets	Notes Pay.	Sal. Pay.	Warr. Oblig.	Adv. Cust. Payments	Shareholders' Equity	
a.	100,000	100,000					
b.			25,500			– 25,500	
c.				150,000		– 150,000	
d.	80,000				80,000		
e.	– 50,000	– 50,000					
f.	– 22,000			– 22,000			
g.					– 30,000	30,000	(Revenue)
h.	– 55,000	– 50,000				– 5,000	
i.	195,000	195,000					
j.	– 200,000	– 195,000				– 5000	

Financial Statement Effects of Warranty Recognition

8-16 Hiram's Hi-Tech Industries assembles specialized electronic interfaces that are used in hand-held computers and communications devices (PDAs). Hiram's has had significant warranty claims on its interfaces and is wondering what liability recognition would be appropriate for 2006. Hiram's 2002 statements showed a warranty liability of $12 million, which was totally exhausted by the end of 2006. Hiram's sales doubled during 2006, while its quality enhancement efforts had little effect. In fact, Hiram's president privately admits that quality may have significantly declined since 2005. The president also wonders whether Hiram's should shorten its typical two-year warranty period.

Hiram's controller is arguing for the recognition of warranty obligations of $12 million because that amount appeared to be adequate for the prior year. Hiram's auditors are arguing for liability recognition of $30 million on the grounds that $12 million is not adequate for the prior year and that, with an increase in sales, more warranty claims are likely.

Hiram's balance sheet equation, without any liability recognition, is as follows:

ASSETS	=	LIABILITIES	+	SHAREHOLDERS' EQUITY
$100M		$35M		$65M

Required

a. Indicate the effect of the controller's recommendation on the balance sheet equation.

b. Indicate the effect of the auditor's recommendation on the balance sheet equation.

c. Calculate the debt to total assets ratio under each recommendation.

d. How do you think an external user of these financial statements will view the differences between a 35% debt to assets ratio and the ratios that you calculated in part c?

e. Now assume that the actual warranty costs in 2007 were $25 million. Show the effects on the balance sheet equation under both the controller's recommendation and the auditor's recommendation.

f. Although the controller has obviously underestimated these warranty claims, do you feel that the auditor has conversely overestimated the warranty claims? Why?

g. What other recommendations regarding quality and warranty issues might you make to Hiram's Hi-Tech Industries?

h. Why might managers want to underestimate warranty liabilities? Discuss both balance sheet and income effects. Discuss the business reasons underlying Hiram's treatment of its warranty obligations.

CHAPTER 9

NONCURRENT LIABILITIES

Learning Objectives

1. *Recognize the types of noncurrent obligations that are reported by business firms.*
2. *Describe the different features of long-term borrowing contracts, such as notes and bonds payable.*
3. *Determine periodic interest expense and the value of noncurrent obligations in financial reports.*
4. *Understand how managers can "smooth" fluctuations in earnings by bond repurchases.*
5. *Distinguish between the effect that bond interest and gains and losses from early retirement have on operating cash flows as opposed to net income.*
6. *Appreciate why income is measured differently for income tax and financial reporting purposes.*
7. *Understand why the tax basis and the financial reporting basis of assets and liabilities may differ.*
8. *Interpret financial statement measurements of income tax expense and deferred income tax liability.*
9. *Distinguish between the operating cash flow and the income statement effects of bonds and deferred taxes.*

INTRODUCTION

Obligations that generally are not required to be paid or settled within one year of the balance sheet date are classified as **noncurrent liabilities**. *This distinction is important because knowing a firm's current liabilities versus its noncurrent liabilities is necessary in assessing the firm's liquidity.* Common examples of noncurrent liabilities include notes and bonds payable. In addition, deferred income tax payments are an important component of liabilities for many companies. Each of these types of liabilities is discussed in the following sections. Note that this chapter relies on the present value concepts developed later in TOPICMOD-I.

Other types of noncurrent liabilities shown in financial statements can be more controversial. The accounting and reporting methods used to report these controversial items have changed substantially, and may continue to evolve. For this reason, two TOPICMOD's (II and III) are devoted to these controversial liabilities including leases, pensions, and post-retirement benefits.

LONG-TERM NOTES PAYABLE

Firms often borrow money by signing notes payable to banks or other lending institutions. Such **notes** can either be interest-bearing or discounted notes. This section describes the essential features of both types.

Interest-Bearing Notes

One way a firm borrows funds is by signing an **interest-bearing note.** A bank or other lender will loan the face amount, or principal, of the note for a specified period. The borrower will then pay interest periodically and repay the principal when the note becomes due (or at its **maturity date**).

If Random Enterprises, Inc., for example, borrows $10 million at the beginning of 2006 for two years at a market interest rate of 12% per year; the financial statements would reflect the following events.

Upon receipt of the loan proceeds at the beginning of 2006, cash and long-term notes payable are each increased by $10 million:

ASSETS	=	LIABILITIES	+	SHAREHOLDERS' EQUITY
Cash + $10 million		Long-term notes payable + $10 million		

In each of the years 2006 and 2007, as the periodic interest payments are made, cash is decreased by $1.2 million ($10 million × 12% = $1.2 million) and interest expense is recognized.

ASSETS	=	LIABILITIES	+	SHAREHOLDERS' EQUITY
Cash – $1.2 million				Retained earnings – $1.2 million (interest expense)

When the loan is repaid at maturity at the end of 2007, cash and long-term notes payable are each decreased by $10 million:

ASSETS	=	LIABILITIES	+	SHAREHOLDERS' EQUITY
Cash – $10 million		Long-term notes payable – $10 million		

The net result of these three transactions is that $10 million cash has been borrowed, and later $12.4 million was repaid. The firm has incurred interest expense of $1.2 million each year, or a total interest expense of $2.4 million, for the privilege of using the $10 million for two years. For illustration purposes we showed the notes payable classification as long-term each year. In reality, the notes payable should be reclassified as a current obligation at the end of 2006 because it is due and payable at the end of 2007.

Discounted Notes

In the previous example, Random Enterprises borrowed $10 million by signing an interest-bearing note. Suppose that the note did not require periodic payments of interest. Instead, assume that Random Enterprises signs a note on January 1, 2006, promising to pay the lender $10 million in two years, and will not make periodic interest payments. In this case, the lender will be unwilling to provide Random the full $10 million face value of the note. *No one is willing to loan money without interest and all long-term financing arrangements involve interest, even if it is not separately identified and paid periodically.*

How much would a lender be willing to loan in exchange for Random's **non-interest-bearing note** of $10 million? To answer this question, if a prospective lender wants to earn 12% interest on the note for two years, we must discount the note. In other words, the interest is taken out of the $10 million to arrive at the amount that Random will receive at the inception of the loan. This is accomplished by calculating the **present value** of the note (see Appendix C), at the current lending rate of 12%. The present value of the note is $7,970,000, computed as follows:

$$P = A \times PVF^{i}_{n}$$

$$= \$10 \text{ million} \times PVF, i = 12\%, n = 2 \text{ years}$$

$$= \$10 \text{ million} \times (.797) \text{ (from Exhibit C-2)}$$

$$= \$7{,}970{,}000$$

The discount of $2,030,000 between the $10 million and the $7,970,000 is the interest expense incurred by Random and interest income earned by the lender on the note over the two-year period. Looking at this transaction another way, if the prospective lender instead deposited \$7,970,000 at the beginning of 2006 in a bank account for two years to earn 12% per year, the initial deposit would grow to \$10 million by the end of 2007. In each year, interest to be recognized is 12% of the value of the note at the start of the year. The yearly interest amounts are calculated as follows:

Amount received from lender,	
January 1, 2006	\$ 7,970,000
Interest during 2006 (\$7,970,000 × .12)	956,400
Loan balance, December 31, 2006	\$ 8,926,400
Interest during 2007 (\$8,926,400 × .12)	1,073,600**
Loan balance, December 31, 2007	\$10,000,000

**Rounded (because the factor from the present value table was rounded)

Notice that the interest expense increases between 2006 and 2007. This occurs because Random Enterprises makes no interest payment to the lender in 2006. As a result, the loan balance (**carrying value**) increases to include the unpaid interest. In other words, the lender is earning **compound interest** (interest on interest) in 2007. These events would affect Random Enterprise's financial statements in the following manner.

The receipt of cash from the lender at the beginning of 2006 in exchange for Random's note payable will increase cash and noncurrent liabilities:

ASSETS	=	LIABILITIES	+	SHAREHOLDERS' EQUITY
Cash + \$7,970,000		Long-term notes payable + \$7,970,000		

Interest expense during 2006 and 2007 will decrease retained earnings and increase the reported value of noncurrent liabilities:

ASSETS	=	LIABILITIES	+	SHAREHOLDERS' EQUITY
		Long-term notes payable + \$956,400		Retained earnings – \$956,400 (interest expense)

On January 1, 2007, the carrying value of the note is $8,926,400 ($7,970,000 + $956,400). In 2007, interest is again added to the loan balance:

ASSETS	=	LIABILITIES	+	SHAREHOLDERS' EQUITY
		Long-term notes payable + $1,073,600		Retained earnings − $1,073,600** (interest expense)

**Rounded

On December 31, 2007 (the maturity date of the note), the carrying value of the note has been increased to $10,000,000 ($8,926,400 + $1,073,600). This liability is eliminated, and the lender is paid cash of $10 million.

ASSETS	=	LIABILITIES	+	SHAREHOLDERS' EQUITY
Cash − $10 million		Long-term notes payable − $10 million		

The net result of these transactions is that slightly less than $8 million has been borrowed and used by Random Enterprises for two years, and interest expense of slightly more than $2 million has been incurred for the privilege of using the $8 million for two years. In the end, Random has repaid $10 million, which included both principal and interest.

BONDS PAYABLE

Bonds payable represents a major source of borrowed capital for U.S. firms. **Bonds** are notes, sold to individual investors as well as to financial institutions. For a variety of reasons, managers may prefer to issue bonds to investors rather than borrowing directly from financial institutions. Bond financing can also offer advantages in terms of the availability and cost of borrowing and the managers' subsequent flexibility in making business decisions. For example, the amount that financial institutions are willing to loan to a single firm may be limited because the lender aims to diversify its risks by loaning smaller amounts to many different borrowers. The sale of bonds, on the other hand, enables the borrower to obtain access to a much larger pool of funds available from large institutional investors and also from thousands of individual investors.

In addition, for some firms, bond financing may be less expensive. The interest rates that prevail in the bond market can be less than the rate available from financial institutions. Finally, bond financing may also offer managers greater flexibility in the future. A direct lending agreement often imposes various restrictions on managers' investing and financing activities until the loan is repaid. As examples, a lending agreement can restrict the firm's dividend payments or limit the amounts that the firm can borrow from other lenders until the debt is repaid. Although bond issuances can also entail similar restrictions, they can be less onerous than the restrictions imposed by financial institutions.

A bond is also a contract that is sold to investors. Bonds obligate the borrower (the issuing corporation) to make periodic interest payments, usually every six months, and to pay the principal or face value of the bond at a specified maturity date. Prior to issuing bonds, managers meet with financial advisers to decide on the maturity value and other terms of the bond contract, as well as to predict the market interest rate at which the bonds can be sold. The predicted interest rate usually becomes the **coupon rate** (also called the face rate or **nominal interest rate**) that is contained in the bond contract. *This rate, in conjunction with the face value, determines the cash interest to be paid periodically to bondholders.*

The **market rate** of interest cannot be known with certainty until the date on which the bonds are sold. Market interest rates are the "cost of money" and are determined by the forces of supply and demand in the financial markets. The federal government, through the actions of the Federal Reserve, also influences interest rates. Because the market rate constantly changes, and the coupon rate is fixed when the bonds are printed, it is rare that the bond coupon rate will coincide exactly with the market interest rate when the bonds are sold. The following sections illustrate the issuance and reporting for bonds when the market interest rate in turn equals, exceeds, or falls below the coupon rate of interest.

Issuance of Bonds at Par

If the coupon rate of a bond coincides with the market rate of interest when the bonds are actually sold to investors, then the bonds will sell at **par value** or face value. The price at which a bond is trading is usually quoted as a percentage of the bond's par value, so that a bond that sells at par has a price of 100. To illustrate the sale of bonds at par, assume Marley Company issues bonds on January 1, 2007, with a principal amount of $100 million, to be repaid in 10 years and a 12% coupon rate of interest payable semiannually. The bond contract obligates Marley to make the following payments:

Principal: $100,000,000 due in 10 years (after 20 six-month periods),

Interest: $6,000,000 due at the end of each six-month period, for 10 years (20 six-month periods) ($100,000,000 × 12% × 6/12 = $6,000,000).

Because the market rate and the coupon rate of interest are the same, the bonds sell at their face value of $100 million. The quoted annual interest rate of 12% is actually 6% each six-month period because the bonds pay interest each six months. When interest is paid each six months, the interest rate is **compounded semi-**

annually. To use the present value tables, bonds with a 12% semiannual interest coupon are regarded as outstanding for a number of six-month periods (20 in this case), and the interest rate is 6% per period. In general, when interest is compounded n times each year, the periodic interest rate is i/n, and the number of periods is $n \times$ years. In the present case, the periodic interest rate is 6% (i/n or 12% / 2 = 6%), and the number of periods is 20 ($n \times$ years or $2 \times 10 = 20$).

The following table illustrates the present value calculation of this bond:

Principal, due in 20 six-month periods at 6% semi-annual market interest rate:

Amount	×	Present value factor (Exhibit I-2) $n = 20$, $i = 6\%$		
$100 million	×	0.312	=	$ 31,200,000

Interest payments, due each six months for 20 periods:

Amount	×	Present value factor (Exhibit I-3) $n = 20$, $i = 6\%$		
$6 million	×	11.47	=	68,800,000***
		Total present value	=	$100,000,000

***Rounding (factors have been rounded)

The following events would be reported in the financial statements over the life of the bond. On January 1, 2007, Marley Company receives $100 million in cash, and bonds payable are recorded in this amount:

ASSETS	=	LIABILITIES	+	SHAREHOLDERS' EQUITY
Cash + $100 million		Bonds payable + $100 million		

Each six months for 10 years, Marley Company recognizes interest expense and pays $6 million to the bondholders each June 30 and December 31 from 2007 through 2016:

ASSETS	=	LIABILITIES	+	SHAREHOLDERS' EQUITY
Cash – $6 million				Retained earnings – $6 million (interest expense)

On the maturity date, December 31, 2016, Marley Company pays $100 million in bond principal and retires the bonds:

ASSETS	=	LIABILITIES	+	SHAREHOLDERS' EQUITY
Cash – $100 million		Bonds payable – $100 million		

To recap, Marley Company received $100 million from investors when the bonds were issued and paid a total of $220 million to bondholders over the life of the bond issue. The total interest expense was, therefore, $120 million ($220 million in payments minus $100 million in receipts), and the interest expense each year was $12 million (2 × $6 million).

Sale or Issuance of Bonds at a Discount

In cases where the coupon rate of interest differs from the market rate on the date that bonds are sold, the present value of the bond issue will not equal the face amount of the bond. Consider, for example, an investor buying a bond when the *coupon rate is below the market rate of interest.* Because the coupon rate does not provide the investor with a rate of return equal to that available on other similar investments, the investor will buy the bonds only if they are sold at a **discount from the par or face value**. *Bear in mind that the bond contract represents a fixed series of cash payments to bondholders. The present value of any fixed series of cash payments depends on the* ***discount rate,*** *which in this case is the market rate of interest.*

To illustrate the accounting for bonds sold at a discount, assume that the Marley Company bonds described earlier were sold on January 1, 2007, and that the market rate of interest was 16% (compounded semiannually) on that date. Investors will discount the bonds' cash flows at the current market rate of interest. Because the coupon rate is only 12%, the bonds will sell at a discount. Note, however, that the interest coupon payments will still be $6 million because that is the amount stated in the bond contract. The present value is computed as follows.

Principal, due in 20 six-month periods at 6% semi-annual market interest rate:

Amount	×	Present value factor (Exhibit I-2) $n = 20, i = 8\%$		
$100,000,000	×	0.215	=	$21,500,000

Interest payments, due each six months for 20 periods:

		(Exhibit I-3) $n = 20, i = 8\%$		
$6,000,000	×	9.818	=	58,908,000**
		Total present value	=	$80,408,000

**Rounded (Present value factors have been rounded).

Consequently, the bonds will sell at $80,408,000 ($100 million face value, minus $19,592,000 discount), i.e., at a price of 80.408. This discount amount is valid because the bond is paying $6,000,000 whereas the semiannual market interest rate of 8% would have required a payment of $8,000,000. The difference of $2,000,000 × present value annuity factor 9.818 equals the discount amount of $19,592,000 (note: there are some rounding differences because the present value factors in the table have been rounded). If prospective bondholders were to deposit $80,408,000 in an account earning interest at 16% compounded semi-annually, they would be able to withdraw $6 million each six months and $100 million at the end of 10 years. For this reason, bond investors would be unwilling to pay more than $80,408,000 for the Marley Company bonds.

Upon issuing the bonds, Marley Company's cash and bonds payable (net of the bond discount) will increase by $80,408,000:

ASSETS	=	LIABILITIES	+	SHAREHOLDERS' EQUITY
Cash + $80,408,000		Bonds payable + $80,408,000		

Many firms record the bonds payable account at face value and the discount to a contra-liability account as follows:

ASSETS	=	LIABILITIES		+	SHAREHOLDERS' EQUITY
Cash		Bond payable	Discount on bonds payable		
+ 80,408,000		+ $100,000,000	– 19,592,000		

The discount represents additional interest to the bondholders. This compensates for the fact that the coupon interest payments are lower than those provided by competing investments. The total interest expense is determined as follows:

Total explicit interest payments	$120,000,000
Add: Bond discount	19,592,000
Total interest expense	$139,592,000

The amount of the interest expense to be recognized each interest period (an interest period is six months in this example) is based on the reported value of the bonds, also known as the carrying value, at the start of the interest period and the market rate of interest when the bonds were issued. Because Marley Company's bonds were sold on January 1, 2007, when the market rate of interest was 16% compounded semiannually, or 8% each six-month period, the interest expense during 2007, 2008, and the last year, 2016, would be determined as shown in Exhibit 9-1.

Whenever the periodic interest expense differs from the periodic cash payments to the bondholders, the reported value of the bonds will be adjusted for the difference. This adjustment is termed **amortization**. In Exhibit 9-1, note that the interest expense recorded in each period exceeds the cash interest ($6,000,000) that is paid to the bondholders. Because the actual interest expense incurred each period is greater than the amount that is paid currently to the bondholders, the reported value of the bonds (bonds payable net of the discount) increases each period. In fact, as shown in Exhibit 9-1, the reported value of the bonds will increase to exactly $100,000,000, the principal amount of the bonds, by the date that the bond issue matures (at the end of the year 2013). In other words,

EXHIBIT 9-1 CALCULATION OF INTEREST EXPENSE

Marley Company
Calculation of Interest Expense
Bonds Sold at a Discount

INTEREST PAYMENT DATE	(1) INTEREST EXPENSE	(2) INTEREST PAYMENT	(3) INCREASE IN REPORTED VALUE "DISCOUNT AMORTIZATION"	(4) REPORTED VALUE OF BONDS
January 1, 2007				$ 80,408,000
June 30, 2007	6,432,640	6,000,000	432,640	80,840,640
December 31, 2007	6,467,251	6,000,000	467,251	81,307,891
June 30, 2008	6,504,631	6,000,000	504,631	81,812,522
December 31, 2008	6,545,000	6,000,000	545,000	82,357,523
.	.	.	.	.
.	.	.	.	.
.	.	.	.	.
December 31, 2015	.	.	.	96,433,440
June 30, 2016	7,714,674	6,000,000	1,714,674	98,148,114
December 31, 2016	7,851,886	6,000,000	1,851,886	100,000,000

(1) Interest expense = market semi-annual interest rate 8% × reported value of bonds at beginning of the period
(2) Interest payment = coupon semi-annual interest rate 6% × face value of bonds
(3) Increase in reported value = column (1) interest expense minus column (2) interest payment
(4) Reported value of bonds at the end of the period = reported value of bonds at beginning of period + column (3) increase in reported value: discount amortization

Note: The reported value of the bonds increases each period because the interest expense exceeds the amount paid to the bondholders, which increases the company's obligation to the bondholders. At the maturity date of the bonds, the reported value will equal the principal (face) amount of $100 million.

the discount on the bonds will be completely amortized by that date, so the bonds will be reported at their face value of $100 million. The interest expense and bond coupon payment for the first six months in 2007 would be recorded in the following way:

ASSETS	=	LIABILITIES	+	SHAREHOLDERS' EQUITY
Cash – $6,000,000		Bonds payable + $432,640		Retained earnings – $6,432,640 (interest expense)

If a discount account is used, the accounting entry is as follows:

ASSETS	=	LIABILITIES		+	SHAREHOLDERS' EQUITY
Cash		Bond payable	Discount on Bonds Payable		Retained earnings
– $6,000,000			+ 432,640		– $6,432,640 (interest expense)

As you can see, because the cash payment required by the coupon rate of interest is less than the actual interest expense for the period, the amount of the liability must be increased for the difference. During the first interest period (January 1 to June 30, 2007), $432,640 of the bond discount has been amortized. The reported value of the bond has grown by $432,640 from $80,408,000 to $80,840,640.

Sale or Issuance of Bonds at a Premium

Suppose the market rate of interest on January 1, 2007, when the Marley Company bonds were sold, is below the coupon rate of 12%. In this case, investors would find the bonds to be quite attractive because the *coupon rate is higher than the market interest rate* available on other investments of equivalent risk. As a result, the market price of Marley's bonds increases. The bonds are issued at a **premium**, in other words, at an amount greater than the principal amount of $100 million. For example, if the market interest rate is 8% when the bonds are issued, investors will be willing to pay $127,140,000, a price of 127.14, determined as follows.

Principal, due in 20 six-month periods at 4% (half the 8% annual rate):

Amount	×	Present value factor (Exhibit I-2) $n = 20$, $i = 4\%$		
$100,000,000	×	0.456	=	$45,600,000

Interest payments, due each six months for 20 periods:

		(Exhibit I-3) $n = 20$, $i = 4\%$		
$6,000,000	×	13.590	=	81,540,000**
		Total present value	=	$127,140,000

**Rounded (Present value factors have been rounded).

Consequently, the bonds will sell at $127,140,000 ($100,000,000 face value + $27,140,000 premium). This premium is to compensate for the disparity in the interest rates. The bond is paying $6,000,000 every six months based on the coupon semi-annual rate of 6%. If the bond paid the market interest rate of 4%, the semi-annual interest payment would have been $4,000,000. This additional $27,140,000 ($2,000,000 payment × present value annuity factor 13.590) is the premium that the bond will command on the date of issue. Note that some rounding differences occur because the present value factors in the table are rounded.

Upon issuing the bonds, Marley Company's cash and bonds payable (net of the bond premium) will increase by $127,140,000:

ASSETS	=	LIABILITIES	+	SHAREHOLDERS' EQUITY
Cash + $127,140,000		Bonds payable + $127,140,000		

Many firms record the bonds payable account at face value and the premium to its own liability account as follows:

ASSETS	=	LIABILITIES		+	SHAREHOLDERS' EQUITY
Cash		Bond payable	Premium on bonds payable		
+ 127,140,000		+ $100,000,000	+ 27,140,000		

The total interest expense is determined as follows:

Total explicit interest payments	$120,000,000
Less: Bond premium	– 27,140,000
Total interest expense	$ 92,860,000

The amount of interest expense to be recognized each interest period (each six months in this example) is based on the reported value of the bonds at the start of the interest period. Exhibit 9-2 shows how the interest expense during 2007, 2008, and the last year of the bond, 2016, would be determined.

EXHIBIT 9-2 CALCULATION OF INTEREST EXPENSE

Marley Company
Calculation of Interest Expense
Bonds Sold at a Premium

INTEREST PAYMENT DATE	(1) INTEREST EXPENSE	(2) INTEREST PAYMENT	(3) DECREASE IN REPORTED VALUE "PREMIUM AMORTIZATION"	(4) REPORTED VALUE OF BONDS
January 1, 2007				$127,140,000
June 30, 2007	5,085,600	6,000,000	(914,400)	126,225,600
December 31, 2007	5,049,024	6,000,000	(950,976)	125,274,624
June 30, 2008	5,010,985	6,000,000	(989,015)	124,285,609
December 31, 2008	4,971,424	6,000,000	(1,028,576)	123,257,033
.	.	.	.	.
.	.	.	.	.
.	.	.	.	.
December 31, 2015	.	.	.	103,772,411
June 30, 2016	4,150,896	6,000,000	(1,849,104)	101,923,307
December 31, 2016	4,076,693	6,000,000	(1,923,307)	100,000,000

(1) Interest expense = market semi-annual interest rate 4% × reported value of bonds at beginning of the period
(2) Interest payment = coupon semi-annual interest rate 6% × face value of bonds
(3) Decrease in reported value = column (1) interest expense minus column (2) interest payment
(4) Reported value of bonds at the end of the period = reported value of bonds at beginning of period − column (3) decrease in reported value: premium amortization

Note: The reported value of the bonds decreases each period because the amount paid to the bondholders exceeds the interest expense, which decreases the company's obligation to the bondholders. On the maturity date of the bonds, the reported value will equal the principal (face) amount of $100 million.

The amount of this interest expense to be recognized in each period would be determined as before; the reported value of the bonds at the start of each interest period would be multiplied by the market rate of interest when the bonds were issued. The logic of this calculation is the same as that shown in Exhibit 9-1 for the case of bonds sold at a discount. The total interest expense incurred by Marley Company over the life of bonds sold at a premium will be less than the total interest coupons paid. In effect, the premium represents a reduction in interest paid to the bondholders, to compensate for the fact that the coupon rate is too high.

The interest expense and bond coupon payment for the first six months in 2007 would be recorded in the following way:

ASSETS	=	LIABILITIES	+	SHAREHOLDERS' EQUITY
Cash – $6,000,000		Bonds payable – $914,400		Retained earnings – $5,085,600 (interest expense)

If the initial entry was recorded to the premium account the accounting entry would be as follows:

ASSETS	=	LIABILITIES		+	SHAREHOLDERS' EQUITY
Cash		Bond payable	Premium on bonds payable		Retained earnings
– $6,000,000			– $914,400		– $5,085,600 (interest expense)

As you can see, because the cash payment required by the coupon rate of interest is more than the actual interest expense for the period, the amount of the liability must be decreased for the difference. During the first interest period (January 1 to June 30, 2007), $914,400 of the bond premium has been amortized. The reported value of the bond has decreased by $914,400 from $127,140,000 to $126,225,600.

Early Retirement of Bonds

After bonds are sold to investors, they are often subsequently traded (bought and sold) among investors. The market value of bonds that are traded among investors varies from day to day as prevailing interest rates rise and fall. This occurs because the bond contract specifies the cash payments that will be made to bondholfers, and the present value of a given set of future cash flows changes whenever there is a change in the rates used to make the present value calculations. From early 2001 to mid-2004 the Federal Reserve, our monetary authority, consistently decreased interest rates in an attempt to boost the economy. During that time, the decline in interest rates greatly impacted the bond market because existing corporate bonds paying higher coupon interest payments substantially increased in value. Since that time, the Federal Reserve has steadily increased interest rates, which in turn has decreased the value of these same corporate bonds.

Bear in mind, though, that *fluctuations in the market prices of outstanding bonds do not result in additional cash inflows and outflows for the issuing company.* Consistent with the historical cost principle, the reported value of bonds in the financial statements of the issuing company is not revised to reflect changes in market interest rates and market prices of the outstanding bonds. Changing interest rates may motivate firms to buy back their outstanding bonds prior to their scheduled maturity dates.

For example, in the mid 1970s interest rates were extremely high. At that time many companies had outstanding bond issues with very low coupon interest paying rates because these bonds were issued in the 1960s when interest rates were very low. This disparity in the market and coupon interest rates caused a significant decline in the market value of these bonds. Keep in mind that a decline results because the remaining cash payments (principal and interest coupons) are discounted by lenders at the higher market interest rates. Companies decided to retire their bonds early by repurchasing them in the market place. The purchase price paid was less than the reported value (carrying value) of these bonds thus creating large accounting gains on these companies' income statements.

Similarly, managers can use bond repurchases as a means of "smoothing" fluctuations in income. For example, in periods of poor operating performance, managers can improve reported income merely by repurchasing outstanding bonds with market values below their reported values. Moreover, firms that retire bonds early often issue additional bonds in order to replace the retired debt. This practice has the appearance of "paper shuffling" because the firm's debt position is essentially unchanged, but substantial gains have been included in income. Also, because firms must issue new debt at higher interest rates in order to retire older debt bearing lower interest rates, future periods will report higher interest expenses and lower net income.

It is interesting to note that with the large number of companies recording gains from early retirement of bonds in the mid-1970s, the FASB jumped in and prevented companies from reporting these material gains as part of their ordinary income from continuing operations and required, instead, that these types of gains/losses be classified as extraordinary items. Recall from our discussion of the income statement in Chapter 4, that extraordinary gains and losses are reported in a separate section of the income statement, separate from the calculation of the firm's income from ongoing or recurring operations.

With the decline of market interest rates in the early 2000's, companies had begun to repurchase their higher paying coupon interest rate bond issues and extinguishing them. This early retirement caused the recognition of losses but it also allowed companies to issue new bonds at much lower interest rates. Of note is that in 2002, with losses being recognized by companies in this manner, the FASB rescinded its requirement of classifying material gains/losses from early extinguishment of bonds are extraordinary items. Such gains and losses are instead shown as part of ordinary income.

Illustration of Early Extinguishment

Assume that Marley Company issued bonds at par early in 2007, and that interest rates have risen subsequently. When interest rates rise, the market values of outstanding bonds decline because the remaining cash payments (principal and interest coupons) are discounted by lenders at higher rates. If we assume that Marley repurchases bonds with a $100 million reported value at a market value of $85 million, the firm would report a gain of $15 million:

Reported value of bonds payable	$100,000,000
Cost to repurchase bonds payable	– 85,000,000
Gain on repurchase of bonds	$ 15,000,000

This transaction would be recognized in Marley's financial statements in the following way:

ASSETS	=	LIABILITIES	+	SHAREHOLDERS' EQUITY
Cash – $85,000,000		Bonds payable – $100,000,000		Retained earnings + $15,000,000 (gain)

The now notorious company, WorldCom, Inc., in May 2001, had the largest U.S. corporate bond issue in history topping out at a whopping $11.9 billion. Due to the risky telecommunications industry that WorldCom was a part of, the company had to pay 7.6% interest rate, which was more than 2.5 percentage points higher than the U.S. Treasury rate. Less than one year later World Com was charged with erroneously capitalizing as assets $3.8 billion in expenses for local phone access charges. WorldCom's bonds were subsequently downgraded to junk bond status and in the summer of 2002, the company filed for bankruptcy, the largest bankruptcy ever declared in the United States. (SOURCE: Gregory Zuckerman, "WorldCom's $11.9 Billion Bond Offering Draws Investors Woes of Telecoms," *The Wall Street Journal,* May 10, 2001, p. C1).

A list of the top 10 U.S. corporate bond deals in history is shown in Exhibit 9-3 (Ibid.).

Reality Check 9-1 shows the composition of long-term debt for a major company that has debt issued at a variety of different interest rates.

EXHIBIT 9-3 TOP 10 U.S. CORPORATE BOND DEALS

ISSUER	DATE	AMOUNT (IN BILLIONS)
WorldCom	May 9, 2001	$11.9
Ford Motor	July 9, 1999	8.6
AT&T	March 23, 1999	8.0
Daimler-Chrysler	January 11, 2001	6.6
AT&T Wireless Services	March 1, 2001	6.5
RJR Holdings	May 12, 1989	6.1
WorldCom	August 6, 1998	6.1
AT&T	July 10, 2000	6.0
Ford Motor Credit	July 26, 2000	6.0
Morgan Stanley	April 18, 2001	6.0

REALITY CHECK 9-1

Johnson & Johnson Corporation, a global pharmaceutical company, includes the following information in a footnote describing the long-term debt reported in its 2005 financial statements:

Long-term debt (partial)	*(Dollars in millions)*
4.95% Debentures due 2033 (4.95% effective rate)	$500
6.73% Debentures due 2023 (6.73% effective rate)	250
3% Zero Coupon Convertible Subordinated Debentures due 2020 (3% effective rate)	202
Notes payable –	
6.95% Notes due 2029, (7.14% effective rate)	293
6.625% Notes due 2009 (6.80% effective rate)	198

Required

a. Why do the interest rates differ among the various debt issues reported by Johnson & Johnson?
b. Why is the information concerning the due dates of J&J's debt useful to the analyst?
c. Note that the coupon rates and effective interest rates differ for some of J&J's debt issues. Based on the information provided above, which, if any, of these issues was sold at par or face value; at a discount; at a premium?
d. Assume that the market rate of interest on similar debt is 7% at the balance sheet date. If so, would the market values of the first two issues listed above be greater or less than their book values? Explain.
e. Based on your answer to part d, if J&J's management wished to report a gain on early debt retirement, which of the issues would be retired?

SOLUTION

a. The primary reason that interest rates differ among debt issues is that interest rates prevailing in financial markets change over time. Consequently, some debt is issued when interest rates in general are relatively high, and other debt is issued when interest rates in general are relatively low.

In addition, interest rates may differ because of the features of individual debt issues. For example, J&J's zero coupon convertible subordinated debentures have a very low interest rate (3%). A convertible debenture allows the investor to trade in the bond certificates for a predetermined amount of the company's stock certificates. This feature is attractive to investors, so lenders are willing to accept a lower rate of interest.

b. The information about the maturity dates of J&J's outstanding debt is useful to the analyst in predicting the firm's future cash flows. The company must generate sufficient cash to retire the debt from operating cash flows and/or from additional borrowings and shareholders' investments.

c. All three of the debentures were issued at par because the coupon paying interest rate and the effective (market) interest rate (locked in at date of issue) are the same. The effective interest rates on the two notes, due 2009 and due 2029, are higher than the coupon rates implying that these two issues were sold at a discount.

There were no debentures or notes sold at a premium. If there had been the coupon rate would have shown a higher interest rate than the effective interest rate.

d. A market rate of interest of 7% would exceed the 4.95% and 6.73% effective rates of the issues due 2033 and 2023, respectively, so both issues would have a market price that is below its book value. Conversely, a market rate of interest of 6% would be less than the 6.73% effective rate of the issue due 2023, so this issue would have a market price that is above its book value.

e. In order to report a gain, management could retire either the issue due 2033 or due 2023. The reported gain would be the difference between the book value and the (lower) market value (the buy back price) of the issue.

WHERE'S THE CASH?

We have discussed so far how bond issues impact earnings with the recording of periodic interest expense and at early retirement with the recognition of gains and losses. Keep in mind, though, that interest expense is not necessarily what a firm actually pays and gains/losses are noncash items.

Let's revisit our earlier example where the Marley Company issued $100 million bonds at a premium. Recall that the coupon annual interest rate was 12% and the effective market interest rate was 8%. Below is a partial amortization table for this bond: (Refer to Exhibit 9-2.)

Interest payment date	*Interest expense*	*Interest payment*	*Increase in reported value: Premium amortization*	*Reported value of bonds*
January 1, 2007				$127,140,000
June 30, 2007	5,085,600	6,000,000	(914,400)	126,225,600
December 31, 2007	5,049,024	6,000,000	(950,976)	125,274,624

Assume that after the interest payment made on December 31, 2006, Marley retired its bonds early by repurchasing them at 98% of face value, $98,000,000. Note that the prevailing market interest rate at the time of buy back has risen above the coupon annual rate of 12% causing the market value of the bond to fall below its face value. Now Marley only has to pay 98% of face value for bonds that were originally issued on January 1, 2006 at approximately 127% of face value because the market interest rate was well below the coupon rate. The large gain on the buy back is shown below (assume the premium is netted into the bonds payable):

ASSETS	=	LIABILITIES	+	SHAREHOLDERS' EQUITY
Cash – $98,000,000		Bonds payable – $125,274,624		Retained earnings + $27,274,624 (gain)

Now, assume that Marley's 2007 income before interest expense and the gain consisted of revenues all received in cash of $200 million and operating expenses all paid in cash of $20 million. Ignoring income taxes, the net income reported on the income statement would be:

Revenues	$200,000,000
Operating expenses	– 20,000,000
Income before interest expense and gain on early extinguishment	180,000,000
Less: interest expense (5,085,600 + 5,049,024)	– 10,134,624
Plus: gain on early extinguishment	+ 27,274,624
Net income	$197,140,000

Aside from the cash received and the cash paid from issuing and subsequently retiring the bond, which are financing activities, what were Marley's cash flows from operating activities for 2007?

Cash received from customers	$200,000,000
Cash paid for operating expenses	– 20,000,000
Cash paid for interest June 30, 2007	– 6,000,000
Cash paid for interest December 31, 2007	– 6,000,000
Cash flow provided by operating activities	$168,000,000

Note that the net income shows $29,140,000 more income than the actual cash flows from operations. An investor might be mistaken into believing that this is really income produced from its operations when in reality the majority of the difference stems from the fact that the firm timed the buy back of its bonds so that it paid far less by re-purchasing the bonds than it had received when originally issuing the bonds.

Early Extinguishment of Debt: Target Corporation

Target took advantage of declining interest rates by repurchasing a portion of its debt and reissuing new debt at much lower interest rates. During 2004, according to Target's long-term debt footnote (Appendix C), in addition to required principal payments of $945 million, Target repurchased $542 million of its long-term debt at an average interest rate of almost 7%. The repurchase resulted in a $89 million loss. According to the newly revised accounting rules, this loss was reported as part of income from continuing operations instead of an extraordinary item, as the superceded rules would have required.

Other Aspects of Borrowing Agreements

In addition to specifying payments of principal and interest, borrowing agreements (indentures) can include a variety of other provisions that are important to users of financial statements. These provisions are added to make the debt issues more attractive to prospective lenders. Common provisions include restrictive covenants, collateral, and convertibility.

Restrictive Covenants

Borrowers may agree to various restrictions on management's ability to invest, pay dividends, incur additional debt, or take other actions that can affect the firm's ability to meet its repayment obligations. Such **restrictive covenants** are often based on accounting measures of assets, liabilities, and/or income. Violation of these restrictions constitutes technical default on the debt and may allow lenders to increase interest rates or impose other penalties on the borrower.

Exhibit 9-4 shows a portion of the footnote disclosures included in The Sherwin-Williams Company's financial statements, describing restrictive covenants related to the company's long-term debt. These agreements require Sherwin-Williams to maintain certain financial ratios and limits Sherwin-Williams capital asset expenditures and its payment of dividends.

The existence and the nature of restrictive covenants are an important concern to analysts of financial reports. *Restrictions that are based directly on accounting measurements, such as working capital (current assets minus current liabilities) and net worth (total assets minus total liabilities, which we have already described as net assets), can affect the choice of accounting methods in use by the firm.*

To illustrate, recall that in periods of rising costs the FIFO method of inventory costing results in higher reported profits and inventory valuations than does LIFO. Also, the straight-line method of depreciating plant and equipment results in lower depreciation charges and higher asset valuations than do accelerated methods of depreciation. Consequently, managers who face restrictive covenants that are based on asset values, income, or net worth would be more likely to choose FIFO rather than LIFO costing for inventories, despite possibly paying higher taxes. They would also probably choose straight-line rather than accelerated depreciation methods for long-lived assets.

Debt covenant restrictions can be affected by changes in GAAP, such as new FASB statements. For instance, if a firm is approaching the minimum limits of

EXHIBIT 9-4 SAMPLE OF FOOTNOTE DISCLOSURES OF RESTRICTIVE COVENANTS

The Sherwin-Williams Company
2005 Annual Report

Note 7—Debt (Partial)

Maturities of long-term debt are as follows for the next five years (in thousands of dollars): $10,493 in 2006; $197,405 in 2007; $65 in 2008; $65 in 2009, and $65 in 2010. Interest expense on long-term debt was $37,201, $37,315, and $37,460 for 2005, 2004 and 2003, respectively.

Among other restrictions, the Company's Notes, Debentures and revolving credit agreements contain certain covenants relating to liens, rating changes, merger and sale of assets, consolidated leverage and change of control as definied in the agreements. In the event of default under any one of these arrangements, acceleration of the maturity of any one or more of these borrowings may result. The Company was in compliance with all convenants for all years presented.

working capital or net worth specified in its lending agreements, management is likely to favor accounting standards that increase reported asset valuations and net worth. Management is also likely to oppose prospective new accounting standards that would make violations of these restrictions more likely. Some debt contracts provide for exceptions or adjustments to the restrictions if there are subsequent changes in GAAP. Another example of restrictive covenants on long-term borrowings is provided in Reality Check 9-2.

Collateral

Debt agreements sometimes require that specific assets of the firm be pledged as security in the event of default by the borrower. These assets are termed **collateral.** Mortgages on office buildings, plant, and equipment are frequent examples, especially in transportation industries such as airlines, railroads, and trucking companies. On the other hand, lenders are sometimes reluctant to accept as collateral a business asset that has limited resale value or alternative use. In these cases, the lender may require that a **sinking fund** be established to secure the debt. The sinking fund is segregated cash and/or other liquid temporary investments, usually administered by an independent trustee or financial institution and pledged as collateral to retire a specific bond or note.

REALITY CHECK 9-2

The following information concerning restrictive covenants has been adapted from footnotes to the financial statements of Nucleum Metallurgy, Inc., a metallurgical technology firm:

The Industrial Revenue Bonds (IRBs) outstanding consist of two note issues. The interest rates on these notes range from 66.5% to 70% of the bank's prime interest rate. These notes are secured by property, plant, and equipment. The IRBs contain restrictive covenants including, among others, a requirement to maintain minimum working capital, consolidated net worth, and a minimum current ratio.

The following amounts appear on the year-end balance sheet:

Current assets	$18,633,000
Total assets	35,118,000
Current liabilities	9,384,000
Total liabilities	10,878,000

Required

a. Assume for purposes of illustration that Nucleum Metallurgy, Inc.'s restrictive covenants require minimum working capital of $7,000,000, consolidated net worth of not less than $20,000,000, and current assets greater than 150% of current liabilities. Would the firm be in compliance with these covenants at the end of the year?

b. By how much might the firm's current assets decrease and still not violate the working capital restriction? (Assume that current liabilities remain constant.)

c. By how much might the firm's current assets decrease and still not violate the current ratio constraint? (Assume that current liabilities remain constant.)

d. Why might lenders restrict both the current ratio and the dollar amount of working capital in restrictive covenants?

SOLUTION

a. Evaluation of compliance with restrictive covenants:

Minimum working capital of $7,000,000:

Current assets	$18,633,000
Less: Current liabilities	– 9,384,000
Working capital	$ 9,249,000

Therefore, the firm complies with the minimum working capital restriction.

Current ratio of 150% (or 1.5):

$$\text{Current ratio} = \frac{\text{Current assets}}{\text{Current liabilities}}$$

$$198.6\% \text{ (or } 1.986) = \frac{\$18{,}633{,}000}{\$9{,}384{,}000}$$

Therefore, the firm complies with the current ratio restriction.

Net worth of $20,000,000:

Net worth	=	Total assets less total liabilities
$24,240,000	=	$35,118,000 – $10,878,000

Therefore, the firm complies with the net worth restriction.

b. The firm's current assets might decrease up to $2,249,000 before violating the working capital restriction:

Actual working capital (see calculation in part a)	$9,249,000
Working capital restriction	– 7,000,000
Excess over restriction	$2,249,000

c. The firm's current assets might decrease to $4,557,000 before violating the current ratio restriction:

Actual current assets	$18,633,000
Current liabilities × 150% ($9,384,000 × 1.5)	– 14,076,000
Difference	$ 4,557,000

d. Lenders may restrict both the current ratio and the dollar amount of working capital for the following reason. Long-term borrowings extend over many years and during that time the firm's operating level may change substantially. For lower levels of output, the firm may have relatively small amounts of current assets and liabilities, and a high current ratio would not provide much protection for long-term lenders. In this case, the dollar amount of working capital is an important feature. At higher levels of output, when current assets and liabilities are relatively large, a high current ratio offers stronger protection to the long-term creditors.

Convertibility

An attractive feature to many investors is the right to exchange debt instruments for other securities, usually common stock of the borrowing firm. **Convertible bonds** give the bondholder the option to exchange bonds for a predetermined number of shares of stock. If the stock price subsequently increases above the value of the bonds, the bondholders will likely convert their holdings to stock. Conversely, if the stock price remains below the value of the debt, the bondholders will continue to collect interest and will receive the bond principal at maturity. Convertible debt is described in more detail in Chapter 10, which discusses shareholders' equity.

FINANCIAL REPORTING FOR INCOME TAXES

Corporations measure income for financial reporting and income tax purposes, and the objectives of these measurements differ. *Income measures for financial reporting purposes should help financial analysts to assess the firm's future ability to generate cash. Income measures for income tax purposes, on the other hand, must comply with the relevant provisions of the Internal Revenue Service (IRS) tax code.* IRS regulations reflect the objectives of government fiscal policy, rather than the objectives of financial analysis and reporting.

Book and Tax Differences

Because of these differing objectives, revenue and expense measurements that are used to determine taxable income may differ from those used in financial reporting. Accountants distinguish between book and tax measurements, such that book measurements are used for financial reporting purposes, while tax measurements must comply with income tax laws.

In most cases, differences between book and tax measurements create **temporary** differences in asset and/or liability values. In order to stimulate purchases of property, plant, and equipment, for example, the U.S. government allows firms to depreciate such assets quickly for tax purposes. Firms can thereby reduce their income taxes in the earlier years after purchasing such assets. This accelerated depreciation usually exceeds the amount of depreciation expense that is used for financial accounting measurements of income. In later years, however, the situation is reversed. Financial statements continue to report depreciation expense, although the asset is already fully depreciated for tax purposes.

Accounting standards for reporting income tax expenses and liabilities reflect a basic premise: *all events that affect the tax impact of temporary differences should be recognized currently in the financial statements.* Broadly, two types of events can affect these expected tax impacts: (1) a change in the amount of temporary differences between the book and the tax bases of a firm's assets (or liabilities) and (2) a change in tax rates that will apply to those temporary differences.

To illustrate the measurement of income tax expenses and liabilities, consider the information provided in Exhibit 9-5 about the financial statement and income tax accounting used by Dorian Company to account for its plant and equipment. As shown in Exhibit 9-5, Dorian uses the straight-line method of depreciation for financial reporting purposes and an accelerated method of depreciation for income tax purposes. As a result, the financial statement carrying value, or book basis, of these assets is $700 million at December 31, 2007, and the **tax basis** of these assets is $300 million. The book and tax bases of Dorian's plant and equipment differ by $400 million:

Book basis of plant and equipment	$700 million
Tax basis of plant and equipment	300 million
Difference	$400 million

EXHIBIT 9-5 DEPRECIATION FOR BOOK AND TAX PURPOSES

Dorian Company
Depreciation of Plant and Equipment for Book and Tax Purposes, 2008

ON DECEMBER 31, 2007:	**BOOK**	**TAX**
Plant and equipment, original cost	$ 900 million	$900 million
Accumulated depreciation	200 million[a]	600 million[b]
Basis	$ 700 million	$300 million
During 2008:		
Income tax rate	35%	35%
Income before depreciation	$ 250 million	$250 million
Depreciation	60 million	150 million
Pre-tax income	$ 190 million	$100 million

ON DECEMBER 31, 2008:	**BOOK**	**TAX**
Plant and equipment, original cost	$ 900 million	$900 million
Accumulated depreciation	260 million	750 million
Basis	$ 640 million	$150 million
Income tax actually payable for 2008:		
Income before depreciation	$ 250 million	
Tax depreciation	– 150 million	
Taxable income	100 million	
Income tax rate	× 35%	
Tax actually payable	$ 35 million	

[a] Straight-line depreciation is used for financial reporting.
[b] Accelerated depreciation is used for tax reporting.

Note that the $400 million difference represents depreciation expense already recorded on the firm's tax records whereas it has not yet been reflected on the GAAP books. This temporary difference will turn around in the future such that the tax records will show $400 million less depreciation than the GAAP books. This will require more taxes to be paid in the future. This results in a deferred tax liability.

Deferred Tax Liability

Because temporary differences such as those resulting from accelerated tax depreciation only allow a firm to postpone its tax payments to later years, the postponed taxes will be paid eventually. For this reason, accounting standards require that firms recognize a **deferred income tax liability** for such future income taxes.

The measurement of a firm's deferred income tax liability is obtained by multiplying the difference between the asset's book and tax bases by the appropriate income tax rate.

Dorian Company's income tax rate is expected to be 35% over the relevant future. Consequently, Dorian's deferred tax liability at December 31, 2007, is $140 million, computed as follows:

Excess of book over tax basis of plant and equipment	$400 million
Income tax rate	× 35%
Deferred tax liability, December 31, 2007	$140 million

Income tax expense reported in the financial statements is computed in the following manner:

Income tax actually payable		$XXX
Increase (decrease) in deferred tax liability	+(–)	YYY
Total income tax expense		$ZZZ

To illustrate, refer again to Exhibit 9-5, which shows that during 2008 Dorian's tax depreciation exceeds the book depreciation of the plant and equipment by $90 million ($150 million – $60 million). As a result, the difference between the tax and book bases of these assets has increased by $90 million, and the amount of the deferred tax liability has increased by $31.5 million, computed as follows:

Book basis of plant and equipment, December 31, 2008	$ 640 million
Less: Tax basis of plant and equipment, December 31, 2008	– 150 million
Difference at December 31, 2008	490 million
Income tax rate	× 35%
Deferred tax liability, December 31, 2008	$ 171.5 million
Less: Deferred tax liability, December 31, 2007	– 140.0 million
Increase in deferred tax liability during 2008	$ 31.5 million

Dorian's 2008 income tax expense is the sum of the amount actually payable, $35 million (shown in Exhibit 9-5), and the increase in the deferred tax liability during 2008 computed above:

Income tax payable (Exhibit 9-5)	$35.0 million
Plus: Increase in deferred tax liability	31.5 million
Total income tax expense	$66.5 million

This tax expense would affect Dorian's financial statements in the following manner:

ASSETS	=	LIABILITIES	+	SHAREHOLDERS' EQUITY
Cash – $35 million		Deferred taxes + $31.5 million		Retained earnings – $66.5 million (income tax expense)

Note that the income tax expense of $66.5 million is equal to 35% of Dorian's reported pre-tax income of $190 million. This relationship occurs because our example assumes that tax rates remain stable at 35%. On the other hand, the percentage relationship of the income tax actually payable, $35 million, to Dorian's pre-tax income is just 18.4% ($35 million / $190 million). If this amount were to be reported as income tax expense on the income statement, investors might be misled about Dorian's true tax burden. For this reason, deferred tax accounting appears to provide a better matching of expenses on the income statement, at least when tax rates are expected to be stable over time. Reality Check 9-3 illustrates the relationships between income tax expenses, tax payments, and effective tax rates for a large U.S. firm.

Historically, tax rates in the U.S. have been relatively stable. In the third quarter of 1993, however, a new deficit-reduction law raised the corporate tax rate from 34 to 35%. This apparently minor adjustment in tax rates required that firms revalue their deferred tax liabilities upward by about 2.9% (1% rate increase / 34% old rate). Because accounting standards require this adjustment to be included in the calculation of tax expense for the quarter in which the new tax law is signed, many firms experienced a considerable drop in the forecast for third-quarter profits. As examples, International Paper's profit forecast fell by 50.8%, and Georgia Pacific's forecasted profits were revised to a forecasted loss.

WHERE'S THE CASH?

The income tax expense or benefit (for losses) on the income statement is a combination of the income taxes currently owed as well as any deferred income taxes. As such, this expense is not the actual cash paid for income taxes. Since it can be difficult for a financial statement user to determine the actual cash paid for income taxes the FASB requires firms to report this amount either at the bottom of the cash flow statement or in a supplemental schedule.

Other Aspects of Income Tax Reporting

The discussion thus far of income tax reporting has emphasized the issue of accelerated depreciation. This focus is appropriate because the predominant portion of temporary differences between the book and the tax bases of U.S. firms' corporate assets is due to differences in tax and book depreciation.

REALITY CHECK 9-3

Alcoa (Aluminum Company of America) reported the following information in its 2005 financial report:

	(Dollars in millions) 2005	2004
Income before income taxes	$1,933	$2,165
Provision (expense) for income tax	441	543
Income taxes paid currently	413	294
Deferred tax liabilities related to depreciating assets at December 31, 2004 and 2005	1,432	1,434

Required

Based solely on the information provided above

a. Determine Alcoa's effective income tax rate during 2005.

b. Determine the percentage relation between Alcoa's actual tax payments and income before taxes during 2005.

c. Provide a likely reason for the difference between the percentages determined in parts a and b above.

d. Assume that Alcoa's statutory tax rate is 35 percent. What would you estimate as the difference between the tax basis and the book basis of Alcoa's depreciable assets at the end of 2005?

SOLUTION

a. Alcoa's effective tax rate during 2005 is the percentage relation of the provision for income tax ($441 million) to income before income tax ($1,933 million), which equals 22.81% or 23% ($413/$1,933).

b. Alcoa's tax payments of $413 million are 21% percent of income before taxes ($413/$1,933).

c. A likely reason for the fact that Alcoa's effective tax rate is above the percentage of income actually paid in income taxes during 2005 is that Alcoa's 2005 income is more than its income reported in 2004. In addition, taxable income may be less than the amount of income recognized in Alcoa's financial statements. This may be due to timing differences in recognizing revenues (such as lower revenues recognized for tax purposes) or in recognizing expenses (such as higher expenses recognized for tax purposes).

d. If Alcoa's statutory tax rate is 35%, the differences between the tax and book bases of the depreciating assets may be estimated as follows:

Deferred tax liabilities related to depreciation	$1,933
Tax rate of 35%	÷ 35%
Difference in tax basis and book basis of depreciable assets	$5,523

Tax and book income measurements differ, however, for many other reasons. For example, revenue and expense measurements in areas such as leasing, warranties, debt refinancing, exchanges of assets, and various other areas are treated differently for tax and book purposes. In some cases, the differences result in postponements of taxable income (as with accelerated depreciation). In other cases, however, the different treatments result in earlier recognition of taxable income. As a result, some firms may report deferred tax assets, rather than deferred tax liabilities. Exhibit 9-6 shows the reasons why the tax and book bases of various assets and liabilities differ for a major U.S. firm. Although further discussion of these other types of temporary differences is too specialized for this text, the basic framework that was used in calculating tax differences due to differences in depreciation methods applies in many other areas.

In addition to timing differences that give rise to deferred tax assets and liabilities, there are various other reasons why the percentage relation between a firm's reported pre-tax income and its income tax expense may differ from the Federal statutory corporate tax rate, which is currently 35%. For this reason, firms are required to disclose the causes of any significant differences between the statutory and the **effective tax rate** in the footnotes to the financial statements. *The effective*

EXHIBIT 9-6 **COMPOSITION OF DEFERRED TAX ASSETS AND LIABILITIES**

Timberland Corporation
(known for its rugged footwear products)
Footnote disclosures of deferred tax items

(Adapted from the 2005 annual report)

	DOLLARS IN THOUSANDS			
DECEMBER 31,	**2005**		**2004**	
CURRENT:	**ASSETS**	**LIABILITIES**	**ASSETS**	**LIABILITIES**
Inventory difference	$ 5,163	$ —	$ 3,754	$ —
Receivable allowance	14,877	—	14,254	—
Employee benefits accruals	4,210	—	2,261	—
Forward currency contracts	—	(302)	5,868	—
Other	2,986	—	2,800	—
Total current	$27,236	$ (302)	$28,937	$ —
NONCURRENT:				
Accelerated depreciation and amortization	$ 301	$ —	$ 4,025	$ —
Puerto Rico tollgate taxes	—	(2,470)	—	(2,470)
Undistributed foreign earnings	—	(5,554)	—	(7,985)
Other	1,471	—	—	(4,345)
Net operating loss carryforwards	806	—	512	—
Less valuation allowance	(806)	—	(512)	—
Deferred compensation	5,177	—	3,507	—
Total noncurrent	$ 6,949	$(8,024)	$ 7,532	$(14,800)

tax rate is the reported income tax expense as a percentage of reported income before tax. Exhibit 9-7 provides an example of such a disclosure. Note that for a given firm, effective tax rates can be either above or below the federal **statutory rate.** Some differences between these rates may be relatively stable over time (such as state and local taxes), and other causes may vary in their effects over time (such as settlements and adjustments of prior years' taxes).

EXHIBIT 9-7 **RECONCILIATION OF STATUTORY AND EFFECTIVE TAX RATE**

Timberland Corporation
Footnote disclosures of income tax rates

(Adapted from the 2005 annual report)

The provision for income taxes differs from the amount computed using the statutory federal income tax rate of 35% due to the following:

DECEMBER 31	2005	2004
Federal income tax at statutory rate	35.0%	35.0%
Federal tax exempt operation in Puerto Rico	(1.6)	(1.5)
State taxes, net of applicable federal benefit	2.7	3.1
Other	(2.2)	(1.1)
Effective income tax rate	33.9%	35.5%

Effective Tax Rate: Target Corporation

According to Target's income tax footnote (Appendix C), the effective tax rate for all three years: 2003–2005 was approximately 38%. The main difference between the effective tax rate and the Federal statutory tax rate of 35% was due to state income taxes of approximately 3%.

Deferred Taxes and the Liability Concept

Present financial reporting standards emphasize that deferred tax obligations are liabilities. In some respects, however, the manner in which deferred tax obligations are classified and measured is inconsistent with liability reporting.

Generally, business liabilities are classified as current or noncurrent based on the length of time to repayment. Deferred tax obligations, in contrast, are classified based on the current versus noncurrent classification of the related asset. Depreciating assets are classified as noncurrent assets, for example, and the related deferred tax obligations are also classified as noncurrent for this reason. Accounting literature does not provide any compelling reason for this practice.

Generally, long-term obligations are reported at their present values; in other words, the future payments are discounted to the present at an appropriate rate of interest. Deferred tax obligations are not discounted, however, even in cases where the temporary differences are not expected to reverse for many years. Consequently, managers and investment analysts often argue that the amounts reported as deferred tax obligations are substantial overstatements of these liabilities' economic value.

SUMMARY OF CASH FLOW IMPACT OF BONDS AND DEFERRED TAXES

Bonds

It is important to remember that the periodic cash payments made by a firm to its bondholders are based on the coupon interest rate stated in the bond contract. The interest expense, though, is based on the market interest rate determined at the time the bonds are issued. A disparity in these two interest rates will result in periodic operating cash flow payments differing from the periodic interest expense recognized on the income statement. In addition, since market interest rates are constantly changing, the fair value of a firm's bonds fluctuates. A firm can buy back its bonds before maturity and time the re-purchase so that the market value of the bonds is less than the carrying value of the bonds. This can create accounting gains that boost a firm's net income but the gain does not increase the firm's operating cash flows.

Deferred Taxes

Because firms must keep two "sets of books", one for financial accounting and one for income tax accounting, temporary differences can result in the assets and/or liability balances. Generally accepted accounting principles (GAAP) require that the income tax effect of these temporary differences be recognized currently. As a result, the income tax expense on the income statement can be very different from what a firm actually pays in income taxes during the year.

In terms of cash flows, a firm must disclose the income taxes it actually pays during the year. Remember to review this information along with the firm's income tax footnote disclosure. Also, keep in mind that the income tax expense on the income statement may never equal what a firm has to pay because temporary differences will constantly arise that affect income tax expense but do not affect operating cash flows.

Summary of Learning Objectives

1. **Recognize the types of noncurrent obligations that are reported by business firms.**
   The major portion of long-term debt that is reported on corporate balance sheets consists of notes and bonds payable. Many corporations also report substantial obligations for deferred income taxes.

2. **Describe the different features of long-term borrowing contracts, such as notes and bonds payable.**
   Notes payable represent direct borrowings by the firm from banks or other lenders. The note is a formal contract to repay a specific amount at a definite future date. Most notes require interest payments periodically over the life of the loan. Some notes do not entail periodic interest payments and instead are sold at a discount to compensate lenders for the use of their funds. Bonds payable constitute a major form of borrowed capital for business corporations. They are contracts that obligate the issuing corporation to make periodic interest payments and to repay the principal at a specified maturity date. Bonds are sold to investors and are actively traded among investors subsequent to their issuance. The amount that the issuing firm receives for its bonds depends on the relationship between the coupon or face rate of interest and the market rate of interest when the bonds are issued. Bonds will sell at par (face) value if the coupon and market rates are equal; they will sell at a discount if the market interest rate exceeds the coupon rate or at a premium if the coupon rate exceeds the market rate.

3. **Determine periodic interest expense and the value of noncurrent obligations in financial reports.**
   Firms use compound interest calculations to determine the periodic interest expense and balance sheet valuation of bonds payable. Fluctuations in the market prices of bonds payable that occur subsequent to their issuance are not reflected in the financial statements. If firms retire bonds early, or before the maturity date, any difference between the carrying value and the cost to retire the bonds is reported as a gain or loss.

4. **Understand how managers can "smooth" fluctuations in earnings by bond repurchases.**
   Managers can improve reported earnings in periods of poor operating performance by merely repurchasing outstanding bonds with market values below their reported values and recording gains. Likewise, they can lower reported earnings in periods of abnormally high operating performance by repurchasing outstanding bonds with market values above their reported values and recording losses.

5. **Distinguish between the effect that bond interest and gains and losses from early retirement have on operating cash flows as opposed to net income.**
   When bonds are issued at a premium or discount, the interest paid each period will not equal the interest expense because of the amortization of the discount or premium. When bonds are repurchased early and retired, any recognized gain or loss on the buy back affects net income but not operating cash flows.

6. **Appreciate why income is measured differently for income tax and financial reporting purposes.**
   Income measurement for tax purposes must comply with income tax laws, and income measurement for financial reporting purposes must comply with

current accounting standards. Because these two income measures serve different purposes, the resulting pre-tax book (financial reporting) income and tax (tax return) income will differ.

7. **Understand why the tax basis and the financial reporting basis of assets and liabilities may differ.**
   Differences between book and tax income imply differences in the book and tax bases (or carrying values) of the related assets. These differences are usually temporary in nature because total taxable income over the entire useful life of an asset will usually be the same for tax and book purposes. In other words, timing differences may allow a firm to postpone tax payments to future years, but not to avoid the tax payments. Consequently, firms must recognize an obligation for deferred (postponed) taxes.

8. **Interpret financial statement measurements of income tax expense and deferred income tax liability.**
   Income tax expense reported in the financial statements is computed by adding income tax payable and any change in the total amount of deferred tax liability:

Income tax actually payable		$XXX
Increase (decrease) in deferred tax liability	+(−)	YYY
Total income tax expense		$ZZZ

   Deferred tax obligations are reported in the balance sheet as part of a firm's total debt. Unlike other long-term obligations, however, they are not shown at their present values and therefore may reflect an overstatement of a firm's liabilities.

9. **Distinguish between the operating cash flow and the income statement effects of bonds and deferred taxes.**
   Bonds require a firm to make periodic interest payments but these operating cash flow payments do not usually equal the interest expense reported on the income statement because of differences between the coupon and market interest rates. In addition, a firm can re-purchase its bonds and affect its net income by timing the re-purchase so that accounting gains are recorded. These gains, though, are noncash items so they do not affect operating cash flows.

   Because taxes can be deferred, firms must keep two "sets of books": financial reporting and income tax reporting. Temporary differences may result in differences in the assets and/or liability balances on each set of books due to timing differences in revenue and expense transactions. GAAP requires that the income tax effect of these temporary differences be recognized currently. The resulting income tax expense on the income statement can be very different from what a firm actually pays in income taxes during the year. In fact, temporary differences tend to arise year after year and this can create an income tax expense that may never reflect what a firm will have to pay in income taxes. Reviewing a firm's income tax footnote disclosure and the amount of income taxes it actually paid during the year are important in obtaining a complete picture of a firm's income taxes.

KEY TERMS

Amortization
Annuity
Bonds
Bond discount
Bonds payable
Bond premium
Carrying value
Collateral
Compound interest
Compounded semiannually
Convertible bonds
Coupon rate
Deferred income tax liability
Discount on bonds
Discount rate
Effective income tax rate
Explicit interest payments
Implicit interest payments
Indentures
Interest-bearing notes
Market rate
Maturity date
Nominal interest rate
Noncurrent liabilities
Noninterest-bearing note
Note
Par value (bonds)
Premium on bonds
Present value
Present value factor
Restrictive covenants
Sinking fund
Statutory rate
Tax basis
Temporary differences

Exercises and Problems

9-1 Identify some of the reasons why a firm may prefer to have both current and noncurrent liabilities.

9-2 If a firm has noncurrent liabilities with a fixed interest rate, what will happen to the firm's liabilities when market interest rates increase? Decrease? Although interest rates on a firm's financial instruments may be fixed, actual current market interest rates can vary on a daily basis. Why don't accountants value liabilities using current market rates?

9-3 Describe the major differences between a bond discount and a bond premium. Discuss the distinctions between coupon (or nominal) interest rates and market interest rates at the bond issuance date.

9-4 Discuss why lenders include various restrictive covenants in a lending agreement. Provide several examples of restrictive covenants.

9-5 Most firms keep at least two "sets of books", in the sense that a given transaction can be interpreted differently for "book" (financial reporting) and "tax" (income tax calculations) purposes. Is this ethical? Discuss.

9-6 Explain the nature of temporary differences between book and tax measurements of assets and liabilities. Why is this concept important for financial reporting of income tax expense? Why is it important for reporting a firm's liabilities?

9-7 Assume U.S. maximum income tax rates are increased from 35 to 40%. How would this increase affect a firm that presently reports a deferred tax liability of $700 million? Specifically, how would the firm's net income be affected in the period when the rate increase is enacted, and how would the carrying value of the deferred tax liability be changed? Do you agree with these financial statement effects? Discuss.

9-8 If a firm has noncurrent liabilities with floating (variable) interest rates, what will happen to a valuation of the firm's liabilities when the market rate of interest increases? Decreases? Why is there more consistency in this case than in the case of fixed interest rates?

Bond Terms

9-9 Describe the key features of long-term bonds. Include the following terms in your description: par or face value, collateral, restrictive covenants, coupon rate, maturity date, and semiannual compounding.

Issuing Noninterest-Bearing Notes

9-10 Calculate the financial statement effects at the date of issue for each of the following discounted notes (also, refer to Chapter 8):

a. $10,000,000 note for one year at a 10% market interest rate.

b. $20,000,000 note for three years at a 12% market interest rate.

c. $5,000,000 note for 10 years at a 10% market interest rate.

d. What amount of cash is necessary to repay these notes at maturity, assuming no other changes during the term of the notes? (Hint: No further calculations are necessary to answer this part.)

Transaction Analysis: Bond Principal and Interest

9-11 Use the balance sheet equation to analyze the financial statement effects of the following transactions involving long-term bonds. Assume semiannual compounding. Set up separate columns as necessary. Use a separate cash column.

a. Issue $10,000,000 of five-year bonds carrying a coupon annual interest rate of 8% (paid semiannually). The market annual rate of interest at the time of issuance for similar bonds was 4%.

b. Record interest due and paid after the first six months.

c. Record interest due and paid at the end of the first year.

d. Record interest due and paid during each six-month period during the second year.

e. How much cash will be paid at maturity (at the end of the fifth year)?

f. Show the effects of the bond repayment on the financial statements at the end of the fifth year. (Ignore any amortization of premium or discount in the last year.)

g. Discuss why these bonds were issued and recorded at a premium or discount.

Transaction Analysis: Notes Payable and Simple Interest

9-12 Use the balance sheet equation to analyze the effects of the following transactions involving noncurrent liabilities. Set up separate accounts for each liability and use a separate column for cash.

1. Sally Shrimpton wanted to expand her pottery business, but had a negative cash flow. She borrowed $150,000 from her local bank and signed a note upon receipt of the cash.
2. Sally purchased a new kiln for $50,000 cash.
3. Sally purchased clay, paint, and other supplies for $20,000 cash.
4. Sally was paid a bonus of $25,000. She needed the cash to remodel her kitchen.
5. Interest for the first six months is due at an annual rate of 15%.
6. Sally paid the interest due.
7. Interest for the second six months is due.
8. Interest for the third six-months is due.
9. Sally paid the interest for both six-month periods and made partial payment of $50,000 on the loan.
10. Interest for the fourth six-month period is due.
11. Interest for the final year (two six-month periods) is due.
12. Sally fully paid the note, along with all accumulated interest.

Issuing Bonds: Premium or Discount

9-13 Maggie Markel's Moving Emporium needs to acquire additional capital in order to purchase new trucks and warehouse storage space, and to conduct a national advertising campaign. Maggie has heard of bonds and thinks that her friends and relatives would buy them if they were especially attractive. Although bonds issued by similar moving companies are currently yielding about 8% compounded semiannually, she decided to be kind to her friends and relatives and offer an interest rate of 10% compounded semiannually on the bonds. Maggie has never heard of premiums or discounts on bonds and intends to sell the bonds at their face amount (par).

Required

a. How many $1,000 bonds must Maggie issue at par in order to raise $1,000,000?

b. Explain the possible effects and consequences of selling $1,000,000 of 10% bonds at par when similar bonds yield 8%.

c. If Maggie sells the bonds at their market value, including an appropriate premium or discount, how much would Maggie receive for the $1,000,000 bonds? (Assume five-year bonds.) How realistic is this assumption? Why?

d. Summarize your recommendations to Maggie about issuing these bonds.

e. Now assume that bonds similar to those issued by Maggie Markel's Moving Emporium are very risky and require an interest rate of 12% compounded semiannually (6% each six months) before they can be sold to anyone, even to Maggie's friends and relatives. Recalculate the issue price and any discount or premium.

Evaluating Liabilities: Restrictive Covenants

9-14 Tall Tree Timber, Inc., issued $10 million in long-term bonds that contained the following restrictive covenants:

- Current ratio must exceed 2.0.
- Return on assets must exceed 2%.
- Net income ratio must exceed 2%.
- Debt composition ratio must be less than 60%.

Tall Tree Timber's most recent financial results (dollars in millions) follow:

Current assets	$ 40	Current liabilities	$ 10
Property, plant, and equipment	55	Long-term debt	9
Other assets	10	Stockholders' equity	86
Total assets	$105	Total liabilities and stockholders' equity	$105
Net revenues	$600	Income tax rate	20%
Net income	$ 30	Interest expense	$ 5

Required

a. Compute the appropriate ratios described in the loan covenants and evaluate whether they have been met. Use ending total assets for average total assets.

b. Suppose the auditors find that revenues have been overstated by $38 million, thereby reducing revenues and reducing net income by $28 million net of tax. This new calculation will reduce stockholders' equity and current assets by $28 million. Recalculate the appropriate ratios and test whether the loan covenants have been met.

c. Alternatively, suppose Tall Tree changes its depletion allowance calculations (of natural trees). This new calculation will reduce stockholders' equity (net income) and property, plant, and equipment by $50 million. Again, recalculate the appropriate ratios and test whether the loan covenants have been met.

d. Alternatively, suppose Tall Tree Timber decides to switch from FIFO to LIFO and that such a switch will reduce current assets and stockholders' equity (net income) by $30 million. Again, recalculate the appropriate ratios and test whether the loan covenants have been met.

e. Which of the above scenarios would cause the greatest concern to bondholders? Would any of these likely result in default proceedings to redeem or "call" the bonds? Why?

Tax Expense, Tax Payable, and Deferred Tax Liability: Effects of Tax Rate Changes

9-15 Rosty Co. began operations in 2007. The firm recognized $30 million of depreciation expense on its income statement and reported $50 million as depreciation on its 2007 tax return. The firm's income was taxed at 30%, and pre-tax income was $25 million.

Required

Determine the following:

a. Tax liability.

b. Deferred tax liability at the end of the year.

c. Difference between the book and tax bases of Rosty's assets at the end of the year.

d. Income tax expense.

e. During 2008, Rosty Co. recognized an additional $30 million of depreciation expense on its income statement and reported $40 million as depreciation on its tax return. During 2008, the statutory income tax rate applicable to firms such as Rosty Co. increased from 30 to 40%. Pre-tax income in 2008 was $12 million. Determine the following amounts:

(1) Difference between the book and tax bases of Rosty's assets at the end of 2008.

(2) Deferred tax liability at the end of 2008.

(3) Tax liability for 2008.
(4) Income tax expense for 2008.
(5) Percentage relationship between pre-tax income and income tax expense reported in the 2008 income statement.

Financial Statement Effects of Deferred Taxes

9-16 Taylor Corporation's statement of operations is summarized below (dollars in thousands):

	2007	*2006*	*2005*
Net sales	$357,850	$282,403	$286,206
Costs and expenses:			
Cost of sales	256,195	221,024	223,826
Selling, general, and administrative expense	103,402	57,972	55,667
Interest expense, net	3,820	487	608
Total costs and expenses	363,417	279,483	280,101
Income (loss) before income tax (benefit)	(5,567)	2,920	6,105
Income tax (benefit)			
Current	(859)	2,649	4,051
Deferred	(7)	(1,067)	(1,181)
	(866)	1,582	2,870
Income (loss) before cumulative changes	(4,701)	1,338	3,235
Cumulative effect of changes in accounting principles		(3,601)	
Net income (loss)	$ (4,701)	$ (2,263)	$ 3,235

Required

1. Explain the item "Income tax (benefit)". How can income tax be positive? That is, how can income tax be deducted from income before tax in 2005 and 2006, and added in 2007?
2. Calculate the following ratios for 2007 and 2006:
   a. Operating income ratio.
   b. Net income ratio.
   c. ROE. Assume that average stockholders' equity for 2007 and 2006 are $114,000 and $117,000 (dollars in thousands). Note: You may want to take out nonrecurring items before calculating the ratios.
3. Evaluate Taylor's performance during 2006 and 2007.

CHAPTER 10

SHAREHOLDERS' EQUITY

Learning Objectives

1. *Appreciate why large business firms prefer to organize as corporations.*
2. *Evaluate transactions and events that affect the components of shareholders' equity.*
3. *Interpret shareholders' equity ratios that are helpful in analyzing financial statements.*
4. *Understand the cash flow implications of shareholder transactions.*

INTRODUCTION

Corporations are the dominant form of business organization in advanced industrial nations such as the United States. Although they only represent about 25% of business firms, they generate about 80% of business revenues. A corporation, like a sole proprietorship and a partnership, obtains its resources from creditors through debt financing (liabilities) and from its investors/owners through **equity financing (owners' capital).** An important distinction exists, though, between a corporation and these other types of entities. *A corporation is a separate legal entity and as such, issues stock certificates to investors/owners in exchange for the equity resources it receives.* Each share of stock represents a fractional ownership interest in the issuing firm. From an accounting equation standpoint, the resources received from investors increase a corporation's assets and/or decrease its liabilities and increase its shareholders' equity component called invested capital or paid-in capital. It is important to note that invested capital is not like a liability to be repaid at a future date.

Most major corporations' stock is traded (bought and sold) on major security exchanges, such as the New York and American Stock Exchanges. For business managers, a primary advantage of the corporate form of organization is the capability to raise large amounts of cash by selling shares of stock to many different individuals and institutions (such as mutual funds, insurance companies, and pension plans), rather than relying on the investments of a few owners and lenders.

A corporation comes into existence when its **charter** is approved by the state in which it chooses to locate and incorporate. State laws vary; consequently many features of corporations depend on the state in which a firm incorporates. Among other things, the charter indicates the corporation's business purpose and authorizes the firm to issue one or more types of ownership shares. The most basic type of ownership share is **common stock.** Common shareholders are the true **residual owners** of a corporation. After all other claims against a firm's assets have been satisfied, the common shareholders own what remains. This view of shareholders' equity is apparent when we write the accounting equation in the following way:

SHAREHOLDERS' EQUITY = ASSETS − LIABILITIES

This expression shows that the value of shareholders' equity (also called stockholders' equity) reported on a firm's balance sheet is determined by the valuation of its assets and liabilities. Recall that financial accounting reports use historical costs rather than current market prices in evaluating the firm's assets and liabilities. For this reason, *the reported value of shareholders' equity does not attempt to measure the* ***market value*** *of the firm's outstanding shares of stock.*

Stockholders expect to earn returns on their investments in the form of dividends and capital gains. **Dividends** are generally distributions of assets, usually cash, that the corporation elects to make periodically to its stockholders. **Capital gains** (or losses) result from increases (or decreases) in the market price of stocks over the period during which an investor holds them. Neither the payment of dividends nor the appreciation in stock prices is guaranteed to the equity investor. Instead, the capability of a corporation to generate cash through profitable operations determines its capability to pay dividends and also influences the market price of its stock.

As we discussed above, corporations receive resources from debt and equity financing. The corporation employs these resources in its operations to generate profits. The profits reinvested in the corporation year after year that have not been paid out to shareholders as dividends are called **retained earnings.** In summary, *there are two major components of shareholders' equity: invested capital and retained earnings.* **Invested capital** represents the resources contributed by the shareholders in exchange for stock and usually includes two components: capital stock at **par value** and **additional paid-in capital.** Invested capital is also sometimes referred to as **contributed capital.** For our purposes, we will concentrate on the sum of these parts, not on the individual components.

Exhibit 10-1 shows the shareholders' equity section from the 2005 balance sheet of Johnson & Johnson, Inc. Note that Johnson & Johnson's total shareholders' equity on January 1, 2006 was $37,871 million. Of that amount, $3,120 million was received from the sale of stock to investors, $41,471 million represented past earnings that were reinvested in the firm's operations, and $755 million represented net reductions in shareholders' equity from various other sources. For most profitable firms, retained earnings represent the major part of shareholders' equity.

EXHIBIT 10-1 SHAREHOLDERS' EQUITY COMPONENTS

Johnson & Johnson Corporation
2005 Annual Report
Shareholders' Equity (Partial)
(Dollars in millions)

	JANUARY 1, 2006	JANUARY 5, 2005
Shareholders' equity:		
Preferred stock—without par value (authorized and unissued 2,000,000 shares)	—	—
Common Stock—$1.00 par value: (authorized 4,340,000,000 shares, issued 3,119,842,000 shares	$ 3,120	$ 3,120
Retained earnings	41,471	35,223
Treasury shares, at cost, 145,364,000 and 148,819,000 shares	(5,965)	(6,004)
Other items (net)	(755)	(526)
Total shareholders' equity	$37,871	$31,813

The description of Johnson & Johnson's common stock in Exhibit 10-1 distinguishes between the number of common shares that are authorized and issued. **Authorized shares** are those that the firm is permitted to issue according to its corporate charter. **Issued shares** are the authorized shares that have been sold to investors. Note that some issued shares may have been repurchased and held as treasury stock, as is explained later in the chapter.

Exhibit 10-1 also shows that Johnson & Johnson's common stock has been assigned a par value of $1.00 per share, and the total par value of the outstanding shares is reported separately on the balance sheet. Although for legal purposes the shares of most firms have a designated par or stated value, this value is usually a minor amount compared to the actual market price of the stock. For example, although Johnson & Johnson's common stock has a par value of just $1.00 per share, the stock had a market price per share of about $60 at the end of 2005.

In addition, Johnson & Johnson has 2 million shares of another type of stock, preferred stock that are authorized for issuance but notice that no shares have been issued to date. Johnson & Johnson is required to disclose this information so that financial statement readers are aware that at any point in time, the company could raise additional funds through selling these shares. We will discuss the features of preferred stock later in the chapter.

BASIC TRANSACTIONS AFFECTING STOCKHOLDERS' EQUITY

Three basic transactions account for most of the changes that occur in shareholders' equity:

1. Sale of stock to investors,
2. Recognition of periodic net income or loss, and
3. Declaration of cash dividends to shareholders.

Each of these transactions is examined in this section. Other less frequent types of transactions are discussed in a subsequent section.

Sale of Stock to Investors

Suppose that Johnson & Johnson's management decides to issue an additional 10 million shares of stock to investors, and the market price is $60 per share of stock. In this case, Johnson & Johnson would receive a total of $600 million from investors. In this example, note that we are ignoring any transactions costs, such as fees and commissions incurred by the issuing firm. The transaction would increase cash and invested capital by $600 million. The invested capital would consist of $10 million of capital stock (common stock could be used) at par value (10 million shares × $1 par value per share), and $590 million in additional paid-in capital ($600 million total invested minus $10 million recorded as par value).

ASSETS	=	LIABILITIES	+	SHAREHOLDERS' EQUITY	
Cash				Capital Stock	Additional Paid-in capital
+ $600 million				+ $10 million	+ $590 million

Managers would immediately put these funds to work to earn returns for the shareholders, such as investing in additional plant and equipment. In other words, the transaction to issue shares of stock is immediately followed by many other transactions in which the money is used for some corporate purpose.

In some instances, items other than cash can be received when stock is issued to investors. Examples include noncash assets, such as property or intangible assets, and services, such as work from a company's attorneys. In addition, a corporation may issue stock to a creditor for payment of a liability instead of paying cash.

Recognition of Periodic Net Income or Loss

Business firms must periodically determine the amount of net income (or loss) from their activities. Net income (loss) represents an increase (or decrease) in a firm's shareholder equity, or net assets, due to its revenues, expenses, gains, and losses during the period. For example, Johnson & Johnson earned $10,411 million of net income during 2005 and paid $3,793 million in dividends. Note the amounts of Johnson & Johnson's retained earnings shown in Exhibit 10-1 at the beginning and the end of 2005. These amounts (millions of dollars) are related in the following way:

Retained earnings, January 5, 2005	$35,223
Add: Net income during 2005	+10,411
Less: Dividends declared during 2005	– 3,793
Other reductions	– 370
Retained earnings, January 1, 2006	$41,471

Notice (Exhibit 10-1) that Johnson & Johnson's fiscal year-end does not fall on December 31. The company has adopted a 52–53 week year that ends on the last Sunday nearest the end of the month of December.

Declaration and Payment of Cash Dividends

Three important dates exist pertaining to dividends: date of declaration, date of record, and date of payment. Referring to our example above, on the **date of declaration,** Johnson & Johnson's Board of Directors declared a dividend and this action caused a liability to be incurred because Johnson & Johnson obligated itself to make the dividend payment. On that date, retained earnings were decreased and liabilities were increased by $3,793 million:

ASSETS	=	LIABILITIES	+	SHAREHOLDERS' EQUITY
		Dividends payable + $3,793 million		Retained earnings – $3,793 million (dividends)

Next, the Board of Directors set a **date of record.** On that date all shareholders owning the company's stock were entitled to receive the dividends. After that date the stock was considered **ex dividend,** which means that subsequent purchasers were not entitled to receive the previously declared dividend. On the **date of payment,** Johnson & Johnson's cash and dividends payable (liability) were reduced by $3,793 million:

ASSETS	=	LIABILITIES	+	SHAREHOLDERS' EQUITY
Cash – $3,793 million		Dividends payable – $3,793 million		

Observe that the change in retained earnings over a period is due primarily to the difference between a firm's net income and dividends during the period. The ending balance in retained earnings is comprised of the total net income of the firm in all past periods, less the total amount of dividends to shareholders, plus or minus the effects of any other adjustments. *A firm may show a negative balance in retained earnings, which is really called a retained or accumulated deficit.* This **deficit** does not bode well for a firm because it generally indicates that the firm has incurred overall net losses since inception.

ADDITIONAL TRANSACTIONS AFFECTING STOCKHOLDERS' EQUITY

In addition to the three basic transactions discussed in the last section, a variety of other, less frequent occurrences may affect the reported amount and composition of shareholders' equity. This section examines several of these additional types of transactions and events.

Stock Dividends

On occasion, firms distribute additional shares of stock to shareholders in proportion to the number of shares presently owned. If a firm declares a one percent **stock dividend,** for example, this means that existing shareholders will receive additional shares equal to one percent of their present holdings. In this case, a shareholder with 100 shares would receive one additional share (1% × 100 shares) as a stock dividend.

Stock dividends reduce retained earnings in an amount equal to the value of the stock that is distributed. As an example, assume that the Flotsam Company has 10 million common shares issued and outstanding and declares a two percent stock dividend when the market price of its stock is $45 per share. The firm will distribute an additional 200,000 shares (2% × 10 million shares = 200,000 shares), and the total value of the dividend is $9 million ($45 × 200,000 shares = $9 million). Retained earnings will decrease, and invested or paid-in capital will increase, by $9 million. The number of shares outstanding will also increase by two percent.

ASSETS	=	LIABILITIES	+	SHAREHOLDERS' EQUITY	
				Invested capital	Retained earnings
				+ $9 million	– $9 million

Notice that this transaction does not affect the firm's assets and liabilities, and therefore does not affect total shareholders' equity. It does not affect cash, as do normal dividends. The individual components of shareholders' equity are affected, however. The transaction decreases retained earnings and creates an offsetting increase in invested capital.

As a stockholder of 100 shares of Flotsam Company, would you be better off as a result of the stock dividend? Although it is true that you have received two additional shares of stock, *your proportionate interest in Flotsam remains unchanged.* Moreover, because the company's assets and liabilities are unchanged, the stock dividend has no direct effect on Flotsam's operating capability. In fact, the market price of each share of stock could decline just enough to leave the total value of your investment unchanged (100 shares × old price = 102 shares × new price).

Surprisingly, *stock dividends do appear to benefit existing shareholders.* The market price per share of existing shares usually does not decline sufficiently to offset the effect of issuing additional shares. Some analysts suggest that this otherwise puzzling result may be due to the use of stock dividends as a "signal to the market" by managers that the firm expects higher profits and cash flows in the future. Managers may be reluctant to make public forecasts about future earnings increases, however, and may instead prefer to communicate their favorable expectations by less direct action such as stock dividends.

Stock Splits

Stock splits are distinct from stock dividends and involve an exchange of multiple shares of stock for existing outstanding shares. In a two-for-one stock split, for example, each "old" share held by existing shareholders can be exchanged for two "new" shares. As an example, assume that a firm with 15,000 shares of $10 par value common stock outstanding and a market price of $80 per share, declares and issues a two-for-one stock split The firm will issue 15,000 additional common shares to its shareholders. *Managers may split a firm's stock when they believe that the price per share has risen beyond the range that is attractive to smaller investors. Therefore, splitting the shares is expected to reduce the share price and increase demand.* Similar to stock dividends, stock splits also seem to be interpreted by investors as favorable signals by management about future operating performance. In our example above, the two-for-one stock split theoretically should cut the market price in half to $40 per share since there are twice as many shares outstanding but since stock splits are viewed favorably by investors the total market value of the firm's outstanding shares is usually higher because the price per share typically does not decline sufficiently to offset the increase in the number of shares.

Unlike stock dividends, stock splits usually do not entail a reduction in retained earnings or an increase in the invested or paid-in capital. In fact, stock splits usually do not change any of the elements in the financial statements. Only the description of the firm's stock is amended to reflect the new number of shares authorized, issued, and outstanding. In our example, before the stock split the firm had a total par value of $150,000 (15,000 shares × $10 par value) and after the stock split the firm had $150,000 (30,000 shares × $5 par value) with no overall impact on stockholders' equity. Note the par value is split in half because there are twice as many shares outstanding.

Reality Check 10-1 shows how a stock split is reported by Johnson & Johnson Corporation.

Treasury Stock

Firms sometimes repurchase their own outstanding shares and hold them for future use. Such *repurchased shares are termed treasury stock and are no longer outstanding, although they continue to be labeled as "issued".*

A variety of motives lead managers to acquire **treasury stock.** The following are some examples.

1. Managers may consider the stock to be undervalued in the stock market and to be a "good buy" that can be resold later at a higher price.
2. Treasury stock purchases may boost the company's earnings per share because they reduce a firm's shareholders' equity.
3. Treasury stock purchases can enable managers to "buy out" certain groups of shareholders in order to re-align votes on future issues of corporate policy.
4. Treasury stock can be distributed to employees under an employee stock option plan.

REALITY CHECK 10-1

A footnote to the 2001 financial statements of Johnson & Johnson Corporation includes the following information:

> On April 26, 2001, the Board of Directors declared a 2-for-1 stock split. Shareowners of record on May 22, 2001 were issued one additional share of Johnson & Johnson common stock on June 12, 2001 for each share held as of the record date. All shares and per share data for all periods presented in these financial statements have been adjusted to reflect the stock split.

Required

a. Why does Johnson & Johnson give retroactive recognition to the stock split in all related financial statement references?
b. Why do you suppose Johnson & Johnson's management decided to split the company's stock?
c. As an existing Johnson & Johnson shareholder, would you be pleased by management's decision to split your stock? Explain.

SOLUTION

a. Johnson & Johnson gives retroactive recognition to the stock split in order to aid analysts in making comparisons with prior years. For example, if net income is unchanged from the prior year and the number of shares is not retroactively adjusted, the earnings per share would appear to decrease by 50%.
b. The company may have split the stock in order to reduce the per-share price, thereby making the stock more accessible for smaller investors. Alternatively, management may use stock splits as an indirect way to signal investors that management expects higher per share earnings and dividends in the future.
c. Generally, existing shareholders benefit from stock splits. Although each shareholder's fractional interest in Johnson & Johnson is not changed by the stock split, the total value of existing shares usually increases around the date of such announcements. The increase in stock prices may reflect investor expectations of higher future cash flows.

The acquisition of treasury stock reduces both cash and shareholders' equity. In this sense, treasury stock acquisitions are the opposite of a shareholders' investment. The cost of treasury shares is usually subtracted from total shareholders' equity. For this reason, the purchase price of treasury stock is a **contra-equity account.**

To illustrate the reporting of treasury stock, Exhibit 10-2 shows the shareholders' equity portion of Handel Corporation's balance sheet at the end of 2007. As of that date, Handel has paid $6,722,000 to acquire its treasury stock.

EXHIBIT 10-2 TREASURY STOCK REPORTING

Handel Corporation
2007 Annual Report
Treasury Stock Reporting
(Dollars in thousands)

	DECEMBER 31, 2007	DECEMBER 31, 2006
Shareholders' equity:		
Common stock: $.01 par value, 50,000,000 shares authorized, 21,309,277 shares issued	$ 213	$ 213
Capital surplus	48,587	49,109
Retained earnings	68,220	72,921
	117,020	122,243
Less 1,450,178 treasury shares in 2007 and 1,011,046 treasury shares in 2006, at cost	6,722	4,279
Total shareholders' equity	$110,298	$117,964

This amount is subtracted when computing Handel's total shareholders' equity. We can infer that the treasury stock purchase had the following effect on Handel's balance sheet:

ASSETS	=	LIABILITIES	+	SHAREHOLDERS' EQUITY
Cash – $6,722,000				Treasury stock – $6,722,000

Although treasury stock has been increased by $6,722,000, this represents a decrease in shareholders' equity because treasury stock is a contra-equity account. Also note that the common stock account has not changed because the repurchased stock has not been retired. It is being held for future use.

Suppose that Handel sold the treasury stock at a greater amount, say $10 million, at a future date. *Generally accepted accounting principles (GAAP) do not allow the recognition of gains or losses due to transactions in a firm's own stock.* Consequently, Handel's cash increases by $10 million, the treasury stock is eliminated, and invested or paid-in capital increases by the difference of $3,278,000 ($10,000,000 – 6,722,000).

Employee Stock Options

Stock options are rights to purchase a firm's stock at a specific price during a designated future period. Although **stock options** are sometimes sold directly to investors, they are usually granted as part of the compensation paid to key executives and other employees. Stock options, as a means of compensation, offer several distinct benefits to firms and employees. Because the value of stock options depends on the future market price of the firm's stock, option holders are highly motivated to improve the performance of the firm. Actions that benefit the firm's stockholders also directly benefit the option holders. As a result, managers and other employees who hold stock options have the same objective as company shareholders: to make the firm's equity securities more valuable. In addition, although option holders gain if the price of the optioned stock subsequently rises, they avoid the "downside risk" of loss if the stock price declines. If the stock price is below the option price, the option simply will not be exercised.

A more arguable advantage of stock options from the firm's point of view has been the manner in which options have been handled in financial statements. *GAAP rules allowed firms to choose between two different ways of reporting the cost of employee stock options, based either on intrinsic values or fair values of the options at the date of grant.* The **intrinsic value** method (Accounting Principles Board Opinion 25—APB25) measures the compensation cost of stock options as the excess of the stock's market price over the option price at the date of the grant. Because most employee options are usually granted at or above market value, firms that elected this method did not recognize any compensation expense associated with the options. Under the alternative elective **fair value** method (Statement of Financial Accounting Standard 123—SFAS 123), compensation expense is measured at the grant date based on the estimated fair market value of the award. Fair values of options must be estimated based on a theoretical model and various assumptions. Estimated stock option values and related compensation expenses can vary significantly, depending on the assumptions used and the model selected. As you might imagine, the resulting impact on net income could be significantly different depending upon which standard a firm chose to use. After years of controversy, the FASB issued revised SFAS 123R in 2005 making it mandatory that firms adopt the fair value method. Gone are the days of allowing firms to use the intrinsic value method.

To illustrate how stock options for employees are treated using the fair value method, assume that Jetsom Inc. issued options to its key employees to purchase one million shares of its common stock in 2007 at an option price of $10 per share, equal to the market price at the date of the grant. Assume that the options themselves are valued at $4 per option using a statistical option pricing model and the vesting period is two years (2007–2008). Subsequently, at the end of 2008, assume that all the options were exercised when Jetsom's market price per share had risen to $90.

For financial statement purposes, Jetsom records \$2 million compensation expense (\$4 million ÷ 2 years) in 2007 and 2008 as follows:

	ASSETS	=	LIABILITIES	+	SHAREHOLDERS' EQUITY	
2007					Additional paid-in capital + 2 million	+ Retained earnings − 2 million compensation expense
2008					Additional paid-in capital + 2 million	+ Retained earnings − 2 million compensation expense

In 2008, when the options are exercised, Jetsom records the cash proceeds of \$10 million (\$10 × 1 million shares) as an issuance of common stock for cash.

ASSETS	=	LIABILITIES	+	SHAREHOLDERS' EQUITY
Cash + \$10 million				Invested capital + \$10 million

The value of employee stock options has been substantial in specific industries. In high-technology companies that rely heavily on stock options to attract and retain talented employees, it is estimated that before the mandatory requirement of SFAS 123R net income was overstated anywhere from 10 to 100% ("Options' Effect On Earnings Sparks Debate," *Wall Street Journal,* May 13, 1998) due to the fact that companies followed the intrinsic value method and were not required to recognize compensation expenses for stock options of key employees. Companies that elected not to recognize compensation expense using the fair value method had to show net income and earnings per share in a footnote to the financial statements as if the fair value method had been used. Reality Check 10-2 shows a portion of such a footnote for a major retail clothing company for 2005 prior to implementing SFAS 123R.

REALITY CHECK 10-2

Abercrombie and Fitch Corporation, a prominent retail clothing company, reports the following information in its 2005 financial statements:

Stock options granted during 2005: 499,900 shares at an average exercise price of \$59.67 per share.

Stock options exercised during 2005: 3,288,612 shares at an average exercise price of \$23.16 per share.

Net income (loss) applicable to common shareholders, as reported in the income statement:

	2005	*2004*
Total	$333,986,000	$216,376,000
Per common share	$ 3.83	$ 2.33

Net income (loss) applicable to common shareholders if stock options granted during the year were valued at fair value:

	2005	*2004*
Total	$312,013,000	$195,014,000
Per common share	$ 3.58	$ 2.10

Required

a. By how much does the market value of the shares after the exercise of the stock options during 2005 differ from the exercise proceeds received by the company? Would this difference affect your assessment of Abercrombie's compensation expense for 2005?

b. Abercrombie uses the intrinsic value method to account for the cost of employee stock-based compensation. As a result, Abercrombie did not recognize any expenses related to these stock options in 2005. How much would the compensation expense have differed in each year if the firm used the fair value method to measure this compensation expense?

SOLUTION

a. The market value of the shares issued by Abercrombie after the exercise of options during 2005 was $196,231,478 (3,288,612 shares × $59.67 per share). The exercise proceeds received by the company was $76,164,254 (3,288,612 shares × $23.16 per share). The difference between these amounts is $120,067,224 ($196,231,478 – $76,164,254). This difference represents the additional economic value of Abercrombie's shares above the amounts received from the option holders. Some analysts suggest that this additional value should be regarded as compensation cost.

b. The differences in compensation costs can be determined by comparing the net income amounts reported in the income statements and the amounts in the footnotes. In 2005 the compensation expense would be higher by $21,973,000 ($333,986,000 – 312,013,000), and in 2004 the compensation expense would be higher by $21,362,000 ($216,376,000 – $195,014,000). Note that in both years the additional expenses related to the stock options are substantially higher than the amounts computed.

Stock Option Examples

Refer to eBay's footnote 1—Stock-based compensation contained in the annual report in Appendix B. Since companies were not required to follow SFAS 123R until 2006, eBay chose to account for stock options using the intrinsic value method. The company decided not to voluntarily elect to follow the fair value method and for good reason. According to eBay's footnote for 2005, the company disclosed the following information: "The impact of recognizing the fair value of option grants and stock grants under our employee stock purchase plan as an expense under FASB Statement No. 148 would have substantially reduced our net income." The company's reported net income for 2005 was $1,082,043,000. If the options were expensed according to the fair value method, the net income would be revised down to only $852,532,000, more than a $200 million reduction!

The FASB chairman, Robert H. Herz, in a meeting held in Denver, Colorado, April 7, 2003, emphasized that stock option accounting (pensions and leases are the other two areas) would likely undergo major changes. Now that companies have to recognize stock option based compensation expense for their key employees, we are likely to see companies follow what Microsoft decided to do.

Microsoft Corporation decided to no longer grant employee stock options. Instead, the company will issue stock to employees only if they meet certain performance objectives. In the New York Times.com, July 14, 2003, article, "Eliminating Stock Options," the author discusses Microsoft's decision regarding stock options,

> "Options, however, have lost some of their luster because in the mania of the late-1990s financial bubble, they were sometimes abused. Some corporations relied on them excessively as a form of compensation, a practice that in some cases led to creative accounting. Some executives sought to manipulate quarterly earnings to cash out their options at a favorable price, with little regard for the long-term welfare of their company. They were also able to load up on options because accounting rules allowed them to be treated as though they were cost free and needn't be expensed."

Preferred Stock

In addition to common stock, *firms often issue preferred stock, which has a priority claim over common stock with respect to dividends.* In addition, if the firm should liquidate its assets and cease to exist, *preferred shareholders' claims would be satisfied before any assets are distributed to the common stockholders.*

The description of **preferred stock** in corporate financial reports discloses the special features of the stock issue. To illustrate, Exhibit 10-3 shows the description of Sequer Corporation's preferred stock contained in its 2007 annual report. Sequer's preferred shares have an annual dividend of $5 per share. Analysts would also note that Sequer's preferred shares are **cumulative** and convertible. *Cumulative indicates that if the firm does not declare a dividend in any year, the amount accumulates*

EXHIBIT 10-3 REPORTING OF PREFERRED STOCK

Sequer Corporation
2007 Annual Report
Footnote Disclosures of Preferred Stock (Partial)

CAPITAL STOCK

The Company's capital stock consists of Class A and Class B common stock, and $5.00 cumulative convertible preferred stock.

Each share of $5.00 cumulative convertible preferred stock is convertible into 1.322 shares of Class A common stock. On December 31, 2007, 4,543,636 shares of Sequer Class A common stock were reserved for conversion of preferred and Class B common stock and stock options. On December 31, 2007, 5,724 Class B common shares were reserved for stock options. There are 797,000 shares of preferred stock outstanding. The preferred stock is redeemable, at the option of the Company, at $100 per share.

and must be paid to the preferred shareholders before any dividends are paid to common stockholders. If Sequer did not pay dividends for three years, for example, then a cumulative dividend of $15 per share ($5 × 3 years) must be paid to preferred shareholders before dividends are paid to common shareholders.

Convertible preferred shares might be exchanged for common shares at the preferred shareholders' option. To illustrate, each share of Sequer's preferred stock is converted into 1.322 shares of common stock. Presently, 797,000 shares of preferred stock have been issued. If the entire issue were to be converted to common stock, then Sequer would issue 1,053,634 common shares (797,000 preferred shares × 1.322 exchange ratio) and would retire the preferred stock. In this case, the preferred stock component of shareholders' equity is eliminated and transferred to common stock. *Note that the conversion of preferred stock does not change total shareholders' equity. Assets and liabilities are also unaffected.* The number of common shares outstanding increases and the preferred stock's dividend requirement is eliminated.

Convertible Debt

Firms that borrow by issuing bonds frequently include a conversion privilege in the bond contract. **Convertible bonds** allow the bondholder to exchange the bonds for a specified number of shares of stock. As an example, let's assume that in 2007 the Aloha Company's long-term debt included $150 million principal in convertible bonds payable, exchangeable for common stock at $15 per share at any time before the year 2008. If all the bondholders elected to convert to common stock, Aloha would then issue 10 million shares of common stock ($150 million bond principal / $15 conversion price). Aloha's bonds payable would be reduced, and invested or paid-in capital would be increased by $150 million:

ASSETS	=	LIABILITIES	+	SHAREHOLDERS' EQUITY
		Bonds Payable − $150 million		Invested capital + $150 million

Note that the conversion of debt to common stock reduces the firm's liabilities and increases shareholders' equity. It does not impact cash flows except for the reduction in interest payments. The number of common shares outstanding is increased, and the periodic interest expense is eliminated. Convertible securities are often translated into **common stock equivalent** amounts, based on the number of common shares that would be issued in the conversion.

Convertible bonds such as those issued by Aloha are **hybrid securities.** *A hybrid security is neither clearly debt nor clearly equity. Instead, it combines certain features of both types of securities.* In the case of convertible bonds, the bondholder is in one sense a lender and owns the firm's promise to make future interest and principal payments. In another sense, the holder of a convertible bond holds an option to acquire a specified number of common shares at a fixed price at any time over the life of the bond issue. In fact, investors in convertible bonds are willing to pay for this combination of debt and equity features. Convertible bonds generally are issued at higher prices (in other words, at lower interest rates) than nonconvertible debt.

The proper way to account for hybrid securities is a matter of debate. Present accounting standards reflect the view that convertible debt is to be reported as debt until it is actually converted and as equity thereafter. No recognition is given in the financial statements to the likelihood that conversion will actually occur, or to the relative values to investors of the hybrid security's debt and equity features.

Opponents of present practice argue that it is misleading to ignore the hybrid nature of convertible securities. In the case of debt, they argue that the issue price should be apportioned between the amount the investor is paying for the debt features and the additional amount being paid for the conversion privilege. Ignoring these separate elements, they contend, causes the financial statements to overvalue the firm's reported liabilities, undervalue its shareholders' equity, and overstate periodic interest expense. To address these and related issues, the FASB is pursuing a comprehensive financial instruments project. The project aims to identify the component claims that are bundled in hybrid financial assets and liabilities and to develop appropriate methods of valuation for these components.

Keep in mind that firms with outstanding bonds must generally pay periodic interest payments to the bondholders. These payments cannot be avoided. On the other hand, firms with outstanding preferred stock are never obligated to pay dividends. Even if the stock is cumulative a firm is not required to pay any dividends in arrears or current dividends to these stockholders unless the Board of Directors declares a dividend.

EARNINGS PER SHARE

Perhaps the most widely cited number in corporate financial reports is **earnings per share (EPS).** *EPS focuses on the common stock and indicates the portion of total company income that is applicable to a single share of common stock.* The reporting of EPS depends upon whether the firm has a simple or a complex capital structure. A **simple capital structure** includes no "potential" common equity securities other than common stock outstanding. A **complex capital structure** includes, in addition to common stock, other securities or agreements that represent potential issues of common stock. Examples of potential issues of common stock include outstanding stock options as well as convertible bonds and convertible preferred stocks. Firms with a simple capital structure report a measure of **basic EPS,** and firms with a complex capital structure report measures of basic and **diluted EPS.** The calculations of basic and diluted EPS are explained and illustrated on the following pages.

Basic EPS

Basic EPS is computed by dividing income available to the common stockholders by the average number of shares outstanding:

$$\text{EPS} = \frac{\text{Net income available for common shareholders}}{\text{Average number of common shares outstanding}}$$

For example, Starbright Company reported net income of \$99 million in 2007 and had 45 million shares of common stock outstanding throughout the entire year. Starbright's 2007 EPS is \$2.20, calculated as follows:

$$\text{EPS} = \frac{\$99\text{ million}}{45\text{ million shares}}$$

$$= \$2.20$$

Basic EPS Calculations with Changes in Shares Outstanding

It is unusual for a large firm's **outstanding shares** to remain constant throughout the year. Additional stock transactions cause the number of shares to vary over the year. In these cases, the denominator in the EPS calculation is the **weighted average** of the common shares outstanding during the year. To illustrate, assume that Starbright reported net income of \$118 million during 2007 and that the firm's common shares changed as shown in Exhibit 10-4.

To calculate Starbright's EPS for 2007, we need first to determine the firm's weighted average shares outstanding during the year. The calculation appears in Exhibit 10-5 and shows that each level of outstanding shares is weighted by the fraction of the year that it stayed constant.

EXHIBIT 10-4 COMMON SHARES OUTSTANDING

Starbright Company
Common Shares Outstanding During 2007

Outstanding shares, January 1, 2007	45 million
Add: Additional shares issued May 1, 2007	+ 15 million
Balance, May 1, 2007	60 million
Less: Treasury shares purchased July 1, 2007	− 10 million
Balance, July 1, 2007	50 million
Add: Additional shares issued October 1, 2007	+ 16 million
Outstanding shares, December 31, 2007	66 million

Exhibit 10-5 shows that Starbright's average shares outstanding in 2007 were 54 million. Accordingly, the firm's EPS in 2007 was

$$\text{EPS} = \frac{\text{Net income, \$118 million}}{\text{Weighted average shares, 54 million}}$$

$$= \text{\$2.19 per share}$$

Basic EPS Calculations with Preferred Stock Outstanding

When a firm has both preferred and common stock outstanding, the preferred stock's share of net income must be subtracted in order to determine the basic EPS of the common stock. This is required because dividends must be paid to preferred shareholders before any earnings are available to common shareholders. Cumulative preferred stock always must be allocated its portion of net income. Noncumulative preferred stock is assigned a portion of income only in years

EXHIBIT 10-5 WEIGHTED AVERAGE COMMON SHARES

Starbright Company
Weighted Average Common Shares During 2007

PERIOD	LENGTH	FRACTION OF A YEAR		SHARES OUTSTANDING		SHARES
January 1–April 30, 2007	4 months	4/12	×	45 million	=	15.0 million
May 1–June 30, 2007	2 months	2/12	×	60 million	=	10.0 million
July 1–Sept 30, 2007	3 months	3/12	×	50 million	=	12.5 million
October 1–Dec 31, 2007	3 months	3/12	×	66 million	=	16.5 million
Totals	12 months					54.0 million

when the firm actually declares a dividend on the preferred stock.

To illustrate, assume that Avalon Company reports net income of $120 million in 2007 and has both preferred and common stock outstanding. Pertinent details about the stock issues appear in Exhibit 10-6.

Diluted EPS

Diluted EPS considers the effects on EPS of all the potential common shares that were outstanding during the year. If inclusion of these shares in the EPS calculation reduces the amount of EPS, then these potential common shares are **dilutive** and will be included in the calculation of diluted EPS. Otherwise, they are **anti-dilutive** and will be omitted from the calculation of diluted EPS. Including dilutive potential common shares in the EPS calculation may require adjustments to the numerator and the denominator of the basic EPS calculation. We will illustrate these adjustments for convertible preferred stock.

Recall from our earlier discussion that the dividends declared or accumulated during the period on preferred stock must be subtracted from net income in order to obtain the income applicable to the common shares. If the convertible preferred stock had been converted at the start of the period, however, the preferred dividends would not be subtracted from net income, and the denominator of the EPS calculation would include the additional shares that were issued on conversion. Keep in mind that we "pretend" that the preferred stock was converted to common stock at the beginning of the period even though, in reality, no conversion has actually taken place. We use the "as if converted" assumption when calculating diluted EPS to determine if the basic EPS would have been

EXHIBIT 10-6 STOCK ISSUE DETAILS

Avalon Company
Descriptions of Preferred and Common Stock
Outstanding During 2007

Preferred stock, cumulative annual dividend of $10 per share, two million shares outstanding throughout all of 2007.

Common stock, 40 million shares outstanding throughout 2007.

Avalon's income available for common stock is determined as follows:

Net income, 2007	$120 million
Less: Income applicable to preferred shares ($10 per share × 2 million shares)	– 20 million
Income applicable to common shares	$100 million

Consequently, the basic EPS of the common stock is $2.50 ($100 million of income / 40 million common shares outstanding).

EXHIBIT 10-7 BASIC EPS CALCULATION

Groucho Company
Basic EPS Calculation During 2007

Preferred stock, cumulative annual dividend of $3 per share, one million shares outstanding throughout 2007, convertible to one million shares of common stock.

Common stock, 9 million shares outstanding throughout 2007.

Net income during 2007:	$48 million
Less: Preferred dividend	$ 3 million
Income applicable to common stock	$45 million

Basic EPS: $5.00 ($45 million / 9 million shares)

diluted by this potential conversion. To illustrate, assume that Groucho Company has a basic EPS of $5.00 per share, computed as shown in Exhibit 10-7.

Inclusion of the potential common shares associated with the convertible preferred stock in the EPS calculation would result in a diluted EPS of $4.80, as follows:

$$\text{Diluted EPS} = \frac{\text{Net Income}}{\text{Common shares outstanding} + \text{shares issuable upon conversion of preferred stock}}$$

$$= \frac{\$48 \text{ million}}{9 \text{ million shares} + 1 \text{ million shares}}$$

$$= \$4.80 \text{ per share}$$

In this case, Groucho would report on the face of the 2007 income statement a basic EPS of $5.00 and a diluted EPS of $4.80. Reality Check 10-3 shows the calculation of basic and dilutive EPS for a firm with potential common shares related to convertible preferred stock in its capital structure.

REALITY CHECK 10-3

Proctor and Gamble, a major consumer products manufacturer, reports the following amounts of basic and diluted EPS in its 2005 financial statements:

	Basic EPS	*Diluted EPS*
Net income	$7,257,000,000	$7,391,000,000
Less: Preferred dividends	(136,000,000)	(135,000,000)
Net income applicable to common stock/	$7,121,000,000/	$7,256,000,000/
Average shares outstanding	2,515,600,000	2,726,200,000
= EPS	$ 2.83	$ 2.66

Required

a. Explain why the amounts of preferred dividends that are subtracted in order to determine net income applicable to the common shares differ between the basic and diluted EPS calculations. Why are some preferred dividends included in the diluted EPS calculation?

b. Determine the total number of potential common shares and the total preferred dividends that are associated with P&G's dilutive convertible preferred stock.

c. Based on your answer to b, determine the preferred stock dividend per potential common share, and explain why this relation causes these preferred shares to be dilutive.

d. Explain why you would consider either basic or diluted EPS to be a more useful measure of P&G's per share earnings.

SOLUTION

a. The calculation of basic EPS requires the subtraction of all preferred stock dividends. In computing diluted EPS, the dividends on dilutive preferred stock are added back because the related potential common shares are treated as if outstanding during the period; in other words the potential common shares are added to the denominator. Some of P&G's preferred dividends remain in the calculation of diluted EPS, either because those preferred shares are not convertible to common stock, or because the EPS effects would be anti-dilutive (EPS would be higher if these shares were converted).

b. The numbers of potential common shares and the dividends on dilutive preferred stock can be determined by comparing the amounts used in computing basic and diluted EPS. The potential common shares are 210,600,000 (2,726,200,000 − 2,515,600,000), and the preferred dividend is $1,000,000 ($136,000,000 − $135,000,000).

c. The preferred stock dividend per potential common share for the dilutive preferred stock is less than $0.01 per share ($1,000,000/210,600,000 = $0.0047). Note that this amount is well below the firm's basic EPS of $2.83. For this reason, the inclusion of these shares in the EPS calculation reduces the measured EPS.

d. Whether basic or diluted, EPS is more useful depending in part on the likelihood that the preferred shares will be converted to common shares. This in turn depends on many factors, including the future profitability of the company.

ANALYSIS BASED ON SHAREHOLDERS' EQUITY

The starting point in any analysis of a corporation's borrowed and equity capital is a careful reading of the descriptions provided in the body of the financial statements and the accompanying footnotes. As you have seen in this chapter, terms such as *convertible, cumulative, preferred,* and many others are critical in understanding the relative rights and priorities of the debt and equity claims on corporate assets.

The number and type of financial ratios that are based on shareholders' equity are constrained only by the imagination of the analyst. New ratios are continually being developed and tested by the "gurus of the day" quoted in the business press. This section discusses three ratios that seem to have stood the test of time: the financial leverage ratio, the market-to-book value ratio, and the price-to-earnings ratio.

The Financial Leverage Ratio

A basic decision faced by financial managers is the extent to which a firm should rely on borrowed capital. Shakespeare's adage "neither a borrower nor a lender be" is poor business advice. *It is beneficial for most corporations to rely on debt to some extent, because the interest expense on debt is tax deductible, while dividends paid to stockholders are not.* The degree of reliance on debt, or **financial leverage,** is measured as the ratio of debt to assets:

$$\text{Financial leverage} = \frac{\text{Total liabilities}}{\text{Total assets}}$$

Exhibit 10-8 shows financial leverage ratio calculations for two firms, based on financial reports for 2005. Target Corporation's debt is equal to about 59% of its total assets. This reflects Target's reliance mainly on the retention of its earnings

EXHIBIT 10-8 FINANCIAL LEVERAGE RATIO CALCULATIONS

Financial Leverage Ratios
Two Firms Measured
(Dollars in millions)

TARGET CORPORATION (JANUARY 28, 2006)	
(Retail)	
Debt	$20,790
Equity	14,205
Total assets (debt plus equity)	$34,995

Financial leverage ratio: $20,790 / $34,995 = .59

JP MORGAN CHASE & COMPANY (DECEMBER 31, 2005)	
(Banking)	
Debt	$1,091,731
Equity	107,211
Total assets (debt plus equity)	$1,198,942

Financial leverage ratio: $1,091,731 / $1,198,942 = 0.91

to finance its growth. JP Morgan Chase & Company provides a dramatic contrast; borrowed capital is equal to more than 91% of its total assets. This reflects the fact that JP Morgan Chase is engaged in the banking industry. Banks accept deposits from customers and report substantial liabilities for future withdrawals.

The lesson to be learned in comparing Target and JP Morgan Chase in Exhibit 10-8 is that comparisons of financial leverage ratios across companies in different industries must be undertaken with caution. To some extent, differences in financial leverage reflect management's willingness (or reluctance) to rely on borrowed capital. To a large extent, however, financial leverage is determined by industry characteristics and practices.

Financial leverage ratios are widely used by analysts to assess the risks of debt and equity securities. Firms with debt percentages that are substantially above their industry averages tend to have a higher likelihood of default on debt payments. As a result, high financial leverage is associated with lower bond quality ratings and therefore higher borrowing (interest) costs. Equity investments have also been found to be riskier for firms with high financial leverages. The share prices of highly leveraged firms tend to be more volatile than the share prices of firms with lower financial leverage.

Exhibit 10-9 shows the variances in the financial leverage ratio among competitor firms within the same industry. Target's 2005 financial leverage ratio is 59% while its competitors: Sears and Wal-Mart have financial leverage ratios of 62% and 61%, respectively. Target's financial leverage ratio is not much lower

EXHIBIT 10-9 FINANCIAL LEVERAGE RATIO CALCULATIONS

Financial Leverage Ratios
Two Competitor Firms of Target Corporation
(Dollars in millions)

SEARS HOLDING CORPORATION (JANUARY 28, 2006)

(Retail)	
Debt	$18,962
Equity	11,611
Total assets (debt plus equity)	$30,573

Financial leverage ratio: $18,962 / $30,573 = 0.62

WAL-MART STORES, INC. (JANUARY 31, 2006)

(Retail)	
Debt	$ 85,016
Equity	53,171
Total assets (debt plus equity)	$138,187

Financial leverage ratio: $85,016 / $138,187 = 0.615

than Wal-Mart's ratio. Target's management stresses that the company's debt levels are needed for growth and will increase only modestly to support store expansion and for its credit card operations.

Market-to-Book Value Ratio

Analysts often compare the market value of a firm's outstanding common stock to the reported value (book value) of common shareholders' equity. For example, at the end of 2005, Wal-Mart Stores, Inc. had 4,165,000,000 shares of stock outstanding, and the market price per share was about $46. Wal-Mart reported total shareholders' equity at $53,171,000,000, or $12.77 book value per share ($53,171,000,000 total shareholders' equity / 4,165,000,000 shares outstanding). Accordingly, Wal-Mart's market-to-book value ratio is computed as follows:

$$\text{Market-to-book value ratio} = \frac{\text{Market price per share}}{\text{Book value per share}}$$

$$= \frac{\$46}{\$12.77}$$

$$= 3.6$$

Why would investors be willing to buy Wal-Mart's stock at over three times its underlying book value? The answer rests on the fact that the current market price of Wal-Mart's stock depends on the future cash flows (dividends and resale price) that stockholders expect. In this sense, market price measures the **economic value** of Wal-Mart's stock. The book value of Wal-Mart's stock, on the other hand, reflects the methods used to identify and measure Wal-Mart's assets and liabilities. Accounting measurements are based largely on historical costs and do not purport to reflect contemporary expectations about future cash flows. Despite its popularity, the market-to-book value ratio appears to be comparing apples to oranges.

Price-to-Earnings Ratio

The ratio of a stock's market price per share to its EPS is termed **price-to-earnings (P/E) ratio.** The P/E ratio of large U.S. firms has averaged about 21 during the last decade. As an example, Wal-Mart's market price per share at the end of 2005 was $46, and its 2005 EPS was reported at $2.68. The resulting P/E ratio is:

$$\text{P/E} = \frac{\text{Price per share}}{\text{EPS}}$$

$$= \frac{\$46}{\$2.68}$$

$$= 17.2$$

This result indicates that Wal-Mart's stock was selling at a price that is 17.2 times its earnings per share. In other words, investors are willing to pay $17.20 for every dollar of earnings.

P/E ratios are often used to assess growth, risk, and earnings quality. How would we expect Wal-Mart's P/E ratio to compare to those of other firms? To answer this question, we must consider the effects of growth, risk, and earnings quality on inter-firm comparisons of P/E ratios.

Growth

P/E ratios vary directly with expected future growth rates in earnings. If investors expect a firm's future earnings to grow rapidly, then the current earnings understate the future earning power of the firm. Stock price, on the other hand, reflects investor expectations of future earnings and cash flows. Consequently, *the ratio of prices to earnings will be relatively high for firms with high expected rates of earnings growth.*

Risk and Earnings Quality

It is well established among investors that riskier investments require higher returns. Lenders require higher interest payments from borrowers with lower credit ratings, and equity investors demand greater returns and therefore pay lower prices for the stocks of risky firms. For this reason, high-risk firms are expected to have lower-than-average P/E multiples, and low-risk firms are expected to exhibit higher-than-average P/E multiples.

Along this line, P/E ratio is often viewed as a measure of how expensive a stock is. The EPS stream is assumed to continue indefinitely into the future, and the P/E ratio reflects how many dollars investors are willing to pay for a $1 EPS stream. For example, the stock of a firm that has a 15 P/E ratio would be viewed as less expensive than one with a P/E ratio of 20 because investors are paying $15 versus $20 for every dollar of earnings.

Some investors recommend purchasing low P/E stocks. The rationale is that these stocks are cheap and have a great deal of upside potential. However, as you might guess, the research evidence regarding the success of this strategy is mixed. In any event, recognize that P/E ratios may vary among firms for several reasons.

First, the sustainability of currently reported earnings in future periods, referred to as **earnings quality**, can affect the P/E ratio. Firms use different accounting principles, which systematically affect EPS. Firms that use conservative methods of income measurement (LIFO inventory costing and accelerated depreciation and amortization) are more likely to be viewed as having higher earnings quality than firms that use more liberal income measurement methods. The securities market is likely to place a higher share price on firms with quality earnings. In other words, P/E multiples should vary directly with firms' earnings quality. The market price is based on the expectations of investors about a company's future performance.

Second, variations in earnings growth can cause P/E ratios to differ among firms. Recall the assumption that the EPS stream is expected to continue indefinitely. This assumption is not valid for many firms. In particular, firms with a large array of favorable investment prospects are likely to grow at relatively fast rates. The current EPS number for these growth firms understates the future EPS stream (the stream for which investors are actually paying), and the P/E ratio is therefore overstated for such growth firms.

Third, in any given year, a firm's EPS might contain a transitory component, one that is not expected to persist into the future. For example, a firm will occasionally take a restructuring charge, which is a special charge that reduces net income. Accordingly, the current year's EPS understates the future earnings stream, and the P/E ratio is higher than it otherwise would be.

Interfirm differences in P/E ratios can be questionable guides for investment selection, however. Instead, differences in P/E ratios might simply reflect differences in accounting methods, earnings growth rates, and transitory earnings components.

An interesting illustration is provided by Electronic Data Systems (EDS). A dispute arose between EDS and one of its major customers regarding amounts due EDS for providing network management services. Litigation ensued and EDS took a charge of $200 million. Based on actual EPS of $1.50, its P/E ratio was:

$$\text{P/E} = \frac{\$52}{\$1.5} = 34.7$$

Eliminating the effect of this one-time charge results in an EPS of approximately $1.74. The "adjusted" P/E ratio would be 29.9.

$$\text{P/E} = \frac{\$52}{\$1.74} = 29.9$$

This is a more reasonable figure and illustrates how P/E ratios can be affected by transitory components of net income.

Reality Check 10-4 illustrates the effect accounting changes can have on P/E ratios.

P/E Ratio—eBay, Inc.

As we discussed above, the P/E ratio is used to assess growth, risk and earnings quality. In stark contrast to Wal-Mart's P/E ratio of 17.2, eBay's P/E ratio is extremely high. At the end of 2005, eBay's stock price per share was $43, its EPS was $0.35, and the P/E ratio was 122.9 ($43/$0.35). Why would investors be willing to pay over one hundred twenty-three times the company's earnings for

REALITY CHECK 10-4

Seaport Corporation reported the following financial information (dollars in thousands):

	2007	*2006*	*2005*
Earnings before cumulative effect of accounting change	$30,574	$2,840	$20,202
Cumulative effect of changing the accounting for inventories, net of tax expense of $1,922	—	3,006	—
Net earnings	$30,574	$5,846	$20,202

Assume that other than the cumulative effect, earnings were not materially affected by the change.

Required

Identify the earnings number for each year that would permit valid comparisons.

SOLUTION

Because 2006 was the only year affected by the change, reported earnings for 2007 and 2005 can be used. For 2006, earnings before the cumulative effect should be used. The valid comparisons involve the following:

2007	$30,574
2006	2,840
2005	20,202

the company's stock? Apparently, investors expect incredibly high rates of earnings growth for eBay. In fact, looking at analyst's expectations, the company is projected to generate earnings per share of over $1.00 at the end of 2006, a very impressive growth, indeed!

CASH FLOW IMPLICATIONS

As we have stressed in previous chapters, many transactions may impact a firm's net income and not its cash flows or vice versa. Shareholder transactions are no exception. As an example, analysts and investors place great emphasis on the EPS ratio. In fact, this ratio has historically been instrumental in influencing the market price of firms' stocks. Bear in mind, though, that EPS is based on net income.

Remember that firms may offer stock options to their employees. Moreover, these stock options represent a form of compensation to the firms' employees. Firms record compensation expense based on the value of the options, not the value of the stock. As our previous example of Jetsom Company showed, the firm granted $10 million of stock options to employees and recorded compensation expense of $4 million over the two-year vesting period. The stock options were exercised when the market value of the stock was $90 million. The firm forfeited $80 million of cash in-flows from selling the stock directly to investors. Had a total of $80 million instead of $4 million been reflected as compensation expense, Jetsom's net income and EPS would have been substantially lower during the stock option period.

In addition, shareholder transactions generally affect a firm's cash flows from financing activities. Recall from Chapter 5 (Cash Flow), a healthy firm will show negative cash flows from financing activities over a period of time. It is important to study the trends in a firm's financing cash flows because a firm might engage in shareholder transactions to enhance its shareholder ratios temporarily but such activities may have a long-term detrimental effect on the firm's overall financial health.

Summary of Learning Objectives

1. **Appreciate why large business firms prefer to organize as corporations.** Major business firms prefer to organize as corporations. The capability of a corporation to sell its ownership shares to a large number of individual and institutional investors allows the firm to invest in large-scale operations. The basic ownership shares in a corporation are referred to as common stock, which represents a residual interest in the firm's assets. Some corporations also issue preferred stock, which has priority over common stock in receiving dividends and other distributions of assets.

2. **Evaluate transactions and events that affect the components of shareholders' equity.**
   Corporate shareholders' equity arises from both the sale of ownership shares and the retention of profits in the business. Most changes that occur in shareholders' equity arise from three basic transactions:

   a. Issuing stock to investors, which increases invested or paid-in capital.
   b. Recognizing periodic income (loss), which increases (decreases) retained earnings.
   c. Declaring cash dividends, which decrease retained earnings.

   Other events that affect shareholders' equity include the following:

   d. Stock dividends are distributions of additional shares to investors. These dividends decrease retained earnings and increase invested or paid-in capital, but they have no effect on total shareholders' equity or total assets.
   e. Stock splits occur when each "old" share of a stock is exchanged for multiple "new" shares. These exchanges do not change any of the components of shareholders' equity.

f. Purchasing treasury shares, the cost of which is subtracted from shareholders' equity, and the subsequent resale of treasury shares.
g. Issuing stock options, which are the rights to purchase the firm's stock at a specified price over a designated future period.
h. Converting securities, such as bonds payable or preferred stock, which allows the holder to exchange the securities for a predetermined number of common shares.

3. **Interpret shareholders' equity ratios that are helpful in analyzing financial statements.**
   Shareholders' equity is used extensively in ratio analysis of financial statements. Four widely employed measures are the following:

$$\text{Earnings per share} = \frac{\text{Net income}}{\text{Weighted average number of common shares outstanding}}$$

$$\text{Debt-to-assets or financial leverage ratio} = \frac{\text{Total debt}}{\text{Total assets}}$$

$$\text{Market-to-book value ratio} = \frac{\text{Market price per share}}{\text{Book value per share}}$$

$$\text{Price-to-earnings ratio} = \frac{\text{Market price per share}}{\text{EPS}}$$

   The proper interpretation of each of these ratios requires that you be familiar with the conventions and limitations of historical-cost-based financial accounting methods.

4. **Understand the cash flow implications of shareholder transactions.**
   Accounting rules require firms to record compensation expense when granting employee stock options at the value of the options, not the value of the stock. This can lead to the appearance of higher net income and earnings per share. However, when the employees exercise these options and purchase the firm's stock, the firm may forfeit substantial cash in-flows because it has to sell the stock to the employees at the option price of the stock, which can be much lower than the market price on the exercise date.

   Shareholder transactions generally affect a firm's financing cash flows. As we discussed in Chapter 5, healthy firms tend to show negative financing cash flow activities. It is important to study the trends in a firm's financing cash flows because a firm might engage in shareholder transactions to enhance shareholder ratios temporarily but such activities may have a long-term detrimental effect on the firm's overall financial health.

KEY TERMS

Additional paid-in capital
Anti-dilutive
Authorized shares
Basic EPS
Book value per share
Capital gains
Charter
Common stock
Common stock equivalent
Complex capital structure
Contra-equity account
Contributed capital
Convertible bonds
Convertible preferred shares
Cumulative preferred stock
Date of declaration
Date of payment
Date of record
Deficit
Diluted
Dilutive
Dividends
Earnings per share (EPS)
Earnings quality
Economic value
Equity capital
Equity financing
Ex dividend
Fair value
Financial leverage ratio
Hybrid securities
Intrinsic value
Invested capital
Issued shares
Leverage
Market-to-book value ratio
Market value
Outstanding shares
Paid-in capital
Par value
Preferred stock
Price-to-earnings (P/E) ratio
Residual owners
Retained earnings
Simple capital structure
Stock dividend
Stock option
Stock split
Treasury stock
Weighted average

Exercises and Problems

10-1 Describe the differences between shareholders' equity and liabilities.

10-2 Identify three components of shareholders' equity and describe each component.

10-3 Describe the differences between common and preferred stock.

10-4 Describe the differences between an equity or ownership interest in a corporation as compared to a creditor interest. What different rights does each have?

10-5 Describe why retained earnings is not cash. Why can't shareholders withdraw their portion of shareholders' equity as cash?

10-6 With regard to common stock, distinguish among authorized, issued, and outstanding shares. Why would a firm never have more outstanding shares than authorized and issued shares?

10-7 What are cumulative dividends as compared to noncumulative dividends?

10-8 **a.** Describe how earnings per share (EPS) are computed.
b. Why is EPS such an important ratio?
c. Describe what EPS represents. Describe what it does not represent.

10-9 Assume that a firm uses relatively conservative methods of accounting (LIFO inventory costing and/or accelerated depreciation methods). Describe how this would affect your interpretation of the following measures: EPS, financial leverage ratio, and price-to-earnings ratio.

Transaction Analysis: Shareholders' Equity

10-10 DWN Corporation began operations in 2007. Calculate the balances in each component of shareholders' equity at the end of 2007, after recognizing the following transactions:

1. Issue one million shares of $5.00 par value common stock at a price of $15.00.
2. Earn net income of $450,000.
3. Declare and pay dividends of $200,000.
4. Purchase 10,000 shares of its common stock as treasury stock at $25.00.
5. Sell 5,000 shares of treasury stock for $30.00.

Comprehensive Exercise: Stockholders' Equity

10-11 Swan and Duboner Corporation has the following stockholders' equity on December 31, 2007:

Six percent preferred stock: $100 par value, 20,000 shares authorized, 5,000 shares issued and outstanding	$ 500,000
Common stock: $5 par value, 1,000,000 shares authorized, 250,000 shares issued	1,250,000

Additional paid-in capital	1,740,000
Total contributed capital	$3,490,000
Retained earnings	850,000
Total stockholders' equity	$4,340,000

The corporation had the following transactions during 2008:

1. *February 1:* Declared a dividend of $6 per share on the preferred stock, and $0.50 per share on the common stock.
2. *February 10:* The board of directors established this as the record date.
3. *February 25:* The dividends were paid.
4. *March 31:* A two-for-one stock split on the common stock was declared and issued.
5. *April 30:* The corporation bought back 100,000 shares of its common stock for $6 per share. These shares will be reissued in the future.
6. *June 30:* Employee stock options were granted for 10,000 shares and the stock option period (vesting period) is two years (2008–2009). Using an option statistical modeling program, the value of the options equals $2/option. The current market price of the stock is $5.50 per share and the exercise price is $6.00 per share.
7. *August 15:* The corporation sold 20,000 shares of its treasury stock for $7.00 per share.
8. *October 31:* Employees exercised their stock options. The current market price is $7.50 per share.
9. *December 31:* The income for the year is $600,000 before the transactions above and before income taxes. The tax rate is 30%.

Required

a. Set up an accounting equation and record the above transactions.

b. Calculate EPS, assuming a weighted average of 380,000 common shares outstanding.

c. Why do companies, in general, declare and issue a stock split?

Comprehensive Dividend Problem: Stockholders' Equity

10-12 Macintosh Browning Corporation has the following stockholders' equity at December 31, 2007:

7% cumulative preferred stock: $120 par, 50,000 shares authorized, 20,000 shares issued and outstanding	$2,400,000
Common stock: $10 par, 500,000,000 shares authorized, 300,000 shares issued	3,000,000
Additional paid-in capital	900,000
Total contributed capital	6,300,000
Retained earnings	1,200,000
Treasury stock (74,000 shares of common stock)	(1,110,000)
Total stockholders' equity	$6,390,000

Required

a. Why did Macintosh issue preferred stock? What does the seven percent cumulative term indicate?

b. Assume that the board of directors has not declared a dividend in the past three years (the preferred stock was outstanding during these years). What is the amount of dividends outstanding for the previous three years on these cumulative shares?

c. Why might Macintosh prefer preferred stock rather than additional debt?

d. If the board declared and paid dividends to the preferred and common shareholders during the year, show the effects (use + and – and ignore $ amounts) on stockholders' equity on the date of declaration, date of record, and date of payment.

Financial Statement Impact: Debt versus Equity

10-13 The Open Sesame Company has assets of $300,000,000, long-term debts of $100,000,000, common stock of $100,000,000, and retained earnings of $100,000,000. Most of the long-term debt consists of convertible debt carrying fairly high interest rates that are about five points above the current prevailing market. Open Sesame wants to issue $100,000,000 of new debt at current market rates. It will then "call", or retire, the existing convertible debt, using the money from the new debt. Because its share prices have also increased 40% over the past several years, Open Sesame is also considering raising additional funds by issuing new shares of common stock. Funds from the common stock issue would then be used to refinance the debt.

Required

a. If Open Sesame issued new debt, what would be the impact on its balance sheet? On its income statement?

b. If Open Sesame issued new common stock, what would be the impact on its balance sheet? What assumption is crucial to answering this question?

c. What other considerations might drive Open Sesame's decision about this possible refinancing of its long-term debt?

d. How might the current creditors be affected if Open Sesame tries to "call", or retire, its convertible debt? How might they feel? What actions might they take immediately after hearing about the call?

Comparing Financial Ratios of Two Firms Using Differing Accounting Methods

10-14 Two firms provided the following information at the end of 2007 (dollars in millions):

	Adam Co.	*Zachary Co.*
Total assets	$ 105	$ 210
Total liabilities	$ 70	$ 120
Shareholders' equity	$ 35	$ 0
Net income during 2007	$ 15	$ 25
Shares outstanding during 2007	1 million	1.2 million
Market price per share	$ 125.00	$ 150.00

Required

a. Based on the information above, determine the following items for each firm:
- Earnings per share
- Price-to-earnings ratio
- Financial leverage ratio

b. Adam used LIFO inventory costing and accelerated depreciation of plant and equipment costs, while Zachary used FIFO costing and straight-line depreciation. If Adam had been using the same inventory costing and depreciation methods as Zachary, then Adam's net income during 2007 would have been higher by $20 million, and the carrying value of Adam's total assets would have been higher by $85 million. Based on this information, re-compute the three ratios above as if Adam and Zachary used the same accounting methods for inventory and depreciation.

c. Describe your overall conclusions regarding the two firms.

Stock Options as Executive Compensation

10-15 Late in 2007, Natalie Attired, a recent MBA graduate, signed a four-year employment contract with Generic Co. that provides her with an annual salary of $90,000. In addition, at the start of *each year,* 2008 through 2011, Natalie received options to purchase 3,000 shares of Generic's common stock at the market price when the options were received. These options are immediately exercisable and expire after five years from the date of receipt. Assume the following information related to these options:

Year	*Market Price per Option*	*Market Price per Share at Beginning of Year*	*Options Exercised During the Year*
2008	$ 5	$ 50	None
2009	$ 8	$ 80	3,000*
2010	$13	$130	2,000**
2011	$ 9	$ 90	None

*3,000 options at $50 option price of stock.
**2,000 options at $80 option price of stock.

Required

a. Determine the total compensation expense that would be reported by Generic in each year from 2008 through 2011.

b. Determine the total economic benefit that Natalie has received (salary plus value of stockholding and options) from Generic over this same period.

c. Comment on any difference between the results in parts a and b.

Conceptual Discussion: Exchanges of Debt or Equity

10-16 Many U.S. firms have completed exchanges or swaps of stock for debt. Collectively, such swaps often retire more debt than the value of the stock that is exchanged. In other words, the face value of the debt often exceeds the market value of the stock that is exchanged. Typical swaps might include:

- Convertible preferred stock for common stock
- Debt for convertible preferred stock
- Convertible debt for common stock
- Debt for cash and common stock

Required

a. What do you suppose are the incentives or motivations for such swaps? Why would an investor or owner give up something with a historical cost higher than its current market value?

b. What is the effect of such swaps on a firm's balance sheet?

Interpreting Financial Statements: Shareholders' Equity

10-17 DUD Computer is a private company. DUD's major product lines are CAD/CAM computer vision design systems, midrange computers, and computer services. DUD had $1.26 billion in debt at the end of 2007, its losses were more than half a billion dollars, and its net worth (retained earnings) was a negative $674.9 million. It will be in default on its loan covenants if it fails to secure new financing by the end of 2009. Its summary financial trends were:

	2007	*2006*
Revenue (in billions)	$1.44	$1.55
Net (loss) (in millions)	($562.8)*	($172.8)
Loss per share	($9.02)	($3.21)

*Includes nonrecurring charges ("write-downs") of $352.2 million.

Required

a. A business editor claimed, "DUD is in peril with too much debt". On what basis was this comment made?

b. Construct a scenario with high debt levels where such a comment would be premature.

c. Using the data given above, calculate the net loss and loss per share after excluding the nonrecurring charges.

d. The company's president and CEO suggested that DUD had a positive cash flow and would have been profitable if it weren't for huge debt payments and write-downs. Critique the president's conclusions. Is it possible for a company with such huge losses to have positive cash flows? Why? Is it also possible for a company's debt payments to affect its net income? Why?

Transfer of Cash to Related Companies

10-18 Philip Morris was the founder and chairman of Lollipops, Inc. until his death in 2007. The company's performance had been sharply declining during the late 1990s. Because Morris owned the majority of the shares in the company, he was very concerned about the resultant decline in the share prices and market value of Lollipops. To protect his investments, he secretly funneled $300,000,000 from other companies that he owned into purchases of additional Lollipops shares. These new shares were used by the other companies as collateral for bank loans, for financing the purchase of the shares, and for supporting the operations of the other companies. After his death, this series of stock purchases and bank loans was revealed in the financial press, and Lollipops' shares plummeted in value!

Required

a. In what ways were these transactions unethical?

b. How might Lollipops have survived this calamity?

CHAPTER 11

A FRAMEWORK FOR FINANCIAL STATEMENT ANALYSIS

Learning Objectives

1. *Understand why financial statements are analyzed.*
2. *Know where to obtain financial information.*
3. *Determine when financial information is comparable and alternatively learn how to enhance the comparability of financial information that may appear to be noncomparable.*
4. *Identify, calculate, use, and interpret appropriate ratios.*
5. *Identify limitations of financial statement analyses.*
6. *Be able to "Follow the Cash".*

INTRODUCTION

Accountants produce and distribute financial information in financial statements. We have shown excerpts from many annual financial reports earlier in this book. In this chapter, we link many of the ratios and analytical concepts that have been previously introduced. The purpose of this chapter is to show how a comprehensive financial statement analysis can be conducted. To accomplish this purpose, we will use the entire set of financial statements from Wal-Mart Stores, Inc., which is one of the United States' largest retailers, with more than 4,500 stores.

In order for financial information to be useful, it must be interpreted. A comprehensive set of ratios in an organized framework enhances the usefulness and interpretability of financial statements and eases the communication of financial information between firms and users.

USERS OF FINANCIAL STATEMENTS

Users of financial statements can be found in many sectors of the economy. Typical users include a firm's owners, creditors, managers, employees, customers, and suppliers. Users of financial statements include those who already have an economic link to the firm as well as those who may want to have a future economic relationship.

Most users have, or intend to have, a transactional relationship with the firm and some users may be able to obtain information directly from the firm. For example, a lender can request that a credit application be prepared according to its own specifications. Potential customers or potential suppliers may also request special information as they see fit. Most users, however, will use the annual financial statements as well as other reports.

Each of these users may have different objectives while analyzing financial statements:

- *Investors* use financial statement information to help decide whether to increase or decrease their ownership interests in the firm. These decisions are based on projections of investment risks and returns. Financial ratios are widely used in making these projections.
- *Managers* use financial statement information in many different ways, but one of the most important is in setting goals. Managerial goals can be stated in terms of increasing various profitability ratios. Goals can be stated in terms of maintaining or increasing the firm's liquidity, or they can be stated in terms of changing the capital structure in favor of more debt or more equity.
- *Customers* often use annual financial statements to evaluate the firm's stability and its capability to deliver on a timely basis the quantity and quality of goods or services that may be purchased.
- *Potential suppliers and creditors* often are most interested in whether the firm can pay its bills.
- *Other users* of financial statements have a more distant relationship with the firm. These users include government regulators in areas such as securities trading, taxation, environmental protection, occupational health and safety, insurance and other financial markets, and foreign trade. Other

interactions could occur with employee trade unions or other community groups. Finally, various economic and public policy analysts might review a firm's financial statements in their quest to create or improve legislation affecting many broad areas of commerce and social welfare. Any of these groups might want to explore how the firm has affected various components of society.

Each user may have a slightly different objective when analyzing financial statements. The user's objectives will help guide the analysis, such that a creditor might focus more on liquidity ratios, and an investor might concentrate more on profitability ratios.

SOURCES OF FINANCIAL INFORMATION

In addition to the basic business financial statements and disclosures that we have described in earlier chapters, other kinds of financial information are available to financial analysts that can be used in combination with financial statements. Most regulatory agencies, for example, require firms to prepare special-purpose regulatory reports, such as tax returns or environmental impact statements. The SEC also requires special reports each year and each quarter. The SEC's annual report is called a **Form 10K,** which is discussed more thoroughly in TOPICMOD-VIII. The Form 10K is an expanded version of the firm's annual report, which can frequently be used to clarify issues of concern or ambiguity in the annual report.

In addition to annual reports filed with the SEC, public companies must also file quarterly reports, **Form 10Q,** which are less detailed than the annual reports. Furthermore, whenever major events require public disclosure, public firms are also required to file special reports with the SEC, designed to provide immediate information to any interested party. Events that must be reported include replacement of the firm's auditor, a major acquisition or disposition of a business segment, or any major news announcement.

Other sources of public information that are more readily available include various business periodicals such as the *Wall Street Journal, Business Week, Forbes, Fortune, Barron's,* or various newsletters that specialize in certain industries or locales. Even your local newspaper will often have a business section at least weekly.

Investment advisory services also publish summary information about specific firms and industries. Some of the more well known of these include Standard & Poors, Moody's, Value Line, Dun & Bradstreet's, and Robert Morris and Associates. Such services provide condensed information from company annual reports. This information is usually prepared in a standardized format. The process of "homogenizing" the information from the annual report, however, may obscure some of the important insights that could have been obtained from the report itself. One advantage of these services is that they provide interpretations of the financial results and their opinions regarding the future prospects of the companies.

The major source of financial information we are concerned with is the firm's **annual report.** A major portion of Wal-Mart's annual report for 2005 is included in Appendix A and will be referenced throughout our discussion. Such reports usually contain the following elements (see annual reports for Wal-Mart, Target, and eBay).

1. **Management discussion and analysis (MDA),** which is a narrative report providing a qualitative description of the year's highlights. This section may also include a letter from the CEO.
2. Independent accountant's report (auditor's report), which is usually presented as an unqualified opinion or as some version of a qualified opinion regarding the financial statements. A **qualified audit opinion** is one of the most severe signals to conduct a more thorough examination of the financial statements. Annual reports generally include the management's statement of responsibility for the information contained in the financial statements. Under the Sarbanes-Oxley Act, managers (CEO and CFO) are now required to sign sworn personal statements agreeing with the financial statement numbers. This should align the managers' personal interests with the shareholders' interests!
3. Primary financial statements, which include the balance sheet, the income statement, and the statement of cash flows.
4. Secondary financial statements, which may include the statement of shareholders' equity, other reconciliations related to the cash flow statement, and other disclosures regarding the primary financial statements.
5. Notes to the financial statements, which include a variety of supplementary disclosures such as quarterly data, business segment information, and *trend information* in the form of five- or 10-year comparisons of selected financial data or key ratios.

This information in the annual report provides the basis for much of the analysis conducted by users of financial statements. Little formal analysis can be applied to the narrative statements in the management discussion sections and in the notes, but these subjective and qualitative comments can provide much insight into the relationships revealed by the ratio calculations. The conscientious analyst must review both the quantitative and qualitative information in the firm's annual financial reports.

Later in this chapter, we provide a framework for reviewing this information in order to assess the firm's past performance and its future potential. For the remainder of the chapter, we focus exclusively on analyzing financial statements from the perspective of an equity investor. Although creditors and other financial analysts use many of the same ratios identified earlier, we will take an investor focus as we develop and illustrate our framework.

BASIS OF COMPARISON

One of the analyst's first decisions is to identify the **basis of comparison.** That is, what data will be used to compare and evaluate the target firm? It's also important to note that financial data do not exist in a vacuum. Analyzing financial statements from one firm for a single year is like reporting only part of a football score (14)! Therefore, financial statement analysis is often concerned with comparing the current year's results with other related results. The choices include:

1. The prior year(s) results;
2. Another similar firm in the same industry;
3. Another firm in which the analyst may invest;
4. All firms in the same industry and/or industry averages; and
5. Benchmarks or targets that have been previously established, such as lending or investing criteria.

The analyst must determine that one of these choices is a comparable and useful reference with which to compare the target firm. Usually, the prior year or years are a good reference point with which to begin. Any statements that include the effects of a major financial restructuring or merger would generally be noncomparable. In other words, before comparing a firm's results with the prior year, the analyst must examine both sets of statements and notes to determine whether a significant unusual event occurred.

If significant unusual events have occurred that would distort comparisons, then the financial statements may need to be restated or rearranged to make them more comparable. Restatements may be necessary in the following situations:

- Mergers or major acquisitions,
- Discontinued operations or major dispositions,
- Changes in accounting principles or estimates,
- Extraordinary items (on the income statement),
- Changes in account classifications,
- Changes in reporting periods (such as fiscal periods),
- Shifts in industry structure or classification, or
- Any other unusual or nonrecurring event.

Note that we have already shown you how to conduct similar restatements in earlier chapters dealing with sustainable income and with converting LIFO statements to FIFO. The general approach to any restatement is to show the data as originally prepared by the company, and then make rough approximations to what might have been reported (pro forma) under an alternative approach. For example, if net income was reported at $4M, but this figure included a $10M special charge for restructuring; then the restated net income (pro forma) would be $14M ($4M + $10M). Generally, the tax effects of these restated figures can be ignored as they are beyond the scope of this text.

It is also beyond the scope of this text to illustrate all of these possible restatements, but several examples are shown in other chapters throughout the book. The primary guideline is that "more comparability is better". Financial information from firms might be comparable if the firms:

- operate in the same country,
- follow similar accounting practices,
- are of similar size (revenues and/or assets),
- produce similar products or services, and
- have a similar capital structure.

Although other important dimensions of comparability may be available, size, capital structure, and product mix are the most important for our purposes. The analyst must decide whether differences in these areas are material or whether they might have an impact on the final conclusions. Comparability is a subjective and qualitative issue that can never be quantified by a numerical index.

Thus far, we have identified four major steps that must be accomplished before starting to calculate financial statement ratios:

1. Identify the purpose and objectives of the analysis.
2. Review the Management's Discussion and Analysis (MDA), the financial statements, notes, and audit opinion to identify any unusual events or characteristics and become familiar with the nature of the firm's operations.
3. Determine whether any restatements due to mergers, discontinued operations, and so on, are necessary to enhance the comparability of the firm's financial statements.
4. Determine whether the firm's size, capital structure, and product mix are sufficiently comparable (between firms or time periods) to proceed with the ratio calculations.

FINANCIAL STATEMENT ANALYSIS RATIOS AND FRAMEWORK

The next major step is to conduct horizontal and vertical analyses of the financial statements. Usually this analysis begins with the income statement, including all its major revenue and expense items. A **horizontal analysis** focuses on year-to-year changes or growth for each major element in the income statement. Common-size financial statements, a tool employed in a **vertical analysis,** examine the percentage composition of the income statement. Percentages are calculated on the basis of net revenues, where each item on the income statement is separately analyzed. In other words, the dollar amounts on each line are converted into percentages (of net revenues).

Horizontal and vertical analyses of the balance sheet statement should also be conducted. (Horizontal and vertical analysis of the major subtotals on the cash flow statement might also be conducted. We view these as optional and do not show any formal analysis of Wal-Mart's cash flow statement.) The results of these analyses will focus attention on areas of significant change. Identify any consistent trends in revenues or major categories of related expenses. Such analyses do not provide complete answers. Rather, they *indicate areas of concern* that require further investigation. Therefore, step 5 in our framework is:

5. Conduct horizontal and vertical analyses of each financial statement. Identify any unusual trends.

Categories of Financial Ratios

Analysts find it useful to classify ratios into broad groupings, based on the characteristics that particular ratios are intended to measure. In this section, we discuss ratios under four major headings that are widely employed by analysts: liquidity, profitability, capital structure, and investor ratios.

Liquidity Ratios

Liquidity ratios indicate the firm's short-term solvency. They also indicate how effectively the firm is managing its **working capital.** Exhibit 11-1 shows the formulas used in computing a representative set of liquidity ratios. Each of these ratios has been described earlier in the text, as indicated by the chapter references in the exhibit. The **current ratio** and **quick ratio** are measures of solvency. Other measures of cash availability can also be used to indicate how long the firm could operate using only its current cash balances. A limitation of these ratios is that they do not reflect the availability of short-term credit. Many firms operate with decreasing levels of liquidity as they rely more heavily on "lines of credit" that

EXHIBIT 11-1 SUMMARY OF LIQUIDITY RATIOS

$$\text{Current ratio} = \frac{\text{Current assets}}{\text{Current liabilities}}$$

(Chapter 3)

$$\text{Quick ratio} = \frac{\text{Cash + cash equivalents + accounts receivable (net)}}{\text{Current liabilities}}$$

(Chapter 3)

$$\text{Average sales per day} = \frac{\text{Sales revenue}}{365}$$

(Chapter 6)

$$\text{Collection period} = \frac{\text{Accounts receivable (gross)}}{\text{Average sales per day}}$$

(Chapter 6)

$$\text{Cost of goods sold per day} = \frac{\text{Cost of goods sold}}{365}$$

(Chapter 6)

$$\text{Number of days' sales in ending inventory (NDS)} = \frac{\text{Ending inventory}}{\text{Cost of goods sold per day}}$$

(Chapter 6)

can be used, or repaid, on a daily basis. Humana, Inc. (a health care insurance and hospital company), for example, reported zero cash on its balance sheet for three years (1990–1992)! In many cases, high current or quick ratios indicate mismanagement or wasteful investment in working capital. Some firms may just have too much liquidity. Either paying off liabilities, paying dividends to shareholders, or buying treasury shares, might be a more effective use of excess cash.

Another view of working capital suggests that it is as important as cash! "Among the most important items . . . inventory, accounts receivable and accounts payable. These are important elements of a company's working capital. Analysts look at *working capital as a sign of the company's efficiency and financial strength.* It is, in effect, the *cash a company uses* to finance the conversion of raw materials into finished goods, then to sell those goods and collect the money owed it (emphasis added)." (Ken Brown, "How to Spot the Dirt in Rosy Annual Reports," *The Wall Street Journal,* February 14, 2003, p. C1).

Accounts receivable management can be evaluated relative to the amount of credit sales, using **accounts receivable as a percentage of sales,** or using the average collection period.

$$\text{Accounts receivable as a percentage of sales} = \frac{\text{Accounts receivable (gross)}}{\text{Sales}}$$

The **collection period** is the average length of time it takes to collect a receivable. It is calculated in two steps by first calculating the average sales per day:

$$\text{Average sales per day} = \frac{\text{Sales}}{365}$$

Next, the collection period is calculated by dividing gross accounts receivable by average sales per day.

$$\text{Collection period} = \frac{\text{Accounts receivable (gross)}}{\text{Average sales per day}}$$

This ratio indicates the number of day's sales in accounts receivable. The collection period indicates how long it takes to collect an average customer's account.

The **number of days in inventory** indicates how quickly the firm is "turning" its inventory. Comparative industry statistics can often be used to evaluate the days in inventory. Certainly, comparisons with the prior periods will indicate whether the turnover has increased or decreased, and changes in product mix will dramatically affect the inventory ratios.

Step 6 in our framework encompasses liquidity ratios

6. Calculate the basic liquidity ratios. In cases where liquidity seems to be too high or too low, conduct further analyses as necessary.

Profitability Ratios

Profitability ratios are the second major focus of analysis for any investor. Without profits, there will be no return to the investor or no one will want to invest. The primary profitability ratios are defined in Exhibit 11-2; note references to earlier chapters where they were initially discussed.

The **gross profit percentage** is the first source of profitability for a manufacturing or merchandising firm. The data for the gross profit margin are found in the first sections of the income statement. These data indicate the level of profits earned from buying and reselling goods. A decreasing gross profit percentage may indicate decreased sales prices, higher costs of production, or a shift from high-profit to low-profit products.

The **operating income ratio** is the second indicator of profitability because it includes all the other normal and recurring operating costs. Increasing or stable levels of operating income indicate sustainability of the firm's profits. Decreasing operating income ratios usually indicate a need for the firm to examine its production efficiency, its marketing strategies, and its control of administrative costs.

The most important profitability ratio from an investor's viewpoint is the **return on equity (ROE) ratio.** It is often called ROI, return on investment ratio,

EXHIBIT 11-2 SUMMARY OF PROFITABILITY RATIOS

Gross profit percentage	=	$\frac{\text{Gross profit}}{\text{Net sales revenue}}$ (Chapter 6)
Operating income percentage	=	$\frac{\text{Operating income}}{\text{Net sales revenue}}$ (Chapter 4)
Return on equity	=	$\frac{\text{Net income}}{\text{Average shareholders' equity}}$ (Chapter 4)
Return on assets	=	$\frac{\text{Net income}}{\text{Average total assets}}$ (Chapter 4)
Cash return on assets	=	$\frac{\text{Cash flow from operating activities}}{\text{Average total assets}}$ (Chapter 5)
Quality of income	=	$\frac{\text{Cash flow from operating activities}}{\text{Net income}}$ (Chapter 5)

because it indicates the annual rate of return to the firm's investors or owners. Return on equity represents the residual return that is available to owners after deducting all other financing costs.

The **return on assets (ROA) ratio** indicates the rate of return on the firm's assets. It can be used to compare rates of return with alternative investments that could be undertaken. It can also be used to compare profitability across firms and over different time periods. (ROA is sometimes calculated with an adjustment for the effects of debt financing by removing the after-tax effects of interest expense. We are not following this convention.)

Some analysts may prefer to analyze the firm's profitability and financial returns in terms of cash and not in terms of accrual-based net income. The **cash return on assets ratio** should be compared with the corresponding profitability ratios based on net income and ROA. Results that appear to be inconsistent should be examined carefully. These ratios look at financial returns to the firm in terms of cash, not in terms of accrual-based net income. As such, analysts often view cash-based profitability ratios as more objective measures.

The final profitability ratio, **quality of income,** is a direct comparison between cash flows from operating activities (CFOA) and net income (NI). The analyst must examine trends within the same company to determine that CFOA is not decreasing relative to NI. Therefore, step 7 in our financial statement analysis framework follows:

7. Calculate profitability ratios based on net income and on cash flows from operating activities. Evaluate trends in profitability and compare the appropriate NI and CFOA ratios for consistency. Compare profitability ratios across similar companies and against industry averages.

Capital Structure

Capital structure analysis assesses the firm's strategies for financing its assets and indicates the relative amounts of debt and equity capital. The analyst evaluates how those sources change and how they compare with other firms in the same industry. The analyst then tries to gain insight into the firm's decisions about capital sources in order to predict future capital financing decisions. An investor would surely like to know whether the firm is likely to issue new debt or sell additional shares of stock. Identifying shifts in capital structure over time may indicate how the firm will make future decisions about sources of capital. The major ways to examine capital structure are summarized in Exhibit 11-3.

The **percentage composition analysis** is the starting point for any analysis of capital structure. It describes the relative amounts of capital obtained from each major source of financing. The analyst can examine the percentage composition results to highlight changes from the prior year as well as compare percentage composition ratios with similar firms and with industry averages.

EXHIBIT 11-3 SUMMARY OF CAPITAL STRUCTURE RATIOS

Percentage composition	=	The results of the vertical analysis of the right side of the balance sheet, such that the sum of all sources of capital must be 100% (Chapter 3)
Suggested % subtotals	=	$\frac{\text{Current liabilities}}{\text{Total liabilities and shareholders' equity}}$
		$\frac{\text{Long-term debt}}{\text{Total liabilities and shareholders' equity}}$
		$\frac{\text{Deferred taxes + other similar liabilities}}{\text{Total liabilities and shareholders' equity}}$
		$\frac{\text{Shareholders' equity}}{\text{Total liabilities and shareholders' equity}}$
Financial leverage (also called debt to assets)	=	$\frac{\text{Total liabilities}}{\text{Total assets}}$ (Chapters 3, 9)
Times interest earned	=	$\frac{\text{Earnings before interest and taxes (EBIT)}}{\text{Interest expense}}$ (Chapter 4)

Note that the **financial leverage ratio** is simply a variation on percentage composition analysis. All liabilities are added and are then divided by total assets (which, by definition, must equal total liabilities and shareholders' equity). It is not always clear whether to include deferred taxes and other similar liabilities, however. In many cases, the analyst will find that this category of liabilities may be a dominant source of capital because of recent changes in accounting rules regarding deferred taxes. The various capital structure ratios (and trends) are also informative about the financing strategies that the firm has chosen.

The **times interest earned ratio** is an indicator of relative risk. The lower the times interest earned, the higher is the risk of bankruptcy or other default. Times interest earned indicates the "cushion" or margin of safety that the firm enjoys in meeting its interest expenses. A ratio close to 1.0 indicates that the firm is barely covering its interest expenses. Any slight decrease in earnings would then result in an inability to cover the interest expenses. As usual, trends in this ratio should be monitored. Therefore, step 8 in our financial statement analysis framework is

8. Evaluate the firm's capital structure with special emphasis on trends in the percentage composition ratios.

Investor Ratios

Investor ratios were introduced in Chapter 10. These ratios all relate to an external dimension of ownership interest. Most indicate how the firm is performing with regard to the market value of its shares. A listing of investor ratios appears in Exhibit 11-4.

The **earnings-per-share (EPS) ratio** indicates the net income earned by each share of outstanding stock. Investors often use EPS as a primary comparison of performance and profitability across different companies. However, *we believe that it is overemphasized.* It should not be used in isolation outside the context of other dimensions of financial performance. Furthermore, EPS's should be used only in conjunction with EPS's from prior years and/or with EPS's from other comparable firms.

The **market-to-book value ratio** indicates the relationship between the market's valuation of the firm and the book values shown in the firm's financial statements. Investors often use the market-to-book ratio to select targets of opportunity where the market is thought to undervalue a particular firm. It can also be used to influence an investor's decision to sell shares in a firm when the market may overvalue the firm's assets. We are concerned that this ratio really includes two diverse factors ("apples and oranges"). The analyst must focus mostly on the separate elements of the numerator and denominator. The numerator reflects a variety of external market perceptions and expectations. The denominator reflects a variety of generally accepted accounting principles (GAAP) applied to the firm's assets and equities. When market values are increasing and book values are declining, this might reflect the fact that GAAP is undervaluing the firm's recorded assets; many valuable economic resources of the firm may not even appear on the balance sheet.

The **price-to-earnings (P/E) ratio** indicates the relationship between market prices and earnings and is widely used to compare firms. Investors often establish guidelines, or cutoffs, such that they only purchase shares with a P/E of less

EXHIBIT 11-4 SUMMARY OF INVESTOR RATIOS

Earnings per share	=	$\frac{\text{Net income available to common}}{\text{Weighted average number of shares outstanding}}$ (Chapter 10)
Market-to-book value	=	$\frac{\text{Market price per share}}{\text{Book value per share}}$ (Chapter 10)
Price-to-earnings (P/E)	=	$\frac{\text{Market price per share}}{\text{Earnings per share}}$ (Chapter 10)

than 30. In any event, the P/E ratio indicates the interaction between stock market prices and the income statement. As such, it is a convenient and widely accessible way to compare alternative investment opportunities.

In order to better understand the effects of the firm's performance relative to the stock market, we normally ask our students to conduct a trend analysis comparing the firm's stock prices to the market trends exhibited by the stock exchange on which that firm's shares are traded. For example, a firm traded on the New York Stock Exchange could be compared to the Dow Jones Industrial Average or to the NYSE market trends. These share price trend data can be found on Yahoo.com (finance) or similar websites. It is important to identify whether the fluctuations in the firm's stock prices are due to unique factors affecting only that firm, or whether the changes are mostly due to external market forces that are uncontrollable by the firm.

Finally, step 9 in our financial statement analysis framework is:

9. Examine the firm's market performance, using EPS, P/E, and market-to-book value ratios.

Final Steps

After assembling this myriad of ratios, the astute analyst must ask a series of questions, such as, So what? What's missing? How do we predict the firm's future performance?

Obviously, there are no easy recipes in this area. The analyst must look for inconsistencies and ambiguities that are evidenced in peculiar trends or unusual ratio results. Many ratios merely provide clues that require the analyst to look further at the notes to determine events and accounting treatments that are the cause of the numbers in the financial statements. The thoughtful analyst will always go back and forth between the numerical calculations and the underlying information in the notes while trying to decipher reality. Therefore, the last step is:

10. Examine any inconsistencies in the ratio results and review the notes for further clarification. Then recalculate the ratios based on new insight and information obtained from the notes. Finally, try to estimate how the firm's liquidity, profitability, capital structure, and investor performance may change in the future.

Financial Statement Analysis Framework

In summary, our entire financial statement analysis framework is:

1. Identify the purpose and objectives of the analysis. Who are the users and what decisions are to be made after the analysis?

2. Review the management's discussion and analysis (MDA), the financial statements, notes, and audit opinions to identify any unusual events or characteristics.
3. Determine whether any restatements due to mergers, discontinued operations, accounting changes, or other factors are necessary to enhance the comparability of the statements.
4. Determine whether the firm's size, capital structure, and product mix are appropriate to proceed with the ratio calculations.
5. Conduct horizontal and vertical analyses of each financial statement. Identify any unusual trends.
6. Calculate the basic liquidity ratios. In cases where liquidity seems to be too high, or too low, conduct further analyses as necessary.
7. Calculate profitability ratios based on net income and on CFOA. Evaluate trends in profitability and compare the appropriate NI and CFOA ratios for consistency. Then compare profitability ratios across similar companies and against industry averages.
8. Evaluate the firm's capital structure with special emphasis on trends in the percentage composition ratios.
9. Examine the firm's market performance using EPS, P/E, and market-to-book value ratios.
10. Examine any inconsistencies in the ratio results. Review the notes for further clarification. Recalculate the ratios based on new insight and information obtained from the notes. Try to estimate how the firm's liquidity, profitability, capital structure, and investor performance may change in the future.

FINANCIAL STATEMENT ANALYSIS, WAL-MART STORES, INC.

In this section, we apply our financial statement analysis framework to Wal-Mart Stores, Inc. We chose the Wal-Mart statements because they are representative of how most large companies present their financial data and because their statements include a variety of interesting but typical complications, where we can concentrate as much on the sources of information as on the numerical calculations. We have taken an investor focus to this analysis, concentrating on information that might be useful to someone contemplating purchasing shares of Wal-Mart's common stock.

Initial Review of Wal-Mart Stores, Inc.

The independent auditor's report by Ernst & Young is a fairly typical, unqualified opinion (see Appendix A). It indicates no particular concerns, or issues that should alarm investors.

Although some unique events occurred during each year, the statements have sufficient detail to permit comparison across the two fiscal years. Note that all the dollar amounts, except the per-share amounts, are *stated in millions of dollars.*

As you have already seen, this type of rounding is quite typical in financial reporting. Such rounding will make no significant difference in the ratio results.

Wal-Mart's MDA highlights several useful results, including a 9.5% growth in sales and a 3% growth in "same-store" sales. Cost of sales as a percentage of sales decreased by a small percentage (0.31%). Net income increased by 9.4%, which is significant. Some of these positive results might be due to the firm's inventory valuation methods, to the change in goodwill amortization, and to the use of straight-line depreciation methods. Review Wal-Mart's MDA (www.walmartstores.com, 2005 Annual Report, p. 23) and Note 1 Appendix A to the financial statements for other clues to help explain the ratio results. We assume that the focus of investigation is to make an investment decision on Wal-Mart's stock.

Horizontal and Vertical Analyses of Wal-Mart Stores, Inc. Income Statements

Horizontal and vertical analyses of Wal-Mart's income statements for fiscal 2005 and 2004 appear in Exhibits 11-5 and 11-6, respectively. The horizontal analysis for Wal-Mart's income statement, Exhibit 11-5, indicates that net sales grew about 9.5% in fiscal 2005, while cost of sales and operating expenses grew slightly more than net sales (9.6% versus 9.5%). The more interesting comparison relates to net income, which increased 9.4% in 2005.

Normally earnings grow faster than sales because at least some of the firm's expenses, such as depreciation and administrative costs, do not vary directly with sales from year to year. The comparisons in Exhibit 11-5 indicate that Wal-Mart's income and revenues have both increased, and in proportion to one another. The vertical analysis of Wal-Mart's income statement in Exhibit 11-6 reinforces the observation that all the operating expenses were stable relative to sales, indicating effective cost control and efficient operations. Note also the increase in interest expense which appears to be related to an increase in the overall debt of the company as well as rising interest rates. If any other material or unexplained changes were noted on the income statement, the analyst would refer to the notes and other financial disclosures to determine the reasons for this change. Wal-Mart's entire financial report for 2005 is included in Appendix A, and problems at the end of this chapter will enable you to explore these statements further.

Horizontal and Vertical Analyses of Wal-Mart Stores, Inc. Balance Sheets

Analysts generally expect that a firm's working capital balances will increase proportionally to the change in revenues during the period. This is because most components of working capital are directly affected by the firm's operating level. On the other hand, changes in noncurrent assets and liabilities are more sporadic in nature and result from episodic events such as capital spending and

EXHIBIT 11-5 HORIZONTAL ANALYSIS OF AN INCOME STATEMENT

Wal-Mart Stores, Inc.
Income Statement: Horizontal Analysis
Fiscal years ended January 31
(Dollars in millions, except per share data)

	2006	PERCENT* CHANGE	2005
Revenues			
Net sales	$312,427	+ 9.5%	$285,222
Other income	3,227	+ 10.9	2,910
	315,654	+ 9.6	288,132
Costs and expenses			
Cost of sales	240,391	+ 9.4	219,793
Operating, selling, and administrative expenses	56,733	+ 10.7	51,248
	297,124	+ 9.6	271,041
Operating income	18,530	+ 8.4	17,091
Interest			
Debt	1,171	+ 25.4	934
Capital leases	249	− 1.6	253
Interest income	− 248	+ 23.4	− 201
Interest, net	1,172	+ 18.9	986
Income before income taxes and minority interest	17,358	+ 7.8	16,105
Provision for income taxes			
Current	5,932	+ 11.4	5,326
Deferred	− 129	−149.0	263
	5,803	+ 3.8	5,589
Income before minority interests	11,555	+ 9.9	10,516
Minority interests	− 324	+ 30.1	− 249
Net income	$ 11,231	+ 9.4%	$ 10,267
Net income per common share			
Basic net income per common share:			
Net income per common share	$ 2.68	+ 11.2	$ 2.41
Average number of common shares	4,183		4,259
Diluted net income per common share:			
Net income per common share	$ 2.68	+ 11.2	$ 2.41
Average number of common shares	4,188		4,266

*Percentage could also be calculated as FY2005/FY2004.

issuances of debt and equity securities. The horizontal analysis of Wal-Mart's balance sheet, shown in Exhibit 11-7, indicates an overall increase in current assets of 12.8% and an increase in total assets of 15.0%. Although several individual items on the balance sheet show large percentage changes, the dollar amounts of

EXHIBIT 11-6 VERTICAL ANALYSIS OF AN INCOME STATEMENT

Wal-Mart Stores, Inc.
Income Statement: Vertical Analysis
Fiscal years ended January 31
(Dollars in millions, except per share data)

	2006	PERCENTAGE	2005	PERCENTAGE
Revenues				
Net sales	$312,427	99.0%	$285,222	99.0%
Other income	3,227	1.0	2,910	1.0
	315,654	100.0	288,132	100.0
Costs and expenses				
Cost of sales	240,391	76.1	219,793	76.3
Operating, selling, and administrative expenses	56,733	18.0	51,248	17.8
	297,124	94.1	271,041	94.1
Operating income	18,530	5.9	17,091	5.9
Interest				
Debt	1,171	0.4	934	0.3
Capital leases	249	0.1	253	0.1
Interest income	– 248	– 0.1	– 201	– 0.1
Interest, net	1,172	0.4	986	0.3
Income before income taxes and minority interest	17,358	5.5	16,105	5.6
Provision for income taxes				
Current	5,932	1.8	5,326	1.8
Deferred	– 129	0.0	263	0.1
	5,803	1.8	5,589	1.9
Income before minority interests	11,555	3.7	10,516	3.7
Minority interests	– 324	– 0.1	– 249	– 0.1
Net income	$ 11,231	3.6%	$ 10,267	3.6%

the changes are relatively minor. The percentage changes are large because the amounts for these items in the base year (2005) are rather small. Overall, the percentage changes shown in Exhibit 11-7 appear reasonable and consistent with the changes noted in the income statement.

The vertical analysis of Wal-Mart's balance sheet in Exhibit 11-8 shows that the composition of the assets and the overall mix of liabilities and shareholder's equity have remained very stable. The firm appears to keep a large portion (23.3%) of its assets in inventories. Also the larger portion of the firm's financing is from borrowing, rather than from shareholder's investments or retained earnings.

One interesting component of Wal-Mart's capital structure is the 100 million authorized shares of preferred stock that have not been issued. This represents a huge capacity for additional capital financing.

EXHIBIT 11-7 HORIZONTAL ANALYSIS OF THE BALANCE SHEET

Wal-Mart Stores, Inc.
Balance Sheet: Horizontal Analysis
Fiscal years ended January 31
(Dollar amounts in millions)

	2006	PERCENT CHANGE	2005
Assets			
Current assets			
Cash and cash equivalents	$ 6,414	+ 16.9%	$ 5,488
Receivables	2,662	+ 55.2	1,715
Inventories	32,191	+ 8.2	29,762
Prepaid expenses and other	2,557	+ 35.4	1,889
Total Current Assets	43,824	+ 12.8	38,854
Property, plant, and equipment, at cost			
Land	16,643	+ 15.0	14,472
Building and improvements	56,163	+ 20.6	46,574
Fixtures and equipment	22,750	+ 6.0	21,461
Transportation equipment	1,746	+ 14.1	1,530
	97,302	+ 15.8	84,037
Less accumulated depreciation	21,427	+ 15.0	18,637
Net property, plant, and equipment	75,875	+ 16.0	65,400
Property under capital lease			
Property under capital lease	5,578	+ 22.4	4,556
Less accumulated amortization	2,163	+ 17.7	1,838
Net property under capital lease	3,415	+ 25.6	2,718
Other assets and deferred charges			
Goodwill	12,188	+ 12.8	10,803
Other assets and deferred charges	2,885	+ 21.3	2,379
Total Assets	$138,187	+ 15.0%	$120,154
Liabilities and shareholders' equity			
Current liabilities			
Commercial paper	$ 3,754	− 1.5%	$ 3,812
Accounts payable	25,373	+ 15.4	21,987
Accrued liabilities	13,465	+ 11.1	12,120
Accrued income taxes	1,340	+ 4.6	1,281
Long-term debt due within one year	4,595	+ 22.2	3,759
Obligations under capital leases due within one year	299	+ 34.1	223
Total Current Liabilities	48,826	+ 13.1	43,182
Long-term debt	26,429	+ 31.6	20,087
Long-term obligations under capital leases	3,742	+ 18.0	3,171
Deferred income taxes and other	4,552	+ 52.9	2,978

EXHIBIT 11-7 (continued)

Wal-Mart Stores, Inc.
Balance Sheet: Horizontal Analysis
Fiscal years ended January 31
(Amounts in millions)

	2006	PERCENT CHANGE	2005
Minority interests	1,467	+ 9.5	1,340
Shareholders' equity			
Preferred stock ($.010 par value; 100 shares authorized, none issued)	—	—	—
Common stock: ($0.10 par value; 11,000 shares authorized, 4,165 and 4,234 shares issued and outstanding in 2006 and 2005, respectively)	417	− 1.4	423
Capital in excess of par value	2,596	+ 7.1	2,425
Retained earnings	49,105	+ 12.0	43,854
Accumulated other comprehensive income	1,053	− 60.1	2,694
Total Shareholders' Equity	53,171	+ 7.6	49,396
Total Liabilities and Shareholders' Equity	$138,187	+ 15.0	$120,154

Liquidity Analysis of Wal-Mart Stores, Inc.

Wal-Mart's liquidity ratios for each fiscal year are calculated in Exhibit 11-9 and provide the following insights. Wal-Mart's current ratio remained unchanged during the year, while the quick ratio increased slightly over the year. The collection period of the accounts receivable has increased from 2.2 to 3.1 days, and the number of days' sales in inventory has decreased from 49.4 days to 48.8 days. Since most of Wal-Mart's sales to customers are for cash, it is not surprising that their accounts receivable are not significant or that the collection period is very short. On the other hand, inventories are a very major component of Wal-Mart's balance sheet, so any deterioration in inventory-related ratios could be important. A small decrease in number of days' sales is probably an improvement, not a negative. On the whole, Wal-Mart's liquidity ratios have improved. An analyst must consider these liquidity improvements in the context of profitability and other ratios.

Profitability Analysis of Wal-Mart Stores, Inc.

Wal-Mart's profitability ratios are calculated in Exhibit 11-10. The operating income ratio indicates no change in profitability. Return on equity has increased while return on assets has decreased. These trends in profitability ratios must be interpreted cautiously, however, until the analyst obtains a better understanding

EXHIBIT 11-8 VERTICAL ANALYSIS OF THE BALANCE SHEET

Wal-Mart Stores, Inc.
Balance Sheet: Vertical Analysis
Fiscal years ended January 31
(Dollar amounts in millions)

	2006 DOLLARS	%	2005 DOLLARS	%
Assets				
Current assets				
Cash and cash equivalents	$ 6,414	+ 4.6%	$ 5,488	+ 4.5
Receivables	2,662	+ 1.9	1,715	+ 1.4
Inventories	32,191	+ 23.3	29,762	+ 24.8
Prepaid expenses and other	2,557	+ 1.9	1,889	+ 1.6
Total Current Assets	43,824	+ 31.7	38,854	+ 32.3
Property, plant, and equipment, at cost				
Land	16,643	+ 12.0	14,472	+ 12.0
Building and improvements	56,163	+ 40.6	46,574	+ 38.8
Fixtures and equipment	22,750	+ 16.5	21,461	+ 17.9
Transportation equipment	1,746	+ 1.3	1,530	+ 1.3
	97,302	+ 70.4	84,037	+ 69.9
Less accumulated depreciation	21,427	+ 15.5	18,637	+ 15.5
Net property, plant, and equipment	75,875	+ 54.9	65,400	+ 54.4
Property under capital lease				
Property under capital lease	5,578	+ 4.0	4,556	+ 3.8
Less accumulated amortization	2,163	+ 1.5	1,838	+ 1.5
Net property under capital lease	3,415	+ 2.5	2,718	+ 2.3
Other assets and deferred charges				
Goodwill	12,188	+ 8.8	10,803	+ 9.0
Other assets and deferred charges	2,885	+ 2.1	2,379	+ 2.0
Total Assets	$138,187	+100.0%	$120,154	+100.0%
Liabilities and shareholders' equity				
Current liabilities				
Commercial paper	$ 3,754	+ 2.7%	$ 3,812	+ 3.2%
Accounts payable	25,373	+ 18.4	21,987	+ 18.3
Accrued liabilities	13,465	+ 9.7	12,120	+ 10.1
Accrued income taxes	1,340	+ 1.0	1,281	+ 1.1
Long-term debt due within one year	4,595	+ 3.3	3,759	+ 3.1
Obligations under capital leases due within one year	299	+ 0.2	223	+ 0.2
Total Current Liabilities	48,826	+ 35.3	43,182	+ 36.0
Long-term debt	26,429	+ 19.1	20,087	+ 16.7
Long-term obligations under capital leases	3,742	+ 2.7	3,171	+ 2.6
Deferred income taxes and other	4,552	+ 3.3	2,978	+ 2.5

EXHIBIT 11-8 (continued)

Wal-Mart Stores, Inc.
Balance Sheet: Vertical Analysis
January 31
(Amounts in millions)

	2006 DOLLARS	%	2005 DOLLARS	%
Minority interests	1,467	+ 1.1	1,340	+ 1.1
Shareholders' equity				
Preferred stock ($.010 par value; 100 shares authorized, none issued)	—		—	
Common stock: ($0.10 par value; 11,000 shares authorized, 4,165 and 4,234 shares issued and outstanding in 2006 and 2005, respectively)	417	+ 0.3	423	+ 0.4
Capital in excess of par value	2,596	+ 1.9	2,425	+ 2.0
Retained earnings	49,105	+ 35.5	43,854	+ 36.5
Accumulated other comprehensive income	1,053	+ 0.8	2,694	+ 2.2
Total Shareholders' Equity	53,171	+ 38.5	49,396	+ 41.1
Total Liabilities and Shareholders' Equity	$138,187	+100.0%	$120,154	+100.0%

of the reasons for the increase in interest expenses. Note that Wal-Mart's interest-bearing debt has increased, which has contributed to the increase in interest expense. There also has been a rise in interest rates as indicated in the MDA.

Similarly, the cash-based profitability ratios also indicate consistent, positive trends. The statement of cash flows (see Appendix A) shows that operating cash flows increased from $15,044 in fiscal 2004 to $17,633 in fiscal 2005. Wal-Mart's cash return on assets increased from 13.5% to 13.8%. Its quality of income also increased from 146.5% to 157%. All of these trends are positive.

These results dictate that the investor look more closely at the sources of cash flow from operations to determine whether they are likely to continue at these same levels. The analyst must look carefully at the major sources of cash inflows and outflows, and estimate trends in each. Wal-Mart's cash flow based ratios seem strong, and all of the major trends in cash seem positive.

As we indicated earlier, most investors prefer cash flows to net income, if they have to make a choice. To Wal-Mart's credit, it also exhibits an increase in profitability, based on net earnings and accrual-based calculations.

EXHIBIT 11-9 LIQUIDITY ANALYSIS

Wal-Mart Stores, Inc.
Liquidity Ratios
Fiscal years ended January 31
(Dollar amounts in millions)

RATIO		FORMULA		2006	2005
Current ratio	=	Current assets / Current liabilities	=	$43,824 / $48,826	$38,854 / $43,182
			=	0.90	0.90
Quick ratio	=	Cash and equivalents, and accounts receivable / Current liabilities	=	$6,414 + 2,662 / $48,826	$5,488 + 1,715 / $43,182
			=	0.19	0.17
Average sales per day	=	Sales revenue / Days in the year*	=	$315,654 / 365	$288,132 / 365
			=	$865	$789
Collection period**	=	Accounts receivable / Average sales per day	=	$2,662 / $865	$1,715 / $789
			=	3.1 days	2.2 days
Cost of goods sold per day	=	Cost of goods sold / Days in the year*	=	$240,391 / 365	$219,793 / 365
			=	$659	$602
Number of days' sales in ending inventory	=	Ending inventory / Cost of goods sold per day	=	$32,191 / $659	$29,762 / $602
			=	48.8 days	49.4 days

* The number of days in the reporting years is 365 days (assumed).
** Because gross receivables are used in this ratio, the balances in the allowance for uncollectible accounts usually must be added to the net accounts receivable. Because this adjustment is not material for Wal-Mart, we have used net accounts receivable in the calculation.

Capital Structure Analysis of Wal-Mart Stores, Inc.

Wal-Mart's capital structure can be described by the ratios in Exhibit 11-11. The vertical analysis of Wal-Mart's liability and shareholders' equity indicates a modest increase in the relative percentages of long-term debt. Deferred taxes and other similar liabilities were minor, relative to total debt in both years. Current liabilities and shareholders' equity increased in absolute amounts, but decreased in percentage terms. Overall, Wal-Mart's changes in debt and equity balances are typical for a growing company. Wal-Mart's times interest earned decreased from

EXHIBIT 11-10 PROFITABILITY ANALYSIS

Wal-Mart Stores, Inc.
Profitability Ratios
Fiscal years ended January 31
(Dollar amounts in millions)

RATIO		FORMULA		2006	2005
Operating income percentage	=	Operating income / Sales revenue	=	$18,530 / $315,654	$17,091 / $288,132
			=	5.9%	5.9%
Return on equity	=	Net income / Shareholders' equity*	=	$11,231 / $53,171	$10,267 / $49,396
			=	21.1%	20.8%
Return on assets	=	Net income + [Interest expense × (1 –* tax rate)]** / Total assets	=	$12,154 / $138,187	$11,039 / $120,154
			=	8.8%	9.2%
Cash return on assets	=	Cash flow from operating activities + Interest paid / Total assets	=	$17,633 + 1,390 / $138,187	$15,044 + 1,163 / $120,154
			=	13.8%	13.5%
Quality of income	=	Cash flow from operating activities / Net income	=	$17,633 / $11,231	$15,044 / $10,267
			=	157%	146.5%

* For convenience we have used end-of-year balance sheet amounts in these ratio calculations. If the balance sheet amounts fluctuate markedly during the year, analysts would instead use averages rather than year-end amounts.

** Calculated using Wal-Mart's federal statutory tax rate of 35%. In 2006, the numerator is $12,154 [$11,231 + $1,420 × (1 – .35)], and in 2005 the numerator is $11,039 [$10,267 + $1,187 × (1 – .35)].

14.6 to 13.2, but still is a healthy margin of safety. On the whole, after considering the increase in debt and associated increase in interest expense, Wal-Mart's capital structure analysis does not indicate any major concerns.

Investor Ratios, Wal-Mart Stores, Inc.

Wal-Mart's investor ratios are calculated in Exhibit 11-12. Based on the ratios shown, it appears that the market is not reassured by Wal-Mart's performance in 2005. Its market-to-book value ratio has decreased. Further evaluations based on trends should also be conducted. The P/E ratio decreased from 21.7 to 17.2. To some extent, this decrease in the P/E ratio may reflect the market's view that Wal-Mart's market price was somewhat inflated and a correction was needed even though

EXHIBIT 11-11 CAPITAL STRUCTURE ANALYSIS

Wal-Mart Stores, Inc.
Capital Structure Ratios
Fiscal years ended January 31
(Dollar amounts in millions)

Composition analysis: Percentage of total financing provided by each type of debt and shareholders' equity.

	2006		2005	
	AMOUNT	%	AMOUNT	%
Total assets (equals total liabilities and shareholders' equity)	$138,187	100.0%	$120,154	100.0%
Financed by:				
Current liabilities	48,826	35.3	43,182	36.0%
Long-term debt and capital leases	30,171	21.8	23,258	19.3
Deferred income taxes and other	4,552	3.3	2,978	2.5
Minority interests	1,467	1.1	1,340	1.1
Total liabilities	85,016	61.5	70,758	59.9
Shareholders' equity	53,171	38.5	49,396	41.1
	$138,187	100.0%	$120,154	100.0%

ADDITIONAL RATIO ANALYSIS:

RATIO	FORMULA		2006	2005
Financial leverage	$\frac{\text{Total liabilities}}{\text{Total assets}}$	=	61.5%	58.9%
Times interest earned	$\frac{\text{Earnings before interest and taxes}}{\text{Interest expense}}$	=	$\frac{\$17,358 + \$1,420}{\$1,420}$	$\frac{\$16,105 + \$1,187}{\$1,187}$
		=	13.2 times	14.6 times

2005 earnings were highter. In any event, the analyst would need to separate out the effects of economy-wide influences on P/E ratios (such as changes in interest rates or other factors causing changes in the overall market prices of equity securities) in order to interpret this change in Wal-Mart's P/E ratio.

Summary, Wal-Mart Stores, Inc.

Our analysis of Wal-Mart's financial statements is positive. The primary weak indicator is in the area of investor ratios, and this result may be due to transitory effects of the stock market that may not persist in the future. There were significant positive trends in liquidity, and stability in profitability ratios. Further examination of supplementary information, as well as subsequent quarterly results, could be used to support or challenge these conclusions.

EXHIBIT 11-12 INVESTOR ANALYSIS

Wal-Mart Stores, Inc.
Investor Ratios
Fiscal years ended January 31
(Dollar amounts in millions)

RATIO	FORMULA		2006	2005
Earnings per share	Provided directly on the income statement (Exhibit 11-5)			
Basic			$ 2.68	$ 2.41
Diluted			$ 2.68	$ 2.41
Book value per share	Shareholders' equity / Number of shares	=	$53,171 / 4,165	$49,396 / 4,234
		=	$12.77	$11.67
Market-to-book value*	Market price per share / Book value per share	=	$46.11 / $12.77	$52.40 / $11.67
		=	3.61	4.49
Price-to-earnings*	Market price per share / Earnings per share	=	$46.11 / $ 2.68	$52.40 / $ 2.41
		=	17.2	21.7

* We have used the fiscal year-end market price per share, and computed book value per share using the number of shares shown on the balance sheet.

LIMITATIONS OF FINANCIAL STATEMENT ANALYSIS

Financial statement analysis is limited on several dimensions. GAAP, and its underlying accounting conventions and measurement rules and principles, present some limits. Managers often have the ability to select favorable accounting methods. They can make choices as to the timing for reporting favorable or unfavorable results. A close reading of the notes can indicate where some of these choices have had an impact on the financial ratios, yet many of these managerial choices will not be revealed to external users of financial statements. Investors, in particular, must rely on independent accountants' assessments of the suitability of management's accounting choices.

Refer to TOPICMOD VI "EARNINGS MANAGEMENT" for a detailed discussion of how an analysis of the firm's cash flows can illustrate the "checks and balances" on management's potential income manipulating activities. Analyzing cash flows helps focus on "real" events that are often hard to distinguish from the effects of alternative accounting methods or principles. By focusing more on cash flows, the investor or other analyst can identify cases where financial reports based on accrual accounting may diverge from the cash flows or inadequately reflect other pertinent economic events.

A second major limitation of financial statement analysis concerns the "What's Missing?" factor. Many major factors affecting profitability and survival of the firm are just not included in accrual accounting, or in the financial statements. Examples of such omissions include changes in the firm's market share, changes in customer relations or preferences, changes in the firm's labor productivity, other changes in its human resources or human resource management systems, innovations or structural changes in technology, changes in the environment, changes in legislation or public policy, changes in competitors, or changes in substitute products or services. Sometimes these factors are discussed in the narrative sections of the annual report. They are often mentioned in the CEO's letter. Wal-Mart's Management Review section alludes to some of these qualitative factors.

A third and final limitation of financial statement analysis concerns predictability. The past may not be a reliable indicator of the future. Stable trends may be reversed tomorrow! Financial statements are just one of the important inputs that the investor must use as a basis for investing decisions. Further study of finance and accounting will give you additional tools on which to rely. TOPIC-MOD X of this text gives you some ideas on how you might pursue your study of these important topics.

Summary of Learning Objectives

1. **Understand why financial statements are analyzed.**
   Investors comprise the primary audience of financial reporting. Financial analysts use financial accounting reports in order to assess the potential risks and returns from investing in debt and equity securities.

2. **Know where to obtain financial information.**
   Although financial statement analysis begins with the set of financial statements included in published financial reports, analysts gather additional information from a variety of sources, including the financial sections of major newspapers, specialized business periodicals, reports of changes in governmental fiscal and monetary policies, conferences and addresses by business leaders, and many other sources.

3. **Determine when financial information is comparable and alternatively learn how to enhance the comparability of financial information that may appear to be noncomparable.**
   The analyst must determine that a comparable and useful reference is available with which to compare the target firm. Usually, the prior year or years are a good reference point with which to begin. Before comparing a firm's results with the prior year, the analyst must examine both sets of statements and notes to determine whether an unusual event occurred. If significant unusual events have occurred that would distort comparisons, then the financial statements for any of these years may need to be restated or rearranged to make them more comparable. The primary guideline is "more comparability is better". Financial information is more comparable between two firms if they

- operate in the same country,
- follow similar accounting practices,
- are of similar size (revenues and/or assets),
- produce similar products or services, and
- have a similar capital structure.

4. **Identify, calculate, use, and interpret appropriate ratios.**
   We have operationalized this objective by developing a general framework that can be used to conduct a comprehensive financial statement analysis. Financial analysis relies on both qualitative and quantitative analyses, and cannot be reduced to a simple set of recipes. The techniques summarized in this chapter merely provide a point of departure for the analyst in assessing the investment worth of a given firm.

   A summary of our financial statement analysis framework follows:

   a. Identify the purpose and objectives of the analysis.
   b. Review the financial statements, accompanying notes, management letters, and other commentary, and the report of the independent auditor. Be alert to any unusual events that may affect your interpretations of the numerical items in the financial statements.
   c. Determine whether any adjustments are needed to make the financial statements comparable to those of the previous year, or to financial statements of other, supposedly similar firms. Be especially aware of mergers, discontinued operations, changes in methods of accounting, or major shifts in product mix.
   d. Conduct horizontal and vertical analyses of the balance sheet and income statement. The horizontal analysis will aid you in discussing major changes in financial statement items compared to previous periods. The vertical analysis will help you focus on variations in the composition of the firm's assets, and the relative proportions of its debt and equity financing. A vertical analysis will also help you focus on causes of variation in net income.
   e. Organize your ratio calculations under the broad headings of liquidity, profitability, capital structure, and investor performance. Compute the standard financial ratios in each of these categories.
   f. Compare the financial ratios to prior years and to industry norms. If the firm's ratios depart from its past history or prevailing norms, attempt to explain these departures by reviewing other supplementary disclosures in the financial statements. Remember that there are often excellent reasons why a firm will differ from its competitors and may alter its policies over time. These steps have been illustrated using Wal-Mart's financial statements.

5. **Identify limitations of financial statement analyses.**
   A variety of judgments are used to decide how to calculate a given financial ratio. Rarely do the line items that are reported in the financial statements fit

neatly into a standard formula. Often the results of the ratio calculations provide more questions than answers. The most useful product of ratio analysis may well be the list of intelligent questions that result.

6. **Be able to "Follow the Cash".**
   We have shown how analysts might obtain slightly different interpretations of Wal-Mart's performance by looking at income statement ratios vs. cash-based ratios. These differences were not significant for Wal-Mart. However, in other circumstances, there could be drastic differences such that the cash-based analyses would be more prominent.

KEY TERMS

Accounts receivable as a percentage of sales revenue
Annual report
Auditor's report
Basis of comparison
Capital structure
Cash return on assets ratio
Collection period
Composition analysis
Current ratio
Earnings-per-share (EPS) ratio
Financial leverage ratio
Form 10K
Form 10Q
Gross profit percentage
Horizontal analysis
Investor ratios
Liquidity ratios
Management discussion and analysis (MDA)
Market-to-book value ratio
Number of days in inventory
Operating income ratio
Percentage composition analysis
Price-to-earnings (P/E) ratio
Profitability ratios
Qualified audit opinion
Quality of income ratio
Quick ratio
Return on assets (ROA) ratio
Return on equity (ROE) ratio
Times interest earned ratio
Vertical analysis
Working capital

Exercises and Problems

11-1 Discuss the basic goals of financial statement analysis. Indicate those goals with which you agree or disagree. Identify any additional goals that may be added.

11-2 Identify several users of financial statement analysis. Discuss the differences between users who have regular interaction with the firm versus those who may have less frequent interactions.

11-3 Identify and describe several sources of financial information for publicly traded U.S. companies.

11-4 Discuss why it is so important that financial information be comparable before conducting analysis and computing ratios.

11-5 Discuss several ways that comparability between firms can be enhanced.

11-6 Discuss several aspects of non-comparability that the analyst cannot overcome.

11-7 Why must both cash and accounts receivable be analyzed as part of a liquidity analysis?

11-8 Why must both cash flows and net income be analyzed as part of a profitability analysis?

11-9 Discuss the differences between cash flow from operating activities (CFOA) and cash collections from customers.

11-10 Discuss why the "What's missing?" question is so crucial during all phases of financial statement analysis.

11-11 Describe several limitations of financial statement analysis. What can be done to minimize these limitations?

11-12 Describe several possible choices of accounting methods that managers may make in an effort to manipulate or influence reported earnings. What can the analyst do to combat these earnings manipulation possibilities?

11-13 Describe how managers can affect the timing of earnings recognition. What can the analyst do to combat these earnings manipulation possibilities?

11-14 Describe how managers may make biased estimates that will cause net income to be overstated or understated. What can the analyst do to combat these earnings manipulation possibilities?

Comprehensive Financial Statement Analysis

11-15 Dairy King, LTD., reported the following results for 2007 (dollars in millions):

	2007	*2006*
Revenues:		
Net sales	$268.8	$241.6
Service fees	54.2	51.6
Franchise sales (fees)	8.6	7.6

Property management	8.1	9.0
Other	1.1	1.3
	340.8	311.1
Costs and expenses:		
Cost of sales	242.4	217.2
Property management expenses	7.6	8.4
Selling, general, and administrative	40.5	37.5
Interest expense (income)	(1.6)	(1.4)
	288.9	261.7
Income before income taxes	51.9	49.4
Income taxes	20.5	19.5
Net income	$ 31.4	$ 29.9
Earnings per common share	$ 1.30	$ 1.19

Dairy King's Consolidated Balance Sheet is shown below:

	2007	*2006*
Assets		
Current assets:		
Cash and cash equivalents	$ 31.8	$ 21.2
Marketable securities	7.0	10.0
Notes receivable, net	7.4	3.4
Accounts receivable, net	25.1	23.2
Inventories	5.4	4.6
Prepaid expenses	2.4	1.1
Miscellaneous	1.2	1.5
Total current assets	80.3	65.0
Other assets:		
Notes receivable, net	14.4	21.4
Miscellaneous	1.3	1.6
Total other assets	15.7	23.0
Other revenue-producing assets:		
Franchise rights, net	87.8	83.8
Rental properties, net	2.9	3.2
Total other assets	90.7	87.0
Property, plant, and equipment, Net	9.8	9.3
Total assets	$196.5	$184.3

	2007	2006
Liabilities and Stockholders' Equity		
Current liabilities:		
Drafts and accounts payable	$ 17.1	$ 16.8
Committed advertising	1.1	2.1
Other liabilities	7.5	6.8
Income taxes payable	.4	1.1
Current maturities (L-T debt)	.4	1.8
Total current liabilities	26.5	28.6
Deferred franchise income	.4	.3
Deferred income taxes	15.0	15.0
Long-term debt	23.3	23.7
Contingencies and commitments (Note 4)		
Total liabilities	65.2	67.6
Stockholders' equity:		
Class A common stock	.1	.1
Class B common stock	.1	.1
Paid-in capital	4.1	4.0
Retained earnings	129.2	114.4
Equity adjustments	(2.2)	(1.9)
Total stockholders' equity	131.3	116.7
Total liabilities and shareholders' equity	$196.5	$184.3

Dairy King's cash flow statement is summarized as follows (dollars in millions):

	2007	2006
Net cash provided by operating activities	$ 33.8	$ 35.0
Net cash provided by (used in) investing activities	(4.6)	(17.3)
Net cash used in financing activities	(18.5)	(27.5)
Net (decrease) increase in cash	$ 10.7	($ 9.8)
Cash payments for income taxes	$ 21.1	$ 18.8
Cash payments for interest	$ 1.9	$ 2.5

Required

a. Identify any unusual terms in Dairy King's financial statements.
b. Prepare a horizontal analysis of Dairy King's income statement.
c. Prepare a vertical analysis of Dairy King's income statement.

d. Calculate the appropriate liquidity ratios from Dairy King's balance sheet.
e. Conduct a profitability analysis.
f. Prepare a capital structure analysis.
g. Write a short memo summarizing your conclusions. Indicate why Dairy King might be facing financial threats or opportunities. Also indicate any additional data necessary to refine your analyses or conclusions.

Introductory Financial Analysis

11-16 General Cinema Companies, Inc., reported the following results for 2007 and 2006 as summarized below (dollars in thousands except for per-share amount):

Years Ended October 31	*2007*	*2006*
Revenues	$452,563	$495,031
Costs applicable to revenues	188,616	214,653
Selling, general, and administrative expenses	241,435	260,128
Corporate expenses	5,646	1,900
Operating earnings (loss)	16,866	18,350
Investment income	1,640	96
Interest expense	(648)	(605)
Other income (expense), net	5,188	(600)
Earnings (loss) before income taxes, and cumulative effect of accounting change	23,046	17,241
Income tax expense	9,449	6,738
Net earnings (loss)	$ 13,597	$ 10,503
Amounts applicable to common shareholders:		
Earnings per share	$ 1.73	NA

General Cinema's consolidated balance sheet is summarized below (dollars in thousands):

October 31	*2007*	*2006*
Assets		
Current assets:		
Cash and equivalents	$ 85,021	$ 7,790
Deferred income taxes	2,090	0
Other current assets	5,722	2,622
Total current assets	92,833	10,412

Property and equipment:		
Land, buildings, and improvements	32,411	38,675
Equipment and fixtures	130,016	131,710
Leasehold improvements	151,442	159,289
	313,869	329,674
Less accumulated depreciation and amortization	136,174	130,349
Total property and equipment, net	177,695	199,325
Other assets:		
Other	26,130	798
Total assets	$296,658	$210,535

October 31	*2007*	*2006*
Liabilities		
Current liabilities:		
Current maturities of long-term liabilities	$ 722	$ 637
Trade payables	39,065	34,028
Other current liabilities	59,972	53,956
Total current liabilities	99,759	88,621
Long-term liabilities:		
Capital lease obligations	4,179	4,756
Other long-term liabilities	28,016	27,551
Total long-term liabilities	32,195	32,307
Deferred income taxes	15,181	17,376
Commitments and contingencies	—	—
Total liabilities	147,135	138,304
Shareholders' Equity		
Common stock: $0.01 par value; authorized 25,000,000; issued and outstanding 7,802, 078	78	—
Paid-in capital	135,848	—
Retained earnings	13,597	—
Investment by Harcourt General	—	72,231
Total shareholders' equity	149,523	72,231
Total liabilities and equity	$296,658	$210,535

General Cinema's cash flow statement is summarized below (dollars in thousands):

Year ended October 31	*2007*	*2006*
Net cash provided by operations	$28,512	$53,849
Net cash used by investment activities	(14,949)	(16,322)
Net cash (used) provided by financing transactions	63,668	(35,288)
Net increase (decrease) in cash during the year	$77,231	$ 2,239
Supplemental schedule of cash flow information		
Cash paid for interest	$ 610	$ 720
Cash paid for income taxes	$13,100	$ 9,500

Required

a. Identify any unusual terms in General Cinema's summarized financial statements.
b. Prepare a horizontal analysis of General Cinema's income statement.
c. Prepare a vertical analysis of General Cinema's income statement.
d. Calculate the appropriate liquidity ratios.
e. Conduct a profitability analysis.
f. Conduct a capital structure analysis. Discuss why General Cinema reported no EPS in 2006.
g. With regard to your analysis of General Cinema Companies, Inc., write a short memo summarizing your conclusions. Indicate why the company might be facing financial threats or opportunities. Also indicate if additional data is necessary to refine your analyses or conclusions.

Comprehensive Financial Statement Analysis

11-17 Electronic Fab Technology (EFT) is a leader in information technology. EFT reported the following results for 2007 and 2006, as summarized below (dollars in thousands):

Year Ended December 31	*2007*	*2006*
Net sales	$52,541,842	$29,816,626
Cost of goods sold	47,123,066	25,688,263
Gross profit	5,418,776	4,128,363
Selling, general and administrative	2,395,164	1,842,442
Operating income	3,023,612	2,285,921
Other income (expense):		
Interest expense	(175,400)	(236,917)

Interest income	78,933	0
Other, net	31,187	(11,723)
Total other income (expense)	(65,280)	(248,640)
Income before income taxes	2,958,332	2,037,281
Income tax expense	1,041,415	736,612
Net income	$ 1,916,917	$ 1,300,669
Weighted average shares outstanding	3,626,845	2,483,000

EFT reported the following consolidated balance sheets, as summarized below (dollars in thousands):

December 31	*2007*	*2006*
Assets		
Current assets:		
Cash and cash equivalents	$ 153,483	$ 43,879
Accounts receivable, net	3,858,523	2,480,421
Inventories	7,479,374	4,639,969
Income taxes receivable	64,655	0
Deferred income taxes	85,847	85,490
Prepaids and others	49,467	49,165
Total current assets	11,691,349	7,298,924
Property and equipment:		
Land	662,098	161,903
Buildings	4,779,049	1,589,865
Machinery and equipment	8,395,468	3,763,995
Furniture and fixtures	1,043,098	328,555
	14,879,713	5,844,318
Less accumulated depreciation	3,162,155	2,188,893
Property plant and equipment (net)	11,717,558	3,655,425
Other assets:		
Cash surrender value of life insurance	36,248	41,750
Other assets	33,929	176,067
	70,177	217,817
Total assets	$23,479,084	$11,172,166

December 31	*2007*	*2006*
Liabilities and Shareholders' Equity		
Current liabilities:		
Notes payable	$ —	$ 300,000
Current portion of long-term debt	170,000	244,433

Accounts payable	3,606,645	3,273,461
Income taxes payable	—	611,790
Accrued compensation	813,788	326,869
Other accrued expenses	356,598	138,827
Total current liabilities	4,947,031	4,895,380
Long-term debt, net of current portion	3,230,000	2,539,337
Deferred income taxes	312,660	190,918
Commitments and contingencies	—	—
	8,489,691	7,625,635
Shareholders' equity:		
Preferred stock: $0.01 par value, authorized 5,000,000 shares	—	—
Common stock; $0.01 par value, authorized 45,000,000 shares, issued 3,891,000 and 2,368,500 shares	38,911	23,685
Additional paid-in capital	10,016,035	505,316
Retained earnings	4,934,447	3,017,530
Total shareholders' equity	14,989,393	3,546,531
Total liabilities and shareholders' equity	$23,479,084	$11,172,166

EFT's consolidated statements of cash flow disclosed the following summary information:

December 31	*2007*	*2006*
Net cash provided (used) by operating activities	$ (697,000)	$814,000
Net cash used in investing activities	(9,035,000)	(870,000)
Net cash provided by financing activities	9,842,000	59,000
Net increase (decrease) in cash	$ 110,000	$ 3,000
Cash paid for:		
Income taxes (refund)	$1,596,475	$ (16,591)
Interest	$ 175,400	$236,917

Required

a. Identify any unusual terms in EFT's summarized financial statements.
b. Prepare a horizontal analysis of EFT's income statement.
c. Prepare a vertical analysis of EFT's income statement.
d. Calculate the appropriate liquidity ratios.
e. Conduct a profitability analysis.
f. Conduct a capital structure analysis.

g. Write a short memo summarizing your conclusions. Indicate why EFT might be facing financial threats or opportunities. Also indicate what additional data you might need to refine your analyses or conclusions.

Using the 10-Step Framework

11-18 Conduct a comprehensive financial analysis of Target's financial statements (see Appendix C).

Required

a. Review Target's financial statements (see Appendix C) to determine whether any unusual or noteworthy events may limit the scope or comparability of financial statement analysis. Review Ernst & Young's audit report. Determine whether any restatements might be necessary and whether any barriers would restrict the comparability of Target's performance. In other words, conduct the first four steps in the financial statement analysis framework.

b. Prepare horizontal and vertical analyses of Target's income statement for fiscal 2005 and 2004 (step 5 of our financial statement analysis framework).

c. Conduct an analysis of Target's liquidity for fiscal 2005 and 2004 (step 6 of our financial statement analysis framework).

d. Conduct an analysis of Target's profitability for fiscal 2005 and 2004 (step 7 of our financial statement analysis framework).

e. Analyze Target's capital structure for fiscal 2005 and 2004 (step 8 of our financial statement analysis framework).

f. Calculate Target's investor ratios for fiscal 2005 and 2004 (step 9 of our financial statement analysis framework).

g. Review your results from the previous six items, state your overall conclusions regarding Target's performance in fiscal 2005 and 2004, and then determine whether your results are consistent (step 10 of the financial statement analysis framework). Recalculate, as necessary, any ratios that should be restated based on new information found in the notes. Identify any additional information that you may require before making an investment in Target.

Financial Statement Analysis (first 4 steps in 10-Step Framework: Reviewing the Notes)

11-19 Review Wal-Mart's financial statements in Appendix A to determine whether any unusual or noteworthy events may limit the scope or comparability of financial statement analysis. Review the audit report and determine whether any restatements might be necessary. Also determine whether any barriers would restrict the comparability of Wal-Mart's performance. In other words, conduct the first four steps of the financial statement analysis framework.

Reviewing the Results of Financial Statement Analysis

11-20 This assignment is based on the computations and exhibits shown in Chapter 11 that are based on Wal-Mart's financial statements. In each case, refer to the relevant exhibits and review the results.

Required

a. Review and summarize the horizontal and vertical analyses of Wal-Mart's income statement for fiscal 2005 and 2004 (step 5 of the financial statement analysis framework).

b. Review and summarize the results of Wal-Mart's liquidity analysis for fiscal 2005 and 2004 (step 6 of the financial statement analysis framework).

c. Review and summarize the results of Wal-Mart's profitability analysis for fiscal 2005 and 2004 (step 7 of the financial statement analysis framework.

d. Review and summarize the results of Wal-Mart's capital structure analysis for fiscal 2005 and 2004 (step 8 of the financial statement analysis framework).

e. Review and summarize Wal-Mart's investor ratios for fiscal 2005 and 2004 (step 9 of the financial statement analysis framework).

f. Conduct step 10 of the financial analysis framework, as may be necessary. Recalculate, as necessary, any ratios that could be restated based on new information found in the notes.

g. On the basis of these results, evaluate the various dimensions of Wal-Mart's performance in fiscal 2005 and 2004. How do any restatements in the previous step change your conclusions about Wal-Mart's profitability? Identify any additional information needed before making an investment in Wal-Mart's.

Ethics Problem Involving Number of Subscribers

11-21 America Online had significant losses in its customer base during 2002 and 2003. It may have been hyping its subscriber numbers by not maintaining accurate customer records. "Its parent, AOL Time Warner, hinted at that this week when Don Logan, the executive who oversees America Online, said one reason for AOL's unexpectedly high subscriber losses was the result of "cleaning up the files." (Julia Angwin, "A Bulk-Sales Initiative by AOL May Have Inflated Subscriptions," *The Wall Street Journal,* July 25, 2003, p. A1)

1. Comment on the relationship between numbers in the financial statements and customer data.

2. Why would investors and creditors be interested in customer data?

3. Who should evaluate customer data, like AOL's subscriber base?

4. Why would AOL management have an incentive to hype its subscriber base?

TOPICMOD I

THE TIME VALUE OF MONEY

Learning Objectives

1. *Determine the future value, or compound amount, of dollars that are invested or borrowed today.*
2. *Determine the value today, or present value, of dollars that are to be received or paid in the future.*

INTRODUCTION

Many business transactions create financial assets and liabilities that represent cash inflows and outflows that will occur in future periods. For this reason, it is necessary to consider the concept of present and future values, or the time value of money, in order to determine how such transactions should be reported in the financial statements.

Future Value

Money deposited to an interest-earning bank account will "grow" over time. For example, \$1,000 deposited in an account earning 8% per year will amount to \$1,080 (\$1,000 × 1.08 = \$1,080) after one year. If the total amount is left on deposit for a second year, it will grow to \$1,166 rounded (\$1,080 × 1.08 = \$1,166). Because the interest is not withdrawn from the account, in each successive year the account earns "interest on interest", and the account grows by a larger dollar amount each year. This notion of earning interest on interest is referred to as **compound interest.** The growth in the account balance can be depicted in the following way:

Initial deposit		\$1,000
Amount in one year		$\$1,000 \times (1.08) = \$1,080$
Amount in two years		$\$1,080 \times (1.08) = \$1,166$
	or	$\$1,000 \times (1.08)^2 = \$1,000 \times (1.166) = \$1,166$

More generally, let P represent the initial deposit, let i represent the interest rate, let n represent the number of periods (e.g., years) over which the deposit is allowed to grow, and let A represent the future value of the deposit. The relationship may be written in the following way.

$$A = P \times (1 + i)^n$$

In our earlier example, $P = \$1,000$, $i = 8\%$, and $n = 2$, so

$$\begin{aligned} A &= P \times (1 + i)^n \\ &= \$1000 \times (1.08)^2 \\ &= \$1000 \times (1.166) \\ &= \$1,166 \end{aligned}$$

If the deposit were allowed to grow for 10 years, the future value would be \$2,159, i.e.,

$$\begin{aligned} A &= P \times (1 \times i)^n \\ &= \$1,000 \times (1.08)^{10} \\ &= \$1,000 \times (2.159) \\ &= \$2,159 \end{aligned}$$

This simple formula may be used for any values of P (the initial deposit), i (the interest rate), and n (the number of periods) in order to obtain the **future value** of the deposit. The expression $(1 \times i)^n$ is referred to as the **future value factor** because it converts the initial deposit to its future value for given values of i and n.

Future values frequently must be computed in business and finance, and special tables have been prepared showing the future value factors for various interest rates and numbers of periods. As a practical matter, financial calculators or personal computers are used to make these calculations. The tables included in this text are useful as a way of introducing you to the concepts of future values and present values. Exhibit I-1 contains future value factors, and you can use this table to verify the calculations that were made earlier. For example, refer to the 8% column in Exhibit I-1; the entries in this column show the future amounts for $1 invested today at 8% per period. The factors for 1, 2, and 10 periods are 1.080, 1.166, and 2.159, respectively; these are the same factors as used in our previous calculations.

Present Value

In the preceding examples, we determined the future value of a cash deposit made today. Business decisions often require that we determine the value today, or present value, of an amount to be received or paid in the future. For example, suppose that we need $10 million in three years to pay for new plant and equipment. How much would we need to deposit today in order to have $10 million in three years, assuming that the interest rate is 10% per year? In this case we know the future amount ($10 million), the interest rate (10%), and the number of periods (three years). We need to determine the value today, or the present value, of $10 million to be paid three years in the future. Recall our earlier expression for calculating future values:

$$A = P \times (1 + i)^n$$

If we know A, the future value, and wish to determine P, the present value, we need only rearrange the expression as follows:

$$P = A \times 1/(1 + i)^n$$

In the present example, the future payment is known to be $10 million. The time period is three years, and the interest rate is 10%.

$$\begin{aligned} P &= A \times 1/(1 + i)^n \\ &= \$10{,}000{,}000 \times 1/(1.10)^3 \\ &= \$10{,}000{,}000 \times (.751) \\ &= \$7{,}510{,}000 \end{aligned}$$

EXHIBIT I-1 FUTURE VALUE OF $1

PERIODS	1%	2%	4%	6%	8%	10%	12%	14%	16%	18%	20%
1	1.010	1.020	1.040	1.060	1.080	1.100	1.120	1.140	1.160	1.180	1.200
2	1.020	1.040	1.082	1.124	1.166	1.210	1.254	1.300	1.346	1.392	1.440
3	1.030	1.061	1.125	1.191	1.260	1.331	1.405	1.482	1.561	1.643	1.728
4	1.041	1.082	1.170	1.262	1.360	1.464	1.574	1.689	1.811	1.939	2.074
5	1.051	1.104	1.217	1.338	1.469	1.611	1.762	1.925	2.100	2.288	2.488
6	1.062	1.126	1.265	1.419	1.587	1.772	1.974	2.195	2.436	2.700	2.986
7	1.072	1.149	1.316	1.504	1.714	1.949	2.211	2.502	2.826	3.186	3.583
8	1.083	1.172	1.369	1.594	1.851	2.144	2.476	2.853	3.278	3.759	4.300
9	1.094	1.195	1.423	1.689	1.999	2.358	2.773	3.252	3.803	4.436	5.160
10	1.105	1.219	1.480	1.791	2.159	2.594	3.106	3.707	4.411	5.234	6.192
11	1.116	1.243	1.539	1.898	2.332	2.853	3.479	4.226	5.117	6.176	7.430
12	1.127	1.268	1.601	2.012	2.518	3.138	3.896	4.818	5.936	7.288	8.920
13	1.138	1.294	1.665	2.133	2.720	3.452	4.363	5.492	6.886	8.599	10.699
14	1.149	1.319	1.732	2.261	2.937	3.798	4.887	6.261	7.988	10.147	12.839
15	1.161	1.346	1.801	2.397	3.172	4.177	5.474	7.138	9.266	11.974	15.407
16	1.173	1.373	1.873	2.540	3.426	4.595	6.130	8.137	10.748	14.129	18.499
17	1.184	1.400	1.948	2.693	3.700	5.054	6.866	9.276	12.468	16.672	22.186
18	1.196	1.428	2.026	2.854	3.996	5.560	7.690	10.575	14.463	19.673	26.623
19	1.208	1.457	2.107	3.026	4.316	6.116	8.613	12.056	16.777	23.214	31.948
20	1.220	1.486	2.191	3.207	4.661	6.728	9.646	13.743	19.461	27.393	38.338
21	1.232	1.516	2.279	3.400	5.034	7.400	10.804	15.668	22.575	32.324	46.005
22	1.245	1.546	2.370	3.604	5.437	8.140	12.100	17.861	26.186	38.142	55.206
23	1.257	1.577	2.465	3.820	5.871	8.954	13.552	20.362	30.376	45.008	66.247
24	1.270	1.608	2.563	4.049	6.341	9.850	15.179	23.212	35.236	53.109	79.497
25	1.282	1.641	2.666	4.292	6.848	10.835	17.000	26.462	40.874	62.669	95.396

In other words, if you were to deposit $7,510,000 into an account earning 10% interest, then the account balance would accumulate to $10 million at the end of three years. You can verify this result by using the future value factors in Exhibit I-1. Note that the future value factor at 10% for three periods is 1.331:

$$\begin{aligned} A &= P \times (1 \times i)^n \\ &= \$7{,}510{,}000 \times (1.10)^3 = \$7{,}510{,}000 \times (1.331) \\ &= \$10{,}000{,}000 \text{ (rounded)} \end{aligned}$$

In financial terms, you would be equally as well off if you were to receive (or pay) $10 million in three years or to receive (or pay) $7,510,000 today. In this case, the future value, A, is multiplied by a **present value factor,** $1/(1 + i)^n$, in order to obtain its present value. Exhibit I-2 contains present value factors. Notice that the future value factors in Exhibit I-1 and the present value factors in Exhibit I-2 have a reciprocal relationship, i.e., present value factors are the inverses of future value factors.

EXHIBIT I-2 PRESENT VALUE OF $1

PERIODS	1%	2%	4%	6%	8%	10%	12%	14%	16%	18%	20%
1	0.990	0.980	0.962	0.943	0.926	0.909	0.893	0.877	0.862	0.847	0.833
2	0.980	0.961	0.925	0.890	0.857	0.826	0.797	0.769	0.743	0.718	0.694
3	0.971	0.942	0.889	0.840	0.794	0.751	0.712	0.675	0.641	0.609	0.579
4	0.961	0.924	0.855	0.792	0.735	0.683	0.636	0.592	0.552	0.516	0.482
5	0.951	0.906	0.822	0.747	0.681	0.621	0.567	0.519	0.476	0.437	0.402
6	0.942	0.888	0.790	0.705	0.630	0.564	0.507	0.456	0.410	0.370	0.335
7	0.933	0.871	0.760	0.665	0.583	0.513	0.452	0.400	0.354	0.314	0.279
8	0.923	0.853	0.731	0.627	0.540	0.467	0.404	0.351	0.305	0.266	0.233
9	0.914	0.837	0.703	0.592	0.500	0.424	0.361	0.308	0.263	0.225	0.194
10	0.905	0.820	0.676	0.558	0.463	0.386	0.322	0.270	0.227	0.191	0.162
11	0.896	0.804	0.650	0.527	0.429	0.350	0.287	0.237	0.195	0.162	0.135
12	0.887	0.788	0.625	0.497	0.397	0.319	0.257	0.208	0.168	0.137	0.112
13	0.879	0.773	0.601	0.469	0.368	0.290	0.229	0.182	0.145	0.116	0.093
14	0.870	0.758	0.577	0.442	0.340	0.263	0.205	0.160	0.125	0.099	0.078
15	0.861	0.743	0.555	0.417	0.315	0.239	0.183	0.140	0.108	0.084	0.065
16	0.853	0.728	0.534	0.394	0.292	0.218	0.163	0.123	0.093	0.071	0.054
17	0.844	0.714	0.513	0.371	0.270	0.198	0.146	0.108	0.080	0.060	0.045
18	0.836	0.700	0.494	0.350	0.250	0.180	0.130	0.095	0.069	0.051	0.038
19	0.828	0.686	0.475	0.331	0.232	0.164	0.116	0.083	0.060	0.043	0.031
20	0.820	0.673	0.456	0.312	0.215	0.149	0.104	0.073	0.051	0.037	0.026
21	0.811	0.660	0.439	0.294	0.199	0.135	0.093	0.064	0.044	0.031	0.022
22	0.803	0.647	0.422	0.278	0.184	0.123	0.083	0.056	0.038	0.026	0.018
23	0.795	0.634	0.406	0.262	0.170	0.112	0.074	0.049	0.033	0.022	0.015
24	0.788	0.622	0.390	0.247	0.158	0.102	0.066	0.043	0.028	0.019	0.013
25	0.780	0.610	0.375	0.233	0.146	0.092	0.059	0.038	0.024	0.016	0.010

For example, when $i = 8\%$ and $n = 2$

Present value factor = 0.857
Future value factor = 1.166

$$\text{Present value factor} = \frac{1}{\text{Future value factor}} \text{ and } .857 = 1/1.166$$

Let's use the present value factors in Exhibit I-2 to determine the present value of $100,000 to be received in five periods, assuming alternatively that the appropriate interest rate is 4%, 8%, or 12%. When interest rates are used to compute present values instead of future values, the interest rate is usually referred to as the **discount rate.**

Discount Rate	Future Cash Receipts	×	Present Value Factor (for n = 5, Exhibit I-2)	=	Present Value
4%	$100,000	×	.822	=	$82,200
8	100,000	×	.681	=	68,100
12	100,000	×	.567	=	56,700

As you might expect, the same future cash flow ($100,000 in this example) has differing present values, depending on the discount rate used. A larger discount rate produces a smaller present value. This is a sensible result because a higher interest rate indicates that interest earnings will be greater. Accordingly, the required initial deposit is smaller. The choice of a suitable discount rate to use in finding the present value of expected future cash flows requires considerable judgment. In general, discount rates that are used by lenders and investors vary directly with risk. For instance, riskier loans and investments require higher discount rates.

Present Value and Series of Future Payments

Imagine for a moment that you have won a million-dollar lottery and will receive payments of $200,000 at the end of each year for five years (5 years × $200,000 = $1 million). Could you use your lottery prize immediately to pay for a million-dollar house? You soon would realize that the lottery prize is worth less than $1 million because the payments will be received at various future dates. To find the prize's real value, you would need to determine the present value of each payment. Then you would add the present values of the individual payments in order to obtain the total present value. Assuming a 10% interest rate, the calculation is as follows:

Date of Payment	Cash Flow	×	Present Value Factor (Exhibit I-2)	=	Present Value
End of:					
Year 1	$200,000	×	.909	=	$181,800
Year 2	200,000	×	.827*	=	165,400
Year 3	200,000	×	.751	=	150,200
Year 4	200,000	×	.683	=	136,600
Year 5	200,000	×	.621	=	124,200
Totals			3.791		$758,200

*Rounded.

This result shows that the series of five payments of $200,000 has a value today of $758,200, even though the total of the five payments is $1 million. In other words, if you were to receive $758,200 today and deposit this amount in a bank account earning 10% per year, you would be able to withdraw $200,000 at the end of each year for five years. In this sense, you would be just as well off receiving $758,200 immediately as if you received the five lottery payments (totaling $1 million) over five years. Instead of buying a million-dollar house today, you can only afford to spend $758,200.

In this lottery example, the cash flows are equal in dollar amount and are paid at the end of each period. The term **annuity** is used to describe equal cash flows over uniform time intervals. Such cash flow patterns are found frequently in business contracts. For this reason, special present value tables have been prepared for evaluating annuities. Exhibit I-3 contains present value factors for this purpose.

If we use the notation *S* to indicate the dollar amount of each of a series of cash flows and PVAF (*i* percent, *n* periods) to indicate the present value factor for an annuity of *n* periods at interest rate *i*, and if the interest rate is 10%, then your lottery winnings may be valued as follows using Exhibit I-3:

$$P = S \times \text{PVAF } (i \text{ percent}, n \text{ periods})$$
$$= \$200{,}000 \times \text{PVAF } (10\%, 5 \text{ periods})$$
$$= \$200{,}000 \times 3.791 \text{ (from Exhibit I-3)}$$
$$= \$758{,}200$$

This is the same result as the one we obtained earlier by finding the present values of each payment and adding them to obtain the total present value of the series of five payments. In fact, the present value factors for annuities are equal to the sum of the present value factors for the individual cash flows. Refer to our previous calculation. The total of the five present value factors from Exhibit I-2 is the same as the present value factor for a five-period annuity from Exhibit I-3.

EXHIBIT I-3 PRESENT VALUE OF AN ANNUITY

PERIODS	1%	2%	4%	6%	8%	10%	12%	14%	16%	18%	20%
1	0.990	0.980	0.962	0.943	0.926	0.909	0.893	0.877	0.862	0.847	0.833
2	1.970	1.942	1.886	1.833	1.783	1.736	1.690	1.647	1.605	1.566	1.528
3	2.941	2.884	2.775	2.673	2.577	2.487	2.402	2.322	2.246	2.174	2.106
4	3.902	3.808	3.630	3.465	3.312	3.170	3.037	2.914	2.798	2.690	2.589
5	4.853	4.713	4.452	4.212	3.993	3.791	3.605	3.433	3.274	3.127	2.991
6	5.795	5.601	5.242	4.917	4.623	4.355	4.111	3.889	3.685	3.498	3.326
7	6.728	6.472	6.002	5.582	5.206	4.868	4.564	4.288	4.039	3.812	3.605
8	7.652	7.325	6.733	6.210	5.747	5.335	4.968	4.639	4.344	4.078	3.837
9	8.566	8.162	7.435	6.802	6.247	5.759	5.328	4.946	4.607	4.303	4.031
10	9.471	8.983	8.111	7.360	6.710	6.145	5.650	5.216	4.833	4.494	4.192
11	10.368	9.787	8.760	7.887	7.139	6.495	5.938	5.453	5.029	4.656	4.327
12	11.255	10.575	9.385	8.384	7.536	6.814	6.194	5.660	5.197	4.793	4.439
13	12.134	11.348	9.986	8.853	7.904	7.103	6.424	5.842	5.342	4.910	4.533
14	13.004	12.106	10.563	9.295	8.244	7.367	6.628	6.002	5.468	5.008	4.611
15	13.865	12.849	11.118	9.712	8.559	7.606	6.811	6.142	5.575	5.092	4.675
16	14.718	13.578	11.652	10.106	8.851	7.824	6.974	6.265	5.669	5.162	4.730
17	15.562	14.292	12.166	10.477	9.122	8.022	7.120	6.373	5.749	5.222	4.775
18	16.398	14.992	12.659	10.828	9.372	8.201	7.250	6.467	5.818	5.273	4.812
19	17.226	15.678	13.134	11.158	9.604	8.365	7.366	6.550	5.877	5.316	4.844
20	18.046	16.351	13.590	11.470	9.818	8.514	7.469	6.623	5.929	5.353	4.870
21	18.857	17.011	14.029	11.764	10.017	8.649	7.562	6.687	5.973	5.384	4.891
22	19.660	17.658	14.451	12.042	10.201	8.772	7.645	6.743	6.011	5.410	4.909
23	20.456	18.292	14.857	12.303	10.371	8.883	7.718	6.792	6.044	5.432	4.925
24	21.243	18.914	15.247	12.550	10.529	8.985	7.784	6.835	6.073	5.451	4.937
25	22.023	19.523	15.622	12.783	10.675	9.077	7.843	6.873	6.097	5.467	4.948

Future Value and Series of Future Payments

Firms sometimes arrange to make a series of cash payments over several periods to a special fund referred to as a **sinking fund.** The ending balance of the sinking fund is usually designated for a special purpose, such as the retirement of outstanding debt or the replacement of operating assets. To illustrate, let us continue with your imagined lottery winnings. Assume that you deposit in a retirement fund the $200,000 payments received at the end of each of the next five years. You expect to earn 10% each year. At the end of the fifth year, what would be the balance in your retirement fund? To find the future value of the fund, you would determine the future value of each deposit. Then you would add these future values in order to determine the total future value of your fund in the following manner:

Date of Deposit	Cash Flow	×	Present Value Factor (Exhibit I-1)	=	Future Value
End of:					
Year 1	200,000	×	1.464	=	292,800
Year 2	200,000	×	1.331	=	266,200
Year 3	200,000	×	1.210	=	242,000
Year 4	200,000	×	1.100	=	220,000
Year 5	200,000	×	1.000	=	200,000
Totals			6.105		$1,221,000

Because each deposit is made at the end of the year, the first deposit earns interest for four years; the second deposit earns interest for three years, and so on. The last deposit is made at the end of the fifth (and last) year and so earns no interest at all. Since each of the cash flows is the same ($200,000), the cash flows are an annuity. That is, they are equal in dollar amount and are deposited each period. Because sinking funds with equal annual deposits are found frequently in business contracts, special future value tables have been prepared containing the appropriate annuity factors. Exhibit I-4 contains such factors.

If we use the notation S to indicate the dollar amount of each of a series of future cash flows and FVAF (i percent, n periods) to indicate the future value factor for an annuity of n periods at interest rate i, and if the interest rate is 10%, then after five periods your retirement fund will amount to $1,221,000, computed as follows using Exhibit I-4:

$$\begin{aligned}\text{Future value} &= S \times \text{FVAF } (i \text{ percent}, n \text{ periods}) \\ &= \$200{,}000 \times \text{FVAF } (10\%, 5 \text{ periods}) \\ &= \$\ 200{,}000 \times 6.105 \text{ (from Exhibit I-4)} \\ &= \$1{,}221{,}000\end{aligned}$$

EXHIBIT I-4 FUTURE VALUE OF AN ANNUITY

PERIODS	1%	2%	4%	6%	8%	10%	12%	14%	16%	18%	20%
1	1.000	1.000	1.000	1.000	1.000	1.000	1.000	1.000	1.000	1.000	1.000
2	2.010	2.020	2.040	2.060	2.080	2.100	2.120	2.140	2.160	2.180	2.200
3	3.030	3.060	3.122	3.184	3.246	3.310	3.374	3.440	3.506	3.572	3.640
4	4.060	4.122	4.246	4.375	4.506	4.641	4.779	4.921	5.067	5.215	5.368
5	5.101	5.204	5.416	5.637	5.867	6.105	6.353	6.610	6.877	7.154	7.442
6	6.152	6.308	6.633	6.975	7.336	7.716	8.115	8.536	8.978	9.442	9.930
7	7.214	7.434	7.898	8.394	8.923	9.487	10.089	10.731	11.414	12.142	12.916
8	8.286	8.583	9.214	9.897	10.637	11.436	12.300	13.233	14.240	15.329	16.499
9	9.369	9.755	10.583	11.491	12.488	13.579	14.776	16.085	17.519	19.089	20.799
10	10.462	10.950	12.006	13.181	14.487	15.937	17.549	19.337	21.322	23.521	25.959
11	11.567	12.169	13.486	14.972	16.645	18.531	20.655	23.045	25.733	28.755	32.150
12	12.683	13.412	15.026	16.870	18.977	21.384	24.133	27.271	30.850	34.931	39.581
13	13.809	14.680	16.627	18.882	21.495	24.523	28.029	32.089	36.786	42.214	48.497
14	14.947	15.974	18.292	21.015	24.215	27.975	32.393	37.581	43.672	50.818	59.196
15	16.097	17.293	20.024	23.276	27.152	31.772	37.280	43.842	51.660	60.965	72.035
16	17.258	18.639	21.825	25.673	30.324	35.950	42.753	50.980	60.925	72.939	87.442
17	18.430	20.012	23.698	28.213	33.750	40.545	48.884	59.118	71.673	87.068	105.931
18	19.615	21.412	25.645	30.906	37.450	45.599	55.750	68.394	84.141	103.740	128.112
19	20.811	22.841	27.671	33.760	41.446	51.159	63.440	78.969	98.603	123.414	154.740
20	22.019	24.287	29.778	36.786	45.762	57.275	72.052	91.025	115.380	146.628	186.688
21	23.239	25.783	31.968	39.993	50.423	64.002	81.699	104.768	134.841	174.021	225.026
22	24.472	27.299	34.248	43.396	55.457	71.402	92.503	120.436	157.415	206.345	271.031
23	25.716	28.845	36.618	46.996	60.893	79.543	104.603	138.297	183.601	244.487	326.237
24	26.973	30.422	39.083	50.812	66.765	88.497	118.155	158.659	213.978	289.494	392.484
25	28.243	32.030	41.646	54.865	73.106	98.347	133.334	181.811	249.214	342.603	471.981

In other words, $200,000 per year for five years at 10% interest has the same value as a single receipt of $1,221,000 at the end of five years. Recall from our earlier example that a five-year $200,000 annuity has a present value of $758,200. From this, it follows that a single payment of $1,221,000 to be received in five years has the same value as $758,200 to be received immediately.[1]

At this point, you have acquired a useful set of tools for dealing with the **time value of money.** You are able to determine the future amount, or compound value, of an amount deposited today at a specified interest rate and number of time periods. Conversely, you are able to determine the value today, or present value, of an

[1] The future value factor for five periods at 10% is 1.611 (from Exhibit I-1).

$$\begin{aligned} A &= P \times (1 + i)^n \\ &= \$758{,}200 \times (1.10)^5 \\ &= \$758{,}200 \times 1.611 \\ &= \$1{,}221{,}000 \text{ (rounded)} \end{aligned}$$

amount to be received at a specified future date, given the prevailing interest rate. Also, you are able to determine both the present value and the future value of an ordinary annuity or a series of periodic cash flows that are equal in dollar amount. The financial reporting of noncurrent liabilities (discussed in Chapter 9) uses these present value factors to calculate the value of long-term liabilities.

This TOPICMOD has explained the time value of money and has illustrated the techniques of compound interest that are used widely in accounting for long-term financial assets and liabilities. Present value is the term used to denote the value today of cash to be received or paid in future periods. Future value is the term used to denote the expected maturity value of cash that is deposited (or otherwise invested) today at a specified rate of interest for a given number of future periods. Special tables have been constructed containing present value and future value factors for single cash flows, and the use of these tables has been illustrated in this TOPICMOD.

Business cash flows are often in the form of annuities, which are a series of cash flows that are equal in dollar amount and occur over uniform time intervals. Present value and future value calculations for annuities have been explained in the TOPICMOD. Special tables also have been constructed for evaluating annuities, and their use has been illustrated.

Summary of Learning Objectives

1. **Determine the future value, or compound amount, of dollars that are invested or borrowed today.**

   Compound interest calculations were explained using the following notations:

   A = future value
   P = present value
   S = dollar amount of each of a series of cash flows (an annuity)
   i = periodic interest rate
   n = number of time periods

   Future value, single cash deposit:

   $$A = P \times (1 + i)^n \text{ (requires use of Exhibit I-1)}$$

   Future value, series of equal cash flows (an annuity):

   $$A = S \times FVAF_n^i \text{ (} i \text{ percent, } n \text{ periods) (requires use of Exhibit I-4)}$$

2. **Determine the value today, or present value, of dollars that are to be received or paid in the future.**

   Present value, single future cash flow:

   $$P = A \times 1/(1 + i)^n \text{ (requires use of Exhibit I-2)}$$

   Present value, series of equal cash flows (an annuity):

   $$P = S \times \text{PVAF } (i \text{ percent}, n \text{ periods}) \text{ (requires use of Exhibit I-3)}$$

KEY TERMS

Annuity
Compound interest
Discount rate
Future value
Future value factor
Present value
Present value factor
Sinking fund
Time value of money

Exercises and Problems

I-1 Describe the concept of compound interest. In your own terms, why is a dollar today worth more than a dollar to be received three years from now?

I-2 Compare and contrast the concepts of future value and present value. Why might a decision maker prefer to use present values? Under what circumstances might future values be preferred?

I-3 Define an annuity. Under what circumstances is an annuity a liability? Why might an analyst prefer to use the annuity concept in analyzing different liabilities?

I-4 In analyzing the benefits of two different annuities, will present values and future values yield a different ranking of the two annuities? Why? Describe the differences between each set of comparisons.

I-5 What basic information must be known before calculating the discounted cash flows associated with any liability?

I-6 Explain the concept of compound interest. In your discussion, explain why an initial deposit left in an interest-earning bank account for several years would earn larger amounts of interest in each successive year.

I-7 Discuss the different perspectives used to analyze the time value of money:

a. Future value versus present value of a single amount

b. Future value versus present value of a series of future payments (annuities)

I-8 When calculating a future value, if the interest rate increases from 12 to 18%, what happens to the future value? Why?

I-9 **a.** When calculating a present value, if the interest rate increases from 12 to 18%, what happens to the present value? Why?

b. Is there any inconsistency between your answer to this question and your answer to Question I-8? Why or why not?

I-10 **a.** Identify the basic types of information that you must have in order to calculate the time value of money.

b. Which of these information elements is more objective (can be determined with greater precision)?

c. How will subjective estimates of some of these factors affect your interpretation and use of present and future values?

I-11 Could an analyst use either present or future values and still get the same rankings or preferences for two alternative projects? Why?

I-12 Assuming that an analyst's conclusions or investment decisions will be the same under either present or future values, why are present values preferred for most analytical purposes?

Future Value Calculations

I-13 Calculate the future value of the following cash flow streams, assuming a 10% annual interest rate in each case:

a. Deposit $10,000 in a certificate of deposit for three years.
b. Deposit $10,000 in a savings account at the end of year 1 and an additional $10,000 at the end of year 2. What is the balance in the account at the end of the second year?
c. Make five deposits of $10,000 in a savings account on December 31 of each year. What is the balance at the end of the fifth year? At the end of the fourth year?

Present Value Calculations

I-14 Calculate the present value of the following cash flow streams, assuming a 12% interest rate in each case:
a. A certificate of deposit will mature in one year that will be worth $10,000 at that time.
b. A $100,000 bond will mature in three years.
c. An insurance payout agreement will provide $30,000 at the end of each of the next three years.

Future Value Calculations

I-15 You have just discovered a 1957 Corvette that the owner will sell you in three years for $25,000. How much must you deposit in your savings account each year for three years in order to be able to buy the Corvette? Assume that all deposits are at the end of the year and that the Corvette will be purchased at the end of the third year. Also, assume an interest rate of eight percent.

Present Value Calculations

I-16 At the end of five years, you are guaranteed to receive $20,000. At each of the specified interest rates, what is the present value of this future promise?
a. Assume annual compounding at 12%.
b. Assume annual compounding at 6%.
c. Why is the present value different at different interest rates? Discuss these differences. Without making any further calculations, would the present value at 16% be higher or lower than the present value at 12%. Discuss why this must be so.

Present Value Calculations

I-17 A firm expects to make future payments on its warranty obligations of $300,000 per year for the next five years. What is the present value of this liability?
a. Assume an interest rate of 12%.
b. Assume an interest rate of 6%.
c. Why should a reader of financial statements be concerned about the interest rate that the firm may have used in calculating the present values of various financial contracts?

Time Value Calculations

I-18 Evaluate each independent situation using the appropriate table and an interest rate of 12%.

a. You would like to relax and not work for the next six years, but you would like to withdraw $25,000 at the end of each year. How much must you have in your investment account now to be able to do this?

b. You would like to have $100,000 upon graduation. How much should you invest in a fund at the end of each year for the next four years?

c. Your firm signs a contract to repay $1,000,000 in five years. How much will the firm receive today in exchange for this promised future payment?

d. You have found some wonderful mountain property. You're thinking if you could invest a single sum of $50,000 for five years you might be able to buy a parcel of land that costs $70,000. However, the land cost is expected to appreciate compounded at four percent per year. Can you afford the land?

Time Value Calculations

I-19 Evaluate each independent situation, using the appropriate table and an interest rate of eight percent.

a. A retirement fund is set up to pay $15,000 per year for the next 20 years. How much must be in the fund at the beginning?

b. A company is required, as part of their loan restrictions, to set up a sinking fund account (an investment account) and invest $5,000 at year-end for four years. How much will be in the fund at the end of four years to provide for the debt payoff? Identify two alternative ways of using the tables to calculate your answer.

c. How much should you invest now to have $60,000 at the end of nine years? Would your answer be different if interest is compounded semi-annually during these nine years?

d. How much will your fund grow to in 10 years if you invest $20,000 today? Would your answer be different if interest is compounded semi-annually during these 10 years?

Annuity Necessary to Meet Future Cash Objective

I-20 A firm promises to pay its CEO a bonus of $1,000,000 on her retirement at the end of eight years. How much must the firm put aside at the end of each year at an interest rate of 10% in order to meet its commitment? Identify two alternative ways of using future value tables to analyze this problem.

Future Value of Annuity Deposits

I-21 A large chemical firm has just lost a major lawsuit and now must make 20 payments of $1,000,000 at year-end to the survivors of its chemical factory explosion. Using an eight percent interest factor, how much must be in the fund to provide for these payments?

Present Value Calculations

I-22 Calculate the present value of the following cash flows, using a 10% interest rate:

a. Your rich uncle promises to give you $1,000,000 in 10 years, when you are more mature and able to handle such sums.

b. Your rich aunt promises to give you $3,000,000 in 20 years, when she is sure you are mature enough to handle such sums.

c. Evaluate which of the two promises you prefer, and describe why you prefer it.

Present Value Calculations

I-23 Calculate the present value of the following cash flows, using an 8% interest rate:

a. Your rich uncle promises to give you $100,000 for each of the next five years, and $1,000,000 at the end of the tenth year.

b. Your rich aunt promises to give you $3,000,000 in 20 years, when she is sure that you will need the money!

c. Evaluate which of the two promises you prefer, and describe why you prefer it.

Present Value Calculations

I-24 Calculate the present value of the following cash flows, using a 12% rate of interest:

a. Your rich uncle promises to give you $100,000 for each of the next five years, $200,000 for the following five years, and $1,000,000 at the end of the tenth year.

b. Your rich aunt promises to give you $3,000,000 in 20 years, when she is sure that she will have enough money to afford this gift.

c. Evaluate which of the two promises you prefer, and describe why you prefer it.

Present Value Calculations

I-25 Calculate the present value of the cash flows associated with a life insurance policy that you inherited, using a 10% interest rate.

a. The life insurance policy offers a payout option of $300,000 at the end of each of the next three years.

b. A second option, under the same policy, is to receive $100,000 at the end of each year, for the next 12 years.

c. Identify which option you prefer, and describe why you prefer it.

Present Value Calculations

I-26 Calculate the present value of the cash flows associated with the retirement options under your pension plan, using an 8% interest rate.

a. One retirement option under the pension plan is to receive 90% of your current annual salary of $80,000 at the end of the year, for life, which is expected to be 20 years.

b. Another option is to receive a lump sum distribution of $1,300,000 immediately.

c. A third option is to receive five annual (year-end) payments of $300,000.

d. Evaluate which option you prefer and describe why you prefer it.

Present Value Calculations

I-27 Calculate the present value of the cash flows associated with the retirement options under your pension plan, using a 10% interest rate.

a. One retirement option under the pension plan is to receive 90% of your current annual salary of $100,000 at the end of the year, for life, which is expected to be 20 years.

b. Another option is to receive a lump sum distribution of $1,000,000 immediately.

c. A third option is to receive five annual (year-end) payments of $250,000.

d. Evaluate which option you prefer and describe why you prefer it.

Present Value Calculations

I-28 Calculate the present value of the cash flows associated with a life insurance policy that you inherited, using a 12% interest rate.

a. The life insurance policy offers a payout option of $500,000 at the end of each of the next four years.

b. A second option, under the same policy, is to receive $245,000 per year, for each of the next 12 years.

c. Identify which option you prefer and describe why you prefer it.

Present Values: Interpreting Financial Statements

I-29 Refer to Wal-Mart's financial statements in Appendix A. Review the financial statements and notes to determine how and where present value calculations may have been used.

Required

a. Were present value calculations disclosed?

b. If the present value calculations were not separately disclosed, discuss areas where you infer that such calculations must have been used.

Present Values: Interpreting Financial Statements

I-30 Refer to Target's financial statements in Appendix C. Review the financial statements and notes to determine how and where present value calculations may have been used.

Required

a. Were present value calculations disclosed?

b. If the present value calculations were not separately disclosed, discuss areas in which you would infer that such calculations must have been used.

TOPICMOD II

LEASES

Learning Objectives

1. *Distinguish between leases that are ordinary rentals and those that are in substance a purchase of assets.*
2. *Determine how leases impact the measurement of financial position and operating performance.*
3. *Understand the cash flow implications of leasing versus purchasing a fixed asset with cash or with debt.*

INTRODUCTION TO PART I: FINANCIAL REPORTING OF LEASE OBLIGATIONS

Business firms obtain the right to use property, plant, and equipment by means of either a purchase or a lease. A **lease** is an agreement between an owner (or **lessor**) and a renter (or **lessee**) that conveys the right to use the leased property for a designated future period (typically several years). The lessee makes periodic payments, usually of the same dollar amount each time, over the term of the lease. Leases can be relatively short term, such as three or four years, or can extend over the entire economic life of the leased asset.

Leasing is an increasingly popular way of obtaining business assets. In fact, leasing is one of the fastest growing industries in the United States. In recent years, leasing has accounted for more than one-third of all new equipment investment in this country. The U.S. Department of Commerce projects that leasing will grow more quickly than other types of asset acquisition throughout the next decade.

Benefits of Leasing

From a lessee's perspective, there are many potential advantages to leasing, rather than purchasing, an asset. Some of these advantages are based on sound economic incentives, and others are based on the methods used to report leases in financial statements.

Financial Flexibility

Leases offer financial flexibility beyond terms available with other borrowing arrangements. For example, loan agreements sometimes impose considerable restrictions on borrowers. These restrictions may concern key financial ratios, profitability requirements, dividend payments, and other financial actions. Lease agreements, on the other hand, do not generally give the lessor the power to impose such restrictions. Instead, the leased asset secures the lessor's claim.

Protection Against Obsolescence

Leasing can also reduce the lessee's risks of equipment obsolescence. A lessor, on the other hand, can have less risk than a lessee if the asset has a well-developed secondary market so that the lessor can resell or re-lease the used equipment. The economic life of an asset depends on its uses; national airlines, for example, cannot use outdated airplanes, but many regional carriers regularly use them for short-haul flights. Consequently, new passenger airplanes are usually first leased to major airlines, and after the initial leasing period, they are then leased to regional carriers.

Reduction of Financial Risk

Unlike some forms of debt financing that carry variable interest rates, lease payments normally are uniform each month or year. This feature insulates the lessee from the effects of interest rate increases. In addition, lease arrangements generally do not require the lessee to make a cash down payment, as most debt financing arrangements require.

Comparison of Installment Purchases versus Leases

To provide a framework for discussing the financial statement effects of leasing, we first consider the case in which a firm borrows in order to purchase a long-lived asset.

Exhibit II-1 provides pertinent information about a jet aircraft to be acquired by the Exec Perk Company.

The company finances the purchase by installment debt and will make a series of $2 million repayments at the end of each of the next six years. This payment pattern is an ordinary annuity, which can be evaluated using present value methods.

Present value = Periodic loan payment × Annuity present value factor, six periods at 12%

= $2 million × 4.111 (Exhibit I-3; i = 12%, n = six periods)

= $8,222,000

Because the present value of the loan payments is $8,222,000, this is a suitable measure of the aircraft's cost to Exec Perk Company. Upon purchasing the aircraft, Exec Perk would increase both its noncurrent assets and noncurrent liabilities by $8,222,000.

ASSETS	=	LIABILITIES	+	SHAREHOLDERS' EQUITY
Equipment + $8,222,000		Installment debt + $8,222,000		

Over the six-year estimated useful life of the aircraft, the cost will be systematically expensed. Assuming a straight-line benefit pattern, the annual depreciation expense is $1,370,333 ($8,222,000 cost / 6 years).

ASSETS	=	LIABILITIES	+	SHAREHOLDERS' EQUITY
Equipment (accumulated depreciation) – $1,370,333				Retained earnings – $1,370,333 (depreciation expense)

EXHIBIT II-1 PURCHASE OF A LONG-LIVED ASSET

Exec Perk Company
Information Regarding Installment Purchase of an Asset

Asset to be purchased:	Jet aircraft
Estimated useful life:	Six years
Benefit pattern:	Straight-line
Residual value:	Zero
Method of financing:	Installment debt
Annual payments (end of year):	$2 million
Borrowing rate:	12%

In addition, Exec Perk has borrowed the money ($8,222,000) from the seller in order to purchase the asset at an interest rate of 12%. For this reason, the firm must also recognize an interest expense of $986,640 ($8,222,000 × 12% = $986,640) during the first year of the loan.

ASSETS	=	LIABILITIES	+	SHAREHOLDERS' EQUITY
		Installment debt + $986,640		Retained earnings – $986,640 (interest expense)

Exec Perk will also make the first installment payment at the end of the year:

ASSETS	=	LIABILITIES	+	SHAREHOLDERS' EQUITY
Cash – $2,000,000		Installment debt – $2,000,000		

As a result of these events, Exec Perk has recognized total aircraft-related expenses of $2,356,973:

Depreciation expense	$1,370,333
Interest expense	986,640
Total expense	$2,356,973

The reported value of the installment debt at year-end, after the first installment payment, is $7,208,640:

Installment debt, beginning of the year	$8,222,000
Add: Interest expense	986,640
Less: debt payment	(2,000,000)
Installment debt, end of the year	$7,208,640

In each of the remaining five years, Exec Perk would continue to record a depreciation expense of $1,370,333 and an interest expense computed at 12% of the installment debt's carrying value. Because the debt is being repaid in installments, the interest expense would be smaller in each successive year.

In summary, the installment purchase of the aircraft has affected Exec Perk's financial statements in the following ways: *long-term assets and long-term debt have increased* to reflect the cost of the asset and the firm's obligation to make installment payments. Also, the *income statement includes both depreciation expense and the interest expense* on the amount borrowed.

It is also important to note that when a firm purchases an asset with installment debt the lender generally requires an upfront cash down payment as security on the loan. In our example above, we ignored any down payment requirement.

Analyzing Leases

Referring to our previous example, assume instead of purchasing the aircraft with installment debt, Exec Perk decided to lease the asset. Could the lease agreement be structured so that Exec Perk, the lessee, must capitalize the asset and the liability as if it were an installment purchase? Let's assume that Exec Perk signed a noncancelable lease contract to pay $2,000,000 at the end of each year for six years, the same payment schedule as above. Refer to Exhibit II-2.

EXHIBIT II-2 PROSPECTIVE LEASE INFORMATION

Exec Perk Company
Information Regarding Prospective Lease Agreement

Property to be leased	Jet aircraft
Lessor's fair value of property	$9 million
Economic life of property	6 years
Annual lease payment (due at the end of each year)	$2 million
Term of lease	6 years
Lessee's incremental borrowing rate	12%
Renewal or purchase options	None
Ownership transfer to lessee	No

Note that the lease covers the entire economic life of the asset and that title to the asset will not transfer to Exec Perk at the end of the lease term. Is there really any difference between this lease agreement and the installment purchase agreement other than the technicality of who owns the title to the asset? Even if Exec Perk has to return the asset at the end of the lease period, isn't the substance of the transaction the same? Isn't Exec Perk enjoying the rewards of ownership over the entire economic life of the asset? Should Exec Perk be required to record an asset and liability as if the lease were an installment purchase? What if the lease period was only three years, or what if the lease payments were not large enough to cover the fair value of the asset? Does this change the substance of the transaction?

To answer these questions and to provide consistent treatment for leases, rules have been established by the FASB that must be followed and require that leases be classified as either capital leases or operating leases.

A **capital lease** is interpreted as if it is essentially a purchase of an asset, financed by debt to be repaid in installments. *Consequently, a capital lease affects the financial statements the same way as an installment purchase. It increases the amounts of reported long-term assets and long-term debts, as shown earlier.* An **operating lease,** on the other hand, is interpreted as an ordinary rental, where the asset is merely used by the lessee. *Operating leases do not entail increases in reported long-term assets and debt. Instead, the lease payments are merely reported as rent or lease expense.*

A lease is classified as a capital lease if it meets *one or more of the following criteria:*

1. The lease transfers ownership of the property (title transfer) to the lessee by the end of the lease.
2. The lease gives the lessee an option to purchase the leased asset at a bargain price (bargain purchase option) at the end of the lease.
3. The lease term is equal to 75% or more of the estimated economic life of the leased property.
4. The present value of the lease payments is 90% or more of the fair value of the property at the inception of the lease.

Note that any *one* of these criteria recognizes that ownership rights have, in substance, been transferred from the lessor to the lessee. *Only if a lease fails all four criteria will it be classified as an operating lease.*

In our example pertaining to Exec Perk, the first two criteria are not met because there is no transfer of title at the end of the lease (first criterion) and there is no bargain purchase option (second criterion). The third criterion is met because the lease period of six years is equal to the estimated economic life of six years. Note that the fourth criterion would not have to be evaluated because one criterion has already been met. This lease would be classified as a capital lease and Exec Perk would be required to record a noncurrent asset and noncurrent liability of $8,222,000 (present value of the lease payments) when the lease is signed exactly as was recorded in the installment purchase example.

What if we changed the facts so that the economic life of the aircraft is ten years instead of six years? Does this change the accounting treatment? The first two criteria are again not met and now the third criterion is not met because the lease term of six years is less than 75% of the estimated economic life (75% of 10 years = 7.5 years) of the leased property.

To evaluate the fourth criterion, the present value of the lease payments must equal or exceed 90% of the leased property's fair value, the lease payments must be discounted using Exec Perk's (the lessee's borrowing rate of 12%). Note that the lease obligates Exec Perk to make payments of $2 million to the lessor at the end of each year for six years. As shown above for the installment purchase, the present value of the payments equals $8,222,000. If we assume that the aircraft's fair market value is $9 million at the inception of the lease, we can see that the present value of the lease payments exceeds the 90% test ($8,222,000 / $9,000,000 = 91.3%). Consequently, Exec Perk must capitalize the lease. Capitalization will increase both the firm's noncurrent assets and noncurrent liabilities by $8,222,000 when the lease is signed.

ASSETS	=	LIABILITIES	+	SHAREHOLDERS' EQUITY
Leased assets + $8,222,000		Lease obligation + $8,222,000		

The subsequent entries for depreciation, interest, and lease payments will be the same as were shown for the installment purchase. The asset's cost will be depreciated for six years instead of its ten-year economic life because Exec Perk will have to return it to the leasing party (the lessor) at the end of the lease term. Note that if either of the first two criteria (transfer of title or bargain purchase option) were present in the lease, the asset would be depreciated over its economic life because it is assumed that the lessee will own the asset during this entire period.

For illustrative purposes the entries for the first year pertaining to the lease are shown below:

Depreciation:

ASSETS	=	LIABILITIES	+	SHAREHOLDERS' EQUITY
Leased assets – $1,370,333				Retained earnings – $1,370,333 (depreciation expense)

Interest and Lease Payment:

ASSETS	=	LIABILITIES	+	SHAREHOLDERS' EQUITY
Cash		Lease obligation + $986,640		Retained earnings – $986,640 (interest expense)
– $2,000,000		– $2,000,000		

As a result of these events, Exec Perk has recognized total lease-related expenses during the first year of $2,356,973:

Depreciation expense	$1,370,333
Interest expense	986,640
Total expense	$2,356,973

The reported value of the lease obligation at year-end, after the first lease payment, is $7,208,640:

Lease obligation, beginning of the year	$8,222,000
Add: Interest expense	986,640
Less: Lease payment	(2,000,000)
Lease obligation, end of the year	$7,208,640

The reported value of the leased asset at the end of this first year is $6,851,667 ($8,222,000 original cost less $1,370,333 depreciation).

Note that the leased asset is oftentimes viewed as an intangible asset. Instead of recording depreciation expense, amortization expense is recorded. Either treatment is acceptable. In addition, for comparison purposes we showed the lease payments as being made at the end of each period. In practice, most leases require payments to be made at the beginning of each period starting with the first lease payment when the lease is signed. This payment pattern is called an annuity due instead of an ordinary annuity and would give slightly different results.

What if Exec Perk's lease contract was structured so that it failed to meet any of the four criteria of a capital lease? The lease would be classified as an operating lease and no asset or liability would be recognized at the inception of the lease. Instead, the firm would record a rent or lease expense of $2,000,000, paid in cash to the lessor at year-end.

ASSETS	=	LIABILITIES	+	SHAREHOLDERS' EQUITY
Cash – $2,000,000				Retained earnings – $2,000,000 (rent expense)

Exhibit II-3 contrasts the impact of capital versus operating lease treatments on Exec Perk's balance sheet and income statement over the life of the lease. Note the following:

1. Capital and operating leases both result in a total expense of $12 million over the entire term of the lease because this is the total amount to be paid to the lessor ($2 million × 6 years = $12 million).
2. Under a capital lease, the total yearly expense (depreciation plus interest) is higher in the earlier years and lower in the later years. This occurs because the interest expense declines as the lease debt is partially repaid in installments. In contrast, the operating lease shows a constant annual expense of $2 million.
3. The capital lease is reported as a leased asset on the balance sheet. The asset is systematically depreciated over the lease term. A lease obligation, to be repaid in installments, is also reported as a liability. In contrast, the operating lease treatment reports neither an asset nor a liability.

EXHIBIT II-3 CAPITAL VERSUS OPERATING LEASE TREATMENTS

Exec Perk
Comparison of Capital and Operating Leases Effects on Selected Financial Statement Items

CAPITAL LEASE EFFECTS:

	Balance Sheet		Income Statement, Year Ended				
Date	**Leased Assets**	**Lease Obligation**	**Depreciation Expense**	**+**	**Interest Expense**	**=**	**Total**
Inception (Jan. 1)	$8,222,000	$8,222,000					
December 31,							
year 1	6,851,667	7,208,640	$1,370,333	+	$ 986,640	=	$ 2,356,973
year 2	5,481,334	6,073,677	1,370,333	+	865,037	=	2,235,370
year 3	4,111,001	4,802,518	1,370,333	+	728,841	=	2,099,174
year 4	2,740,668	3,378,820	1,370,333	+	576,302	=	1,946,635
year 5	1,370,335	1,784,278	1,370,333	+	405,458	=	1,775,791
year 6	-0-	-0-	1,370,335*	+	215,722*	=	1,586,057
Totals			$8,222,000	+	$3,778,000	=	$12,000,000

OPERATING LEASE EFFECTS:

Balance Sheet		Income Statement, Year Ended	
Leased Assets	**Lease Obligation**	**Rental Expense each year**	**$2,000,000 × 6 years**
-0-	-0-	Total over 6 years $12,000,000	

*Differs due to rounding.

IMPACT OF LEASES ON RATIO RELATIONSHIPS

The differences in the financial reporting of capital and operating leases may have a major impact on financial ratios for firms with many leases. Recall that for lessees capital leases result in higher asset values and greater amounts of debt than do operating leases. Also, capital leases initially result in lower incomes (because total lease expenses are higher in the earlier years of the lease). Consequently, ratios that use net income, total assets, or debt in their calculations will be affected. As examples, return on assets, the debt-to-assets ratio, and earnings per share will all appear less favorable in the earlier years under capital leases because capital leases must be shown as both an asset and a liability.

Operating leases, on the other hand, are accounted for as rentals, so that neither the leased property nor the liability for future lease payments is shown on the balance sheet. For this reason, *operating leases are often referred to as "off-balance-sheet" financing.* Accounting standards, however, require that footnotes to the financial statements include substantial disclosures about operating leases. Financial analysts, if they desire, can use this supplementary information to recast the balance sheet as if the operating leases are treated similarly to capital leases.

Reality Check II-1 illustrates how financial analysts can use supplementary information regarding operating leases in evaluating Delta Air Lines indebtedness.

Refer to Exhibit II-4 pertaining to Target Corporation. You will notice that the company has both capital and operating leases but the financial impact of these leases is far less for this retail company compared to Delta Air Lines.

It is interesting to note that even though supplementary information must be disclosed in the footnotes for operating leases many firms that lease property (lessees) will go to great lengths to negotiate leases that violate all four of the capital lease criteria causing the leases to be classified as operating leases. Some creative lease arrangements have emerged over the years to ensure operating lease treatment so that lessees do not have to report debt. One such arrangement is called a **third party guarantee.** Insurance companies and investments firms have made this a lucrative business by acting as third party guarantors for lessees in certain lease contracts causing an otherwise capital lease to violate the four capital lease criteria and be classified as an operating lease for the lessee. Even though the details of this type of lease arrangement are beyond the scope of this text it is worth noting that *many leases that probably should be capital leases are recorded as operating because some creative "gimmick" has been arranged causing the lease contract to violate the capital lease criteria,* something that the FASB did not intend. In fact, as we previously mentioned, accounting for leases is one of the "hot topics" along with pensions and stock options that the FASB has either revised recently or intends on revising.

Cash Flow Implications of Leasing versus Purchasing a Fixed Asset

One of the biggest advantages of leasing a fixed asset versus purchasing it with cash or with debt is that leasing generally does not require any large upfront cash payment. In other words, leasing requires periodic payments spread out over

REALITY CHECK II-1

Delta Air Lines is one of the largest airlines in the world. It provides scheduled passenger service, airfreight, mail, and other related aviation services. Selected balance sheet information from Delta's 2004 annual report is given here along with Note 7 to the financial statements, describing Delta's lease obligations.

Like most airlines, Delta leases the major portion of its assets. Most of these leases are structured as operating leases by violating the FASB's criteria for capital leases. Accounting standards require that the minimum annual rental commitments under both capital and operating leases be disclosed for the ensuing five years and in the aggregate for later years.

DELTA AIR LINES, INC.
SELECTED FINANCIAL INFORMATION, 2004 ANNUAL REPORT
(DOLLARS IN MILLIONS)

Balance sheet	
Current assets	$ 3,606
Property and equipment	16,556
Other assets	1,639
Total	$21,801
Current liabilities	$ 5,941
Noncurrent liabilities and other credits	21,379
Total liabilities	27,320
Total stockholders' equity	(5,519)
Total	$21,801
Net (loss) income	$(5,198)

DELTA AIR LINES, INC.
FOOTNOTE DISCLOSURES OF LEASE OBLIGATIONS
(ADAPTED FROM THE 2004 ANNUAL REPORT)

Note 7. Lease Obligations (partial):

The Company leases certain aircraft, airport terminal and maintenance facilities, ticket offices, and other property from third parties. Rental expense for operating leases, which is recorded on a straight-line basis over the life of the lease, totaled $1.3 billion for each year ended December 31, 2004, 2003, 2002. Amounts due under capital leases are recorded as liabilities. Interest in assets acquired under capital leases is recorded as property and equipment on the Consolidated Balance Sheet.

As of December 31, 2004, the Company's minimum rental commitments under capital leases and noncancelable operating leases with initial or remaining terms of more than one year were as follows:

Years Ending June 30	*Capital Leases*	*Operating Leases*
	(In millions)	
2005	$ 158	$ 1,091
2006	162	1,017
2007	134	915
2008	112	980
2009	146	836
After 2009	410	4,823
Total minimum lease payments	$1,122	$9,662
Less: Amounts representing interest	674	
Present value of future minimum capital lease payments	448	
Less: Current obligations under capital leases	58	
Long-term capital lease obligations	$ 390	

SOURCE: Delta Air Lines, Inc., 2004 Annual Report.

Required

a. Assume that for purposes of financial analysis, you wish to treat Delta's operating leases as if they were capital leases. Develop an approximation of the capitalized value of Delta's leases, based on the information provided in Note 7.

b. Show how your approximation of the capitalized values of Delta's operating leases would affect your measurements of total assets, total liabilities, property and equipment, the ratio of liabilities to assets, the ratio of property, plant, and equipment to assets, net income (loss), and the ratio of net income (loss) to total assets.

SOLUTION

a. The present values of Delta's capital leases are included in the asset and liability totals reported in its balance sheet (and in our summary balance sheet information). If financial analysts also desire to incorporate Delta's operating leases as if they were capital leases, it is necessary first to discount the future minimum lease payments at Delta's borrowing rate. The borrowing rate is not disclosed in the financial statements, however. If it may be assumed that Delta's capital and operating leases have relatively similar cash flow patterns, then an approximate present value for the operating leases may be computed as follows:

	(millions of dollars):
Present value of capital lease payments (Note 7)	$ 448
Total minimum capital lease payments (Note 7)	$ 1,122
Percentage of present value to total payments:	

$$\frac{\$448}{\$1,122} = 39.9\%$$

Total minimum operating lease payments	$ 9,662
Percentage of present value to total payments (above)	× 39.9%
Estimated present value of operating lease payments	$ 3,855

b. This approximation indicates that capitalization of the operating leases would increase Delta's reported property, plant, and equipment, as well as debt, by about $3.855 billion. Selected financial statement relationships would be affected by capitalizing leases as follows:

DELTA AIR LINES, INC.
SELECTED FINANCIAL RATIOS BEFORE AND AFTER CAPITALIZATION OF OPERATING LEASES
(DOLLARS IN MILLIONS)

	Before Capitalization (See Reality Check II-1)	*After Capitalization**	*Percent Change*
Total assets	$21,801	$25,656	+ 18%
Total liabilities	$27,320	$31,175	+ 14%
Property and equipment	$16,556	$20,411	+ 23%
Liabilities/assets	125.3%	121.5%	
Property and equipment/assets	75.9%	79.6%	
Net loss	$(5,198)	$(5,198)**	
Net loss divided by total assets	(23.8)%	(20.3)%**	(15)%**

* The amounts after capitalization are determined by adding $3.855 billion to debt and property and equipment, based on the approximate present value of the operating lease commitments computed earlier.

** For convenience, we assume that net loss is the same before and after capitalization. Lease expense is generally higher in the earlier years of capital leases. Although the income effect is not readily calculable given the information in Delta's financial report, Delta's reported net loss would likely have increased if the operating leases had been capitalized.

As shown in the preceding calculations, the capitalization of Delta's operating leases would increase the reported amount of total assets, liabilities, and property and equipment by 18%, 14%, and 23%, respectively.

EXHIBIT II-4 CAPITAL AND OPERATING LEASE DISCLOSURES

Target Corporation
Footnote Disclosures of Lease Obligations
(Adapted from the 2005 Annual Report)

Lease Obligations (partial):

As of January 28, 2006, the Company's minimum rental commitments under capital leases and noncancelable operating leases with initial or remaining terms of more than one year were as follows:

YEARS ENDING DECEMBER 31	CAPITAL LEASES	OPERATING LEASES
	(IN MILLIONS)	
2006	$ 12	$ 137
2007	12	132
2008	13	123
2009	13	114
2010	13	107
After 2010	160	2,484
Total future minimum lease payments	$223	$3,097
Less: interest	122	1,703
Present value of minimum lease payments	$101	$1,394

Target Corporation
Selected Financial Ratios Before and After
Capitalization of Operating Leases
(Dollars in millions)

	BEFORE CAPITALIZATION	AFTER CAPITALIZATION	PERCENT CHANGE
Total assets	$34,995	$36,389	+ 4%
Total liabilities	$20,790	$22,184	+ 7%
Property and equipment	$19,038	$20,432	+ 7%
Liabilities/assets	59.4%	61.0%	
Property and equipment/assets	54.4%	56.2%	

As shown in the preceding calculations, the capitalization of Target's operating leases would increase the reported amount of total assets, liabilities, and property and equipment by 4%, 7%, and 7%, respectively.

some specified lease term. Purchasing, on the other hand, requires a firm to either use a lot of its cash immediately to pay for the asset or if the firm borrows the cash to purchase the asset, the lender generally requires a cash down payment as security on the loan.

In addition, lease payments generally are uniform from year to year whereas debt financing oftentimes carries variable interest rates that create fluctuating loan payments.

Summary of Learning Objectives

1. **Distinguish between leases that are ordinary rentals and those that are in substance a purchase of assets.**
   A lease is an agreement between an owner (or lessor) and a renter (or lessee) that conveys the right to use the leased property for a designated future period. Accountants classify leases as either capital leases or operating leases. A capital lease is interpreted as essentially a purchase of the leased asset, while an operating lease is reported on the same basis as an ordinary rental. Accounting standards provide a set of explicit criteria to identify capital leases. Essentially, a capital lease transfers the potential risks and rewards of ownership to the lessee. A capital lease is reported as an asset financed by installment debt.

2. **Determine how leases impact the measurement of financial position and operating performance.**
   Capital leases affect the balance sheet and income statement in the same manner as an installment purchase of the asset would. Noncurrent assets and lease obligations are reported based on the present value of the series of lease payments. The annual expense (lease amortization expense and interest expense) is relatively higher in the earlier years and declines as the lease obligation is reduced over time. By contrast, operating leases are reported as ordinary rentals. Neither assets nor liabilities are recognized in the balance sheet when the lease is signed. The annual expense is generally equal to the annual lease payments. Extensive disclosures in the Notes to Financial Statements are provided for all long-term leases, both capital and operating, indicating the amount and timing of future minimum lease payments. Financial statement analysts must use these "off-balance-sheet" amounts in order to aid in assessments of liquidity and solvency of lessee firms.

3. **Understand the cash flow implications of leasing versus purchasing a fixed asset with cash or with debt.**
   From a cash flow standpoint, leasing provides advantages over purchasing a fixed asset with cash or with debt because it generally does not require an upfront cash payment and unlike debt financing, which tends to carry varying interest rates and fluctuating loan payments, lease payments are generally uniform from year to year.

KEY TERMS

Capital lease
Lease
Lessee
Lessor
Operating lease
Third party guarantees

Exercises and Problems

II-1 Discuss several reasons why a firm's managers might choose to lease rather than purchase operating assets (such as buildings and equipment).

II-2 Distinguish between capital leases and operating leases as the terms are used in financial reporting. Is the distinction meaningful? Discuss.

II-3 Contrast the effects that capital leases and operating leases have on the following financial statement elements and relationships. Discuss how each of these effects might influence a manager's decision about how to design a lease contract.

a. Total assets
b. Total liabilities
c. Net income, earlier years
d. Net income, later years
e. Ratio of debt to total assets
f. Ratio of operating income to total assets

Operating or Capital Lease

II-4 Determine the first year's financial statement impact of the following lease terms:

- Annual payments, at year-end, $15,000
- Five-year useful life
- 10% borrowing rate
- Straight-line benefit pattern
- Zero residual value
- Five-year lease term
- Lessor's fair value of property, $60,000

Lease versus Purchase

II-5 Consider the following terms:

- Annual payments, end of each year, $40,000
- 10-year useful life
- 10% borrowing rate
- Straight-line benefit pattern
- Zero residual value
- Lease purchase
- Initial deposit upon signing agreement, $20,000, refundable upon satisfying all purchase terms
- Five-year lease terms
- Lessor's fair value of property, $170,000

Required

a. What lease terms should be changed to insure this purchase would be reported as a capital lease?

b. Using the accounting equation, show the first year's financial statement impact of your revised terms, and compare it to the financial statement impact of the original terms.

Ratio Effects: Lease versus Purchase

II-6 Consider the following summary financial statements at the beginning of the period:

Current assets	$1,050,000	Current liabilities	$ 650,000
Other assets	2,450,000	Other liabilities	1,500,000
		Capital stock	100,000
		Retained earnings	1,250,000
Total	$3,500,000	Total	$3,500,000

Net income during the period (exclusive of the lease) was $250,000. Also consider the following lease terms:

- Annual payments, at year-end, $25,000
- 10-year useful life
- 12% borrowing rate
- Straight-line benefit pattern
- Zero residual value
- Lease purchase
- Eight-year lease term
- Lessor's fair value of property, $225,000

Required

Use beginning balance sheet data to calculate the following requirements:

a. Calculate the ROE ratio and the financial leverage ratio for this company, assuming that this new asset is reported on the financial statements as a capital lease.

b. Calculate the ROE ratio and the financial leverage ratio for this company, assuming that this new asset is reported on the financial statements as an operating lease.

c. Discuss the relative impact of acquiring this asset under an operating lease versus a capital lease on these financial statements. Demonstrate these effects using the accounting equation.

Interpreting Financial Statements: Leases

II-7 Review Target's financial statements in Appendix C.

Required

a. Read the Leases footnote. Identify any unfamiliar or unusual terms. Match the terms presented in this chapter to the terms used by Target.

b. Do the firm's capital leases (the firm is the lessee) have any significant effect on its balance sheet? How?

c. Do the firm's operating leases (the firm is the lessee) have any significant effect on its balance sheet? How?

d. What proportion of the firm's total assets were financed by capital leases?

e. What other impact might leases have on the long-term success or failure of this firm?

Leases

II-8 The following note was taken from Abercrombie & Fitch's annual report:

NOTE 6:

Leased Facilities and Commitments

Annual store rent is comprised of a fixed minimum amount, plus contingent rent based on a percentage of sales exceeding a stipulated amount. Store lease terms generally require additional payments covering taxes, common area costs and certain other expenses.

A summary of rent expense follows (thousands):

	2005	**2004**
Fixed minimum rent	$170,009	$141,450
Contingent rent	16,178	6,932
Total	186,187	148,382
Building, equipment and other	3,241	1,663
Total rent expense	$189,428	$150,045

At January 28, 2006, the Company was committed to non-cancelable leases with remaining terms of one to 15 years. A summary of operating lease commitments under non-cancelable leases follows (thousands):

Fiscal years:	**Future Minimum Lease Obligations**
2006	$187,674
2007	187,397
2008	178,595
2009	169,856
2010	155,670
Thereafter	538,635

Required

a. Abercrombie's total liabilities in 2005 and 2004, respectively, were $794,601 and $717,465 (in thousands). Based on the information in Note 5, does it seem that the leases were a material component of these liabilities? If not, did the choice to capitalize or expense the lease payments have any material effect on Abercrombie's debt/asset ratios? Liquidity ratios? Asset turnover ratios?

b. Abercrombie's net income in 2005 and 2004, respectively, was $333,986 and $216,376 (in thousands). Again, based on the information in Note 5, was the rent expense a material component of net income? If so, did the choice of capitalizing or expensing the leases have a significant effect on Abercrombie's EPS? Net income as a percentage of net sales? ROE?

c. Discuss the differing effects of capitalized leases on balance sheet ratios, as compared to profitability ratios.

Leases

II-9 The Kroger Company reported the following information about leases in its 2005 annual report:

The Kroger Company
Notes to Consolidated Financial Statements

(10) Leases and Lease-Financed Transactions (partial)

The Company operates primarily in leased facilities. Lease terms generally range from 10 to 20 years with options to renew for varying terms. Terms of certain leases include escalation clauses, percentage rent based on sales or payment of executory costs such as property taxes, utilities or insurance and maintenance. Rent expense for leases with escalation clauses, capital improvement funding or other lease concessions is accounted for on a straight-line basis beginning with the earlier of the lease commencement date or the date the Company takes possession. Portions of certain properties are subleased to others for periods generally ranging from one to 20 years.

Minimum annual rentals and payments under capital leases for the five years subsequent to 2006 and in the aggregate are:

	Capital Leases	Operating Leases
2006	$61	$ 784
2007	57	732
2008	54	684
2009	52	635
2010	51	588
Thereafter	344	4,075
	619	$7,498
Less estimated executory costs included in capital leases	(3)	
Net minimum lease payments under capital leases	616	
Less amount representing interest	(270)	
Present value of net minimum lease payments under capital leases	$346	

Total future minimum rentals under noncancellable subleases at January 28, 2006, were $431.

Required

a. For the purpose of financial analysis, it may be necessary to treat Kroger's operating leases as if they were capital leases. Develop an approximate capitalized value of Kroger's leases based on the information provided in Note 10.

b. Discuss in narrative terms how this amount will affect the results of various ratio calculations, including the debt to assets ratio, the net income ratio, ROA, and ROE.

c. Download Abercrombie and Fitch's annual report and read Note 6. Compare and contrast Kroger's disclosure of its leases with the disclosures provided by Abercrombie (see Problem II-8). Which company provides more information? What factors might have resulted in these differences in lease disclosures?

TOPICMOD III

PENSIONS AND OTHER POSTRETIREMENT BENEFITS

Learning Objectives

1. *Know the difference between defined contribution and defined benefit pension plans.*
2. *Appreciate the impact of pension and non-pension postretirement benefit liabilities on reported financial position and operating results.*
3. *Understand the key assumptions necessary to measure postretirement obligations and expenses.*
4. *Comprehend the cash flow implications of underfunded pension and other postretirement benefit plans.*

POSTRETIREMENT BENEFIT OBLIGATIONS

Most medium- and larger-sized business firms provide retired employees with pensions and other postretirement benefits, mainly medical insurance coverage. The costs of these postretirement benefits are a component of employee expenses incurred during the **service lives** of the retirees, which are the working years prior to retirement. For this reason, the periodic expenses and obligations for postretirement benefits must be estimated to measure the operating performance and financial position of the employer firms.

Standards for the measurement and reporting of postretirement expenses and obligations have tightened considerably during the past decade or so. Separate standards govern reporting for pensions and reporting for other (nonpension) postemployment benefits. The following sections describe and contrast the financial reporting standards for both types of retiree benefits.

PENSION EXPENSES AND OBLIGATIONS

Pension plans are either defined contribution plans or defined benefit plans. A **defined contribution pension plan** specifies the periodic amount, usually a percentage of an employee's current salary, that the firm must contribute to a pension fund. The employee's retirement benefit depends on how well the pension fund invests the contributions that it has received. In any event, the employer's only obligation is to make the agreed-on contributions to the plan. *In effect, the employee bears all the risks and rewards of the investment performance of the pension fund.* The financial reporting effects of defined contribution plans are straightforward and noncontroversial. The accounting entry for employer contributions to a defined contribution retirement plan is as follows:

ASSETS	=	LIABILITIES	+	SHAREHOLDERS' EQUITY
– Cash				(Retained earnings) – Pension expense

Defined benefit pension plans, in contrast, specify the benefits that employees will receive at retirement. The employer makes periodic contributions to a pension fund in order to set aside funds to pay these benefits. Income tax rules and other government regulations influence the amounts of these periodic contributions.

Because defined benefit plans specify the dollar amounts of the pensions to be paid to retirees, the employer assumes all the risks and rewards associated with the pension fund investments. For instance, if pension fund assets are insufficient to pay the agreed-upon benefits, then the employer must make additional payments. On the other hand, if the pension fund's assets exceed the amounts required for benefits, the employer can reduce its contributions and in some cases can even withdraw the excess funds from the pension fund.

Defined benefit pension plans have proven to be especially popular in U.S. industries that have strong labor union representation. Unions usually favor labor agreements that offer security and low risk to their members. Managers in these industries also have tended to favor labor contracts that postpone the cash impact of labor costs. Defined benefit plans, therefore, are prevalent in the automobile, chemical, machinery, steel, paper, and transportation industries. Among firms with less labor union representation, the current trend has been away from defined benefit plans to defined contribution plans. In fact, defined contribution plans have become the more preferred type of retirement plan among firms today because they involve less paperwork, and the risks associated with these plans are borne by the employees, not the employer.

Exhibit III-1 shows the relationships among the employer, the pension plan, and the retirees in a typical defined benefit pension plan. The employer makes contributions to the pension fund, and the pension fund ultimately makes payments to retirees as specified in the employer's labor agreements. Unlike a defined contribution plan, however, the employer's pension obligation is to pay the benefits promised by the pension plan. In substance, the employer has an obligation to the beneficiaries, and the pension fund itself is just an intermediary.

THE BASIC ACCOUNTING EQUATION

To illustrate financial reporting for a defined benefit pension plan, refer to Exhibits III-2 and III-3, which contain portions of the pension footnote disclosures from U.S. Steel's annual report for 2005. U.S. Steel has more than one defined benefit pension plan and the pension benefits specified in these plans are based both on the employees' years of service and highest earnings levels in the years preceding retirement. Special attention should be given to the measurements of annual pension cost and pension obligations. Both items are discussed in the following sections.

EXHIBIT III-1 DEFINED BENEFIT PENSION PLANS

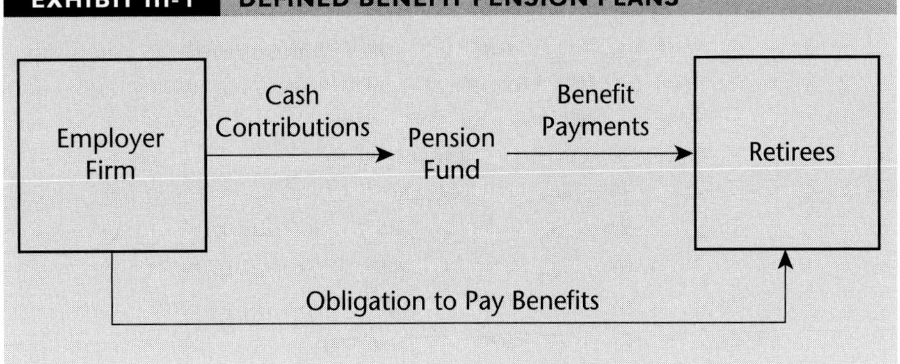

EXHIBIT III-2 PENSION EXPENSE FOOTNOTE DISCLOSURES

U.S. Steel Corporation
Pension Expense (Benefit) Recognized in Consolidated Income Statement
(Adapted from the 2005 Annual Report)

The assumptions used in each year and the components of the annual pension cost follow:

(DOLLARS IN MILLIONS)	2005	2004	2003
Assumptions:			
Expected return on plan assets	8.00%	8.00%	8.14%
Discount rate	5.75%	6.00%	6.25%
Pension cost:			
Service cost—benefits earned during the period	$ 95	$ 94	$ 103
Interest on projected benefit obligation	430	459	460
Expected return on plan assets	(548)	(570)	(635)
Other items	303	271	628
Total cost (benefit)	$ 280	$ 254	$ 556

EXHIBIT III-3 PENSION LIABILITY FOOTNOTE DISCLOSURES

U.S. Steel Corporation
Pension Liability Footnote Disclosures
(Adapted from the 2005 Annual Report)

POSTRETIREMENT PENSION BENEFITS

U.S. Steel has noncontributory defined benefit pension plans covering the majority of domestic employees. Benefits under these plans are based upon years of service and final average pensionable earnings, or minimum benefit based upon years of service, whichever is greater.

The following sets forth the plans' actuarial assumptions used and funded status at the valuation date of December 31 together with amounts recognized in the consolidated balance sheets:

(DOLLARS IN MILLIONS)	2005	2004
Assumptions:		
Discount rate	5.50%	5.75%
Average rate of compensation increase	4.00%	4.00%
Projected benefit obligation	$(7,784)	$(7,935)
Plan assets at fair value	7,178	7,554
Projected benefit obligation in excess of plan assets	(606)	(381)
Various adjustments (net)	2,860	2,731
Prepaid pension cost at December 31	$2,254	$2,350

Measurement of Pension Expenses

Exhibit III-2 shows the components of the pension expense (benefit) reported in U.S. Steel's income statement, defined as follows:

- **Service cost,** also called the "normal cost", is the value of future pension benefits that employees have earned during the current year.
- **Interest cost** is the interest on the projected benefit obligation (PBO) for the year. The **projected benefit obligation** measures the amount of pension benefits that employees have earned to date, based on the expected future salary levels that will determine these pension benefits. The projected benefit obligation is a present value, the discounted value of future payments. Each year this present value increases because the payment date is closer. The details of PBO are discussed in the next section.
- **Return on plan assets** is a reduction in pension expense for the return that is expected on the plan's assets (resources invested by the firm in income-producing assets that will be used to pay retirement benefits). The anticipated or expected, not actual, return on the plan assets is used as a component of pension expense so that the expense is not severely influenced by actual variations in investment values.
- **Other items (net),** include the systematic amortization of liabilities existing when present pension reporting standards were adopted, the obligations resulting from subsequent changes in pension benefits, the revisions in various assumptions underlying the pension valuation, and other factors.

Measurement of Benefit Obligations

Exhibit III-3 explains the measurement of U.S. Steel's pension obligations. Because pension benefits will be paid in future years, it is necessary to estimate the future payments and discount these to present values using an appropriate rate of interest. U.S. Steel uses a discount rate of 5.50% to measure its pension obligations for 2005.

The choice of a discount rate is crucial in evaluating pension obligations because minor variations in discount rates cause large variations in present values. Analysts often use the following rule of thumb: A one percent variation in the assumed discount rate causes about a 20% variation in the valuation of pension obligations.

Observe that U.S. Steel reports the actuarial present value of its pension obligation called projected benefit obligation (PBO). Recall that the projected benefit obligation measures the amount of pension benefits that employees have earned to date, based on the expected future salary levels that will determine these pension benefits. Two other present value measurements of pension obligation exist and are discussed at length later in the TOPICMOD.

U.S. Steel reported a pension expense for 2005 of $280 million. The cost resulted because the expected return on plan assets was less than the service cost plus the interest cost and other items incurred on the projected benefit obligation during the year. It is interesting to note that three years earlier in 2002 U.S. Steel reported pension benefit (income) instead of an expense. A benefit can result when the expected return on plan assets is much larger than the service cost plus the interest cost and other items incurred on the projected benefit obligation during the year. You may think that reporting pension income instead of pension expense is very unusual. However, it is important to understand that many assumptions and estimates are used in accounting for pensions, which can result in pension income as opposed to pension expense.

EVALUATION OF PENSION REPORTING

Pension reporting continues to be an area of controversy in financial accounting. The basic issues center on (1) the assumptions used in measuring pension obligations and expenses, (2) the appropriate definition of pension obligations, and (3) whether pension funds are entities distinct from the employer firms.

Assumptions

As shown in U.S. Steel's pension footnote, a myriad of actuarial and economic assumptions underlie the estimation of pension obligations. **Actuarial assumptions** (employee turnover, service lives, longevity, and so on) are fairly standardized and noncontroversial. The major controversies concern **economic assumptions,** particularly the assumed interest rate used to discount future pension benefits, and the anticipated rate of return on pension plan assets.

Employers are required to re-evaluate all potentially material assumptions when they perform annual measurements of pension and other postretirement benefit obligations. Many corporations have needed to re-assess the adequacy of the assumed discount rates as a result of the declines in interest rates on high-quality bonds that have occurred in recent years. Using lower interest rates to measure these obligations increases their present values, but on the other hand, related assumptions may also need to be revised because they are based on the same set of expectations about future economic conditions. For example, lower long-term interest rates are usually associated with lower rates of expected inflation, and this may suggest that the assumed rates of salary progression and health-care-cost trend rates should be revised downwards also. If so, these changes reduce the related liabilities. Consequently, the effects of interest rate changes may create revisions of several related assumptions that have offsetting (positive and negative) effects on pension and other postretirement obligations.

Corporations have primarily invested a large portion of their pension plan assets in the stocks of other companies. The returns earned on these stock investments historically have been strong. In fact, many companies set their anticipated or expected return rate on their plan assets at a much higher rate than the interest rate anticipated on the pension benefit obligation (PBO). Bear in mind that interest costs on the PBO increase pension expense whereas expected returns on plan assets reduce pension expense. With the declines in the stock market in the years 2000 through 2002, employers had to re-evaluate their stock portfolios and consider lowering their expected return rates of their pension plan assets.

Exhibit III-3 shows that the total market value of U.S. Steel's pension plan assets was $7.18 billion at the end of 2005. This amount is less than the projected benefit obligation (PBO) of $7.78 billion and indicates that U.S. Steel's pension plans were underfunded by $606 million at that date. You may think that this underfunded amount should be reported as a pension liability on the firm's balance sheet. However, accounting standards have allowed delayed recognition for various items such as gains and losses that may occur when actual results differ from estimated results. For example, when the actual return earned on plan assets differs from the expected return this may cause a gain or loss because pension expense reflects expected returns not actual returns. Should the gain or loss be an adjustment to pension expense? The FASB, after much debate, decided that because pension accounting involves many estimates and assumptions, the impact on pension expense should be minimized by deferring gains and losses and allowing them to be amortized into pension expense over future periods (rather than immediately recognized).

U.S. Steel's pension plans for 2005 were underfunded by $606 million but as the footnotes indicate, the net effect on the balance sheet was not a liability but an overall asset balance of $2,254 million. How can this be? The difference between the underfunded amount of $606 million and the net asset of $7,178 million was due to unrecognized losses (due to delayed recognition) most likely resulting from actual returns on plan assets being less than the expected returns of 8.00%.

As you can see by this example of U.S. Steel, companies have actually been able to report a pension asset (prepaid pension cost) instead of a pension liability even though the pension plan shows that it is underfunded. This is due to the delayed recognition of gains/losses in both the income statement via the pension expense account and in the balance sheet. As you can imagine pension accounting has been extremely controversial. The FASB has wanted to revise the accounting for defined benefit pension plans. It has been working on this project for sometime and as of the end of 2006, it issued a new standard, SFAS 158 "Employers' Accounting for Defined Benefit Pension and Other Postretirement Plans—an amendment of FASB Statements No. 87, 88, 106, and 132(R)." This standard will require companies like U.S. Steel to adjust their balance sheet pension account to equal the underfunded amount (difference between the PBO and Plan Assets) at year-end (beginning after December 15, 2006). Looking at the U.S. Steel disclosure in Exhibit III-3, if the new standard were in place at that time, U.S. Steel would have had to report a pension liability of $606 million, not the prepaid pension asset of $2,254. With the new standard, the difference of $2,860 representing the delayed gains/losses will now be required to be reported as part of the other comprehensive income of the company. Note, though, pension expense remains the same under the new standard.

Measurements of Pension Obligations

Three separate measures of pension obligation exist: projected (previously discussed), vested, and accumulated benefit obligations. **Vested benefit obligation** indicates amounts to which employees have irrevocable rights, even if they leave the firm prior to retirement. **Accumulated benefit obligation (ABO)** shows the amount of pension benefits that employees have earned to date, based on current salary levels. In essence, if the pension plan were curtailed today, the *ABO represents what would be owed to the employees since it is the actuarial present value of the future cash payments based on current salary levels.*

Managers and analysts often disagree about which of these best represents the firm's pension obligation. Managers sometimes assert that vested benefits are the best measure of the obligation, because this is the amount that must be paid to employees, even if the firm discontinues its operations immediately. Bear in mind, however, that financial statements reflect a "going concern" assumption, unless the firm is actually expected to liquidate in the near-term future. Alternatively, some firms argue that the accumulated benefit amount is a suitable measure, because it assumes continuity of the firm but does not incorporate salary increases that have yet to occur.

Finally, analysts frequently argue that the projected benefit obligation is most realistic, because it is based on expected pension payments (assuming normal rates of salary increase). In contrast, the accumulated benefit obligation is not meaningful because future salary increases are ignored.

Referring back to our example, U.S. Steel reported an underfunded status of its pension plans of $606 million (PBO – fair value of plan assets) in the pension footnotes for 2005. However, recall that the balance sheet effect was a net asset of $2,254 million due to the deferred recognition of losses. With the adoption of the new standard, SFAS 158, U.S. Steel will no longer be able to "hide" its underfunded amount in the footnotes but will now be required to report this amount as a liability on its balance sheet.

Pension Fund as a Distinct Entity

The pension fund is merely an intermediary between the employer and the pension beneficiary, as depicted in Exhibit III-1. The employer is ultimately liable for all pension benefits and bears all of the risks associated with the pension fund's investments. Consequently, many analysts do not regard the pension fund as an entity distinct from the employer firm and suggest that pension plan assets and obligations should be included (consolidated) with those of the employer for financial reporting purposes.

The consolidation of the employer firm and its pension plan would dramatically alter the financial statements of most industrial firms. For example, U.S. Steel's pension plans had $7.18 billion in assets and $7.78 billion in obligations at the end of 2005. U.S. Steel itself had about $10 billion in assets (exclusive of pension amounts) at that date and only $3 billion in shareholders' equity.

In this case, inclusion of the pension fund assets and obligations on U.S. Steel's balance sheet would almost double the apparent size of the company and more than double its reported debt financing.

OTHER POST-RETIREMENT EXPENSES AND OBLIGATIONS

Approximately one-third of all U.S. workers are covered by employer medical plans that continue the employee's coverage after retirement. The costs of retiree medical benefits are substantial and are expected to continue to increase as people live longer. Inflation and improvements in medical technology will also likely contribute to rising health costs.

Until 1993, the predominant way of reporting these nonpension postretirement benefits was on a **pay-as-you-go** basis, in which expenses were reported on a cash basis and no obligations were recognized for future payments. Current accounting standards, however, require that firms report their obligations to provide future benefits and accrue the expenses during the years that employees provide service (SFAS No. 106, "Employers' Accounting for Postretirement Benefits Other Than Pensions," December, 1990). For most affected firms, conversion to an accrual basis increased the amount of expenses recognized for medical benefits by two to three times (200 to 300%).

Illustration of Nonpension Postretirement Benefit Disclosures

Exhibits III-4 and III-5 contain excerpts of U.S. Steel's other postretirement benefit disclosures and will serve as a basis for our discussion. Observe that the overall format and content of these disclosures parallels that shown earlier for pension benefits (refer to Exhibits III-2 and III-3). The analyst would focus on the measurement of the firm's obligation and the determination of the annual expense. Note that Exhibit III-4 shows that U.S. Steel reports a liability of $1.935 billion for nonpension postretirement benefits at the end of 2005. This amount represents the difference between the present value of these benefits ($2.81 billion) and the plan assets at fair value ($532 million) plus other items, net ($339 million). As with the new revisions to pension accounting described earlier, nonpension postretirement accounting will also require the liability on the balance sheet to equal the underfunded amount. For U.S. Steel this would mean that the accrued benefit cost of $1,935 million plus $339 million of other items, totalling $2,274 million would be shown as a component of other comprehensive income.

Although this measurement is similar to the measurement of pension obligations shown earlier (refer to Exhibit III-3), there are two notable differences. First, the **accumulated postretirement benefit obligation** measures the present value of the future benefits that employees and retirees have earned to date. The calculation incorporates future medical cost changes, based on an assumed average health care trend rate. The future price of medical inflation is admittedly hard to predict, and U.S. Steel also provides the analyst with an estimate of the sensitivity of the measurements to a one percent increase (decrease) in the assumed rate.

EXHIBIT III-4 NONPENSION POSTRETIREMENT OBLIGATION

U.S. Steel Corporation
Postretirement Benefits Other Than Pensions
Obligations and Expenses Recognized in Financial Statements
(2005 Annual Report)

POSTRETIREMENTS BENEFIT OBLIGATION:

U.S. Steel also has defined benefit retiree health care and life insurance plans (other benefits) covering most domestic employees upon their retirement.

The following sets forth the plans' actuarial assumptions used and funded status at the valuation date of December 31, together with the amounts recognized in the consolidated balance sheets:

(DOLLARS IN MILLIONS)	2005	2004
Assumptions:		
Discount rate	5.50%	5.75%
Accumulated postretirement benefit obligation	$(2,806)	$(2,730)
Plan assets at fair value	532	466
Accumulated postretirement benefit obligation in excess of plan assets	(2,274)	(2,264)
Other items, net	339	143
Accrued benefit cost	$(1,935)	$(2,121)

A one percent point change in assumed health care cost trend rates would have the following effects.

(DOLLARS IN MILLIONS)	1-PERCENTAGE POINT INCREASE	1-PERCENTAGE POINT DECREASE
Effect on total of service and interest cost components	$ 8	$ (7)
Effect on other postretirement benefit obligations	140	(117)

Second, the fair values of the plan assets are minor, relative to the accumulated benefit obligation. Few firms fund any of their nonpension retirement benefits. There are no regulatory funding requirements or income tax advantages to motivate early funding, and most firms opt instead to simply pay the medical and life insurance premiums when they become due.

Measurement of Nonpension Postretirement Benefit Expense

The cost components shown in Exhibit III-5 for the nonpension expenses follow the same format as those for pension costs (refer to Exhibit III-2). The service cost represents the amount of the accumulated benefit obligation that was earned

EXHIBIT III-5 POSTRETIREMENT BENEFITS EXPENSE FOOTNOTE DISCLOSURES

U.S. Steel Corporation
Postretirement Benefit Expense Recognized in Consolidated Income Statement
(Adapted from the 2005 Annual Report)

POSTRETIREMENT BENEFITS EXPENSE:

The assumptions used in each year and the components of our postretirement benefit cost follow:

(DOLLARS IN MILLIONS)	2005	2004	2003
Assumptions:			
Expected return on plan assets	8.00%	8.00%	8.00%
Discount rate	5.75%	6.00%	5.98%
Postretirement benefit cost:			
Service cost	$ 12	$ 12	$ 16
Interest on accumulated postretirement benefit obligation	150	153	181
Expected return on plan assets	(36)	(35)	(39)
Other (net)	(17)	(24)	83
Total cost	$ 109	$ 106	$ 241

Assumed health care cost trend rates no longer have a significant effect on the majority of the liabilities reported for our health care plants, other than the benefit plan offered to retired mineworkers, due to the cost cap that was negotiated in 2003 with the USWA that freezes all retiree medical costs after the 2006 base year.

SOURCE: Excerpts from Note 20 to U.S. Steel Corporation's 2005 Annual Report.

by employees over the current year. The interest cost is the beginning of the year obligation multiplied by the discount rate. For firms like U.S. Steel, with mature employee groups, interest cost is the largest component of the net expense because the benefit obligation is so large. Because the benefits are not substantially funded, the expected return on plan assets provides only a minor offset to the other cost components.

A comparison of the financial statement effects of pension and nonpension benefits for U.S. Steel indicates that both types of postretirement benefits have significant effects on the firm's financial position and operating results. Even though both postretirement benefit plans show an underfunded status, the nonpension benefits are notably higher (over $1.9 billion) than the pension benefits (about $606 million) at the end of 2005. Similarly, the firm's pension benefit plan produced a pension expense of $280 million in 2005 whereas the nonpension benefits produced an expense of $109 million.

Reality Check III-1 contrasts the disclosures related to pensions and nonpension postemployment benefits for a large U.S. corporation.

REALITY CHECK III-1

PRA Industries, Inc. is a major supplier of specialty glass and special chemicals. The following information has been abstracted from the notes to PRA's 2007 financial statements:

	Pension Benefits		*Other Postretirement Benefits*	
	2007	*2006*	*2007*	*2006*
	(Dollars in millions)		*(Dollars in millions)*	
Funded status of benefit plans:				
Plan assets at market value	$2,308	$2,006	$ —	$ —
Accumulated benefit obligation	1,857	1,704	704	676
Projected benefit obligation	2,023	1,859	—	—
Components of annual expense:				
Service cost	36	36	7	7
Interest cost	134	124	48	43
Return on assets	(212)	(189)	—	—
Other	17	30	6	4
Total cost	$ (25)	$ 1	$ 61	$ 54
Underlying assumptions:				
Discount rate	7.0%	7.5%	7.0%	7.5%
Expected return on plan assets	10.9%	10.9%	—	—
Future compensation increases	4.6%	4.6%	—	—
Health care cost trend	—	—	7.0%	7.3%

Required

a. Do you consider PRA's pension benefits and other postemployment benefits to be overfunded or underfunded at the end of 2007? Explain.

b. Distinguish between the "accumulated benefit obligation" amounts reported for each type of plan.

c. With respect to the components of the annual costs, why is interest expense included? Why does the return on plan assets appear as a negative component?

d. The disclosure of assumptions reveals two changes between 2007 and 2006: (1) the discount rate has been decreased from 7.5% to 7.0%, and (2) the health care cost trend rate has been changed from 7.3% to 7.0%. Explain how each of these changes would affect your comparisons of postemployment liabilities and costs between 2007 and 2006.

SOLUTION

a. *Pension plans:* PRA's plan assets at market value exceed the accumulated benefit obligation by $451 million ($2,308 million less $1,857 million), and PRA's plan assets exceed the projected benefit obligation by $285 million ($2,308 million less $2,023 million). By either measure, PRA's plans are fully funded at the end of 2007. The projected benefit obligation, which includes projected rates of compensation increases, is a more meaningful definition of the pension obligation.

Other (nonpension) plans: PRA's accumulated benefit obligation is $704 million, which is entirely unfunded at the end of 2007.

All plans combined: In the aggregate, PRA's postretirement plans appear to be underfunded by $419 million ($704 unfunded nonpension benefits less $285 overfunded pension benefits).

b. The "accumulated benefit obligation" has a different interpretation for pension obligations than for other postretirement obligations. For pension obligations, the accumulated benefit obligation *assumes that present salary levels continue through the employee retirement dates;* in other words, future rates of compensation increases are ignored. For nonpension obligations, on the other hand, future rates of medical cost inflation are formally incorporated in the calculation of the accumulated benefit obligations. The financial statement analyst must be alert to the different meanings of "accumulated benefits."

c. Interest expense is a component of the annual cost of postretirement benefits because the obligations are reported at present value; the expected future benefit payments are discounted at an appropriate interest rate. As time passes, the present value of future payments increases. *This increase in the value of a liability is due to interest expense.*

The *return on plan assets represents amounts that have been earned* on the invested plan assets. Increases in the value of the plan's investments reduce the amount of the unfunded pension obligation. For this reason, these returns constitute income (or a reduction in expense) related to pensions.

d. *Discount rate:* Expected future benefit payments are discounted to determine the present value of the pension obligation. *Reductions in the discount rate increase the present value of the pension obligation.*

Health care cost trend rate: A decrease in this rate reduces the firm's estimated future payments for medical benefits and thereby reduces the firm's obligation.

Cash Flow Implications of Pensions and Other Postretirement Benefit Plans

Firms with defined benefit pension plans must make a minimum cash contribution to the pension fund assets each year based on regulatory requirements. Note, though, this is a minimum amount each year and oftentimes does not equal the pension costs incurred during the year. Firms with postretirement benefit plans other than pensions have no regulatory requirement to fund annual contributions. Therefore, in terms of postretirement benefits, many firms have highly underfunded plans. Even though the bulk of benefit payments will not have to be made for years, the looming obligation to pay these benefits with very little funding in place does not bode well for many firms. As we discussed in the TOPICMOD, firms who offer these types of plans will be responsible to cover any deficiencies in benefit payments. In essence, the future cash flow requirements on these firms may very well cripple their operating capabilities and ultimately cause their demise.

Summary of Learning Objectives

1. **Know the difference between defined contribution and defined benefit pension plans.**
Pension plans are either defined contribution or defined benefit plans. Defined contribution plans specify the employer's required payments to the pension fund and do not present any special reporting issues. Defined benefit plans, on the other hand, specify the future pension payments to which an employee will be entitled. Both types of plans require that the employer make periodic payments to a pension fund, but under a defined benefit plan the employer assumes all of the risks associated with pension fund investments.

2. **Appreciate the impact of pension and non-pension postretirement benefit liabilities on reported financial position and operating results.**
Firms with defined benefit pension plans must compare their projected benefit obligation (PBO) to the fair value of their plan assets. When PBO exceeds the plan assets' fair value, the difference must be reported as a pension liability on the firm's balance sheet, per the newly issued standard, SFAS 158. Pension expense reported on the income statement consists mainly of current service costs plus interest on the pension obligation minus returns expected to be earned on the pension fund's assets. When expected returns on plan assets are larger than the service and interest costs on the project benefit obligation this can cause recognition of pension benefit income instead of pension expense.

3. **Understand the key assumptions necessary to measure postretirement obligations and expenses.**
Measurements of pension obligations and expenses are based on a variety of assumptions, including assumptions about future earnings of pension fund investments and future salary increases of covered employees. The critical assumptions are disclosed in footnotes to the financial statements. Financial analysts must be alert to variations in assumptions used by different firms to measure pension obligations and expenses.

   Standards for the financial reporting of nonpension postretirement benefits have been adopted recently and are similar to the standards used for reporting pensions. The future trend of medical costs must be considered in predicting future benefits. Such costs are difficult to predict due to changes in medical technology, medical cost inflation, changing standards of medical care, the potential impact of a national health plan, and other factors. For this reason, the liabilities and expenses associated with nonpension retiree benefits are difficult to measure. Financial analysts must be creative as well as cautious when incorporating these measurements in financial ratio analysis.

4. **Comprehend the cash flow implications of underfunded pension and other postretirement benefit plans.**
   The future cash flow requirements could be quite demanding on firms that provide pension and other postretirement benefit plans because these firms are paying little to no annual contributions to the funds' plan asset accounts compared to the growing retirement benefit fund obligations.

KEY TERMS

Accumulated benefit obligation
Accumulated postretirement benefit obligation
Actuarial assumptions
Defined benefit pension plan
Defined contribution pension plan
Economic assumptions
Interest cost
Other items (net)
Pay-as-you-go
Pension plan
Projected benefit obligation (PBO)
Return on plan assets
Service cost
Service lives
Vested benefit obligation

Exercises and Problems

III-1 Distinguish between defined contribution and defined benefit pension plans. Which arrangement is riskier for the employee? Which is riskier for the employer? Explain.

III-2 Newly issued accounting standards require that firms report their underfunded balances as pension liabilities on the balance sheet. Describe what is meant by an underfunded pension. Explain why such an amount should (or should not) be included on the balance sheet.

III-3 Pension expense includes three main components: service cost, interest cost, and a reduction in expense for the return on plan assets. Explain how each of these amounts is determined.

Interpreting Financial Statements: Retirement Benefits

III-4 Review Wal-Mart's financial statements in Appendix A.

Required

a. Scan the notes and the rest of the financial statements for information pertaining to Wal-Mart's retirement benefits. Identify any unfamiliar or unusual terms. Match the terms presented in this TOPICMOD to the terms used by Wal-Mart.

b. Ignoring the United Kingdom and subsidiaries retirement plan information, answer the following questions:

i. Why does Wal-Mart have no pension liability?

ii. What was the expense recorded for retirement plans?

c. Why do you suppose Wal-Mart's United Kingdom and Japan subsidiaries have a defined benefit pension plan whereas its United States' subsidiaries do not have defined benefit pension plans?

d. Does the United Kingdom subsidiary and the Japan subsidiary show an over or underfunded pension? What was the amount?

Postretirement Benefits

III-5 Access the EDGAR archives (http://www.sec.gov/edgar/searchedgar/webusers.htm) and locate the most recent 10K filing by Kmart. Information about Kmart's pension plan can be found in the Notes to the Financial Statements.

Required

a. What are the total pension assets and liabilities?

b. What is the funding status of the pension plan?

c. What discount rate and average rate of return have been adopted by the company?

d. Identify total assets and total debt as reported on the balance sheet and calculate the debt-to-assets ratio. Then, including all retirement plan-related assets and liabilities, recalculate the values of total assets, total liabilities, and the debt-to-assets ratio. What do you observe?

e. Now examine the latest 10K for Wal-Mart (available at EDGAR). Should you make the same adjustments for Wal-Mart that you made for Kmart? State your reasons.

TOPICMOD IV

INTERNATIONAL ASPECTS OF FINANCIAL ACCOUNTING

Learning Objectives

1. *Understand how foreign exchange rate fluctuations affect the financial reporting of transactions conducted in foreign currencies.*
2. *Determine how financial statements prepared initially in foreign currencies are translated to U.S. dollars.*
3. *Appreciate the wide diversity of international accounting practices.*

Prepared with the assistance of L. A. Martin, Associate Professor of Accounting, University of Colorado at Denver and Health Sciences Center.

INTRODUCTION

Business activities are increasingly international. As tariff barriers dissolve through regional trade arrangements, such as the North American Free Trade Agreement (NAFTA) and the European Union (EU), domestic business firms rely more extensively on international trade both for sources of supply and as markets for their products. Many firms also are forced to rely on cross-border investments. The political and economic reshaping of Eastern Europe and the increasing modernization of China ensure that international trade will be a substantial and rapidly growing component in the business affairs of firms who focus mainly on the domestic market.

As foreign suppliers and customers become more essential to business activities, companies frequently establish or acquire subsidiary companies that operate in foreign nations. Most financial managers will regularly need to review and interpret financial statements produced in other countries. To report financial statements on a consolidated basis to U.S. investors, the foreign operations of those affiliates need to be translated into U.S. dollars. Because most *foreign currency exchange rates fluctuate over time,* a variety of issues arise in the preparation of dollar-denominated financial reports.

This TOPICMOD discusses three related aspects of financial reporting for firms engaged in international business:

1. the reporting of transactions between foreign and domestic firms, when the transactions are valued on the basis of the foreign currency;
2. the method used in translating the financial statements of foreign affiliates that have been prepared in other currencies into U.S. dollars; and
3. the diversity of accounting practices that exists among nations and the emerging efforts to achieve international harmonization of accounting practices.

FOREIGN CURRENCY TRANSACTIONS

If a U.S. company either buys from or sells to a foreign company, the firms must specify the currency that will be used to settle the resulting accounts receivable or payable. If the contract specifies payment in U.S. dollars, the foreign firm bears the risk of changes in the exchange rate. If the contract specifies payment in foreign (non-U.S.) currency, the U.S. firm bears the risk. To illustrate, consider the case where a U.S. firm bears the risk under a contract specifying payment in the foreign currency. If **foreign currency transactions** create receivables or payables that must be settled in a foreign currency, these balances are **denominated** in the foreign currency.

When a U.S. firm collects an account receivable that is paid in a foreign currency, it then *converts the foreign currency to dollars.* Conversely, in order for a U.S. firm to make payment of an account that is payable in a foreign currency, it may have to first convert U.S. dollars into the foreign currency. In either case, the U.S. firm must buy or sell foreign currency at the current **foreign exchange rate** between the U.S. dollar and the foreign currency. The foreign exchange rate specifies the number of U.S. dollars needed to obtain one unit of a specific foreign currency. Note that **direct rates** for foreign exchange quote the number of U.S. dollars required for one unit of a foreign currency. **Indirect rates** indicate the number of foreign currency units required for one U.S. dollar. The *discussion in this TOPICMOD uses only direct quotations.*

As a basis for discussion, hypothetical foreign exchange rates between the U.S. dollar ($) and the British pound (£) for various dates are provided in Exhibit IV-1. These rates show the number of U.S. dollars required to buy one British pound at the dates indicated. If we assume the rate is 1.80 on April 1, 2006, then U.S. $1.80 is needed to buy one British pound.

The information in Exhibit IV-1 includes **spot rates** and **forward rates.** A spot rate is the rate of exchange for the immediate delivery of foreign currencies. A forward rate is the rate of exchange for the future delivery of foreign currencies, and the market in which foreign currencies are bought and sold for future delivery is referred to as a **currency forward market.** Exhibit IV-1 indicates that the 60-day forward exchange rate of dollars to pounds is 1.68. If a U.S. firm needs British pounds in 60 days, it could contract today with a foreign exchange broker to buy pounds 60 days hence at a price of U.S. $1.68 per pound. Alternatively, the firm could simply wait and buy the pounds in 60 days at the prevailing spot rate on that date.

Firms frequently contract to buy or sell foreign currencies in the forward market in order to protect against the risks of foreign exchange rate fluctuations. The exchange rates between most pairs of currencies change frequently in response to the forces of supply and demand. As the number of U.S. dollars that is needed to buy a unit of foreign currency increases (or decreases), that foreign currency is said to strengthen (or weaken) against the dollar. As a result, if a U.S. firm has a foreign currency-denominated receivable or payable, then the equivalent dollar value of the account will vary as foreign currency exchange rates fluctuate.

The existence of forward markets for the foreign currencies of most major U.S. trading partners allows managers to **hedge,** or protect against the risks of exchange rate fluctuations. To illustrate, assume that on April 1, 2006, the Reagan Company, a U.S. firm, sells merchandise to Thatcher, Ltd., a British firm. The sales agreement specifies that Thatcher will make a payment of £150,000 to Reagan in 60 days, on May 30, 2006. Sales are recorded using the spot rate on the date of sale, rather than the forward rate for the date of anticipated collection. Because the spot rate of exchange at the transaction date, April 1, 2006, is 1.80 (see Exhibit IV-1), Reagan would record the account receivable and sale at $270,000 ($1.80 × 150,000).

ASSETS	=	LIABILITIES	+	SHAREHOLDERS' EQUITY
Accounts receivable + $270,000				Retained earnings + $270,000 (sales revenue)

Exhibit IV-1 shows that the spot rate of exchange on May 30, 2006, when Thatcher, Ltd., pays the receivable balance has fallen to 1.70. This indicates that the U.S. dollar has strengthened against the British pound and it requires fewer dollars to buy British pounds. Conversely, because the Reagan Company has a pound-denominated account receivable, the dollar value of the receivable has declined to $255,000 ($1.70 × £150,000). Reagan's collection of the receivable would increase cash by $255,000, but the entire receivable must be eliminated, so an exchange rate loss would be recognized for $15,000 ($270,000 − $255,000).

ASSETS		=	LIABILITIES	+	SHAREHOLDERS' EQUITY
Cash	Accounts receivable				Retained earnings
+ $255,000	− $270,000				− $15,000 (foreign currency loss)

In this example, the Reagan Company was exposed to the risk of exchange rate fluctuations over the 60-day collection period. The firm held an accounts receivable denominated in a foreign currency and incurred a loss because that foreign currency weakened against the dollar. Consequently, the dollar value of the receivable declined. Reagan could instead have chosen to protect itself against rate fluctuations at the date of sale by contracting on April 1 with a foreign exchange broker to sell 150,000 British pounds in 60 days at the 60-day forward exchange rate of 1.68.

Upon signing such a **hedging contract**, the Reagan Company would recognize an account receivable from the currency broker for $252,000 ($1.68 forward rate × 150,000) to be received in 60 days. Reagan would also recognize an account payable to the broker for $270,000 ($1.80 spot rate × 150,000), to be paid in British pounds in 60 days, and a hedging expense of $18,000 ($270,000 account payable less $252,000 account receivable).

EXHIBIT IV-1 HYPOTHETICAL FOREIGN EXCHANGE RATES

"Hypothetical Foreign Exchange Rates" between the U.S. Dollar ($) and the British Pound (£), Spot and Forward Rates

DATE			$/£
April 1, 2006	Spot rate:		1.80
	Forward rate:	30 days	1.695
		60 days	1.68
		90 days	1.67
May 30, 2006	Spot rate:		1.70

ASSETS	=	LIABILITIES	+	SHAREHOLDERS' EQUITY
Accounts receivable + $252,000		Accounts payable + $270,000		Retained earnings – $18,000 (hedging expense)

In effect, Reagan would have paid $18,000 to protect itself from exposure to foreign currency rate fluctuations over the collection term of the account receivable. They would have an account receivable from Thatcher, Ltd. in British pounds that is offset by a liability to the foreign exchange broker that also is denominated in British pounds.

In summary, when a U.S. firm contracts either to receive or to pay future accounts that are denominated in foreign currencies, there is an attendant risk of gains or losses from fluctuations in foreign exchange rates. Usually, firms are able to insulate themselves from risk by hedging, which is accomplished by entering into contracts with foreign exchange brokers to buy or sell foreign currencies at future dates.

The example in this section has shown how a firm would hedge a foreign currency account receivable by contracting to sell foreign currency in the future. Firms with foreign currency accounts payable, however, would hedge in the opposite fashion. They would hedge by contracting to buy foreign currency in the future. In either case, the objective is the same: *to have offsetting receivables and payables in the foreign currency.* Besides hedging foreign currency-denominated accounts receivable or payable, firms often hedge commitments to engage in future transactions. These can include purchase commitments, sales agreements, employment contracts, and so on.

Hedging one's exposure to foreign exchange rate fluctuations is similar in concept to the payment of an insurance premium in order to avoid risk. Firms engaged in international trade may have significant amounts of foreign currency-denominated financial assets and liabilities. If these are left unhedged, gains and losses caused by changes in exchange rates might account for a substantial portion of periodic profits and losses. Rather than speculate on the future strength or weakness of the dollar, most managers of industrial trading firms hedge to avoid exposure to exchange rate fluctuations. Reality Check IV-1 describes how one firm hedges its exposures to foreign exchange rate fluctuations.

TRANSLATION OF FOREIGN CURRENCY FINANCIAL STATEMENTS

Foreign subsidiaries of U.S. firms usually prepare their financial statements in the currencies in which they transact their business, which is referred to as their **functional currency.** The U.S. parent firm prepares its financial reports in U.S. dollars and, as a consequence, the financial statements of the foreign subsidiaries must be translated into U.S. dollars in order to be consolidated with those of the parent company.

REALITY CHECK IV-1

General Motors Company is a major automotive producer. The company included the following disclosures related to the management of its foreign exchange exposures in its financial statements (edited):

> "GM is an international corporation with operations in over 50 countries and has foreign currency exposures at these operations related to buying, selling, and financing in currencies other than the local currency. The magnitude of these exposures significantly varies over time depending on the strength of local automotive markets and sourcing decisions.
>
> GM enters agreements in order to manage certain foreign exchange exposures in accordance with established policy guidelines. These agreements primarily hedge cash flows such as debt, firm commitments, and anticipated transactions involving vehicles, components, fixed assets, and subsidiary dividends. GM uses foreign exchange forward contracts as well as purchased and written foreign exchange options. Foreign exchange forward contracts are legal agreements between two parties to purchase or sell a foreign currency for a price specified on the contract date with delivery and settlement in the future."

Required

a. The Note discussion indicates that the firm attempts to hedge debt, firm commitments, and anticipated transactions. Commitments and anticipated transactions are not formally recognized in the body of the financial statements, however. Discuss the advisability of hedging events that have not yet been recorded for financial statement purposes.

b. Provide an example of both a commitment and an anticipated transaction that exposes a firm to foreign currency risk. In each case, describe how the risk might be hedged.

SOLUTION

a. In attempting to insulate the firm from changes in foreign exchange rates, managers need not be bound by the completed transaction convention in financial accounting. Commitments are firm agreements to engage in future transactions at specific amounts of foreign currency and, if unhedged, represent exposure in an economic sense. Anticipated transactions, on the other hand, represent intentions rather than firm agreements, and in many cases these anticipated transactions eventually might not occur. For this reason, it is arguable whether they represent economic exposures to future exchange rate changes.

b. An example of a foreign currency commitment is a future purchase agreement made to a supplier, to be paid in a specified amount of foreign currency. An example of an anticipated transaction would be budgeted sales to customers abroad, with the sales proceeds to be received in foreign currencies. Regarding the purchase commitment, if future exchange rates change, the cost of the inventory and the liability to the supplier will both be changed in terms of U.S. dollars. The commitment could be hedged by selling the foreign currency for future delivery (by creating an offsetting account receivable denominated in the foreign currency). Regarding the future sales transactions, it is not easily known whether the terms or the equivalent dollar amounts of those sales will be changed as a consequence of future changes in foreign exchange rates. Because future sales represent expected future receipts of a foreign currency, the selling firm might hedge by contracting for a future sale of the foreign currency. It would be difficult to determine whether the foreign currency risks had been fully hedged, however, because the actual future sales amounts are not presently known.

To illustrate the process of translating foreign currency financial statements, consider the balance sheets and income statements of Perot, Inc., a subsidiary of a U.S. company, at the end of 2004, as shown in Exhibit IV-2. Perot, Inc., operates in Taiwan and prepares its financial statements in New Taiwan dollars, or NT$. Because Perot, Inc., is a subsidiary of a U.S. company, its financial statements must be translated into U.S. dollars prior to consolidation with those of the U.S. parent.

Foreign exchange rates between U.S. and New Taiwan dollars must be used to translate the various elements of Perot's financial statements into U.S. dollars. Accounting standards require the use of different rates for different financial statement elements. The FASB specifies the following rates for translation (SFAS No. 52, "Foreign Currency Translation"):

- The **average exchange rate** during the reporting period is used to translate income statement items. Average rates are appropriate when operating activities have been level throughout the year, and changes in exchange rates have occurred evenly throughout the year. Exhibit IV-2 shows that the average rate during 2004 was $0.04. Thus, on average it required US$0.04 to buy one NT dollar during 2004.
- The **current exchange rate** (the spot rate at the balance sheet date) is used to translate asset and liability items. Exhibit IV-2 shows that the current exchange rate was US$0.038 on December 31, 2004.
- Various **historical exchange rates** are used to translate the balances of invested capital, beginning retained earnings, and dividends. Exhibit IV-2 shows that the exchange rate when Perot's stock was issued was $.05, and the rate when dividends were declared in 2004 was US$0.039. The balance of Perot's retained earnings, translated into U.S. dollars, was $40.5 million at the beginning of 2004.

EXHIBIT IV-2 TRANSLATION OF FOREIGN CURRENCY FINANCIAL STATEMENTS

Perot, Inc.
Summary Income Statement and Balance Sheet
Year Ended December 31, 2004
(All currencies in millions)

INCOME STATEMENT, YEAR ENDED DECEMBER 31, 2004

ACCOUNT	NT$	TRANSLATION RATE	US$
Revenues	5,000	.04[a]	200.0
Expenses	(4,200)	.04[a]	(168.0)
Net income	800		32.0

BALANCE SHEET, DECEMBER 31, 2004

ACCOUNT	NT$	TRANSLATION RATE	US$
Assets	8,500	.038[b]	323.0
Liabilities	4,600	.038[b]	174.8
Invested capital	2,500	.050[c]	125.0
Retained earnings	1,400	—	60.8
Translation adjustment	—	—	(37.6)
Total	8,500		323.0

ANALYSIS OF RETAINED EARNINGS CHANGES DURING 2004

ACCOUNT	NT$	TRANSLATION RATE	US$
Beginning balance	900	—[d]	40.5
Net income	800	—[e]	32.0
Dividends	(300)	.039[f]	(11.7)
Ending balance	1,400		60.8

Notes: [a] Average exchange rate during 2004.
[b] Current (spot) rate on December 31, 2004
[c] Historical rate when capital stock was issued.
[d] Beginning balance in U.S. dollars is obtained from the translated balance sheet on January 1, 2004.
[e] See translated income statement above.
[f] Historical rate when dividends were declared.

The ending balance in retained earnings is not translated directly from Perot Inc.'s foreign currency balance sheet. Instead, it is computed in the following manner:

	millions of US$
Retained earnings, beginning balance (January 1, 2004)	$40.5
Add: Translated amount of net income (Exhibit IV-2)	32.0
Less: Translated amount of dividends (Exhibit IV-2)	(11.7)
Retained earnings, ending balance (December 31, 2004)	$60.8

Note in Exhibit IV-2 that the translated balance sheet for Perot, Inc. requires a **translation adjustment** in order to remain in balance. This adjustment is required because not all balance sheet elements are translated at the same exchange rate. In Perot's case, the translated amounts of total assets are less than the translated amounts of total liabilities and shareholders' equity (exclusive of the translation adjustment) by $37.6 million. For this reason, $37.6 million must be subtracted from shareholders' equity to restore the balance.

The interpretation of this translation adjustment is a matter of continuing controversy. The FASB suggests the following interpretation: When a foreign subsidiary of a U.S. firm has assets in excess of its liabilities, this is similar to a partially unhedged investment in a foreign currency. If a *foreign currency strengthens (or weakens) against the U.S. dollar, then this unhedged investment gives rise to an unrealized gain (or loss)*. In Perot's case, the foreign currency (NT$) has weakened against the U.S. dollar, and the translation adjustment can be interpreted as an unrealized loss. Because the parent company intends to maintain its investment in Perot, Inc. over the foreseeable future, and because foreign currency exchange rates are likely to continue to fluctuate, it would be premature to recognize such unrealized gains or losses in income.

Some analysts question the view that a firm's net asset position should be viewed as an unhedged foreign currency investment. Instead, they argue that investments in nonmonetary items, such as inventories, property, plant, equipment, and other assets, should be accounted for based on the historical cost concept that underlies the parent company's financial statements. Translation of asset costs at current exchange rates causes the U.S. dollar book values of the assets to change whenever the translation rate fluctuates. For this reason, the translated book values do not represent historical costs. In a partial recognition of this problem, the FASB requires that the books of US subsidiaries in foreign countries with high inflation be kept in US Dollars.

Many analysts who otherwise accept the FASB's interpretation of the net assets reported in foreign currency financial statements object to the exclusion of translation gains or losses from net income. These critics suggest that financial accountants have no special expertise in identifying temporary versus permanent changes in currency exchange rates. If current exchange rates are determined in a well-functioning foreign exchange market based on the trading activities of informed investors, these analysts argue that the gains or losses that result from unhedged net assets or liabilities should be reported as part of net income when they occur.

INTERNATIONAL VARIATIONS IN ACCOUNTING STANDARDS

Diversity pervades the world community. Variations in language, custom, cuisine, and architecture, as well as in business, political, and social organizations, give truth to the adage that "travel is broadening". Although tour books routinely ignore the fact, accounting standards also vary among nations. International diversity in accounting standards complicates the task for investor analysts when attempting to evaluate risks and returns based on comparable financial information. Moreover, disparate accounting standards and disclosure requirements impede the capability of firms to raise debt and equity capital across national boundaries.

The accounting standards that have developed in a given nation or region reflect to some extent the unique characteristics of the society and business community in which they have evolved. Accordingly, as business firms become more international in their activities, and as investors aim for greater international diversification of their investments, it becomes essential to understand the differences in accounting standards that exist among nations.

UNDERLYING CAUSES OF ACCOUNTING DIVERSITY

Differences in accounting standards originate mainly from differences in the objectives of financial reporting across nations. In turn, different objectives exist for financial reporting due to the differing characteristics of cultures, of legal systems, of the financial structure of business firms, of the relation between financial and tax accounting, and other factors. Obviously, many of these influences overlap and may have a similar effect on accounting structure and rules.

Cultural Influences

Much research has been done that indicates cultural characteristics play a role in shaping the regulatory environment of a country. Cultures that center on close knit family groupings within a community or evolve in scattered geographical settings that force families to be self-sufficient tend to keep information to themselves and are less likely to develop systems of accounting focused on providing information to outsiders. These cultures often have a dominant individual or group of individuals who determine the structure of information collection and/or distribution. Examples of these types of cultures are Saudi Arabia and Mexico. Both have accounting systems that collect information but distribute it to very few. On the other hand, other cultures tend to be less dominated by individuals or groups of individuals who set the societal and regulatory norms. These cultures have less of a tendency to restrict access to information and more of a tendency to willingly share information. Examples include the U.S. and Great Britain. These cultures tend to be more interested in widespread access to information that is reflected in accounting information that is widely distributed and provided in a readable, understandable manner.

Legal System Influences

The legal system of a nation influences the extent to which accounting standards establish general, flexible guides for reporting practices, as opposed to providing a complete set of detailed, rigid rules with minimal scope for professional judgment by reporting firms. Countries such as the United States and the United Kingdom, for example, are common or case law countries and have legal systems that rely on statutes, which are then interpreted by the courts in a flexible manner to deal with the unique circumstances in individual cases. Other nations, such as France and Germany, are code law countries and have legal systems in which laws are designed to cover most circumstances.

Corresponding to these differing legal systems, accounting rules in France and Germany are written into national law and are very detailed and explicit, leaving no scope for judgment. On the other hand, both countries are part of the European Union which subscribes to the IFRS and, in fact, are approved as part of French law. IFRS are "principle-based" and are not "rule-based"; hence, professional judgment is required in both countries. Similarly, but with some notable exceptions, U.S. and British accounting standards tend to establish broad frameworks and allow considerable room for interpretations and assumptions in individual cases.

Financial Structure Influences

The financial structure of a firm refers to the sources from which its investment capital is obtained. In the United States and the United Kingdom, a major portion of financing is obtained by the sale of equity shares on security exchanges. These securities are typically held by a wide variety of individuals and institutions that rely on published financial reports for investment-relevant information. For this reason, the focus of financial accounting standards is on the decision-making usefulness and high level of disclosure and clarity of published financial reports.

In many other nations, including Germany and Japan, corporate financing is obtained primarily from direct borrowings and from sales of equity securities to banks and other financial institutions. In these cases, the lenders and investors are able to demand relevant and timely financial information directly from the firm. Because major lenders and investors do not depend on public financial reports, accounting standards for public financial reports are determined by factors other than investor information, such as conformity with the tax rules or the information needs of government economic planners.

Taxation Influences

In countries such as Germany, Italy, France, and Japan, there is a very close correspondence between financial reporting standards and the rules used to determine taxable income. In these nations, there is no distinction made between the possibly different measurements needed for purposes of government fiscal policy and the information needs of investors. When revenues and expenses are reported to investors, they also must be included in the tax reports. Note also that price-to-earnings multiples (the ratio of market price per share to earnings per share) are much higher in Germany and Japan than in the United States. This comparison suggests that investors consider German and Japanese earnings numbers to be of higher quality (more conservative) than reported earnings of U.S. firms.

INTERNATIONAL DIFFERENCES IN SELECTED ACCOUNTING PRACTICES

This section considers five specific areas of accounting practice: accounting for goodwill in business acquisitions, consolidation policy, accounting for leases, pension reporting, and departures from historical cost in valuing assets. In each case, U.S. standards are compared to those in several major industrial nations.

Goodwill

As discussed in Chapter 10, goodwill arises in a business acquisition when the buyer pays an amount that exceeds the fair value of the identifiable net assets of the seller. The amount assigned to goodwill often accounts for a major portion of the purchase price. In several European nations, including Germany, the Netherlands, and Italy, goodwill was charged immediately to shareholders' equity. As a result, the asset (goodwill) did not appear on the balance sheet, and subsequent earnings were not reduced by goodwill amortization. Before the recent changes in U.S. treatment of goodwill, purchased goodwill had to be capitalized and amortized over an estimated useful life (not to exceed 40 years). Managers of U.S. firms often claimed that this difference in accounting standards caused an "uneven playing field," because their European counterparts were able to report higher profits subsequent to business combinations. Under IFRS #3, these differences have been eliminated. EU countries now require that goodwill be capitalized as an asset with an indefinite life. The goodwill asset is evaluated annually to see if it is impaired.

This is consistent with U.S. standards, SFAS 142, which requires U.S. firms to report goodwill if it arises during an acquisition, but they are no longer required to systematically amortize the amount recorded. Goodwill must, however, be examined annually or more often for impairment and appropriate adjustments to earnings must be made in that year.

Consolidations

Firms in the United States are required to consolidate all majority-owned subsidiaries. Except for Australia, most major industrial nations do not require the consolidation of **nonhomogeneous subsidiaries,** which are those whose major operating activities take place in industries that differ from those of the parent company. U.S. automobile manufacturers, for example, are required to consolidate their financing subsidiaries, even though the activities are quite distinct from those of the parent companies. American managers argue that a substantial portion of the assets and debt controlled by foreign parent companies can easily be hidden on the books of unconsolidated, controlled subsidiaries. As a consequence, financial ratio calculations that are based on published financial statements can appear to be less favorable for U.S. firms. This difference will be resolved in 2008 under a Memorandum of Understanding between the FASB and the EU countries to develop a consistent approach to consolidations (see Exhibit IV-3).

EXHIBIT IV-3 **MEMORANDUM OF UNDERSTANDING WITH THE FASB**

A Roadmap for Convergence between IFRSs and U.S. GAAP—2006–2008

Memorandum of Understanding between the FASB and the IASB 27 February 2006

FOR THE MOST CURRENT INFORMATION

ON THIS MEMO OF UNDERSTANDING

GO TO:

http://www.iasb.org/Current+Projects/Memorandum+of+Understanding+with+the+FASB.htm

Leases

As discussed in TOPICMOD-II, U.S. accounting standards require that long-term leases be **capitalized,** or recorded as assets and liabilities based on present value measurements, when the lessee acquires both the risks and the rewards of ownership. Although many advanced industrial nations have similar standards, the criteria they use to identify a capital lease are considerably more flexible than those in the United States. As a result, most leases are interpreted as operating leases, in other words, as ordinary rentals of assets, rather than capital leases. In Japan, most leases are designed as operating leases in order to minimize taxes. In Italy, all leases are reported as operating leases. Therefore, lease disclosures are not comparable between firms in these countries, until an expected (2008) exposure draft identifies how to resolve these differences.

Pensions

The defined benefit type of pension plan that has been widely adopted by U.S. firms, as discussed in TOPICMOD-III, is relatively less important in other nations. In many countries, government-sponsored pension arrangements are more prominent than are company-sponsored plans, and most of the latter are defined contribution plans. Even in cases where defined benefit plans do exist, only the U.S. requires an annual evaluation of the discount rate that is used to estimate the value of the pension liability. This annual evaluation has in recent years caused the amounts of unfunded pension liabilities, and also the reported pension expense, to be more volatile for mature U.S. firms. Moreover, U.S. standards require much greater detail in the footnote disclosures of pension assumptions, funding status, cost components, and other items. An interim standard is expected in 2010 to improve both presentation and disclosure of pension data under IFRS.

Asset Valuations

American accounting standards generally require that assets be valued at historical cost unless they are impaired. Exceptions to this are the lower of cost or market (LCM) rules, which are applied to the most current assets and the fair market value rules for investments in marketable securities. In contrast, most European companies may choose to revalue tangible and intangible noncurrent assets at the current replacement cost. Tangible noncurrent assets can be valued at current market values even if the new value is above the previous one. France allows current cost revaluations of tangible assets, but not intangibles. Because of extremely high inflation rates, South American countries require that the historical costs of most noncurrent assets be adjusted by a purchasing power index to reflect inflation.

INTERNATIONAL HARMONIZATION OF ACCOUNTING STANDARDS

Recent years have seen a burgeoning demand by foreign firms for debt and equity capital, which has been obtained by selling securities in other nations. This demand is partly attributable to the wave of privatization in Eastern Europe and in South America. **Privatization** is the act of selling government-owned or controlled enterprises to private investors, and the resultant demands for investment capital often exceed what is available in the local economies.

The demand for access to investment capital in other nations is also due in part to international differences in the cost of capital. For example, because of a rigorous and comprehensive set of financial reporting standards and well-regulated securities markets, the cost of investment capital in U.S. financial markets is generally lower than that in other Western nations. It can be quite costly, however, for foreign companies to initially prepare their financial statements in their domestic currency using domestic accounting standards, and then to recast their financial reports before listing their shares on foreign stock exchanges. The costs of meeting the foreign exchange listing requirements include monetary costs of restating the financial statements and the disclosure of competitive information that might have been "secret" in their domestic reports. However, the benefits from listing on a major exchange often outweigh these costs. As an example, in 1993, Daimler-Benz AG, a German automaker, decided to list its shares on the New York Stock Exchange. To comply with U.S. financial reporting standards, the company incurred expenses that were estimated to exceed $500 million ("Foreign

Firms Raise More and More Money in the U.S. Markets," *The Wall Street Journal*, October 5, 1993).

The considerable amount of expense incurred by firms in preparing financial reports to comply with multiple sets of accounting standards, as well as the difficulties encountered by investor analysts in evaluating investment opportunities across national boundaries, has given impetus to efforts for creating a set of international accounting standards. This would require that financial statements worldwide conform to a single set of accounting standards.

To promote harmonization of accounting standards throughout the world business community, the International Accounting Standards Committee (IASC) was formed in 1973. This committee, now the International Accounting Standards Board (IASB), is a joint effort, initially undertaken by professional accounting groups in 10 Western nations (including the AICPA in the United States). The IASB issues accounting pronouncements termed International Accounting Standards (IAS). To date, more than 41 such standards, along with 8 IFRS, have been issued. Exhibit IV-4 contains a statement by IASC of the reasons why international accounting standards are desirable.

EXHIBIT IV-4 PURPOSES OF INTERNATIONAL ACCOUNTING STANDARDS

The Need for International Accounting Standards

At present, financial reports prepared for shareholders and other users involve principles and procedures that can vary widely from country to country, and sometimes even within a country. Accounting reports, therefore, can lack comparability. This is highly unsatisfactory because

- it can cause preparation costs for financial reports that are much higher than necessary. A multinational company may have to prepare different reports on its operations for use in different countries; and
- businesses will want to have a uniform system for assessing financial performance in their operations in different countries. They will also want their external reports to be consistent with internal assessments of performance. These two objectives are not achievable if accounting standards vary from country to country.

Investment analysts and other users of financial reports incur extra costs of analysis when the reports are prepared according to different standards in different countries. They may be confused in their interpretation of the reports. Effective competition among the capital markets of the world may be impaired and companies may have to bear higher costs of capital because of the difficulties involved in financial analysis. The credibility of accounting suffers. Accounting reports will significantly lose credibility if a company reports different profit numbers in different countries for given transactions.

International Accounting Standards are also of great usefulness for developing countries or other countries, which do not have a national standard setting body or do not have the resources to undertake the full process of preparing accounting standards. The preparation of accounting standards involves considerable cost and, quite apart from the advantages of uniformity, it would not be economic for each country to have a separate process.

The magnitude of cross-border financing transactions, securities trading, and direct foreign investment is enormous, often in smaller as well as larger countries. The need of a single set of rules by which assets, liabilities, and income are recognized and measured is urgent.

SOURCE: International Accounting Standards Committee (IASC) www.iasc.org.uk

The effectiveness of the IASB as a force for international harmonization is limited by several factors. First, the committee has no power to enforce its standards. Recall that in the United States, the authority of the FASB is backed by the endorsement of the SEC, and firms must follow FASB pronouncements in order to list and sell securities. No similar authority exists to give credibility to IASB standards.

A second reason why IASB standards have failed to achieve harmonization is the fact that the standards enacted usually fail to create a single method of accounting. Instead, most standards enumerate and endorse a variety of accounting methods that are used by member nations. Only in this manner has the IASB been able to achieve the consensus needed to issue its standards. There is no agreement that exists among IASB members regarding the set of accounting standards that is "best" for the international financial market. For example, there is wide acknowledgment that U.S. accounting standards require more elaborate and comprehensive disclosures than do the standards in other nations. Yet accounting groups in other nations argue, "More is not necessarily better." They claim that financial reporting in the United States might be unduly complicated and expensive, thereby putting extra burdens on preparers and users alike.

It is *questionable whether any international group, whatever its composition, will be able to achieve worldwide harmonization of accounting standards.* Throughout the earlier chapters of this book we have considered many of the FASB standards that govern financial reporting in the United States. As you have seen, such standards are the result of a political process that attempts to balance the economic impact of accounting rules across a variety of different constituencies. Similar processes exist in other nations. Accordingly, existing accounting standards can vary from those in the United States because a different political environment exists in those nations. It may be naive to believe that the FASB, or its counterpart groups in other countries, will modify their standards purely in the interest of international harmonization.

THE CHANGING INTERNATIONAL ECONOMIC CLIMATE

Financial reporting does not exist in a vacuum, and major international developments, both planned and unplanned, will inevitably affect the form and content of financial statements. Changes in international monetary arrangements, capital markets, governmental fiscal policies, and business risks will ultimately affect the types of information that investors require from financial reports. Two major changes in the recent international environment include the adoption of a supranational currency by several major European nations and the economic upheavals experienced by a number of Asian nations.

A Supra-National Currency

In the early 1990s, the European Union (EU) agreed to introduce a single European currency in an effort to create a European Monetary Union. The Euro, which was introduced in early 1999, coexisted with existing national currencies for three years. Some EU members (e.g., the U.K. and Denmark) have retained their national currencies as legal tender. The conversion rates for former national currencies and the Euro were fixed as of the date each country adopted the Euro and these rates will never change. For example, one Euro was worth 5.94573 Finnish marks, 340.750 Greek drachmas, and 0.787564 Irish punts.

The expected advantages of this single currency include:

- the elimination of risks due to foreign currency fluctuations,
- savings in transactions costs, which will stimulate trade and investment, and
- the potential of lower inflation and interest rates for some member nations.

A single currency, however, implied a coordination of the monetary policies of the member countries. Because monetary policy is very closely tied to fiscal (taxation and government spending) policy, this also implied an evolving similarity across nations in terms of political and social policies. Some of these expectations are not being realized as nationalism and world economic events affect the Euro countries.

The introduction of the Euro has had various direct and indirect effects on accounting. Member nations now prepare financial reports in the common currency, and recast their historical data in terms of the new currency. Firms' pricing policies, wage levels, tax regulations, and overall business strategies all were affected by the introduction of the Euro.

In December 2006, the Euro became more widely circulated than the U.S. dollar! Will the Euro also displace the U.S. dollar as the world's leading currency? Governments, firms, and individuals may reconsider the prominence of the U.S. dollar as the currency in which to keep reserves and issue debt. Potentially strong shifts in international capital flows could change costs of capital (and the values of publicly traded debt and equity securities) in ways that are difficult to predict.

The Asian Crisis

Many Asian economies have experienced significant economic upheaval during the last two decades, which has led to precipitous declines in the trading value of stocks and bonds and the failures of many banks, industrial corporations, and other entities. As the U.S. dollar has strengthened against most Asian currencies, the price of imports from other nations has declined in the U.S., while the cost of U.S. exports of goods and services has increased to customers in other nations.

The ultimate impact of the Asian crisis on U.S. firms and on their financial reports has not resulted in financial catastrophes around the world. Major factors that are still affecting firms doing business in Asia are currency devaluation and political instability in the region, as well as declining share prices leading to higher costs of local financing. The stronger U.S. dollar makes it harder for U.S. firms to market their now relatively more expensive products and services in this area, while at the same time it increases the degree of domestic competition from now relatively less expensive imports. In addition, the financial statements of many firms may have had to record substantial write-downs of asset values. As Asian market values have tumbled, the market values of debt and equity securities carried on the balance sheets of many U.S. firms fell well below their carrying values. Moreover, even the recorded values of investments in long-lived tangible assets in Asian countries needed to be reduced. Managers expanded their disclosures of significant risks and uncertainties to assure that they adequately communicate the increased business, financial, and political risks in their international activities.

Summary of Learning Objectives

1. **Understand how foreign exchange rate fluctuations affect the financial reporting of transactions conducted in foreign currencies.**
   Companies engaged in international trade often have accounts receivable or accounts payable that are denominated in foreign currencies. Fluctuations in foreign currency exchange rates affect the dollar value of such receivables and payables, resulting in gains or losses. The existence of forward markets for foreign currencies allows managers to hedge and thereby protect against the risks of exchange rate fluctuations. Firms with foreign currency receivables may contract to sell foreign currency in the future, and firms with foreign currency payables may contract to buy foreign currency in the future. In either case, the firm's goal is to have offsetting amounts of receivables and payables denominated in a given foreign currency.

2. **Determine how financial statements prepared initially in foreign currencies are translated to U.S. dollars.**
   Foreign subsidiaries of U.S. firms usually prepare their financial statements in the currencies in which they transact their business. For financial reporting purposes, these foreign currency financial statements must be translated into U.S. dollars in order to be consolidated with the U.S. parent. Generally, an average exchange rate for the period is used to translate the income statement; the current exchange rate on the balance sheet date is used to translate assets and liabilities, and historical exchange rates are used to translate most components of shareholders' equity. As a consequence of using a variety of exchange rates, the balance sheet requires a translation adjustment in order to balance. Currently, accounting standards do not recognize changes in this translation adjustment as gains or losses in the income statement. Instead, the adjustment is reported as a separate component of shareholders' equity.

3. **Appreciate the wide diversity of international accounting practices.**
   Many different sets of accounting standards coexist in the world economy. In any given nation, local accounting standards are influenced by the unique characteristics of the society and business community. Differences in cultural

values and legal systems contribute to the differences in accounting and reporting standards. Because international diversity in accounting standards complicates the task of investment analysis and impedes the international flow of capital, there is widespread interest in the establishment of uniform worldwide accounting standards. Such efforts have had only limited success to date, however. There is no consensus internationally that any existing set of national standards would be best for all nations.

KEY TERMS

Average exchange rate
Capitalize
Currency forward market
Current exchange rate
Denominated
Direct rates
Foreign currency transactions
Foreign exchange rate
Forward rate
Functional currency
Hedge
Hedging contract
Historical exchange rates
Indirect rates
Nonhomogeneous subsidiaries
Privatization
Spot rate
Translation adjustment

Exercises and Problems

IV-1 Describe what is meant by a foreign currency transaction.

IV-2 Which of the following events is a foreign currency transaction from the point of view of the U.S. firm?

- **a.** A U.S. firm purchases inventory from a British firm, with payment to be made in British pounds.
- **b.** A U.S. firm sells to an Italian firm, with payment to be made in U.S. dollars.
- **c.** A U.S. firm purchases from a Taiwanese firm, with payment to be made in Japanese yen.

IV-3 Distinguish between spot rates and forward rates of foreign currency exchange. Which rate would a U.S. firm use in order to report its balance sheet accounts receivable in foreign currencies? Why?

IV-4 Explain why the financial statements of U.S. firms' foreign subsidiaries must be translated to U.S. dollars in order to prepare consolidated financial statements.

IV-5 The balance sheets of foreign firms, prepared in their local currencies, must be in balance (assets equal liabilities plus shareholders' equity). Yet when such balance sheets are translated to U.S. dollars, they usually require a "translation adjustment" in order to balance. Explain why this is so.

IV-6 Identify the exchange rate (current, historical, or average) that would be used to translate each of the following elements of a foreign subsidiary's financial statements to U.S. dollars:

- **a.** Accounts receivable
- **b.** Property, plant, and equipment
- **c.** Total liabilities
- **d.** Paid-in capital
- **e.** Sales
- **f.** Net income
- **g.** Dividends

Foreign Currency Transactions

IV-7 In each of the following examples, determine the gain or loss resulting from foreign exchange transactions. All exchange rates are shown as the number of U.S. dollars required to obtain one unit of foreign currency.

- **a.** Bancroft Company purchases supplies and records an account payable of 100,000 Japanese yen. The exchange rate on the purchase date is \$0.007. When the account payable is paid, the exchange rate has risen to \$0.008.
- **b.** Vaughn Enterprises sells services and records an account receivable of 12,000 British pounds when the exchange rate is \$1.55. Vaughn receives payment in pounds from the British buyer when the exchange rate is \$1.60.

c. Bishop Chess Company records an account payable of 60,000 Swiss francs when the exchange rate is $0.65. At payment date, the exchange rate has fallen to $0.62.

Foreign Currency Transactions

IV-8 In each of the following examples, determine the gain or loss resulting from foreign exchange transactions. All exchange rates are shown as the number of U.S. dollars required to obtain one unit of foreign currency.

a. Shipley Company purchases supplies and records an account payable of 82,000 Japanese yen. The exchange rate on the purchase date is $0.009. When the account payable is paid, the exchange rate has fallen to $0.006.

b. Cameron Enterprises sells services and records an account receivable of 38,200 British pounds when the exchange rate is $1.38. Cameron receives payment in pounds from the British buyer when the exchange rate is $1.44.

c. Bishop Chess Company records an account payable of 82,000 French francs when the exchange rate is $0.56. At payment date, the exchange rate has fallen to $0.51.

d. Describe how each firm might have hedged its foreign currency exposure by transactions to buy or sell foreign currencies in futures markets.

Foreign Currency Transactions: Unhedged Accounts Receivable and Payable

IV-9 In each of the following cases, determine the amount of gain or loss to be reported in 2007 due to unhedged accounts receivable or payable that are denominated in foreign currencies. All exchange rates are stated as the number of U.S. dollars required to obtain one unit of foreign currency.

a. Asebrook Company recorded an account receivable of 10,000 British pounds in 2007 when the exchange rate was $1.50. At year-end, the exchange rate had risen to $1.60.

b. Baker Company recorded an account payable of 1,000,000 New Taiwan dollars in 2007 when the exchange rate was $0.04. At year-end, the exchange rate had risen to $0.05.

c. Hanno Company recorded an account receivable of 100,000 Canadian dollars in 2007 when the exchange rate was $0.75. At year-end, the exchange rate had fallen to $0.68.

d. Pfeiffer Company recorded an account payable of 50,000 Swiss francs in 2007 when the exchange rate was $0.60. At year-end, the exchange rate had fallen to $0.57.

e. In each of these cases (a through d), describe how the U.S. firm might have insulated itself from foreign exchange gains and losses by transactions in the foreign exchange forward market.

Foreign Currency Transactions and Hedging Activities

IV-10 On October 1, 2007, the Keaton Company, a U.S. firm, sold merchandise to Chaplin, Inc., a British firm. The sales agreement specifies that Chaplin will make a payment of £500,000 to Keaton in 120 days on February 1, 2008. Relevant exchange rates are shown in the following table:

Date	*Rate*	*$/£*
October 1, 2007	Spot	$1.50
	30-day forward	1.48
	60-day forward	1.46
	90-day forward	1.42
	120-day forward	1.40
December 31, 2007	Spot	1.46
February 1, 2008	Spot	1.51

Required

a. Determine the amount of the account receivable and sales revenue to be recorded (in U.S. dollars) by the Keaton Company in the year acquired.

b. What gain or loss would Keaton report in 2007 and in 2008 if the foreign currency receivables were not hedged?

c. Describe how Keaton might hedge the above transaction in the forward market for British pounds. What is the amount of income or expense associated with the hedging transaction?

d. In retrospect on February 1, 2008, would it have been wise for Keaton to hedge the account receivable? Explain.

Interpreting Financial Statements: Foreign Currency Translation

IV-11 Review Wal-Mart's financial statements in Appendix A.

Required

a. Read Notes 1 and 3. Identify any unfamiliar or unusual terms. Match the terms presented in this TOPICMOD to the terms used by Wal-Mart.

b. Does the firm's treatment of foreign currency translations seem to have any significant effect on its balance sheet? On its income statement?

c. What other impact might foreign currency translations have on the long-term success or failure of this firm? On other aspects of its financial statements? On other aspects of the firm's performance?

Translation of Foreign Currency Financial Statements

IV-12 The balance sheet and income statement of Buchanen, Inc., a subsidiary of a U.S. company, is shown below. Buchanen, Inc. operates in New Zealand and prepares its financial statements in New Zealand dollars (NZ$).

BUCHANEN, INC.
BALANCE SHEET AND INCOME STATEMENT
DECEMBER 31, 2008
(NZ$ IN MILLIONS)

Income Statement			*Balance Sheet*		
Revenues	NZ$ 1,200	Assets	NZ$ 1,500	Liabilities	NZ$ 600
Expenses	(900)			Paid-in capital	150
Net income	NZ$ 300			Retained earnings	750
			NZ$ 1,500		NZ$ 1,500

Supplementary information:

Exchange rates (US$/NZ$):	
Average during 2008	.55
Spot rate, December 31, 2008	.60
Historical rate when capital stock was issued	.75
Beginning balance in retained earnings, in US$	$500.00

No dividends to shareholders were declared during 2008.

Required

a. Translate Buchanen's financial statements into U.S. dollars so that they can be consolidated with those of the U.S. parent firm.

b. Has the U.S. dollar strengthened or weakened relative to the New Zealand dollar during 2008? Explain how this change has affected Buchanen's translated balance sheet.

c. Explain why a translation adjustment is required in order to bring the translated balance sheet into balance.

Reconciliation of Income and Shareholders' Equity: The United States and Chile

IV-13 Foreign companies whose shares are registered on U.S. security exchanges must file a description of significant differences between U.S. and domestic accounting principles with the SEC as well as a reconciliation of net income and shareholders' equity under domestic and U.S. GAAP.

Goldplate Company, Inc., a Chilean firm, included the following information:

1. *Differences in Measurement Methods*

The principal methods applied in preparing the accompanying financial statements that have resulted in amounts that differ from those that would have otherwise been determined under U.S. GAAP, are as follows:

(a) *Inflation Accounting*

The cumulative inflation rate in Chile, as measured by the Consumer Price Index, for the three-year period ended December 31, 2008, was approximately 85%.

Chilean accounting principles require that financial statements be restated to reflect the full effects of loss in the purchasing power of the Chilean peso on the financial position and the results of reporting entities' operations. The method is based on a model in which net inflation gains or losses caused by monetary assets and liabilities exposed to changes in the purchasing power of local currency are calculated by restating all nonmonetary accounts of the financial statements.

The inclusion of price-level adjustments in the accompanying financial statements is considered appropriate under the prolonged inflationary conditions affecting the Chilean economy.

(b) *Revaluations of Property, Plant, and Equipment*
Certain property, plant, and equipment are reported in the financial statements at amounts determined in accordance with a technical appraisal carried out in 2008. Revaluation of property, plant, and equipment is an accounting principle not generally accepted in the United States.

(c) *Vacation Expense*
The cost of vacations earned by employees is generally recorded by the Company on a pay-as-you-go basis. Accounting principles generally accepted in the United States require that this expense be recorded on the accrual basis as the vacations are earned.

(d) *Inventory Valuation*
Finished and in-process products are reported on the financial statements at the replacement cost of the raw materials included therein and therefore exclude labor and overhead, the practice of which is contrary to U.S. GAAP.

(e) *Write-Up of Noncurrent Asset*
Net income reported in the Chilean GAAP financial statements as of December 31, 2008, includes the effects of the reversal of a valuation allowance recorded in prior years to writing down the carrying value of disposable land to estimated market value.

2. *Reconciliations of Net Income and Shareholders' Equity:*

Net Income Reconciliation For the year ended March 31, 2008 (CH$ in thousands)		*Shareholders' Equity Reconciliation For the year ended March 31, 2008 (CH$ in thousands)*	
Net income, Chilean GAAP	CH$ 14,201,342	Shareholders' equity	CH$ 36,773,825
Depreciation on revaluation	43,188	Property revaluations	(4,259,726)
Provision for vacations	(58,984)	Inventory costing	67,592
Reverse asset write-up	(1,744,402)	Other	(2,154,501)
Other	627,904		
Net income, U.S. GAAP	CH$ 13,069,048	Shareholders' equity, U.S. GAAP	CH$ 30,427,190

Required

a. For each of the individual differences between U.S. and Chilean GAAP, indicate which method of accounting you consider to be the most useful to investor analysts. Explain your reasoning.

b. Based on the information provided above, do you consider Chilean or U.S. GAAP to be more conservative? Explain.

c. Discuss why each of the individual reconciling items is added (or subtracted) in converting from Chilean to U.S. GAAP.

IV-14 Foreign Currency Effects: McDonald's Corporation

McDonald's Corporation is a global corporation and primarily operates and franchises quick-service restaurant businesses. Access the EDGAR archives (www.sec.gov/edaux/searches.htm) to locate McDonald's 2002 10K. Answer the following questions based on its Financial Information about Foreign and Domestic Operations:

a. What is the dollar impact on foreign currency transactions included in consolidated net income?

b. How does the company translate the financial statements of foreign operations other than those in hyper-inflationary economics?

c. How does the company translate monetary assets (accounts receivable and cash) of subsidiaries located in hyper-inflationary economies?

d. How did weaker Latin American currencies impact McDonald's foreign currency translation and revenue growth rate in 2002?

TOPICMOD V

REPORTING ISSUES FOR AFFILIATED COMPANIES

Learning Objectives

1. *Understand the reasons for reporting consolidated financial statements.*
2. *Appreciate the consolidation process and various forms of business combinations.*
3. *Understand GAAP for reporting consolidated entities.*

INTRODUCTION

Most financial statements you read will contain the term "Consolidated" in the heading. What does this mean? Even small companies often report financial results that include certain consolidated entities. In part, this is a function of a company's organization—many firms will establish a separate legal entity in order to perform a specific process. For example, General Motors, the large American automobile manufacturer, has a **subsidiary,** GMAC, to provide auto loans for GM customers. GM is the **parent company** of GMAC. GM consolidates the results of GMAC with its own, and what appears in the consolidated balance sheet in the cash account, for example, is the sum of all the cash belonging to GM and GMAC (as well as other consolidated entities).

Another common business activity which gives rise to the need for consolidated financial statements is **M&A,** or **mergers and acquisitions.** Quite often when a business acquires another firm it continues to treat the subsidiary as a separate legal entity. Throughout the year each entity will report its own results and maintain its own financial statements. For reporting purposes, however, the parent company will consolidate the subsidiary's results with its own.

Most large firms grow by a combination of internal and external expansion. **Internal expansion** occurs as firms invest in new plant and equipment, research, and other productive assets in order to serve growing markets or to extend the scope of their operations into new products and markets. **External expansion** occurs as firms take over, or merge with, other existing firms. This TOPICMOD discusses the reasons why corporate takeovers may be preferable to internal expansion. Financial reporting for affiliated firms is also explained as of the date of acquisition and for subsequent periods.

MOTIVATIONS FOR BUSINESS COMBINATIONS

Business firms often expand by taking over existing corporations. Such actions, known as **business combinations,** can be more attractive than direct investments in new plant and equipment for several reasons. The buyer firm, for example, may believe that external expansion is less costly than purchasing new assets and competing for customers in new markets. Also, the acquired firm may offer other advantages, such as a stable and reliable network of suppliers, a seasoned workforce, and proven methods of production and distribution. As a consequence, expansion by combination may avoid many of the uncertainties and start-up costs encountered under internal expansion.

There are two common themes when a business intends to expand its operations through external acquisition. **Vertical integration** occurs when a company acquires another firm involved in its supply or delivery chain. For example, a beverage bottler may acquire a distributor in order to have more control over its delivery method to customers. **Horizontal integration** occurs when a company expands its operations geographically by acquiring a similar business in another market. An example of horizontal expansion would be Gart Sports, a regional sporting goods retailer in the Rocky Mountain west, acquiring The Sports Authority, another regional retailer, primarily operating in the northeast.

A third strategy for external growth through acquisition is **diversification.** Diversification is when a firm acquires another company operating in a completely unrelated field. This can be common for a business in a cyclical industry wanting to reduce the volatility of its revenues and earnings. Diversification gives rise to **conglomerates,** such as General Electric, which operates businesses in industries as diverse as jet engine manufacturing and television broadcasting.

When existing firms are combined, it enables them to eliminate duplicate facilities or yield economies of scale in production, distribution, marketing, finance, and/or general corporate administration. A buyer company believes that the acquired firm's assets are poorly managed and that more profits could be earned by improving its asset management. A purchaser hopes that new management may introduce operating efficiencies that yield higher profits.

Business combinations permit a firm to diversify quickly. A buyer firm in a declining industry can re-deploy its resources into other products and markets. As cigarette smoking has declined among informed adults, for example, many larger tobacco firms have diversified by acquiring firms in other industries. By combining their businesses, firms attempt to diversify their cyclical or seasonal risks.

A major factor in recent business combinations is the rapid pace of technological change in communications, which permits links between industries that were previously considered to be unrelated. The **Internet** has inspired combinations of firms in areas as disparate as cable television, telecommunications, banking, cinema, and catalog retail sales. The ongoing information revolution promises to redefine the boundaries among industries and provide impetus to many additional unconventional business combinations.

FORMS OF BUSINESS COMBINATIONS

Business combinations occur in a variety of different ways. In a **merger,** a buyer firm acquires either the stock or the assets and liabilities of an investee firm. The ***investee** is then dissolved and no longer exists* as a separate corporation. Alternatively, firms can combine by **consolidation.** In a consolidation, a *new corporation is created* to acquire the stock or the net assets of two or more existing companies. The *original companies then cease to exist* as separate corporations. Finally, a business combination can occur as an acquisition. In an **acquisition,** a buyer firm acquires more than 50% of an investee firm's voting stock and thereby controls the investee. The buyer firm is referred to as the **parent company,** and the *acquired firm continues to exist and operate as a subsidiary* of the parent company.

Acquisitions comprise a major portion of the business combinations that occur among larger corporations. This type of business combination offers several advantages over mergers and consolidations. Because the parent may obtain effective control of a subsidiary without the need to acquire 100% of the seller's shares, the required investment by the parent may be reduced substantially. Also, because the subsidiary continues to exist as a legally separate entity, the parent has only limited liability for the debts of the subsidiary. In addition, it is relatively easy for the parent to increase or decrease its investment at future dates by purchasing or selling the subsidiary's shares; this is known as **piecemeal acquisition** or **divestiture.**

A parent company and the other firms that it influences or controls are referred to as **affiliated companies.** Two other types of business entities that generally bring up consolidation issues are **joint ventures** and **special purpose entities,** or **SPE's.** Often, these are businesses set up for a specific purpose and are formed through investments from two or more otherwise unrelated companies. Joint ventures and SPE's give rise to some interesting reporting issues, but are beyond the scope of this text. The remainder of the discussion in this TOPICMOD will explain financial reporting for affiliated companies.

FINANCIAL REPORTING FOR CONTROLLING INTERESTS IN AFFILIATED FIRMS

When one firm acquires the stock of another firm, the fair market value of the acquired firm's resources (cash, fixed assets, shares of stock, or debt, for example) paid by the parent is used to set the value of the acquired assets. *Because the parent's investment exceeds 50% of the affiliate's voting shares, the parent is assumed to control the affiliate.* Subsequent accounting and reporting for the affiliated firm are based on historical costs as explained in earlier chapters

Note that the fair market value of the acquired firm's assets will often differ from their net book value. For example, consider a building acquired on January 1, 2004 for $200,000, with a useful life of 20 years and a salvage value of $0; the depreciation expense recognized annually would be $10,000. So by January 1, 2009, the net book value of the building would be $150,000. However, consider that the fair market value of the building has increased to $250,000 (i.e., a third-party buyer would be willing to pay that amount to acquire the building). Assuming that the acquiring company purchases 100% of the outstanding common stock in the subsidiary, the parent company would then value the building on its books at the fair market value of $250,000.

Such differences between the book value and fair market value of various assets help explain the difference between the purchase price of a company and its net book value (the shareholder's equity on the balance sheet). The other reason why companies often pay more to acquire another firm is the need to pay a premium in order to convince the shareholders of the acquired company to accept the acquisition.

Goodwill is created when the total purchase price for the acquired company exceeds the fair market value of its net assets. Goodwill is an **intangible asset** on the balance sheet and it *will remain unchanged at its historical cost from year to year.* However, companies with goodwill on their balance sheets must perform an annual **impairment test** to measure whether the recorded goodwill has lost any of its value. If the result of the impairment test determines that the goodwill is overstated then the parent company must take an **impairment charge,** or write down the value of its goodwill. After the stock market bubble burst in 2000, one result was that many companies soon found that they had severely overpaid for their acquisitions. The result has been some quite large write-downs of goodwill (e.g., AOL and Time Warner).

Accounting for the Acquisition of a Subsidiary Firm

To illustrate a typical acquisition, refer to Exhibit V-1, which shows the **pre-acquisition balance sheets** and other pertinent information for Pepper Company and Shaker Inc., on January 1, 2008. On that date, Pepper Company paid a total of $400 million ($100 million in cash and $300 million in common stock) to acquire 100% of Shaker's outstanding shares from the existing shareholders.

Note that Shaker's balance sheet at the date of combination shows net assets (and therefore shareholders' equity) of $310 million. Pepper's willingness to pay $400 million indicates that the carrying value of Shaker's net assets at the combination date is less than the economic value of those net assets by at least $90 million ($400 million – $310 million). Indeed, the note to Exhibit V-1 reveals that the firm has $90 million of internally generated goodwill that does not appear on the balance sheet.

The acquisition of Shaker's stock increases Pepper's investment in affiliated companies by $400 million; cash decreases by $100 million, and invested capital increases by $300 million. Pepper's net assets increase by $300 million.

ASSETS		=	LIABILITIES	+	SHAREHOLDERS' EQUITY
Cash	Investments in affiliates				Invested capital
– $100 million	+ $400 million				+ $300 million

Shaker's balance sheet is unaffected by the acquisition. Because Pepper Company bought Shaker's shares directly from existing shareholders, Shaker was not a party to the transaction. Shaker Company has neither received any resources nor issued any additional shares of stock.

Reality Check V-1 illustrates the effect of acquiring a subsidiary company at a cost in excess of the acquired net assets' fair value.

Financial Reporting Subsequent to the Acquisition

Because Pepper Company has effective control of Shaker through ownership of all their voting shares, generally accepted accounting practices require that Pepper Company's financial statements be prepared on a consolidated basis. **Consolidated financial statements** report the combined financial position, cash flows, and operating results for all firms that are under the parent company's control. Consolidation looks beyond the fact that affiliated firms are distinct legal entities and focuses on the fact that they constitute a single economic entity. Consolidation is mainly a process of adding together the financial statement elements of the parent and its controlled subsidiaries with certain necessary **consolidation adjustments** that will be described later.

EXHIBIT V-1 PRE-ACQUISITION BALANCE SHEETS

Pepper Company and Shaker Inc.
Pre-acquisition Balance Sheets and Other Information, on January 1, 2008
(Dollars in millions)

PEPPER COMPANY
BALANCE SHEET AT JANUARY 1, 2008

Assets		Liabilities and Equity	
Current assets:		Current liabilities	$ 420
Cash	$ 150		
Other current assets	520	Long-term debt	540
Total	670	Total liabilities	960
Noncurrent assets			
Property, plant, and equipment, (net)	1,230	Shareholders' equity: Invested capital	280
Other	450	Retained earnings	1,110
Total	1,680	Total equity	1,390
Total assets	$2,350	Total liabilities and equity	$2,350

SHAKER, INC.
BALANCE SHEET AT JANUARY 1, 2008

Assets		Liabilities and Equity	
Current assets:		Current liabilities	$ 50
Cash	$ 20		
Other current assets	1,260	Long-term debt	1,280
Total	1,280	Total liabilities	1,330
Noncurrent assets			
Property, plant, and equipment, (net)	320	Shareholders' equity: Invested capital	150
Other	40	Retained earnings	160
Total	360	Total equity	310
Total assets	$1,640	Total liabilities and equity	$1,640

Note: An independent appraisal of Shaker Inc.'s assets and liabilities on January 1, 2008, indicates that book values and fair market values are equal, except that Shaker has $90 million of internally generated goodwill that does not appear on the balance sheet.

REALITY CHECK V-1

The Du Pont Company, one of the world's largest chemical companies, provides the following information about a business combination (edited; dollars in millions):

> Protein Technologies International was purchased on December 1, 1997. PTI is a global supplier of soy proteins and applied technology to the food and paper processing industries. Du Pont common stock shares totaling 22,500,000, with a fair value of $1,297, were issued in this transaction. In addition, related costs of $4 were incurred. For accounting purposes, the acquisition has been treated as a purchase. Based on preliminary estimates that are subject to revision, the purchase price has been allocated as follows: cash, $47; other current assets, $158; noncurrent assets, $897; and liabilities assumed, $301, including $188 of debt.

Required

a. Based on the above information, show how Du Pont's balance sheet was affected by the acquisition of Protein Technologies. (Assume that Protein Technologies continues in existence as a legally distinct company.)

b. Determine the excess of Du Pont's purchase price over the fair value of Protein Technologies' net assets (in other words, the goodwill) implicit in the Protein Technologies acquisition.

c. Why do you suppose that Du Pont was willing to pay a substantial premium over the net assets' fair value in order to acquire protein technologies?

d. Assume that Du Pont prepares a consolidated balance sheet immediately following the acquisition of protein technologies. Show how the balance sheet of Du Pont would differ before and after consolidation.

SOLUTION

a. The total value of the consideration (cash plus common stock) paid by Du Pont is $1,301 million, which would affect Du Pont's balance sheet as follows on the acquisition date:

ASSETS		=	LIABILITIES	+	SHAREHOLDERS' EQUITY
Cash	Investment in PTI				Common stock
– $4 million	+ $1,301 million				+ $1,297 million

b. The goodwill implicit in the acquisition price is computed as follows (dollars in millions):

Cost of investment in PTI (see above)		$1,301
Fair value of net assets:		
Fair value of assets acquired	$1,102	
Less: Fair value of liabilities assumed	(301)	
Net		801
Excess of cost over fair value of net assets (goodwill)		$ 500

c. Du Pont's managers believe that the value of the future cash flows to be earned from the PTI acquisition justify the substantial acquisition premium. The economic values of many firms exceed the fair values of their identifiable net assets. This is especially true for firms such as PTI that have substantial investments in research and development, highly skilled employees, and a well-developed customer base.

d. Du Pont's balance sheet would be adjusted in order to be consolidated with PTI at the acquisition date. The entire investment account would be eliminated and PTI 's assets and liabilities would be added to Du Pont's assets and liabilities, and the goodwill would be recognized on the consolidated balance sheet.

ASSETS		=	LIABILITIES	+	SHAREHOLDERS' EQUITY
Investment in PTI:	– $1,301 million		+ $301 million		
Other assets:	+ $1,102 million				
Goodwill:	+ $500 million				

A consolidation of Pepper Company and Shaker Inc. at the acquisition date would entail only the preparation of a consolidated balance sheet because no combined operations or cash flows have yet occurred at that date. Exhibit V-2 shows the consolidation process. Note the following:

1. The **pre-acquisition balance sheet** of each firm is listed side by side in a vertical format to facilitate adding the elements across each row.
2. A firm does not report an investment in its own shares as an asset on the balance sheet. Therefore, the balance of the investment account that appears on the separate (unconsolidated) balance sheet of the parent company must be eliminated because the investee firm is included in the consolidated entity.
3. Shaker's shareholders' equity must be eliminated because, from a consolidated point of view, its stock is not outstanding. Pepper holds all of Shaker's stock, and none is held by outside investors.
4. Shaker's net assets are revalued in the process of consolidation in order to reflect their appraised values at the acquisition date. Recall that Pepper Company paid $400 million to acquire Shaker's shareholders' equity, which has a carrying value of $310. The $90 million difference is attributed to goodwill. From a consolidated perspective, Shaker's net assets are $90 million higher than they are from the perspective of Shaker as a separate company. Pepper incurred this additional cost by buying Shaker's shares at an amount in excess of book value.

EXHIBIT V-2 **CONSOLIDATION OF PEPPER AND SHAKER**

Pepper Company and Shaker Inc.
Consolidation at the Acquisition Date, January 1, 2008
(Dollars in millions)

	PEPPER COMPANY[a]	SHAKER, INC.	ADJUSTMENTS	CONSOLIDATED
Current assets				
Cash	$ 50	$ 20		$ 70
Other current assets	520	1,260		1,780
Total current assets	570	1,280		1,850
Noncurrent assets				
Property, plant, and equipment (net)	1,230	320		1,550
Investment in Shaker Inc.	400	—	−400[b]	—
Goodwill	—	—	+90[b]	90
Other	450	40		490
Total noncurrent assets	2,080	360		2,130
Total assets	$2,650	$1,640		$3,980
Current liabilities	$ 420	$ 50		$ 470
Long-term debt	540	1,280		1,820
Total liabilities	960	1,330		2,290
Shareholders' equity				
Invested capital	580	150	−150[b]	580
Retained earnings	1,110	160	−160[b]	1,110
Total shareholder's equity	1,690	310		1,690
Total liabilities and equity	$2,650	$1,640		$3,980

[a] Pepper Company's balance sheet differs from Exhibit V-1 because cash was reduced by $100 million and invested capital was increased by $300 million in order to acquire the investment in Shaker Inc. for $400 million.

[b] Pepper's investment in Shaker is eliminated, as well as Shaker's shareholders' equity. The difference of $90 million ($400 less $310 million) resulted from Shaker's goodwill ($90 million).

As a result of these consolidating adjustments, the consolidated balance sheet of Pepper Company, shown on the right side of Exhibit V-2, shows consolidated assets of $3.98 billion and consolidated liabilities of $2.29 billion. Both of these amounts are greater than those shown on Pepper's separate balance sheet. The shareholders' equity of Pepper, $1.69 billion, is the same before and after consolidation, however, because the shareholders' equity of the subsidiary has been eliminated in the consolidation process.

A further complication can occur whenever the parent does not own 100% of the subsidiary's stock. Because Pepper Company owns 100% of Shaker Inc., the subsidiary's entire shareholders' equity is eliminated. In cases where a parent achieves control by acquiring less than 100% of a subsidiary's stock, the book value of the remaining outstanding shares of the subsidiary will appear on the consolidated financial statements with the label **non-controlling interest in consolidated subsidiaries.** This term often appears either as another category of shareholders' equity or as a separate item between liabilities and shareholders' equity.

Equity Method of Accounting for Affiliate Subsequent to the Acquisition Date

After the acquisition date, a parent company will often account for its investment in affiliated firms, using the **equity method of accounting.** The equity method requires that Pepper recognize its share of Shaker's subsequent reported income (or loss). Moreover, any dividends paid by Shaker to Pepper will be considered as a reduction of Pepper's investment cost. Because Pepper recognizes Shaker's income as it is earned, Pepper cannot also count Shaker's dividend payments as additional income. To do so would be "double-counting". Another consolidation method is the **cost method of accounting,** where the parent only recognizes dividends from the subsidiary as they are received.

To illustrate the equity method, assume that Shaker Inc. earned $12 million in 2008 and paid dividends of $6 million. All the dividends are paid to Pepper, which owns all of Shaker's stock. Pepper Company would recognize Shaker's income as an increase in the carrying value of the investment and as income of $12 million:

ASSETS	=	LIABILITIES	+	SHAREHOLDERS' EQUITY
Investment in subsidiary + $12 million				Retained earnings + $12 million (income from investments)

Upon receipt of the dividend, Pepper Company would increase cash and reduce the investment balance by $6 million:

ASSETS		=	LIABILITIES	+	SHAREHOLDERS' EQUITY
Cash	Investment in subsidiary				
+ $6 million	– $6 million				

Recall that Pepper Company paid an amount that was $90 million in excess of the book value of Shaker's shareholders' equity at the acquisition date. This amount was attributed to goodwill. This asset is being used in Shaker's operations, and from Pepper Company's point of view, the additional asset cost must be evaluated annually (**impairment test**) for impairment over the useful life of the asset. Any impairment in goodwill will result in further reductions in Pepper's "Investment in subsidiary" account. If the goodwill **impairment charge** for the current year were $5 million, then Pepper's investment account would only increase by $1 million ($12 million income less $6 million dividends and $5 million goodwill impairment charge).

Other Types of Consolidation Adjustments

The consolidation of Pepper Company and its subsidiary Shaker Inc. requires relatively few adjustments because we assume that the operations of both firms are completely independent. In many cases, however, numerous transactions take place between affiliated firms, and these transactions require further adjustments as part of the consolidation process. Consider, for example, a parent firm that has acquired controlling ownership of a major supplier. After the acquisition, the firms would certainly continue their existing business relationship and, as a result, the subsequent consolidated financial statements of the parent firm would require the following types of adjustments:

1. The accounts payable of the parent would include amounts owed to the subsidiary. Correspondingly, the accounts receivable of the subsidiary would include amounts due from the parent. These **intercompany receivables and payables** would be eliminated in consolidation. It makes no sense to report amounts owed to and from oneself on a consolidated balance sheet.
2. The sales among companies included in a consolidation do not constitute sales to outside entities. As a result, unless these **intercompany sales** are eliminated in preparing the consolidation, both consolidated sales and cost of goods sold would be overstated in the financial statements.
3. The inventories reported by the parent would very likely include items purchased from the subsidiary at a profit to the subsidiary. From a consolidated point of view, however, these inventories have not been sold to outside entities at the balance sheet date. As a result, these **unrealized inventory profits** would be removed from the carrying value of the inventory and from the subsidiary's income in the process of consolidation.

Various other transactions between affiliated firms occur frequently and must be adjusted appropriately in preparing a set of consolidated financial statements. Bear in mind that a set of legally distinct companies is consolidated as a single economic or reporting entity. As a result, financial statement elements, such as receivables, payables, revenues, and expenses, must involve transactions only with other, outside entities.

FINANCIAL RATIOS AND CONSOLIDATED FINANCIAL STATEMENTS

Consolidated financial statements are prepared primarily to serve investors and financial analysts. A useful starting point in the analysis of financial statements is the calculation of a set of key financial ratios. Note that many of these ratios were first introduced in earlier chapters and were summarized in Chapter 11. This section illustrates how the consolidation of affiliated companies affects selected financial statement ratios.

As seen earlier, some financial statement elements change dramatically as a result of consolidating subsidiary firms, while other items are unaffected. To illustrate the effects of consolidation on selected financial ratios, Exhibit V-3 repeats the financial statements of Pepper Company before and after consolidation, as developed earlier in the TOPICMOD. Exhibit V-3 also shows the calculation of two widely used financial ratios.

EXHIBIT V-3 FINANCIAL RATIOS

Selected Financial Ratios Before and After Consolidation
Pepper Company and Shaker Inc.
on January 1, 2008
(Dollars in millions)

	PEPPER COMPANY, UNCONSOLIDATED (FROM EXHIBIT V-2)	PEPPER COMPANY, CONSOLIDATED (FROM EXHIBIT V-2)
Current assets	$ 570	$1,850
Noncurrent assets	2,080	2,130
Total assets	$2,650	$3,980
Current liabilities	$ 420	$ 470
Long-term debt	540	1,820
Total liabilities	960	2,290
Shareholders' equity	1,690	1,690
Total liabilities and equity	$2,650	$3,980

Net income during 2005: $30 million

RATIO	UNCONSOLIDATED	CONSOLIDATED
Debt-to-assets	$960/$2,650 = 36.2%	$2,290/$3,980 = 57.5%
Current ratio	$570/$420 = 1.36	$1,850/$470 = 3.94

Note the following:

1. Pepper's debt-to-assets ratio increased markedly from 36.2 to 57.5 percent as a result of consolidation. This ratio increases whenever a consolidated subsidiary has debt financing.
2. In Pepper Company's case, the current ratio increased from 1.36 to 3.94 percent as a result of consolidation. This occurs because Shaker Inc., the subsidiary, has a higher current ratio than the parent company.

These illustrative ratio calculations show that many of the ratios used by analysts will differ before and after consolidation. Analysts must be careful when examining ratio trends that cover periods when new subsidiaries are being consolidated (or when subsidiaries are being sold or divested).

EVALUATION OF CONSOLIDATION ACCOUNTING

Financial accounting standards require the reporting of consolidated financial statements, based on a presumption that investor analysts need to evaluate the total set of economic resources that are controlled by the parent company, as well as the total liabilities and other claims against those resources. Correspondingly, the consolidated income statement measures the total revenues and expenses attributed to these economic resources and claims.

The FASB has initiated a comprehensive reexamination of the principles and assumptions that underlie consolidated financial statements. Two key issues are (1) developing a meaningful measure of "control" for purposes of including an investee in the consolidation, and (2) the extent to which consolidation may in some cases impair rather than enhance the usefulness of financial statements.

With respect to the issue of control, it is unclear that owning a majority of an investee's outstanding shares is a necessary means of establishing control. For example, a substantial portion of the outstanding shares in widely held companies is not voted at stockholders' meetings. Smaller investors with minor shareholdings may lack the incentive to study the issues and participate in the governance of a corporation. As a consequence, a parent company owning much less than 50% of an affiliate's outstanding stock can still regularly cast a majority of the votes on matters of company policy. The issue of control is further muddied by the existence of convertible securities (such as convertible bonds and convertible preferred stock as discussed in Chapter 10). If the holders of such securities can convert their holdings to voting common stock at any time, then the ownership percentages in an investee can shift dramatically on short notice.

The usefulness of consolidated financial statements has also been questioned on grounds that aggregations of information cause a loss of information. Some analysts and company managers argue that, because consolidation often entails adding together financial statements from companies of diverse industries, the resulting totals are very difficult to interpret. For example, most automotive companies and other durable goods manufacturers have subsidiary companies that extend consumer credit to the parent company customers. It had been a longstanding practice for the parent firms to exclude finance subsidiaries from their consolidations, which is defended on the grounds that analysts would be misled by an aggregation of manufacturing and financial companies. Subsequently, the FASB issued a standard that requires the consolidation of all majority-owned subsidiaries (see SFAS No. 92, "Consolidation of All Majority-Owned Subsidiaries," October, 1987).

Summary of Learning Objectives

1. **Understand the reasons for reporting consolidated financial statements.** Business firms often expand by taking over existing firms. Most takeovers occur as acquisitions, in which a buyer firm acquires a majority of the voting shares of a seller firm. The buyer is thereafter referred to as the parent company, and

the seller as a subsidiary company. Both firms continue to exist as legally distinct corporations. Because they are under common control, their financial statements must be consolidated for financial reporting purposes.

2. **Appreciate the consolidation process and various forms of business combinations.**
   Consolidation requires adding together the assets, liabilities, revenues, and expenses of the parent and subsidiary firms. A variety of consolidation adjustments must be made to reflect the fact that both firms are now a single economic entity. The following adjustments characterize most consolidations:
   a. The balance of the parent's investment account in the subsidiary must be eliminated because, from a consolidated perspective, the subsidiary is not a distinct economic entity. The subsidiary's shareholders' equity also must be eliminated because its shares are not held outside the consolidated entity.
   b. The subsidiary's individual assets and liabilities may require revaluation in the process of consolidation in order to reflect differences between the parent's cost of acquisition and their carrying values at the acquisition date. In subsequent periods, these revaluations may require adjustments to the revenues and expenses used in computing consolidated income.
   c. Intercompany borrowing and lending might result in accounts receivable and payable on the balance sheets of a parent and its consolidated subsidiaries. If so, these amounts must be eliminated.
   d. Revenues and expenses reported on the consolidated income statement must reflect only transactions with outside entities, which are firms that are not included in the consolidation. Similarly, the carrying values of assets must exclude any unrealized profits for assets that have been transferred among the affiliated firms.

3. **Understand GAAP for reporting consolidated entities.**
   Financial accounting standards require the reporting of consolidated financial statements so that analysts may evaluate the total set of economic resources that are controlled by the parent company, as well as the total liabilities and other claims against those resources. The consolidated income statement measures the total revenues and expenses attributed to these economic resources and claims.

   With respect to the issue of control, it is unclear whether the ownership percentage is the best way to measure control. A parent company owning much less then 50% of an affiliate's outstanding stock can still regularly cast a majority of votes on matters of company policy. The issue of control is further muddied by the existence of convertible securities which can be converted to voting common stock at any time, such that the ownership precentages in an investee can shift dramatically on short notice.

   The usefulness of consolidated financial statements has also been questioned on grounds that aggregations of information cause a loss of information. Some analysts and company managers argue that, because consolidation often entails adding together financial statements from companies of diverse industries, the resulting totals are very difficult to interpret. The FASB issued a standard that requires the consolidation of all majority-owned subsidiaries (see SFAS No. 92, "Consolidation of All Majority-Owned Subsidiaries," October, 1987).

KEY TERMS

Acquisition
Affiliated companies
Business combination
Conglomerates
Consolidated financial statements
Consolidation
Consolidation adjustments
Cost method of accounting
Diversification
Divestiture
Equity method of accounting
External expansion
Goodwill
Horizontal integration
Impairment charge
Impairment test
Intangible asset
Intercompany receivables and payables
Intercompany sales
Internal expansion
Internet
Investee
Joint venture
Merger
Mergers and acquisitions (M&A)
Non-controlling interest in consolidated subsidiaries
Nonhomogeneous subsidiaries
Parent company
Piecemeal acquisition
Pre-acquisition balance sheet
Special purpose entity (SPE)
Subsidiary
Unrealized inventory profits
Vertical integration

Exercises and Problems

V-1 Distinguish between business growth through internal and external expansion. Discuss several reasons why a firm might seek to expand externally, rather than internally.

V-2 Business combinations usually occur in the form of mergers, consolidations, or acquisitions. How does each of these types of combinations differ?

V-3 Suppose that Psycho Company buys all of Somatic Inc.'s outstanding shares directly from Somatic's existing shareholders. Describe how Somatic's balance sheet would be affected by the acquisition.

V-4 What is meant by consolidated financial statements? In what circumstances should a parent company's financial statements be prepared on a consolidated basis?

V-5 Which of the following items would differ on a firm's financial statements before and after consolidation of its subsidiaries? Explain your answers.

a. Total assets
b. Total liabilities
c. Shareholders' equity
d. Sales
e. Expenses
f. Net income

V-6 Indicate how each of the following financial ratios changes after a consolidation of a parent firm and its subsidiaries:

a. Debt-to-total assets ratio
b. Net income-to-shareholders' equity ratio
c. Net income-to-total assets ratio
d. Net income-to-sales ratio
e. Current ratio

V-7 Respond to the following remarks: I just read in the financial pages that Whale company owns 60% of Minnow Inc.'s shares. Whale Company includes all of Minnow's assets and liabilities and all of Minnow's revenues and expenses in its consolidated financial statements. It seems to me that this is a misrepresentation. If Whale owns 60% of Minnow, then it should only reflect 60% of Minnow in its financial statements.

Purchased Goodwill

V-8 The following excerpt is from the acquisitions note contained in Tyler Corporation's 2007 annual report:

> On January 7, 2007, the company completed the purchase of Institutional Financing Services, Inc. (IFS) . . . IFS was acquired for approximately $50,000,000 and the assumption of seasonal working capital debt of $12,800,000. The purchase price and

expenses associated with the acquisition exceeded the fair value of IFS's net assets by approximately $40,854,000, which has been assigned to goodwill.

Required

a. Why did Tyler Corporation pay over $40 million more than the fair value of IFS's net assets?

b. Under prior GAAP, Tyler amortized goodwill over 40 years; what was the impact on net income under such an annual amortization?

c. Under current GAAP, what is the potential impact of Tyler's recognition of $40 million in goodwill?

Consolidation

V-9 Goliath Corporation purchased all of Masonry Corporation's outstanding stock on January 1, 2007, for $6,000,000. The purchase price was paid as follows: Goliath Corporation issued 40,000 shares of its own common stock, par $1, with a market price of $102/share, and cash paid of $1,920,000. The acquisition was accounted for as a purchase. Therefore, Masonry's income statement has been included with Goliath's since the acquisition date. The estimated fair value and carrying value of the assets purchased and the liabilities assumed totaled $7,600,000 and $2,100,000.

Required

a. Use the balance sheet equation to show how Goliath's financial statements will be affected by its acquisition of Masonry. (Assume that Masonry continues as a separate corporation.)

b. Determine any goodwill inherent in this acquisition.

c. Why did Goliath pay more than the fair value of Masonry's net assets?

Consolidation and Goodwill

V-10 On January 1, 2007, Maple Grove Deli, Inc. purchased all of the outstanding stock of Bizno's Sub Shops, Inc. for $4,500,000. Maple Grove paid $2,000,000 cash and issued 25,000 shares of its common stock, no par value, currently selling for $100 per share. The estimated fair value and carrying value of Bizno's assets (purchased by Maple Grove) and liabilities (assumed by Maple Grove) approximated $6,200,000 and $1,920,000 respectively. The excess of the purchase price over the fair value of the assets is being amortized over 40 years on a straight-line basis. During 2007, Bizno's earned a net income of $3,400,000 and paid dividends of $230,000.

Required

a. Use the balance sheet equation to show how Maple Grove's financial statements are affected at the date of acquisition.

b. How is Maple Grove affected by Bizno's net income and dividends?

c. How much goodwill would Maple Grove amortize under prior GAAP? Show the effect on Maple Grove's balance sheet equation.

d. What is the correct treatment of goodwill under current GAAP, assuming no impairment?

e. What is the net amount Maple Grove earned from owning Bizno's during the year? How much would net income increase using current GAAP treatment of goodwill, vs. using prior GAAP? What are the implications of this increase in net income?

Consolidation: Adjustment to the Income Statement

V-11 Presented below are condensed income statements for the MHL Company and its wholly owned subsidiary, PTE Inc., for the year ended December 31, 2007 (dollars in millions). MHL acquired its ownership of PTE in 2006.

	MHL Company	*PTE Inc.*
Sales	$260	$180
Cost of sales	(110)	(75)
Other operating expenses	(145)	(85)
Net income*	5	20

*MHL has not recognized any income during 2007 related to its ownership of PTE's shares.

Required

Explain how each of the following items would affect your preparation of a consolidated income statement for MHL and PTE:

a. During 2007, PTE made sales to MHL totaling $40 million.

b. At the end of 2007, MHL's inventory includes $10 million for items purchased from PTE. The cost of these sales incurred by PTE was $4.5 million.

c. At the beginning of 2007, none of MHL's inventory consisted of goods purchased from PTE.

d. Prepare a consolidated income statement for MHL Company for the year 2007.

Consolidation: Adjustments to the Balance Sheet

V-12 Presented below are condensed balance sheets for the ASAP Company and its wholly owned subsidiary, BYOB Inc., at December 31, 2007 (dollars in millions):

	ASAP Company	*BYOB Inc.*
Current assets	$ 30	$ 55
Noncurrent assets	210	95
Total	$240	$150
Liabilities	$110	$ 85
Shareholders' equity	130	65
Total	$240	$150

Required

Explain how each of the following items would affect your preparation of a consolidated balance sheet for ASAP and BYOB:

a. The noncurrent assets of ASAP include its investment in BYOB at a value of $65 million.

b. The current assets of BYOB include an account receivable from ASAP of $9 million.

c. The noncurrent assets of BYOB include land purchased from ASAP for $25 million. The cost of the land to ASAP was $7 million.

d. Prepare a consolidated balance sheet for ASAP Company on December 31, 2007.

Consolidation of Balance Sheets

V-13 Selected items from the unconsolidated financial statements of Tipton Financial Services, Inc., and its wholly owned subsidiary are provided below. Tipton uses the equity method to account for its investment in Smartcom, Inc. Its investment cost is equal to Smartcom's net asset book value (shareholders' equity).

	Tipton	*Smartcom*
	(Dollars in thousands)	
Total assets (including the investment)	$ 420,000	$210,000
Total liabilities	230,000	190,000
Total shareholders' equity	190,000	20,000
Sales	1,200,000	575,000
Interest expense	40,000	30,000
Net income	24,000	100

Required

a. Combine the two unconsolidated companies' financial statements and show the consolidated financial statements of Tipton, similar to Exhibit V-2. Remember to eliminate Tipton's investment against Smartcom's shareholders' equity.

b. Calculate the following ratios for Tipton before and after consolidation:

(1) Debt-to-total assets ratio.

(2) Return on shareholders' equity ratio (use ending shareholders' equity to approximate the average).

c. Comment on any differences in these ratios before and after consolidation.

Interpreting Financial Statements: Affiliated Firms

V-14 Review Wal-Mart's financial statements in Appendix A.

Required

a. Read Notes 1 and 11. Identify any unfamiliar or unusual terms. Match the terms presented in this TOPICMOD to the terms used by Wal-Mart.

b. Determine whether Wal-Mart's relationships with its subsidiaries seem to have a significant effect on the firm's liquidity, profitability, capital structure, or other important dimensions of the firm's performance.

c. Does the firm use the equity method of accounting for its ownership of affiliated companies? How does the firm's choice of method affect its results? To the extent possible, characterize the method used as conservative, aggressive, or "in-between" in terms of its impact on net income.

Allocation of Acquisition Cost in a Purchase

V-15 Ronco, Inc. purchased all of the outstanding voting stock of Nanco, Ltd. on January 1, 2007, at a cost of $750 million paid in cash. On the acquisition date, Nanco had the following assets and liabilities (dollars in millions):

	Book Value	*Fair Market Value*
Cash	$ 55	$ 55
Other assets	820	950
Liabilities	430	364

Required

a. Explain why the fair market values of Nanco's identifiable assets and liabilities may differ from their book or carrying values at the acquisition date.

b. Determine the excess of Ronco's investment cost over the book value of Nanco's net assets.

c. Determine the excess of Ronco's investment cost over the fair market value of Nanco's net assets.

d. Is goodwill implicit in the investment cost incurred by Ronco? If so, what amount would be reported as goodwill in Ronco's consolidated balance sheet on January 1, 2007?

Preparation of Consolidated Balance Sheet at Acquisition Date

V-16 On January 1, 2007, Tipper Company purchased all of Albert Inc.'s outstanding stock. The post-combination balance sheets of both firms are listed below (dollars in millions):

	Tipper Company	*Albert Inc.*
Cash	$ 20	$ 5
Accounts receivable	120	65
Other assets	950	330
Investment in Albert, Inc.	410	—
Total assets	$1,500	$400
Liabilities	$650	160
Shareholders' equity	850	240
Total liabilities and shareholders' equity	$1,500	$400

Additional information:

1. On the date of acquisition, Albert Inc.'s other assets had a fair market value of $380 million. All other components of net assets had fair market values approximately equal to book values.
2. Albert's accounts receivable include $25 million that is due from Tipper Company.

Required

a. Assume that Tipper Company will report a consolidated balance sheet on January 1, 2007. Indicate how each of the following items would be valued in the consolidated statement:

(1) Accounts receivable
(2) Other assets
(3) Investment in Albert Inc.
(4) Goodwill
(5) Liabilities
(6) Shareholders' equity

Business Acquisition: ALLTEL Corporation

V-17 Access the EDGAR archives (www.sec.gov/edaux/searches.htm) and locate the S-4/A report filed by ALLTEL Corp. on June 21, 2005. This report was filed on the successful acquisition of one of the largest rural wireless communications services in the United States. Examine the report and answer the following questions:

a. Which company did ALLTEL acquire?

b. What were the separate revenue and operating incomes for each company prior to the acquisition (for the three months ended March 31, 2005)?

c. Refer to the Pro Forma Combined Condensed Statement of Income and identify the revenue and operation income for the same period had the companies been combined.

d. Separately calculate the operating income percentage and net income percentage (of sales) for each company and for the combined company. What are your observations?

e. What were the total assets and total liabilities of each company and of the combined company? What do you observe when comparing the data?

TOPICMOD VI

EARNINGS MANAGEMENT

Learning Objectives

1. *Describe the purpose of financial accounting and how it is used in earnings management.*
2. *Describe the motivations for and methods of earnings management.*
3. *Understand the need to look beyond the accrual basis numbers and focus on the cash basis numbers in assessing a firm's overall financial health.*

INTRODUCTION

Throughout this text, we have emphasized that a major **informational role** of financial accounting is to *provide information useful for economic decision-making.* For example, we saw how financial accounting information can be used in a variety of decision contexts, such as granting credit. *Financial accounting also serves as a basis for engaging in contracts.* That is, many legal contracts are based on financial statement numbers. The compensation of top executives, for example, is often tied to reported net income. As another example, loan agreements require firms to maintain specified levels of various accounting numbers, such as the debt-to-assets ratio.

Given that many legal contracts require certain financial statement results, changing the accounting principles used to prepare those statements will affect whether the contract terms are met. Of course, changing contract terms affects the wealth of the contracting parties. Thus, the adoption of a new, income-decreasing accounting principle may, for example, reduce the compensation paid to a firm's executives. This adversely affects their wealth, and since the corporation pays out less cash, the shareholders are benefited.

It is no surprise, then, that corporate managers are particularly interested in the selection of accounting principles and the earnings numbers reported by their firms. In fact, because acceptable alternative accounting principles exist within GAAP, corporate managers play a key role in selecting accounting principles. Bear in mind that although managers may have some interest in providing information useful for decision making, *financial statement readers need to be acutely aware of conflicting managerial motivations.* Managers may be motivated to engage in **earnings management,** which involves making accounting related decisions that will result in favorable consequences for themselves and/or their firms.

Remember that a firm's reported accounting earnings (net income) might affect the firm's stock price and influence analyst or investor expectations. As a result, managers are more inclined to manipulate this number than any other number on the financial statements. Recall that accounting earnings (net income), according to GAAP, is based on accrual accounting. Revenues and expenses are recorded when earned and incurred not necessarily when the cash is received or paid. Oftentimes, it is not clear when revenues have been earned and expenses incurred. It is ultimately the managers' judgments and estimations that influence the timing and dollar amount to be recognized in the financial statements. Moreover, it is the managers' personal motivations that play a large part in influencing their judgments and estimates.

In the following sections we will explore in depth what motivates managers to engage in earnings management. Next, we will discuss how managers can undertake actions that will affect the accrual income number reported on the financial statements and finally, we will demonstrate how cash basis accounting can act as a check and balance on the accrual accounting numbers.

Motivations for Earnings Management

Reported earnings can affect corporate wealth, and the wealth of their managers, in the following ways:

1. Lending agreements typically place restrictions on borrowers by using accounting numbers and ratios. Restrictions include minimum levels of retained earnings and current ratios, and maximum levels of debt-to-equity ratios. Higher reported net income reduces the likelihood that an agreement would be violated. Since violations can result in higher interest rates or other adverse consequences to the borrower, managers have an incentive to inflate reported earnings.
2. Managers' bonuses are often based on reported accounting earnings. Managers' can increase their personal wealth by making accounting decisions that maximize their bonus.
3. Governments have the power to significantly affect corporate wealth through taxes, subsidies, antitrust actions, and a variety of other regulations and restrictions. Reported accounting earnings can affect the likelihood that a firm will reap a benefit or incur the cost of a governmental intervention. Because of this, some firms and their managers have an incentive to reduce reported income.
4. Stock market analysts pay close attention to a firm's earnings and the trend in earnings. Most valuation models place a positive weight on earnings growth. Consequently, corporations are motivated to report higher earnings, year after year. Also, analysts seek to minimize risk. Since highly variable earnings reflect increased risk, corporations seek to smooth peaks and troughs in reported earnings.
5. Earnings are also used as a basis for bargaining. When negotiating with an employees' union over wages and benefits, for example, a corporation's best interest might be served by reporting low earnings. The corporation can then claim that it doesn't have the financial resources to meet demands for higher employee compensation.

Methods of Earnings Management

GAAP provides corporate managers with a tremendous amount of discretion regarding accounting-related decisions and estimates. Managers may use this latitude to shift income across years in order to achieve the objectives outlined in the previous section. Corporations can also time certain transactions in order to manage earnings. Specific **earnings management tools** include the following:

1. GAAP often permits a firm to choose its accounting methods from several acceptable alternatives. For example, earlier chapters of this book discussed three ways to account for inventory and three methods of depreciation. Managers seeking to maximize reported earnings would likely

choose the FIFO inventory method (assuming a period of rising prices) and the straight-line method of depreciating fixed assets.

2. A variety of assumptions and estimates are needed to implement GAAP. For example, to actually calculate depreciation charges, estimates of useful lives and salvage values are needed. Other estimates required by GAAP include uncollectible accounts and product warranty liabilities. Managers often know considerably more about these issues than do the firm's auditors. Although managers' estimates must be reasonable, the range of possibilities is fairly large.
3. Newly promulgated FASB standards usually provide a period of time, often two or three years, during which firms can initially adopt the new rules. Adoption dates selected by individual firms depend on the projected effects of the standard on the firm's financial statements (which could be in the billions of dollars), and on the firm's earnings management objectives.
4. During the past decade, numerous firms have taken large restructuring charges. These charges arise when firms revamp operations. They mostly include writing down assets and recognizing the severance benefits liability to employees who have been (or will be) terminated. Most restructurings take several years to complete. Restructuring charges can be an earnings management tool because of the ability to spread these costs over several years.
5. Earnings can also be managed by cleverly timing certain transactions. For example, recall the accounting for securities classified as available-for-sale. Changes in the market value of these securities are not reflected in earnings while the securities are held. At the time securities are sold, the entire gain or loss (the difference between the historical cost and the selling price) is recorded. By carefully selecting to sell certain securities from its portfolio, a firm can predetermine if a gain or loss will be included in earnings.

What Would You Do?

As the chief financial officer for Bullet Enterprises, the chief executive officer (CEO) has asked your advice regarding an accounting principle change she is considering. Many firms in your industry have recently adopted LIFO. These adoptions were motivated by substantial increases in inventory costs. Under such conditions, LIFO can provide significant tax savings. Bullet's inventory costs have also risen, but not as much as your competitor's prices.

However, another issue concerns you. Your compensation package includes a bonus based on reported net income and the bonus is not activated unless net income exceeds $500,000. Your analysis shows that if LIFO is not adopted, net income will approximate $750,000. If LIFO is adopted, net income will be about $475,000. What would you tell the CEO?

Implications of Earnings Management

Accounting-related decisions (the selection of accounting principles and the development of accounting estimates) affect corporate wealth and the wealth of their managers. With the wide latitude provided by GAAP it is a safe bet that corporate managers will continue to choose accrual accounting methods and adjustments that will help them achieve their earnings management objectives. *The manipulation of income can degrade the quality of a firm's reported earnings and highlights the need to look beyond the accrual numbers.* In other words, as we have stressed throughout this text, *financial statement readers should ask the question:* ***"Where's the Cash?"***

Examination of a firm's cash flows, namely understanding the changes in a firm's operating cash flows as well as understanding the trends in a firm's investing and financing cash flow activities are important. Remember, **"Cash Is King."** If, for example, a firm has a sluggish year, it may be tempted to prematurely recognize revenues before they are actually earned and justify this action as a change in an accounting estimate.

Recall from our discussion in Chapter 5, Xerox Corporation prematurely recorded revenues during 1997–2000 by adjusting lease contracts, and manipulating their accounts receivable by relaxing credit terms for customers and not recording sales returns. A detailed analysis of the company's operating cash flows during this same period would have revealed that accounts receivable were increasing at a rather alarming rate, causing a severe drain on the company's operating cash flows. To make up for their cash drain, Xerox borrowed heavily as shown by an increase in the company's financing cash flows. In reality, Xerox was not collecting cash from many of its accounts receivable customers because they were uncollectible. Merchandise that was returned by customers was secretly hidden in warehouses so that the company could avoid having to record sales returns. Xerox was having trouble keeping pace with other copier manufacturers in the industry so it had to manage its earnings by playing with the accrual accounting numbers to make up for its sluggish operations.

In the article, "The Ins and Outs of Cash Flow", the author describes the importance of reviewing a company's operating cash flows.

> "At the heart of evaluating cash from operations are consideration of changes in assets and liabilities. Accounting experts pay a lot of attention to accounts receivable, representing what customers owe the company. When receivables rise at a faster pace than sales, the company may be having trouble collecting what it is owed. Since cash isn't flowing in as it should be, a rise shows up as a negative on the cash-flow statement . . . if operating cash doesn't pick up, bail out. Eventually, lenders lose patience with companies whose operations hemorrhage cash. . . . When inventories grow faster than sales, it might mean demand is softening. Since buying inventory requires cash, an increase here causes cash to fall. Conversely, when liabilities such as accounts payable increase, so do a

company's cash balances. By delaying payments to creditors, management frees up cash." (Anne Tergesen, "The Ins and Outs of Cash Flow", *BusinessWeek Investor*, Jan. 22, 2003.)

Delaying payments isn't necessarily good: "If accounts payable grows every year, you have to be suspicious that they are stringing out their customers," says Jack Ciesielski, author of the *Analyst's Accounting Observer*, a Baltimore-based publication."(Ibid.)

In summary, as part of a thorough financial analysis of a firm, it is critically important to pay close attention to the firm's trends in cash flows. Managers will continue to manage their firms' earnings to achieve personal and firm earnings objectives. As we have witnessed during recent accounting scandals, some managers have pushed earnings management to the point of fraudulent deception by reporting erroneous earnings numbers.

With the myriad of judgments and estimations required by accrual accounting, the temptation to manipulate earnings will continue to exist. Asking the question, "**Where's the Cash?**" will remain an important check and balance on a company's reported earnings. In addition, a thorough examination of the detailed disclosures in a firm's financial statement notes and a thorough knowledge of the firm and its industry are essential in "developing a complete picture" of a firm's overall financial health.

Summary of Learning Objectives

1. **Describe the purpose of financial accounting and how it is used in earnings management.**
   Financial accounting is designed to provide useful information for economic decision making. Second, many contracts are written in terms of accounting numbers. Because different accounting principles result in different accounting numbers, contract terms can be altered simply by changing accounting principles. Thus, corporate managers develop preferences for certain accounting principles. As a result, financial statement numbers are not necessarily unbiased, and they should be interpreted accordingly.

2. **Describe the motivations for and methods of earnings management.**
   Reported accounting earnings can significantly affect corporate wealth, and their managers' wealth. Because of this, corporations have an incentive to select accounting principles and make other accounting-related decisions in order to achieve their earnings management objectives.

3. **Understand the need to look beyond the accrual basis numbers and focus on the cash basis numbers in assessing a firm's overall financial health.**
   Because corporate managers have the ability to manipulate their firms' reported earnings through selected accrual accounting methods and adjustments, financial statement readers should ask the question, "**Where's the**

Cash?" In other words, a thorough examination of a firm's cash flows is important. Likewise, examination of the detailed disclosures in the financial statement notes and a thorough knowledge of the firm and its industry are essential in assessing a firm's overall financial health.

KEY TERMS

Cash Is King
Earnings management
Earnings management tools
Informational role
Where's the Cash?

Exercises and Problems

VI-1 Describe financial accounting's two primary roles. Discuss the major criteria that financial accounting must adopt as part of its informational role. What other roles or criteria would you suggest? Why?

VI-2 How do a firm's accounting principles affect contracts that are based on the financial statements?

VI-3 Discuss how economic consequences can affect various users of financial statements. How should those who are affected by economic consequences participate in the development of accounting principles?

VI-4 Why should financial analysts not be willing to accept all the information in a firm's financial statements at face value?

VI-5 What is earnings management? Why would a manager engage in earnings management? Would an investor or creditor approve of such activities? Under what circumstances would an investor or creditor approve? Why?

VI-6 Discuss each of the motivations for earnings management. Under what circumstances would you support the use of these techniques? Why?

VI-7 Identify some methods that might be used to manage earnings that were not described in this TOPICMOD. Are these new methods more appropriate or more ethical than the methods already described in the TOPICMOD? Why?

VI-8 What are the implications of earnings management? As an external financial analyst, what can be done to combat earnings management?

VI-9 Iomega Corporation designs and markets data management drives such as the magnetic disk drive known as the Zip drive. The Company reported the following income statement:

IOMEGA CORPORATION AND SUBSIDIARIES
CONSOLIDATED STATEMENTS OF OPERATIONS
(IN THOUSANDS)
YEAR ENDED DECEMBER 31,

	2002	*2001*	*2000*
Sales	$614,363	$831,094	$1,300,184
Cost of sales	378,239	645,504	810,500
Goss margin	236,124	185,590	489,684
Operating Expenses:			
Selling, general, and administrative	133,506	210,001	290,333
Research and development	36,249	49,522	58,577

Restructuring charges (reversals)	(2,423)	38,946	(4,814)
Bad debt expense (credit)	(3,068)	7,121	(2,637)
Total operating expenses	164,264	305,590	341,459
Operating income (loss)	71,860	(120,000)	148,225
Interest income	8,641	15,806	21,907
Interest expense	(1,108)	(432)	(4,176)
Other expense	(3,504)	(1,499)	(3,638)
Income (loss) before income taxes	75,889	(106,125)	162,318
Benefit (prevision) for income taxes	(41,170)	12,846	7,312
Net income (loss)	$ 34,719	$(93,279)	$ 169,630

Required

a. Point out key areas managers may have engaged in earnings management.

b. Do you believe earnings management has been an effective tool for Iomega?

TOPICMOD VII

ACCOUNTING CHANGES

Learning Objective

1. *Interpret financial statements for firms making accounting changes.*

ACCOUNTING CHANGES

The term **accounting changes** includes three types of accounting events:

- **A change in accounting principle,**
- **A change in accounting estimate, and**
- **A change in reporting entity.**

Since the accounting for each type of change is different, they are discussed separately.

Change in Accounting Principle

In many situations, corporate managers are free to choose from several acceptable accounting methods. For example, LIFO or FIFO can be used for inventory valuation, and an accelerated or straight-line method can be used to calculate depreciation expense. Although managers can choose between alternative GAAP, *once a method is selected, it should be used consistently from period to period.* This enhances the **inter-period comparability** of financial statements. In other words, if a firm consistently uses the same accounting principles from one period to another, changes in the financial statement numbers over time will likely reflect changes in the underlying economics of the firm, rather than the effect of an accounting principle change.

Although the consistent use of accounting principles is desirable, firms do occasionally change from one principle to another. Because financial statement readers do not usually expect such changes, these changes are highlighted in the auditor's report. Since the existence of an accounting change dramatically alters the interpretation of financial statements, a review of the auditor's report should always be one of the first steps in the analysis of financial statements.

An accounting principle change (change from one GAAP principle to another GAAP principle) such as a change from FIFO to Average Cost inventory cost method compromises the comparability of financial statements because of the inconsistent application of GAAP. According to the FASB's Statement of Financial Accounting Concepts, financial information should be (1) relevant and reliable and (2) consistent and comparable.

How, then, should a change in one acceptable accounting principle to another acceptable accounting principle be accomplished so that comparable and consistent financial statements can be maintained? Many believe that in the year of the change, the account balances should be restated to show the amounts that would have appeared if the new method had been used all along. In other words, the cumulative effect of the change is reported in the adoption year's income. No comparable amount appears in prior or subsequent years' income. This causes inconsistencies because the new accounting principle is used in the current and future years but not in prior years. Proponents of this treatment believe that the public confidence is maintained because the earnings reported in prior years are not affected. This is important because imagine the contractual agreements that exist that are impacted by company reported earnings (i.e., bonus and profit sharing plans). Until recently, the "cumulative effect treatment" has been the generally accepted method for accounting principle changes.

The FASB has been working on a project with the IASB (International Accounting Standards Board) to resolve differences between U.S. GAAP and IFRS (International Financial Reporting Standards). One big difference between the two has been in the area of accounting principle changes. FASB recently issued SFAS 154, "Accounting Changes and Error Corrections—A Replacement of APB Opinion No. 20 and FASB Statement No. 3" as part of its goal of converging U.S. GAAP with IFRS.

With this new standard, accounting principle changes are accounted for retroactively. Under this approach prior years' financial statements are restated to reflect the use of the new method. The obvious advantage of making **retroactive changes** is that the financial statements of the current and prior years are based on a common set of accounting principles. However, there is always the lingering question, "will reissuing financial statements with numbers different from those that originally appeared dilute the public's confidence in financial reporting?"

Retroactive Application General Rule

To illustrate the general rule, Exhibit VII-1 a and b contain a condensed income statement and a note from the 2007 financial statements of CA Aerospace, Inc. (CA), a manufacturer of commercial aircraft cabin interior products, such as aircraft seats, food and beverage preparation and storage equipment, and in-flight entertainment systems. In 2006, CA evaluated its accounting policy of capitalizing (recording as an asset) engineering costs incurred before a contract had been signed with a customer. This policy is rather liberal and results in higher reported asset values and higher reported income. In 2006, CA adopted the more conservative policy of expensing these costs. CA's new policy is more consistent with that used by most of its rivals. CA appropriately accounted for this accounting principle change by retroactively adjusting the income statement for 2005 to show the reader what net income would have been had the expensing of engineering costs been applied all along. Therefore, the retained earnings and inventory accounts would contain the effects of the newly adopted standard and these two accounts would be adjusted at the beginning of 2005 to reflect the cumulative effect of the application of the newly adopted accounting principle on years prior to 2005.

A change from any inventory costing method to LIFO is not retroactively applied due to the nature of LIFO (old good still here). A change in depreciation, amortization, or depletion method is now considered a change in accounting estimate. The following section discusses changes in accounting estimates.

Exceptions

FASB has provided exceptions to the retroactive application treatment. A change from any inventory costing method to LIFO is not retroactively applied due to

EXHIBIT VII-1a ACCOUNTING PRINCIPLES CHANGE BEFORE RETROACTIVE APPLICATION OF THE CHANGE

CA Aerospace, Inc.
Consolidated Statement of Operation (Condensed)
(Dollars in thousands)

	2007	2006	2005
Net sales	$412,379	$232,582	$229,347
Cost of sales	270,557	160,031	154,863
Gross profit	141,822	72,551	74,484
Other expenses	126,591	132,632	93,356
Earnings (loss) before income taxes	15,231	(60,081)	(18,872)
Income taxes	1,522	—	(6,806)
Net earnings (loss)	$ 13,709	$(60,081)	$(12,066)

EXHIBIT VII-1b ACCOUNTING PRINCIPLES CHANGE AFTER RETROACTIVE APPLICATION OF THE CHANGE

CA Aerospace, Inc.
Consolidated Statement of Operation (Condensed)
(Dollars in thousands)

	2007	2006	2005
Net sales	$412,379	$232,582	$229,347
Cost of sales	270,557	160,031	154,863
Gross profit	141,822	72,551	74,484
Other expenses	126,591	132,632	**116,688**
Earnings (loss) before income taxes	15,231	(60,081)	(42,204)
Income taxes	1,522	—	*(6,806)
Net earnings (loss)	$ 13,709	$(60,081)	$(35,398)

* Income taxes would have changed but for clarity in illustrating the retroactive charge we have kept the income taxes the same.

Note 2. Accounting Change. In 2006, the Company undertook a comprehensive review of the engineering capitalization policies followed by its competitors and others in its industry peer group. The results of this study and an evaluation of the Company's policy led the company to conclude that it should adopt the accounting method that it believes is followed by most of its competitors and certain members of its industry peer group. Previously, the Company had capitalized pre-contract engineering costs as a component of inventories, which were then amortized to earnings as the product was shipped. The Company now expenses such costs as they are incurred. While the accounting policy for pre-contract engineering expenditures previously followed by the Company was in accordance with generally accepted accounting principles, the changed policy is preferable.

The effect of expensing engineering costs only in 2006 was a charge of $42,114 and the effect in 2005 as if the accounting principle of expensing engineering costs were applied was a charge of $23,332. The cumulative effect of this change on years prior to 2005 was $17,456 and the inventory and retained earnings accounts at the beginning of 2005 were adjusted by this amount.

the nature of LIFO (old goods' costs still in inventory). In the year of the change, the company simply uses the beginning balance of its inventory (based on the old costing method) as its adoption year LIFO beginning balance. No retroactive adjustments are required.

A change in depreciation, amortization or depletion method is now considered a change in accounting estimate. The following section discusses changes in accounting estimates.

Change in Accounting Estimate

Many financial statement figures are based on estimates. Depreciation expense and the book value of fixed assets, for example, are determined by estimates of useful lives and salvage values. As another example, uncollectible accounts expense and the net value of accounts receivable are based on estimates of the number of customers that will not honor their obligations to the firm.

An inherent aspect of estimates is that they do not always prove to be correct. Conceptually, changes in accounting estimates could be accounted for retroactively. That is, when an estimate proves faulty, prior years' financial statements could be restated. However, the accounting profession has *rejected the concept of restating prior years' financial statements for changes in accounting estimates.* For most firms of even modest size, a large number of estimates will miss their mark. The retroactive approach would result in firms continually restating financial statements, which would seriously compromise the credibility and usefulness of financial reporting.

Instead, changes in accounting estimates are accounted for **prospectively** by including them in the year of the change and in future years, if appropriate. To illustrate **prospective changes,** assume that a machine is acquired for $14,000 in 2007. It has a salvage value of $2,000 and an estimated life of five years. Straight-line depreciation is used and the annual depreciation charge is $2,400:

$$\text{Annual depreciation expense} = \frac{(\$14{,}000 - \$2{,}000)}{5} = \$2{,}400$$

Assume that at the beginning of 2009 the machine's total useful life is now estimated to be eight years. Depreciation expense for 2007 and 2008 is not changed. The remaining depreciable base is depreciated over the remaining useful life of six years. Annual depreciation expense for 2009 through 2014 is $1,200:

Cost	$14,000
Less salvage value	(2,000)
Less depreciation to date	(4,800)
Remaining depreciable base	$ 7,200

$$\text{Annual depreciation expense} = \frac{\text{Remaining depreciable base}}{\text{Remaining life}}$$

The effect of changes in accounting estimates on net income must be disclosed in the notes to the financial statements.

As an example, Sears, Roebuck & Company reported the following information in its 2002 annual report:

> In 2002, the Company increased its allowance for uncollectible accounts as a percentage of credit card receivables to 5.79% from 4.04% in 2001 and 4.03% in 2000. In the second quarter of 2002, the Company refined its methodology for determining the uncollectible portion of current accounts and credit card fee balances, resulting in an increase to the allowance for uncollectible accounts in the amount of $300 million. In accordance with Accounting Principles Board Opinion No. 20, "Accounting Changes", the effect of this change in accounting was recorded as a change in accounting estimate.

Bear in mind, though, that virtually all firms experience changes in accounting estimates but they are usually too small (immaterial) to require disclosure.

Change in Reporting Entity

A change in a reporting entity occurs when a firm changes the specific subsidiaries included in its consolidated financial statements (see TOPICMOD-V). This situation often arises when the parent first acquires the majority share of a subsidiary's voting stock.

The acquisition and consolidation of a new subsidiary essentially result in a different reporting entity. The new subsidiary might substantially change the consolidated group's size, scope, and scale of operations, as well as the nature of the products and services provided. Accordingly, the results of the new consolidated group cannot be validly compared to the results of the old group as previously reported.

A change in a reporting entity is accounted for ***retroactively.*** Prior years' financial statements are *restated to reflect the past results of the new consolidated group.* This approach ensures the comparability of the financial statements.

Summary of Learning Objective

1. **Interpret financial statements for firms making accounting changes.**
   Given that acceptable alternatives exist within GAAP, firms sometimes change accounting principles. Most changes are accounted for retroactively. That is, prior years' financial statements are restated to reflect the new principle, which ensures that the firm's financial statements are comparable across time periods. Changes in accounting estimates are accounted for prospectively. That is, prior years' financial statements are not altered. The effect of the estimate change is reflected in the current and future years' income. Finally, changes in reporting entities are accounted for retroactively.

KEY TERMS

Accounting changes
Change in accounting principle
Change in accounting estimate
Change in reporting entity
Cumulative effect
Cumulative estimate
Inter-period comparability
Pro forma amounts
Prospective changes
Prospectively
Retroactive changes
Retroactively

Exercises and Problems

VII-1 Describe three different types of accounting changes. Under what circumstances should each be reported?

VII-2 Discuss why financial statement users prefer a firm to consistently use the same accounting principles.

VII-3 What is the financial statement user's first indication that an accounting change has occurred? Why should this source be examined first when reading a financial statement?

VII-4 Discuss the general rule in reporting the effects of an accounting principle change.

VII-5 Under the general rule dealing with accounting principle changes, have the firm's retained earnings changed? How has the firm gained or lost some of its prior (accumulated) retained earnings? Why?

VII-6 Discuss the controversy over the change to FASB Standard 154 pertaining to accounting principle changes.

VII-7 When the effects of a change in an accounting estimate are recognized, can prior financial statements be restated retroactively? Why?

VII-8 Where are the effects of changes in accounting estimates reported? Why should the financial statement user often not be aware of many of these changes?

VII-9 Why is a change in reporting entity shown as a retroactive adjustment and not as a prospective adjustment?

Accounting Principle Change

VII-10 Mesple Music, Inc. purchased musical instrument equipment on January 1, 2006, for $25,000. Mesple depreciated it on the straight-line basis over five years with no salvage value. However, on January 1, 2008, the company realized that the productive capacity of this equipment is declining, so it decided to change to the double-declining balance method of depreciation. Recall that change in depreciation method is not considered a change in accounting principle.

Required

a. Calculate depreciation expense for 2006 and 2007, using the straight-line method.

b. Calculate depreciation expense for 2006 and 2007, using the double-declining balance method. (Refer to Chapter 7 for details on double-declining balance depreciation.)

Accounting Principle Change

VII-11 Central Air Conditioning, Inc. purchased machinery for installing air conditioners. The purchase price of the machine on July 1, 2007, was $35,000. The company chose a seven-year life, sum-of-the-years' digits (SYD) depreciation, and no salvage value. Unfortunately, the weather during 2007, 2008, and 2009 was extremely mild and the machinery was not used as much as the company had thought. Therefore, it decided that the straight-line method would be more representative of the productive capacity of the machine, so it switched to the straight-line method on July 1, 2010.

Required (Ignore Income Tax)

a. Calculate depreciation expense, using SYD for the annual periods ending June 30, 2008, 2009, and 2010. (See Chapter 7 for a review of SYD depreciation.)

b. Calculate depreciation expense, using the straight-line method for the annual periods ending June 30, 2008, 2009, and 2010.

Ratios: Accounting Change

VII-12 Polymer Corporation presented the following (partial) income statements (dollars in thousands, except EPS):

		December 31	
	2007	*2006*	*2005*
Income from continuing operations after tax	$ 207,500	$195,400	$189,600
Net income	$ 207,500	$195,400	$ 189,600
Weighted-average common shares outstanding	146,000	146,000	146,000
Market price of stock	$20	$18	$16

What if the company told you that it changed inventory cost methods in 2006 from FIFO to average cost and the effect on 2005 would have been $11,000 reduction in net income and the cumulative effect on years prior to 2005 would have been $25,000? The financial statements for 2006 and 2007 are based on the new accounting principle, average cost, but 2005 was based on FIFO.

Required

a. Correct the income statement for 2005. (Ignore income tax effects.)

b. Explain how the cumulative effect on years prior to 2005 would be accounted for.

c. Calculate earnings per share (EPS) and calculate the P/E ratio for each year, both before and after correcting the 2005 income statement.

d. Comment on the impact these results might have on an investor's preferences or risks.

Calculating Bad Debt Expense

VII-13 Dandy's Discount Duds offers credit to all customers. It estimated that 15% of all such customers will not be able to pay their accounts. Dandy's credit sales in 2007 were $4,000,000. Its estimated bad debt expense was calculated at 15% of annual credit sales.

Required

a. What is the effect of estimated bad debts on net income in 2007?

b. In early 2008, Dandy discovered that half of its customers have been laid off because a major automaker closed two of its plants. Dandy found that 25 percent of its customers will not be able to pay their accounts. What impact will this new realization have on Dandy's income for 2008?

c. If a retroactive adjustment to 2007's net income were necessary, what other information is needed that is not shown in this problem?

d. Why is it appropriate that such adjustments to estimates be shown on a prospective basis?

Interpreting Financial Statements: Accounting Changes and Restructuring

VII-14 Listed below are the income statements for Alto Corporation, a large distributor of copiers in North America (dollars in thousands):

	September 30	
	2007	*2006*
Revenues:		
Net sales	$7,925,784	$6,387,078
Dividends, interest, and other income	3,537	6,332
Finance subsidiaries	66,731	51,149
	7,996,052	6,444,559
Costs and Expenses: Cost of goods sold	5,884,819	4,799,757
Selling and administrative	1,765,483	1,378,814
Interest	43,802	40,189
Finance subsidiaries interest	27,978	23,662
Restructuring costs		175,000
	7,722,082	6,417,422
	273,970	27,137
Loss from unconsolidated affiliate	(117,158)	(2,538)
Income from continuing operations before taxes	156,812	24,599

Taxes on income	86,203	16,984
Income from continuing operations	70,609	7,615
Loss from discontinued operations, net of tax		(7,515)
Net Income	$ 70,609	$ 100

Required

a. Study Alto's income statement. Identify any unfamiliar or unusual terms.

b. Discuss Alto's different reporting treatment in 2006 for its loss from discontinued operations and its restructuring costs.

c. As an investor, evaluate the two items in part b. What impact might they have on the company's future operations?

Recognizing the Effects of Accounting Changes

VII-15 The Keller Company reported the following financial information (dollars in millions):

	2007	*2006*	*2005*
Earnings before cumulative effect of accounting change	$680.7	$682.8	$606.0
Cumulative effect of change in method of accounting for postretirement benefits other than pensions (net of tax benefits)*	—	(251.6)	—
Net earnings	$680.7	$431.2	$606.0

Assume that other than the cumulative effect, earnings for 2006 and 2005 were not materially affected by the change.

*The cumulative effect of the change:	2005	$(149.6)
	Prior to 2005	(102.0)
		$(251.6)

Required

a. Correct the company's income statement using retroactive application. (Ignore any income tax effects.)

b. These earnings figures, stated on a per share basis, are as follows:

	2007	*2006*	*2005*
Earnings before cumulative effect of accounting change	$ 2.94	$2.86	$ 2.51
Cumulative effect of change in method of accounting for postretirement benefits other than pensions (net of tax benefits)	—	(1.05)	—

Net earnings	$ 2.94	$ 1.81	$ 2.51
Price per share	$56.75	$67.00	$65.33

i. Compute the P/E ratio for each year before and after retroactive application.
ii. Discuss your results from i.

Interpreting Financial Statements: Restructuring

VII-16 Iomega Corporation designs and markets data management drives such as the magnetic disk drive known as the Zip drive. The company's income statement and partial footnotes pertaining to bad debt and restructuring expenses are presented below.

IOMEGA CORPORATION AND SUBSIDIARIES
CONSOLIDATED STATEMENTS OF OPERATIONS
(In thousands, except per share data)

	Years Ended December 31,		
	2002	**2001**	**2000**
Sales	$614,363	$831,094	$1,300,184
Cost of sales	378,239	645,504	810,500
Gross margin	236,124	185,590	489,684
Operating Expenses:			
Selling, general and administrative	133,506	210,001	290,333
Research and development	36,249	49,522	58,577
Restructuring charges (reversals)	(2,423)	38,946	(4,814)
Bad debt expense (credit)	(3,068)	7,121	(2,637)
Total operating expenses	164,264	305,590	341,459
Operating income (loss)	71,860	(120,000)	148,225
Interest income	8,641	15,806	21,907
Interest expense	(1,108)	(432)	(4,176)
Other expense	(3,504)	(1,499)	(3,638)
Income (loss) before income taxes	75,889	(106,125)	162,318
Benefit (provision) for income taxes	(41,170)	12,846	7,312
Net income (loss)	$ 34,719	$(93,279)	$ 169,630
Basic	$ 0.68	$ (1.74)	$ 3.13
Diluted	$ 0.68	$ (1.74)	$ 3.07*
Weighted average common shares outstanding	51,214	53,489	54,110
Weighted average common shares outstanding—assuming dilution	51,363	53,489	55,998

*As reported by Iomega but cannot be calculated.

IOMEGA CORPORATION AND SUBSIDIARIES
NOTES TO CONSOLIDATED FINANCIAL STATEMENTS (Continued)

Allowance for Doubtful Accounts

The Company records its trade receivables at sales value and establishes a non-specific allowance for estimated doubtful accounts by applying specified percentages to the different receivable aging categories. The percentage applied against the aging categories increases as the accounts become further past due. Accounts in excess of 180 days past due are fully reserved. In addition, specific reserves are established for specific customer accounts identified, as known collection problems occur due to insolvency, disputes or other collection issues. The amounts of these specific reserves are estimated by management based on the following assumptions/variables: customer's financial position, age of the customer's receivables and changes in payment schedules. The allowance for doubtful accounts is charged with the write-off of uncollectible customer accounts whether due to insolvency, settlement or disputes.

Restructuring Charges

The Company's 1999 and 2001 restructuring charges were recorded under EITF issue No. 94-3, "Liability Recognition for Certain Employee Termination Benefits and Other Costs to Exit an Activity (including Certain Costs Incurred in a Restructuring)" ("EIFT 94-3"). EITF 94-3 states that restructuring charges, other than amounts for severance and benefits, can be recorded when a detailed restructuring plan to exit specific activities has been approved by management prior to the financial reporting date and the Company has the ability to reasonably estimate costs. Estimated amounts for severance and benefits are accrued once the potentially affected employees have been notified of the termination and severance benefits have been communicated. The communication must include, at a minimum, the number of impacted employees, the job functions and the locations that are affected. The Company revised some of its estimates for the restructuring charges during 2002 under the guidance provided by EITF 94-3 (see Note 5 for more detail).

(5) Restructuring Charges/Reversals

During 2001, the Company recorded approximately $39.0 million in net pre-tax restructuring charges. These charges were comprised of approximately $1.1 million related to restructuring actions initiated during the second quarter of 2001, $33.1 million (net of a $0.2 million fourth quarter 2001 reversal) related to restructuring actions initiated during the third quarter of 2001 and $4.8 million related to restructuring actions initiated during the fourth quarter of 2001. These restructuring charges consisted of cash and non-cash charges of approximately $28 million and $11 million, respectively.

During 2002, the Company had a net reversal or adjustment of $2.4 million of previously recorded restructuring reserves. This $2.4 million net reversal was comprised of $2.0 million related to charges recorded for the 1999 restructuring actions and $0.4 million related to charges recorded for the third quarter 2001 restructuring actions. The detail of each of these restructuring actions follows along with an update on the current status of each of these actions as of December 31, 2002.

Required

a. Review Iomega's income statement and footnotes above. Why does Iomega's bad debt and restructuring expenses show positive amounts for 2001 and negative amounts for 2002 and 2000?

b. Why shouldn't these expenses be reported as retroactive adjustments so that the years are more comparable?

Interpreting Financial Statements: Restructuring

VII-17 Bergen Corporation reported the following information (dollars in thousands) in its 2007 consolidated earnings statement:

Operating earnings from continuing operations	$70,983
Net interest expense	22,723
Earnings from continuing operations before taxes	48,260
Taxes on income from continuing operations	19,653
Earnings from continuing operations	28,607
Extraordinary loss from tornado damage, net of income tax benefit	(2,570)
Net earnings	$26,037

Required

a. Comment on any unusual items in this income statement. Has Bergen reported any accounting changes?

b. Bergen's statements disclosed an item, earlier in the income statement, "Restructuring charge, $33,000,000." This item appeared only in the 2007 column, with nothing reported in the prior years. How do you suppose that this item related to operations of 2007 and to its continuing operations?

c. Note 12, Restructuring and Other Unusual Charges, disclosed the following new information: During the fourth quarter of fiscal 2007, the Company embarked on a restructuring plan which consists of accelerated consolidation of domestic facilities into larger, more efficient regional distribution centers, the merging of duplicate operating systems, the reduction of administrative support in areas not affecting valued services to customers and the discontinuance of services and programs that did not meet the Company's strategic and economic return objective. The pre-tax cost incurred pertaining to the restructuring plan is $33.0 million. The restructuring charge represents the costs associated with restructure, primarily abandonment and severance.

Briefly explain, in your own words, the actions taken by the company as described in the note.

d. Why do you suppose Bergen decided to incur restructuring costs in the later part of 2007 instead of waiting until 2008?

e. How will the restructuring charges in 2007 affect Bergen's future operations? How will these effects be reported in future years?

f. The same note disclosed another unusual charge: On June 18, 2007, the Company announced that a joint bid which the Company had made in April 2007 with the French Company, Pharmaceutique Francaise, to acquire the largest French pharmaceutical distribution company, Office Pharmaceutique, had been withdrawn. Accordingly, expenses of $2.5 million, before income tax benefit of $1.0 million associated with the transaction, have been recorded in the fourth quarter of fiscal 2007. These expenses are not listed anywhere as a separate item in Bergen's income statement. Why? Why must these costs be reported in 2007 and not in 2006 or 2008? Would your conclusions about the reporting of these costs change if you later found that Bergen's had reported in earlier years a separate section in its income statement called "Discontinued Operations"?

g. Bergen's earnings from continuing operations in 2006 and 2005 were, respectively, $53,012,000 and $58,061,000. How has this trend been affected by the $33,000,000 restructuring charge? If the company had not taken this charge in 2007, what would its earnings from continuing operations have been for 2007, and how would this affect the earlier trend?

Effects of Retroactive Adjustment: Percentage-of-Completion Method

VII-18 Ace Construction Company accounted for all its long-term contracts on a deferred basis; that is, all revenue and expenses were deferred until the completion of the contract when all the costs were known with certainty. Although this is a conservative approach, Ace has been having difficulty with its auditors and with the IRS over this approach. It now desires to shift to a percentage-of-completion method. Assume that only one such contract is to be changed at this time. This contract for $5,000,000 was initiated four years ago, and an equal amount of work was done each year. The contract work cost the firm $4,000,000.

Required

a. Show the effects of the $5,000,000 on the accounting equation, assuming that it was all reported as income in the final year.

b. Show the effects on the accounting equation of a retroactive adjustment to the firm's financial statements for each of the contract years. To answer this question, you may need to review Chapter 4.

c. Does this set of adjustments seem important to investors or financial analysts? Does it seem to be a useful adjustment that would be viewed as helpful by the readers of the firm's financial statements? Why?

Discussion of Accounting Changes

VII-19 Identify an accounting change that requires a retroactive adjustment. Create a numerical example of this accounting change and show the effects on net income and retained earnings.

Discussion of Accounting Changes

VII-20 Why would a change from FIFO, or some other inventory method, to LIFO not require a retroactive adjustment of a firm's financial statements? What would be the cumulative effect of such an adjustment?

Discussion of Accounting Changes

VII-21 Discuss why the effects of a change in an accounting estimate are not reported using the "retroactive application" rule.

Various Accounting Changes

VII-22 Match the following terms to the correct description. For each situation, describe in words (ignore the dollar amounts) what accounting treatments are required.

a. Change in accounting principle, accounted for prospectively
b. Change in reporting entity
c. Change in accounting estimate
d. Change in accounting principle, retroactive effect reported

_____ 1. Shipley Office Products, Inc. used equipment for three years and depreciated it on the straight-line basis. The original useful life was seven years, but after three years the company decided to change the original life to five years.

_____ 2. American Shoe Corporation purchased all the outstanding stock of Faborini, Inc. in early 2007. American Shoe Corporation is preparing its comparative financial statements for the year ended December 2007.

_____ 3. Sportscards USA decided to change its inventory costing method from LIFO to FIFO.

_____ 4. Homer Sampson owned the Second Time Through apparel shop. He wanted to raise capital to expand, so he decided to "go public" and offer the company stock for sale in the open market. At the same time, the company implemented an accounting change for postretirement benefits and calculated the cumulative effect of going from "pay-as-you-go" to estimating retirement benefits and accruing an expense each year.

TOPICMOD VIII

FINANCIAL REPORTING ISSUES (SEC)

Learning Objectives

1. *Analyze information about operating segments.*
2. *Describe annual and interim reports.*
3. *Identify reports filed with the Securities and Exchange Commission (SEC).*

SEGMENT REPORTING

Many large corporations engage in a variety of different business activities and operate in various economic and geographic environments. They also serve many customers, both large and small, and financial statements provide figures covering all such groups. Many analysts, however, feel that they would benefit from more detailed information. They suggest that **segment reporting** could assist them in making better estimates of a firm's risk and expected return. For example, a firm that generates 10% of its revenue and profit from software development and 90% from manufacturing breakfast cereal will have a different risk and return outlook than one that generates 10% of its revenue and profit from breakfast cereal and 90% from software development.

Accordingly, all publicly held corporations are required to make certain disclosures in financial statement notes. These disclosure requirements are summarized in the following sections.

Operating Segments

An **operating segment** is a component of a firm (1) that engages in business activities from which it can earn revenues and incur expenses, (2) whose operating results are regularly reviewed by the firm's chief operating decision maker, and (3) for which financial information is available. This definition is intentionally broad and recognizes that firms are organized in different ways. Some firms are organized around the products that are produced and distributed, which is the way many large diversified corporations are organized. Other firms are organized based on the type of customer. An auto parts distributor, for example, could have separate divisions to sell to professionals (repair shops) and to individual car owners (via its own retail outlets). Still other firms could be organized based on geography, with each region or country constituting its own segment.

Operating segments correspond to the organizational subunits that the firm's top management uses in evaluating performance and allocating resources. The advantage of this approach is that financial statement readers are provided with the same view of the firm and the same information that is used by top management. The disadvantage is that operating segment classifications across firms are not uniform, and inter-firm comparisons of segment information are difficult.

For each major segment, firms must report:

1. Profit or loss,
2. Total assets, and
3. A number of other amounts, such as revenue from external customers and depreciation expense, but only if those amounts are included in the profit or loss measure used by the chief operating decision maker.

The measurement of each segment item (listed above) is the *amount used by the chief operating decision maker. These amounts need not comply with GAAP.* Recall that for internal purposes, managers can use whatever information they find relevant. The FASB has now mandated that these internal measures be reported to the public (which includes a firm's competitors). Firms must also explain how the measurements are made and some of them must be reconciled to figures appearing on the GAAP-based financial statements.

Geographic Areas

A firm is also required to report information about its activities in different geographic areas. In particular, a firm must *separately report revenue generated from its country of domicile and revenue generated in all foreign countries.* A firm must also report long-lived assets located in the country of domicile and long-lived assets located in all foreign countries. If any of the above amounts attributed to an individual foreign country is material, separate disclosure is required.

Because political stability varies considerably from country to country, information about foreign activities is particularly helpful in assessing a firm's risk. The safety of a firm's assets in a relatively unstable country or the continuity of sales in such a country might be highly uncertain. This is an important consideration in estimating risk. For example, ICN Pharmaceuticals, Inc. reported $147,351,000 impairment charges as part of its loss from discontinued operations in 2002 relating to its Russian, Hungary, and Czech Republic operations. These impairment charges were required because the carrying value of the long-lived assets pertaining to these operations exceeded their fair market values. ICN Pharmaceutical's income from continuing operations was $84,245,000 but with the impairment charges and other smaller items the company reported a net loss of over $134,000,000.

Major Customers

A customer is considered to be a **major customer** if it accounts for 10 percent or more of a firm's revenue. *Total revenue generated by each major customer must be disclosed as well as the operating segment that services the client; the customer need not be identified.* This information provides insights into the *risk associated with a firm's revenue stream.* Greater risk is indicated if a few customers from one segment account for a large portion of revenue. If customers from that segment concurrently experience economic difficulties, the firm's revenue may suffer significantly. Moreover, a customer who accounts for a sizable portion of revenue may be able to demand significant concessions, which could have an unfavorable effect on the firm's future financial performance.

An Illustration

Exhibit VIII-1 contains segment information for Global Enterprises, Inc., which has three operating segments:

EXHIBIT VIII-1 INTERNATIONAL ENTERPRISES, INC, SEGMENT REPORTING DISCLOSURE

Operating Segment and Geographic Area Disclosures
(Dollars in millions)

	CHEMICAL SPECIALTIES	FOOD & FUNCTIONAL PRODUCTS	AEROSPACE	CORPORATE & OTHER	TOTAL
OPERATING SEGMENTS					
2007					
Net Sales	$900	$800	$700	$200	$2,600
Profit (Loss) from Operations	150	100	120	(50)	320
Total Assets	650	700	600	250	2,200
Depreciation	60	50	55	20	185
2006					
Net Sales	825	770	650	180	2,425
Profit (Loss) from Operations	130	80	60	(45)	225
Total Assets	630	675	580	225	2,110
Depreciation	55	45	50	15	165

GEOGRAPHIC AREA	U.S.	FOREIGN	TOTAL
2007			
Net Sales	$1,600	$1,000	$2,600
Long-Lived Assets	1,000	500	1,500
2006			
Net Sales	1,400	1,025	2,425
Long-Lived Assets	970	480	1,450

1. Chemical Specialties produces chemicals for use by paper manufacturers and water-soluble polymers that enhance the storage and usage of liquid products.
2. Food and Functional Products produces items such as food gums used in processed meats and baked goods as well as fat substitutes.
3. Aerospace provides propulsion systems for virtually all space and military programs.

Based on sales and assets, the segments are generally of comparable size. To assess the relative profitability of the three segments, divide operating profit by assets. This is similar to the return on assets calculation discussed in Chapter 4. The results for 2007 are:

- Chemical Specialties 23.1%
- Food and Functional Products 14.3%
- Aerospace 20.0%

Segment data can also help analysts assess risks and future trends. For example, the success of Global's low-fat products will depend on consumer attitudes regarding their diets and their efforts to "eat right." In contrast, the aerospace segment's success will be determined by its capability to adapt to a post-Cold War environment. The trend in the profitability of the aerospace segment is quite favorable; its profit doubled in 2007 over the previous year.

Exhibit VIII-1 also contains disclosures by geographic area. The majority of Global's sales take place in the United States, although about 38 percent of its sales occur in other countries. Thus, for example, the attitudes of consumers in both the United States and abroad will affect the success of Global's low-fat products.

ANNUAL REPORTS

All publicly held corporations and many closely held ones issue their financial statements as part of an **annual report** to shareholders. Because these reports are a major means of communicating with shareholders, corporations take great care in their preparation. The reports are usually prepared on glossy paper, contain interesting photographs, and are sometimes quite lengthy. The 2005 annual report of Amgen, Inc., a global biotechnology company, for example, is over 100 pages long. Excerpts from annual reports for Wal-Mart, Inc., eBay, Inc., and Target, Inc. are provided in the appendices (Appendices A, B, C).

In addition to the financial statements and the related notes, annual reports include the following information:

1. an introductory letter by the chief executive officer highlighting the year's performance and commenting on prospects for the future,
2. a review of the types of businesses in which the firm is involved,
3. a financial summary (sales, net income, and so on) for each of the five or 10 most recent years,
4. management's discussion and analysis of the firm's liquidity, capital resources, and operations,
5. a statement by management acknowledging its responsibility to prepare the financial statements and maintain an adequate system of internal controls. In addition, certification statements signed by the chief executive and chief financial officers are included acknowledging their personal responsibility for the accuracy of the financial statements.
6. the auditor's report expressing an opinion on the fairness of the financial statements,
7. quarterly financial data,
8. stock price and dividend data, and
9. a listing of officers and directors, along with a limited description of their backgrounds.

Management's discussion and analysis (MDA) is one of the newest and most informative sections of the annual report. As noted in item 4, it includes a discussion of liquidity, capital resources, and operations. MDA contains an analysis of past performance and known trends. It also identifies the underlying economic causes of the observed trends.

In addition, MDA provides two types of information about the future. First, management may know of existing circumstances that will have an impact on future operations. For example, the planned sale of a firm's subsidiary will affect both operations and liquidity. Second, management might also comment on anticipated trends and their effect on the firm's future. An illustration of this type of analysis might be a sales forecast based on macroeconomic factors, such as an impending recession or higher interest rates.

Refer to the MDA section in Wal-Mart's annual report in Appendix A, which includes a discussion on trends in revenues, expenses, and income, as well as expectations about sales levels in 2005. A discussion of financial condition and liquidity is also provided by most companies in their MDA section.

INTERIM REPORTING

Annual financial statements are usually issued between one and three months after a firm's fiscal year-end. Given that firms' transactions occur on an ongoing basis throughout the year, many analysts feel that annual financial statements do not report information in a timely manner. Because of this, all publicly held corporations and many closely held companies report financial information on an interim basis throughout the year. Most firms undertaking such **interim reporting** do so quarterly.

Interim financial statements are usually highly abbreviated and contain only limited disclosures in notes. Moreover, they are not audited. Thus, although interim financial statements are more timely, they are not as comprehensive or as reliable as annual financial statements.

In general, interim financial statements are prepared based on the same accounting principles as a firm's annual financial statements. However, two exceptions exist. First, interim financial statements frequently require the use of additional estimates. For example, many firms do not undertake a physical count of inventory at the close of each quarter. Instead, the ending inventory amount and cost of goods sold are estimated.

The second exception concerns expense recognition. Some costs that are expensed for annual purposes are not immediately expensed for interim reporting if they clearly benefit more than one interim period. Instead, these costs are deferred (treated as an asset) and subsequently allocated as an expense to future interim periods.

The ski industry offers a good example. It would be reasonable for a ski area to have a fiscal year that runs from June 1 to May 31. Since May 31 is a low point in their operations, it is a natural time to tally results. Much of a ski area's repair and maintenance activities, however, take place over the ensuing summer months. In general, we know that repairs and maintenance costs are expensed immediately. However, given that the ski industry earns little revenue in the summer months and the repairs and maintenance costs will clearly benefit operations during the upcoming season, immediately expensing such costs will not result in the most useful interim financial information. Instead, these costs are deferred and allocated as an expense to future interim periods based on the revenue generated in those periods.

As the ski area example illustrates, the nature of some businesses is quite seasonal. Consequently, care must be exercised in projecting annual results from interim periods. The accounting profession encourages firms to include in their interim reports the results for the most recent 12-month period.

Refer to Target's annual report contained in Appendix C. You will notice that for the year ended January 28, 2006, the company reported sales revenues of $52,620 million. You might initially think that Target earned a proportionate amount of revenue of $52,620/4 = $13,155 each quarter. However, remember that Target is in the highly seasonal retail business and looking at the company's 2005 quarterly results, the company earned more of its sales revenue ($16,947) in the fourth quarter (November–January).

REPORTS FILED WITH THE SEC

As you know from Chapter 1 the SEC has the legislative authority to regulate the financial disclosures of publicly held corporations. Although the SEC requires firms to file a number of different reports, two of these are of the most interest to us: 10K reports and 10Q reports.

A firm's **10K report** includes virtually all the information contained in its annual report, plus some additional disclosures. These disclosures include information about litigation, executive compensation, and shareholdings by officers and directors. Because 10K reports include such detailed disclosures, they are intended to meet the information needs of rather sophisticated investors. Accordingly, most firms send annual reports to shareholders and make 10K reports available on request.

The second SEC report, the **10Q report,** includes a firm's quarterly financial statements, plus some additional disclosures. These disclosures include information on litigation and defaults on debt securities. Firms usually send quarterly financial statements to shareholders and send 10Q reports on request.

Summary of Learning Objectives

1. **Analyze information about operating segments.**
   Firms are required to make disclosures in financial statements about their major operating segments. This information is intended to help analysts assess the risks and expected returns associated with each business segment.

2. **Describe annual and interim reports.**
   Although this text focuses on financial accounting and the resultant financial statements, the broader context of financial reporting should be considered.

Financial reporting includes financial statements as well as other financial information. Some of this information is contained in annual and interim reports, and includes the president's letter, management's discussion and analysis, and the auditor's report.

3. **Identify reports filed with the Securities and Exchange Commission (SEC).** The most common reports filed with the SEC are 10K and 10Q reports. These reports contain, respectively, a firm's annual and quarterly financial statements, as well as more detailed disclosures. Relatively sophisticated analysts are the primary users of these reports.

KEY TERMS

Annual report
Interim reporting
Major customer
Management discussion and analysis (MDA)
Operating segment
Segment reporting
10K report
10Q report

Exercises and Problems

VIII-1 Describe an industry "segment" and the types of information that must be reported for each segment.

VIII-2 Why are the identifiable assets for each segment shown as part of segment reporting?

VIII-3 Why are profits for each segment shown as part of segment reporting?

VIII-4 Why are domestic and foreign operations separately disclosed? How would this information be helpful to an investor or creditor?

VIII-5 Why is information about a firm's major customers reported as part of the notes on the firm's segment? Why not use a threshold higher than 10% as the criterion for determining who is a major customer?

VIII-6 Describe why a firm with more foreign operations or more large customers (greater than 10% of its volume) might be viewed as having higher risk than a domestic company with many small customers (less than 10%).

VIII-7 Why does a firm's annual report contain so much information in such a variety of formats? Under what circumstances is a more condensed format more useful?

VIII-8 Why are interim reports less reliable and less useful than annual reports? In what major ways do interim reports differ from annual reports?

Segment Reporting

VIII-9 The following (partial) information was provided in the industry segment note in American Household Corporation's 2007 financial statements (dollars in millions):

	Years Ended December 31	
	2007	*2006*
Net sales:		
Health care products	$ 7,885.6	$7,369.1
Food products	997.3	935.8
Agricultural products	83.3	—
Consolidated total	$ 8,966.2	$8,304.9
Income before taxes health care products	$ 1,839.9	$1,836.7
Food products	155.6	152.4
Agricultural products	16.8	—
Corporate	17.5	3.6
Consolidated total	$ 2,029.8	$1,992.7

Total assets on December 31:		
Health care products	$ 8,118.4	$5,165.3
Food products	558.8	504.4
Agricultural products	1,173.9	—
Corporate	11,823.7	2,017.7
Consolidated total	$21,674.8	$7,687.4
Net sales by geographic region:		
United States	$ 5,908.0	$5,695.8
Canada and Latin America	1,022.4	897.7
Europe and Africa	1,422.7	1,196.6
Asia and Australia	613.1	514.8
Consolidated total	$ 8,966.2	$8,304.9

Required

a. For each segment, calculate the return on assets (use end-of-year assets and operating profit) and calculate income before tax as a percent of sales.

b. Evaluate the performance of each segment. Regarding the products and services sold by each segment, comment on concerns and outlooks that an investor might have.

c. Comment on the company's sales in the different geographic regions. How could this impact the investor's evaluation of American Household Corporation's potential future performance?

Evaluation of Segment Disclosure for Two Firms

VIII-10 Examine notes from the financial statements of two different companies to determine how they report segments of their operations. Evaluate the level of disclosure for each firm in terms of the usefulness and relevance of the notes provided by each firm.

Identification of Industry Segments

VIII-11 Locate the most recent 10K filing by Johnson & Johnson Corporation from the EDGAR archives (http://www.sec.gov/edgar/searchedgar/webusers.htm). The 'Notes to the Financial Statements' contain detailed segment information.

Required

a. Identify the major business (industry) segments in which Johnson & Johnson is involved.

b. What is the percentage contribution of each segment to the company's net sales and profit from operations? Which is the most important business segment?

c. For which geographic areas does Johnson & Johnson have a material presence in terms of net sales?

d. In your opinion, is Johnson & Johnson a U.S. company or a global company?

Interim Reporting

VIII-12 Review Note 12 pertaining to the quarterly financial data for Wal-mart Corporation located in Appendix A.

Required

a. Review the annual income statement for the fiscal year ended 1/31/06 and the financial data for the four quarters and evaluate any seasonal trends in these quarterly numbers.

b. Discuss why Wal-Mart would choose January 31 as its fiscal year-end.

TOPICMOD IX

ACCOUNTING RESEARCH AND THE EFFICIENT MARKET HYPOTHESIS

Learning Objectives

1. *Explain the efficient market hypothesis (EMH) and its implications for accounting.*
2. *Understand why accounting researchers are concerned with the EMH.*

ACCOUNTING INFORMATION AND THE EFFICIENT MARKET HYPOTHESIS

Although accounting and finance researchers have now studied the **efficient market hypothesis (EMH)** for several decades, it remains rather controversial. This section describes the EMH and summarizes its implications for accounting. We included this TOPICMOD as an example of the linkages between accounting research and business practice. We do not expect you to solve any numerical problems in this area!

The Efficient Market Hypothesis

The EMH states that publicly available information is fully reflected in share prices. That is, once a corporation releases information (for example, quarterly net income), that information is quickly and unbiasedly reflected in share prices. This implies that a trading strategy based on publicly available information will not be particularly successful.

Considerable evidence exists indicating that share prices react very quickly to accounting information. Exhibit IX-1 shows the results of a study that examined the number of extreme price changes that occurred when a sample of firms released their earnings announcements. As can be seen, most of the price changes occurred within a few hours of the announcement. Thus, unless one acts very quickly, no especially large profits are available by trading based on reported earnings announcements.

Not all research evidence, however, is consistent with the EMH. Some studies have shown that sizable abnormal returns can be earned from an analysis of publicly available financial statements. These returns exceed typical transaction costs (such as brokerage commissions), suggesting that a net profit could be made.

Overall, the research evidence regarding the EMH is conflicting. As you progress through your business education, pay particular attention to new evidence that pertains to this issue.

Implications of the EMH

The EMH has important messages for corporate managers and individual investors. Acceptance of the EMH should suggest to corporate managers that any attempt to affect their share price by using accounting ploys to influence reported earnings is not likely to be successful. For example, inflating earnings by selecting an income-increasing accounting principle will not fool financial statement readers. They will recognize that the increase in income was not due to improvements in the underlying profitability of the firm. Of course, rejection of the EMH could lead to a different inference.

Individual investors who accept the EMH would conclude that they are unable to earn abnormal profits by developing trading strategies based on publicly available information. Accordingly, selecting investments by analyzing annual reports will not prove profitable. The information in these reports is already reflected in share prices by the time the investor is able to obtain the

EXHIBIT IX-1 MARKET REACTION TO EARNINGS ANNOUNCEMENTS

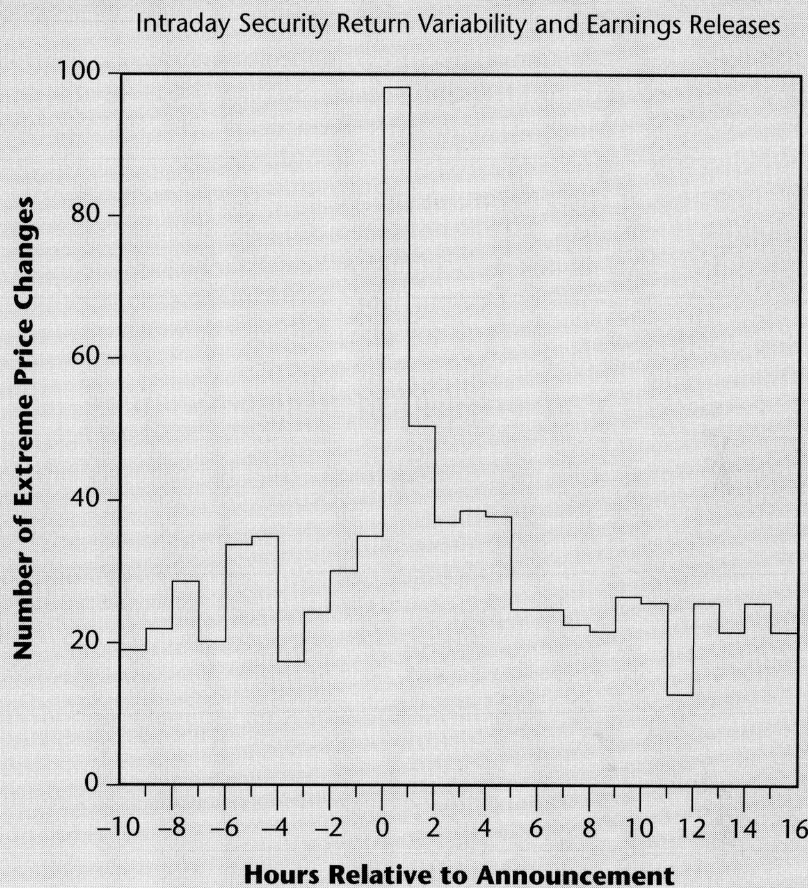

SOURCE: J. M. Patell and M. A. Wolfson, "The Intraday Speed of Adjustment of Stock Prices to Earnings and Dividend Announcements," *Journal of Financial Economics,* 1984, p. 240.

report. These investors would be inclined to diversify their investments, perhaps by choosing mutual funds, which are investment vehicles that own shares in hundreds of corporations. By owning a small part of many companies, an investor's risk is reduced.

Investors who reject the EMH do not feel that share prices necessarily reflect all publicly available information. They feel that a careful analysis of financial statements and other information permits them to identify underpriced securities. Assuming that prices eventually gravitate to their "true values", these stocks represent a favorable investment opportunity.

Accepting the EMH may raise a question about the usefulness of financial statements. If financial statements cannot be used to identify profitable investments, are they of any use? The answer is clearly yes. Even though no individual will be able to earn abnormal profits by trading on the information contained in financial statements, all investors benefit from the disclosure of that information. Financial statements help stock markets identify relatively efficient companies. Capital resources can then be allocated to those firms, and overall wealth is expanded. Financial statements can also be used in corporate buyouts. By identifying inefficient firms (those firms whose managers are not effectively utilizing assets), takeover firms can select targets.

Also keep in mind that the EMH applies mostly to large, organized stock markets. Financial statements can be very useful in valuing closely held companies that are not publicly traded. Financial statements can also be used in credit-granting decisions, labor negotiations, and a variety of other situations.

Summary of Learning Objectives

1. **Explain the efficient market hypothesis (EMH) and its implications for accounting.**
   Despite considerable research effort, the validity of the EMH remains unsettled. Proponents believe that managers cannot fool the stock market with accounting gimmicks, and that investors cannot reap abnormal profits by using trading strategies based on publicly available information. Critics of the EMH believe that share prices do not reflect all publicly available information, and that investors can develop profitable strategies based on a variety of information sources.

2. **Understand why accounting researchers are concerned with the EMH.**
   Accounting researchers test whether new accounting rules have an impact on share prices. Under the EMH, the announcement of new policies should have more impact on share prices than the effective date of the new policies. Financial statements help stock markets efficiently adjust stock prices.

KEY TERM

Efficient market hypothesis (EMH)

Exercises and Problems

IX-1 Describe the efficient market hypothesis (EMH). How does it affect financial statement analysis as described in this text?

IX-2 Assume that a firm changes from FIFO to LIFO during a period of rising prices. Would a proponent of the EMH predict an increase or decrease in the firm's share price as a result of the change in inventory valuations? Why?

IX-3 Why do price-to-earnings (P/E) ratios differ between firms?

TOPICMOD X

CAREERS IN ACCOUNTING

Learning Objectives

1. *Describe the major industry segments in accounting.*
2. *Describe several career options in accounting.*

INTRODUCTION

The field of accounting offers a variety of interesting and challenging career opportunities. In fact, Money magazine ranked accounting one of the most popular occupations. Accounting was rated high in short-term outlook, job security, and prestige. It was rated low in stress and strain. (Try telling that to a tax accountant on April 14!) This TOPICMOD describes possible accounting career choices.

Many people, who begin their careers as accountants, remain accountants throughout their work lives. Others use accounting as a stepping- stone. For example, some members of congress are accountants, and at least one TV star (Bob Newhart) is a former accountant. Moreover, many chief executive officers have accounting backgrounds.

The American Institute of CPAs (AICPA) has compiled a summary of the placement results of recent college graduates. It shows the following:

	Bachelor's	Master's
Public accounting	29%	53%
Business/industry	21	15
Government	3	2
Nonprofit	2	1
Other areas	2	2
Graduate school	17	1
Unknown	26	26
Total	100%	100%

SOURCE: *The Supply of Accounting Graduates and the Demand for Public Recruits—2005,* AICPA.

Although this text concentrates on financial accounting, a wide array of accounting careers is possible.

PUBLIC ACCOUNTING

CPA firms are the most visible employer of accountants. This visibility, in part, stems from the auditing relationship that CPA firms have with the very largest corporations. The financial statements of all publicly held companies are accompanied by an auditor's report, thereby providing CPA firms with significant publicity. Additionally, CPA firms have recently undertaken advertising campaigns costing millions of dollars. These firms regularly place advertisements in business publications such as *The Wall Street Journal* and *Fortune.* They also utilize television commercials. One firm has even aired a commercial during the Super Bowl!

CPA firms provide three primary services: auditing, tax preparation and planning, and management consulting. These services and the associated career opportunities are discussed in the following sections.

Auditing

As you know, a major role of CPA firms is to audit financial statements. The purpose of an audit is to ascertain if the statements comply with generally accepted accounting principles (GAAP). In essence, audits enhance the reliability of financial statements.

CPA firms generally have four hierarchical levels:

1. partners,
2. managers,
3. senior accountants, and
4. staff accountants.

Most CPA firms hire recent college graduates as staff accountants. These individuals have excellent educational backgrounds, but usually little or no practical experience. Accordingly, firms provide both formal and on-the-job training.

Staff accountants perform the "pick and shovel" work on an audit. Typical tasks include conducting test counts of inventory, sending letters to the client's customers to confirm accounts receivable, preparing and reviewing bank reconciliation's, and verifying payroll withholdings. Computer-based tests and analyses have replaced much of the drudgery associated with these tasks.

After two or three years of experience, many staff accountants are promoted to senior accountant. Senior accountants' responsibilities are much more interesting than those of staff accountants. Seniors play a major role in planning the audit. This entails specifying the audit tests necessary for a particular client. Seniors also supervise the fieldwork. That is, they oversee the staff accountants who perform the audit tests at the client's place of business.

After a total of five or six years of experience, some candidates are promoted to manager. Managers, along with senior accountants, participate in planning the audit. They supervise senior accountants and review the work of both senior and staff accountants. Managers also have significant interactions with the client's upper-level management. The auditor and the client must make many joint decisions, such as the timing of fieldwork.

After a total of about 12 years of employment in large firms, successful candidates are promoted to partner. Less time is usually needed in smaller firms. Partners are ultimately responsible for the quality of an audit. They confer with the manager and senior accountant regarding difficult or sensitive problems. They are also the primary liaison with the client's top executives. In addition, a major part of their job entails practice development, such as getting new clients and retaining current clients. CPA firms are, after all, businesses that need clients in order to generate revenues and profits.

Tax

A major function of CPA firms is to assist clients with their taxes. Both individuals and business organizations, such as corporations, need this help. In general, CPAs provide two types of tax services. One is tax compliance, which entails completing tax returns at year-end. The other service is **tax planning** which involves structuring transactions in order to minimize their tax effects.

Staff accountants and senior accountants are highly involved in **tax compliance.** Managers and partners review the work of staff and seniors and also provide clients with tax planning advice.

An increasingly important area is international tax. The globalization of business is prompting many corporations to conduct their affairs in more than one country. This requires knowledge of the tax laws of those countries, and the tax treaties among those countries.

Management Consulting

Members of CPA firms are widely recognized not only for their expertise in accounting, auditing, and taxes, but also for their overall business knowledge. Because of this, CPA firms offer a wide variety of consulting services to their clients. Perhaps the most prominent service is the installation of computerized information systems. Other services include employee benefits, mergers and acquisitions, and health care consulting.

CPA firms have been extremely successful in their consulting endeavors. For example, a recent survey by the AICPA showed that small businesses were three times more likely to seek advice from their CPA than from any other source.

Characteristics of CPA Firms

CPA firms can be described based on several characteristics. This section summarizes many important aspects of CPA firms.

Organizational Form

CPA firms have traditionally been organized as sole proprietorships or partnerships. Recall that the owners of these organizations have unlimited legal liability. That is, their personal assets are available to meet all obligations of the business.

The individual states, which regulate the accounting profession, have been reluctant to permit accounting firms to organize as corporations. Many regulators feel that professionals (doctors, lawyers, accountants) should be fully responsible for their actions and should not enjoy the shield of limited liability provided by corporations.

An excellent counterargument exists, however. Consider a national CPA firm with offices in many cities. Let's assume that one of the firm's owners in the Boston office conducts a faulty audit and that the firm is sued. Should the personal assets of the firm's owners who work in, say, the Seattle office be available to satisfy any claims that may arise? These owners had nothing to do with the faulty audit, and might have only a passing acquaintance with the owner from the Boston office.

The accounting profession is currently seeking ways to limit the exposure of CPAs for damages arising from the actions of others. In many states, several organizational forms have recently become available to CPAs. Two of these are professional corporations and limited liability partnerships. Both of these organizational forms place limits on the liability of owners for acts committed by other owners. Owners, however, are still fully responsible for the consequences of their own acts. Accounting firms that conduct business in only one state typically use professional corporations. Firms that operate in two or more states use limited liability partnerships.

Size

CPA firms vary dramatically in size. Many CPA firms consist of only an owner and maybe a few employees. In contrast, a number of CPA firms are extremely large international organizations. Exhibit X-1 contains a listing of the eight largest public accounting firms in the United States. The largest four firms are often referred to as the "Big Four" (prior to Arthur Andersen's demise, they were the "Big Five"). To gain an appreciation for their size, examine the columns labeled "Number of Professional Staff" and "Number of Offices". You can see that they are considerably larger than the other firms listed.

Of course, many medium-sized CPA firms exist. Without doubt, the public's best interest is served by a wide array of firm sizes. For example, small individual taxpayers (like us) might appreciate the personal attention (and relatively low fees) of a small or midsize firm. In contrast, a large international corporation will need the services of a large CPA firm that has multiple offices and specializes in international and domestic taxes and auditing.

The last three columns of Exhibit X-1 show the services emphasized by each firm. Most firms focus on accounting, auditing, and taxes. Most firms now earn a small portion of their revenues from consulting services.

EXHIBIT X-1 **LARGEST U.S. PUBLIC ACCOUNTING FIRMS**

		REVENUE FYE						Revenue Split (%)		
	Firm	U.S. Net	% Chg. vs. Prev. Year	No. of Partners	No. of Prof. Staff	No. of Offices	No. of SEC Clients	A&A	Tax	MCS
1	Deloitte	$6,876.0	5.6	2,568	20,273	107	3,597	40	26	30
2	Ernst & Young	5,511.0	4.0	2,000	16,489	95	2,856	67	30	0
3	PricewaterhouseCoopers	5,180.0	11.0	1,983	17,754	99	3,303	63	29	0
4	KPMG	3,808.0	8.5	1,585	11,866	95	1,893	72	28	0
5	Grant Thornton	718.0	27.0	407	2,843	48	367	53	30	18
6	RSM McGladrey	661.0	12.8	453	2,801	103	106	42	34	22
7	BDO Seidman	440.0	20.5	238	1,495	35	358	62	26	12
8	CBIZ/Mayer Hoffman McGann	373.5	6.7	231	1,610	35	30	23	27	50

SOURCE: *Public Accounting Report,* Copyright © 2005 by CCH Incorporated, 4025 W. Peterson Ave., Chicago, IL 60646. 800-449-8114.

Compensation

Exhibit X-2 summarizes salary information for several U.S. cities and the nation as a whole. Salaries vary considerably based on location. This variation reflects both the cost of living differences and supply and demand factors.

Based on levels within the firm, the biggest jump in compensation occurs between manager and partner. This makes sense, given that a manager is simply an employee of the firm, whereas a partner is an owner.

Exhibit X-2 contains averages for firms of all sizes. Compensation is usually higher in the larger firms. For example, partners in Big Four firms earn in excess of a quarter of a million dollars annually.

Overtime

Employees of CPA firms have very demanding work schedules, largely due to the needs of their clients. All individual taxpayers must file their returns by April 15. Calendar year-end corporations must file their returns by March 15, and publicly held corporations with a calendar year-end must submit their audited financial statements by March 31.

Clearly, January through April are busy months for CPA firms. Employees of CPA firms work substantial overtime during this period. Average work weeks of 60 hours (or more) are common.

Fortunately, there can be a silver lining to the overtime cloud. Some firms provide a leisure bank. Overtime hours worked during busy seasons enable employees to take additional vacation days during slow seasons. Most firms also provide the option of monetary compensation for overtime hours.

Travel

Large CPA firms have large clients, who have a number of geographic locations. Many employees of large CPA firms undertake some out-of-town travel. The auditing and management consulting staffs do most of the traveling. Although

EXHIBIT X-2 ACCOUNTING SALARIES

TITLE & EXPERIENCE	LARGE FIRMS	SMALL FIRMS
Entry level (Up to 1 year)	$41,750–$47,000	$34,000–$39,250
Staff (1–3 years)	47,000–55,000	38,000–45,000
Senior (3–5 years)	55,000–69,000	45,000–57,000
Manager (6–9 years)	68,000–92,000	57,750–69,000
Partner	Data not available	

Adapted from: *2005 Salary Guide,* Robert Half International, Inc., Menlo Park, CA, 2005, p. 16.

generalizations are difficult, two or three weeks of travel each year is a reasonable average. The tax staff usually travels considerably less.

CORPORATE (INDUSTRY) ACCOUNTING

Accountants who work in corporate settings perform a wide array of functions. The following sections describe general accounting, internal auditing, taxes, cost accounting, and budgeting.

General Accounting

Corporations are, of course, responsible for the preparation of their financial statements. This is a significant task, particularly for large corporations. Because of this, corporations employ many accountants to generate the information needed for financial statements.

Corporations are also subject to other reporting requirements. For example, lenders will sometimes ask for more detailed information than that found in financial statements. As another example, corporations must prepare SEC registration statements when they sell securities to the public. These and other requirements increase the need for general accounting personnel.

Internal Auditing

Virtually all large corporations, and many midsize ones, have **internal audit** staffs. A primary objective of an internal audit is the same as that of an external audit performed by public accountants: to help ensure the reliability of financial statements.

However, the role of internal auditing is somewhat broader. It also includes operational auditing, which assesses the effectiveness and efficiency of the corporation's operations. In part, this entails determining if internal policies are being followed. For example, many firms have a policy of paying quickly for purchases so that favorable discounts can be taken. Internal audits periodically assess if this policy is actually followed. Internal audits can also deal with much more complex issues, such as compliance with environmental laws and regulations.

Taxes

Tax accountants who work for corporations participate in the two primary tax-related activities of compliance and planning. Compliance can be quite complex for large corporations that operate in a number of jurisdictions. Federal tax returns must be completed, as well as multiple state returns. If the corporation operates in other nations, foreign returns must be compiled. Tax accountants are also responsible for returns related to payroll taxes, sales taxes, real estate taxes, and personal property taxes.

Tax planning is also a major responsibility for corporate tax accountants. The area of mergers and acquisitions is an increasingly important one for tax planning. It involves important issues such as these:

1. Should the target corporation's stock or the underlying assets be acquired?
2. Should the acquisition be funded by issuing stock, using available cash, or incurring new debt?

Careful attention to these questions can have a large impact on the amount of taxes paid.

Cost Accounting

It is crucially important for corporations to know the cost of the products and services that they produce. Without such knowledge, the profitability of different products and customers cannot be measured. This could result in unwise business decisions.

Calculating product costs in single-product firms is relatively straightforward. All manufacturing costs are related to that one product and are included in its cost. **Cost accounting** becomes much more difficult in multi-product firms. In these firms, the same manufacturing facility is frequently used to produce several (perhaps many) products. Because of this, the cost of the facility must be allocated to the various products. The basis for such allocations is frequently not obvious, and cost accountants must decide how the costs are to be assigned to each product.

Cost accountants also accumulate information to help in controlling costs. For example, an important cost in many organizations is inventory handling costs, which include receiving, shipping, and storage costs. Knowing the amount spent on these activities is an essential ingredient to controlling the costs.

Budgeting

To be successful, corporations must identify goals and develop plans to achieve those goals. Budgets are quantitative expressions of corporate plans and reflect a corporation's expectations regarding future results. Realistic budgets help identify profitable opportunities. Moreover, the departure of actual results from budget targets will suggest areas in need of corrective action. Accountants play a major role in **budgeting.** In conjunction with operating personnel, they develop forecasts of future operations. Accountants then trace through the effects of these forecasted operations on various financial statement items. For example, forecasts of sales and costs are a prerequisite for cash flow planning. That is, accountants will assess the impact and timing of forecasted sales and costs on cash to ascertain if future borrowings will be needed or if excess cash will be generated.

Personnel Policies

Corporations differ considerably regarding overtime, travel, training, and so on. Every situation is different, and job candidates should be careful to ask the necessary questions.

Compensation also varies, but surveys have been done that provide average salary figures. Exhibit X-3 contains entry-level averages for several types of corporate accounting positions. There is little variation across position categories, although there are considerable geographic differences. The exhibit also contains average salaries for controllers, who are the chief accounting officers in corporations.

OTHER OPPORTUNITIES

Accountants are employed by many different organizations. Virtually all governmental units (federal, state, and local) rely on accountants to monitor their flow of funds. The Internal Revenue Service (IRS) employs a large number of tax accountants to interpret tax laws, provide assistance to taxpayers, and audit returns. Not-for-profit organizations, such as certain hospitals and charitable organizations, also need the services of accountants, who perform many of the same tasks in these organizations as those undertaken in corporations.

CERTIFICATION

Potential employers and the public at large have an interest in identifying competent accountants. To assist in this process, several professional organizations have established certification programs. For example, the Institute of Management Accountants operates the **Certified Management Accountant (CMA)** program.

EXHIBIT X-3 CORPORATE ACCOUNTING SALARIES

	COMPANY SIZE		
TITLE	**Large**	**Medium**	**Small**
CFO, Treasurer	$296,000	$133,000	$ 98,000
Vice President, Finance	$241,000	$139,000	$ 87,000
Director of Finance	$150,000	$106,000	$ 85,000
Director of Accounting	$136,000	$ 99,000	$ 78,000
Controller	$127,000	$ 94,000	$ 67,000
Assistant Controller/Assistant Treasurer	$102,000	$ 75,000	$ 55,000
General, Audit, Tax, and Cost Accountants	$ 38,000	$ 36,000	$ 33,000
Financial, Budget, Treasury, and Cost Analysts	$ 37,000	$ 36,000	$ 33,000
Bookkeepers	$ 30,000	$ 30,000	$ 30,000
Accounts Receivables/Payables Manager	$ 50,000	$ 42,000	$ 36,000
Accounts Receivables/Payables Clerk	$ 31,000	$ 29,000	$ 28,000
Payroll Manager/Supervisor	$ 53,000	$ 44,000	$ 36,000
Payroll Clerk	$ 31,000	$ 30,000	$ 28,000

Adapted from: *2005 Salary Guide*, Robert Half International, Inc., Menlo Park, CA, 2005, pp. 8–15.

Other certification programs include **Certified Internal Auditor (CIA)** and **Certified Fraud Examiner (CFE).** Some certificate programs outside of the accounting field (Certified Financial Analyst) also require knowledge of accounting. To become certified, accountants submit their credentials for evaluation against standardized criteria established by the sponsoring organization. Most certificate programs require candidates to have a specified educational background, pass a rigorous exam, and have a certain amount of work experience. The following sections describe the two most well known certificates: CPA and CMA.

Certified Public Accountant

The most widely known and widely held certificate is the **Certified Public Accountant (CPA).** In fact, becoming a CPA involves more than receiving the blessing of a private organization. CPAs, like doctors and lawyers, are licensed by the individual states. Each state has its own specific licensing requirements. This section provides a general overview of these requirements.

Education

Most states require at least a bachelor degree and a specified array of accounting and related business courses. Many states require at least 24 semester hours of accounting. Courses might include intermediate financial accounting, intermediate managerial accounting, auditing, and taxes. Approximately 24 semester hours in other business courses, such as management, economics, finance, business law, and information systems, are also required.

There is a strong movement among the states to require 150 semester hours, rather than 120, for licensing. The rationale for this change is that both business in general, and accounting in particular, are becoming so complex that an adequate introduction to these topics requires 150 hours. The AICPA recommends the following allocation of semester hours:

General education	60–80
Education in business administration	35–50
Accounting education	25–40

The 150-hour requirement has been implemented or is being phased in by more than 40 states. Some states, including Colorado, have rescinded the 150-hour requirement. Of course, CPAs who have 120 semester hours and are licensed prior to adoption of the 150-hour provision retain their licenses.

The CPA Exam

All states require candidates to pass the Uniform CPA Exam, developed by the AICPA. The exam used to be given twice a year, on the first Wednesday and

Thursday in May and November. It was an exhausting experience, taking exams for two full days!

As of April 5, 2004, the Uniform CPA Examination is now offered on a computer-based format at Prometric and state-board authorized test centers across the United States. The test is offered up to six days a week, during two out of every three months throughout the year. Eligible candidates are able to take any or all sections of the exam during any of the testing windows, but are not be allowed to take the same section of the exam twice during any testing window.

The exam has four parts:

1. Auditing and Attestation (4½ hours)
2. Financial Accounting and Reporting (4 hours)
3. Regulation (3 hours)
4. Business Environment and Concepts (2½ hours)

In addition to the new computer-based format, the exam now emphasizes more information technology and general business knowledge. The exam also has a new component called "simulations" which are condensed case studies designed to test the candidates research and writing skills. For example, a candidate researching an income tax question may be required to perform an electronic search of the Internal Revenue Code and income tax regulations to answer questions within the simulation and to provide the answers in the form of a brief business memo or letter. Refer to www.cpa-exam.org for more information on the CPA exam.

Work Experience

Most states require one to three years of public accounting experience as a condition of licensing. Some states permit alternative work experiences, such as internal auditing. A few states have no experience requirement.

Other Requirements

Many states require CPA candidates to pass an ethics exam. Most candidates complete a self-study course to prepare for this exam. Some states also have residency or employment requirements.

Nearly all states also require that their certificate holders engage in ongoing continuing professional education. This requirement usually involves 40 hours of training per year that is designed to enhance the competence of CPAs.

Career Implications

Individuals are precluded from practicing public accounting without being a CPA. Thus, a CPA certificate is public accounting's entry requirement. (Keep in mind that you can work for a CPA firm without being a CPA.) However, in evaluating job candidates, many employers use easily implemented screening criteria, of which a CPA license is one. As a result, corporations, governmental units, and other organizations employ many CPAs.

Ethical decisions can have a significant impact on an accountant's career. "Whistle-blowers" are often stigmatized and have trouble getting a job at the same level as before they "went public." We are only trying to suggest that there is a significant cost associated with maintaining a high ethical standard. On the other hand, there is a high cost of not doing so. Reality Check X-1 illustrates how one person's career was destroyed over some "cover-ups" at Tyco.

Certified Management Accountant

The CMA program has four objectives:

1. to establish management accounting as a recognized profession by identifying the role of the management accountant and financial manager, the underlying body of knowledge, and a course of study by which such knowledge is acquired;
2. to encourage higher educational standards in the management accounting field;
3. to establish an objective measure of an individual's knowledge and competence in the field of management accounting; and
4. to encourage continued professional development by management accountants.

Education

To become a CMA, a candidate must hold a bachelor's degree or a CPA certificate. Although the CMA program does not designate specific course work, the CMA exam, as a practical matter, effectively requires candidates to take a certain array of courses.

The CMA Exam

The CMA exam is a four-part exam intended to measure candidates' knowledge of management accounting and financial management. In addition, the exam assesses candidates' abilities to analyze information and to communicate the results of that analysis. Ethical responsibilities are also addressed throughout the exam. The CMA exam's four parts are

1. Economics, Finance, and Management
2. Financial Accounting and Reporting
3. Management Reporting, Analysis, and Behavioral Issues
4. Decision Analysis and Information Systems

REALITY CHECK X-1

Example of a Poor Ethical Decision Ruining an Accountant's Career

Auditor's career ruined after not disclosing details of Tyco's accounts!

The public expects independent auditors to carefully review the financial statements and accounts of companies they oversee, partly to protect shareholders from fraud. Auditing careers can be effectively constrained or terminated by the SEC when it determines that a public accountant is not protecting the public's interests.

Richard P. Scalzo, a partner at PricewaterhouseCoopers who was the chief outside auditor for *Tyco International*, was accused by the Securities and Exchange Commission (SEC) of *issuing fraudulent reports and engaging in improper professional conduct* over a five-year period from 1997–2001. For example, the SEC alleges that he did not require disclosure of bonus details and other perquisites paid to Tyco executives and he did not object to Tyco's use of an undisclosed reserve fund to absorb unexpected expenses. The SEC banned Mr. Scalzo from practicing before the Commission as an accountant, effectively ruining his auditing career.

"Investors rely on auditors and are betrayed when auditors fail to conduct diligent audits," said Thomas C. Newkirk, associate director for enforcement at the S.E.C. "In this case, senior management was looting the company, and Scalzo was confronted with numerous warning signs about management's integrity. Scalzo is not being sanctioned because he did not discover the looting; he is being charged because he did not look despite these warnings. (p. C1)"

Mr. Scalzo apparently did not raise alarms about Tyco's accounting and he failed to inform Tyco's audit committee. The SEC claimed Mr. Scalzo knew that Tyco maintained a general reserve that it used to offset unanticipated expenses over a five-year period. Such reserves are not allowed under generally accepted accounting principles because they can be used to manipulate profits.

According to the SEC, Mr. Scalzo did not require disclosure of bonuses and loans given to top executives at Tyco. During the 1999 audit, Mr. Scalzo did not require disclosure of a $35.5 million interest-free loan to L. Dennis Kozlowski, Tyco's chief executive, or a similar $8 million interest free loan to Mark H. Swartz, the company's chief financial officer. Although the PricewaterhouseCoopers audit team recommended that Tyco disclose the loans, Tyco argued that the loans were not material and Mr. Scalzo agreed with the company's position and did not require disclosure of the loans.

Mr. Kozlowski granted $96 million in bonuses to 51 Tyco officers and managers after an initial public offering of Tyco's shares in TyCom Ltd. (cable communications). While Mr. Kozlowski and Mr. Swartz received almost $50 million in bonuses, none were disclosed because the company claimed they were not material. Mr. Scalzo agreed.

> Tyco paid Frank E. Walsh, a Tyco director, an undisclosed finder's fee of $20 million in 2001 after spending $10 billion to acquire CIT, a financial services firm. Again Mr. Scalzo was told the fee was immaterial and it was not discussed with Tyco's audit committee.
>
> Mr. Newkirk of the S.E.C. said: "The cumulative impact of all the warning signs that Scalzo missed really is quite astonishing. By the time you get to 2000, it really is quite a sad performance. (p. C4)"
>
> This scenario illustrates how an audit partner of a large CPA firm could have been more diligent in reporting questionable transactions to Tyco's audit committee and to the SEC. Failing to disclose is apparently the major sin of omission that led to Mr. Scalzo's downfall.
>
>

Candidates may register for any number of parts and take the parts in any order; the entire exam must be passed within three years. Each part takes four hours and the entire exam is given over a two-day period in mid-June and mid-December. Candidates who have passed the CPA exam are given credit for Part 2, Financial Accounting and Reporting.

Other Requirements

CMA candidates must have two continuous years of management accounting experience or three years of auditing experience in public accounting. Holders of CMA certificates must meet a continuing professional education requirement that consists of 30 hours per year. Qualifying subjects include management accounting, corporate taxation, finance, computer science, systems analysis, statistics, management skills, insurance, marketing, business law, or other subjects relevant to the certificate holder's career development or employer needs.

WEB SITES

Numerous Web sites are available that provide information and advice about career opportunities and job search strategies. Many of these sites also provide lists of jobs and offer you the opportunity to put your resume on file. Some of these sites are

www.accountingnet.com
www.careerbuilder.com
www.careermag.com
www.craigslist.com
www.hotjobs.com

Each of the Big Four firms has a Web site that describes, among other things, their career opportunities. These sites are

www.us.deloitte.com (Deloitte & Touche)
www.ey.com (Ernst & Young)
www.us.kpmg.com (KPMG)
www.pwcglobal.com/us (Price Waterhouse Coopers)

Finally, several very interesting sites regarding the accounting profession are available.

www.imanet.org
www.aicpa.org
www.fasb.org

THE FUTURE

As with many fields of endeavor, accounting faces continual change. Robert Half International, a leading employment agency specializing in accounting, has identified several factors that will affect accounting as we enter the 21st century. The following sections discuss these factors.

Computers

Computers are a fact of life for every accountant. Even very small organizations have computerized their accounting functions. The widespread use of computers is due to (1) the rapidly declining cost of computers, (2) the increased power of such computers, and (3) the availability of low-cost accounting software.

Accountants must be familiar with both hardware and software. College courses and continuing professional education classes address these issues. Since many computers operate in a similar fashion, most courses focus on software. Most software packages are user-friendly and require no knowledge of computer programming languages. These packages usually include readable instruction manuals, as well as on screen tutorials and help functions.

Although employers often provide training, they also look quite favorably on job candidates who already have some computer expertise. In fact, some employers pay a 5 to 10% premium to candidates who have experience with certain software packages.

Globalization

Businesses are now looking at the entire world as their marketplace. Both corporations and public accounting firms are expanding their international operations, creating the need for accountants with a global view. Accountants need to know the business practices, accounting procedures, language, and social customs of the countries in which their firms operate. Much of this knowledge is gained through experience, but some of it, including language training, can be obtained through formal classes.

Demographics and Personnel Policies

Perhaps the most noteworthy demographic trend in accounting is the increasing number of female accountants. More than half of recent accounting graduates were women. This suggests an increase in two-career couples. Managing two demanding work schedules and a family life is quite difficult. Because of this, organizations are becoming more flexible in their terms of employment. Part-time employment and job-sharing are more commonplace. Some public accounting firms have a partnership track that entails less than full-time work.

Although women comprise a majority of recent accounting graduates, men still dominate the upper levels in most firms (the "glass ceiling" effect). However, the trend is towards more equality. Although a few years ago only 6% of partners in large public accounting firms were female, current statistics indicate that women hold approximately 10% of partnership positions. Firms ensure that their female staff do not feel alienated and are given proper career guidance, due to the formal mentoring programs implemented at most large firms.

Summary of Learning Objectives

1. **Describe the major industry segments in accounting**
   Accounting offers a variety of career opportunities, many of which are rather lucrative. Public accounting firms, corporations, governmental units, and not-for-profit organizations employ accountants.
   Certification is an important step in an accountant's career path. It is an indication of a candidate's qualifications. The most recognized certificate is the CPA. The CMA is, perhaps, the second most recognized certification.

2. **Describe several career options in accounting.**
   The future outlook for accounting jobs is good. Demand for accountants is expected to be strong, and accountants continue to be respected by the business community. Accounting professionals engage in a variety of functions, such as financial accounting, taxes, cost accounting, and budgeting. Ethics have become one of the most important issues that can affect an accountant's career. Accounting is also a road to the top of business organizations; many chief executive officers began their careers as accountants.

KEY TERMS

Budgeting
Certified Fraud Examiner (CFE)
Certified Internal Auditor (CIA)
Certified Management Accountant (CMA)
Certified Public Accountant (CPA)
Cost accounting
Internal audit
Tax compliance
Tax planning

TOPICMOD XI

ACCOUNTING PROCEDURES

Learning Objectives

1. *Prepare and post journal entries.*
2. *Calculate account balances.*
3. *Prepare and post adjusting entries.*
4. *Prepare and post closing entries.*
5. *Generate balance sheets and income statements from general ledger accounts.*

INTRODUCTION

This text focuses on conceptual accounting issues and the uses of accounting information. In contrast, this TOPICMOD summarizes the detailed procedures used by accountants to generate financial statements. Although, in theory, the basic accounting equation can be used to prepare financial statements, virtually all firms would find that approach to be extremely cumbersome. Firms need far more efficient processes when they have hundreds of different assets and liabilities and engage in thousands (or millions!) of transactions.

The General Ledger

Recall from Chapter 2 that the core of financial accounting is the analysis of transactions in terms of the basic accounting equation:

ASSETS = LIABILITIES + OWNERS' EQUITY

The purpose of this analysis is to summarize the effects of different types of transactions on the equation's elements. In real business settings, this summarization is done in the general ledger. Although most accounting systems are computerized, at this stage we will illustrate a manual system. In such a system, the general ledger often takes the form of a loose-leaf notebook. Each page is assigned to a particular equation item (such as cash, inventory, accounts payable, or invested capital) and is referred to as an account.

Debits and Credits

To show increases and decreases in account amounts, plus (+) and minus (−) signs could be used. For several reasons, however, the accounting profession has discarded this alternative. Instead, each account is divided into a left-hand side and a right-hand side; increases are recorded on one side and decreases are recorded on the other.

For all accounts, the left-hand side is the debit (Dr) side and the right-hand side is the credit (Cr) side. For accountants, debit and credit have no meanings other than left and right, respectively. This can be a source of confusion. Many nonaccountants associate the term credit with something good. The accountant does not. Debits and credits are terms that are commonly used under **double-entry accounting.** Entries are made at least twice; at least one debit and at least one credit.

In actual business practice, general ledger accounts can take many forms. For simplicity, they are illustrated here using **T-accounts.** T-accounts for cash and accounts payable are shown as follows:

Cash	
Dr	Cr

Accounts Payable	
Dr	Cr

The side of an account in which increases and decreases are recorded depends on the nature of the account. Increases in assets are recorded by debits, and decreases are recorded by credits. The rules for liabilities and shareholders' equity are the reverse: increases are recorded as credits, and decreases are recorded as debits. These rules are summarized in Exhibit XI-1.

The debit and credit rules are largely arbitrary. Accordingly, with one exception, do not look for any special logic in them. One aspect of the rules does make sense, however. Because assets appear on the opposite side of the basic accounting equation from liabilities and shareholders' equity, the debit and credit rules for assets are the opposite of the rules for liabilities and shareholders' equity. The reasoning for this is discussed later.

An Example

Consider two illustrative transactions. First, shareholders invest $10,000 in a firm. In terms of the basic equation, this transaction increases cash and increases shareholders' equity (invested capital):

In the general ledger, an increase in cash is recorded as a debit, and an increase in shareholders' equity is recorded as a credit. After the analysis, the amounts would appear as follows:

ASSETS	=	LIABILITIES	+	SHAREHOLDERS' EQUITY
Cash + $10,000				Invested capital + $10,000

In the general ledger, an increase in cash is recorded as a debit, and an increase in shareholders' equity is recorded as a credit. After the analysis, the amounts would appear in T-accounts in the ledger as follows:

Cash			Invested Capital	
$10,000				$10,000

EXHIBIT XI-1 DEBIT AND CREDIT RULES

Assets		=	Liabilities		+	Shareholders' Equity	
Dr	Cr		Dr	Cr		Dr	Cr
+	–		–	+		–	+

The second transaction involves a purchase of inventory for $2,000. This transaction increases inventory and decreases cash:

ASSETS		=	LIABILITIES	+	SHAREHOLDERS' EQUITY
Cash	Inventory				
– $2,000	+ $2,000				

The decrease in cash is recorded as a credit, and the increase in inventory is recorded as a debit, as shown in these T-accounts:

Cash	
$10,000	$2,000

Inventory	
$2,000	

As previously mentioned, the rules for assets (which appear on the left side of the equation) are the opposite of the rules for liabilities and shareholders' equity (which appear on the right side of the equation). This is no coincidence. By reversing the rules, the equality of debits and credits for each transaction (and in total) is assured. For example, when inventory is purchased for cash, inventory is debited and cash is credited for $2,000. The equality of debits and credits helps accountants identify and eliminate errors from the accounting process.

Balancing Accounts

To determine the net amount of cash, inventory, and so on at the end of an accounting period, the accounts must be **balanced.** This is done by totaling the debits and credits in each account and calculating their difference. This difference is shown on the side of the account that has the larger amount. These balances are the basis for the financial statements. The balanced cash account shows an $8,000 debit balance:

	Cash	
	10,000	2,000
Bal	8,000	

Chart of Accounts

Firms have a great deal of discretion in choosing their account titles and the number of accounts they employ. Accordingly, most firms develop a **chart of accounts,** which is essentially an index to the general ledger. It lists account titles and account numbers. Account numbers are often employed because they provide a firm's personnel with an efficient and unambiguous way to communicate. Exhibit XI-2 illustrates a chart of accounts.

EXHIBIT XI-2 JACOBS GOLF AND TENNIS CHART OF ACCOUNTS

ACCOUNT	ACCOUNT NUMBER
Cash	110
Accounts Receivable	120
Prepaid Rent	130
Inventory	140
Equipment	150
Accumulated Depreciation	160
Accounts Payable	210
Unearned Revenue	220
Utilities Payable	230
Interest Payable	240
Notes Payable	250
Invested Capital	310
Retained Earnings	320

THE GENERAL JOURNAL

In the general ledger, the information about a given transaction is spread across two or more accounts. This makes it difficult for auditors and others to review all the information about a given transaction. The general journal is another major accounting record. It provides a chronological listing of all transactions and events. This enables the auditor to easily see all the accounts affected by a single transaction. As with the general ledger, the general journal in a manual system consists of a loose-leaf notebook.

Journal Entries

General journal entries are actually the first step in the formal financial accounting process. This step occurs after the accountant has conceptually analyzed the transaction in terms of the basic accounting equation, ascertained which accounts have increased or decreased, and translated the increases and decreases into debits and credits. A transaction's **journal entry** consists of:

1. the date,
2. the account(s) to be debited,
3. the account(s) to be credited,
4. the amounts, and
5. an explanation.

For example, if shareholders invest $10,000 in a firm on January 1, cash is increased and shareholders' equity is increased. Translated into **debits** and **credits,** cash is debited and invested capital is credited. In journal entries, the debits are shown first, and the credits are indented and shown after the debits. The journal entry for the $10,000 investment would be:

January 1

Cash	10,000	
Invested Capital		10,000
To record shareholders' investment		

Notice that the journal contains two separate columns for dollar amounts. The one to the left is for debits and the one to the right is for credits.

Posting

To determine account balances, the amounts in the journal entries need to be placed in the general ledger. Transcribing the amounts from journal entries into the general ledger is called **posting.** From a procedural standpoint, transactions, events, and so on, are never initially entered into the general ledger. **General journal** entries are always prepared and are then posted to the general ledger.

EXHIBIT XI-3 THE ACCOUNTING PROCESS

1. Identify transactions and events.
2. Analyze transactions and events in terms of the basic accounting equation.
3. Translate the transaction analysis into debits and credits.
4. Prepare journal entries and post to the general ledger.
5. Prepare and post adjusting entries.
6. Prepare the income statement.
7. Prepare and post closing entries.
8. Prepare the balance sheet.

Summary

The accounting process includes the steps summarized in Exhibit XI-3. We have covered the first four steps. Later in this TOPICMOD, we will cover the other steps in the accounting process.

AN ILLUSTRATION OF ACCOUNTING PROCEDURES

Chapter 2 provided a comprehensive example involving Jacobs Golf and Tennis (JG&T). JG&T began operations in January 2006 and engaged in a number of transactions. That example is used here to demonstrate the accounting procedures just discussed. The only difference between Chapter 2 and the treatment here is that we now assume that JG&T is organized as a corporation.

Transaction 1: Shareholders invest $50,000.
Analysis: Increase cash; increase invested capital.
Debits and credits: Increase cash (an asset) by a debit: increase invested capital (shareholders' equity) by a credit.
Journal entry:

January 1	Cash	50,000	
	Invested Capital		50,000
	To record investment by shareholders		

Transaction 2: Borrowed $20,000 from a bank.
Analysis: Increase cash; increase notes payable.
Debits and credits: Increase cash by a debit; increase notes payable by a credit.
Journal entry:

January 1	Cash	20,000	
	Notes Payable		20,000
	To record note payable		

Transaction 3: Paid in advance one year's rent of $12,000.
Analysis: Increase prepaid rent; decrease cash.
Debits and credits: Increase prepaid rent by a debit; decrease cash by a credit.
Journal entry:

January 1	Prepaid Rent	12,000	
	Cash		12,000
	To record prepayment of one year's rent		

Transaction 4: Purchased inventory on account, $30,000.
Analysis: Increase inventory; increase accounts payable.
Debits and credits: Increase inventory by a debit; increase accounts payable by a credit.
Journal entry:

January 1	Inventory	30,000	
	Accounts Payable		30,000
	To record the purchase of inventory on account		

Transaction 5: Purchased equipment for $25,000.
Analysis: Increase equipment; decrease cash.
Debits and credits: Increase equipment by a debit; decrease cash by a credit.
Journal entry:

January 1	Equipment	25,000	
	Cash		25,000
	To record purchase of equipment for cash		

At this point, journal entries have been prepared for all of JG&T's preliminary transactions. The next step is to post these entries to general ledger accounts. Exhibit XI-4 contains general ledger accounts that reflect these postings.

EXHIBIT XI-4 JACOBS GOLF AND TENNIS GENERAL LEDGER

Cash

1) 50,000	3) 12,000
2) 20,000	5) 25,000
Bal 33,000	

Prepaid Rent

3) 12,000	

Inventory

4) 30,000	

Equipment

5) 25,000	

Notes Payable

	2) 20,000

Accounts Payable

	4) 30,000

Invested Capital

	1) 50,000

REVENUE AND EXPENSE ACCOUNTS

Revenue and expense transactions affect the retained earnings component of shareholders' equity. For example, if a firm renders services in the amount of $100 to clients, on account, accounts receivable increases and retained earnings increases:

ASSETS	=	LIABILITIES	+	SHAREHOLDERS' EQUITY
Accounts receivable + $100				Retained earnings + $100 (sales)

As you know from Chapter 2, the income statement summarizes the many types of revenue and expense transactions that affect retained earnings during a period. If all revenue and expense transactions were commingled in that one account, ascertaining the detailed amounts for each line item on the income statement would be quite difficult.

Consequently, general ledger accounts are established for each revenue and expense item desired on the income statement. Instead of initially debiting or crediting retained earnings for revenue and expense transactions, the revenue and expense accounts are used. These accounts are best viewed as temporary accounts, which are really components of retained earnings. Increases in revenues are shown as credits, while increases in expenses are treated as debits. Note that expenses reduce retained earnings. Increasing the debit balance in an expense account actually decreases retained earnings. Exhibit XI-5 summarizes the debit and credit rules for revenue and expense accounts.

EXHIBIT XI-5 **DEBIT AND CREDIT RULES FOR REVENUE AND EXPENSE ACCOUNTS**

Revenue		Expense	
Dr	Cr	Dr	Cr
−	+	+	−

To illustrate JG&T's revenue and expense transactions for January 2006, assume that all transactions occur on January 15.

Transaction 6:	Rendered services to customers for $200 plus a promised $400 future payment.		
Analysis:	Increase cash; increase accounts receivable; increase service revenue.		
Debits and credits:	Debit cash by $200; debit accounts receivable by $400; Credit service revenue by $600.		
Journal Entry:			
January 15	Cash	200	
	Accounts Receivable	400	
	Service Revenue		600
	To record service revenue		

The preceding entry is referred to as a **compound journal entry.** Its distinguishing characteristic is that more than one account is either debited or credited (or both). As with all journal entries, the total dollar amount of debits equals the total dollar amount of credits.

Transaction 7:	Received $100 from customers for services to be performed at a later date.		
Analysis:	Increase cash; increase unearned revenue (remember that unearned revenue is a liability).		
Debits and credits:	Debit cash; credit unearned revenue.		
Journal entry:			
January 15	Cash	100	
	Unearned Revenue		100
	To record customers' prepayment of revenue		
Transaction 8:	Paid workers' salaries of $700.		
Analysis:	Decrease cash; decrease retained earnings via salary expense.		
Debits and credits:	Debit salary expense; credit cash		
Journal entry:			
January 15	Salary Expense	700	
	Cash		700
	To record payment of salary expense		
Transaction 9:	Received a $120 utility bill for services already used. Payment was not immediately made.		
Analysis:	Utilities expense increases; utilities payable increases.		
Debits and Credits:	Debit utilities expense; credit utilities payable.		
Journal entry:			
January 15	Utilities Expense	120	
	Utilities Payable		120
	To record January utilities expense		
Transaction 10:	Sold, for $4,000 on account, inventory costing $2,200.		
Analysis:	Accounts receivable increases; sales increase; inventory decreases; cost of goods sold (COGS) increases.		
Debits and credits:	Debit accounts receivable; credit sales; debit COGS; credit inventory.		
Journal entry:			
January 15	Accounts Receivable	4,000	
	Sales		4,000
	To record a credit sale on account		
	COGS	2,200	
	Inventory		2,200
	To record COGS on credit sale		

Exhibit XI-6 contains ledger accounts reflecting the posting of these entries.

ADJUSTING ENTRIES

As you know from Chapter 2, adjustments to the accounting records are typically needed before financial statements are prepared. The adjustments are needed to ensure that the account balances are correct and up to date. These adjustments result from interest accruals, depreciation, and a variety of other matters. **Adjustments** to the account balances are accomplished by journal entries, referred

EXHIBIT XI-6 JACOBS GOLF AND TENNIS GENERAL LEDGER

Cash	
1) 50,000	3) 12,000
2) 20,000	5) 25,000
6) 200	8) 700
7) 100	
Bal 32,600	

Accounts Receivable	
6) 400	
10) 4,000	
Bal 4,400	

Prepaid Rent	
3) 12,000	

Inventory	
4) 30,000	10) 2,200
Bal 27,800	

Equipment	
5) 25,000	

Notes Payable	
	2) 20,000

Accounts Payable	
	4) 30,000

Unearned Revenue	
	7) 100

Utilities Payable	
	9) 120

Invested Capital	
	1) 50,000

Retained Earnings	

Service Revenue	
	6) 600

Sales	
	10) 4,000

Salary Expense	
8) 700	

Utilities Expense	
9) 120	

Cost of Goods Sold	
10) 2,200	

to as **adjusting entries.** We now analyze the adjustments needed to correctly show JG&T's accounts as of January 31.

Transaction 11: Incurred but did not pay interest expense of $133.
Analysis: Increase interest expense; increase interest payable.
Debits and credits: Debit interest expense; credit interest payable.
Journal entry:

January 31	Interest Expense	133	
	Interest Payable		133
	To record January interest expense		

Transaction 12: Used $1,000 of prepaid rent.
Analysis: Increase rent expense; decrease prepaid rent.
Debits and credits: Debit rent expense; credit prepaid rent.
Journal entry:

January 31	Rent Expense	1,000	
	Prepaid Rent		1,000
	To record January rent expense		

Transaction 13: Depreciation on equipment amounted to $208.
Analysis: Increase depreciation expense; decrease equipment by increasing the balance in the contra-asset account, accumulated depreciation.
Debits and credits: Debit depreciation expense; credit accumulated depreciation.
Journal entry:

January 31	Depreciation Expense	208	
	Accumulated Depreciation		208
	To record January depreciation expense		

Transaction 14: Earned $50 of the $100 advance payment previously made by customers.
Analysis: Decrease unearned revenue; increase service revenue.
Debits and credits: Debit unearned revenue; credit service revenue.
Journal entry:

January 31	Unearned Revenue	50	
	Service Revenue		50
	To record revenue earned		

General ledger accounts with these postings appear in Exhibit XI-7. The balances in the revenue and expense accounts are now correct and the income statement, contained in Exhibit XI-8, can be prepared based on the revenue and expense accounts.

CLOSING ENTRIES

At this point, a problem exists in preparing JG&T's balance sheet. Since the revenue and expense transactions, which really affect retained earnings, were not recorded in that account, the balance sheet will not balance. Therefore, the amounts in the revenue and expense accounts must be transferred to retained earnings. This is done via **closing entries.**

JG&T's closing entries at the end of January appear in Exhibit XI-9. Viewed in isolation, closing entries do not make a great deal of sense. However, keep in mind their purpose: to transfer balances from revenue and expense accounts to retained earnings. General ledger accounts that reflect the posting of these entries appear in Exhibit XI-10. The balance now in retained earnings is that which would have been there if all the revenue and expense transactions were initially recorded in that account.

Note that after posting the closing entries, the balance in each revenue and expense account is zero. This is why they are called **temporary (or nominal) accounts.** Moreover, since the balances are zero, next month they will only reflect the revenue and expense amounts for February and not a cumulative amount beginning with January. This will enable the easy preparation of an income statement for the month of February.

DIVIDENDS

JG&T engaged in one more transaction in January. It declared and paid a $100 dividend to the shareholders. The analysis is as follows:

Transaction 17:	Paid dividend of $100.		
Analysis:	Cash decreases; retained earnings decreases.		
Debits and credits:	Debit retained earnings; credit cash.		
Journal entry:			
January 31	Retained Earnings	100	
	Cash		100
	To record dividend		

This entry is also posted in the general ledger accounts appearing in Exhibit XI-10. At this point, all transactions have been journalized and posted, and the revenue and expense accounts have been closed to retained earnings. A balance sheet based on the account balances in Exhibit XI-10 can be prepared as shown in Exhibit XI-11.

EXHIBIT XI-7 JACOBS GOLF AND TENNIS GENERAL LEDGER

Cash

Debit	Credit
1) 50,000	3) 12,000
2) 20,000	5) 25,000
6) 200	8) 700
7) 100	
Bal 32,600	

Accounts Receivable

Debit	Credit
6) 400	
10) 4,000	
Bal 4,400	

Prepaid Rent

Debit	Credit
3) 12,000	12) 1,000
Bal 11,000	

Inventory

Debit	Credit
4) 30,000	10) 2,200
Bal 27,800	

Equipment

Debit	Credit
5) 25,000	

Accumulated Depreciation

Debit	Credit
	13) 208

Notes Payable

Debit	Credit
	2) 20,000

Accounts Payable

Debit	Credit
	4) 30,000

Unearned Revenue

Debit	Credit
14) 50	7) 100
Bal	50

Utilities Payable

Debit	Credit
	9) 120

Interest Payable

Debit	Credit
	11) 133

Invested Capital

Debit	Credit
	1) 50,000

Retained Earnings

Debit	Credit

Service Revenue

Debit	Credit
	6) 600
	14) 50
Bal	650

Sales

Debit	Credit
	10) 4,000

Salary Expense

Debit	Credit
8) 700	

Utilities Expense

Debit	Credit
9) 120	

Cost of Goods Sold

Debit	Credit
10) 2,200	

Interest Expense

Debit	Credit
11) 133	

Rent Expense

Debit	Credit
12) 1,000	

Depreciation Expense

Debit	Credit
13) 208	

EXHIBIT XI-8 INCOME STATEMENT

Jacobs Golf and Tennis
Income Statement
For the month ended January 31, 2006

Revenue	
Sales	$4,000
Services	650
Total revenue	$4,650
Expenses	
Cost of goods sold	2,200
Rent	1,000
Salary	700
Depreciation	208
Interest	133
Utilities	120
Total expenses	4,361
Net income	$ 289

EXHIBIT XI-9 CLOSING ENTRIES

Jacobs Golf & Tennis
General Journal
January 31

	DR	CR
15) Retained earnings	4,361	
Salary expense		700
Utilities expense		120
Cost of goods sold		2,200
Interest expense		133
Rent expense		1,000
Depreciation expense		208
To close expense accounts		
16) Service revenue	650	
Sales	4,000	
Retained earnings		4,650
To close revenue accounts		

EXHIBIT XI-10 JACOBS GOLF AND TENNIS GENERAL LEDGER

BALANCE SHEET ACCOUNTS

Cash

1) 50,000	3) 12,000
2) 20,000	5) 25,000
6) 200	8) 700
7) 100	17) 100
Bal 32,500	

Accounts Receivable

6) 400	
10) 4,000	
Bal 4,400	

Prepaid Rent

3) 12,000	12) 1,000
Bal 11,000	

Inventory

4) 30,000	10) 2,200
Bal 27,800	

Equipment

5) 25,000	

Accumulated Depreciation

	13) 208

Notes Payable

	2) 20,000

Accounts Payable

	4) 30,000

Unearned Revenue

14) 50	7) 100
Bal	50

Utilities Payable

	9) 120

Interest Payable

	11) 133

Invested Capital

	1) 50,000

Retained Earnings

15) 4,361	16) 4,650
17) 100	
Bal	189

INCOME STATEMENT ACCOUNTS

Service Revenue

	6) 600
16) 650	14) 50
	Bal 0

Sales

16) 4,000	10) 4,000
	Bal 0

Salary Expense

8) 700	15) 700
Bal 0	

Utilities Expense

14) 120	15) 120
Bal 0	

EXHIBIT XI-10 (continued)

Interest Expense

	Debit		Credit
11)	133	15)	133
Bal	0		

Depreciation Expense

	Debit		Credit
13)	208	15)	208
Bal	0		

Rent Expense

	Debit		Credit
12)	1,000	15)	1,000
Bal	0		

Cost of Goods Sold

	Debit		Credit
10)	2,200	15)	2,200
Bal	0		

EXHIBIT XI-11 BALANCE SHEET

Jacobs Golf and Tennis
Balance Sheet
January 31, 2006

ASSETS			**LIABILITIES AND SHAREHOLDERS' EQUITY**	
Cash		$ 32,500	Liabilities	
Accounts receivable		4,400	Accounts payable	$ 30,000
Prepaid rent		11,000	Utilities payable	120
Inventory		27,800	Interest payable	133
Equipment	$25,000		Unearned revenue	50
Less: Accumulated			Notes payable	20,000
depreciation	(208)	24,792	Total liabilities	50,303
			Shareholders' equity	
			Invested capital	50,000
			Retained earnings	189
				50,189
			Total liabilities and	
Total assets		$100,492	shareholders' equity	$100,492

OTHER PROCEDURAL MATTERS

One TOPICMOD cannot cover all of accounting's detailed procedures. However, a few additional items deserve attention.

Trial Balances and Worksheets

The equality of debits and credits implies that the total of all accounts with debit balances should equal the total of all accounts with credit balances. As a check on this, accountants prepare trial balances at various points in the accounting process.

A **trial balance** is simply a listing of general ledger accounts and their amounts. Two columns are used: one for accounts with debit balances and one for accounts with credit balances. Exhibit XI-12 contains an illustration of a trial balance based on the account balances in Exhibit XI-10. Note that the totals in the two columns balance.

An extended form of the trial balance is the **worksheet.** The worksheet serves two purposes. First, it includes a trial balance, so, accordingly, it provides a check on certain errors. Second, it serves as a testing ground for adjusting and closing entries. That is, prior to inserting the adjusting and closing entries into the general journal and ledger, many accountants test these entries in the worksheet, which is not a formal part of the accounting records. By doing this, errors in these entries can hopefully be eliminated before they are entered in the formal books of account. Worksheets are highly mechanical, so they are not considered further in this text.

Subsidiary Ledgers

This TOPICMOD has discussed only two formal accounting records: the **general ledger** and **general journal.** In actual practice, there are many more. One type of record is a **subsidiary ledger.** The purpose of a subsidiary ledger is to provide detailed information regarding a particular general ledger account.

EXHIBIT XI-12 TRIAL BALANCE

Jacobs Golf & Tennis
Trial Balance
January 31, 2006

	DEBIT	CREDIT
Cash	32,500	
Accounts receivable	4,400	
Prepaid rent	11,000	
Inventory	27,800	
Equipment	25,000	
Accumulated depreciation		208
Notes payable		20,000
Accounts payable		30,000
Unearned revenue		50
Utilities payable		120
Interest payable		133
Invested capital		50,000
Retained earnings		189
	100,700	100,700

Consider, for example, accounts receivable. This account indicates the total amount due from customers. Of course, firms also need to know the amount owed by each individual customer. Unfortunately, the accounts receivable account does not easily provide this information. The accounts receivable subsidiary ledger is designed to do this. Envision the subsidiary ledger as a separate loose-leaf notebook with a page (account) assigned to each customer.

To illustrate, assume that the Pine Company is owed a total of $700 from its three customers. Customer A owes $400, Customer B owes $200, and Customer C owes $100. As shown in Exhibit XI-13, Pine's accounts receivable general ledger account shows a balance of $700. The subsidiary ledger, appearing in the lower half of the exhibit, shows the detail of each customer's indebtedness. Notice that the total of the subsidiary ledger accounts is $700, which agrees with the accounts receivable general ledger account. Several other general ledger accounts, such as accounts payable and equipment, have subsidiary ledgers.

Special Journals

Preparing general journal entries for each transaction is a laborious, time-consuming process; account titles must be written and often the same amount must be written twice in the same entry. Because of this, accountants have devised streamlined journalizing procedures that make use of special journals. **Special journals** are constructed to achieve great efficiencies in journalizing transactions. Examples of special journals include sales journals, cash receipts journals, and cash payments journals.

Computerization

This TOPICMOD has emphasized manual (pen-and-ink) accounting systems, which are simple and straightforward. Accordingly, they help you envision the flow of information. However, the vast majority of actual accounting systems are

EXHIBIT XI-13 PINE COMPANY GENERAL AND SUBSIDIARY LEDGERS

GENERAL LEDGER

Accounts Receivable	
700	

ACCOUNTS RECEIVABLE SUBSIDIARY LEDGER

Customer A		Customer B		Customer C	
400		200		100	

computerized and such systems have several advantages. First, they are able to process large numbers of transactions more quickly than manual systems. Consequently, they provide financial statements and other reports in a more timely manner. Second, they achieve a greater degree of accuracy than manual systems. Finally, they permit a greater amount of information (different reports) to be generated.

Computerized accounting systems require both hardware and software. Hardware consists of a computer's physical components, such as storage disks, monitors, keyboards, and central processing units. Computers range in size from laptop models to mainframe computers that can occupy an entire floor.

Software refers to coded instructions given to the computer, telling it how to process information. A set of instructions concerning one or more related tasks is called a program. Some firms develop their own programs for accounting tasks. Other firms rely on programs developed by software specialists. Many programs currently exist that enable small- and medium-sized firms to computerize their accounting functions quickly and inexpensively.

Summary of Learning Objectives

1. **Prepare and post journal entries.**
   Journal entries translate a transaction's basic accounting equation analysis into debits and credits. Because journal entries do not summarize the effects of transactions on the various financial statement elements, journal entries must be posted to general ledger accounts.

2. **Calculate account balances.**
   Account balances are determined by summing the debits in an account, summing the credits, and taking the difference.

3. **Prepare and post adjusting entries.**
   Adjusting entries are prepared at the end of a time period (usually a month, quarter, or year). Adjusting entries are needed because certain events might not have been reflected in the account balances. Typical examples include interest expense and depreciation expense. Adjusting entries update the account balances so that correct financial statements can be prepared.

4. **Prepare and post closing entries.**
   Revenue and expense transactions are initially recorded in revenue and expense accounts. This permits the preparation of a detailed income statement. Because these transactions ultimately affect retained earnings, closing entries are needed to transfer the balances in revenue and expense accounts to retained earnings.

5. **Generate balance sheets and income statements from general ledger accounts.**
   Financial statements can be prepared by simply transcribing the balances from the relevant general ledger accounts onto the appropriate financial statement.

KEY TERMS

Adjusting entries
Adjustments
Balanced
Chart of accounts
Closing entries
Compound journal entry
Double-entry accounting
Entry
Credit (Cr)
Debit (Dr)
General journal
General ledger
Journal entry
Posting
Special journals
Subsidiary ledger
T-accounts
Temporary (nominal) accounts
Trial balance
Worksheet

Exercises and Problems

XI-1 Define the terms debit and credit.

XI-2 Draw a diagram reflecting the parts of the accounting cycle, showing how journals, ledgers, and so on, are used to record transactions.

XI-3 Define the term posting.

XI-4 Discuss why a firm might use subsidiary ledgers.

XI-5 Why are adjusting entries used?

XI-6 Would a cash-based system have a need for adjusting entries? Why?

XI-7 Why are closing entries used?

XI-8 If a firm never prepared periodic financial statements, would it need to prepare adjusting or closing entries? Why?

XI-9 What are some of the conditions that might cause a trial balance not to be "in balance"?

XI-10 Describe each of the steps in the accounting process, as shown below:

1. Identify transactions and events.
2. Analyze transactions and events in terms of the basic accounting equation.
3. Translate the transaction analysis into debits and credits.
4. Prepare journal entries and post to the general ledger.
5. Prepare and post adjusting entries.
6. Prepare the income statement.
7. Prepare and post-closing entries.
8. Prepare the balance sheet.

XI-11 John Hasty opened his bakery on March 1, 2007. The following transactions took place in early March:

1. Deposited $10,000 into a checking account in the name of the Hasty Bakery.
2. Leased a small kitchen for one year at $500 per month. One month's rent was paid at this time.
3. Purchased kitchen equipment for $3,000 cash.
4. Purchased baking ingredients for $6,000 on account.
5. Obtained a $2,000, nine percent, one-year loan.
6. Rented a delivery truck for three years. The monthly payment of $200 is due at the end of each month. Nothing was paid in March.
7. Obtained a one-year insurance policy on the kitchen equipment. Paid the entire premium of $500.

Required

a. Prepare the journal entries to record these transactions.
b. Prepare any necessary adjusting entries (such as interest expense).
c. Post all journal entries to T-accounts.
d. Prepare a trial balance.
e. Prepare a balance sheet for the Hasty Bakery as of March 31, 2007.

XI-12 The following account balances are shown on November 30, 2006, for the Clever Bookstore:

Cash	$ 8,000	Accounts payable	$ 4,000
Accounts receivable	9,000	Salaries payable	2,000
Inventory	60,000	Notes payable	35,000
Supplies	3,000	J. Clever, capital	39,000
Total	$80,000	Total	$80,000

The following transactions occurred during December.

1. Paid workers the $2,000 owed them on November 30.
2. Made sales totaling $40,000. One-half of the sales were for cash. The other half was on account. The cost of goods sold was $25,000.
3. Purchased inventory on account, $15,000.
4. Collected in cash $22,000 of receivables.
5. Used supplies totaling $800.
6. Paid accounts payable of $12,000.
7. Paid December's interest on the note payable in the amount of $300.

Required

a. Prepare the journal entries to record these transactions.
b. Prepare any necessary adjusting entries.
c. Post all journal entries to T-accounts.
d. Prepare a trial balance.
e. Prepare a balance sheet for Clever Bookstore as of December 31, 2007.

XI-13 The following transactions all occurred on January 2 of the current year:

1. A company paid a $2,000 bill for a fire insurance policy that covers the current year and next year.
2. A company purchased for $200 a trash compactor that has an expected life of five years.
3. Two attorneys, working under a corporate structure, decide that a ski chalet at Vail is necessary to entertain current and prospective clients. At the same time, they are considering the addition of a third attorney. This new attorney has a ski chalet that she purchased five years ago for $120,000. Its current market value is $200,000.

Required

a. Prepare the journal entries to record these transactions. Record the acquisition of the ski chalet when the new attorney is hired and it is transferred to the corporation.
b. Prepare any necessary adjusting entries for the company's December 31 year-end (such as depreciation expense).
c. Post all journal entries to T-accounts.

XI-14 On June 1, a sole proprietorship was formed to sell and service personal computers. During the first six months, the following transactions occurred:

1. On June 1, invested $50,000 in the business.
2. On July 1, purchased a four-wheel-drive pickup truck for $22,000 (on account) that will be used in the business.
3. On September 1, paid fuel and repairs costs of $1,750 for the truck.
4. On December 31, the truck proves to be a "lemon" and it is sold to a used car dealer for $1,000.

Required

a. Prepare the journal entries to record these transactions.
b. Prepare any necessary adjusting entries for the company's December 31 year-end (such as depreciation expense).
c. Post the journal entries and accruals to T-accounts.
d. Prepare a trial balance.
e. Prepare a balance sheet for the December 31 year-end.

XI-15 Seaver & Co., a CPA firm, prepares their own financial statements with a December 31 year-end.

1. As of December 31, Seaver & Co. have rendered $20,500 worth of services to clients for which they have not yet billed the client, and for which they have not made any accounting entry.
2. Seaver & Co. owns equipment (computers, etc.) having an original cost of $12,000. The equipment has an expected life of six years.
3. On January 1, 2006, Seaver borrowed $15,000. Both principal and interest are due on December 31, 2007. The interest rate is 11%.
4. On January 1, 2006, Seaver rented storage space for three years. The entire three-year charge of $15,000 was paid at this time. Seaver correctly created a prepaid rent account in the amount of $15,000.
5. As of December 31, workers have earned $10,200 in wages that are unpaid and unrecorded.

Required

a. Record any necessary adjusting entries for 2006.
b. Post the journal entries to T-accounts.

XI-16 Susan Sweet opened a candy shop on January 1.

1. Susan Sweet invested $100,000 in cash on January 1, 2006, and began business as a sole proprietorship under the same name.
2. Susan Sweet paid $20,000 for a six-month lease. The lease is renewable for another six months on July 1.
3. Susan Sweet purchased candy and other "sweetments" at a cost of $40,000 in cash.
4. Susan Sweet purchased store fixtures at a cost of $15,000, paying $5,000 in cash. These store fixtures have a useful life of five years, with no expected salvage value.

5. During the first month of operations, Susan Sweet's sales totaled $32,000. At the end of the first month, her outstanding accounts receivable were only $1,500. Her cost of sales was $9,500.
6. During the first month, her other operating expenses were $37,300 on account. Susan Sweet also paid Susan a "salary" of $10,000, which was really a withdrawal.
7. Susan Sweet recorded depreciation for the first year.

Required

a. Prepare the journal entries to record these transactions.
b. Prepare any necessary adjusting entries (such as rent expense).
c. Post the entries to T-accounts.
d. Prepare a trial balance.
e. Prepare an income statement and balance sheet for Susan Sweets to "tell the story" of the first month's operations.

XI-17 Susan's Shoe Shop opened on January 1. The following transactions took place during the first month:

1. Deposited $30,000 in the firm's checking account.
2. Purchased shoes, boots, socks, and other inventory for $45,000 on account.
3. Purchased display shelving, chairs, and other fixtures for $10,000 cash and $40,000 on account. Assume a useful life of five years.
4. Obtained a three-year, $20,000 bank loan at 8% annual interest.
5. Paid $10,000 to two different creditors.
6. Signed an application for a one-year insurance policy and paid the year's premium of $2,400.
7. Paid three employees a monthly salary of $2,000 each.
8. Collected $35,000 from customers on account.

Required

a. Prepare the journal entries to record these transactions.
b. Prepare any necessary adjusting entries.
c. Post all journal entries to T-accounts.
d. Prepare a trial balance.
e. Prepare an income statement and balance sheet for Susan's Shoe Shop on January 31.

XI-18 Matt's Ski Shop is in the process of acquiring a vehicle for the business. The following transactions took place in December 2006:

1. Verbally agreed to purchase a used car from Slee-Z-Auto for $3,500.
2. Paid $400 for a warranty on the used car.
3. Took the car on a test drive, found it faulty, and told the salesperson to deliver a different car.

4. The sales manager kindly transferred the warranty to the second vehicle.
5. Paid $7,500 for the vehicle, which has a useful life of five years, and no salvage value.
6. Paid license and taxes of $475.
7. Bought new tires for $550.
8. On a cold winter morning, the car failed to start.
9. Purchased a new battery for $85.
10. Filed a warranty claim for the new battery.
11. Received $65 payment under the warranty.

Required

a. Prepare the journal entries to record these transactions.
b. Prepare any necessary adjusting entries.
c. Post all journal entries to T-accounts.

XI-19 Matt, the sole proprietor of Matt's Ski Shop, traveled to Switzerland to attend the Alpine Equipment Exposition. The following transactions occurred:

1. Paid $2,000 for airline tickets, hotel accommodations, and tour guidance from Hugo's U-Go Travel.
2. Changed the airline reservation.
3. Paid a $35 fee to change the reservation.
4. Arrived at the hotel and checked in.
5. Found his room to be next to the hotel laundry and facing the noisy loading zone. Furthermore, the room only had two cheap radios and no television!
6. Asked the hotel manager for a more suitable room.
7. Tipped the bellhop $5 after his luggage was moved.
8. Upon checking out of the hotel at the end of the week, found a $50 per day upgrade charge on his hotel bill.
9. Paid $257 for meals and phone charges on his hotel bill, but denied liability and responsibility for the upgrade charges.
10. The hotel manager insisted that the upgrade charges were Matt's responsibility, and that they would be added to his credit card balance.
11. Filed a complaint with Hugo's U-Go Travel and with the credit card issuer.
12. Received a refund of $200 from Hugo.
13. Received a credit for the upgrade charges from the credit card issuer.
14. Took films from the exposition to a photo shop for developing. Charges for developing and printing these films were expected to be $45.
15. Paid the $45 two weeks later.

Required

Prepare the journal entries for these related transactions.

XI-20 John's Anti-Mediation League (JAML) engaged in the following transactions in 2006:

1. On January 1, JAML borrowed $100,000 at 6% per year with interest due quarterly.
2. JAML paid a $1,000 kickback to a good friend who helped obtain the loan.
3. JAML had not yet paid any interest after the loan had been in effect for three months.
4. On June 30, JAML paid the interest due.
5. On July 1, JAML renegotiated the terms of the loan, which increased the interest rate to 9% per year.
6. At the end of September, John paid the interest on the loan from his personal account.
7. At the end of December, JAML accrued the interest due.
8. On January 1, 2007, JAML paid the interest due to the lender and to John's personal account.

Required

a. Prepare the journal entries to record these transactions.
b. Post all journal entries to T-accounts.

XI-21 Sue's Mediation League (SML) engaged in the following transactions in 2006:

1. On January 1, SML borrowed $250,000 at 9% per year with interest due quarterly.
2. SML paid $1,000 to a good friend who helped obtain the loan.
3. SML had not yet paid any interest after the loan had been in effect for three months.
4. On June 30, SML paid the interest due.
5. On July 1, SML renegotiated the terms of the loan, which decreased the interest rate to 6% per year.
6. At the end of September, Sue paid the interest on the loan from her personal account.
7. At the end of December, SML accrued the interest due.
8. On January 1, 2007, SML paid the interest due to the lender and to Sue's personal account.

Required

a. Prepare the journal entries to record these transactions.
b. Post all journal entries to T-accounts.

XI-22 Sharon's Affairs and Parties (SAAP) engaged in the following transactions in 2006:

1. SAAP borrowed $150,000 at 10% per year to begin operations.
2. SAAP accrued the first month's interest on the loan.

3. SAAP accrued the second month's interest.
4. SAAP paid the interest due at the end of the second month.
5. Sharon loaned SAAP $10,000 at 24% interest per year.
6. SAAP accrued interest for the next month on both loans.
7. SAAP paid accrued interest at the end of the third month.
8. SAAP repaid Sharon's loan, along with a loan "cancellation" fee of $2,500.
9. SAAP accrued interest for the next month.
10. SAAP repaid the original loan, along with nine months accrued interest at the end of 2006.

Required

a. Prepare the journal entries to record these transactions.
b. Post all journal entries to T-accounts.

XI-23 Hilger's Intimate Promises (HIP) engaged in the following transactions in 2006:

1. HIP borrowed $50,000 at 8% per year to begin operations.
2. HIP accrued the first month's interest on the loan.
3. HIP accrued the second month's interest.
4. HIP paid the interest due at the end of the second month.
5. Hilger loaned HIP $10,000 at 24% interest per year.
6. HIP accrued interest for the next month on both loans.
7. HIP paid accrued interest at the end of the third month.
8. HIP repaid Hilger's loan, along with a loan "cancellation" fee of $1,500.
9. HIP accrued interest for the next month.
10. HIP repaid the original loan, along with nine months accrued interest at the end of 2006.

Required

a. Prepare the journal entries to record these transactions.
b. Post all journal entries to T-accounts.

APPENDIX A

WAL-MART STORES, INC.

Eleven-Year Financial Summary

WAL-MART

(Dollar amounts in millions except per share data)

Fiscal Year Ended January 31,	2006	2005	2004
Operating Results			
Net sales	**$312,427**	$285,222	$256,329
Net sales increase	**9.5%**	11.3%	11.6%
Comparative store sales increase in the United States [1]	**3%**	3%	4%
Cost of sales	**$240,391**	$219,793	$198,747
Operating, selling, general and administrative expenses	**56,733**	51,248	44,909
Interest expense, net	**1,172**	986	832
Effective tax rate	**33.4%**	34.7%	36.1%
Income from continuing operations	**$ 11,231**	$ 10,267	$ 8,861
Net income	**11,231**	10,267	9,054
Per share of common stock:			
Income from continuing operations, diluted	**$ 2.68**	$ 2.41	$ 2.03
Net income, diluted	**2.68**	2.41	2.07
Dividends	**0.60**	0.52	0.36
Financial Position			
Current assets of continuing operations	**$ 43,824**	$ 38,854	$ 34,421
Inventories	**32,191**	29,762	26,612
Property, equipment and capital lease assets, net	**79,290**	68,118	59,023
Total assets of continuing operations	**138,187**	120,154	105,405
Current liabilities of continuing operations	**48,826**	43,182	37,840
Long-term debt	**26,429**	20,087	17,102
Long-term obligations under capital leases	**3,742**	3,171	2,997
Shareholders' equity	**53,171**	49,396	43,623
Financial Ratios			
Current ratio	**0.9**	0.9	0.9
Return on assets [2]	**8.9%**	9.3%	9.2%
Return on shareholders' equity [3]	**22.5%**	22.6%	21.3%
Other Year-End Data			
Discount stores in the United States	**1,209**	1,353	1,478
Supercenters in the United States	**1,980**	1,713	1,471
SAM'S CLUBs in the United States	**567**	551	538
Neighborhood Markets in the United States	**100**	85	64
Units outside the United States	**2,285**	1,587	1,355

(1) Comparative store sales are considered to be sales at stores that were open as of February 1 of the prior fiscal year and have not been expanded or relocated since that date.

(2) Income from continuing operations before minority interest divided by average total assets.

(3) Income from continuing operations before minority interest divided by average shareholders' equity.

Financial information for all years has been restated to reflect the sale of McLane Company, Inc. ("McLane") that occurred in fiscal 2004. McLane is presented as a discontinued operation. All years have been restated for the fiscal 2004 adoption of the expense recognition provisions of Statement of Financial Accounting Standards No. 123, "Accounting and Disclosure of Stock-Based Compensation." In fiscal 2005, we adopted Statement of Financial Accounting Standards No. 123R, "Share-Based Payment," which did not result in a material impact to our financial statements.

In fiscal 2003, the Company adopted Financial Accounting Standards Board Statement No. 142, "Goodwill and Other Intangible Assets." In years prior to adoption, the Company recorded amortization expense related to goodwill.

18

2003	2002	2001	2000	1999	1998	1997	1996
$229,616	$204,011	$180,787	$156,249	$130,522	$112,005	$99,627	$89,051
12.6%	12.8%	15.7%	19.7%	16.5%	12.4%	11.9%	13.7%
5%	6%	5%	8%	9%	6%	5%	4%
$178,299	$159,097	$140,720	$121,825	$102,490	$ 88,163	$78,897	$70,485
39,983	35,147	30,822	26,025	21,778	18,831	16,437	14,547
927	1,183	1,196	840	598	716	807	863
35.2%	36.2%	36.5%	36.8%	37.4%	37.0%	36.8%	36.8%
$ 7,818	$ 6,448	$ 6,087	$ 5,394	$ 4,240	$ 3,424	$ 2,978	$ 2,689
7,955	6,592	6,235	5,324	4,397	3,504	3,042	2,737
$ 1.76	$ 1.44	$ 1.36	$ 1.21	$ 0.95	$ 0.76	$ 0.65	$ 0.58
1.79	1.47	1.39	1.19	0.98	0.77	0.66	0.59
0.30	0.28	0.24	0.20	0.16	0.14	0.11	0.10
$ 29,543	$ 26,615	$ 25,344	$ 23,478	$ 20,064	$ 18,589	$17,385	$16,779
24,401	22,053	20,987	19,296	16,361	16,005	15,556	15,667
51,374	45,248	40,461	35,533	25,600	23,237	19,935	18,554
92,900	81,549	76,231	68,983	48,513	44,221	38,571	36,621
32,225	26,795	28,366	25,525	16,155	13,930	10,432	10,944
16,597	15,676	12,489	13,653	6,887	7,169	7,685	8,483
3,000	3,044	3,152	3,000	2,697	2,480	2,304	2,089
39,461	35,192	31,407	25,878	21,141	18,519	17,151	14,757
0.9	1.0	0.9	0.9	1.2	1.3	1.7	1.5
9.2%	8.4%	8.6%	9.8%	9.5%	8.5%	8.0%	7.9%
20.9%	19.4%	21.3%	22.9%	21.4%	19.2%	18.7%	19.6%
1,568	1,647	1,736	1,801	1,869	1,921	1,960	1,995
1,258	1,066	888	721	564	441	344	239
525	500	475	463	451	443	436	433
49	31	19	7	4	—	—	—
1,272	1,154	1,054	991	703	589	314	276

The consolidation of The Seiyu, Ltd., had a significant impact on the fiscal 2006 financial position amounts in this summary. The acquisition of the ASDA Group PLC and the Company's related debt issuance had a significant impact on the fiscal 2000 amounts in this summary.

Years prior to 1998 have not been restated for the effects of the change in accounting method for SAM'S CLUB membership revenue recognition as the effects of this change would not have a material impact on this summary. The cumulative effect for this accounting change recorded in fiscal 2000 amounted to $198 million net of tax.

Certain reclassifications have been made to prior periods to conform to current presentations.

Table of contents

Management's Discussion and Analysis of
Results of Operations and Financial Condition

WAL-MART

Overview

Wal-Mart Stores, Inc. ("Wal-Mart" or the "Company") is a global retailer committed to improving the standard of living for our customers throughout the world. We earn the trust of our customers every day by providing a broad assortment of quality merchandise and services at every day low prices ("EDLP") while fostering a culture that rewards and embraces mutual respect, integrity and diversity. EDLP is our pricing philosophy under which we price items at a low price every day so that our customers trust that our prices will not change erratically under frequent promotional activity. Our focus for SAM'S CLUB is to provide exceptional value on brand-name merchandise at "members only" prices for both business and personal use. Internationally, we operate with similar philosophies. Our fiscal year ends on January 31.

We intend for this discussion to provide the reader with information that will assist in understanding our financial statements, the changes in certain key items in those financial statements from year to year, and the primary factors that accounted for those changes, as well as how certain accounting principles affect our financial statements. The discussion also provides information about the financial results of the various segments of our business to provide a better understanding of how those segments and their results affect the financial condition and results of operations of the Company as a whole. This discussion should be read in conjunction with our financial statements and accompanying notes as of January 31, 2006, and the year then ended.

Throughout this Management's Discussion and Analysis of Results of Operations and Financial Condition, we discuss segment operating income and comparative store sales. Segment operating income refers to income from continuing operations before net interest expense, income taxes and minority interest. Segment operating income does not include unallocated corporate overhead. Comparative store sales is a measure which indicates the performance of our existing stores by measuring the growth in sales for such stores for a particular period over the corresponding period in the prior year. For fiscal 2006 and prior years, we considered comparative store sales to be sales at stores that were open as of February 1st of the prior fiscal year and had not been expanded or relocated since that date. Stores that were expanded or relocated during that period are not included in the calculation. Comparative store sales is also referred to as "same-store" sales by others within the retail industry. The method of calculating comparative store sales varies across the retail industry. As a result, our calculation of comparative store sales is not necessarily comparable to similarly titled measures reported by other companies. Beginning in fiscal 2007, we changed our method of calculating comparative store sales. These changes are described in our Current Report on Form 8-K that we furnished to the SEC on February 2, 2006.

On May 23, 2003, we consummated the sale of McLane Company, Inc. ("McLane"), one of our wholly-owned subsidiaries, for $1.5 billion. As a result of this sale, we classified McLane as a discontinued operation in the financial statements for fiscal 2004. McLane's external sales prior to the divestiture were $4.3 billion in fiscal 2004. McLane continues to be a supplier to the Company.

Operations

Our operations are comprised of three business segments: Wal-Mart Stores, SAM'S CLUB and International.

Our Wal-Mart Stores segment is the largest segment of our business, accounting for approximately 67.2% of our fiscal 2006 net sales. This segment consists of three traditional retail formats, all of which are located in the United States, and Wal-Mart's online retail format, Walmart.com. Our traditional Wal-Mart Stores retail formats include:

- Supercenters, which average approximately 187,000 square feet in size and offer a wide assortment of general merchandise and a full-line supermarket;
- Discount stores, which average approximately 102,000 square feet in size and offer a wide assortment of general merchandise and a limited assortment of food products; and
- Neighborhood Markets, which average approximately 42,000 square feet in size and offer a full-line supermarket and a limited assortment of general merchandise.

Our SAM'S CLUB segment consists of membership warehouse clubs in the United States and the segment's online retail format, samsclub.com. SAM'S CLUB accounted for approximately 12.7% of our fiscal 2006 sales. Our SAM'S CLUBs in the United States average approximately 129,000 square feet in size.

As of January 31, 2006, our International operations were located in nine countries and Puerto Rico. Internationally, we generated approximately 20.1% of our fiscal 2006 sales. Outside the United States, we operate several different formats of retail stores and restaurants, including supercenters, discount stores and SAM'S CLUBs. Additionally, at January 31, 2006, we owned an unconsolidated 33.3% minority interest in Central American Retail Holding Company ("CARHCO"), a retailer operating in five Central American countries. In February 2006, we acquired a controlling interest in CARHCO.

The Retail Industry

We operate in the highly competitive retail industry in both the United States and abroad. We face strong sales competition from other discount, department, drug, variety and specialty stores and supermarkets, many of which are national chains. Additionally, we compete with a number of companies for prime retail site locations, as well as in attracting and retaining quality employees ("associates"). We, along with other retail companies, are influenced by a number of factors including, but not limited to: cost of goods, consumer debt levels, economic conditions, interest rates, customer preferences, employment, labor costs, inflation, currency exchange fluctuations, fuel prices, weather patterns and insurance costs. Our SAM'S CLUB segment faces strong sales competition from other wholesale club operators, as well as other retailers. Further information on risks to our Company can be located in Item 1A, Risk Factors, in our Annual Report on Form 10-K for the year ended January 31, 2006.

Management's Discussion and Analysis of
Results of Operations and Financial Condition

WAL-MART

Key Items in Fiscal 2006

Significant financial items during fiscal 2006 include:

- Net sales increased 9.5% from fiscal 2005 to $312.4 billion in fiscal 2006, and net income increased 9.4% to $11.2 billion. Foreign currency exchange rates favorably impacted sales and operating income by $1.5 billion and $64 million, respectively, in fiscal 2006.
- Net cash provided by operating activities was $17.6 billion for fiscal 2006. During fiscal 2006, we repurchased $3.6 billion of our common stock under our share repurchase program and paid dividends of $2.5 billion. Additionally during fiscal 2006, we issued $7.7 billion in long-term debt, repaid $2.7 billion of long-term debt and funded a net decrease in commercial paper of $704 million.
- Total assets increased 15.0%, to $138.2 billion at January 31, 2006, when compared to January 31, 2005. During fiscal 2006, we made $14.6 billion of capital expenditures which was an increase of 13.0% over capital expenditures of $12.9 billion in fiscal 2005.
- When compared to fiscal 2005, our Wal-Mart Stores segment experienced an 8.2% increase in operating income and a 9.4% increase in net sales in fiscal 2006.
- SAM'S CLUB's continued focus on our business members helped drive an 8.2% increase in operating income on a 7.2% increase in net sales when comparing fiscal 2006 with fiscal 2005.
- Our International segment generated a net sales and operating income increase of 11.4% compared to fiscal 2005.

Company Performance Measures

Management uses a number of metrics to assess the Company's performance. The following are the more frequently used metrics:

- Comparative store sales is a measure which indicates the performance of our existing stores by measuring the growth in sales for such stores for a particular period over the corresponding period in the prior year. Our Wal-Mart Stores segment's comparative store sales were 3.0% for fiscal 2006 versus 2.9% for fiscal 2005. Our SAM'S CLUB segment's comparative club sales were 5.0% in fiscal 2006 versus 5.8% in fiscal 2005.
- Operating income growth greater than net sales growth has long been a measure of success for us. For fiscal 2006, our operating income increased by 8.4% when compared to fiscal 2005, while net sales increased by 9.5% over the same period. Our SAM'S CLUB segment met this target; however, the Wal-Mart Stores segment fell short of the target, while the International segment grew operating income at the same rate as net sales.
- Inventory growth at a rate less than that of net sales is a key measure of our efficiency. However, our increased purchases of imported merchandise and recent acquisition activity impact this measure. Total inventories at January 31, 2006, were up 8.2% over levels at January 31, 2005, and net sales were up 9.5% when comparing fiscal 2006 with fiscal 2005. Approximately 150 basis points of the fiscal 2006 increase in inventory was from increased levels of imported merchandise, which carries a longer lead time, and an additional 170 basis points was from the consolidation of The Seiyu, Ltd. and the purchase of Sonae Distribuição Brasil S.A.
- With an asset base as large as ours, we are focused on continuing to make certain our assets are productive. It is important for us to sustain our return on assets. Return on assets is defined as income from continuing operations before minority interest divided by average total assets. Return on assets for fiscal 2006, 2005 and 2004 was 8.9%, 9.3% and 9.2%, respectively. Return on assets in fiscal 2006 was impacted by acquisition activity in the fourth quarter.

Results of Operations

The Company and each of its operating segments had net sales (in millions), as follows:

	2006			2005			2004	
Fiscal Year Ended January 31,	Net sales	Percent of total	Percent increase	Net sales	percent of total	Percent increase	Net sales	Percent of total
Wal-Mart Stores	**$209,910**	**67.2%**	**9.4%**	$191,826	67.3%	10.1%	$174,220	68.0%
SAM'S CLUB	**39,798**	**12.7%**	**7.2%**	37,119	13.0%	7.5%	34,537	13.5%
International	**62,719**	**20.1%**	**11.4%**	56,277	19.7%	18.3%	47,572	18.5%
Total net sales	**$312,427**	**100.0%**	**9.5%**	$285,222	100.0%	11.3%	$256,329	100.0%

Our total net sales increased by 9.5% and 11.3% in fiscal 2006 and 2005 when compared to the previous fiscal year. Those increases resulted from our expansion programs and comparative store sales increases in the United States. Comparative store sales increased 3.4% in fiscal 2006 and 3.3% in fiscal 2005. As we continue to add new stores in the United States, we do so with an understanding that additional stores may take sales away from existing units. We estimate that comparative store sales in fiscal 2006, 2005 and 2004 were negatively impacted by the opening of new stores by approximately 1% per year. We expect that this effect of opening new stores on comparable store sales will continue during fiscal 2007 at a similar rate.

During fiscal 2006 and 2005, foreign currency exchange rates had a $1.5 billion and $3.2 billion favorable impact, respectively, on the International segment's net sales, causing an increase in the International segment's net sales as a percentage of total net sales relative to the Wal-Mart Stores and SAM'S CLUB segments. Additionally, the decrease in the SAM'S CLUB segment's net sales as a percent of total Company sales in fiscal 2006 and 2005 when compared to the previous fiscal years resulted from the more rapid development of new stores in the International and Wal-Mart Stores segments than the SAM'S CLUB segment. We expect this trend to continue for the foreseeable future.

Our total gross profit as a percentage of net sales (our "gross margin") was 23.1%, 22.9% and 22.5% in fiscal 2006, 2005 and 2004, respectively. Our Wal-Mart Stores and International segment sales yield higher gross margins than our SAM'S CLUB segment. Accordingly, the greater increases in net sales for the Wal-Mart Stores and International segments in fiscal 2006 and 2005 had a favorable impact on the Company's total gross margin.

Operating, selling, general and administrative expenses ("operating expenses") as a percentage of net sales were 18.2%, 17.9% and 17.5% for fiscal 2006, 2005 and 2004, respectively. The increase in operating expenses as a percentage of total net sales was primarily due to a faster rate of growth in operating expenses in our Wal-Mart Stores and International segments, which have higher operating expenses as a percentage of segment net sales than our SAM'S CLUB segment. Operating expenses in fiscal 2006 were higher as a percentage of net sales because of increases in utilities, maintenance and repairs and advertising. Increases in these expenses in fiscal 2006 were partially offset by reduced payroll costs as a percentage of net sales. Operating expenses in fiscal 2005 were impacted by the Wal-Mart Stores and SAM'S CLUB segments' implementation of a new job classification and pay structure for hourly field associates in the United States. The job classification and pay structure, which was implemented in the second quarter of fiscal 2005, was designed to help maintain internal equity and external competitiveness.

Operating expenses in fiscal 2004 were impacted by the adoption of Emerging Issues Task Force Issue No. 02-16, "Accounting by a Reseller for Cash Consideration Received from a Vendor" ("EITF 02-16"). The adoption of EITF 02-16 resulted in an after-tax reduction in fiscal 2004 net income of approximately $140 million.

Interest, net, as a percentage of net sales increased from fiscal 2004 through fiscal 2006. The increase was due to higher borrowing levels and higher interest rates during the period from fiscal 2004 through fiscal 2006. The $186-million increase in interest, net, in fiscal 2006 consisted of a $221-million increase due to higher borrowing levels and $99 million due to higher interest rates, partially offset by a benefit from refund of IRS interest paid, reversal of interest on income tax accruals for prior years, and reduced levels of interest on fiscal 2006 income tax accruals. The $154-million increase in interest, net, in fiscal 2005 consisted of a $139-million increase due to higher borrowing levels, a $26-million decrease due to changing interest rates and a $41-million increase in interest on income tax accruals.

Our effective income tax rates for fiscal 2006, 2005 and 2004 were 33.4%, 34.7% and 36.1%, respectively. The fiscal 2006 rate was less than the fiscal 2005 rate due primarily to adjustments in deferred income taxes and resolutions of certain federal and state tax contingencies. The fiscal 2005 rate was less than the fiscal 2004 rate due to the October 2004 passage of the Working Families Tax-Relief Act of 2004, which retroactively extended the work opportunity tax credit for fiscal 2005. In addition, the fiscal 2004 effective tax rate was impacted by an increase in the deferred tax asset valuation allowance as a result of tax legislation in Germany. This legislation required us to reevaluate the recoverability of deferred tax assets in Germany, resulting in a $150 million increase in the fiscal 2004 provision for income taxes.

In fiscal 2006, we earned net income of $11.2 billion, a 9.4% increase over fiscal 2005. In fiscal 2005, we earned income from continuing operations of $10.3 billion, a 15.9% increase over fiscal 2004. Net income in fiscal 2005 increased 13.4% from fiscal 2004 largely as a result of the increase in income from continuing operations described above, net of the $193 million provided from the discontinued operations and sale of McLane in fiscal 2004.

Wal-Mart Stores Segment

Fiscal Year	Segment Net Sales Increase from Prior Fiscal Year	Segment Operating Income (in millions)	Segment Operating Income Increase from Prior Fiscal Year	Operating Income as a Percentage of Segment Sales
2006	**9.4%**	**$15,324**	**8.2%**	**7.3%**
2005	10.1%	14,163	9.7%	7.4%
2004	10.9%	12,916	9.1%	7.4%

The segment net sales increases in fiscal 2006 and fiscal 2005 from the prior fiscal years resulted from comparative store sales increases of 3.0% in fiscal 2006 and 2.9% in fiscal 2005, in addition to our expansion program. Market development strategies in fiscal 2006 continued to put pressures on comparative stores sales increases as new stores were opened within the trade area of established stores. We have developed several initiatives to help mitigate this pressure and to grow comparable store sales through becoming more relevant to the customer by creating a better store shopping experience, continual improvement in product assortment and an aggressive store upgrade program to be instituted over the next 18 months.

Management's Discussion and Analysis of
Results of Operations and Financial Condition

WAL-MART

Our expansion programs consist of opening new units, converting discount stores to supercenters, relocations that result in more square footage, as well as expansions of existing stores. Segment expansion during fiscal 2006 included the opening of 24 discount stores, 15 Neighborhood Markets and 267 supercenters (including the conversion and/or relocation of 166 existing discount stores into supercenters). Two discount stores closed in fiscal 2006. During fiscal 2006, our total expansion program added approximately 39 million of store square footage, an 8.6% increase. Segment expansion during fiscal 2005 included the opening of 36 discount stores, 21 Neighborhood Markets and 242 supercenters (including the conversion and/or relocation of 159 existing discount stores into supercenters). Two discount stores closed in fiscal 2005. During fiscal 2005, our total expansion program added approximately 36 million of store square footage, an 8.6% increase.

Fiscal 2006 segment operating income was down 0.1% as a percentage of segment net sales. This decrease was driven by a 4 basis point decline in gross margin and an 8 basis point increase in operating expenses, partially offset by a slight increase in other income as a percentage of segment net sales. This gross margin decrease from fiscal 2005 can be attributed to the continued increase in sales of our lower-margin food items as a percentage of total segment net sales, rising transportation costs, and the unfavorable impact of an adjustment to our product warranty liabilities in fiscal 2006. The segment's operating expenses as a percentage of segment net sales in fiscal 2006 were higher than fiscal 2005 primarily due to expense pressures from utilities and advertising costs.

While our fiscal 2005 segment operating income as a percentage of segment net sales was unchanged from fiscal 2004, segment gross margin and operating expenses as a percentage of segment net sales were each up 0.4% for the year. Our gross margin improvement in fiscal 2005 can be primarily attributed to our global sourcing effort and reductions in markdowns and shrinkage as a percentage of segment net sales for fiscal 2005 when compared to fiscal 2004. The segment's operating expenses in fiscal 2005 as a percentage of segment net sales were higher than fiscal 2004 primarily due to expense pressures from associate wages and accident costs. Wages primarily increased due to our new job classification and pay structure, which was implemented in the second quarter of fiscal 2005.

SAM'S CLUB Segment

Fiscal Year	Segment Net Sales Increase from Prior Fiscal Year	Segment Operating Income (in millions)	Segment Operating Income Increase from Prior Fiscal Year	Operating Income as a Percentage of Segment Sales
2006	**7.2%**	**$1,385**	**8.2%**	**3.5%**
2005	7.5%	1,280	13.7%	3.4%
2004	8.9%	1,126	10.1%	3.3%

Growth in net sales for the SAM'S CLUB segment in fiscal 2006 and fiscal 2005 resulted from comparative club sales increases of 5.0% in fiscal 2006 and 5.8% in fiscal 2005, along with our expansion program. Comparative club sales in fiscal 2006 increased at a slower rate than in fiscal 2005 primarily due to lower growth rates in certain fresh and hardline categories. The impact of fuel sales contributed 130 basis points and 121 basis points to fiscal 2006 and 2005 comparative club sales, respectively. We believe that a greater focus on providing a quality in-club experience for our members will improve overall sales, including sales in these categories. Segment expansion consisted of the opening of 17 new clubs in fiscal 2006 and 13 clubs in fiscal 2005. One club closed in fiscal 2006. Our total expansion program added approximately 3 million of additional club square footage, or 3.8%, in fiscal 2006 and approximately 3 million, or 3.7%, of additional club square footage in fiscal 2005.

Segment operating income as a percentage of segment net sales increased slightly in fiscal 2006 when compared to fiscal 2005. The increase was due to an improvement in operating expenses and other income as a percentage of segment net sales, partially offset by a slight decrease in gross margin as a percentage of segment net sales. Operating expenses as a percentage of segment net sales improved primarily due to lower wage and accident costs in fiscal 2006 when compared to fiscal 2005, partially offset by the impact of increased utility costs. The increase in other income as a percentage of segment net sales was primarily the result of income recognized from higher membership sales in fiscal 2006. Gross margin as a percentage of net sales decreased due to strong sales in certain lower margin categories, including fuel and tobacco, during fiscal 2006.

Segment operating income as a percentage of segment net sales increased slightly in fiscal 2005 when compared to fiscal 2004 due to an improvement in gross margin, partially offset by an increase in operating expenses as a percentage of segment net sales and the impact of the adoption of EITF 02-16 in fiscal 2004. The improvement in gross margin was primarily a result of strong sales in higher margin categories. Operating expenses as a percentage of segment net sales increased due to higher wage costs resulting from our new job classification and pay structure, which was implemented in the second quarter of fiscal 2005. The adoption of EITF 02-16 resulted in a decrease to the segment's operating income in fiscal 2004 of $44 million.

International Segment

Fiscal Year	Segment Net Sales Increase from Prior Fiscal Year	Segment Operating Income (in millions)	Segment Operating Income Increase from Prior Fiscal Year	Operating income as a Percentage of Segment Sales
2006	**11.4%**	**$3,330**	**11.4%**	**5.3%**
2005	18.3%	2,988	26.1%	5.3%
2004	16.6%	2,370	18.6%	5.0%

At January 31, 2006, our International segment was comprised of wholly-owned operations in Argentina, Brazil, Canada, Germany, South Korea, Puerto Rico and the United Kingdom, the operation of joint ventures in China and the operations of majority-owned subsidiaries in Japan and Mexico.

The fiscal 2006 increase in the International segment's net sales primarily resulted from improved operating execution, our international expansion program and the impact of changes in foreign currency exchange rates. In fiscal 2006, the International segment opened 698 units, net of relocations and closings, which added 52 million, or 39.2%, of additional unit square footage. This includes the acquisition of Sonae Distribuição Brasil S.A., ("Sonae") in Southern Brazil, which added 139 stores and 11 million square feet in December 2005, and the consolidation of The Seiyu, Ltd. in Japan, which added 398 stores and 29 million square feet in December 2005. Additionally, the impact of changes in foreign currency exchange rates favorably affected the translation of International segment sales into U.S. dollars by an aggregate of $1.5 billion in fiscal 2006.

The fiscal 2005 increase in the International segment's net sales primarily resulted from improved operating execution, our international expansion program and the impact of foreign currency exchange rate changes. In fiscal 2005, the International segment opened 232 units, net of relocations and closings, which added 18 million, or 15.6%, of additional unit square footage. This includes the acquisition of Bompreço S.A. Supermercados do Nordeste in Brazil, which added 118 stores and approximately 8 million square feet in February 2004. Additionally, the impact of changes in foreign currency exchange rates favorably affected the translation of International segment sales into U.S. dollars by an aggregate of $3.2 billion in fiscal 2005.

Fiscal 2006 sales at our United Kingdom subsidiary, ASDA, were 42.7% of the International segment net sales. Sales for ASDA included in our consolidated income statement during fiscal 2006, 2005, and 2004 were $26.8 billion, $26.0 billion, and $21.7 billion, respectively.

While fiscal 2006 International segment operating income as a percentage of segment net sales was unchanged from fiscal 2005, segment gross margin was up 0.5%. This improvement in segment gross margin was offset by an increase in operating expenses and a decrease in other income, both as a percentage of segment net sales. The International segment's improvement in gross margin is primarily due to a favorable shift in the mix of products sold toward general merchandise categories which carry a higher margin. The 0.3% increase in operating expenses was driven primarily by increased advertising, utility and insurance expenditures. Other income declined 0.2% in fiscal 2006 primarily due to a reduction in current year rental income in Canada and a payroll tax recovery in Mexico in fiscal 2005. Fiscal 2006 operating income includes a favorable impact of $64 million from changes in foreign currency exchange rates.

The fiscal 2005 increase in segment operating income as a percentage of segment net sales compared with fiscal 2004 resulted primarily from a 0.3% improvement in gross margin. The improvement in gross margin was due to a favorable shift in the mix of products sold toward general merchandise categories. Fiscal 2005 operating income includes a favorable impact of $150 million from changes in foreign currency exchange rates.

Future financial results for our foreign operations could be affected by factors such as changes in foreign currency exchange rates, weak economic conditions, changes in tax law and government regulations in the foreign markets in which we operate.

Liquidity and Capital Resources

Overview

Cash flows provided by operating activities supply us with a significant source of liquidity. Our cash flows from operating activities were $17.6 billion in fiscal 2006 compared with $15.0 billion in fiscal 2005. The increase in cash flows provided by operating activities was primarily attributable to improved income from operations and improved inventory management resulting in accounts payable growing at a faster rate than inventory.

Our cash flows from operating activities of continuing operations were $15.0 billion in fiscal 2005, compared with $15.9 billion in fiscal 2004. This decrease was primarily attributable to differences in the timing of payroll, income and other taxes, supplier payments and the timing of the collection of receivables in fiscal 2005 compared with fiscal 2004.

In fiscal 2006, we paid dividends of $2.5 billion, made $14.6 billion in capital expenditures, paid $3.6 billion to repurchase shares of our common stock, received $7.7 billion from the issuance of long-term debt, repaid $2.7 billion of long-term debt and repaid $704 million of commercial paper (net of issuances).

Working Capital

Current liabilities exceeded current assets at January 31, 2006, by $5.0 billion, an increase of $622 million from January 31, 2005. Our ratio of current assets to current liabilities was 0.9 to 1 at January 31, 2006 and 2005. At January 31, 2006, we had total assets of $138.2 billion compared with total assets of $120.2 billion at January 31, 2005.

Management's Discussion and Analysis of
Results of Operations and Financial Condition

WAL-MART

Company Share Repurchase Program

From time to time, we repurchase shares of our common stock under a $10.0 billion share repurchase program authorized by our Board of Directors in September 2004. During the first half of fiscal 2006, we repurchased $3.6 billion of shares under this repurchase program. No shares of our common stock were repurchased under this program in the third or fourth quarters of fiscal 2006. During fiscal 2005, we repurchased $4.5 billion of shares under the current and past authorizations. At January 31, 2006, approximately $6.1 billion of additional shares may be repurchased under the current authorization.

There is no expiration date for or other restriction limiting the period over which we can make our share repurchases under the program, which will expire only when and if we have repurchased $10.0 billion of our shares under the program. Under the program, repurchased shares are constructively retired and returned to unissued status. We consider several factors in determining when to make share repurchases, including among other things, our current cash needs, the ratio of our debt to our total capitalization, our cost of borrowings, and the market price of the stock.

Common Stock Dividends

We paid dividends totaling approximately $2.5 billion or $0.60 per share in fiscal 2006. The dividends paid in fiscal 2006 represent a 15.4% increase over fiscal 2005. The fiscal 2005 dividend of $0.52 per share represented a 44.4% increase over fiscal 2004. We have increased our dividend every year since the first dividend was declared in March 1974.

On March 2, 2006, the Company's Board of Directors approved an increase in annual dividends to $0.67 per share. The annual dividend will be paid in four quarterly installments on April 3, 2006, June 5, 2006, September 5, 2006, and January 2, 2007 to holders of record on March 17, May 19, August 18 and December 15, 2006, respectively.

Contractual Obligations and Other Commercial Commitments

The following table sets forth certain information concerning our obligations and commitments to make contractual future payments, such as debt and lease agreements, and contingent commitments:

(In millions)	Payments due during fiscal years ending January 31,				
	Total	2007	2008-2009	2010-2011	Thereafter
Recorded Contractual Obligations					
Long-term debt	$31,024	$ 4,595	$ 6,178	$ 7,516	$ 12,735
Commercial paper	3,754	3,754	—	—	—
Capital lease obligations	6,380	592	1,138	1,040	3,610
Unrecorded Contractual Obligations:					
Non-cancelable operating leases	9,683	797	1,461	1,220	6,205
Interest on long-term debt	14,823	1,419	2,374	1,848	9,182
Undrawn lines of credit	5,296	5,296	—	—	—
Trade letters of credit	2,593	2,593	—	—	—
Standby letters of credit	2,800	2,800	—	—	—
Purchase obligations	19,872	10,519	9,023	218	112
Total commercial commitments	$96,225	$32,365	$20,174	$11,842	$ 31,844

Purchase obligations include all legally binding contracts such as firm commitments for inventory purchases, utility purchases, as well as commitments to make capital expenditures, software acquisition/license commitments and legally binding service contracts. Purchase orders for the purchase of inventory and other services are not included in the table above. Purchase orders represent authorizations to purchase rather than binding agreements. For the purposes of this table, contractual obligations for purchase of goods or services are defined as agreements that are enforceable and legally binding and that specify all significant terms, including: fixed or minimum quantities to be purchased; fixed, minimum or variable price provisions; and the approximate timing of the transaction. Our purchase orders are based on our current inventory needs and are fulfilled by our suppliers within short time periods. We also enter into contracts for outsourced services; however, the obligations under these contracts are not significant and the contracts generally contain clauses allowing for cancellation without significant penalty.

The expected timing for payment of the obligation discussed above is estimated based on current information. Timing of payments and actual amounts paid may be different depending on the timing of receipt of goods or services or changes to agreed-upon amounts for some obligations.

Off Balance Sheet Arrangements

In addition to the unrecorded contractual obligations discussed and presented above, the Company has made certain guarantees as discussed below for which the timing of payment, if any, is unknown.

In connection with certain debt financing, we could be liable for early termination payments if certain unlikely events were to occur. At January 31, 2006, the aggregate termination payment was $89 million. These two arrangements expire in fiscal 2011 and fiscal 2019.

In connection with the development of our grocery distribution network in the United States, we have agreements with third parties which would require us to purchase or assume the leases on certain unique equipment in the event the agreements are terminated. These agreements, which can be terminated by either party at will, cover up to a five-year period and obligate the Company to pay up to approximately $233 million upon termination of some or all of these agreements.

There are no recourse provisions which would enable us to recover from third parties any amounts paid under the above guarantees. No liability for these guarantees has been recorded in our financial statements.

The Company has entered into lease commitments for land and buildings for 60 future locations. These lease commitments with real estate developers provide for minimum rentals ranging from five to 35 years, which, if consummated based on current cost estimates, will approximate $95 million annually over the lease terms.

Capital Resources

During fiscal 2006, we issued $7.7 billion of long-term debt. The net proceeds from the issuance of such long-term debt were used to repay outstanding commercial paper indebtedness and for other general corporate purposes.

At January 31, 2006 and 2005, the ratio of our debt to our total capitalization was 42% and 39%, respectively. The fiscal 2006 consolidation of Seiyu and purchase of Sonae increased our debt to total capitalization at January 31, 2006, by 2.5 percentage points. Our objective is to maintain a debt to total capitalization ratio averaging approximately 40%.

Management believes that cash flows from operations and proceeds from the sale of commercial paper will be sufficient to finance any seasonal buildups in merchandise inventories and meet other cash requirements. If our operating cash flows are not sufficient to pay dividends and to fund our capital expenditures, we anticipate funding any shortfall in these expenditures with a combination of commercial paper and long-term debt. We plan to refinance existing long-term debt as it matures and may desire to obtain additional long-term financing for other corporate purposes. We anticipate no difficulty in obtaining long-term financing in view of our credit rating and favorable experiences in the debt market in the recent past. The following table details the ratings of the credit rating agencies that rated our outstanding indebtedness at January 31, 2006.

Rating agency	Commercial paper	Long-term debt
Standard and Poor's	A-1 +	AA
Moody's Investors Service	P-1	Aa2
Fitch Ratings	F1 +	AA
Dominion Bond Rating Service	R-1(middle)	AA

In February 2006, we entered into a £150 million revolving credit facility in the United Kingdom. Interest on borrowings under the credit facility accrues at LIBOR plus 25 basis points.

Future Expansion

Capital expenditures for fiscal 2007 are expected to be approximately $17.5 billion, including additions of capital leases. These fiscal 2007 expenditures will include the construction of 20 to 30 new discount stores, 270 to 280 new supercenters (with relocations or expansions accounting for approximately 160 of those supercenters), 15 to 20 new Neighborhood Markets, 30 to 40 new SAM'S CLUBs (with relocations or expansions accounting for 20 of those SAM'S CLUBs) and 220 to 230 new units in our International segment (with relocations or expansions accounting for approximately 35 of those units). We plan to finance this expansion, and any acquisitions of other operations that we may make during fiscal 2007, primarily out of cash flows from operations.

Market Risk

In addition to the risks inherent in our operations, we are exposed to certain market risks, including changes in interest rates and changes in foreign currency exchange rates.

The analysis presented for each of our market risk sensitive instruments is based on a 10% change in interest or foreign currency exchange rates. These changes are hypothetical scenarios used to calibrate potential risk and do not represent our view of future market changes. As the hypothetical figures indicate, changes in fair value based on the assumed change in rates generally cannot be extrapolated because the relationship of the change in assumption to the change in fair value may not be linear. The effect of a variation in a particular assumption is calculated without changing any other assumption. In reality, changes in one factor may result in changes in another, which may magnify or counteract the sensitivities.

At January 31, 2006 and 2005, we had $31.0 billion and $23.8 billion, respectively, of long-term debt outstanding. Our weighted average effective interest rate on long-term debt, after considering the effect of interest rate swaps, was 4.79% and 4.08% at January 31, 2006 and 2005, respectively. A hypothetical 10% increase in interest rates in effect at January 31, 2006 and 2005, would have increased annual interest expense on borrowings outstanding at those dates by $48 million and $25 million, respectively.

At January 31, 2006 and 2005, we had $3.8 billion of outstanding commercial paper obligations. The rate, including fees, on these obligations at January 31, 2006 and 2005, was 3.9% and 2.9%, respectively. A hypothetical 10% increase in commercial paper rates in effect at January 31, 2006 and 2005, would have increased annual interest expense on the outstanding balances on those dates by $14 million and $11 million, respectively.

Management's Discussion and Analysis of
Results of Operations and Financial Condition

WAL-MART

We enter into interest rate swaps to minimize the risks and costs associated with financing activities, as well as to maintain an appropriate mix of fixed- and floating-rate debt. Our preference is to maintain approximately 50% of our debt portfolio, including interest rate swaps, in floating-rate debt. The swap agreements are contracts to exchange fixed- or variable-rates for variable- or fixed-interest rate payments periodically over the life of the instruments. The aggregate fair value of these swaps was a gain of approximately $133 million and $472 million at January 31, 2006 and 2005, respectively. A hypothetical increase (or decrease) of 10% in interest rates from the level in effect at January 31, 2006, would result in a (loss) or gain in value of the swaps of ($103 million) or $104 million, respectively. A hypothetical increase (or decrease) of 10% in interest rates from the level in effect at January 31, 2005, would result in a (loss) or gain in value of the swaps of ($123 million) or $126 million, respectively.

We hold currency swaps to hedge the foreign currency exchange component of our net investments in the United Kingdom and Japan. In addition, we hold a cross-currency swap which hedges the foreign currency risk of debt denominated in currencies other than the local currency. The aggregate fair value of these swaps at January 31, 2006 and 2005, was a loss of $244 million and $169 million, respectively. A hypothetical 10% increase (or decrease) in the foreign currency exchange rates underlying these swaps from the market rate would result in a (loss) or gain in the value of the swaps of ($96 million) and $78 million at January 31, 2006, and ($90 million) and $71 million at January 31, 2005. A hypothetical 10% change in interest rates underlying these swaps from the market rates in effect at January 31, 2006 and 2005, would have an insignificant impact on the value of the swaps.

In addition to currency swaps, we have designated debt of approximately £2.0 billion as of January 31, 2006 and 2005, as a hedge of our net investment in the United Kingdom. At January 31, 2006, a hypothetical 10% increase (or decrease) in value of the U.S. dollar relative to the British pound would result in a gain (or loss) in the value of the debt of $359 million. At January 31, 2005, a hypothetical 10% increase (or decrease) in value of the U.S. dollar relative to the British pound would result in a gain (or loss) in the value of the debt of $380 million. In addition, we have designated debt of approximately ¥87.1 billion as of January 31, 2006 as a hedge of our net investment in Japan. At January 31, 2006, a hypothetical 10% increase (or decrease) in value of the U.S. dollar relative to the Japanese yen would result in a gain (or loss) in the value of the debt of $75 million.

Summary of Critical Accounting Policies

Management strives to report the financial results of the Company in a clear and understandable manner, although in some cases accounting and disclosure rules are complex and require us to use technical terminology. In preparing our consolidated financial statements, we follow accounting principles generally accepted in the United States. These principles require us to make certain estimates and apply judgments that affect our financial position and results of operations as reflected in our financial statements. These judgments and estimates are based on past events and expectations of future outcomes. Actual results may differ from our estimates.

Management continually reviews its accounting policies, how they are applied and how they are reported and disclosed in our financial statements. Following is a summary of our more significant accounting policies and how they are applied in preparation of the financial statements.

Inventories

We value our inventories at the lower of cost or market as determined primarily by the retail method of accounting, using the last-in, first-out ("LIFO") method for substantially all merchandise inventories in the United States, except SAM'S CLUB merchandise and merchandise in our distribution warehouses, which is based on the cost LIFO method. Inventories for international operations are primarily valued by the retail method of accounting and are stated using the first-in, first-out ("FIFO") method.

Under the retail method, inventory is stated at cost, which is determined by applying a cost-to-retail ratio to each merchandise grouping's retail value. The cost-to-retail ratio is based on the fiscal year purchase activity. The retail method requires management to make certain judgments and estimates that may significantly impact the ending inventory valuation at cost as well as the amount of gross margin recognized. Judgments made include the recording of markdowns used to sell through inventory and shrinkage. Markdowns designated for clearance activity are recorded at the time of the decision rather than at the point of sale, when management determines the salability of inventory has diminished. Factors considered in the determination of markdowns include current and anticipated demand, customer preferences and age of merchandise, as well as seasonal and fashion trends. Changes in weather patterns and customer preferences related to fashion trends could cause material changes in the amount and timing of markdowns from year to year.

When necessary, the Company records a LIFO provision each quarter for the estimated annual effect of inflation, and these estimates are adjusted to actual results determined at year-end. Our LIFO provision is calculated based on inventory levels, markup rates and internally generated retail price indices except for grocery items, for which we use a consumer price index. At January 31, 2006 and 2005, our inventories valued at LIFO approximated those inventories as if they were valued at FIFO.

The Company provides for estimated inventory losses ("shrinkage") between physical inventory counts on the basis of a percentage of sales. The provision is adjusted annually to reflect the historical trend of the actual physical inventory count results. Historically, shrinkage has not been volatile.

Impairment of Assets

We evaluate long-lived assets other than goodwill for indicators of impairment whenever events or changes in circumstances indicate their carrying values may not be recoverable. Management's judgments regarding the existence of impairment indicators are based on market conditions and our operational performance, such as operating income and cash flows. The variability of these factors depends on a number of conditions, including uncertainty about future events, and thus our accounting estimates may change from period to period. These factors could cause management to conclude that impairment indicators exist and require that impairment tests be performed, which could result in management determining that the value of long-lived assets is impaired, resulting in a writedown of the long-lived assets.

Goodwill is not amortized, but is evaluated for impairment annually or whenever events or changes in circumstances indicate that the value of certain goodwill may be impaired. This evaluation requires management to make judgments relating to future cash flows, growth rates, and economic and market conditions. These evaluations are based on discounted cash flows that incorporate the impact of existing Company businesses. Historically, the Company has generated sufficient returns to recover the cost of goodwill and other intangible assets. Because of the nature of the factors used in these tests, if different conditions occur in future periods, future operating results could be materially impacted.

Income Taxes

The determination of our provision for income taxes requires significant judgment, the use of estimates, and the interpretation and application of complex tax laws. Significant judgment is required in assessing the timing and amounts of deductible and taxable items. We establish reserves when, despite our belief that our tax return positions are fully supportable, we believe that certain positions may be successfully challenged. When facts and circumstances change, we adjust these reserves through our provision for income taxes.

Self-Insurance

We use a combination of insurance, self-insured retention and self-insurance for a number of risks, including, without limitation, workers' compensation, general liability, vehicle liability and the Company's portion of employee-related health care benefits. Liabilities associated with the risks that we retain are estimated in part by considering historical claims experience, including frequency, severity, demographic factors, and other actuarial assumptions. In calculating our liability, we analyze our historical trends, including loss development, and apply appropriate loss development factors to the incurred costs associated with the claims made against our self-insured program. The estimated accruals for these liabilities could be significantly affected if future occurrences or loss development differ from these assumptions. For example, for workers' compensation and liability, a 1% increase or decrease to the assumptions for claims costs and loss development factors would increase or decrease our self-insurance accrual by $23 million and $62 million, respectively.

For a summary of our significant accounting policies, please see Note 1 to our consolidated financial statements that appear after this discussion.

Forward-Looking Statements

This Annual Report contains statements that Wal-Mart believes are "forward-looking statements" within the meaning of the Private Securities Litigation Reform Act of 1995. Those statements are intended to enjoy the protection of the safe harbor for forward-looking statements provided by that Act. These forward-looking statements include statements under the caption "Results of Operations" regarding the effect of the opening of new stores on existing stores sales and the trend in the percentages that the net sales of certain of our business segments represent of our total net sales, under the caption "SAM'S CLUB Segment" regarding the improvement in net sales in the SAM'S CLUB Segment and under the caption "Liquidity and Capital Resources" in Management's Discussion and Analysis of Results of Operations and Financial Condition with respect to our capital expenditures, our ability to fund certain cash flow shortfalls by the sale of commercial paper and long-term debt securities, our ability to sell our long-term securities and our anticipated reasons for repurchasing shares of our common stock. These statements are identified by the use of the words "anticipate," "believe," "contemplate," "expect," "plan," and other, similar words or phrases. Similarly, descriptions of our objectives, strategies, plans, goals or targets are also forward-looking statements. These statements discuss, among other things, expected growth, future revenues, future cash flows, future capital expenditures, future performance and the anticipation and expectations of Wal-Mart and its management as to future occurrences and trends. These forward-looking statement are subject to certain factors, in the United States and internationally, that could affect our financial performance, business strategy, plans, goals and objectives. Those factors include the cost of goods, labor costs, the cost of fuel and electricity, the cost of healthcare benefits, insurance costs, catastrophic events, competitive pressures, inflation, accident-related costs, consumer buying patterns and debt levels, weather patterns, transport of goods from foreign suppliers, currency exchange fluctuations, trade restrictions, changes in tariff and freight rates, changes in tax and other laws and regulations that affect our business, the outcome of legal proceedings to which we are a party, unemployment levels, interest rate fluctuations, changes in employment legislation and other capital market, economic and geo-political conditions. Moreover, we typically earn a disproportionate part of our annual operating income in the fourth quarter as a result of the seasonal buying patterns. Those buying patterns are difficult to forecast with certainty. The foregoing list of factors that may affect our performance is not exclusive. Other factors and unanticipated events could adversely affect our business operations and financial performance. We discuss certain of these matters more fully, as well as certain risk factors that may affect our business operations, financial condition and results if operations, in other of our filings with the SEC, including our Annual Report on Form 10-K. We filed our Annual Report on Form 10-K for the year ended January 31, 2006, with the SEC on or about March 29, 2006. Actual results may materially differ from anticipated results described or implied in these forward-looking statements as a result of changes in facts, assumptions not being realized or other circumstances. You are urged to consider all of these risks, uncertainties and other factors carefully in evaluating the forward-looking statements. The forward-looking statements included in this Annual Report are made only as of the date of this report, and we undertake no obligation to update these forward-looking statements to reflect subsequent events or circumstances, except as may be required by applicable law.

Consolidated Statements of Income

WAL-MART

(Amounts in millions except per share data)

Fiscal Year Ended January 31,	2006	2005	2004
Revenues:			
Net sales	**$312,427**	$285,222	$256,329
Other income, net	**3,227**	2,910	2,352
	315,654	288,132	258,681
Costs and expenses:			
Cost of sales	**240,391**	219,793	198,747
Operating, selling, general and administrative expenses	**56,733**	51,248	44,909
Operating income	**18,530**	17,091	15,025
Interest:			
Debt	**1,171**	934	729
Capital leases	**249**	253	267
Interest income	**(248)**	(201)	(164)
Interest, net	**1,172**	986	832
Income from continuing operations before income taxes and minority interest	**17,358**	16,105	14,193
Provision for income taxes:			
Current	**5,932**	5,326	4,941
Deferred	**(129)**	263	177
	5,803	5,589	5,118
Income from continuing operations before minority interest	**11,555**	10,516	9,075
Minority interest	**(324)**	(249)	(214)
Income from continuing operations	**11,231**	10,267	8,861
Income from discontinued operation, net of tax	**—**	—	193
Net income	**$ 11,231**	$ 10,267	$ 9,054
Basic net income per common share:			
Income from continuing operations	**$ 2.68**	$ 2.41	$ 2.03
Income from discontinued operation	**—**	—	0.05
Basic net income per common share	**$ 2.68**	$ 2.41	$ 2.08
Diluted net income per common share:			
Income from continuing operations	**$ 2.68**	$ 2.41	$ 2.03
Income from discontinued operation	**—**	—	0.04
Diluted net income per common share	**$ 2.68**	$ 2.41	$ 2.07
Weighted-average number of common shares:			
Basic	**4,183**	4,259	4,363
Diluted	**4,188**	4,266	4,373
Dividends per common share	**$ 0.60**	$ 0.52	$ 0.36

See accompanying notes.

30

Consolidated Balance Sheets

WAL-MART

(Amounts in millions except per share data) January 31,	2006	2005
Assets		
Current assets:		
Cash and cash equivalents	**$ 6,414**	$ 5,488
Receivables	**2,662**	1,715
Inventories	**32,191**	29,762
Prepaid expenses and other	**2,557**	1,889
Total current assets	**43,824**	38,854
Property and equipment, at cost:		
Land	**16,643**	14,472
Buildings and improvements	**56,163**	46,574
Fixtures and equipment	**22,750**	21,461
Transportation equipment	**1,746**	1,530
Property and equipment, at cost	**97,302**	84,037
Less accumulated depreciation	**21,427**	18,637
Property and equipment, net	**75,875**	65,400
Property under capital lease:		
Property under capital lease	**5,578**	4,556
Less accumulated amortization	**2,163**	1,838
Property under capital lease, net	**3,415**	2,718
Goodwill	**12,188**	10,803
Other assets and deferred charges	**2,885**	2,379
Total assets	**$138,187**	$120,154
Liabilities and shareholders' equity		
Current liabilities:		
Commercial paper	**$ 3,754**	$ 3,812
Accounts payable	**25,373**	21,987
Accrued liabilities	**13,465**	12,120
Accrued income taxes	**1,340**	1,281
Long-term debt due within one year	**4,595**	3,759
Obligations under capital leases due within one year	**299**	223
Total current liabilities	**48,826**	43,182
Long-term debt	**26,429**	20,087
Long-term obligations under capital leases	**3,742**	3,171
Deferred income taxes and other	**4,552**	2,978
Minority interest	**1,467**	1,340
Commitments and contingencies		
Shareholders' equity:		
Preferred stock ($0.10 par value; 100 shares authorized, none issued)	**—**	—
Common stock ($0.10 par value; 11,000 shares authorized, 4,165 and 4,234 issued and outstanding at January 31, 2006 and January 31, 2005, respectively)	**417**	423
Capital in excess of par value	**2,596**	2,425
Accumulated other comprehensive income	**1,053**	2,694
Retained earnings	**49,105**	43,854
Total shareholders' equity	**53,171**	49,396
Total liabilities and shareholders' equity	**$138,187**	$120,154

See accompanying notes.

Consolidated Statements of Shareholders' Equity

WAL-MART

(Amounts in millions except per share data)	Number of Shares	Common Stock	Capital in Excess of Par Value	Accumulated Other Comprehensive Income	Retained Earnings	Total
Balance – January 31, 2003	4,395	$ 440	$ 1,954	$ (509)	$37,576	$39,461
Comprehensive income						
Net income from continuing operations					8,861	8,861
Net income from discontinued operation					193	193
Other comprehensive income:						
Foreign currency translation				1,685		1,685
Net unrealized depreciation of derivatives				(341)		(341)
Minimum pension liability				16		16
Total comprehensive income						10,414
Cash dividends ($0.36 per share)					(1,569)	(1,569)
Purchase of Company stock	(92)	(9)	(182)		(4,855)	(5,046)
Stock options exercised and other	8		363			363
Balance – January 31, 2004	4,311	431	2,135	851	40,206	43,623
Comprehensive income						
Net income from continuing operations					10,267	10,267
Other comprehensive income:						
Foreign currency translation				2,130		2,130
Net unrealized depreciation of derivatives				(194)		(194)
Minimum pension liability				(93)		(93)
Total comprehensive income						12,110
Cash dividends ($0.52 per share)					(2,214)	(2,214)
Purchase of Company stock	(81)	(8)	(136)		(4,405)	(4,549)
Stock options exercised and other	4		426			426
Balance – January 31, 2005	**4,234**	**423**	**2,425**	**2,694**	**43,854**	**49,396**
Comprehensive income:						
Net income from continuing operations					**11,231**	**11,231**
Other comprehensive income:						
Foreign currency translation				**(1,920)**		**(1,920)**
Net unrealized depreciation of derivatives				**228**		**228**
Minimum pension liability				**51**		**51**
Total comprehensive income						**9,590**
Cash dividends ($0.60 per share)					**(2,511)**	**(2,511)**
Purchase of Company stock	**(74)**	**(7)**	**(104)**		**(3,469)**	**(3,580)**
Stock options exercised and other	**5**	**1**	**275**			**276**
Balance – January 31, 2006	**4,165**	**$ 417**	**$ 2,596**	**$ 1,053**	**$49,105**	**$53,171**

See accompanying notes.

32

Consolidated Statements of Cash Flows

WAL-MART

(Amounts in millions)

Fiscal Year Ended January 31,	2006	2005	2004
Cash flows from operating activities			
Income from continuing operations	**$ 11,231**	$ 10,267	$ 8,861
Adjustments to reconcile net income to net cash provided by operating activities:			
Depreciation and amortization	**4,717**	4,264	3,852
Deferred income taxes	**(129)**	263	177
Other operating activities	**620**	378	173
Changes in certain assets and liabilities, net of effects of acquisitions:			
Decrease (increase) in accounts receivable	**(456)**	(304)	373
Increase in inventories	**(1,733)**	(2,494)	(1,973)
Increase in accounts payable	**2,390**	1,694	2,587
Increase in accrued liabilities	**993**	976	1,896
Net cash provided by operating activities of continuing operations	**17,633**	15,044	15,946
Net cash provided by operating activities of discontinued operation	**—**	—	50
Net cash provided by operating activities	**17,633**	15,044	15,996
Cash flows from investing activities			
Payments for property and equipment	**(14,563)**	(12,893)	(10,308)
Investment in international operations, net of cash acquired	**(601)**	(315)	(38)
Proceeds from the disposal of fixed assets	**1,049**	953	481
Proceeds from the sale of McLane	**—**	—	1,500
Other investing activities	**(68)**	(96)	78
Net cash used in investing activities of continuing operations	**(14,183)**	(12,351)	(8,287)
Net cash used in investing activities of discontinued operation	**—**	—	(25)
Net cash used in investing activities	**(14,183)**	(12,351)	(8,312)
Cash flows from financing activities			
Increase (decrease) in commercial paper	**(704)**	544	688
Proceeds from issuance of long-term debt	**7,691**	5,832	4,099
Purchase of Company stock	**(3,580)**	(4,549)	(5,046)
Dividends paid	**(2,511)**	(2,214)	(1,569)
Payment of long-term debt	**(2,724)**	(2,131)	(3,541)
Payment of capital lease obligations	**(245)**	(204)	(305)
Other financing activities	**(349)**	113	111
Net cash used in financing activities	**(2,422)**	(2,609)	(5,563)
Effect of exchange rate changes on cash	**(102)**	205	320
Net increase in cash and cash equivalents	**926**	289	2,441
Cash and cash equivalents at beginning of year	**5,488**	5,199	2,758
Cash and cash equivalents at end of year	**$ 6,414**	$ 5,488	$ 5,199
Supplemental disclosure of cash flow information			
Income tax paid	**$ 5,962**	$ 5,593	$ 4,538
Interest paid	**1,390**	1,163	1,024
Capital lease obligations incurred	**286**	377	252

See accompanying notes.

Notes to Consolidated Financial Statements

WAL-MART

1 Summary of Significant Accounting Policies

Consolidation

The consolidated financial statements include the accounts of Wal-Mart Stores, Inc. and its subsidiaries ("Wal-Mart" or the "Company"). Significant intercompany transactions have been eliminated in consolidation. Investments in which the Company has a 20 percent to 50 percent voting interest and where the Company exercises significant influence over the investee are accounted for using the equity method.

The Company's operations in Argentina, Brazil, China, Germany, Japan, Mexico, South Korea and the United Kingdom are consolidated using a December 31 fiscal year-end, generally due to statutory reporting requirements. There were no significant intervening events which materially affected the financial statements. The Company's operations in Canada and Puerto Rico are consolidated using a January 31 fiscal year-end.

The Company consolidates the accounts of certain variable interest entities where it has been determined that Wal-Mart is the primary beneficiary of those entities' operations. The assets, liabilities and results of operations of these entities are not material to the Company.

Cash and Cash Equivalents

The Company considers investments with a maturity of three months or less when purchased to be cash equivalents. The majority of payments due from banks for third-party credit card, debit card and electronic benefit transactions ("EBT") process within 24-48 hours, except for transactions occurring on a Friday, which are generally processed the following Monday. All credit card, debit card and EBT transactions that process in less than seven days are classified as cash and cash equivalents. Amounts due from banks for these transactions classified as cash totaled $575 million and $549 million at January 31, 2006 and 2005, respectively.

Receivables

Accounts receivable consist primarily of receivables from insurance companies resulting from our pharmacy sales, receivables from suppliers for marketing or incentive programs, receivables from real estate transactions and receivables from property insurance claims. Additionally, amounts due from banks for customer credit card, debit card and EBT transactions that take in excess of seven days to process are classified as accounts receivable.

Inventories

The Company values inventories at the lower of cost or market as determined primarily by the retail method of accounting, using the last-in, first-out ("LIFO") method for substantially all merchandise inventories in the United States, except SAM'S CLUB merchandise and merchandise in our distribution warehouses, which is based on the cost LIFO method. Inventories of foreign operations are primarily valued by the retail method of accounting, using the first-in, first-out ("FIFO") method. At January 31, 2006 and 2005, our inventories valued at LIFO approximate those inventories as if they were valued at FIFO.

Financial Instruments

The Company uses derivative financial instruments for purposes other than trading to manage its exposure to interest and foreign exchange rates, as well as to maintain an appropriate mix of fixed and floating-rate debt. Contract terms of a hedge instrument closely mirror those of the hedged item, providing a high degree of risk reduction and correlation. Contracts that are effective at meeting the risk reduction and correlation criteria are recorded using hedge accounting. If a derivative instrument is a hedge, depending on the nature of the hedge, changes in the fair value of the instrument will either be offset against the change in fair value of the hedged assets, liabilities or firm commitments through earnings or recognized in other comprehensive income until the hedged item is recognized in earnings. The ineffective portion of an instrument's change in fair value will be immediately recognized in earnings. Instruments that do not meet the criteria for hedge accounting, or contracts for which the Company has not elected hedge accounting, are marked to fair value with unrealized gains or losses reported in earnings during the period of change.

Capitalized Interest

Interest costs capitalized on construction projects were $157 million, $120 million, and $144 million in fiscal 2006, 2005 and 2004, respectively.

Long-Lived Assets

Long-lived assets are stated at cost. Management reviews long-lived assets for indicators of impairment whenever events or changes in circumstances indicate that the carrying value may not be recoverable. The evaluation is performed at the lowest level of identifiable cash flows, which is typically at the individual store level. Cash flows expected to be generated by the related assets are estimated over the asset's useful life based on updated projections. If the evaluation indicates that the carrying amount of the asset may not be recoverable, any potential impairment is measured based on a projected discounted cash flow method using a discount rate that is considered to be commensurate with the risk inherent in the Company's current business model.

Goodwill and Other Acquired Intangible Assets

Goodwill is not amortized; rather it is evaluated for impairment annually or whenever events or changes in circumstances indicate that the value of certain goodwill may be impaired. Other acquired intangible assets are amortized on a straight-line basis over the periods that expected economic benefits will be provided. These evaluations are based on discounted cash flows and incorporate the impact of existing Company businesses. The analyses require significant management judgment to evaluate the capacity of an acquired business to perform within projections. Historically, the Company has generated sufficient returns to recover the cost of the goodwill and other intangible assets.

Goodwill is recorded on the balance sheet in the operating segments as follows (in millions):

January 31,	2006	2005
International	$11,883	$10,498
SAM'S CLUB	305	305
Total goodwill	$12,188	$10,803

The fiscal 2006 consolidation of The Seiyu, Ltd. and acquisition of Sonae Distribuição Brasil S.A. and the fiscal 2005 acquisition of Bompreço S.A. Supermercados do Nordeste resulted in increases to goodwill. In addition, changes in the International segment's goodwill result from foreign currency exchange rate fluctuations.

Leases

The Company estimates the expected term of a lease by assuming the exercise of renewal options where an economic penalty exists that would preclude the abandonment of the lease at the end of the initial non-cancelable term and the exercise of such renewal is at the sole discretion of the Company. This expected term is used in the determination of whether a store lease is a capital or operating lease and in the calculation of straight-line rent expense. Additionally, the useful life of leasehold improvements is limited by the expected lease term. If significant expenditures are made for leasehold improvements late in the expected term of a lease, judgment is applied to determine if the leasehold improvements have a useful life that extends beyond the original expected lease term or if the leasehold improvements have a useful life that is bound by the end of the original expected lease term.

Rent abatements and escalations are considered in the calculation of minimum lease payments in the Company's capital lease tests and in determining straight-line rent expense for operating leases.

Foreign Currency Translation

The assets and liabilities of all foreign subsidiaries are translated using exchange rates at the balance sheet date. The income statements of foreign subsidiaries are translated using average exchange rates. Related translation adjustments are recorded as a component of accumulated other comprehensive income.

Revenue Recognition

The Company recognizes sales revenue net of estimated sales returns at the time it sells merchandise to the customer, except for layaway transactions. The Company recognizes revenue from layaway transactions when the customer satisfies all payment obligations and takes possession of the merchandise. Customer purchases of Wal-Mart and SAM'S CLUB shopping cards are not recognized as revenue until the card is redeemed and the customer purchases merchandise by using the shopping card.

SAM'S CLUB Membership Fee Revenue Recognition

The Company recognizes SAM'S CLUB membership fee revenues both in the United States and internationally over the term of the membership, which is 12 months. The following table details unearned revenues, membership fees received from members and the amount of revenues recognized in earnings for each of the fiscal years 2006, 2005 and 2004 (in millions):

Fiscal Year Ended January 31,	2006	2005	2004
Deferred membership fee revenue, beginning of year	$ 458	$ 449	$ 437
Membership fees received	940	890	840
Membership fee revenue recognized	(908)	(881)	(828)
Deferred membership fee revenue, end of year	$ 490	$ 458	$ 449

SAM'S CLUB membership revenue is included in other income, net in the revenues section of the Consolidated Statements of Income.

The Company's deferred membership fee revenue is included in accrued liabilities in the Consolidated Balance Sheets. The Company's analysis of historical membership fee refunds indicates that such refunds have been nominal. Accordingly, no reserve existed for membership fee refunds at January 31, 2006 and 2005.

Cost of Sales

Cost of sales includes actual product cost, change in inventory, the cost of transportation to the Company's warehouses from suppliers, the cost of transportation from the Company's warehouses to the stores and clubs and the cost of warehousing for our SAM'S CLUB segment.

Payments from Suppliers

Wal-Mart receives money from suppliers for various programs, primarily volume incentives, warehouse allowances and reimbursements for specific programs such as markdowns, margin protection and advertising. Substantially all allowances are accounted for as a reduction of purchases and recognized in our Consolidated Statements of Income when the related inventory is sold.

Operating, Selling, General and Administrative Expenses

Operating, selling, general and administrative expenses include all operating costs of the Company that are not related to the transportation of products from the supplier to the warehouse or from the warehouse to the store. Additionally, the cost of warehousing and occupancy for our Wal-Mart Stores segment distribution facilities are included in operating, selling, general and administrative expenses. Because we do not include the cost of our Wal-Mart Stores segment distribution facilities in cost of sales, our gross profit and gross margin may not be comparable to those of other retailers that may include all costs related to their distribution facilities in costs of sales and in the calculation of gross profit and gross margin.

Notes to Consolidated Financial Statements

WAL-MART

Advertising Costs

Advertising costs are expensed as incurred and were $1.6 billion, $1.4 billion and $966 million in fiscal 2006, 2005 and 2004, respectively. Advertising costs consist primarily of print and television advertisements.

Pre-Opening Costs

The costs of start-up activities, including organization costs and new store openings, are expensed as incurred.

Share-Based Compensation

The Company recognizes expense for its share-based compensation based on the fair value of the awards that are granted. The fair value of stock options is estimated at the date of grant using the Black-Scholes-Merton option valuation model which was developed for use in estimating the fair value of exchange traded options that have no vesting restrictions and are fully transferable. Option valuation methods require the input of highly subjective assumptions, including the expected stock price volatility. Measured compensation cost is recognized ratably over the vesting period of the related share-based compensation award.

Share-based compensation awards that may be settled in cash are accounted for as liabilities and marked to market each period.

Insurance/Self-Insurance

The Company uses a combination of insurance, self-insured retention and self-insurance for a number of risks, including, without limitation, workers' compensation, general liability, vehicle liability and the Company-funded portion of employee-related health care benefits. Liabilities associated with these risks are estimated in part by considering historical claims experience, demographic factors, frequency and severity factors and other actuarial assumptions.

Depreciation and Amortization

Depreciation and amortization for financial statement purposes are provided on the straight-line method over the estimated useful lives of the various assets. Depreciation expense, including amortization of property under capital leases for fiscal years 2006, 2005 and 2004 was $4.7 billion, $4.3 billion and $3.9 billion, respectively. For income tax purposes, accelerated methods of depreciation are used with recognition of deferred income taxes for the resulting temporary differences. Leasehold improvements are depreciated over the shorter of the estimated useful life of the asset or the remaining lease term. Estimated useful lives for financial statement purposes are as follows:

Buildings and improvements	5–50 years
Fixtures and equipment	3–12 years
Transportation equipment	3–15 years

Income Taxes

Income taxes are accounted for under the asset and liability method. Deferred tax assets and liabilities are recognized for the estimated future tax consequences attributable to differences between the financial statement carrying amounts of existing assets and liabilities and their respective tax bases. Deferred tax assets and liabilities are measured using enacted tax rates in effect for the year in which those temporary differences are expected to be recovered or settled. The effect on deferred tax assets and liabilities of a change in tax rate is recognized in income in the period that includes the enactment date. Valuation allowances are established when necessary to reduce deferred tax assets to the amounts more likely than not to be realized.

In determining the quarterly provision for income taxes, the Company uses an annual effective tax rate based on expected annual income and statutory tax rates. The effective tax rate also reflects the Company's assessment of the ultimate outcome of tax audits. Significant discrete items are separately recognized in the income tax provision in the quarter in which they occur.

The determination of the Company's provision for income taxes requires significant judgment, the use of estimates, and the interpretation and application of complex tax laws. Significant judgment is required in assessing the timing and amounts of deductible and taxable items. Reserves are established when, despite management's belief that the Company's tax return positions are fully supportable, management believes that certain positions may be successfully challenged. When facts and circumstances change, these reserves are adjusted through the provision for income taxes.

Net Income Per Common Share

Basic net income per common share is based on the weighted-average outstanding common shares. Diluted net income per common share is based on the weighted-average outstanding shares adjusted for the dilutive effect of stock options and restricted stock grants. The dilutive effect of stock options and restricted stock was 5 million, 7 million and 10 million shares in fiscal 2006, 2005 and 2004, respectively. The Company had approximately 57 million, 59 million and 50 million option shares outstanding at January 31, 2006, 2005 and 2004, respectively, which were not included in the diluted net income per share calculation because their effect would be antidilutive as the underlying option price exceeded the average market price of the stock for the period.

Estimates and Assumptions

The preparation of consolidated financial statements in conformity with generally accepted accounting principles requires Management to make estimates and assumptions. These estimates and assumptions affect the reported amounts of assets and liabilities. They also affect the disclosure of contingent assets and liabilities at the date of the consolidated financial statements and the reported amounts of revenues and expenses during the reporting period. Actual results may differ from those estimates.

Reclassifications

Certain reclassifications have been made to prior periods to conform to current presentations.

2 Commercial Paper and Long-term Debt

Information on short-term borrowings and interest rates is as follows (dollars in millions):

Fiscal Year	2006	2005	2004
Maximum amount outstanding at any month-end	**$9,054**	$7,782	$4,957
Average daily short-term borrowings	**5,719**	4,823	1,498
Weighted-average interest rate	**3.4%**	1.6%	1.1%

At January 31, 2006 and 2005, short-term borrowings consisted of $3.8 billion of commercial paper. At January 31, 2006, the Company had committed lines of credit of $5.0 billion with 57 firms and banks, which were used to support commercial paper, and committed and informal lines of credit with various banks totaling an additional $693 million.

Long-term debt at January 31, consists of (in millions)

Interest Rate	Due by Fiscal Year	2006	2005
2.130 – 6.875%	Notes due 2010	**$ 4,527**	$ 4,500
5.250%	Notes due 2036	**4,279**	1,883
1.100 – 13.250%, LIBOR less 0.140%	Notes due 2007	**3,415**	3,164
2.875 – 8.380%, LIBOR less 0.1025%	Notes due 2008	**3,311**	1,500
0.1838 – 0.880%	Notes due 2011[(1)]	**3,308**	500
0.750 – 7.250%	Notes due 2014	**2,885**	2,883
3.000 – 3.375%	Notes due 2009	**2,800**	1,000
1.200 – 4.125%	Notes due 2012	**2,015**	2,000
5.750 – 7.550%	Notes due 2031	**1,890**	1,941
3.150 – 6.630%	Notes due 2016	**767**	—
2.950 – 5.006%	Notes due 2019[(1)]	**516**	500
5.300 – 6.750%	Notes due 2024	**266**	250
2.100 – 2.875%	Notes due 2015	**53**	—
2.000 – 2.500%	Notes due 2017	**41**	—
3.750 – 5.000%	Notes due 2018	**31**	—
5.170%	Notes due 2021	**25**	—
1.000 – 2.300%	Notes due 2013	**23**	—
4.150 – 5.875%, LIBOR less 0.0425%	Notes due 2006	**—**	2,597
	Other[(2)]	**872**	1,128
Total		**$31,024**	$23,846

(1) *Includes put option on $500 million.*

(2) *Includes adjustments to debt hedged by derivatives.*

The Company has two separate issuances of $500 million debt with embedded put options. For the first issuance, beginning June 2001, and each year thereafter, the holders of $500 million of the debt may require the Company to repurchase the debt at face value, in addition to accrued and unpaid interest. The holders of the other $500 million issuance may require the Company to repurchase the debt at par plus accrued interest at any time. Both of these issuances have been classified as a current liability in the Consolidated Balance Sheets.

Under the Company's most significant borrowing arrangements, the Company is not required to observe financial covenants. However, under certain lines of credit totaling $5.0 billion, which were undrawn as of January 31, 2006, the Company has agreed to observe certain covenants, the most restrictive of which relates to minimum net worth levels and amounts of additional secured debt and long-term leases. In addition, one of our subsidiaries has restrictive financial covenants on $2.0 billion of long-term debt that requires it to maintain certain equity, sales, and profit levels. The Company was in compliance with these covenants at January 31, 2006.

Long-term debt is unsecured except for $1.1 billion, which is collateralized by property with an aggregate carrying value of approximately $1.4 billion. Annual maturities of long-term debt during the next five years and thereafter are (in millions):

Fiscal Year Ended January 31,	Annual Maturity
2007	$ 4,595
2008	3,320
2009	2,858
2010	4,639
2011	2,877
Thereafter	12,735
Total	$ 31,024

The Company has entered into sale/leaseback transactions involving buildings while retaining title to the underlying land. These transactions were accounted for as financings and are included in long-term debt and the annual maturities schedule above. The resulting obligations are amortized over the lease terms. Future minimum lease payments during the next five years and thereafter are (in millions):

Fiscal Year Ended January 31,	Minimum Payments
2007	$ 9
2008	10
2009	10
2010	10
2011	10
Thereafter	211
Total	$ 260

Notes to Consolidated Financial Statements

WAL-MART

The Company had trade letters of credit outstanding totaling $2.6 billion at January 31, 2006 and 2005. At January 31, 2006 and 2005, the Company had standby letters of credit outstanding totaling $2.3 billion and $2.0 billion, respectively. These letters of credit were issued primarily for the purchase of inventory and insurance.

3 Financial Instruments

The Company uses derivative financial instruments for hedging and non-trading purposes to manage its exposure to interest and foreign exchange rates. Use of derivative financial instruments in hedging programs subjects the Company to certain risks, such as market and credit risks. Market risk represents the possibility that the value of the derivative instrument will change. In a hedging relationship, the change in the value of the derivative is offset to a great extent by the change in the value of the underlying hedged item. Credit risk related to derivatives represents the possibility that the counterparty will not fulfill the terms of the contract. The notional, or contractual, amount of the Company's derivative financial instruments is used to measure interest to be paid or received and does not represent the Company's exposure due to credit risk. Credit risk is monitored through established approval procedures, including setting concentration limits by counterparty, reviewing credit ratings and requiring collateral (generally cash) when appropriate. The majority of the Company's transactions are with counterparties rated "AA-" or better by nationally recognized credit rating agencies.

Fair Value Instruments

The Company enters into interest rate swaps to minimize the risks and costs associated with its financing activities. Under the swap agreements, the Company pays variable-rate interest and receives fixed-rate interest payments periodically over the life of the instruments. The notional amounts are used to measure interest to be paid or received and do not represent the exposure due to credit loss. All of the Company's interest rate swaps that receive fixed interest rate payments and pay variable interest rate payments are designated as fair value hedges. As the specific terms and notional amounts of the derivative instruments exactly match those of the instruments being hedged, the derivative instruments were assumed to be perfect hedges and all changes in fair value of the hedges were recorded on the balance sheet with no net impact on the income statement.

Net investment Instruments

At January 31, 2006, the Company is party to cross-currency interest rate swaps that hedge its net investments in the United Kingdom and Japan. The agreements are contracts to exchange fixed-rate payments in one currency for fixed-rate payments in another currency. The Company also has outstanding approximately £2.0 billion of debt that is designated as a hedge of the Company's net investment in the United Kingdom and ¥87.1 billion of debt that is designated as a hedge of the Company's net investment in Japan. All changes in the fair value of these instruments are recorded in other comprehensive income, offsetting the foreign currency translation adjustment that is also recorded in other comprehensive income.

Cash Flow Instruments

The Company is party to a cross-currency interest rate swap to hedge the foreign currency risk of certain foreign-denominated debt. The swap is designated as a cash flow hedge of foreign currency exchange risk. The agreement is a contract to exchange fixed-rate payments in one currency for fixed-rate payments in another currency. Changes in the foreign currency spot exchange rate result in reclassification of amounts from other accumulated comprehensive income to earnings to offset transaction gains or losses on foreign-denominated debt. The instrument matures in fiscal 2007.

The Company expects that the amount of gain or loss existing in other accumulated comprehensive income to be reclassified into earnings within the next 12 months will not be significant.

Fair Value of Financial Instruments

Instrument Fiscal Year Ended January 31, (in millions)	Notional Amount **2006**	 2005	Fair Value **2006**	 2005
Derivative financial instruments designated for hedging:				
Receive fixed-rate, pay floating rate interest rate swaps designated as fair value hedges	**$ 6,945**	$ 8,042	**$ 133**	$ 477
Receive fixed-rate, pay fixed-rate cross-currency interest rate swaps designated as net investment hedges (Cross-currency notional amount: GBP 795 at 1/31/2006 and 1/31/2005)	**1,250**	1,250	**(107)**	(14)
Receive fixed-rate, pay fixed-rate cross-currency interest rate swap designated as a cash flow hedge (Cross-currency notional amount: CAD 503 at 1/31/2006 and 1/31/2005)	**325**	325	**(120)**	(87)
Receive fixed-rate, pay fixed-rate cross-currency interest rate swap designated as a net investment hedge (Cross-currency notional amount: ¥52,056 at 1/31/2006 and 1/31/2005)	**432**	432	**(17)**	(68)
Receive floating rate, pay fixed-rate interest rate swap designated as a cash flow hedge	**—**	1,500	**—**	(5)
Total	**$ 8,952**	$11,549	**$ (111)**	$ 303
Non-derivative financial instruments:				
Long-term debt	**$31,024**	$23,846	**$31,580**	$25,016

Notes to Consolidated Financial Statements

WAL-MART

Hedging instruments with an unrealized gain are recorded on the Consolidated Balance Sheets in other current assets or other assets and deferred charges, based on maturity date. Those instruments with an unrealized loss are recorded in accrued liabilities or deferred income taxes and other, based on maturity date.

Cash and cash equivalents: The carrying amount approximates fair value due to the short maturity of these instruments.

Long-term debt: Fair value is based on the Company's current incremental borrowing rate for similar types of borrowing arrangements.

Fair value instruments and net investment instruments: The fair values are estimated amounts the Company would receive or pay to terminate the agreements as of the reporting dates.

4 Accumulated Other Comprehensive Income

Comprehensive income is net income plus certain other items that are recorded directly to shareholders' equity. Amounts included in accumulated other comprehensive income for the Company's derivative instruments and minimum pension liability are recorded net of the related income tax effects. The following table gives further detail regarding changes in the composition of accumulated other comprehensive income during fiscal 2006, 2005 and 2004 (in millions):

	Foreign Currency Translation	Derivative Instruments	Minimum Pension liability	Total
Balance at January 31, 2003	$ (1,125)	$ 822	$ (206)	$ (509)
Foreign currency translation adjustment	1,685			1,685
Change in fair value of hedge instruments		(444)		(444)
Reclassification to earnings		103		103
Subsidiary minimum pension liability			16	16
Balance at January 31, 2004	560	481	(190)	851
Foreign currency translation adjustment	2,130			2,130
Change in fair value of hedge instruments		(235)		(235)
Reclassification to earnings		41		41
Subsidiary minimum pension liability			(93)	(93)
Balance at January 31, 2005	**$ 2,690**	**$ 287**	**$ (283)**	**$ 2,694**
Foreign currency translation adjustment	**(1,920)**			**(1,920)**
Change in fair value of hedge instruments		**157**		**157**
Reclassification to earnings		**71**		**71**
Subsidiary minimum pension liability			**51**	**51**
Balance at January 31, 2006	**$ 770**	**$ 515**	**$ (232)**	**$ 1,053**

5 Income Taxes

The income tax provision consists of the following (in millions):

Fiscal Year Ended January 31,	2006	2005	2004
Current:			
Federal	**$4,646**	$4,116	$4,039
State and local	**449**	640	333
International	**837**	570	569
Total current tax provision	**5,932**	5,326	4,941
Deferred:			
Federal	**(62)**	311	31
State and local	**56**	(71)	2
International	**(123)**	23	144
Total deferred tax provision	**(129)**	263	177
Total provision for income taxes	**$5,803**	$5,589	$5,118

Income from continuing operations before income takes and minority interest by jurisdiction is as follows (in millions):

Fiscal Year Ended January 31,	2006	2005	2004
United States	**$14,447**	$13,599	$12,075
Outside the United States	**$ 2,911**	2,506	2,118
Total income from continuing operations before income taxes and minority interest	**$17,358**	$16,105	$14,193

Notes to Consolidated Financial Statements

WAL-MART

Items that give rise to significant portions of the deferred tax accounts are as follows (in millions):

January 31,	2006	2005
Deferred tax liabilities		
Property and equipment	**$ 2,355**	$2,210
International, principally asset basis differences	**1,141**	1,054
Inventory	**336**	187
Other	**265**	230
Total deferred tax liabilities	**$ 4,097**	$3,681
Deferred tax assets		
International loss carryforwards and asset basis differences	**$ 2,082**	$1,460
Amounts accrued for financial reporting purposes not yet deductible for tax purposes	**1,668**	1,361
Stock-based compensation expense	**248**	258
Other	**353**	263
Total deferred tax assets	**4,351**	3,342
Valuation allowance	**(1,054)**	(526)
Total deferred tax assets, net of valuation allowance	**$ 3,297**	$2,816
Net deferred tax liabilities	**$ 800**	$ 865

The change in the Company's net deferred tax liability is impacted by foreign currency translation.

A reconciliation of the significant differences between the effective income tax rate and the federal statutory rate on pretax income is as follows:

Fiscal Year Ended January 31,	2006	2005	2004
Statutory tax rate	**35.00%**	35.00%	35.00%
State income taxes, net of federal income tax benefit	**1.86%**	2.30%	1.53%
Income taxes outside the United States	**(1.75%)**	(1.81%)	(0.20%)
Other	**(1.68%)**	(0.79%)	(0.27%)
Effective income tax rate	**33.43%**	34.70%	36.06%

Federal and state income taxes have not been provided on accumulated but undistributed earnings of foreign subsidiaries aggregating approximately $6.8 billion at January 31, 2006 and $5.3 billion at January 31, 2005, as such earnings have been permanently reinvested in the business. The determination of the amount of the unrecognized deferred tax liability related to the undistributed earnings is not practicable.

The Company had foreign net operating loss carryforwards of $4.7 billion at January 31, 2006. Of this amount, $1.3 billion related to the December 2005 consolidation of The Seiyu, Ltd. The recording of the related deferred tax asset of $525 million resulted in a corresponding increase in the valuation allowance. Any tax benefit ultimately realized from the Japan net operating loss carryforward will adjust goodwill. Net operating loss carryforwards of $1.4 billion expire in various years through 2011.

6 Acquisitions And Disposal

Acquisitions

During December 2005, the Company purchased an additional interest in The Seiyu, Ltd. ("Seiyu"), for approximately $570 million, bringing the Company's total investment in Seiyu, including adjustments arising from the equity method of accounting, to $1.2 billion. Seiyu is a retailer in Japan, which operates 398 stores selling apparel, general merchandise, food and certain services. Following this additional purchase, the Company owns approximately 53.3% of Seiyu. Beginning on the date of the controlling interest purchase, the Company began consolidating Seiyu as a majority-owned subsidiary using a December 31 fiscal year-end. Seiyu's results of operations were not material to the Company. As a result of the consolidation of Seiyu, total assets and liabilities of $6.8 billion and $5.6 billion, respectively, were recorded in our financial statements. Goodwill recorded in the consolidation amounted to approximately $1.6 billion. The amount of assets and liabilities recorded in the consolidation of Seiyu are preliminary estimates made by management and will be finalized upon completion of the valuation of tangible and intangible assets and liabilities.

The minority interest in Seiyu is represented, in part, by shares of Seiyu's preferred stock which are convertible into shares of Seiyu common stock. If the minority holder of Seiyu's preferred stock proposes to sell or convert its shares of preferred stock, the Company has the right to purchase those shares at a predetermined price.

Through a warrant exercisable through December 2007, the Company can contribute approximately ¥154.6 billion, or $1.3 billion at a January 31, 2006, exchange rate of 117.75 yen per dollar, for approximately 538 million additional common shares of Seiyu stock. If the warrant is exercised, we would own approximately 71% of the stock of Seiyu by the end of December 2007. These calculations assume no conversion of Seiyu's preferred stock into common shares and no other issuances of Seiyu common shares.

In December 2005, the Company completed the purchase of Sonae Distribuição Brasil S.A. ("Sonae"), a retail operation in Southern Brazil consisting of 139 hypermarkets, supermarkets and warehouse units. The purchase price was approximately $720 million. Assets recorded in the acquisition of Sonae were $1.3 billion and liabilities assumed were $566 million. As a result of the Sonae acquisition, we recorded goodwill of $305 million and other identifiable intangible assets of $89 million. Sonae's results of operations, which were not material to the Company, are included in our consolidated financial statements following the date of acquisition using a December 31 fiscal year-end. The amount of assets and liabilities recorded in the purchase of Sonae are preliminary estimates made by management and will be finalized upon completion of the valuation of tangible and intangible assets and liabilities.

In September 2005, the Company acquired a 33.3% interest in Central American Retail Holding Company ("CARHCO"), a retailer with more than 360 supermarkets and other stores in Costa Rica, El Salvador, Guatemala, Honduras and Nicaragua. The purchase price was approximately $318 million, including transaction costs. In fiscal 2006, the Company accounted for its investment in CARHCO under the equity method. Concurrent with the purchase of the investment in CARHCO, the Company entered into an agreement to purchase an additional 17.7% of CARHCO in the first quarter of fiscal 2007 and an option agreement that will allow the Company to purchase up to an additional 24% beginning in September 2010. To the extent that the Company does not exercise its option to purchase the additional 24% of CARHCO, the minority shareholders will have certain put rights that could require the Company to purchase the additional 24% after September 2012. In February 2006, the Company purchased the additional 17.7% of CARHCO for a purchase price of approximately $212 million.

In February 2004, the Company completed its purchase of Bompreço S. A. Supermercados do Nordeste ("Bompreço"), a supermarket chain in northern Brazil with 118 hypermarkets, supermarkets and mini-markets. The purchase price was approximately $315 million, net of cash acquired. The results of operations for Bompreço, which were not material to the Company, have been included in the Company's consolidated financial statements since the date of acquisition.

Disposal

On May 23, 2003, the Company completed the sale of McLane Company, Inc. ("McLane"). The Company received $1.5 billion in cash for the sale. The accompanying consolidated financial statements and notes reflect the gain on the sale and the operations of McLane as a discontinued operation.

Following is summarized financial information for McLane (in millions):

Fiscal Year Ended January 31,	2004
Net sales	$4,328
Income from discontinued operation	$ 67
Income tax expense	25
Net operating income from discontinued operation	42
Gain on sale of McLane, net of $147 income tax expense	151
Income from discontinued operation, net of tax	$ 193

The effective tax rate on the gain from the sale of McLane was 49% as a result of the non-deductibility of $99 million of goodwill recorded in the original McLane acquisition.

7 Share-Based Compensation Plans

As of January 31, 2006, the Company has awarded share-based compensation to executives and other associates of the Company through various share-based compensation plans. The compensation cost recognized for all plans was $244 million, $204 million, and $183 million for fiscal 2006, 2005, and 2004, respectively. The total income tax benefit recognized for all share-based compensation plans was $82 million, $71 million, and $66 million for fiscal 2006, 2005, and 2004, respectively.

On February 1, 2003, the Company adopted the expense recognition provisions of Statement of Financial Accounting Standards No. 123 ("SFAS 123"), restating results for prior periods. In December 2004, the Financial Accounting Standards Board issued a revision of SFAS 123 ("SFAS 123(R)"). The Company adopted the provisions of SFAS 123(R) upon its release. The adoption of SFAS 123(R) did not have a material impact on our results of operations, financial position or cash flows. All share-based compensation is accounted for in accordance with the fair-value based method of SFAS 123(R).

The Company's Stock Incentive Plan of 2005 (the "Plan"), which is shareholder-approved, permits the grant of stock options, restricted (non-vested) stock and performance share compensation awards to its associates for up to 210 million shares of common stock. The Company believes that such awards better align the interests of its associates with those of its shareholders.

Under the Plan and prior plans, stock option awards have been granted with an exercise price equal to the market price of the Company's stock at the date of grant. Generally, outstanding options granted before fiscal 2001 vest over seven years. Options granted after fiscal 2001 generally vest over five years. Shares issued upon the exercise of options are newly issued. Options granted generally have a contractual term of 10 years. The fair value of each stock option award is estimated on the date of grant using the Black-Scholes-Merton option valuation model that uses various assumptions for inputs, which are noted in the following table. Generally, the Company uses historical volatilities and risk free interest rates that correlate with the expected term of the option. To determine the expected life of the option, the Company bases its estimates on historical grants with similar vesting periods. The following tables represents a weighted-average of the assumptions used by the company to estimate the fair values of the Company's stock options at the grant dates:

Fiscal Year Ended January 31,	**2006**	2005	2004
Dividend yield	**1.9%**	1.1%	0.9%
Volatility	**24.9%**	26.2%	32.3%
Risk-free interest rate	**4.2%**	3.5%	2.8%
Expected life in years	**6.1**	5.3	4.5

Notes to Consolidated Financial Statements

WAL-MART

A summary of the stock option award activity for fiscal 2006 is presented below:

Options	Shares	Weighted-Average Exercise Price	Weighted-Average Remaining Life in Years	Aggregate Intrinsic Value
Outstanding at January 31, 2005	68,115,000	$ 46.79		
Granted	4,281,000	50.74		
Exercised	(4,208,000)	23.26		
Forfeited or expired	(8,645,000)	51.92		
Outstanding at January 31, 2006	59,543,000	$ 48.02	6.5	$163,326,000
Exercisable at January 31, 2006	32,904,000	$ 45.20	5.3	$162,240,000

The weighted-average grant-date fair value of options granted during the fiscal years ended January 31, 2006, 2005 and 2004, was $12.29, $11.92 and $14.89, respectively. The total intrinsic value of options exercised during the years ended January 31, 2006, 2005 and 2004, was $108.3 million, $221.6 million and $231.0 million, respectively.

Under the Plan, the Company grants various types of awards of restricted (non-vested) stock to certain associates. These grants include awards for shares that vest based on the passage of time, performance criteria, or both. Vesting periods vary. The restricted stock awards may be settled in stock, or deferred as stock or cash, based upon the associate's election. Consequently, these awards are classified as liabilities in the accompanying balance sheets unless the associate has elected for the award to be settled or deferred in stock. The fair value of the restricted stock liabilities is remeasured each reporting period. The total liability for restricted stock awards at January 31, 2006, was $61.1 million.

A summary of the Company's restricted (non-vested) stock award activity for fiscal 2006 is presented below:

Non-Vested Stock Awards	Shares	Weighted-Average Grant-Date Fair Value
Restricted Stock Awards at January 31, 2005	3,423,000	$ 46.63
Granted	2,955,000	$ 44.81
Vested	(383,000)	$ 44.78
Forfeited	(551,000)	$ 45.02
Restricted Stock Awards at January 31, 2006	5,444,000	$ 46.08

As of January 31, 2006, there was $157.9 million of total unrecognized compensation cost related to restricted stock granted under the Plan, which is expected to be recognized over a weighted-average period of 5.9 years. The total fair value of shares vested during the fiscal years ended January 31, 2006, 2005, and 2004, was $19.9 million, $33.9 million and $8.0 million, respectively.

During fiscal 2005, the Company began issuing performance share awards under the Plan, the vesting of which is tied to the achievement of performance criteria. These awards accrue to the associate based on the extent to which revenue growth and return on investment goals are attained or exceeded over a one- to three-year period. Based on the extent to which the targets are achieved, vested shares may range from 0% to 150% of the original award amount. Because the performance shares may be settled in stock or cash, the performance shares are accounted for as liabilities in the accompanying balance sheets. Outstanding performance shares, the related liability and unrecognized compensation cost as of January 31, 2006 and 2005, were not significant.

The Company's United Kingdom subsidiary, ASDA, also offers two other stock option plans to its associates. The first plan, The ASDA Colleague Share Ownership Plan 1999 ("CSOP"), grants options to certain associates. Options granted under the CSOP Plan generally expire six years from the date of grant, with half vesting on the third anniversary of the grant and the other half on the sixth anniversary of the date of grant. Shares in the money at the vesting date are exercised while shares out of the money at the vesting date expire. The second plan, The ASDA Sharesave Plan 2000 ("Sharesave"), grants options to certain associates at 80% of market value on the date of grant. Sharesave options become exercisable after either a three-year or five-year period and generally lapse six months after becoming exercisable. Outstanding options under these plans as well as the related aggregate intrinsic value as of January 31, 2006, were not significant.

8 Litigation

The Company is involved in a number of legal proceedings. In accordance with Statement of Financial Accounting Standards No. 5, "Accounting for Contingencies," the Company has made accruals with respect to these matters, where appropriate, which are reflected in the Company's consolidated financial statements. The Company may enter into discussions regarding settlement of these matters, and may enter into settlement agreements, if it believes settlement is in the best interests of the Company's shareholders. The matters, or groups of related matters, discussed below, if decided adversely to or settled by the Company, individually or in the aggregate, may result in liability material to the Company's financial condition or results of operations.

The Company is a defendant in numerous cases containing class-action allegations in which the plaintiffs have brought claims under the Fair Labor Standards Act ("FLSA"), corresponding state statutes, or other laws. The plaintiffs in these lawsuits are current and former hourly associates who allege, among other things, that the Company forced them to work "off the clock," or failed to provide work breaks, or otherwise claim they were not paid for work performed. The complaints generally seek unspecified monetary damages, injunctive relief, or both. Class certification has yet to be addressed in a majority of the cases. Class certification has been denied or overturned in cases pending in Arizona, Arkansas, Florida, Georgia, Indiana, Louisiana, Maryland, Michigan, Nevada, New Jersey, North Carolina, Ohio, Texas, West Virginia and Wisconsin. Some or all of the requested classes have been certified in cases pending in California, Colorado, Massachusetts, Minnesota, Missouri, New Mexico, Oregon, Pennsylvania and Washington. Conditional certifications for notice purposes under the FLSA have been allowed in cases in Georgia, Michigan and Texas. The Company cannot estimate the possible loss or range of loss which may arise from these lawsuits.

The Company is a defendant in *Savaglio v. Wal-Mart Stores, Inc.*, a class-action lawsuit in which the plaintiffs allege that they were not provided meal and rest breaks in accordance with California law, and seek monetary damages and injunctive relief. A jury trial on the plaintiffs' claims for monetary damages concluded on December 22, 2005. The jury returned a verdict of $57,216,673 in statutory penalties and $115 million in punitive damages. The Company believes that it has substantial defenses to the claims at issue, and intends to challenge the verdict in post-trial motions and, if necessary, on appeal. Meanwhile, the plaintiffs' claims for injunctive relief have been tentatively set for trial in June 2006.

A putative class action is pending in California challenging the methodology of payments made under various Associate incentive bonus plans, and a second putative class action in California asserts that the Company has omitted to include bonus payments in calculating associates' regular rate of pay for purposes of determining overtime. As to the first case (*Cruz v. Wal-Mart Stores, Inc.*), the Company cannot estimate the possible loss or range of loss which may arise. The parties have entered into an agreement to settle the second case (*Fries v. Wal-Mart Stores, Inc.*), which must be approved by the court in order to become effective. If approved by the court, the settlement will include all class members who do not opt out of the settlement class. The amount to be paid by Wal-Mart under the settlement will not have a material impact on the Company's financial condition or results of operations.

The Company is currently a defendant in five putative class actions brought on behalf of assistant store managers who challenge their exempt status under state and federal laws, which are pending in California, Michigan, New Mexico and Tennessee. Conditional certification for notice purposes under the FLSA has been granted in one of these cases (*Comer v. Wal-Mart Stores, Inc.*). Otherwise, no determination has been made as to class certification in any of these cases. The Company cannot estimate the possible loss or range of loss which may arise from these lawsuits.

The Company is a defendant in *Dukes v. Wal-Mart Stores, Inc.*, a class-action lawsuit commenced in June 2001 and pending in the United States District Court for the Northern District of California. The case was brought on behalf of all past and present female employees in all of the Company's retail stores and warehouse clubs in the United States. The complaint alleges that the Company has engaged in a pattern and practice of discriminating against women in promotions, pay, training and job assignments. The complaint seeks, among other things, injunctive relief, front pay, back pay, punitive damages, and attorneys' fees. Following a hearing on class certification on September 24, 2003, on June 21, 2004, the District Court issued an order granting in part and denying in part the plaintiffs' motion for class certification. The class, which was certified by the District Court for purposes of liability, injunctive and declaratory relief, punitive damages, and lost pay, subject to certain exceptions, includes all women employed at any Wal-Mart domestic retail store at any time since December 26, 1998, who have been or may be subjected to the pay and management track promotions policies and practices challenged by the plaintiffs. The class as certified currently includes approximately 1.6 million present and former female associates.

The Company believes that the District Court's ruling is incorrect. The United States Court of Appeals for the Ninth Circuit has granted the Company's petition for discretionary review of the ruling. The Court of Appeals heard oral argument from counsel in the case on August 8, 2005. There is no indication at this time as to when a decision will be rendered. If the Company is not successful in its appeal of class certification, or an appellate court issues a ruling that allows for the certification of a class or classes with a different size or scope, and if there is a subsequent adverse verdict on the merits from which there is no successful appeal, or in the event of a negotiated settlement of the litigation, the resulting liability could be material to the Company. The plaintiffs also seek punitive damages which, if awarded, could result in the payment of additional amounts material to the Company. However, because of the uncertainty of the outcome of the appeal from the District Court's certification decision, because of the uncertainty of the balance of the proceedings contemplated by the District Court, and because the Company's liability, if any, arising from the litigation, including the size of any damages award if plaintiffs are successful in the litigation or any negotiated settlement, could vary widely, the Company cannot reasonably estimate the possible loss or range of loss which may arise from the litigation.

The Company is a defendant in *Mauldin v. Wal-Mart Stores, Inc.*, a class-action lawsuit that was filed on October 16, 2001, in the United States District Court for the Northern District of Georgia, Atlanta Division. The class was certified on August 23, 2002. On September 30, 2003, the court denied the Company's motion to reconsider that ruling. The class is composed of female Wal-Mart associates who were participants in the Associates Health and Welfare Plan at any time from March 8, 2001, to the present and who were using prescription contraceptives. The class seeks amendment of the Plan to include coverage for prescription contraceptives, back pay for all members in the form of reimbursement of the cost of prescription contraceptives, pre-judgment interest, and attorneys'

Notes to Consolidated Financial Statements

WAL-MART

fees. The complaint alleges that the Company's Health Plan violates Title VII's prohibition against gender discrimination in that the Health Plan's Reproductive Systems provision does not provide coverage for prescription contraceptives. The Company cannot estimate the possible loss or range of loss which may arise from this litigation.

The Company is a defendant in a lawsuit that was filed on August 24, 2001, in the United States District Court for the Eastern District of Kentucky. *EEOC (Janice Smith) v. Wal-Mart Stores, Inc.* is an action brought by the EEOC on behalf of Janice Smith and all other females who made application or transfer requests at the London, Kentucky, distribution center from 1995 to the present, and who were not hired or transferred into the warehouse positions for which they applied. The class seeks back pay for those females not selected for hire or transfer during the relevant time period. The class also seeks injunctive and prospective affirmative relief. The complaint alleges that the Company based hiring decisions on gender in violation of Title VII of the 1964 Civil Rights Act as amended. The EEOC can maintain this action as a class without certification. The Company cannot estimate the possible loss or range of loss which may arise from this litigation.

On November 8, 2005, the Company received a grand jury subpoena from the United States Attorney's Office for the Central District of California, seeking documents and information relating to the Company's receipt, transportation, handling, identification, recycling, treatment, storage and disposal of certain merchandise that constitutes hazardous materials or hazardous waste. The Company has been informed by the U.S. Attorney's Office for the Central District of California that it is a target of a criminal investigation into potential violations of the Resource Conservation and Recovery Act ("RCRA"), the Clean Water Act, and the Hazardous Materials Transportation Statute. This U.S. Attorney's Office contends, among other things, that the use of Company trucks to transport certain returned merchandise from the Company's stores to its return centers is prohibited by RCRA because those materials may be considered hazardous waste. The government alleges that, to comply with RCRA, the Company must ship from the store certain materials as "hazardous waste" directly to a certified disposal facility using a certified hazardous waste carrier. The Company contends that the practice of transporting returned merchandise to its return centers for subsequent disposition, including disposal by certified facilities, is compliant with applicable laws and regulations.

Additionally, the U.S. Attorney's Office in the Northern District of California has initiated its own investigation regarding the Company's handling of hazardous materials and hazardous waste and the Company has received administrative document requests from the California Department of Toxic Substances Control requesting documents and information with respect to two of the Company's distribution facilities. Further, the Company also received a subpoena from the Los Angeles County District Attorney's Office for documents and administrative interrogatories requesting information, among other things, regarding the Company's handling of materials and hazardous waste. California state and local government authorities and the State of Nevada have also initiated investigations into these matters. The Company is cooperating fully with the respective authorities.

The Company cannot estimate the possible loss or range of loss which may arise from this matter.

9 Commitments

The Company and certain of its subsidiaries have long-term leases for stores and equipment. Rentals (including, for certain leases, amounts applicable to taxes, insurance, maintenance, other operating expenses and contingent rentals) under operating leases and other short-term rental arrangements were $1.3 billion, $1.2 billion and $1.1 billion in 2006, 2005 and 2004, respectively. Aggregate minimum annual rentals at January 31, 2006, under non-cancelable leases are as follows (in millions):

Fiscal Year	Operating Leases	Capital Leases
2007	$ 797	$ 592
2008	751	588
2009	710	550
2010	634	526
2011	586	514
Thereafter	6,205	3,610
Total minimum rentals	$ 9,683	6,380
Less estimated executory costs		39
Net minimum lease payments		6,341
Less imputed interest at rates ranging from 3.0% to 29.0%		2,300
Present value of minimum lease payments		$4,041

The Company has entered into sale/leaseback transactions involving buildings and the underlying land that were accounted for as capital and operating leases. Included in the annual maturities schedule above are $429 million of capital leases and $140 million of operating leases.

Certain of the Company's leases provide for the payment of contingent rentals based on a percentage of sales. Such contingent rentals amounted to $27 million, $32 million and $38 million in 2006, 2005 and 2004, respectively. Substantially all of the Company's store leases have renewal options, some of which may trigger an escalation in rentals.

In connection with certain debt financing, we could be liable for early termination payments if certain unlikely events were to occur. At January 31, 2006, the aggregate termination payment was $89 million. These two arrangements expire in fiscal 2011 and fiscal 2019.

In connection with the development of our grocery distribution network in the United States, we have agreements with third parties which would require us to purchase or assume the leases on certain unique equipment in the event the agreements are terminated. These agreements, which can be terminated by either party at will, cover up to a five-year period and obligate the Company to pay up to approximately $233 million upon termination of some or all of these agreements.

Notes to Consolidated Financial Statements

WAL-MART

There are no recourse provisions which would enable us to recover from third parties any amounts paid under the above guarantees. No liability for these guarantees has been recorded in our financial statements.

The Company has entered into lease commitments for land and buildings for 60 future locations. These lease commitments with real estate developers provide for minimum rentals ranging from 5 to 35 years, which if consummated based on current cost estimates, will approximate $95 million annually over the lease terms.

10 Retirement-related Benefits

In the United States, the Company maintains a Profit Sharing and 401(k) Retirement Savings Plan under which most full-time and many part-time associates become participants following one year of employment. The Profit Sharing component of the plan is entirely funded by the Company, with an additional contribution made by the Company to the associates' 401(k) component of the plan. In addition to the Company contributions to the 401(k) Retirement Savings component of the plan, associates may elect to contribute a percentage of their earnings. During fiscal 2006, participants could contribute up to 25% of their pretax earnings, but not more than statutory limits.

Associates may choose from among 13 different investment options for the 401(k) Retirement Savings component of the plan. For associates who did not make an election, their 401(k) balance in the plan is placed in a balanced fund. Associates are immediately vested in their 401(k) funds and may change their investment options at any time. Additionally, fully vested associates have the same 13 investment options for the Profit Sharing component of the plan. Associates are fully vested in the Profit Sharing component of the plan after seven years of service.

Annual contributions made by the Company to the United States and Puerto Rico Profit Sharing and 401(k) Retirement Savings Plans are made at the sole discretion of the Company, and were $827 million, $756 million and $662 million for fiscal 2006, 2005 and 2004, respectively.

Employees in foreign countries who are not U.S. citizens are covered by various post-employment benefit arrangements. These plans are administered based upon the legislative and tax requirements in the country in which they are established. Annual contributions to foreign retirement savings and profit sharing plans are made at the discretion of the Company, and were $244 million, $199 million and $123 million in fiscal 2006, 2005 and 2004, respectively.

The Company's subsidiaries in the United Kingdom and Japan have defined benefit pension plans. The plan in the United Kingdom was underfunded by $332 million and $419 million at January 31, 2006 and 2005, respectively. The plan in Japan was underfunded by $228 million at January 31, 2006.

11 Segments

At January 31, 2006, the Company and its subsidiaries were principally engaged in the operation of retail stores located in all 50 states, Argentina, Brazil, Canada, Germany, South Korea, Puerto Rico and the United Kingdom, through joint ventures in China, and through majority-owned subsidiaries in Japan and Mexico. The Company identifies segments based on management responsibility within the United States and in total for international units.

The Wal-Mart Stores segment includes the Company's supercenters, discount stores and Neighborhood Markets in the United States, as well as Walmart.com. The SAM'S CLUB segment includes the warehouse membership clubs in the United States as well as samsclub.com. At January 31, 2006, the International segment consisted of the Company's operations in Argentina, Brazil, China, Germany, Mexico, South Korea, Japan and the United Kingdom, which are consolidated using a December 31 fiscal year-end, generally due to statutory reporting requirements. There were no significant intervening events which materially affected the financial statements. The Company's operations in Canada and Puerto Rico are consolidated using a January 31 fiscal year-end. The amounts under the caption "Other" in the following table include unallocated corporate overhead. The Company's portion of the results of our unconsolidated minority interest in Seiyu prior to December 20, 2005, and our unconsolidated minority interest in CARHCO are also included under the caption "Other."

Notes to Consolidated Financial Statements

WAL-MART

The Company measures the profit of its segments as "segment operating income," which is defined as income from continuing operations before net interest expense, income taxes and minority interest. Information on segments and the reconciliation to income from continuing operations before income taxes and minority interest are as follows (in millions):

Fiscal Year Ended January 31, 2006	Wal-Mart Stores	SAM'S CLUB	International	Other	Consolidated
Revenues from external customers	**$ 209,910**	**$ 39,798**	**$ 62,719**	**$ —**	**$ 312,427**
Intercompany real estate charge (income)	**3,454**	**547**	**—**	**(4,001)**	**—**
Depreciation and amortization	**1,922**	**296**	**1,043**	**1,456**	**4,717**
Operating income (loss)	**15,324**	**1,385**	**3,330**	**(1,509)**	**18,530**
Interest expense, net					**(1,172)**
Income from continuing operations before income taxes and minority interest					**$ 17,358**
Total assets of continuing operations	**$ 32,809**	**$ 5,686**	**$ 51,581**	**$48,111**	**$ 138,187**

Fiscal Year Ended January 31, 2005	Wal-Mart Stores	SAM'S CLUB	International	Other	Consolidated
Revenues from external customers	$ 191,826	$ 37,119	$ 56,277	$ —	$ 285,222
Intercompany real estate charge (income)	2,754	513	—	(3,267)	—
Depreciation and amortization	1,561	274	919	1,510	4,264
Operating income (loss)	14,163	1,280	2,988	(1,340)	17,091
Interest expense, net					(986)
Income from continuing operations before income taxes and minority interest					$ 16,105
Total assets of continuing operations	$ 29,489	$ 5,685	$ 40,981	$43,999	$ 120,154

Fiscal Year Ended January 31, 2004	Wal-Mart Stores	SAM'S CLUB	International	Other	Consolidated
Revenues from external customers	$ 174,220	$ 34,537	$ 47,572	$ —	$ 256,329
Intercompany real estate charge (income)	2,468	484	—	(2,952)	—
Depreciation and amortization	1,482	249	810	1,311	3,852
Operating income (loss)	12,916	1,126	2,370	(1,387)	15,025
Interest expense, net					(832)
Income from continuing operations before income taxes and minority interest					$ 14,193
Total assets of continuing operations	$ 27,028	$ 4,751	$ 35,230	$38,396	$ 105,405

Certain information for fiscal years 2005 and 2004 has been reclassified to conform to current-year presentation.

In the United States, long-lived assets, net, excluding goodwill and other assets and deferred charges were $55.5 billion and $48.4 billion as of January 31, 2006 and 2005, respectively. In the United States, additions to long-lived assets were $11.8 billion, $9.8 billion and $8.1 billion in fiscal 2006, 2005 and 2004, respectively. Outside of the United States, long-lived assets, net, excluding goodwill and other assets and deferred charges were $23.8 billion and $19.7 billion in fiscal 2006 and 2005, respectively. Outside of the United States, additions to long-lived assets were $2.8 billion, $3.1 billion and $2.2 billion in fiscal 2006, 2005 and 2004, respectively. The International segment includes all real estate outside the United States. The operations of the Company's ASDA subsidiary are significant in comparison to the total operations of the International segment. ASDA sales during fiscal 2006, 2005 and 2004 were $26.8 billion, $26.0 billion and $21.7 billion, respectively. At January 31, 2006 and 2005, ASDA long-lived assets, consisting primarily of property and equipment, net, and goodwill, net, totaled $17.7 billion and $18.9 billion, respectively. The decline in ASDA's long-lived assets from January 31, 2005 to January 31, 2006 was largely due to foreign currency translation.

12 Quarterly Financial Data (Unaudited)

(Amounts in millions except per share information)	Quarters ended April 30,	July 31,	October 31,	January 31,
Fiscal 2006				
Net sales	$70,908	$76,811	$ 75,436	$ 89,273
Cost of sales	54,571	58,787	57,988	69,045
Gross profit	$16,337	$18,024	$ 17,448	$ 20,228
Net income	$ 2,461	$ 2,805	$ 2,374	$ 3,589
Basic and diluted net income per common share	$ 0.58	$ 0.67	$ 0.57	$ 0.86
Fiscal 2005				
Net sales	$64,763	$69,722	$ 68,520	$ 82,216
Cost of sales	49,969	53,533	52,567	63,723
Gross profit	$14,794	$16,189	$ 15,953	$ 18,493
Net income	$ 2,166	$ 2,651	$ 2,286	$ 3,164
Basic and diluted net income per common share	$ 0.50	$ 0.62	$ 0.54	$ 0.75

The sum of quarterly financial data will not agree to annual amounts due to rounding.

13 Subsequent Events

On March 2, 2006, the Company's Board of Directors approved an increase in the Company's annual dividend to $0.67 per share. The annual dividend will be paid in four quarterly installments on April 3, 2006, June 5, 2006, September 5, 2006, and January 2, 2007 to holders of record on March 17, May 19, August 18 and December 15, 2006, respectively.

In February 2006, we entered into a £150 million revolving credit facility in the United Kingdom. Interest on borrowings under the credit facility accrues at LIBOR plus 25 basis points.

Report of Independent Registered Public Accounting Firm

The Board of Directors and Shareholders,
Wal-Mart Stores, Inc.

We have audited the accompanying consolidated balance sheets of Wal-Mart Stores, Inc. as of January 31, 2006 and 2005, and the related consolidated statements of income, shareholders' equity and cash flows for each of the three years in the period ended January 31, 2006. These financial statements are the responsibility of the Company's management. Our responsibility is to express an opinion on these financial statements based on our audits.

We conducted our audits in accordance with the standards of the Public Company Accounting Oversight Board (United States). Those standards require that we plan and perform the audit to obtain reasonable assurance about whether the financial statements are free of material misstatement. An audit includes examining, on a test basis, evidence supporting the amounts and disclosures in the financial statements. An audit also includes assessing the accounting principles used and significant estimates made by management, as well as evaluating the overall financial statement presentation. We believe that our audits provide a reasonable basis for our opinion.

In our opinion, the financial statements referred to above present fairly, in all material respects, the consolidated financial position of Wal-Mart Stores, Inc. at January 31, 2006 and 2005, and the consolidated results of its operations and its cash flows for each of the three years in the period ended January 31, 2006, in conformity with U.S. generally accepted accounting principles.

We also have audited, in accordance with the standards of the Public Company Accounting Oversight Board (United States), the effectiveness of Wal-Mart Stores, Inc.'s internal control over financial reporting as of January 31, 2006, based on criteria established in *Internal Control - Integrated Framework* issued by the Committee of Sponsoring Organizations of the Treadway Commission and our report dated March 27, 2006 expressed an unqualified opinion thereon.

/s/ Ernst & Young LLP

Rogers, Arkansas
March 27, 2006

Report of Independent Registered Public Accounting Firm on Internal Control Over Financial Reporting

The Board of Directors and Shareholders,
Wal-Mart Stores, Inc.

We have audited management's assessment, included in the accompanying Management's Report to Our Shareholders under the caption "Report on Internal Control Over Financial Reporting," that Wal-Mart Stores, Inc. maintained effective internal control over financial reporting as of January 31, 2006, based on criteria established in *Internal Control - Integrated Framework* issued by the Committee of Sponsoring Organizations of the Treadway Commission (the COSO criteria). Wal-Mart Stores, Inc.'s management is responsible for maintaining effective internal control over financial reporting and for its assessment of the effectiveness of internal control over financial reporting. Our responsibility is to express an opinion on management's assessment and an opinion on the effectiveness of the company's internal control over financial reporting based on our audit.

We conducted our audit in accordance with the standards of the Public Company Accounting Oversight Board (United States). Those standards require that we plan and perform the audit to obtain reasonable assurance about whether effective internal control over financial reporting was maintained in all material respects. Our audit included obtaining an understanding of internal control over financial reporting, evaluating management's assessment, testing and evaluating the design and operating effectiveness of internal control, and performing such other procedures as we considered necessary in the circumstances. We believe that our audit provides a reasonable basis for our opinion.

A company's internal control over financial reporting is a process designed to provide reasonable assurance regarding the reliability of financial reporting and the preparation of financial statements for external purposes in accordance with generally accepted accounting principles. A company's internal control over financial reporting includes those policies and procedures that (1) pertain to the maintenance of records that, in reasonable detail, accurately and fairly reflect the transactions and dispositions of the assets of the company; (2) provide reasonable assurance that transactions are recorded as necessary to permit preparation of financial statements in accordance with generally accepted accounting principles, and that receipts and expenditures of the company are being made only in accordance with authorizations of management and directors of the company; and (3) provide reasonable assurance regarding prevention or timely detection of unauthorized acquisition, use, or disposition of the company's assets that could have a material effect on the financial statements.

Because of its inherent limitations, internal control over financial reporting may not prevent or detect misstatements. Also, projections of any evaluation of effectiveness to future periods are subject to the risk that controls may become inadequate because of changes in conditions, or that the degree of compliance with the policies or procedures may deteriorate.

As indicated in the accompanying Management's Report to Our Shareholders, management's assessment of and conclusion on the effectiveness of internal control over financial reporting did not include the internal controls of The Seiyu, Ltd., and Sonae Distribuição Brasil S.A., both of which were acquired in fiscal 2006 and are included in the fiscal 2006 consolidated financial statements of Wal-Mart Stores, Inc. These entities represented, in the aggregate, 5.8% and 0.1% of total assets and total net sales, respectively, of the Company as of, and for the year ended, January 31, 2006. These acquisitions are more fully discussed in Note 6 to the consolidated financial statements for fiscal 2006. Our audit of internal control over financial reporting of Wal-Mart Stores, Inc. also did not include an evaluation of the internal control over financial reporting for these fiscal 2006 acquisitions.

In our opinion, management's assessment that Wal-Mart Stores, Inc. maintained effective internal control over financial reporting as of January 31, 2006, is fairly stated, in all material respects, based on the COSO criteria. Also, in our opinion, Wal-Mart Stores, Inc., maintained, in all material respects, effective internal control over financial reporting as of January 31, 2006, based on the COSO criteria.

We also have audited, in accordance with the standards of the Public Company Accounting Oversight Board (United States), the consolidated balance sheets of Wal-Mart Stores, Inc. as of January 31, 2006 and 2005, and the related consolidated statements of income, shareholders' equity and cash flows for each of the three years in the period ended January 31, 2006 and our report dated March 27, 2006 expressed an unqualified opinion thereon.

/s/ Ernst & Young LLP

Rogers, Arkansas
March 27, 2006

49

Management's Report to Our Shareholders

WAL-MART

Management of Wal-Mart Stores, Inc. ("Wal-Mart" or the "Company") is responsible for the preparation, integrity and objectivity of Wal-Mart's consolidated financial statements and other financial information contained in this Annual Report to Shareholders. Those consolidated financial statements were prepared in conformity with accounting principles generally accepted in the United States. In preparing those consolidated financial statements, management was required to make certain estimates and judgments, which are based upon currently available information and management's view of current conditions and circumstances.

The Audit Committee of the Board of Directors, which consists solely of independent directors, oversees our process of reporting financial information and the audit of our consolidated financial statements. The Audit Committee stays informed of the financial condition of Wal-Mart and regularly reviews management's financial policies and procedures, the independence of our independent auditors, our internal control and the objectivity of our financial reporting. Both the independent auditors and the internal auditors have free access to the Audit Committee and meet with the Audit Committee periodically, both with and without management present.

We have retained Ernst & Young LLP, an independent registered public accounting firm, to audit our consolidated financial statements found in this annual report. We have made available to Ernst & Young LLP all of our financial records and related data in connection with their audit of our consolidated financial statements.

We have filed with the Securities and Exchange Commission ("SEC") the required certifications related to our consolidated financial statements as of and for the year ended January 31, 2006. These certifications are attached as exhibits to our Annual Report on Form 10-K for the year ended January 31, 2006. Additionally, we have also provided to the New York Stock Exchange the required annual certification of our Chief Executive Officer regarding our compliance with the New York Stock Exchange's corporate governance listing standards.

Report on Internal Control Over Financial Reporting

Management has responsibility for establishing and maintaining adequate internal control over financial reporting. Internal control over financial reporting is a process designed to provide reasonable assurance regarding the reliability of financial reporting and the preparation of financial statements for external reporting purposes in accordance with accounting principles generally accepted in the United States. Because of its inherent limitations, internal control over financial reporting may not prevent or detect misstatements. Management has assessed the effectiveness of the Company's internal control over financial reporting as of January 31, 2006. In making its assessment, management has utilized the criteria set forth by the Committee of Sponsoring Organizations ("COSO") of the Treadway Commission in *Internal Control — Integrated Framework*. Management concluded that based on its assessment, Wal-Mart's internal control over financial reporting was effective as of January 31, 2006. Management's assessment of the effectiveness of the Company's internal control over financial reporting as of January 31, 2006, has been audited by Ernst & Young LLP, an independent registered public accounting firm, as stated in their report which appears in this Annual Report to Shareholders.

Management's assessment of the effectiveness of the Company's internal control over financial reporting excluded The Seiyu, Ltd. and Sonae Distribuição Brasil S.A., both of which were acquired in fiscal 2006. These entities represented, in the aggregate, 5.8% and 0.1% of consolidated total assets and consolidated net sales, respectively, of the Company as of and for the year ended January 31, 2006. These acquisitions are more fully discussed in Note 6 to our consolidated financial statements for fiscal 2006. Under guidelines established by the SEC, companies are allowed to exclude acquisitions from their first assessment of internal control over financial reporting following the date of the acquisition.

Evaluation of Disclosure Controls and Procedures

We maintain disclosure controls and procedures designed to provide reasonable assurance that information required to be timely disclosed is accumulated and communicated to management in a timely fashion. Management has assessed the effectiveness of these disclosure controls and procedures as of January 31, 2006, and determined they were effective as of that date to provide reasonable assurance that information required to be disclosed by us in the reports we file or submit under the Securities Exchange Act of 1934, as amended, was accumulated and communicated to management, as appropriate, to allow timely decisions regarding required disclosure and were effective to provide reasonable assurance that such information is recorded, processed, summarized and reported within the time periods specified by the SEC's rules and forms.

Report on Ethical Standards

Our Company was founded on the belief that open communications and the highest standards of ethics are necessary to be successful. Our long-standing "Open Door" communication policy helps management be aware of and address issues in a timely and effective manner. Through the open door policy all associates are encouraged to inform management at the appropriate level when they are concerned about any matter pertaining to Wal-Mart.

Wal-Mart has adopted a Statement of Ethics to guide our associates in the continued observance of high ethical standards such as honesty, integrity and compliance with the law in the conduct of Wal-Mart's business. Familiarity and compliance with the Statement of Ethics is required of all associates who are part of management. The Company also maintains a separate Code of Ethics for our senior financial officers. Wal-Mart also has in place a Related-Party Transaction Policy. This policy applies to Wal-Mart's senior officers and directors and requires material related-party transactions to be reviewed by the Audit Committee. The senior officers and directors are required to report material related-party transactions to Wal-Mart. We maintain an ethics office which oversees and administers an ethics hotline. The ethics hotline provides a channel for associates to make confidential and anonymous complaints regarding potential violations of our statements of ethics, including violations related to financial or accounting matters.

/s/ H. Lee Scott, Jr.
H. Lee Scott, Jr.
President and Chief Executive Officer

/s/ Thomas M. Schoewe
Thomas M. Schoewe
Executive Vice President and Chief Financial Officer

50

APPENDIX B

eBAY, INC.

Report of Independent Registered Public Accounting Firm

To the Board of Directors and Stockholders of eBay Inc:

We have completed integrated audits of eBay Inc.'s 2005 and 2004 consolidated financial statements and of its internal control over financial reporting as of December 31, 2005, and an audit of its 2003 consolidated financial statements in accordance with the standards of the Public Company Accounting Oversight Board (United States). Our opinions, based on our audits, are presented below.

Consolidated financial statements and financial statement schedule

In our opinion, the consolidated financial statements listed in the index appearing under Item 15(a)(1) present fairly, in all material respects, the financial position of eBay Inc and its subsidiaries at December 31, 2005 and December 31, 2004, and the results of their operations and their cash flows for each of the three years in the period ended December 31, 2005 in conformity with accounting principles generally accepted in the United States of America. In addition, in our opinion, the financial statement schedule listed in the index appearing under Item 15(a)(2) presents fairly, in all material respects, the information set forth therein when read in conjunction with the related consolidated financial statements. These financial statements and financial statement schedule are the responsibility of the Company's management. Our responsibility is to express an opinion on these financial statements and financial statement schedule based on our audits. We conducted our audits of these statements in accordance with the standards of the Public Company Accounting Oversight Board (United States). Those standards require that we plan and perform the audit to obtain reasonable assurance about whether the financial statements are free of material misstatement. An audit of financial statements includes examining, on a test basis, evidence supporting the amounts and disclosures in the financial statements, assessing the accounting principles used and significant estimates made by management, and evaluating the overall financial statement presentation. We believe that our audits provide a reasonable basis for our opinion.

As discussed in Note 1 to the Consolidated Financial Statements, effective July 1, 2003 the Company adopted the provisions of Financial Accounting Standards Board Interpretation No. 46, "Consolidation of Variable Interest Entities — an interpretation of ARB 51".

Internal control over financial reporting

Also, in our opinion, management's assessment, included in Management's Report on Internal Control Over Financial Reporting appearing under Item 9A, that the Company maintained effective internal control over financial reporting as of December 31, 2005 based on criteria established in *Internal Control — Integrated Framework* issued by the Committee of Sponsoring Organizations of the Treadway Commission (COSO), is fairly stated, in all material respects, based on those criteria. Furthermore, in our opinion, the Company maintained, in all material respects, effective internal control over financial reporting as of December 31, 2005, based on criteria established in *Internal Control — Integrated Framework* issued by the COSO. The Company's management is responsible for maintaining effective internal control over financial reporting and for its assessment of the effectiveness of internal control over financial reporting. Our responsibility is to express opinions on management's assessment and on the effectiveness of the Company's internal control over financial reporting based on our audit. We conducted our audit of internal control over financial reporting in accordance with the standards of the Public Company Accounting Oversight Board (United States). Those standards require that we plan and perform the audit to obtain reasonable assurance about whether effective internal control over financial reporting was maintained in all material respects. An audit of internal control over financial reporting includes obtaining an understanding of internal control over financial reporting, evaluating management's assessment, testing and evaluating the design and operating effectiveness of internal control, and performing such other procedures as we consider necessary in the circumstances. We believe that our audit provides a reasonable basis for our opinions.

A company's internal control over financial reporting is a process designed to provide reasonable assurance regarding the reliability of financial reporting and the preparation of financial statements for external purposes in accordance with generally accepted accounting principles. A company's internal control over financial reporting includes those policies and procedures that (i) pertain to the maintenance of records that, in reasonable detail, accurately and fairly reflect the transactions and dispositions of the assets of the company; (ii) provide reasonable assurance that transactions are recorded as necessary to permit preparation of financial statements in accordance with generally accepted accounting principles, and that receipts and expenditures of the company are being made only in accordance with authorizations of management and directors of the company; and (iii) provide reasonable assurance regarding prevention or timely detection of unauthorized acquisition, use, or disposition of the company's assets that could have a material effect on the financial statements.

Because of its inherent limitations, internal control over financial reporting may not prevent or detect misstatements. Also, projections of any evaluation of effectiveness to future periods are subject to the risk that controls may become inadequate because of changes in conditions, or that the degree of compliance with the policies or procedures may deteriorate.

/s/ PricewaterhouseCoopers LLP

San Jose, California
February 23, 2006

eBay Inc.

CONSOLIDATED BALANCE SHEET

	December 31, 2004	December 31, 2005
	(In thousands, except par value amounts)	
ASSETS		
Current assets:		
Cash and cash equivalents	$ 1,330,045	$ 1,313,580
Short-term investments	682,004	774,650
Accounts receivable, net	240,856	322,788
Funds receivable from customers	123,424	255,282
Restricted cash and investments	155,405	29,702
Other current assets	379,415	487,235
Total current assets	2,911,149	3,183,237
Long-term investments	1,267,707	825,667
Property and equipment, net	709,773	801,602
Goodwill	2,709,794	6,120,079
Intangible assets, net	362,909	823,280
Other assets	29,719	35,121
	$ 7,991,051	$ 11,788,986
LIABILITIES AND STOCKHOLDERS' EQUITY		
Current liabilities:		
Accounts payable	$ 37,958	$ 55,692
Funds payable and amounts due to customers	331,805	586,651
Accrued expenses and other current liabilities	421,969	578,557
Deferred revenue and customer advances	50,439	81,940
Short-term obligations	124,272	—
Income taxes payable	118,427	182,095
Total current liabilities	1,084,870	1,484,935
Deferred tax liabilities, net	135,971	215,682
Other liabilities	41,869	40,388
Total liabilities	1,262,710	1,741,005
Commitments and Contingencies (Note 8)		
Stockholders' equity:		
Common Stock, $0.001 par value; 3,580,000 shares authorized; 1,338,608 and 1,404,183 shares issued and outstanding	1,339	1,404
Additional paid-in capital	4,855,717	7,272,476
Unearned stock-based compensation	(4,825)	(45,540)
Retained earnings	1,634,468	2,716,511
Accumulated other comprehensive income	241,642	103,130
Total stockholders' equity	6,728,341	10,047,981
	$ 7,991,051	$ 11,788,986

The accompanying notes are an integral part of these consolidated financial statements.

eBay Inc.
CONSOLIDATED STATEMENT OF INCOME

	Year Ended December 31,		
	2003	2004	2005
	(In thousands, except per share amounts)		
Net revenues	$ 2,165,096	$ 3,271,309	$ 4,552,401
Cost of net revenues	416,058	614,415	818,104
Gross profit	1,749,038	2,656,894	3,734,297
Operating expenses:			
Sales and marketing	567,565	857,874	1,230,728
Product development	159,315	240,647	328,191
General and administrative	332,668	415,725	591,716
Payroll tax on employee stock options	9,590	17,479	13,014
Amortization of acquired intangible assets	50,659	65,927	128,941
Total operating expenses	1,119,797	1,597,652	2,292,590
Income from operations	629,241	1,059,242	1,441,707
Interest and other income, net	36,573	77,867	111,148
Interest expense	(4,314)	(8,879)	(3,478)
Income before cumulative effect of accounting change, income taxes and minority interests	661,500	1,128,230	1,549,377
Provision for income taxes	(206,738)	(343,885)	(467,285)
Minority interests	(7,578)	(6,122)	(49)
Income before cumulative effect of accounting change	447,184	778,223	1,082,043
Cumulative effect of accounting change, net of tax	(5,413)	—	—
Net income	$ 441,771	$ 778,223	$ 1,082,043
Per share basic amounts:			
Income before cumulative effect of accounting change	$ 0.35	$ 0.59	$ 0.79
Cumulative effect of accounting change	(0.00)	—	—
Per share basic amounts	$ 0.35	$ 0.59	$ 0.79
Per share diluted amounts:			
Income before cumulative effect of accounting change	$ 0.34	$ 0.57	$ 0.78
Cumulative effect of accounting change	(0.00)	—	—
Per share diluted amounts	$ 0.34	$ 0.57	$ 0.78
Weighted average shares:			
Basic	1,276,576	1,319,458	1,361,708
Diluted	1,313,314	1,367,720	1,393,875

The accompanying notes are an integral part of these consolidated financial statements.

eBay Inc.

CONSOLIDATED STATEMENT OF COMPREHENSIVE INCOME

	Year Ended December 31,		
	2003	2004	2005
		(In thousands)	
Net income	$ 441,771	$ 778,223	$ 1,082,043
Other comprehensive income (loss):			
Foreign currency translation	66,326	139,523	(140,459)
Unrealized gains (losses) on investments, net	(5,497)	(8,703)	1,922
Unrealized gains on cash flow hedges	4,249	5,525	1,297
Estimated tax benefit/(provision)	620	1,102	(1,272)
Other comprehensive income (loss):	65,698	137,447	(138,512)
Comprehensive income	$ 507,469	$ 915,670	$ 943,531

The accompanying notes are an integral part of these consolidated financial statements.

80

eBay Inc.

CONSOLIDATED STATEMENT OF STOCKHOLDERS' EQUITY

	Year Ended December 31,		
	2003	2004	2005
		(In thousands)	
Common stock:			
Balance, beginning of year	$ 1,246	$ 1,299	$ 1,339
Common stock issued	53	40	65
Balance, end of year	1,299	1,339	1,404
Additional paid-in-capital:			
Balance, beginning of year	3,107,508	3,936,510	4,855,717
Common stock issued	694,288	650,985	1,862,199
Common stock repurchased	(79)	(1)	—
Unearned stock-based compensation, net of cancellations	4,155	6,240	107,981
Stock option income tax benefit	130,638	261,983	446,579
Balance, end of year	3,936,510	4,855,717	7,272,476
Unearned stock-based compensation:			
Balance, beginning of year	(5,253)	(2,008)	(4,825)
Unearned stock-based compensation, net of cancellations	(1,079)	(4,068)	(64,726)
Amortization of unearned stock-based compensation	4,324	1,251	24,011
Balance, end of year	(2,008)	(4,825)	(45,540)
Retained earnings:			
Balance, beginning of year	414,474	856,245	1,634,468
Net income	441,771	778,223	1,082,043
Balance, end of year	856,245	1,634,468	2,716,511
Accumulated other comprehensive income:			
Balance, beginning of year	38,498	104,196	241,642
Change in unrealized gain (loss) on investments, net of tax	(3,178)	(5,392)	1,169
Change in unrealized gain on cash flow hedges, net of tax	2,549	3,315	778
Foreign currency translation adjustment	66,327	139,523	(140,459)
Balance, end of year	104,196	241,642	103,130
Total stockholders' equity	$ 4,896,242	$ 6,728,341	$ 10,047,981
Number of Shares			
Common stock:			
Balance, beginning of year	1,245,108	1,298,586	1,338,608
Issuance of common stock for cash and services	53,478	40,022	32,769
Issuance of common stock for acquisitions	—	—	32,806
Balance, end of year	1,298,586	1,338,608	1,404,183

The accompanying notes are an integral part of these consolidated financial statements.

81

eBay Inc.

CONSOLIDATED STATEMENT OF CASH FLOWS

	Year Ended December 31, 2003	2004	2005
		(In thousands)	
Cash flows from operating activities:			
Net income	$ 441,771	$ 778,223	$ 1,082,043
Adjustments:			
Cumulative effect of accounting change	5,413	—	—
Provision for doubtful accounts and authorized credits	46,049	90,942	89,499
Provision for transaction losses	36,401	50,459	73,773
Depreciation and amortization	159,003	253,690	378,165
Amortization of unearned stock-based compensation	5,492	5,832	31,772
Tax benefit on the exercise of employee stock options	130,638	261,983	267,142
Impairment of certain equity investments	1,230	—	—
Minority interests	7,784	6,122	49
Changes in assets and liabilities, net of acquisition effects:			
Accounts receivable	(153,373)	(105,540)	(151,993)
Funds receivable from customers	(38,879)	(44,751)	(132,606)
Other current assets	(13,133)	(312,756)	(49,371)
Other non-current assets	(4,111)	(308)	(4,612)
Deferred tax liabilities, net	69,770	28,652	91,690
Accounts payable	17,348	(33,975)	564
Funds payable and amounts due to customers	56,172	216,967	251,870
Accrued expenses and other liabilities	85,704	39,618	17,013
Deferred revenue and customer advances	8,864	20,061	3,646
Income taxes payable	11,976	30,096	61,247
Net cash provided by operating activities	874,119	1,285,315	2,009,891
Cash flows from investing activities:			
Purchases of property and equipment, net	(365,384)	(292,838)	(338,281)
Proceeds from sale of corporate aircraft	—	—	28,290
Purchases of investments	(2,035,053)	(1,754,808)	(1,324,353)
Maturities and sales of investments	1,297,262	1,079,548	1,928,539
Acquisitions, net of cash acquired	(216,367)	(1,036,476)	(2,732,230)
Other	—	(8,646)	(14,696)
Net cash used in investing activities	(1,319,542)	(2,013,220)	(2,452,731)
Cash flows from financing activities:			
Proceeds from issuance of common stock, net	700,817	650,638	599,845
Payment of headquarters facility lease obligation	—	—	(126,390)
Principal payments on long-term obligations	(11,951)	(2,969)	(1,849)
Net cash provided by financing activities	688,866	647,669	471,606
Effect of exchange rate changes on cash and cash equivalents	28,757	28,768	(45,231)
Net increase (decrease) in cash and cash equivalents	272,200	(51,468)	(16,465)
Cash and cash equivalents at beginning of period	1,109,313	1,381,513	1,330,045
Cash and cash equivalents at end of period	$ 1,381,513	$ 1,330,045	$ 1,313,580
Supplemental cash flow disclosures:			
Cash paid for interest	$ 3,237	$ 8,234	$ 3,478
Cash paid for income taxes	$ 3,519	$ 13,875	$ 40,256
Non-cash investing and financing activities:			
Common stock issued for acquisition	$ —	$ —	$ 1,262,674

The accompanying notes are an integral part of these consolidated financial statements.

eBay Inc.

NOTES TO CONSOLIDATED FINANCIAL STATEMENTS

Note 1 — The Company and Summary of Significant Accounting Policies:

The Company

eBay Inc. ("eBay") was incorporated in California in May 1996, and reincorporated in Delaware in April 1998. eBay, together with its subsidiaries, pioneers new communities around the world, built on commerce, sustained by trust, and inspired by opportunity. eBay brings together millions of buyers and sellers every day on a local, national and international basis through an array of websites. eBay provides online marketplaces for the sale of goods and services, online payment services and online communication offerings to a diverse community of individuals and businesses.

eBay currently has three primary businesses: the eBay Marketplace, Payments and Communications. The eBay Marketplaces segments provide the infrastructure to enable online commerce in a variety of formats, including the traditional auction platform, along with our other online platforms, such as Rent.com, Shopping.com, Kijiji, mobile.de, and Marktplaats.nl. The Payments segment, which consists of our PayPal, Inc. ("PayPal") business, enables individuals or businesses to securely, easily and quickly send and receive payments online. The Communications segment, which consists of our Skype Technologies SA ("Skype") business, enables VoIP calls between Skype users, as well as provides low-cost connectivity to traditional fixed-line and mobile telephones.

When we refer to "we," "our," "us" or "eBay" in this document, we mean the current Delaware corporation (eBay Inc.) and its California predecessor, as well as all of our consolidated subsidiaries.

Use of estimates

The preparation of consolidated financial statements in conformity with generally accepted accounting principles requires management to make estimates and assumptions that affect the reported amounts of assets and liabilities and disclosure of contingent assets and liabilities at the date of the consolidated financial statements and the reported amounts of revenues and expenses during the reporting period. On an ongoing basis, we evaluate our estimates, including those related to provisions for doubtful accounts and authorized credits, the provision for transaction losses, legal contingencies, income taxes, advertising and other non-transaction revenues, and goodwill and intangible assets. We base our estimates on historical experience and on various other assumptions that are believed to be reasonable under the circumstances. Actual results could differ from those estimates.

Principles of consolidation and basis of presentation

The accompanying financial statements are consolidated and include the financial statements of eBay and our majority-owned subsidiaries. All significant intercompany balances and transactions have been eliminated in consolidation.

The consolidated financial statements include 100% of the assets and liabilities of these majority-owned subsidiaries and the ownership interests of minority investors are recorded as minority interests. Investments in entities where we hold more than a 20% but less than a 50% ownership interest and have the ability to significantly influence the operations of the investee are accounted for using the equity method of accounting and the investment balance is included in long-term investments, while our share of the investees' results of operations is included in interest and other income, net. Investments in entities where we hold less than a 20% ownership interest and where we do not have the ability to significantly influence the operations of the investee are accounted for using the cost method of accounting and are included in long-term investments.

Certain prior period balances have been reclassified to conform to the current period presentation.

eBay Inc.

NOTES TO CONSOLIDATED FINANCIAL STATEMENTS — (Continued)

Fair value of financial instruments

Cash and cash equivalents are short-term, highly liquid investments with original or remaining maturities of three months or less when purchased. Our financial instruments, including cash, cash equivalents, accounts receivable, funds receivable, accounts payable, and funds payable are carried at cost, which approximates their fair value because of the short-term maturity of these instruments.

Short and long-term investments, which include marketable equity securities and government and corporate bonds, are classified as available-for-sale and reported at fair value using the specific identification method. Unrealized gains and losses are excluded from earnings and reported as a component of other comprehensive income (loss), net of related estimated tax provisions or benefits. Additionally, we assess whether an other-than-temporary impairment loss on our investments has occurred due to declines in fair value or other market conditions. Declines in fair value that are considered other than temporary are recorded as an impairment of certain equity investments in the consolidated statement of income.

Derivative instruments

We recognize all derivative instruments on the balance sheet at fair value. Changes in the fair value (i.e., gains or losses) of the derivatives are recorded each period in the consolidated statement of income or accumulated other comprehensive income (loss). For a derivative designated as a cash flow hedge, the gain or loss on the derivative is initially reported as a component of accumulated other comprehensive income (loss) and subsequently reclassified into the consolidated statement of income when the hedged transaction affects earnings. For derivatives recognized as a fair value hedge, the gain or loss on the derivative in the period of change and the offsetting loss or gain of the hedged item attributed to the hedged risk, are recognized in accumulated other comprehensive income until the hedge matures, at which time the gain or loss is recognized as interest and other income, net. For derivatives not recognized as hedges, the gain or loss on the derivative in the period of changes is recognized as interest and other income, net.

Concentrations of credit risk

Our cash, cash equivalents, accounts receivable and funds receivable are potentially subject to concentration of credit risk. Cash and cash equivalents are placed with financial institutions that management believes are of high credit quality. Our accounts receivable are derived from revenue earned from customers located in the U.S. and internationally. Accounts receivable balances are settled through customer credit cards, debit cards, and PayPal accounts, with the majority of accounts receivable collected upon processing of credit card transactions. We maintain an allowance for doubtful accounts receivable and authorized credits based upon our historical experience. Historically, such losses have been within our expectations. However, unexpected or significant future changes in trends could result in a material impact to future statements of income or cash flows. Due to the relatively small dollar amount of individual accounts receivable, we generally do not require collateral on these balances. The provision for doubtful accounts is recorded as a charge to operating expense, while the provision for authorized credits is recognized as a reduction of net revenues.

During the years ended December 31, 2003, 2004, and 2005, no customers accounted for more than 10% of net revenues. As of December 31, 2004 and 2005, no customers accounted for more than 10% of net accounts receivable.

Allowances for transaction losses

Our Payments segment is exposed to transaction losses due to fraud, as well as non-performance of customers. We establish allowances for estimated losses arising from processing customer transactions, such as charge-backs for unauthorized credit card use and merchant related charge-backs due to non-delivery of goods or services, Automated Clearing House, or ACH, returns, and debit card overdrafts. These allowances

eBay Inc.

NOTES TO CONSOLIDATED FINANCIAL STATEMENTS — (Continued)

represent an accumulation of the estimated amounts necessary to provide for transaction losses incurred as of the reporting date, including those to which we have not yet been notified. The allowances, which involve the use of actuarial techniques, are monitored monthly and are updated based on actual claims data reported by our claims processors. The allowances are based on known facts and circumstances, internal factors including our experience with similar cases, historical trends involving loss payment patterns and the mix of transaction and loss types. Additions to the allowance, in the form of provisions, are reflected as a general and administrative expense in our consolidated statement of income. At December 31, 2004 and 2005, the allowance for transaction losses totaled $11.0 million and $20.2 million, respectively, and was included in accrued expenses and other current liabilities in our consolidated balance sheet.

Foreign currency

Substantially all of our foreign subsidiaries use the local currency of their respective countries as their functional currency. Assets and liabilities are translated at exchange rates prevailing at the balance sheet dates. Revenues, costs and expenses are translated into United States dollars at average exchange rates for the period. Gains and losses resulting from translation are recorded as a component of accumulated other comprehensive income (loss).

Realized gains and losses from foreign currency transactions are recognized as interest and other income, net.

Funds receivable and funds payable to customers

Funds receivable and payable relate to our Payments segment and arise due to the time taken to clear transactions through external payment networks. When customers fund their account using their bank account or credit card, or withdraw money from their bank account or through a debit card transaction, there is a clearing period before the cash is received or sent by PayPal, usually two or three business days for U.S. transactions, and up to five to eight business days for international transactions. Hence, these funds are treated as a receivable or payable until the cash is settled.

Customer accounts

As an agent on behalf of our customers we deposit all U.S.-based customer funds held in U.S. dollars into Federal Deposit Insurance Corporation (FDIC) insured bank accounts or PayPal's Money Market Fund. FDIC insurance is available to U.S.-based PayPal customers if we (1) place pooled customer funds in bank accounts denominated 'PayPal as Agent for the Benefit of its Customers' or similar caption, (2) maintain records sufficient to identify the claim of each customer in the FDIC-insured account, (3) comply with applicable FDIC recordkeeping requirements, and (4) truly operate as an agent of our customers. These customer funds held by us as an agent on behalf of customers are not reflected on our consolidated balance sheet. Additionally, we receive a custodial credit from our service provider in the form of a reduction in transaction processing fees based upon balances held with each institution. This credit is recognized as a reduction in processing costs in cost of revenues.

Effective February 13, 2004, PayPal customers resident in the European Union began to receive services through PayPal's U.K. subsidiary, which holds an electronic money issuer license. Electronic Money Institution, or ELMI, regulations require that customer balances in the U.K. subsidiary be represented as claims on the subsidiary (held as a principal rather than as an agent) and invested only in specified types of liquid assets. These customer balances are therefore included on our consolidated balance sheet as other current assets with the corresponding amount due to customers reflected as a liability.

eBay Inc.

NOTES TO CONSOLIDATED FINANCIAL STATEMENTS — (Continued)

Property and equipment

Property and equipment are stated at historical cost less accumulated depreciation. Depreciation and amortization are computed using the straight-line method over the estimated useful lives of the assets, generally, one to three years for computer equipment and software, up to 30 years for buildings and building improvements, ten years for aviation equipment, the shorter of five years or the term of the lease for leasehold improvements, three years for furniture and fixtures and three years for vehicles.

Goodwill and intangible assets

Goodwill represents the excess of the purchase price over the fair value of the net tangible and identifiable intangible assets acquired in a business combination. Intangible assets resulting from the acquisitions of entities accounted for using the purchase method of accounting are estimated by management based on the fair value of assets received. Identifiable intangible assets are comprised of purchased customer lists and user base, trademarks and trade names, developed technologies, and other intangible assets. Identifiable intangible assets are being amortized over the period of estimated benefit using the straight-line method and estimated useful lives ranging from one to eight years. Goodwill is not subject to amortization, but is subject to at least an annual assessment for impairment, applying a fair-value based test.

Impairment of Long-lived assets

We evaluate long-lived assets for impairment whenever events or changes in circumstances indicate that the carrying amount of a long-lived asset may not be recoverable. An asset is considered impaired if its carrying amount exceeds the future net cash flow the asset is expected to generate. If an asset is considered to be impaired, the impairment to be recognized is measured by the amount by which the carrying amount of the asset exceeds its fair market value. We assess the recoverability of our long-lived and intangible assets by determining whether the unamortized balances can be recovered through undiscounted future net cash flows of the related assets. The amount of impairment, if any, is measured based on projected discounted future net cash flows.

We evaluate goodwill, at a minimum, on an annual basis and whenever events and changes in circumstances suggest that the carrying amount may not be recoverable. Impairment of goodwill is tested at the reporting unit level by comparing the reporting unit's carrying amount, including goodwill, to the fair value of the reporting unit. The fair values of the reporting units are estimated using a combination of the income, or discounted cash flows, approach and the market approach, which utilizes comparable companies' data. If the carrying amount of the reporting unit exceeds its fair value, goodwill is considered impaired and a second step is performed to measure the amount of impairment loss, if any. We conducted our annual impairment test as of August 31, 2005 and determined there was no impairment. There were no events or circumstances from that date through December 31, 2005 that would impact this assessment.

Revenue recognition

Our net revenues result from fees associated with our transaction, advertising and other non-transaction services in our U.S. Marketplaces, International Marketplaces, Payments and Communications segments. Transaction revenue is derived primarily from listing, feature and final value fees paid by sellers and fees from payment processing services. Revenue from advertising is derived principally from the sale of online banner and sponsorship advertisements for cash and through barter arrangements. Other non-transaction net revenue is primarily composed of our end-to-end services net revenue that is derived principally from contractual arrangements with third parties that provide transaction services to eBay users. Revenue is recognized when evidence of an arrangement exists, the fee is fixed and determinable, no significant obligation remains and collection of the receivable is reasonably assured.

eBay Inc.

NOTES TO CONSOLIDATED FINANCIAL STATEMENTS — (Continued)

Our U.S. and International Marketplaces segments earn listing and feature fee revenues which are recognized ratably over the estimated period of the auction while revenues related to final value fees are recognized at the time that the transaction is successfully concluded. A transaction is considered successfully concluded when at least one buyer has bid above the seller's specified minimum price or reserve price, whichever is higher, at the end of the transaction term. For services offered on Shopping.com, our comparison shopping site, revenue is generated from lead referral fees based on the number of times a user clicks through to a merchant's website from our Shopping.com website. Lead referral fees are recognized in the period in which the user clicks through to the merchant's website.

Our Payments segment earns transaction fees from processing transactions for certain customers. Revenue resulting from a payment processing transaction is recognized once the transaction is complete.

Our Communications segment revenue is recognized when the related offering is provided. The majority of Communications segment revenues are prepaid. We record deferred revenue for prepaid amounts in excess of revenue recognized.

Our advertising revenue is derived principally from the sale of online banner and sponsorship advertisements. To date, the duration of our banner and sponsorship advertising contracts has ranged from one week to five years, but is generally one week to one year. Advertising revenues on both banner and sponsorship contracts are recognized as "impressions" (i.e., the number of times that an advertisement appears in pages viewed by users of our websites) are delivered or ratably over the term of the agreement where such agreements provide for minimum monthly or quarterly advertising commitments or where such commitments are fixed throughout the term. Barter transactions are valued on amounts realized in similar cash transactions occurring within six months prior to the date of the barter transaction. To the extent that significant delivery obligations remain at the end of a period or collection of the resulting account receivable is not considered probable, revenues are deferred until the obligation is satisfied or the uncertainty is resolved. These amounts are included in deferred revenue in our consolidated balance sheet. Revenue from barter arrangements totaled $10.1 million, $13.3 million and $6.7 million for the years ended December 31, 2003, 2004 and 2005, respectively, with the reciprocal arrangements being recognized as an operating expense. In general, the services are received in the same period in which the reciprocal services are provided. In certain circumstances, we are required to record against revenue payments to a party who is also a customer. These payments primarily consist of certain promotional activities which result in payments to our users.

Our end-to-end services revenues are derived principally from contractual arrangements with third parties that provide transaction services to eBay and PayPal users. To date, the duration of our end-to-end services contracts has ranged from one to three years. End-to-end services revenues are recognized as the contracted services are delivered to end users. To the extent that significant obligations remain at the end of a period or collection of the resulting receivable is not considered probable, revenues are deferred until the obligation is satisfied or the uncertainty is resolved.

Provisions for doubtful accounts, transaction losses and authorized credits are made at the time of revenue recognition based upon our historical experience. The provision for doubtful accounts and transaction losses are recorded as charges to operating expense, while the provision for authorized credits is recognized as a reduction of net revenues.

Product development costs

Costs related to the planning and post implementation phases of our website development efforts are recorded as an operating expense. Direct costs incurred in the development phase are capitalized and amortized over the product's estimated useful life of one to three years as charges to cost of net revenues.

eBay Inc.

NOTES TO CONSOLIDATED FINANCIAL STATEMENTS — (Continued)

Advertising expense

We expense the costs of producing advertisements at the time production occurs and expense the cost of communicating advertising in the period during which the advertising space or airtime is used. Internet advertising expenses are recognized based on the terms of the individual agreements, which is generally over the greater of the ratio of the number of impressions delivered over the total number of contracted impressions, pay-per-click, or on a straight-line basis over the term of the contract. Advertising expenses totaled $321.4 million, $459.5 million and $665.1 million during the years ended December 31, 2003, 2004, and 2005, respectively.

Stock-based compensation

We account for stock-based employee compensation issued under compensatory plans using the intrinsic value method, which calculates compensation expense based on the difference, if any, on the date of the grant, between the fair value of our stock and the option exercise price. Generally accepted accounting principles require companies who choose to account for stock option grants using the intrinsic value method to also determine the fair value of option grants using an option pricing model, such as the Black-Scholes model, and to disclose the impact of fair value accounting in a note to the financial statements. In December 2002, the FASB issued Statement of Financial Accounting Standards No. 148, "Accounting for Stock-Based Compensation Transition and Disclosure, an Amendment of FASB Statement No. 123." We did not elect to voluntarily change to the fair value based method of accounting for stock based employee compensation and record such amounts as charges to operating expense. We amortize the stock-based compensation charge in accordance with FASB Interpretation No. 28 over the vesting period of the related options, which is generally four years. The impact of recognizing the fair value of option grants and stock grants under our employee stock purchase plan as an expense under FASB Statement No. 148 would have substantially reduced our net income, as follows (in thousands, except per share amounts):

	Year Ended December 31,		
	2003	2004	2005
Net income, as reported	$ 441,771	$ 778,223	$ 1,082,043
Add: Amortization of stock-based compensation expense determined under the intrinsic value method, net of tax	5,492	1,715	18,749
Deduct: Total stock-based compensation expense determined under fair value based method, net of tax	(201,775)	(190,935)	(248,260)
Pro forma net income	$ 245,488	$ 589,003	$ 852,532
Earnings per share:			
Basic — Reported	$ 0.35	$ 0.59	$ 0.79
Pro forma	$ 0.19	$ 0.45	$ 0.63
Diluted — Reported	$ 0.34	$ 0.57	$ 0.78
Pro forma	$ 0.19	$ 0.43	$ 0.61

The weighted average fair value of options granted in the years ended December 31, 2003, 2004 and 2005, were $8.15, $12.12 and $11.70, respectively.

eBay Inc.

NOTES TO CONSOLIDATED FINANCIAL STATEMENTS — (Continued)

We calculated the fair value of each option award on the date of grant using the Black-Scholes option pricing model. The following weighted average assumptions were used for each respective period:

	Year Ended December 31,		
	2003	2004	2005
Risk-free interest rates	1.9%	2.5%	3.8%
Expected lives	3 years	3 years	3 years
Dividend yield	0%	0%	0%
Expected volatility	64%	49%	36%

We account for stock-based arrangements issued to non-employees using the fair value based method, which calculates compensation expense based on the fair value of the stock option granted using the Black-Scholes option pricing model at the date of grant, or over the period of performance, as appropriate.

Income taxes

We account for income taxes using an asset and liability approach, which requires the recognition of taxes payable or refundable for the current year and deferred tax liabilities and assets for the future tax consequences of events that have been recognized in our financial statements or tax returns. The measurement of current and deferred tax assets and liabilities is based on provisions of enacted tax laws; the effects of future changes in tax laws or rates are not anticipated. If necessary, the measurement of deferred tax assets is reduced by the amount of any tax benefits that are not expected to be realized based on available evidence.

Cumulative Effect of Change in Accounting Principle

In accordance with the provisions of FIN 46, "Consolidation of Variable Interest Entities," we have included our San Jose corporate headquarters lease arrangement in our consolidated financial statements since July 1, 2003. Under this accounting standard, our balance sheet at December 31, 2004 reflects additions for land and buildings totaling $126.4 million, lease obligations of $122.5 million and non-controlling minority interests of $3.9 million. Our consolidated statement of income for the year ended December 31, 2003, reflects the reclassification of lease payments on our San Jose corporate headquarters from operating expense to interest expense, beginning with quarters following our adoption of FIN 46 on July 1, 2003, a $5.4 million after-tax charge for cumulative depreciation for periods from lease inception through June 30, 2003, and incremental depreciation expense of approximately $400,000, net of tax, per quarter for periods after June 30, 2003. We have adopted the provisions of FIN 46 prospectively from July 1, 2003, and as a result, have not restated prior periods. The cumulative effect of the change in accounting principle arising from the adoption of FIN 46 has been reflected in net income in 2003. As of December 31, 2004, we had $126.4 million included within current restricted cash and investments relating to our San Jose headquarters lease facility lease arrangement, which had effectively provided us with full ownership rights to these facilities. In February 2004, we elected not to extend the lease period, which required us to purchase the facility on March 1, 2005. We utilized the $126.4 million in restricted cash and investments to complete the purchase of the facility.

Comprehensive income

Comprehensive income includes all changes in equity (net assets) during a period from non-owner sources. The change in accumulated other comprehensive income for all periods presented resulted from, net of tax foreign currency translation gains and losses, unrealized and realized gains and losses on investments, and unrealized gains and losses on cash flow hedges.

eBay Inc.

NOTES TO CONSOLIDATED FINANCIAL STATEMENTS — (Continued)

Recent Accounting Pronouncements

Share-Based Payments

In December 2004, the FASB issued Statement of Financial Accounting Standards No. 123 (revised 2004), "Share-Based Payment" (FAS 123R) that addresses the accounting for share-based payment transactions in which an enterprise receives employee services in exchange for either equity instruments of the enterprise or liabilities that are based on the fair value of the enterprise's equity instruments or that may be settled by the issuance of such equity instruments. The statement eliminates the ability to account for share-based compensation transactions, as we do currently, using the intrinsic value method prescribed by Accounting Principles Board, or APB, Opinion No. 25, "Accounting for Stock Issued to Employees," and generally requires that such transactions be accounted for using a fair-value-based method and recognized as expenses in our consolidated statement of income. The statement requires companies to assess the most appropriate model to calculate the value of the options. We currently use the Black-Scholes option pricing model to value options and are currently assessing which model we may use in the future under the new statement and may deem an alternative model to be more appropriate. The use of a different model to value options may result in a different fair value than the use of the Black-Scholes option pricing model. In addition, there are a number of other requirements under the new standard that would result in different accounting treatment than currently required. These differences include, but are not limited to, the accounting for the tax benefit on employee stock options and for stock issued under our employee stock purchase plan, and the presentation of these tax benefits within the consolidated statement of cash flows. In addition to the appropriate fair value model to be used for valuing share-based payments, we will also be required to determine the transition method to be used at date of adoption. The allowed transition methods are the prospective and retroactive adoption alternatives. The prospective method requires that compensation expense be recorded for all unvested stock options and restricted stock at the beginning of the first quarter of adoption of FAS 123R, while the retroactive method requires companies to record compensation expense for all unvested stock options and restricted stock beginning with the first disclosed period restated.

In April 2005, the Securities and Exchange Commission announced the adoption of a new rule that amends the effective date of FAS 123R. The effective date of the new standard under these new rules for our consolidated financial statements is January 1, 2006. Adoption of this statement will have a significant impact on our consolidated financial statements as we will be required to expense the fair value of our stock option grants and stock purchases under our employee stock purchase plan rather than disclose the impact on our consolidated net income within our footnotes, as is our current practice (see "The Company and Summary of Significant Accounting Policies").

The amounts disclosed within our footnotes are not necessarily indicative of the amounts that will be expensed upon the adoption of FAS 123R. We expect the compensation charges under FAS 123R to reduce earnings per diluted share by approximately $0.16 to $0.17 per share for the year ending December 31, 2006. Compensation expense calculated under FAS 123R may differ from amounts currently disclosed within our footnotes and may also differ from our expectations based on changes in the fair value of our common stock, changes in the number of options granted or the terms of such options, the treatment of tax benefits and changes in interest rates or other factors. In addition, upon adoption of FAS 123R, we may choose to use a different valuation model to value the compensation expense associated with employee stock options and stock purchases under our employee stock purchase plan.

Note 2 — Net Income Per Share:

Basic net income per share is computed by dividing the net income for the period by the weighted average number of common shares outstanding during the period. Diluted net income per share is computed by dividing the net income for the period by the weighted average number of shares of common stock and potentially dilutive common stock outstanding during the period. Potentially dilutive common stock,

eBay Inc.

NOTES TO CONSOLIDATED FINANCIAL STATEMENTS — (Continued)

composed of unvested restricted common stock and incremental common shares issuable upon the exercise of stock options, are included in diluted net income per share using the treasury stock method to the extent such shares are dilutive. The following table sets forth the computation of basic and diluted net income per share for the periods indicated (in thousands, except per share amounts):

	Year Ended December 31,		
	2003	2004	2005
Numerator:			
Income before cumulative effect of accounting change	$ 447,184	$ 778,223	$ 1,082,043
Cumulative effect of accounting, net of tax	(5,413)	—	—
Net income	$ 441,771	$ 778,223	$ 1,082,043
Denominator:			
Weighted average common shares	1,276,674	1,319,548	1,361,748
Weighted average unvested common stock subject to repurchase	(98)	(90)	(40)
Denominator for basic calculation	1,276,576	1,319,458	1,361,708
Weighted average effect of dilutive securities:			
Weighted average unvested common stock subject to repurchase	98	90	40
Employee stock options	36,640	48,172	32,127
Denominator for diluted calculation	1,313,314	1,367,720	1,393,875
Per share amounts:			
Income before cumulative effect of accounting change	$ 0.35	$ 0.59	$ 0.79
Cumulative effect of accounting change	(0.00)	—	—
Per share basic amounts	$ 0.35	$ 0.59	$ 0.79
Per share amounts:			
Income before cumulative effect of accounting change	$ 0.34	$ 0.57	$ 0.78
Cumulative effect of accounting change	(0.00)	—	—
Per share diluted amounts	$ 0.34	$ 0.57	$ 0.78

The calculation of diluted income per share excludes all anti-dilutive shares. For the years ended December 31, 2003, 2004 and 2005, the number of anti-dilutive shares, as calculated based on the weighted average closing price of our common stock for the period, amounted to approximately 7.0 million, 3.4 million and 26.7 million shares, respectively.

eBay Inc.

NOTES TO CONSOLIDATED FINANCIAL STATEMENTS — (Continued)

Note 3 — Business Combinations, Goodwill and Intangible Assets:

Through both domestic and international acquisitions, we have continued to expand our business. The following table summarizes our purchase acquisitions in 2004 and 2005 with aggregate purchase prices in excess of $50 million (in thousands):

Company Name	Year Acquired	Post Acquisition Ownership	Net Tangible Assets/ (Liabilities)	Identifiable Intangible Assets	Deferred Tax Liabilities	Minority Interest	Unearned Stock-Based Compensation	Goodwill	Aggregate Purchase Price
mobile.de	2004	100%	$ 11,183	$ 30,500	$ (13,115)	$ —	$ —	$ 123,885	$ 152,453
Baazee.com	2004	100%	2,747	2,350	(905)	—	—	46,125	50,317
Marktplaats.nl	2004	100%	(1,902)	38,500	(11,778)	—	—	266,570	291,390
Internet Auction	2004	99.9%	N/A	60,143	(17,864)	43,833	—	438,684	524,796
Rent.com	2005	100%	18,050	61,800	(24,924)	—	—	380,439	435,365
International classified websites	2005	100%	(201)	13,800	(3,786)	—	—	71,771	81,584
Shopping.com	2005	100%	145,898	133,600	(29,683)	—	16,759	418,711	685,285
Skype	2005	100%	(1,610)	280,300	(71,474)		55,249	2,330,961	2,593,426
VeriSign's Payment Gateway Business	2005	100%	(8,804)	106,600	—	—	—	275,989	373,785

Tangible net assets were valued at their respective carrying amounts as we believe that these amounts approximated their current fair values at the respective acquisition dates. The valuation of identifiable intangible assets acquired reflects management's estimates based on, among other factors, use of established valuation methods. Such assets consist of customer lists and user base, trademarks and trade names, developed technologies and other acquired intangible assets including contractual agreements. Identifiable intangible assets are amortized over the period of estimated benefit using the straight-line method and the estimated useful lives of one to eight years. We believe the straight-line method of amortization represents our best estimate of the distribution of the economic value of the identifiable intangible assets. Goodwill represents the excess of the purchase price over the fair value of the net tangible and identifiable intangible assets acquired in each business combination. The following table summarizes our acquired intangible assets by type related to the above purchase acquisitions (in thousands):

Company Name	Year Acquired	Customer List/ User Base	Trade name/ Trademarks	Developed Technologies	Other Intangible Assets	Total Acquired Intangible Assets
mobile.de	2004	$ 20,400	$ 4,600	$ 5,500	$ —	$ 30,500
Baazee.com	2004	600	150	100	1,500	2,350
Marktplaats.nl	2004	—	37,000	1,500	—	38,500
Internet Auction	2004	46,510	12,239	1,394	—	60,143
Rent.com	2005	34,500	18,000	8,200	1,100	61,800
International classified websites	2005	2,600	11,200	—	—	13,800
Shopping.com	2005	73,600	38,700	21,300	—	133,600
Skype	2005	27,700	243,800	8,000	800	280,300
VeriSign's Payment Gateway Business	2005	86,700	400	19,500	—	106,600

The results of operations for periods prior to our acquisition for each acquisition during 2003, 2004 and 2005, both individually and in the aggregate, except for Skype, were not material to our consolidated statement of income and, accordingly, pro forma results of operations have not been presented.

92

eBay Inc.

NOTES TO CONSOLIDATED FINANCIAL STATEMENTS — (Continued)

mobile.de Acquisition

On April 1, 2004, we acquired a 100% interest in mobile.de for a cash purchase price of approximately €121 million. mobile.de is a classifieds advertising website for vehicles in Germany. The total purchase price recorded was approximately $152 million, including approximately $3 million in estimated acquisition-related expenses. We accounted for the acquisition as a purchase transaction and, accordingly, the purchase price has been allocated to the tangible and intangible assets acquired and liabilities assumed on the basis of their respective estimated fair values on the acquisition date.

The estimated useful economic lives of the identifiable intangible assets acquired in the mobile.de acquisition are eight years for the user base, two years for the developed technology and two years for the trade name.

Baazee.com Acquisition

On August 2, 2004, we acquired a 100% interest in Baazee.com for a cash purchase price of approximately $50 million. Baazee.com is an online marketplace in India. Through this acquisition, we have established eBay in India and will open our global online marketplaces to Baazee.com's strong and growing community. The total purchase price recorded was approximately $50 million, including $1 million in estimated acquisition-related expenses. We accounted for the acquisition as a purchase transaction and, accordingly, the purchase price has been allocated to the tangible and intangible assets acquired and liabilities assumed on the basis of their respective estimated fair values on the acquisition date.

The estimated useful economic lives of the identifiable intangible assets acquired in the Baazee.com acquisition are three years for the noncompete agreement, three years for the user base, one year for the trade name, and one year for the developed technology.

Marktplaats.nl Acquisition

On November 10, 2004, we acquired a 100% interest in Marktplaats.nl for a cash purchase price of approximately €226 million. The total purchase price recorded was approximately $291 million. Marktplaats.nl is an online classifieds website in the Netherlands. The acquisition allows us to expand our e-commerce position in the Netherlands while adding to our growing knowledge of classifieds-style commerce. The total purchase price recorded was approximately $291.4 million, including approximately $2.0 million in estimated acquisition-related expenses. We accounted for the acquisition as a purchase transaction and, accordingly, the purchase price has been allocated to the tangible and intangible assets acquired and liabilities assumed on the basis of their respective estimated fair values on the acquisition date.

The estimated useful economic lives of the identifiable intangible assets acquired in the Marktplaats.nl acquisition are five years for the trade name and eighteen months for the developed technology.

Internet Auction Co., Ltd.

On December 17, 2003, we increased our majority interest of Internet Auction Co., Ltd., ("IAC" or "Internet Auction"), from approximately 51% to approximately 62% by the settlement of our tender offer for approximately 1.6 million shares. The total cash consideration for these additional shares was approximately $93.9 million, which includes approximately $2.2 million in estimated acquisition-related expenses. Internet Auction introduced online trading in South Korea when it launched in April 1998. Shares of Internet Auction were listed on the KOSDAQ. Prior to the fourth quarter of 2003, we consolidated our original investment in IAC's common shares and recorded the minority investor's percentage share of income or losses in minority interests in our consolidated statement of income.

eBay Inc.

NOTES TO CONSOLIDATED FINANCIAL STATEMENTS — (Continued)

During September 2004, we purchased additional shares resulting in an aggregate increase of our ownership interest to approximately 97%. We purchased approximately 4.5 million shares for KRW125,000 per share for a total cash amount of approximately KRW557 billion. The total cash consideration for these additional shares was approximately $484.8 million, which includes approximately $1.7 million in estimated acquisition-related expenses.

On October 5, 2004 we closed our tender offer to purchase additional shares of IAC, resulting in an increase of our ownership interest to approximately 99.7%. We purchased approximately 344,000 shares for KRW125,000 per share. The total cash consideration for these additional shares was approximately $37.8 million, which includes approximately $400,000 in estimated acquisition-related expenses.

On December 6, 2004, the delisting of IAC common shares from the KOSDAQ was approved. Under Korean securities regulations, a seven business day period is required prior to the delisting date for on-the-market trade of shares. During that seven day period, from November 25, 2004 through December 3, 2004, we purchased approximately 17,000 additional shares for KRW125,000 per share, to increase our ownership interest to approximately 99.9%. The total cash consideration for these additional shares was approximately $2.2 million, which includes approximately $200,000 of estimated acquisition-related expenses.

Through these purchases, we have continued to expand our presence in South Korea, one of the largest online markets in Asia. This is consistent with our strategy of establishing and expanding our global online marketplaces in countries that represent the majority of the world's e-commerce revenue. The estimated useful economic lives of the identifiable intangible assets acquired in the increase in ownership of IAC are eight years for the user base, five years for the trade name, and two years for the developed technology. The identifiable intangible assets are being amortized using the straight-line method over their useful economic lives. We accounted for this acquisition as purchase transactions and, accordingly, the purchase price has been allocated to the tangible and intangible assets acquired and liabilities assumed on the basis of their respective estimated fair values on the acquisition date.

Rent.com

On February 23, 2005, we acquired Viva Group, Inc., which does business under the name Rent.com, for a cash purchase price of approximately $415 million plus payments for net cash and investments of approximately $18 million. Rent.com is an Internet listing website in the apartment and rental housing industry. The acquisition better enables our expansion into the online real estate market and is consistent with our strategy of growing our global online marketplaces. The total purchase price recorded was approximately $435 million, including approximately $2 million in estimated acquisition-related expenses. We accounted for the acquisition as a non-taxable purchase transaction and, accordingly, the purchase price has been allocated to the tangible and intangible assets acquired and liabilities assumed on the basis of their respective estimated fair values on the acquisition date.

The estimated useful economic lives of the identifiable intangible assets acquired in the Rent.com acquisition are six years for the customer list, five years for the trade name, three years for the developed technology and the advertising relationships, and one year for the user base.

International Classifieds Websites

During the second quarter of 2005, we announced our acquisitions of three international classifieds websites, Gumtree.com, LoQUo, and opusforum, which operate in select international cities. These acquisitions help us expand our global network of classifieds websites to create a more efficient place for local consumers to come together online. The aggregate purchase price recorded for these acquisitions was approximately $81.6 million, including approximately $1.3 million in estimated acquisition-related expenses. We accounted for two of these acquisitions as non-taxable and one as a taxable purchase transaction and,

eBay Inc.

NOTES TO CONSOLIDATED FINANCIAL STATEMENTS — (Continued)

accordingly, the purchase price for each acquisition has been allocated to the tangible and intangible assets acquired and liabilities assumed on the basis of their respective estimated fair values on the applicable acquisition date.

The estimated useful economic lives of the identifiable intangible assets acquired in these acquisitions are five years for both the trade names and for the customer lists. The final purchase price allocation will depend primarily upon the completion of our integration plan.

Shopping.com

On August 30, 2005, we acquired Shopping.com Ltd., or Shopping.com, for a purchase price of approximately $685.3 million. We acquired all outstanding shares of Shopping.com's common stock for $21 per share in cash totaling approximately $634.5 million and we assumed Shopping.com's outstanding common stock options, valued at approximately $43.2 million. The total purchase price also includes approximately $7.6 million in estimated acquisition-related expenses. Shopping.com is a provider of online comparison shopping and consumer reviews. This acquisition is consistent with our strategy of growing our global online marketplaces and we believe that it will create a premier online shopping experience for individuals and businesses of all sizes. We accounted for the acquisition as a taxable purchase transaction and, accordingly, the purchase price has been allocated to the tangible and intangible assets acquired and liabilities assumed on the basis of their respective estimated fair values on the acquisition date.

The intrinsic value of Shopping.com's unvested common stock options assumed in the acquisition totaled approximately $16.8 million and was recorded as unearned stock-based compensation. The unearned stock-based compensation relating to the unvested options is being amortized on an accelerated basis over the remaining vesting period of less than one year to four years, consistent with the graded vesting approach under FASB Interpretation No. 28.

The estimated useful economic lives of the identifiable intangible assets acquired in the Shopping.com acquisition are four years for the customer base and five years for the trade names and the developed technology. The final purchase price allocation will depend primarily upon the completion of our integration plan and the final valuation of certain acquired tax attributes.

Skype

On October 14, 2005, we acquired all of the outstanding securities of Skype Technologies S.A. ("Skype"), for a total initial consideration of approximately $2.6 billion, plus potential performance-based payments of up to approximately $1.3 billion. In addition, we agreed to assume Skype's stock options outstanding as of the closing date and convert them into options to acquire approximately 1.9 million shares of our common stock. The initial consideration of approximately $2.6 billion is comprised of approximately $1.3 billion in cash and 32.8 million shares of our common stock. For accounting purposes, the stock portion of the initial consideration is valued at approximately $1.3 billion based on the average closing price of our common stock surrounding the acquisition announcement date of September 12, 2005. The shares of our common stock issued in connection with the acquisition are subject to certain contractual restrictions on resale. Additionally, the assumed options have been valued at $64.6 million and were included as part of the purchase price. The purchase price will be allocated to the tangible and intangible assets acquired and liabilities assumed based on their respective fair values at the acquisition date.

In addition to the initial consideration, the maximum amount potentially payable under the performance-based earn-out is approximately €1.1 billion, or approximately $1.3 billion, and would be payable in cash or common stock, at our discretion. The earn-out payments are contingent upon Skype achieving certain net revenue, gross profit margin-based targets and active user targets. Base earn-out payments of up to an aggregate of approximately €877 million, or approximately $1.0 billion, weighted equally among the three

eBay Inc.

NOTES TO CONSOLIDATED FINANCIAL STATEMENTS — (Continued)

targets, would be payable if the targets are achieved over any four-quarter period commencing on January 1, 2006 through June 30, 2009. Additional bonus earn-out payments of up to an aggregate of approximately €292 million, or approximately $345 million, weighted equally among the three targets, would be payable if Skype exceeds the targets during calendar year 2008. Any contingent earn-out payments made will be accounted for as additional purchase price and will increase goodwill. As any contingent earn-out payments are to be paid in Euros, the Dollar amounts set forth above were based on the Euro-Dollar exchange rate as of December 31, 2005.

Skype is a Luxembourg-based company that was established in 2003. Skype has developed software that, among other things, enables free calls between Skype users online. Skype's premium offerings, which currently are its primary source of revenue, provide low-cost connectivity to traditional fixed-line and mobile telephones. We believe that Skype can increase the velocity of trade on our websites, especially in categories that require more involved communications, as well as enable us to develop and provide new e-commerce offerings.

The intrinsic value of Skype's unvested common stock options assumed in the acquisition totaled approximately $55.2 million and was recorded as unearned stock-based compensation. The unearned stock-based compensation relating to the unvested options will be amortized on an accelerated basis over the remaining vesting period of approximately three years, consistent with the graded vesting approach under FASB Interpretation No. 28.

The estimated useful economic lives of the identifiable intangible assets acquired in the Skype acquisition are five years for registered user technology and trade names, two years for existing technology, and one year for network access agreements. The final purchase price allocation will depend primarily upon the refinement of certain estimates and analyses and the final valuation of certain tax attributes.

Supplemental information on an unaudited pro forma basis, as if the Skype acquisition were completed at the beginning of the years 2004 and 2005, is as follows (in thousands, except per share amounts):

	December 31,	
	2004	2005
	(Unaudited)	
Revenue	$ 3,277,534	$ 4,594,954
Net income	$ 684,905	$ 944,057
Diluted income per share	$ 0.49	$ 0.66

The unaudited pro forma supplemental information is based on estimates and assumptions, which eBay believes are reasonable. The average foreign exchange rates during years 2004 and 2005 were used in preparing the supplemental information. The unaudited pro forma supplemental information prepared by management is not necessarily indicative of the condensed consolidated financial position or results of income in future periods or the results that actually would have been realized had eBay and Skype been a combined company during the specified periods.

VeriSign's Payment Gateway Business

On November 18, 2005, we acquired VeriSign's payment gateway business for a purchase price of approximately $373.8 million, consisting of $370.0 million in cash and $3.8 million in estimated acquisition-related expenses. The payment gateway is a real-time, scalable Internet payment platform that allows merchants to authorize, process and manage online payments. Additionally, we have signed a multi-year security technology agreement with VeriSign, Inc. that calls for us to invest in the deployment of its

eBay Inc.

NOTES TO CONSOLIDATED FINANCIAL STATEMENTS — (Continued)

technologies that enable and better protect online transactions, including the purchase of up to one million two-factor authentication tokens.

We accounted for the acquisition as a purchase transaction and, accordingly, the purchase price has been allocated to the tangible and intangible assets acquired and liabilities assumed on the basis of their respective estimated fair values on the acquisition date. The estimated useful economic lives of the identifiable intangible assets acquired in the acquisition are five years for registered user base and existing technology and one year for the trade names. The final purchase price allocation will depend primarily upon the completion of our integration plan.

PayPal Acquisition-Related Liabilities

During the year ended December 31, 2003, we finalized our formal plan to exit certain activities and integrate certain facilities of PayPal. This plan included provisions to terminate leases for redundant facilities, dispose of redundant fixed assets and leasehold improvements, resolve certain pre-acquisition legal contingencies, provide various employee-related benefits and exit certain contractual obligations.

The components of the PayPal acquisition related liabilities are as follows (in thousands):

	Balance at December 31, 2004	Cash Payments	Balance at December 31, 2005
Excess facilities and fixed assets	$ 23,746	$ (4,086)	$ 19,660
Other liabilities and contingencies	3,287	—	3,287
Total liability	$ 27,033	$ (4,086)	$ 22,947

Excess facilities and fixed assets liabilities consist primarily of accruals for PayPal's remaining lease obligations, net of estimated sublease income. A substantial portion of the excess facilities and fixed assets liabilities recorded as of December 31, 2005 are expected to settle in cash during future periods.

As of December 31, 2005, other PayPal liabilities and contingencies consist primarily of accruals for certain employee-related tax liabilities.

Goodwill

Goodwill information for each segment is as follows (in thousands):

	December 31, 2004	Goodwill Acquired	Adjustments	December 31, 2005
Segments:				
U.S. Marketplaces	$ 148,703	$ 809,590	$ 2,788	$ 961,081
International Marketplaces	1,516,055	71,771	(62,037)	1,525,789
Payments	1,072,396	275,989	—	1,348,385
Communications	—	2,330,961	(18,777)	2,312,184
	$ 2,737,154	$ 3,488,311	$ (78,026)	$ 6,147,439

The increase in goodwill acquired during the year ended December 31, 2005, resulted primarily from our acquisition of the outstanding shares of Rent.com, International classifieds websites, Shopping.com, Skype, and VeriSign's payment gateway business, as well as certain insignificant acquisitions. Adjustments to goodwill during the year ended December 31, 2005, resulted primarily from foreign currency translation adjustments relating to goodwill and the release of certain acquisition liabilities associated with our current and prior period acquisitions.

eBay Inc.

NOTES TO CONSOLIDATED FINANCIAL STATEMENTS — (Continued)

Investments accounted for under the equity method of accounting are classified on our balance sheet as long-term investments. Such investments include identifiable intangible assets, deferred tax liabilities and goodwill. Goodwill related to our equity method investments totaled approximately $27.4 million as of December 31, 2004 and 2005.

Intangible Assets

The components of acquired identifiable intangible assets are as follows (in thousands):

	December 31, 2004				December 31, 2005			
	Gross Carrying Amount	Accumulated Amortization	Net Carrying Amount	Weighted Average Useful Economic Life	Gross Carrying Amount	Accumulated Amortization	Net Carrying Amount	Weighted Average Useful Economic Life
				(years)				(years)
Intangible assets:								
Customer lists and user base	$300,929	$ (80,097)	$220,832	7	$ 526,657	$ (145,397)	$381,260	6
Trademarks and trade names	139,239	(30,811)	108,428	6	443,565	(75,571)	367,994	5
Developed technologies	40,686	(28,488)	12,198	3	101,971	(45,882)	56,089	4
All other	33,895	(7,534)	26,361	4	36,450	(14,761)	21,689	4
	$514,749	$ (146,930)	$367,819		$ 1,108,643	$ (281,611)	$827,032	

All of our acquired identifiable intangible assets are subject to amortization. Acquired identifiable intangible assets are comprised of customer lists and user base, trademarks and trade names, developed technologies, and other acquired intangible assets including patents and contractual agreements. No significant residual value is estimated for the intangible assets. The increase in intangible assets during the year ended December 31, 2005 resulted primarily from certain intangible assets acquired as part of our acquisition of the outstanding shares of Rent.com, International classifieds websites, Shopping.com, Skype and VeriSign's payment gateway business totaling approximately $61.8 million, $13.8 million, $133.6 million, $280.3 million, and $106.6 million, respectively. The net carrying amount of intangible assets related to our investments totaled approximately $4.9 million and $3.8 million, as of December 31, 2004 and 2005, respectively. Aggregate amortization expense for intangible assets totaled $53.2 million, $70.2 million and $136.4 million for the years ended December 31, 2003, 2004 and 2005, respectively.

Expected future intangible asset amortization from acquisitions completed as of December 31, 2005 is as follows (in thousands):

Fiscal Years:	
2006	$ 198,474
2007	185,929
2008	178,201
2009	159,791
2010	88,479
Thereafter	16,158
	$ 827,032

eBay Inc.

NOTES TO CONSOLIDATED FINANCIAL STATEMENTS — (Continued)

Note 4 — Segments:

Reporting segments are based upon our internal organization structure, the manner in which our operations are managed, the criteria used by our chief operating decision-maker to evaluate segment performance, the availability of separate financial information, and overall materiality considerations.

The U.S. Marketplaces segment includes U.S. online marketplaces commerce platforms. The International Marketplaces segment includes our international online marketplaces commerce platforms. The Payments segment includes our global payments platform consisting of our PayPal subsidiary. The Communications segment includes the VoIP offerings provided by our Skype subsidiary. Results from our Communications segment reflect Skype operations for the post-acquisition period from October 15, 2005 through December 31, 2005.

Direct contribution consists of revenues less direct costs. Direct costs include specific costs of net revenues, sales and marketing expenses, and general and administrative expenses over which segment managers have direct discretionary control, such as advertising and marketing programs, customer support expenses, bank charges, provisions for doubtful accounts, authorized credits and transaction losses. Expenses over which segment managers do not currently have discretionary control, such as certain general and administrative costs, are monitored by management through shared cost centers and are not evaluated in the measurement of segment performance. Prior period amounts have been reclassified to reflect the current management of site operations cost and product development expenses as direct costs.

The following table summarizes the financial performance of our reporting segments (in thousands):

	Year Ended December 31, 2003			
	U.S. Marketplaces	International Marketplaces	Payments	Consolidated
Net revenues from external customers	$ 1,062,834	$ 664,640	$ 437,622	$ 2,165,096
Direct costs	631,154	317,887	355,075	1,304,116
Direct contribution	431,680	346,753	82,547	860,980
Operating expenses and indirect costs of net revenues				231,739
Income from operations				629,241
Interest and other income, net				36,573
Interest expense				(4,314)
Income before cumulative effect of accounting change, taxes and minority interests				$ 661,500

eBay Inc.

NOTES TO CONSOLIDATED FINANCIAL STATEMENTS — (Continued)

	Year Ended December 31, 2004			
	U.S. Marketplaces	International Marketplaces	Payments	Consolidated
Net revenues from external customers	$ 1,399,848	$ 1,173,759	$ 697,702	$ 3,271,309
Direct costs	851,214	574,381	573,500	1,999,095
Direct contribution	548,634	599,378	124,202	1,272,214
Operating expenses and indirect costs of net revenues				212,972
Income from operations				1,059,242
Interest and other income, net				77,867
Interest expense				(8,879)
Income before cumulative effect of accounting change, taxes and minority interests				$ 1,128,230

	Year Ended December 31, 2005				
	U.S. Marketplaces	International Marketplaces	Payments	Communications	Consolidated
Net revenues from external customers	$ 1,804,092	$ 1,695,045	$1,028,455	$ 24,809	$ 4,552,401
Direct costs	1,114,472	829,233	723,875	41,977	2,709,557
Direct contribution	689,620	865,812	304,580	(17,168)	1,842,844
Operating expenses and indirect costs of net revenues					401,137
Income from operations					1,441,707
Interest and other income, net					111,148
Interest expense					(3,478)
Income before cumulative effect of accounting change, taxes and minority interests					$ 1,549,377

The following tables summarize the allocation of net revenues and the long-lived assets based on geography (in thousands):

	December 31,		
	2003	2004	2005
U.S. net revenues	$ 1,406,512	$ 1,889,936	$ 2,471,273
International net revenues	758,584	1,381,373	2,081,128
Net revenues	$ 2,165,096	$ 3,271,309	$ 4,552,401

eBay Inc.

NOTES TO CONSOLIDATED FINANCIAL STATEMENTS — (Continued)

	December 31,	
	2004	2005
U.S. long-lived tangible assets	$ 659,423	$ 750,353
International long-lived tangible assets	80,069	86,370
Total long-lived assets	$ 739,492	$ 836,723

Net revenues attributed to the U.S. and International geographies are based upon the country in which the seller, payment recipient, advertiser or end-to-end service provider is located. Germany accounted for greater than 10% of our total net revenues for the years ended December 31, 2003, 2004, and 2005, respectively. The United Kingdom accounted for greater than 10% of our total net revenues for the years ended December 31, 2004 and 2005. Long-lived assets attributed to the U.S. and International geographies are based upon the country in which the asset is located or owned.

Note 5 —Investments:

At December 31, 2004 and 2005, short and long-term investments were classified as available-for-sale securities, except for restricted cash and investments and equity method investments, and are reported at fair value as follows (in thousands):

	December 31, 2004			
	Gross Amortized Cost	Gross Unrealized Gains	Gross Unrealized Losses	Estimated Fair Value
Short-term investments:				
Restricted cash and investments	$ 156,130	$ 25	$ (750)	$ 155,405
Corporate debt securities	581,058	33	(2,908)	578,183
Government and agency securities	80,274	—	(432)	79,842
Time deposits and other	23,979	—	—	23,979
	$ 841,441	$ 58	$ (4,090)	$ 837,409
Long-term investments:				
Restricted cash and investments	$ 1,397	$ 21	$ —	$ 1,418
Corporate debt securities	827,505	107	(2,137)	825,475
Government and agency securities	397,211	—	(4,733)	392,478
Equity instruments and equity method investments	48,336	—	—	48,336
	$ 1,274,449	$ 128	$ (6,870)	$ 1,267,707

eBay Inc.

NOTES TO CONSOLIDATED FINANCIAL STATEMENTS — (Continued)

	December 31, 2005			
	Gross Amortized Cost	Gross Unrealized Gains	Gross Unrealized Losses	Estimated Fair Value
Short-term investments:				
Restricted cash and investments	$ 29,670	$ 32	$ —	$ 29,702
Corporate debt securities	362,438	4	(2,679)	359,763
Government and agency securities	371,537	—	(3,198)	368,339
Time deposits and other	46,548	—	—	46,548
	$ 810,193	$ 36	$ (5,877)	$ 804,352
Long-term investments:				
Restricted cash and investments	$ 1,065	$ —	$ —	$ 1,065
Corporate debt securities	665,418	115	(1,921)	663,612
Government and agency securities	110,450	—	(1,409)	109,041
Equity instruments and equity method investments	51,949	—	—	51,949
	$ 828,882	$ 115	$ (3,330)	$ 825,667

The following table summarizes the fair value and gross unrealized losses of our short-term and long-term investments, aggregated by type of investment instrument and length of time that individual securities have been in a continuous unrealized loss position, at December 31, 2005 (in thousands):

	Less than 12 Months		12 Months or Greater		Total	
	Fair Value	Gross Unrealized Losses	Fair Value	Gross Unrealized Losses	Fair Value	Gross Unrealized Losses
Corporate debt securities	$ 401,789	$ (1,544)	$ 250,487	$ (3,011)	$ 652,276	$ (4,555)
Government and agency securities	47,184	(38)	398,486	(4,624)	445,670	(4,662)
	$ 448,973	$ (1,582)	$ 648,973	$ (7,635)	$ 1,097,946	$ (9,217)

Our investment portfolio consists of both corporate and government securities that have a maximum maturity of three years. The longer the duration of these securities, the more susceptible they are to changes in market interest rates and bond yields. As yields increase, those securities purchased with a lower yield-at-cost show a mark-to-market unrealized loss. All unrealized losses are due to changes in interest rates and bond yields. We expect to realize the full value of all these investments upon maturity or sale. The losses on these securities have an average duration of approximately 11 months.

eBay Inc.

NOTES TO CONSOLIDATED FINANCIAL STATEMENTS — (Continued)

The estimated fair value of short and long-term investments classified by date of contractual maturity at December 31, 2005 are as follows (in thousands):

	December 31, 2005
One year or less (including restricted cash and investments of $29,702)	$ 804,352
One year through two years (including restricted cash and investments of $989)	491,937
Two years through three years (including restricted cash and investments of $76)	281,781
Equity instruments and equity method investments	51,949
	$ 1,630,019

During 2003, we recorded impairment charges totaling $1.2 million as a result of the deterioration of the financial condition of certain of our private and public equity investees that were considered to be other than temporary. We did not record any impairment charges during 2004 and 2005.

Equity method investments

We have certain investments accounted for using the equity method of accounting of which the total of these investments, including identifiable intangible assets, deferred tax liabilities and goodwill, are classified on our balance sheet as a long-term investments. Our consolidated results of operations include, as a component of other income, our share of the net income or loss of these investments together with amortization expense relating to acquired intangible assets. Our share of the results of investees' results of operations are not significant for any period presented.

Note 6 — Derivative Instruments:

Transaction Exposure

As of December 31, 2005, we had outstanding forward foreign exchange hedge contracts with notional values equivalent to approximately $151.5 million with maturity dates within 31 days. The hedge contracts are used to offset changes in non-US dollar denominated functional currency value of assets and liabilities as a result of foreign exchange rate fluctuations. Transaction gains and losses on the contracts and the assets and liabilities are recognized each period in interest and other income, net.

Translation Exposure

We consolidate the earnings of our international subsidiaries by converting them into U.S. dollars in accordance with Statement of Financial Accounting Standards No. 52 "Foreign Currency Translation" (FAS 52). Such earnings will fluctuate when there is a change in foreign currency exchange rates. From time to time, we enter into transactions to hedge portions of our foreign currency denominated earnings translation exposure using both foreign currency options and forward contracts. All contracts that hedge translation exposure mature ratably over the quarter in which they are executed. During the years ended December 31, 2004 and 2005, the realized gains and losses related to these hedges were not significant.

Economic Exposure

We currently charge our international subsidiaries on a monthly basis for their use of intellectual property and technology and for certain corporate services provided by eBay and by PayPal. These charges are denominated in Euros and these forecasted inter-company transactions represent a foreign currency cash flow exposure. To reduce foreign exchange risk relating to these forecasted inter-company transactions, we entered into forward foreign exchange contracts during the year ended December 31, 2005. The objective of the

eBay Inc.

NOTES TO CONSOLIDATED FINANCIAL STATEMENTS — (Continued)

forward contracts is to better ensure that the U.S. dollar-equivalent cash flows are not adversely affected by changes in the U.S. dollar/Euro exchange rate. Pursuant to Statement of Financial Accounting Standards No. 133 "Accounting for Derivative Instruments and Hedging Activities" (FAS 133), we expect the hedge of certain of these forecasted transactions to be highly effective in offsetting potential changes in cash flows attributed to a change in the U.S. dollar/Euro exchange rate. Accordingly, we record as a component of accumulated other comprehensive income all unrealized gains and losses related to the forward contracts that receive hedge accounting treatment. We record all unrealized gains and losses in interest and other income, net, related to the forward contracts that do not receive hedge accounting treatment pursuant to FAS 133. During the years ended December 31, 2004 and 2005, the realized gains and losses related to these hedges were not significant. The notional amount of our economic hedges receiving hedge accounting treatment and the losses, net of gains, recorded to accumulated other comprehensive income as of December 31, 2004 was $140.2 million and $3.4 million, respectively. The notional amount of our economic hedges receiving hedge accounting treatment and the losses, net of gains, recorded to accumulated other comprehensive income as of December 31, 2005 was $203.0 million and $200,000, respectively.

Note 7 — Balance Sheet Components:

	December 31,	
	2004	2005
	(In thousands)	
Accounts receivable, net:		
Accounts receivable	$ 319,489	$ 396,373
Allowance for doubtful accounts	(67,853)	(62,507)
Allowance for authorized credits	(10,780)	(11,078)
	$ 240,856	$ 322,788

	December 31,	
	2004	2005
	(In thousands)	
Other current assets:		
Customer accounts	$ 270,918	$ 324,595
Prepaid expenses	54,159	44,610
Deferred tax asset, net	10,427	59,274
Other	43,911	58,756
	$ 379,415	$ 487,235

eBay Inc.

NOTES TO CONSOLIDATED FINANCIAL STATEMENTS — (Continued)

	December 31, 2004	December 31, 2005
	(In thousands)	
Property and equipment, net:		
Computer equipment and software	$ 683,716	$ 894,401
Land and buildings, including building improvements	278,709	342,689
Leasehold improvements	99,623	121,306
Furniture and fixtures	43,689	56,854
Aviation equipment and other	30,609	40,968
	1,136,346	1,456,218
Accumulated depreciation	(426,573)	(654,616)
	$ 709,773	$ 801,602

During the years ended December 31, 2003, 2004 and 2005, we capitalized $38.5 million, $41.3 million and $37.1 million of software development costs, respectively, the majority of which relates to major site and other product development efforts. Total depreciation expense on our property and equipment was $105.8 million in 2003, $183.5 million in 2004 and $240.6 million in 2005.

During 2005, we sold a corporate aircraft at net book value for proceeds of $28.3 million. During 2004, we sold the remaining property related to our former Butterfields subsidiary for approximately $12.7 million in cash and recognized a loss of approximately $800,000.

	December 31, 2004	December 31, 2005
	(In thousands)	
Accrued expenses and other current liabilities:		
Acquisition related accrued expenses	$ 17,679	$ 27,513
Compensation and related benefits	110,146	139,080
Advertising	65,499	96,502
Contractors and consultants	21,464	31,904
Professional fees	51,029	61,328
Transaction loss reserve	10,986	20,246
VAT accrual	45,320	43,257
Other current liabilities	99,846	158,727
	$ 421,969	$ 578,557

Note 8 — Commitments and Contingencies:

Lease Arrangements

There were no material capital leases at December 31, 2005. Capital leases consist of various computer and other office leases that totaled $1.8 million at December 31, 2004.

eBay Inc.

NOTES TO CONSOLIDATED FINANCIAL STATEMENTS — (Continued)

We also have lease obligations under certain other non-cancelable operating leases. Future minimum rental payments under our non-cancelable operating leases, at December 31, 2005, are as follows (in thousands):

Year Ending December 31,	Operating Leases
2006	$ 22,988
2007	19,454
2008	17,142
2009	15,259
2010	12,035
Thereafter	53,287
Total minimum lease payments	$ 140,165

Rent expense in the years ended December 31, 2003, 2004 and 2005, excluding payments under our consolidated facilities lease, totaled $8.6 million, $7.7 million, and $14.4 million, respectively.

Litigation and Other Legal Matters

In April 2001, two of our European subsidiaries, eBay GmbH and eBay International AG, were sued by Montres Rolex S.A. and certain of its affiliates in the regional court of Cologne, Germany. The suit subsequently was transferred to the regional court in Düsseldorf, Germany. Rolex alleged that our subsidiaries were infringing Rolex's trademarks as a result of users selling counterfeit Rolex watches through our German website. The suit also alleged unfair competition. Rolex sought an order enjoining the sale of Rolex-branded watches on the website as well as damages. In December 2002, a trial was held in the matter and the court ruled in favor of eBay on all causes of action. Rolex appealed the ruling to the Higher Regional Court of Düsseldorf, and the appeal was heard in October 2003. In February 2004, the court rejected Rolex's appeal and ruled in our favor. Rolex has appealed the ruling to the German Federal Supreme Court and a hearing is expected in December 2006. In September 2004, the German Federal Supreme Court issued its written opinion in favor of Rolex in a case involving an unrelated company, ricardo.de AG, but somewhat comparable legal theories. Although it is not yet clear what the ultimate effect of the reasoning of the German Federal Supreme Court's ricardo.de decision will have when applied to eBay, we believe the Court's decision has resulted in an increase in similar litigation against us in Germany, although we do not currently believe that it will require a significant change in our business practices.

In September 2001, MercExchange LLC filed a complaint against us, our Half.com subsidiary and ReturnBuy, Inc. in the U.S. District Court for the Eastern District of Virginia (No. 2:01-CV-736) alleging infringement of three patents (relating to online consignment auction technology, multiple database searching and electronic consignment systems) and seeking a permanent injunction and damages (including treble damages for willful infringement). In October 2002, the court granted in part our summary judgment motion, effectively invalidating the patent related to online auction technology and rendering it unenforceable. This ruling left only two patents in the case. Trial of the matter began in April 2003. In May 2003, the jury returned a verdict finding that eBay had willfully infringed one and Half.com had willfully infringed both of the patents in the suit, awarding $35 million in compensatory damages. Both parties filed post-trial motions, and in August 2003, the court entered judgment for MercExchange in the amount of approximately $30 million plus pre-judgment interest and post-judgment interest in an amount to be determined, while denying MercExchange's request for an injunction and attorneys' fees. We appealed the verdict and judgment in favor of MercExchange and MercExchange filed a cross-appeal of the granting in part of our summary judgment motion and the denial of its request for an injunction and attorneys' fees.

eBay Inc.

NOTES TO CONSOLIDATED FINANCIAL STATEMENTS — (Continued)

In March 2005, the U.S. Court of Appeals for the Federal Circuit issued a ruling in the appeal of the MercExchange patent litigation suit which, among other things (1) invalidated all claims asserted against eBay and Half.com arising out of the multiple database search patent and reduced the verdict amount by $4.5 million; (2) upheld the electronic consignment system patent; (3) affirmed the district court's refusal to award attorneys' fees or enhanced damages against us; (4) reversed the district court's order granting summary judgment in our favor regarding the auction patent; and (5) reversed the district court's refusal to grant an injunction and remanded that issue to the district court for further proceedings. In May 2005, the Court of Appeals for the Federal Circuit granted our petition to stay the mandate in the case in order to allow us to petition the U.S. Supreme Court for review on certain issues. We filed our petition for review with the U.S. Supreme Court in July 2005, and on November 28, 2005, the Court granted our petition for review. Oral arguments in the case are scheduled for March 29, 2006. In parallel with the federal court proceedings, at our request, the U.S. Patent and Trademark Office is actively reexamining each of the patents in suit, having found that substantial questions exist regarding the validity of the claims contained in them. In January 2005, the Patent and Trademark Office issued an initial ruling rejecting all of the claims contained in the patent that related to online auctions; in March 2005, the Patent and Trademark Office issued an initial ruling rejecting all of the claims contained in the patent that related to electronic consignment systems; and in May 2005, the Patent and Trademark Office issued an initial ruling rejecting all of the claims contained in the patent that related to multiple database searching. Even if successful, our litigation of these matters will continue to be costly. In addition, as a precautionary measure, we have modified certain functionality of our websites and business practices in a manner which we believe would avoid any further infringement. For this reason, we believe that any injunction that might be issued by the district court will not have any impact on our business. We also believe we have appropriate reserves for this litigation. Nonetheless, if we are not successful in appealing or modifying the court's ruling, and if the modifications to the functionality of our websites and business practices are not sufficient to make them non-infringing, we would likely be forced to pay significant additional damages and licensing fees and/or modify our business practices in an adverse manner.

In August 2002, Charles E. Hill & Associates, Inc. filed a lawsuit in the U.S. District Court for the Eastern District of Texas (No. 2:02-CV-186) alleging that we and 17 other companies, primarily large retailers, infringed three patents owned by Hill generally relating to electronic catalog systems and methods for transmitting and updating data at a remote computer. The suit seeks an injunction against continuing infringement, unspecified damages, including treble damages for willful infringement, and interest, costs, expenses, and fees. The case was transferred to the U.S. District Court for the Southern District of Indiana in January 2003, but was transferred back to the U.S. District Court for the Eastern District of Texas in December 2003. A claim construction hearing was held in August 2005. In February 2006, we entered into a settlement agreement with the plaintiffs in the case under which we will be licensed under all of the patents at issue.

In February 2002, PayPal was sued in California state court (No. CV-805433) in a purported class action alleging that its limiting access to customer accounts and failure to promptly restore access to legitimate accounts violates California state consumer protection laws and is an unfair business practice and a breach of PayPal's User Agreement. This action was re-filed with a different named plaintiff in June 2002 (No. CV-808441), and a similar action was also filed in the U.S. District Court for the Northern District of California in June 2002 (No. C-02-2777). In March 2002, PayPal was sued in the U.S. District Court for the Northern District of California (No. C-02-1227) in a purported class action alleging that its limiting access to customer accounts and failure to promptly restore access to legitimate accounts violates federal and state consumer protection and unfair business practice laws. The two federal court actions were consolidated into a single case, and the state court action was stayed pending developments in the federal case. In June 2004, the parties announced that they had reached a proposed settlement. The settlement received approval from the federal court on November 2, 2004, and the state court action was dismissed with prejudice in March 2005. In the settlement, PayPal does not acknowledge that any of the allegations in the case are true. Under the terms of

eBay Inc.

NOTES TO CONSOLIDATED FINANCIAL STATEMENTS — (Continued)

the settlement, certain PayPal account holders are eligible to receive payment from a settlement fund of $9.25 million, less administrative costs and the amount awarded to plaintiffs' counsel by the court. That sum is being distributed to class members who have submitted timely claims in accordance with the settlement's plan of allocation. The plan of allocation for a portion of the settlement fund that remains undistributed must still be approved by the court. That plan was recently approved by the Special Master, who has recommended that the District Court issue its approval. Substantially all of the cost associated with the settlement was reserved in 2003.

In July 2004, a purported class action lawsuit was filed by two eBay users in Superior Court of the State of California, County of Santa Clara (No. 104CV022708) alleging that eBay engaged in improper billing practices as the result of problems with the rollout of a new billing software system in the second and third quarters of 2004. The lawsuit sought damages and injunctive relief. An amended complaint was filed in January 2005, dropping one plaintiff, changing the capacity of the other plaintiff to that of representative plaintiff, and adding seven additional eBay users as plaintiffs. The amended complaint expanded its claim to include numerous alleged improper billing practices from September 2003 until the present. In February 2005, eBay filed a motion to strike and a demurrer seeking to dismiss the complaint. In April 2005, the court sustained portions of the demurrer, but granted the plaintiffs leave to amend their complaint. The plaintiffs filed a second amended complaint, dropping the last original plaintiff and again adding new plaintiffs. We filed a motion to strike and a demurrer regarding the plaintiffs' second amended complaint. In July 2005, the court again sustained a portion of the demurrer and again granted the plaintiffs leave to amend their complaint, and the plaintiffs filed a third amended complaint. In December 2005, the plaintiffs filed a fourth amended complaint, dropping several plaintiffs. In January 2006, the parties reached tentative agreement on the terms of a settlement, though the settlement has not been finalized.

In February 2005, eBay was sued in Superior Court of the State of California, County of Santa Clara (No. 105CV035930) in a purported class action alleging that certain bidding features of our site constitute "shill bidding" for the purpose of artificially inflating bids placed by buyers on the site. The complaint alleges violations of California's Auction Act, California's Consumer Remedies Act, and unfair competition. The complaint seeks injunctive relief, damages, and a constructive trust. In April 2005, we filed a demurrer seeking to dismiss the complaint, and a hearing on the demurrer was held in February 2006. We believe that we have meritorious defenses and intend to defend ourselves vigorously.

In March 2005, eBay, PayPal, and an eBay seller were sued in Supreme Court of the State of New York, County of Kings (No. 6125/05) in a purported class action alleging that certain disclosures regarding PayPal's Buyer Protection Policy, users' chargeback rights, and the effects of users' choice of funding mechanism are deceptive and/or misleading. The complaint alleged misrepresentation on the part of eBay and PayPal, breach of contract and deceptive trade practices by PayPal, and that PayPal and eBay have jointly violated the civil RICO statute (18 U.S.C. Section 1961(4)). In April 2005, eBay and PayPal removed the case to the U.S. District Court for the Eastern District of New York and the plaintiffs filed an amended complaint in the U.S. District Court (No. 05-CV-01720) repeating the allegations of the initial complaint but dropping the civil RICO allegations. The complaint seeks injunctive relief, compensatory damages, and punitive damages. Following several mediation sessions, the parties reached a tentative settlement in December 2005. The parties are still engaged in the process of documenting this settlement. In order for the settlement to become final, the court must preliminarily approve its terms, and the settlement must then receive final approval from the court after a public hearing. The full amount of the proposed settlement was accrued in our consolidated income statement for the year ended December 31, 2005.

In January 2005, 51 former shareholders of Epinions, Inc. common stock including founders and former employees of that company filed a lawsuit in Superior Court of the State of California County of San Francisco (No. CGC 05-437906) related to the April 2003 merger of Epinions and DealTime, Ltd. The lawsuit was filed against certain of Epinions' former officers and directors and preferred shareholders and the

eBay Inc.

NOTES TO CONSOLIDATED FINANCIAL STATEMENTS — (Continued)

company that resulted from the merger, Shopping.com Ltd. eBay completed its acquisition of Shopping.com Ltd. on August 30, 2005. The lawsuit contended that the defendants were responsible for breaches of fiduciary duty and material misstatements and omissions, that defendants undervalued the DealTime stock that Epinions' shareholders received in connection with the merger, and that plaintiffs' common stock of Epinions was wrongfully cancelled without compensation. Defendants disputed the contentions of the case and denied any allegations of wrongdoing. The parties tentatively reached agreement as to the monetary terms for settlement of the dispute in September 2005, and in December 2005, the settlement was finalized and the lawsuit was dismissed. The settlement amount has been accounted for as an assumed liability in connection with our acquisition of Shopping.com.

Other third parties have from time to time claimed, and others may claim in the future, that we have infringed their intellectual property rights. We have been notified of several potential patent disputes, and expect that we will increasingly be subject to patent infringement claims as our services expand in scope and complexity. In particular, we expect to face additional patent infringement claims involving services we provide, including various aspects of our Payments and communications businesses. We have in the past been forced to litigate such claims. We may also become more vulnerable to third-party claims as laws such as the Digital Millennium Copyright Act, the Lanham Act and the Communications Decency Act are interpreted by the courts and as we expand geographically into jurisdictions where the underlying laws with respect to the potential liability of online intermediaries like ourselves are either unclear or less favorable. These claims, whether meritorious or not, could be time consuming and costly to resolve, cause service upgrade delays, require expensive changes in our methods of doing business, or could require us to enter into costly royalty or licensing agreements.

From time to time, we are involved in other disputes or regulatory inquiries that arise in the ordinary course of business. The number and significance of these disputes and inquiries are increasing as our business expands and our company grows larger. Any claims or regulatory actions against us, whether meritorious or not, could be time consuming, result in costly litigation, require significant amounts of management time, and result in the diversion of significant operational resources.

Indemnification Provisions

In the ordinary course of business, we have included limited indemnification provisions in certain of our agreements with parties with whom we have commercial relations, including our standard marketing, promotions and application-programming-interface license agreements. Under these contracts, we generally indemnify, hold harmless, and agree to reimburse the indemnified party for losses suffered or incurred by the indemnified party in connection with claims by any third party with respect to our domain names, trademarks, logos and other branding elements to the extent that such marks are applicable to our performance under the subject agreement. In a limited number of agreements, including agreements under which we have developed technology for certain commercial parties, we have provided an indemnity for other types of third-party claims, substantially all of which are indemnities related to our copyrights, trademarks, and patents. In our PayPal business, we have provided an indemnity to our payments processors in the event of certain third-party claims or card association fines against the processor arising out of conduct by PayPal. To date, no significant costs have been incurred, either individually or collectively, in connection with our indemnification provisions.

Note 9 — Related Party Transactions:

We have entered into indemnification agreements with each of our directors, executive officers and certain other officers. These agreements require us to indemnify such individuals, to the fullest extent permitted by Delaware law, for certain liabilities to which they may become subject as a result of their affiliation with us.

eBay Inc.

NOTES TO CONSOLIDATED FINANCIAL STATEMENTS — (Continued)

A member of our Board of Directors is a general partner of certain venture capital funds that beneficially hold in the aggregate a greater than 10% equity interest in several public and private companies. In 2000, we invested $3.0 million in capital stock of one such private company that provides a real estate solution to home buyers and sellers and received a warrant to purchase additional shares, which if exercised, would bring our total ownership to less than 5% of its capital stock. The member of our Board of Directors referred to above is also a member of such company's Board of Directors. Such company effected an initial public offering of its common stock in 2004 and we sold all of the shares we owned in such company in 2005.

Separately, a member of our Board of Directors is a director and Chairman of the Executive Committee of the Board of Directors of a company with whom PayPal, in September 2000, prior to eBay's acquisition of PayPal, entered into a strategic marketing agreement. The agreement was terminated in December 2002, and PayPal paid the company an early termination fee of $1.3 million in January 2003 in accordance with the terms of the agreement. In addition, in July 2003, such company purchased an entity with which eBay had a pre-existing data licensing agreement. In June 2004, this contract was amended to extend the term of the agreement and to update the fees. Under the terms of eBay's agreement, as amended, with the purchased entity, eBay recognized $156,000 of revenue in 2003, $323,000 of revenue in 2004, and $143,000 of revenue in 2005. The revenues expected to be recognized by us is approximately $35,500 per quarter for the remainder of the term, which is through May 2006.

As of December 31, 2005, there were no significant amounts payable or amounts receivable under these arrangements. All contracts with related parties are at rates and terms that we believe are comparable with those entered into with independent third parties.

Note 10 — Preferred Stock:

We are authorized, subject to limitations prescribed by Delaware law: to issue Preferred Stock in one or more series; to establish the number of shares included within each series; to fix the rights, preferences and privileges of the shares of each wholly unissued series and any related qualifications, limitations or restrictions; and to increase or decrease the number of shares of any series (but not below the number of shares of a series then outstanding) without any further vote or action by the stockholders. At December 31, 2004 and 2005, there were 10 million shares of $0.001 par value Preferred Stock authorized for issuance, and no shares issued or outstanding.

Note 11 — Common Stock:

Our Certificate of Incorporation, as amended, authorizes us to issue 3,580 million shares of common stock. A portion of the shares outstanding are subject to repurchase over a four-year period from the earlier of the issuance date or employee hire date, as applicable. At December 31, 2004 and 2005 there were 140,000 and 40,000 shares subject to repurchase rights, respectively.

At December 31, 2005, we had reserved 222.6 million shares of common stock available for future issuance under our stock option plans, including 129.1 million shares related to outstanding stock options. In addition, as of December 31, 2005, we had reserved approximately 4.0 million shares of common stock available for future issuance under our deferred stock unit plan, and approximately 5.8 million shares of common stock available for future issuance under our employee stock purchase plan.

Note 12 — Employee Benefit Plans:

Employee Stock Purchase Plan

We have an employee stock purchase plan for all eligible employees. Under the plan, shares of our common stock may be purchased over an offering period with a maximum duration of two years at 85% of the lower of the fair market value on the first day of the applicable offering period or on the last day of the six-

eBay Inc.

NOTES TO CONSOLIDATED FINANCIAL STATEMENTS — (Continued)

month purchase period. Employees may purchase shares having a value not exceeding 10% of their gross compensation during an offering period. During the years ended December 31, 2003, 2004, and 2005, employees purchased approximately 1.2 million, 1.2 million, and 1.4 million shares at average prices of $12.79, $20.66 and $25.55 per share, respectively. At December 31, 2005, approximately 5.8 million shares of common stock were reserved for future issuance. Our employee stock purchase plan contains an "evergreen" provision that automatically increases, on each January 1, the number of shares reserved for issuance under the employee stock purchase plan by the number of shares purchased under this plan in the preceding calendar year.

Employee Savings Plans

We have a savings plan, which qualifies under Section 401(k) of the Internal Revenue Code. Participating employees may contribute up to 25% of their annual salary, but not more than statutory limits. We contribute one dollar for each dollar a participant contributes, with a maximum contribution of $1,500 per employee. Our non-U.S. employees are covered by various other savings plans. Our expenses for these plans were $3.9 million in 2003, $5.6 million in 2004 and $8.6 million in 2005.

Stock Unit Plan

We have a deferred stock unit plan under which deferred stock units have been granted to new non-employee directors elected to our Board of Directors after December 31, 2002. Under this plan, each new director receives a one-time grant of deferred stock units equal to the result of dividing $150,000 by the fair market value of our common stock on the date of grant. Each deferred stock unit constitutes an unfunded and unsecured promise by us to deliver one share of our common stock (or the equivalent value thereof in cash or property at our election). Each deferred stock unit award granted to a new non-employee director upon election to the Board vests 25% one year from the date of grant, and at a rate of 2.08% per month thereafter. If the services of the director are terminated at any time, all rights to the unvested deferred stock units shall also terminate. In addition, directors may elect to receive, in lieu of annual retainer and committee chair fees and at the time these fees would otherwise be payable (i.e., on a quarterly basis in arrears for services provided), fully vested deferred stock units with an initial value equal to the amount of these fees. Deferred stock units are payable following the termination of a director's tenure as a director. All eBay officers, directors and employees are eligible to receive awards under the plan, although, to date, awards have been made only to new non-employee directors. As of December 31, 2005, 27,391 units have been awarded under this plan.

Equity Incentive Plans

We have equity incentive plans for directors, officers and employees. Stock options granted under these plans generally vest 25% one year from the date of grant (or 12.5% six months from the date of grant for grants to existing employees) and the remainder vest at a rate of 2.08% per month thereafter, and generally expire 10 years from the date of grant. Stock options issued prior to June 1998, were exercisable immediately, subject to repurchase rights held by us, which lapsed over the vesting period. Shares of restricted stock issued under these plans are subject to repurchase by us at such times as determined by the Board of Directors, typically five years. At December 31, 2005, 93.5 million shares were available for future grant.

eBay Inc.

NOTES TO CONSOLIDATED FINANCIAL STATEMENTS — (Continued)

The following table summarizes activity under our equity incentive plans for the years ended December 31, 2003, 2004 and 2005 (shares in thousands):

	Year Ended December 31,					
	2003		2004		2005	
	Shares	Weighted Average Exercise Price	Shares	Weighted Average Exercise Price	Shares	Weighted Average Exercise Price
Outstanding at beginning of period	148,714	$ 13.43	138,410	$ 16.93	137,208	$ 23.63
Granted and assumed	53,388	22.63	43,628	38.27	34,991	38.36
Exercised	(52,288)	12.96	(38,718)	16.17	(31,458)	17.91
Cancelled	(11,404)	16.18	(6,112)	23.73	(11,632)	32.71
Outstanding at end of period	138,410	16.93	137,208	23.63	129,109	28.19
Options exercisable at end of period	45,010	$ 13.92	49,346	$ 16.77	59,571	$ 21.67

The following table summarizes information about fixed stock options outstanding at December 31, 2005 (shares in thousands):

	Options Outstanding at December 31, 2005			Options Exercisable at December 31, 2005	
Range of Exercise Prices	Number of Shares Outstanding	Weighted Average Remaining Contractual Life	Weighted Average Exercise Price	Number of Shares Exercisable	Weighted Average Exercise Price
$ 0.08 — $13.73	14,106	5.1 years	$ 7.82	11,485	$ 8.02
$13.74 — $15.11	13,026	6.3	14.28	10,104	14.32
$15.13 — $19.39	20,274	6.5	18.24	13,515	17.94
$19.39 — $27.38	15,403	7.2	24.59	8,244	24.25
$27.43 — $34.57	6,927	8.2	31.00	2,435	30.46
$34.62 — $41.50	31,453	8.6	36.17	8,402	35.33
$42.51 — $42.58	15,587	9.2	42.52	2,803	42.54
$42.96 — $58.21	12,333	9.1	46.99	2,583	47.04
	129,109	7.6	$ 28.19	59,571	$ 21.67

	Exercisable		Unexercisable		Total	
	Shares	Weighted Average Exercise Price	Shares	Weighted Average Exercise Price	Shares	Weighted Average Exercise Price
In-the-money	56,952	$ 20.63	60,339	$ 31.61	117,291	$ 26.28
Out-of-the-money	2,452	47.26	9,366	47.14	11,818	47.16
Total options outstanding	59,404	$ 21.73	69,705	$ 33.70	129,109	$ 28.19

In-the-money options are options with an exercise price lower than the $43.22 closing price of our common stock on December 31, 2005. Out-of-the-money options are options with an exercise price greater than the $43.22 closing price of our common stock on December 31, 2005.

In connection with the change in status from an employee to a non-employee, we were required, in accordance with FASB Interpretation No. 44 "Accounting for Certain Transactions Involving Stock Compensation — an interpretation of APB Opinion No. 25" and EITF 00-23 "Issues Related to the

eBay Inc.

NOTES TO CONSOLIDATED FINANCIAL STATEMENTS — (Continued)

Accounting for Stock Compensation under APB Opinion No. 25 and FASB Interpretation No. 44", to remeasure the portion of an individual's options that were unvested at the date of the change in status. The remeasurement is required to be at fair value and will continue to be revalued over the period of performance. The related stock-based compensation amortization recognized during the year ended December 31, 2005 totaled approximately $6.7 million. The fair value of these unvested options have been estimated using the Black-Scholes option pricing model with the following weighted average assumptions: risk-free interest rate, 4.43%; effective contractual life, 3 years; dividend yield, 0%; and expected volatility, 35%.

The following table summarizes additional stock option information related to grants made to our employees and grants made specifically to named officers, which include our chief executive officer and the other four most highly compensated officers during the year (in thousands, except percentages):

	Year Ended December 31,		
	2003	2004	2005
Total outstanding shares of common stock (at period end)	1,298,586	1,338,608	1,404,184
As a percentage of total outstanding shares of common stock:			
Grants during the period	4%	3%	2%
Total outstanding "in-the-money" grants	11%	10%	8%
Total outstanding grants	11%	10%	9%
Grants to named officers during the period	*	*	*
Total outstanding grants to named officers	1%	1%	1%
Total stock option grants during the period	53,388	43,628	34,991
Grants to named officers during the period as a percent of total grants during the period	9%	7%	4%
Total outstanding stock option grants (at period end)	138,410	137,208	129,109
Total outstanding grants to named officers as a percent of total stock option grants outstanding	11%	11%	11%

* Less than half of a percentage point

Non-stockholder approved stock option grants

Prior to our initial public offering in 1998, our Board of Directors approved three stock option grants outside of formally approved stockholder plans to two independent directors upon their joining our Board of Directors and to an executive officer upon his hiring. All of such option grants vested over 25% one year from the date of grant, with the remainder vesting at a rate of 2.08% per month thereafter and expire 10 years from the date of grant. The options granted to the independent directors were immediately exercisable, subject to repurchase rights held by us, which lapse over the vesting period. The terms and conditions of such grants are otherwise identical to nonqualified option grants made under the stock option plan in effect at that time. At the time of such grants, members of our Board of Directors (and their affiliates) beneficially owned in excess of 90% of our then outstanding voting interests. We have previously disclosed such option grants in our Prospectus filed with the Securities and Exchange Commission on September 25, 1998 in connection with our initial public offering under the headings "Management — Director Compensation" and "Management — Compensation Arrangements." Prior to 2004, one director and the executive officer had exercised all available options under their respective grants. At December 31, 2005, one grant remained outstanding to one independent director, with 1,383,000 shares to be issued upon exercise of the outstanding options at an average

eBay Inc.

NOTES TO CONSOLIDATED FINANCIAL STATEMENTS — (Continued)

exercise price of $0.39. There were no shares remaining available under these non-stockholder approved plans for future grants as of December 31, 2005.

Note 13 —Income Taxes:

The components of pretax income before cumulative effect of accounting change and minority interest in consolidated companies for the years ended December 31, 2003, 2004 and 2005 are as follows (in thousands):

	Year Ended December 31,		
	2003	2004	2005
United States	$ 449,078	$ 820,892	$ 943,575
International	212,422	307,338	605,802
	$ 661,500	$ 1,128,230	$ 1,549,377

The provision for income taxes is composed of the following (in thousands):

	Year Ended December 31,		
	2003	2004	2005
Current:			
Federal	$ 124,075	$ 246,795	$ 382,925
State and local	36,646	57,099	89,717
Foreign	10,378	23,546	79,838
	171,099	327,440	552,480
Deferred:			
Federal	40,619	27,836	(37,651)
State and local	(1,041)	(3,565)	(7,106)
Foreign	(3,939)	(7,826)	(40,438)
	35,639	16,445	(85,195)
	$ 206,738	$ 343,885	$ 467,285

The following is a reconciliation of the difference between the actual provision for income taxes and the provision computed by applying the federal statutory rate of 35% for 2003, 2004, and 2005 to income before income taxes (in thousands):

	Year Ended December 31,		
	2003	2004	2005
Provision at statutory rate	$ 228,873	$ 394,881	$ 542,282
Permanent differences:			
Foreign income taxed at different rates	(43,826)	(82,267)	(144,864)
Change in valuation allowance	5,756	2,000	12,587
Tax-exempt interest income	(1,272)	—	—
State taxes, net of federal benefit	23,297	35,008	53,697
Tax credits	(7,943)	(6,975)	(9,136)
Other	1,853	1,238	12,719
	$ 206,738	$ 343,885	$ 467,285

eBay Inc.

NOTES TO CONSOLIDATED FINANCIAL STATEMENTS — (Continued)

Deferred tax assets and liabilities are recognized for the future tax consequences of differences between the carrying amounts of assets and liabilities and their respective tax bases using enacted tax rates in effect for the year in which the differences are expected to reverse. Significant deferred tax assets and liabilities consist of the following (in thousands):

	December 31,	
	2004	2005
Deferred tax assets:		
Net operating loss and credits	$ 165,673	$ 64,905
Accruals and allowances	57,648	78,665
Net unrealized (gains) losses	(6,596)	9,616
Net deferred tax assets	216,725	153,186
Valuation allowance	(158,602)	(16,946)
	58,123	136,240
Deferred tax liabilities:		
Acquisition-related intangibles	(129,310)	(212,702)
Depreciation and amortization	(54,357)	(79,946)
	(183,667)	(292,648)
	$ (125,544)	$ (156,408)

As of December 31, 2005, our federal net operating loss carryforwards for income tax purposes were approximately $123.8 million. If not utilized, the federal net operating loss carryforwards will begin to expire in 2019. As of December 31, 2005, our federal and state tax credit carryforwards for income tax purposes were approximately $70.1 million and $67.5 million, respectively. If not utilized, the federal tax credit carryforwards will begin to expire in 2019, and the state tax credit carryforwards will begin to expire in 2015.

We receive tax deductions from the gains realized by employees on the exercise of certain non-qualified stock options for which the benefit is recognized as a component of stockholders' equity. Historically, we have evaluated the deferred tax assets relating to these stock option deductions along with our other deferred tax assets and concluded that a valuation allowance is not required for that portion of the total deferred tax assets that are not considered more likely than not to be realized in future periods. To the extent that the deferred tax assets with a valuation allowance become realizable in future periods, we will have the ability, subject to carryforward limitations, to benefit from these amounts. When realized, the tax benefits of tax deductions related to stock options are accounted for as an increase to additional paid-in capital rather than a reduction of the income tax provision. Our profitability coupled with the level of stock option deductions generated during 2005 resulted in the utilization of net operating losses related to deferred tax assets for stock option deductions. Accordingly the valuation allowance related to these deferred tax assets was eliminated in 2005, resulting in an increase of $166.3 million in additional paid-in capital. Beginning in 2006, deferred tax assets related to stock option deductions will be recognized in the periods when the benefit is received.

We have not provided for U.S. federal income and foreign withholding taxes on $974.2 million of non-U.S. subsidiaries' undistributed earnings as of December 31, 2005, because such earnings are intended to be indefinitely reinvested in the operations and potential acquisitions of our International Marketplaces segment. Upon distribution of those earnings in the form of dividends or otherwise, we would be subject to U.S. income taxes (subject to an adjustment for foreign tax credits). It is not practicable to determine the income tax liability that might be incurred if these earnings were to be distributed.

eBay Inc.

NOTES TO CONSOLIDATED FINANCIAL STATEMENTS — (Continued)

Supplementary Data — Quarterly Financial Data-Unaudited:

The following tables present certain unaudited consolidated quarterly financial information for each of the eight quarters ended December 31, 2005. This quarterly information has been prepared on the same basis as the Consolidated Financial Statements and includes all adjustments necessary to state fairly the information for the periods presented. The results of operations for any quarter are not necessarily indicative of results for the full year or for any future period. All share and per share amounts included in the following consolidated financial data have been adjusted to reflect all previous stock splits, including our two-for-one stock split, effective February 16, 2005.

Quarterly Financial Data
(Unaudited, in thousands, except per share amounts)

	Quarter Ended			
	March 31	June 30	September 30	December 31
2004				
Net revenues	$ 756,239	$ 773,412	$ 805,876	$ 935,782
Gross profit	$ 621,881	$ 626,881	$ 648,755	$ 759,377
Net income	$ 200,100	$ 190,395	$ 182,349	$ 205,379
Net income per share-basic	$ 0.15	$ 0.14	$ 0.14	$ 0.15
Net income per share-diluted	$ 0.15	$ 0.14	$ 0.13	$ 0.15
Weighted-average shares:				
Basic	1,305,002	1,316,138	1,323,144	1,333,486
Diluted	1,347,596	1,364,842	1,369,954	1,385,694

	Quarter Ended			
	March 31	June 30	September 30	December 31
2005				
Net revenues	$ 1,031,724	$ 1,086,303	$ 1,105,515	$ 1,328,859
Gross profit	$ 845,355	$ 894,463	$ 905,140	$ 1,089,339
Net income	$ 256,291	$ 291,560	$ 254,971	$ 279,221
Net income per share-basic	$ 0.19	$ 0.22	$ 0.19	$ 0.20
Net income per share-diluted	$ 0.19	$ 0.21	$ 0.18	$ 0.20
Weighted-average shares:				
Basic	1,343,442	1,351,375	1,357,239	1,394,566
Diluted	1,382,150	1,379,088	1,387,038	1,426,475

eBay Inc.

FINANCIAL STATEMENT SCHEDULE

The Financial Statement Schedule II — VALUATION AND QUALIFYING ACCOUNTS is filed as part of this Annual Report on Form 10-K.

	Balance at Beginning of Period	Charged/ Credited to Net Income	Charged to Other Account	Charges Utilized/ Write-offs	Balance at End of Period
	(In thousands)				
Allowance for Doubtful Accounts and Authorized Credits					
Year ended December 31, 2003	$ 30,702	$ 46,049	$ —	$ (28,682)	$ 48,069
Year ended December 31, 2004	48,069	90,942	—	(60,378)	78,633
Year ended December 31, 2005	78,633	89,499	—	(94,547)	73,585
Allowance for Transaction Losses					
Year ended December 31, 2003	10,107	36,401	—	(34,500)	12,008
Year ended December 31, 2004	12,008	50,459	—	(51,481)	10,986
Year ended December 31, 2005	10,986	73,773	—	(64,514)	20,245
Tax Valuation Allowance					
Year ended December 31, 2003	145,182	20,649	—	—	165,831
Year ended December 31, 2004	165,831	(7,229)	—	—	158,602
Year ended December 31, 2005	158,602	13,196	—	(154,852)	16,946

117

APPENDIX C

TARGET, INC.

CONSOLIDATED STATEMENTS OF OPERATIONS

(millions, except per share data)	2005	2004	2003
Sales	$ **51,271**	$ 45,682	$ 40,928
Net credit card revenues	**1,349**	1,157	1,097
Total revenues	**52,620**	46,839	42,025
Cost of sales	**34,927**	31,445	28,389
Selling, general and administrative expenses	**11,185**	9,797	8,657
Credit card expenses	**776**	737	722
Depreciation and amortization	**1,409**	1,259	1,098
Earnings from continuing operations before interest expense and income taxes	**4,323**	3,601	3,159
Net interest expense	**463**	570	556
Earnings from continuing operations before income taxes	**3,860**	3,031	2,603
Provision for income taxes	**1,452**	1,146	984
Earnings from continuing operations	**2,408**	1,885	1,619
Earnings from discontinued operations, net of taxes of $46 and $116	—	75	190
Gain on disposal of discontinued operations, net of taxes of $761	—	1,238	—
Net earnings	$ **2,408**	$ 3,198	$ 1,809
Basic earnings per share			
Continuing operations	$ **2.73**	$ 2.09	$ 1.78
Discontinued operations	—	.08	.21
Gain from discontinued operations	—	1.37	—
Basic earnings per share	$ **2.73**	$ 3.54	$ 1.99
Diluted earnings per share			
Continuing operations	$ **2.71**	$ 2.07	$ 1.76
Discontinued operations	—	.08	.21
Gain from discontinued operations	—	1.36	—
Diluted earnings per share	$ **2.71**	$ 3.51	$ 1.97
Weighted average common shares outstanding			
Basic	**882.0**	903.8	911.0
Diluted	**889.2**	912.1	919.2

See Notes to Consolidated Financial Statements throughout pages 28-39.

CONSOLIDATED STATEMENTS OF FINANCIAL POSITION

(millions, except footnotes)	January 28, 2006	January 29, 2005
Assets		
Cash and cash equivalents	$ **1,648**	$ 2,245
Accounts receivable, net	**5,666**	5,069
Inventory	**5,838**	5,384
Other current assets	**1,253**	1,224
Total current assets	**14,405**	13,922
Property and equipment		
Land	**4,449**	3,804
Buildings and improvements	**14,174**	12,518
Fixtures and equipment	**3,219**	2,990
Computer hardware and software	**2,214**	1,998
Construction-in-progress	**1,158**	962
Accumulated depreciation	**(6,176)**	(5,412)
Property and equipment, net	**19,038**	16,860
Other non-current assets	**1,552**	1,511
Total assets	$ **34,995**	$ 32,293
Liabilities and shareholders' investment		
Accounts payable	$ **6,268**	$ 5,779
Accrued liabilities	**2,193**	1,633
Income taxes payable	**374**	304
Current portion of long-term debt and notes payable	**753**	504
Total current liabilities	**9,588**	8,220
Long-term debt	**9,119**	9,034
Deferred income taxes	**851**	973
Other non-current liabilities	**1,232**	1,037
Shareholders' investment		
Common stock (a)	**73**	74
Additional paid-in-capital	**2,121**	1,810
Retained earnings	**12,013**	11,148
Accumulated other comprehensive income	**(2)**	(3)
Total shareholders' investment	**14,205**	13,029
Total liabilities and shareholders' investment	$ **34,995**	$ 32,293

(a) *Authorized 6,000,000,000 shares, $.0833 par value; 874,074,850 shares issued and outstanding at January 28, 2006; 890,643,966 shares issued and outstanding at January 29, 2005.*

Preferred Stock *Authorized 5,000,000 shares, $.01 par value; no shares were issued or outstanding at January 28, 2006 or January 29, 2005.*

See Notes to Consolidated Financial Statements throughout pages 28-39.

CONSOLIDATED STATEMENTS OF CASH FLOWS

(millions)	2005	2004	2003
Operating activities			
Net earnings	$ **2,408**	$ 3,198	$ 1,809
Earnings from and gain on disposal of discontinued operations, net of taxes	**—**	(1,313)	(190)
Earnings from continuing operations	**2,408**	1,885	1,619
Reconciliation to cash flow			
Depreciation and amortization	**1,409**	1,259	1,098
Share-based compensation expense	**93**	60	57
Deferred income taxes	**(122)**	233	208
Bad debt provision	**466**	451	476
Loss on disposal of property and equipment, net	**70**	59	41
Other non-cash items affecting earnings	**(50)**	73	10
Changes in operating accounts providing/(requiring) cash:			
Accounts receivable originated at Target	**(244)**	(209)	(279)
Inventory	**(454)**	(853)	(579)
Other current assets	**(28)**	(37)	(196)
Other non-current assets	**(24)**	(147)	(166)
Accounts payable	**489**	823	721
Accrued liabilities	**351**	319	85
Income taxes payable	**70**	(91)	74
Other	**17**	(17)	19
Cash flow provided by operations	**4,451**	3,808	3,188
Investing activities			
Expenditures for property and equipment	**(3,388)**	(3,068)	(2,738)
Proceeds from disposals of property and equipment	**58**	56	67
Change in accounts receivable originated at third parties	**(819)**	(690)	(538)
Proceeds from sale of discontinued operations	**—**	4,881	—
Cash flow (required for)/provided by investing activities	**(4,149)**	1,179	(3,209)
Financing activities			
Decrease in notes payable, net	**—**	—	(100)
Additions to long-term debt	**913**	10	1,200
Reductions of long-term debt	**(527)**	(1,487)	(1,179)
Dividends paid	**(318)**	(272)	(237)
Repurchase of stock	**(1,197)**	(1,290)	(48)
Stock option exercises	**172**	146	36
Share-based compensation tax benefit	**59**	69	25
Other	**(1)**	—	(10)
Cash flow required for financing activities	**(899)**	(2,824)	(313)
Cash flows of discontinued operations (Revised) *(a)*			
(Required for)/provided by operations	**—**	(549)	545
Required for investing activities	**—**	(44)	(248)
Required for financing activities	**—**	(33)	(5)
Net cash (required for)/provided by discontinued operations	**—**	(626)	292
Net (decrease)/increase in cash and cash equivalents	**(597)**	1,537	(42)
Cash and cash equivalents at beginning of year	**2,245**	708	750
Cash and cash equivalents at end of year	$ **1,648**	$ 2,245	$ 708

(a) We have revised this statement for 2004 and 2003 to separately disclose the operating, investing and financing portions of the cash flows attributable to our discontinued operations. We had previously reported these amounts on a combined basis.

Amounts presented herein are on a cash basis and therefore may differ from those shown in other sections of this Annual Report. Consistent with the provisions of SFAS No.95, "Statement of Cash Flows," cash flows related to accounts receivable are classified as either an operating activity or an investing activity, depending on their origin.

Cash paid for income taxes was $1,448 million, $1,742 million and $781 million during 2005, 2004 and 2003, respectively. Cash paid for interest (net of interest capitalized) was $468 million, $480 million and $542 million during 2005, 2004 and 2003, respectively.

See Notes to Consolidated Financial Statements throughout pages 28-39.

CONSOLIDATED STATEMENTS OF SHAREHOLDERS' INVESTMENT

(millions, except footnotes)	Common Stock Shares	Stock Par Value	Additional Paid-in Capital	Retained Earnings	Accumulated Other Comprehensive Income/(Loss)	Total
February 1, 2003	909.8	$ 76	$ 1,400	$ 8,017	$ 4	$ 9,497
Consolidated net earnings	—	—	—	1,809	—	1,809
Other comprehensive loss	—	—	—	—	(1)	(1)
Total comprehensive income						1,808
Dividends declared	—	—	—	(246)	—	(246)
Repurchase of stock	(1.5)	—	—	(57)	—	(57)
Issuance of stock for ESOP	0.6	—	17	—	—	17
Stock options and awards	2.9	—	113	—	—	113
January 31, 2004	911.8	76	1,530	9,523	3	11,132
Consolidated net earnings	—	—	—	3,198	—	3,198
Other comprehensive loss	—	—	—	—	(6)	(6)
Total comprehensive income						3,192
Dividends declared	—	—	—	(280)	—	(280)
Repurchase of stock	(28.9)	(3)	—	(1,293)	—	(1,296)
Stock options and awards	7.7	1	280	—	—	281
January 29, 2005	890.6	74	1,810	11,148	(3)	13,029
Consolidated net earnings	—	—	—	2,408	—	2,408
Other comprehensive income	—	—	—	—	1	1
Total comprehensive income						2,409
Dividends declared	—	—	—	(334)	—	(334)
Repurchase of stock	(23.1)	(2)	—	(1,209)	—	(1,211)
Stock options and awards	6.6	1	311	—	—	312
January 28, 2006	**874.1**	**$ 73**	**$ 2,121**	**$ 12,013**	**$ (2)**	**$ 14,205**

In June 2004, our Board of Directors authorized the repurchase of $3 billion of our common stock. In November 2005, our Board increased the aggregate authorization by $2 billion, for a total authorization of $5 billion. We expect the repurchase of our common stock to be made primarily in open market transactions, subject to market conditions, and anticipate completion of the aggregate program in the next two to three years. In 2005, we repurchased a total of 23.1 million shares of our common stock for a total investment of $1,197 million ($51.88 per share).

Junior Preferred Stock Rights *In 2001, we declared a distribution of preferred share purchase rights which expire in September 2006. Terms of the plan provide for a distribution of one preferred share purchase right for each outstanding share of our common stock. Each right will entitle shareholders to buy one twelve-hundredth of a share of a new series of junior participating preferred stock at an exercise price of $125.00, subject to adjustment. The rights will be exercisable only if a person or group acquires ownership of 20 percent or more of our common stock or announces a tender offer to acquire 30 percent or more of our common stock.*

Dividends *Dividends declared per share were $.38, $.31 and $.27 in 2005, 2004 and 2003, respectively.*

See Notes to Consolidated Financial Statements throughout pages 28-39.

NOTES TO CONSOLIDATED FINANCIAL STATEMENTS

1. Summary of Accounting Policies

Organization Target Corporation (the Corporation or Target) operates large-format general merchandise discount stores in the United States. Our credit card operation represents an integral component of our core retail business. We also operate Target.com, an online business. We operate as a single business segment.

Consolidation The consolidated financial statements include the balances of the Corporation and its subsidiaries after elimination of material intercompany balances and transactions. All material subsidiaries are wholly owned.

Use of Estimates The preparation of our consolidated financial statements, in conformity with U.S. generally accepted accounting principles (GAAP), requires management to make estimates and assumptions affecting reported amounts in the consolidated financial statements and accompanying notes. Actual results may differ from those estimates.

Fiscal Year Our fiscal year ends on the Saturday nearest January 31. Unless otherwise stated, references to years in this report relate to fiscal years rather than to calendar years. Fiscal years 2005, 2004 and 2003 each consisted of 52 weeks.

Reclassifications Certain prior year amounts have been reclassified to conform to the current year presentation.

Share-Based Compensation We adopted the provisions of Statement of Financial Accounting Standards No.123R, "Share-Based Payment" (SFAS No.123R), in 2004 under the modified retrospective transition method. Therefore, all prior period financial statements have been restated to recognize compensation cost in the amounts previously reported in the Notes to Consolidated Financial Statements under the provisions of SFAS No.123. SFAS No.123R requires that all share-based compensation be accounted for using a fair-value-based method. In 2005, the FASB issued additional guidance on SFAS No.123R in the form of Staff Positions (FSPs). FSP 123(R)-2 clarifies that a share-based compensation award is considered "granted" (and fair value should be estimated) when the employer and its employees have a mutual understanding of the key terms and conditions of the award, and further clarifies that this mutual understanding is presumed to exist at the date the award is approved by the Board of Directors or management with relevant authority, assuming certain conditions are met. We applied this guidance to our share-based awards upon issuance of the FSP.

SFAS No.123R requires companies to determine the amount of an additional paid-in capital (APIC) pool that would be available to absorb deferred tax asset write-offs by calculating the net excess tax benefits credited to APIC as if the company had always been following the provisions of SFAS No.123R. FSP 123(R)-3 provides an elective transition alternative for calculating the beginning balance of the APIC pool, which we have elected to adopt. Our practice with regard to awards that were not fully vested upon our adoption of SFAS No.123R is to treat the entire amount of such awards as partially vested for purposes of calculating the beginning balance of the APIC pool.

Generally, in accordance with SFAS No.123R, we recognize compensation expense for awards on a straight-line basis over the four-year vesting period. However, in certain circumstances under our share-based compensation plans, we allow for the vesting of employee awards to continue post-employment. Accordingly, for awards granted subsequent to our adoption of SFAS No.123R and to the extent those awards continue to vest post-employment because the employee met certain age and service requirements at the date of grant, we accelerate expense recognition, such that the value of the award is fully expensed over the employee's service period instead of over the explicit vesting period. Awards granted prior to the adoption of SFAS No.123R continue to be expensed over the explicit vesting period in accordance with SEC guidelines. Information related to outstanding stock options, performance shares and restricted stock is disclosed in Note 26, pages 35-36.

Derivative Financial Instruments SFAS No.133, "Accounting for Derivative Instruments and Hedging Activities," as amended, defines derivatives and requires that they be carried at fair value on the balance sheet. It also provides for hedge accounting when certain conditions are met. Our derivative instruments are primarily interest rate swaps which hedge the fair value of certain debt by effectively converting interest from a fixed rate to a floating rate. These instruments qualify for hedge accounting and the associated assets and liabilities are recorded in the Consolidated Statements of Financial Position. The change in market value of an interest rate swap as well as the offsetting change in market value of the hedged debt is recognized into earnings in the current period. Ineffectiveness would result when changes in the market value of the hedged debt are not completely offset by changes in the market value of the interest rate swap. There was no ineffectiveness recognized in 2005, 2004 or 2003 related to these instruments. Further information related to interest rate swaps is disclosed in Note 21, page 33.

2. Revenues

Revenues are recognized as sales occur and are net of expected returns. Total revenues do not include sales tax as we consider ourselves a pass-through conduit for collecting and remitting sales taxes. Commissions earned on sales generated by leased departments are included within sales and were $14 million in 2005, $14 million in 2004 and $13 million in 2003.

Revenue from gift card sales is recognized at redemption of the gift card. Our gift cards do not have expiration dates. Based on historical redemption rates, a certain percentage of gift cards will never be redeemed, which is referred to as "breakage." Estimated breakagerevenue is recognized as the remaining gift card values are redeemed.

Net credit card revenues are recognized according to the contractual provisions of each applicable credit card agreement. If an account is written-off, any uncollected finance charges or late fees are recorded as a reduction of net credit card revenues. Target retail store sales charged to our credit cards totaled $3,655 million, $3,269 million and $3,006 million in 2005, 2004 and 2003, respectively.

3. Cost of Sales and Selling, General and Administrative (SG&A) Expenses

The following illustrates the primary costs classified in each major expense category:

Cost of Sales	SG&A Expenses
Total cost of products sold including: • Freight expenses associated with moving merchandise from our vendors to our distribution centers and our retail stores • Vendor income that is not reimbursement of specific, incremental and identifiable costs Inventory shrink Markdowns Shipping and handling expenses Terms cash discount	Payroll and benefit costs Occupancy and operating costs of retail, distribution, and corporate facilities Advertising offset by vendor income that is a reimbursement of specific, incremental and identifiable costs Other administrative costs

The methodology behind the classification of expenses varies across the retail industry.

4. Consideration Received from Vendors

We receive consideration for a variety of vendor-sponsored programs, such as volume rebates, markdown allowances, promotions and advertising and for our compliance programs, referred to as "vendor income." Vendor income reduces either our inventory costs or SG&A expenses based on application of EITF Issue No. 02-16, "Accounting by a Customer (Including a Reseller) for Certain Consideration Received from a Vendor," as amended by EITF Issue No. 03-10, "Application of Issue 02-16 by Resellers to Sales Incentives Offered to Consumers by Manufacturers." Promotional and advertising allowances are intended to offset our costs of promoting and selling the vendor's merchandise in our stores. Under our compliance programs, vendors are charged for merchandise shipments that do not meet our requirements ("violations"), such as late or incomplete shipments. These allowances are recorded when violations occur.

5. Advertising Costs

Advertising costs are expensed at first showing of the advertisement and were $1,028 million, $888 million and $872 million for 2005, 2004 and 2003, respectively. Advertising vendor income that offset advertising expenses was approximately $110 million, $72 million and $58 million for 2005, 2004 and 2003, respectively. Newspaper circulars and media broadcast made up the majority of our advertising costs in all three years.

6. Discontinued Operations

We completed the sale of our Marshall Field's and Mervyn's businesses during 2004. In accordance with SFAS No. 144, "Accounting for the Impairment or Disposal of Long-Lived Assets," the financial results of Marshall Field's and Mervyn's are reported as discontinued operations.

No financial results of discontinued operations are included for the year ended January 28, 2006. For the years ended January 29, 2005 and January 31, 2004, total revenues included in discontinued operations were $3,095 million and $6,138 million, respectively, and earnings from discontinued operations were $75 million and $190 million, net of taxes of $46 million and $116 million, respectively. In addition, we recorded a gain on the sale of discontinued operations of $1,238 million, net of taxes of $761 million, during the year ended January 29, 2005.

There were no assets or liabilities of Marshall Field's or Mervyn's included in our Consolidated Statements of Financial Position at January 28, 2006 or January 29, 2005.

7. Earnings per Share

Basic earnings per share (EPS) is net earnings divided by the average number of common shares outstanding during the period. Diluted EPS includes the incremental shares assumed to be issued on the exercise of stock options and the potentially issuable performance shares.

(millions, except per share data)	Basic EPS			Diluted EPS		
	2005	2004	2003	2005	2004	2003
Net earnings	$ **2,408**	$ 3,198	$ 1,809	$ **2,408**	$ 3,198	$ 1,809
Basic weighted average common shares outstanding	**882.0**	903.8	911.0	**882.0**	903.8	911.0
Stock options and performance shares	—	—	—	**7.2**	8.3	8.2
Weighted average common shares outstanding	**882.0**	903.8	911.0	**889.2**	912.1	919.2
Earnings per share	$ **2.73**	$ 3.54	$ 1.99	$ **2.71**	$ 3.51	$ 1.97

Our diluted EPS calculation excludes any shares related to stock options for which the effect would have been antidilutive. There were no material antidilutive shares issuable upon exercise excluded from the dilutive EPS calculations at January 28, 2006, January 29, 2005 and January 31, 2004, respectively.

8. Other Comprehensive Income/(Loss)

Other comprehensive income/ (loss) includes revenues, expenses, gains and losses that are excluded from net earnings under GAAP and are recorded directly to shareholders' investment. In 2005, 2004 and 2003, other comprehensive income/(loss) primarily included gains and losses on certain hedge transactions and the change in our minimum pension liability, net of related taxes.

9. Cash Equivalents

Cash equivalents include highly liquid investments with an original maturity of three months or less from the time of purchase. We carry these investments at cost, which approximates market value. These investments were $1,172 million and $1,732 million in 2005 and 2004, respectively. Also included in cash equivalents are proceeds due from credit and debit card transactions with settlement terms of less than five days. Credit and debit card receivables included within cash equivalents were $285 million and $242 million, respectively, for 2005 and 2004.

10. Accounts Receivable

Accounts receivable are recorded net of an allowance for expected losses. The allowance, recognized in an amount equal to the anticipated future write-offs based on delinquencies, risk scores, aging trends, industry risk trends and our historical experience, was $451 million at January 28, 2006 and $387 million at January 29, 2005. Substantially all accounts continue to accrue finance charges until they are written off. Accounts are written off when they become 180 days past due.

In 2004, we chartered Target Bank for the purpose of issuing credit cards to qualified businesses, as our Target National Bank charter does not allow for the issuance of commercial credit cards.

As a method of providing funding for our accounts receivable, we sell on an ongoing basis all of our consumer credit card receivables to Target Receivables Corporation (TRC), a wholly-owned bankruptcy remote subsidiary. TRC then transfers the receivables to the Target Credit Card Master Trust (the Trust), which from time to time will sell debt securities to third parties, either directly or through a related trust. These debt securities represent undivided interests in the Trust assets. TRC has also retained an undivided interest in the Trust's assets that are not represented by the debt securities sold to third parties and a 2 percent undivided interest in the Trust assets that is held by Target National Bank, a wholly-owned subsidiary of Target which also services receivables. TRC uses the proceeds from the sale of debt securities and its share of collections on the receivables to pay the purchase price of the receivables to Target.

The accounting guidance for such transactions, SFAS No.140, "Accounting for Transfers and Servicing of Financial Assets and Extinguishments of Liabilities (a replacement of SFAS No.125)," requires the inclusion of the receivables within the Trust and any debt securities issued by the Trust, or a related trust, in our Consolidated Statements of Financial Position. Notwithstanding this accounting treatment, the receivables transferred to the Trust are not available to general creditors of Target. Upon termination of the securitization program and repayment of all debt securities issued from time to time by the Trust, or a related trust, any remaining assets could be distributed to Target in a liquidation of TRC.

11. Inventory

Substantially all of our inventory and the related cost of sales are accounted for under the retail inventory accounting method using the last-in, first-out (LIFO) method. Inventory is stated at the lower of LIFO cost or market. The LIFO provision is calculated based on inventory levels, markup rates and internally-measured retail price indices. We have not recorded any material LIFO provision in 2005 or 2004.

We routinely enter into arrangements with certain vendors whereby we do not purchase or pay for merchandise until that merchandise is ultimately sold to a guest. Revenues under this program are included in the sales line in the Consolidated Statements of Operations, but the merchandise received under the program is not included in our Consolidated Statements of Financial Position because of the simultaneous timing of our purchase and sale of this inventory. Sales made under these arrangements totaled $872 million, $357 million and $142 million for 2005, 2004 and 2003, respectively.

In 2005, we adopted SFAS No.151, "Inventory Costs, an amendment of ARB No. 43, Chapter 4," which clarifies that abnormal amounts of idle facilities expense, freight, handling costs and spoilage are to be recognized as current period charges and provides guidance on the allocation of overhead. This adoption did not have a material impact on our net earnings, cash flows or financial position.

12. Other Current Assets

(millions)	January 28, 2006	January 29, 2005
Vendor income and other receivables	$ **560**	$ 428
Deferred taxes	**344**	344
Other	**349**	452
Total	$ **1,253**	$ 1,224

In addition to vendor income, other receivables relate primarily to pharmacy receivables and merchandise sourcing services provided to third parties.

13. Property and Equipment

Property and equipment are recorded at cost, less accumulated depreciation. Depreciation is computed using the straight-line method over estimated useful lives. Depreciation expense for the years 2005, 2004 and 2003 was $1,384 million, $1,232 million and $1,068 million, respectively. Accelerated depreciation methods are generally used for income tax purposes. Repair and maintenance costs were $474 million, $453 million and $393 million in 2005, 2004 and 2003, respectively, and are expensed as incurred.

Estimated useful lives by major asset category are as follows:

Asset	Life (in years)
Buildings and improvements	8–39
Fixtures and equipment	4–15
Computer hardware and software	4

In accordance with SFAS No.144, "Accounting for the Impairment or Disposal of Long-Lived Assets," all long-lived assets are reviewed when events or changes in circumstances indicate that the asset's carrying value may not be recoverable. No material impairments were recorded in 2005, 2004 or 2003 as a result of the tests performed.

In March 2005, the FASB issued FASB Interpretation No. 47, "Accounting for Conditional Asset Retirement Obligations, an interpretation of FASB Statement No.143" (FIN 47). The primary purpose of FIN 47 is to clarify that an entity is required to recognize a liability for the fair value of a conditional asset retirement obligation when incurred if the liability's fair value can be reasonably estimated. FIN 47 is effective no later than the end of fiscal years ending after December 15, 2005. The adoption of this guidance did not have a material impact on our net earnings, cash flows or financial position.

14. Other Non-Current Assets

(millions)	January 28, 2006	January 29, 2005
Prepaid pension expense	$ **752**	$ 733
Cash value of life insurance	**524**	446
Goodwill and intangible assets	**183**	206
Other	**93**	126
Total	$ **1,552**	$ 1,511

15. Goodwill and Intangible Assets

Goodwill and intangible assets are recorded within other non-current assets at cost less accumulated amortization. Goodwill and intangible assets by major classes were as follows:

	Goodwill		Leasehold Acquisition Costs		Other		Total	
(millions)	Jan. 28, 2006	Jan. 29, 2005	Jan. 28, 2006	Jan. 29, 2005	Jan. 28, 2006	Jan. 29, 2005	Jan. 28, 2006	Jan. 29, 2005
Gross asset	$ **80**	$ 80	$ **182**	$ 185	$ **205**	$ 201	$ **467**	$ 466
Accumulated amortization	**(20)**	(20)	**(70)**	(52)	**(194)**	(188)	**(284)**	(260)
Net goodwill and intangible assets	$ **60**	$ 60	$ **112**	$ 133	$ **11**	$ 13	$ **183**	$ 206

Amortization is computed on intangible assets with definite useful lives using the straight-line method over estimated useful lives that range from three to 29 years. Amortization expense for the years 2005, 2004 and 2003 was $25 million, $27 million and $30 million, respectively. The estimated aggregate amortization expense of our definite-lived intangible assets for each of the five succeeding fiscal years is as follows:

(millions)	2006	2007	2008	2009	2010
Amortization expense	$ 23	$ 20	$ 19	$ 19	$ 17

We have goodwill and certain intangible assets that are not amortized but instead are subject to an annual impairment test. Discounted cash flow models are used in determining fair value for the purposes of the required annual impairment analysis. No material impairments were recorded in 2005, 2004 and 2003 as a result of the tests performed.

During 2004, goodwill with an approximate carrying value of $63 million was disposed of as part of the Marshall Field's transaction.

16. Accounts Payable

Our accounting policy is to reduce accounts payable when checks to vendors clear the bank from which they were drawn. Outstanding checks included in accounts payable were $645 million and $992 million at year-end 2005 and 2004, respectively.

17. Accrued Liabilities

(millions)	January 28, 2006	January 29, 2005
Wages and benefits	$ **506**	$ 422
Taxes payable	**366**	287
Gift card liability	**294**	214
Other	**1,027**	710
Total	$ **2,193**	$ 1,633

Taxes payable consist of real estate, employee withholdings and sales tax liabilities. Gift card liability represents the amount of gift cards that have been issued but have not been redeemed, net of estimated breakage.

18. Commitments and Contingencies

At January 28, 2006, our obligations included notes and debentures of $9,771 million (further discussed in Note 19, page 32), the present value of capital lease obligations of $101 million and total future payments of operating leases with total contractual lease payments of $3,097 million, including certain options for lease term extension that are expected to be exercised in the amount of $1,421 million and $122 million of legally binding minimum lease payments for stores that will open in 2006 (see additional detail in Note 22, pages 33-34). In addition, real estate obligations, including commitments for the purchase, construction, or remodeling of real estate and facilities, were approximately $838 million at January 28, 2006. Purchase obligations, which include all legally binding contracts such as firm commitments for inventory purchases, merchandise royalties, purchases of equipment, marketing-related contracts, software acquisition / license commitments and service contracts and were $1,431 million at January 28, 2006. In the normal course of business we issue purchase orders to purchase inventory, which represent authorizations to purchase and are cancelable by their terms. We do not consider purchase orders to be firm inventory commitments. We also issue letters of credit in the ordinary course of business which are not firm commitments as they are conditional on the purchase order not being cancelled. If under certain circumstances, and at our sole discretion, we choose to cancel a purchase order, we may be obligated to reimburse the vendor for unrecoverable outlays incurred prior to cancellation. Standby letters of credit, which relate primarily to the portion of our insurance claims for which we have retained the risk, totaled $104 million at January 28, 2006.

The terms of a significant portion of the Visa/MasterCard antitrust litigation settlement were finalized during 2005. Consequently, we recorded a $27 million ($.02 per share) gain for our share of the proceeds, which we expect to collect during fiscal 2006. We also expect to receive an additional, smaller payment; however, the amount and timing of that payment are not certain at this time. Accordingly, no additional gain was recorded at January 28, 2006.

We are exposed to claims and litigation arising in the ordinary course of business and use various methods to resolve these matters in a manner that we believe serves the best interest of our shareholders and other constituents. We believe the amounts provided in our consolidated financial statements are adequate in light of the probable and estimable liabilities. Our policy is to disclose pending lawsuits and other known claims that may have a material adverse impact on our results of operations, cash flows or financial condition. We do not believe any of the currently identified claims and litigated matters meet this criterion.

19. Notes Payable and Long-Term Debt

We obtain short-term financing throughout the year under our commercial paper program, which is a form of notes payable. Information on this program is as follows:

Notes Payable

(dollars in millions)	2005	2004
Notes payable outstanding at year-end	$ —	$ —
Maximum amount outstanding during the year	$ 994	$ 1,422
Average amount outstanding during the year	$ 77	$ 55
Weighted-average interest rate	4.0%	1.3%

At January 28, 2006, a committed unsecured credit facility totaling $1.6 billion was in place through a group of banks at specified rates. This 2005 facility replaced our two previous committed credit agreements and is scheduled to expire in June 2010. No balances were outstanding at any time during 2005 or 2004 under any of these agreements.

On November 9, 2005, TRC issued to the public, through the Target Credit Card Owner Trust 2005-1, $900 million of debt backed by credit card receivables. This issue of receivable-backed securities has an expected maturity of five years and a floating interest rate set at 1-month LIBOR plus 0.06 percent. Refer to Note 10, page 30, for further discussion of our accounts receivable financing program. The total amount of long-term debt backed by credit card receivables was $1,650 million at January 28, 2006 and $750 million at January 29, 2005. We did not repurchase any significant amount of long-term debt during 2005.

In 2004, we issued no long-term debt and we called or repurchased $542 million of long-term debt with an average remaining life of 24 years and weighted average interest rate of 7.0 percent, resulting in a pre-tax loss of $89 million (approximately $.06 per share), reflected in net interest expense.

Our debt portfolio, including swap valuation adjustments, was as follows:

Long-Term Debt

	January 28, 2006		January 29, 2005	
(dollars in millions)	Rate (a)	Balance	Rate (a)	Balance
Notes and debentures:				
Due 2005–2009	5.6%	$ 4,249	4.1%	$ 4,818
Due 2010–2014	5.8	3,840	6.2	2,954
Due 2015–2019	5.5	240	3.3	234
Due 2020–2024	9.3	213	9.3	212
Due 2025–2029	6.7	325	6.7	325
Due 2030–2032	6.6	904	6.6	904
Total notes and debentures (b)	5.9%	9,771	5.2%	9,447
Capital lease obligations		101		91
Less: current portion		(753)		(504)
Long-term debt		$ 9,119		$ 9,034

(a) Reflects the weighted average stated interest rate as of year-end, including the impact of interest rate swaps.

(b) The estimated fair value of total notes and debentures, using a discounted cash flow analysis based on our incremental interest rates for similar types of financial instruments, was $10,229 million at January 28, 2006 and $10,171 million at January 29, 2005.

Required principal payments on total notes and debentures over the next five years, excluding capital lease obligations and fair market value adjustments recorded in long-term debt, are:

(millions)	2006	2007	2008	2009	2010
Required principal payments	$ 751	$ 1,321	$ 1,451	$ 751	$ 2,236

Most of our long-term debt obligations contain certain covenants related to secured debt levels. In addition, our credit facility contains a debt leverage covenant. We are, and expect to remain, in compliance with these covenants.

20. Net Interest Expense

(millions)	2005	2004	2003
Interest expense on debt	$ 524	$ 509	$ 543
Interest expense on capital leases	8	9	9
Loss on debt repurchase	—	89	15
Capitalized interest	(42)	(18)	(8)
Interest income	(27)	(19)	(3)
Net interest expense	$ 463	$ 570	$ 556

21. Interest Rate Swaps

Our accounting policy for derivative financial instruments is discussed in Note 1 on page 28.

At January 28, 2006 and January 29, 2005, interest rate swaps were outstanding in notional amounts totaling $3,300 million and $2,850 million, respectively. The increase in swap exposure was executed to convert more of our fixed-rate debt to floating-rate debt to minimize the effect on our earnings of changes in interest rates, given that the majority of interest rates on our credit card receivables re-price based on the changes in the prime rate.

During 2005, we entered into four interest rate swaps with notional amounts of $250 million, $350 million, $325 million and $225 million. We also terminated an interest rate swap with a notional amount of $200 million, resulting in a gain of $24 million that will be amortized into net interest expense over the remaining 13-year life of the hedged debt. During 2004, we entered into two interest rate swaps with notional amounts of $200 million and two interest rate swaps with notional amounts of $250 million. We also terminated an interest rate swap with a notional amount of $200 million, resulting in a loss of $16 million that will be amortized into net interest expense over the remaining 14-year life of the hedged debt. In 2005 and 2004, the gains and losses amortized into net interest expense for terminated swaps were not material to our results of operations.

Interest Rate Swaps
(dollars in millions)

	Notional Amount Outstanding at			Pay Floating Rate at (a)	
Maturity	**Jan. 28, 2006**	**Jan.29, 2005**	**Receive Fixed**	**Jan. 28, 2006**	**Jan.29, 2005**
Feb. 2005	$ —	$ 500	7.5%	—%	2.4%
May 2006	**550**	550	4.6	**4.8**	3.3
Mar. 2008	**250**	—	3.9	**4.4**	—
Mar. 2008	**250**	250	3.8	**4.4**	2.4
Oct. 2008	**500**	500	4.4	**4.8**	3.2
Oct. 2008	**250**	250	3.8	**4.4**	2.5
Nov. 2008	**200**	200	3.9	**4.4**	2.4
Jun. 2009	**400**	400	4.4	**4.8**	3.3
Jun. 2009	**350**	—	4.2	**4.5**	—
Aug 2010	**325**	—	4.8	**4.5**	—
Aug.2010	**225**	—	4.5	**4.5**	—
May 2018	—	200	5.8	—	3.3
	$ 3,300	$ 2,850			

(a) Reflects floating interest rate as of the respective year-end.

The weighted average life of the interest rate swaps was approximately 2.7 years at January 28, 2006.

The fair value of outstanding interest rate swaps and unamortized gains/(losses) from terminated interest rate swaps was $(21) million at January 28, 2006 and $45 million at January 29, 2005. There was no ineffectiveness recognized in 2005, 2004 or 2003 related to these instruments.

22. Leases

We lease certain retail locations, warehouses, distribution centers, office space, equipment and land. Assets held under capital leases are included in property and equipment and lease payments are charged to depreciation and net interest expense over the life of the lease. Operating lease rentals are expensed on a straight-line basis over the life of the lease. Rent expense is recognized beginning with the earlier of the date when we become legally obligated for the rent payments or the date when we take possession of the property. At the inception of a lease, we determine the lease term by assuming the exercise of those renewal options that are reasonably assured because of the significant economic penalty that exists for not exercising those options. The exercise of lease renewal options is at our sole discretion. The expected lease term is used to determine whether a lease is capital or operating and is used to calculate straight-line rent expense. Additionally, the useful life of buildings and leasehold improvements are limited by the expected lease term. Our amortization of leasehold improvements is consistent with the guidance issued by the EITF in 2005 in Issue No. 05-6, "Determining the Amortization Period for Leasehold Improvements Purchased after Lease Inception or Acquired in a Business Combination," which requires that leasehold improvements purchased after the beginning of the initial lease term be amortized over the shorter of the assets' useful lives or a term that includes the original lease term plus any renewals that are reasonably assured at the date the leasehold improvements are purchased. Therefore, our adoption of this guidance did not have an impact in our net earnings, cash flows or financial position.

Rent expense on buildings, which is included in selling, general and administrative expenses, includes percentage rents based on a percentage of retail sales over contractual levels. Total rent expense was $154 million in 2005, $240 million in 2004 and $150 million in 2003. Refer to Note 29, page 39 for discussion of the 2004 lease accounting adjustment. Certain leases require us to pay real estate taxes, insurance, maintenance and other operating expenses associated with the leased premises. These amounts are not included in rent expense but are classified in selling, general and administrative expenses consistent with similar costs for owned locations. Most long-term leases include options to renew, with terms varying from one to 50 years. Certain leases also include options to purchase the property.

Future minimum lease payments required under noncancelable lease agreements existing at January 28, 2006, were:

Future Minimum Lease Payments

(millions)	Operating Leases	Capital Leases
2006	$ 137	$ 12
2007	132	12
2008	123	13
2009	114	13
2010	107	13
After 2010	2,484	160
Total future minimum lease payments	$ 3,097*(a)*	223
Less: Interest *(b)*		(122)
Present value of minimum capital lease payments		$ 101*(c)*

(a) Total contractual lease payments include certain options to extend lease terms, in the amount of $1,421 million, that are expected to be exercised because the investment in leasehold improvements is significant and also includes $122 million of legally binding minimum lease payments for stores that will open in 2006.

(b) Calculated using the interest rate at inception for each lease.

(c) Includes current portion of $2 million.

23. Income Taxes

We account for income taxes under the asset and liability method. We have recognized deferred tax assets and liabilities for the estimated future tax consequences attributable to differences between the financial statement carrying amounts of existing assets and liabilities and their respective tax bases. Deferred tax assets and liabilities are measured using enacted income tax rates in effect for the year in which those temporary differences are expected to be recovered or settled. The effect on deferred tax assets and liabilities of a change in tax rate is recognized into income in the period that includes the enactment date. In the Consolidated Statements of Financial Position, the current deferred tax asset balance is the net of all current deferred tax assets and current deferred tax liabilities. The non-current deferred tax liability is the net of all non-current deferred tax assets and non-current deferred tax liabilities.

To determine our quarterly provision for income taxes, we use annual effective tax rates based on expected annual income and statutory tax rates, adjusted for discrete tax events that occur during the quarter.

Reconciliation of tax rates is as follows:

Tax Rate Reconciliation

	2005	2004	2003
Federal statutory rate	**35.0%**	35.0%	35.0%
State income taxes, net of federal tax benefit	**3.3**	3.3	3.3
Dividends on ESOP stock	**(0.2)**	(0.2)	(0.2)
Work opportunity tax credits	**(0.2)**	(0.2)	(0.2)
Other	**(0.3)**	(0.1)	(0.1)
Effective tax rate	**37.6%**	37.8%	37.8%

The components of the provision for income taxes were:

Income Tax Provision: Expense

(millions)	2005	2004	2003
Current			
Federal	$ **1,361**	$ 908	$ 669
State/other	**213**	144	107
	1,574	1,052	776
Deferred			
Federal	**(110)**	83	184
State/other	**(12)**	11	24
	(122)	94	208
Total	$ **1,452**	$ 1,146	$ 984

The components of the net deferred tax asset / (liability) were:

Net Deferred Tax Asset/(Liability)

(millions)	January 28, 2006	January 29, 2005
Gross deferred tax assets		
Deferred and other compensation	$ **399**	$ 332
Self-insured benefits	**217**	179
Accounts receivable valuation allowance	**167**	147
Inventory	**1**	47
Postretirement health care obligation	**39**	38
Other	**151**	128
	974	871
Gross deferred tax liabilities		
Property and equipment	**(1,080)**	(1,136)
Pension	**(287)**	(268)
Deferred credit card income	**(103)**	(87)
Other	**(11)**	(9)
	(1,481)	(1,500)
Total	$ **(507)**	$ (629)

During the year ended January 29, 2005, $566 million of the proceeds attributable to the real properties sold in the Marshall Field's and Mervyn's dispositions were used to acquire replacement properties which will be used in our business. $373 million of the gain related to the sold real properties was deferred for income tax purposes as allowed by Section 1031 of the Internal Revenue Code until such time as the replacement properties are disposed.

24. Other Non-Current Liabilities

(millions)	January 28, 2006	January 29, 2005
Deferred compensation	$ **596**	$ 528
Worker's compensation and general liability	**362**	317
Other	**274**	192
Total	$ **1,232**	$ 1,037

25. Share Repurchase

In June 2004, our Board of Directors authorized the repurchase of $3 billion of our common stock. In November 2005, our Board increased the aggregate authorization by $2 billion, for a total authorization of $5 billion. In 2005, we repurchased 23.1 million shares at an average price per share of $51.88, for a total investment of $1,197 million. Since June 2004, we have repurchased a total of 51.6 million shares at an average price per share of $47.95, for a total investment of $2,473 million. We expect to complete the aggregate program in the next two to three years.

26. Share-Based Compensation

Our accounting policy for share-based compensation is discussed in Note 1 on page 28.

We maintain a long-term incentive plan for key employees and non-employee members of our Board of Directors. Our long-term incentive plan allows us to grant equity-based compensation awards, including stock options, performance share awards, restricted stock awards, or a combination of awards. A majority of granted awards are non-qualified stock options that vest annually in equal amounts over a four-year period. These options generally expire no later than 10 years after the date of the grant. Options granted to the non-employee members of our Board of Directors become exercisable after one year and have a 10-year term. We have issued performance share or performance share unit awards annually since January 2003. These awards represent shares potentially issuable in the future based upon the attainment of performance criteria including compound annual growth rates in revenue and EPS. The number of unissued common shares reserved for future grants under the share-based compensation plans was 47,659,572 at January 28, 2006 and 51,560,249 at January 29, 2005.

Share-Based Compensation Awards

	Stock Options						
	Total Outstanding			Currently Exercisable			Performance Shares Potentially Issuable
(options and shares in thousands)	Number of Options	Exercise Price(a)	Intrinsic Value(b)	Number of Options	Exercise Price(a)	Intrinsic Value (b)	
February 1, 2003	34,787	$ 25.73	$ 204	21,931	$ 20.89	$ 204	552*(c)*
Granted	4,638	38.34					573*(d)*
Canceled/forfeited	(407)	34.77					—
Exercised	(2,859)	12.58					—
January 31, 2004	36,159	$ 28.28	$ 363	23,689	$ 24.48	$ 326	1,125
Granted	4,072	49.12					629*(e)*
Canceled/forfeited	(513)	35.32					(73)
Exercised/earned	(7,727)	20.95					(73)
January 29, 2005	31,991	$ 32.59	$ 540	22,102	$ 28.79	$ 458	1,608
Granted	4,057	53.94					597*(f)*
Canceled/forfeited	(691)	40.67					(252)
Exercised	(6,643)	26.58					—
January 28, 2006	**28,714**	**$ 36.82**	**$ 505**	**19,229**	**$ 31.64**	**$ 438**	**1,953*(g)***

(a) Weighted average.

(b) Represents stock price appreciation subsequent to the grant date, in millions.

(c) Awards are earned based on performance during four years ending February 3, 2007.

(d) Awards are earned based on performance during four years ending February 2, 2008.

(e) Awards are earned based on performance during three years ending February 2, 2008.

(f) Awards are earned based on performance during three years ending January 31, 2009.

(g) Approximately 34 percent of these potentially issuable performance shares, if and when earned, will be paid in cash or deferred through a credit to the deferred compensation accounts of the participants in an amount equal to the value of any earned performance shares.

Nonvested Options and Performance Share Awards

(options and shares in thousands)	Stock Options	Weighted Average Fair Value at Grant Date	Performance Shares Potentially Issuable	Weighted Average Fair Value at Grant Date
Nonvested at January 30, 2005	9,889	$ 11.83	1,608	$ 38.84
Granted	4,057	16.85	597	53.96
Vested/earned *(a)*	(3,774)	11.75	—	—
Cancelled/forfeited	(687)	11.78	(252)	39.28
Nonvested at January 28, 2006	**9,485**	**$ 14.01**	**1,953**	**$ 44.55**

(a) Based on the explicit vesting period.

The Black-Scholes model was used to estimate the fair value of the options at grant date based on the assumptions noted in the following table. Volatility represents an average of market quotes for implied volatility of 5.5-year options on Target stock. The expected life is estimated based on analysis of options already exercised and any foreseeable trends or changes in behavior. The risk-free interest rate is an interpolation of the relevant U.S. Treasury security maturities as of each applicable grant date. The assumptions disclosed below represent a weighted average of the assumptions used for all of our stock option grants throughout the year.

Valuation of Share-Based Compensation

	2005	2004	2003
Stock option valuation assumptions:			
Dividend yield	**0.7%**	0.7%	0.8%
Volatility	**27%**	22%	29%
Risk-free interest rate	**4.4%**	3.8%	3.0%
Expected life in years	**5.5**	5.5	5.0
Grant date weighted-average fair value	$ **16.85**	$ 13.10	$ 11.04
Performance share grant date weighted-average fair value	$ **53.96**	$ 49.43	$ 38.25
Compensation expense recognized in Statements of Operations *(millions) (a)*	$ **93**	$ 60	$ 57
Related income tax benefit (millions)	$ **37**	$ 23	$ 22
Compensation realized by employees upon option exercises (millions)	$ **180**	$ 201	$ 72
Related income tax benefit (millions)	$ **71**	$ 77	$ 28

(a) Represents the total fair value of options vested and performance shares earned.

As of January 28, 2006, there was $102 million of total unrecognized compensation expense related to nonvested stock options. That cost is expected to be recognized over a weighted average period of 1.4 years. The weighted average remaining life of currently exercisable options is 4.6 years, while total outstanding options have a weighted average remaining life of six years. Future compensation expense related to performance shares depends on future performance and could range from a credit of $39 million for previously recognized amounts up to a maximum of $50 million of expense assuming full payout under all outstanding awards.

27. Defined Contribution Plans

Employees who meet certain eligibility requirements can participate in a defined contribution 401(k) plan by investing up to 80 percent of their compensation, as limited by statute or regulation. Generally, we match 100 percent of each employee's contribution up to 5 percent of total compensation. Our contribution to the plan is initially invested in Target Corporation common stock. These amounts are free to be diversified by the employee three years after initial eligibility in the plan.

In addition, we maintain non-qualified, unfunded deferred compensation plans for highly-compensated employees whose participation in our 401(k) plan is limited by statute or regulation. These employees choose from a menu of crediting rate alternatives which are the same as the investment choices in our 401(k) plan. We credit an additional 2 percent per year to the accounts of active employees, in part to recognize the risks inherent to their participation in a plan of this nature. We also maintain a frozen non-qualified, unfunded plan for certain officers in which deferred compensation earns returns tied to market levels of interest rates plus an additional 6 percent return as determined by the plan's terms. We control some of our risk of offering the non-qualified plans through investing in vehicles that offset a substantial portion of our economic exposure to the returns of those plans. These investment vehicles are marked to market with the related gains and losses recognized in the Consolidated Statements of Operations in the period they occur. At times, adjusting our position in these investment vehicles includes repurchasing shares of Target common stock. In 2005, 2004 and 2003, these repurchases totaled 1.5 million, 0.8 million and 1.5 million shares, respectively.

(millions)	2005	2004	2003
401(k) Defined Contribution Plan			
401(k) matching contributions	$ **118**	$ 118	$ 117
Non-Qualified Deferred Compensation Plans			
Benefits expense	$ **64**	$ 63	$ 86
Related investments	**(34)**	(40)	(58)
Net expense	$ **30**	$ 23	$ 28

In 2005, 2004 and 2003, certain retired executives accepted our offer to exchange our obligation to them under certain frozen non-qualified plans for cash or deferrals in our current non-qualified deferred compensation plan. These exchange transactions resulted in expense of $7 million, $17 million, and $17 million, respectively. We expect lower future expenses as a result of these transactions.

Expenses for Marshall Field's and Mervyn's employees are included in the table above to the extent we retained the related assets and obligations of their plans subsequent to the 2004 divestiture of those businesses.

28. Pension and Postretirement Health Care Benefits

We have a qualified defined benefit pension plan covering all U.S. employees who meet age and service requirements. We also have unfunded non-qualified pension plans for employees with qualified plan compensation restrictions. Benefits are provided based on years of service and the employee's compensation. During fiscal 2004, we merged our three qualified U.S. pension plans into one plan. This merger did not have a material impact on the financial results of the plan. Upon retirement employees also become eligible for certain health care benefits if they meet minimum age and service requirements and agree to contribute a portion of the cost.

We recorded a reduction in our accumulated post-retirement benefit obligation of $7 million in 2004 as a result of the Medicare Prescription Drug, Improvements and Modernization Act of 2003. In addition, the expense amounts shown in the table below for 2004 reflect a $1 million reduction due to the amortization of the actuarial gain and reduction in interest cost due to the effects of the Act.

In 2005, certain non-qualified pension and survivor benefits owed to current officers were exchanged for cash or deferrals in our current non-qualified deferred compensation plan, which resulted in expense of $11 million. The effect of these exchange transactions is included in the pension tables below. There were no such exchange transactions during 2004 or 2003.

Obligations and Funded Status

(millions)	Pension Benefits				Postretirement Health Care Benefits	
	Qualified Plans		Non-qualified Plans			
	2005	2004	2005	2004	2005	2004
Change in Projected Benefit Obligation						
Benefit obligation at beginning of measurement period *(a)*	$ **1,515**	$ 1,333	$ **34**	$ 29	$ **107**	$ 123
Service cost	**66**	78	**1**	1	**2**	3
Interest cost	**85**	82	**2**	2	**6**	7
Actuarial loss	**55**	68	**4**	4	**3**	(6)
Benefits paid	**(94)**	(65)	**(5)**	(3)	**(13)**	(13)
Plan amendments	**(1)**	19	**(3)**	1	**—**	(7)
Benefit obligation at end of measurement period	$ **1,626**	$ 1,515	$ **33**	$ 34	$ **105**	$ 107
Change in Plan Assets						
Fair value of plan assets at beginning of measurement period	$ **1,698**	$ 1,405	$ **—**	$ —	$ **—**	$ —
Actual return on plan assets	**174**	157	**—**	—	**—**	—
Employer contribution	**67**	201	**5**	3	**13**	13
Benefits paid	**(94)**	(65)	**(5)**	(3)	**(13)**	(13)
Fair value of plan assets at end of measurement period	$ **1,845**	$ 1,698	$ **—**	$ —	$ **—**	$ —
Funded status	$ **219**	$ 183	$ **(33)**	$ (34)	$ **(105)**	$ (107)
Unrecognized actuarial loss	**561**	584	**16**	15	**8**	6
Unrecognized prior service cost	**(32)**	(39)	**—**	2	**—**	—
Net amount recognized	$ **748**	$ 728	$ **(17)**	$ (17)	$ **(97)**	$ (101)

(a) Measurement date is October 31 of each year.

Amounts recognized in the Consolidated Statements of Financial Position consist of:

(millions)	Pension Benefits				Postretirement Health Care Benefits	
	Qualified Plans		Non-qualified Plans			
	2005	2004	2005	2004	2005	2004
Prepaid benefit cost	$ **752**	$ 733	$ **—**	$ —	$ **—**	$ —
Accrued benefit cost	**(9)**	(11)	**(22)**	(24)	**(97)**	(101)
Intangible assets	**—**	—	**—**	2	**—**	—
Accumulated OCI	**5**	6	**5**	5	**—**	—
Net amount recognized	$ **748**	$ 728	$ **(17)**	$ (17)	$ **(97)**	$ (101)

Net Pension and Postretirement Health Care Benefits Expense

(millions)	Pension Benefits			Postretirement Health Care Benefits		
	2005	2004	2003	2005	2004	2003
Service cost benefits earned during the period	$ **67**	$ 79	$ 74	$ **2**	$ 3	$ 2
Interest cost on projected benefit obligation	**87**	84	75	**6**	7	8
Expected return on assets	**(137)**	(122)	(114)	**—**	—	—
Recognized losses	**43**	36	18	**1**	1	1
Recognized prior service cost	**(5)**	(7)	(7)	**—**	—	—
Settlement/curtailment charges	**—**	1	—	**—**	(7)	—
Total	$ **55**	$ 71	$ 46	$ **9**	$ 4	$ 11

The amortization of any prior service cost is determined using the straight-line method over the average remaining service period of employees expected to receive benefits under the plan. As a result of freezing the benefits for Marshall Field's and Mervyn's team members at the time of their respective dispositions and retaining the related assets and obligations of the plans, we were required to record curtailment charges in 2004. These charges are also included in the gain on disposal of discontinued operations in the Consolidated Statements of Operations.

Other information related to defined benefit pension plans is as follows:

(millions)	2005	2004
Accumulated benefit obligation (ABO) for all plans *(a)*	$ **1,534**	$ 1,501
Projected benefit obligation for pension plans with an ABO in excess of plan assets *(b)*	**46**	49
Total ABO for pension plans with an ABO in excess of plan assets	**41**	45
Fair value of plan assets for pension plans with an ABO in excess of plan assets	**3**	5

(a) The present value of benefits earned to date assuming no future salary growth.

(b) The present value of benefits earned to date by plan participants, including the effect of assumed future salary increases.

Assumptions

Weighted average assumptions used to determine benefit obligations at October 31:

	Pension Benefits		Postretirement Health Care Benefits	
	2005	2004	2005	2004
Discount rate	**5.75%**	5.75%	**5.75%**	5.75%
Average assumed rate of compensation increase	**3.50%**	2.75%	**n/a**	n/a

Weighted average assumptions used to determine net periodic benefit cost for years ended October 31:

	Pension Benefits		Postretirement Health Care Benefits	
	2005	2004	2005	2004
Discount rate	**5.75%**	6.25%	**5.75%**	6.25%
Expected long-term rate of return on plan assets	**8.00%**	8.00%	**n/a**	n/a
Average assumed rate of compensation increase	**2.75%**	3.25%	**n/a**	n/a

The discount rate used to measure net periodic benefit cost each year is the rate as of the beginning of the year (i.e. the prior measurement date). With an essentially stable asset allocation over the following time periods, our annualized rate of return on qualified plans' assets has averaged 5.1 percent, 9.9 percent and 11.5 percent for the 5-year, 10-year and 15-year periods, respectively, ending October 31, 2005.

An increase in the cost of covered health care benefits of 10 percent was assumed for 2005. The rate is assumed to be 9 percent in 2006 and is reduced by 1 percent annually to 5 percent in 2010 and thereafter.

A 1 percent change in assumed health care cost trend rates would have the following effects:

	1% Increase	1% Decrease
Effect on total of service and interest cost components of net periodic postretirement health care benefit cost	$ —	$ —
Effect on the health care component of the postretirement benefit obligation	$ 5	$ (4)

Additional Information

Our pension plan weighted average asset allocations at October 31, 2005 and 2004 by asset category were as follows:

Asset Category

	2005	2004
Domestic equity securities	**36%**	37%
International equity securities	**20**	21
Debt securities	**26**	26
Other	**18**	16
Total	**100%**	100%

Our asset allocation strategy for 2006 targets 35 percent in domestic equity securities, 20 percent in international equity securities, 25 percent in debt securities and 20 percent in other assets. Equity securities include our common stock in amounts substantially less than 1 percent of total plan assets at October 31, 2005 and 2004. Other assets include private equity, mezzanine and distressed debt and timber and less than a 5 percent allocation to real estate. Our expected long-term rate of return assumptions as of October 31, 2005 were 8.5 percent, 8.5 percent, 5 percent and 10 percent for domestic equity securities, international equity securities, debt securities and other assets, respectively.

Contributions

Given the qualified pension plan's funded position, we are not required to make any contributions in 2006, although we may choose to make discretionary contributions of up to $80 million. We expect to make contributions in the range of $5 million to $15 million to our postretirement health care benefit plan in 2006.

Estimated Future Benefit Payments

Benefit payments by the plans, which reflect expected future service as appropriate, are expected to be paid as follows:

(millions)	Pension Benefits	Postretirement Health Care Benefits
2006	$ 64	$ 11
2007	72	12
2008	80	13
2009	86	13
2010	90	14
2011—2015	$ 540	$ 79

29. Quarterly Results (Unaudited)

Due to the seasonal nature of our business, fourth quarter operating results typically represent a substantially larger share of total year revenues and earnings because it includes the holiday shopping season. We follow the same accounting policies for preparing quarterly and annual financial data. The table below summarizes quarterly results for 2005 and 2004:

	First Quarter		Second Quarter		Third Quarter		Fourth Quarter		Total Year	
(millions, except per share data)	**2005**	**2004**	**2005**	**2004**	**2005**	**2004**	**2005**	**2004**	**2005**	**2004**
Total revenues	**$11,477**	$10,180	**$11,990**	$10,556	**$12,206**	$10,909	**$16,947**	$15,194	**$52,620**	$46,839
Gross margin	**$ 3,615**	$ 3,140	**$ 3,839**	$ 3,268	**$ 3,829**	$ 3,300	**$ 5,061**	$ 4,529	**$16,344**	$14,237
Earnings from continuing operations	**$ 494**	$ 392	**$ 540**	$ 360	**$ 435**	$ 324	**$ 939**	$ 809	**$ 2,408**	$ 1,885
Earnings from discontinued operations, net of taxes of $25, $19, $2 and $46	**$ —**	$ 40	**$ —**	$ 31	**$ —**	$ 4	**$ —**	$ —	**$ —**	$ 75
Gain/(loss) on disposal of discontinued operations, net of taxes of $650, $132, $(21) and $761 *(a)*	**$ —**	$ —	**$ —**	$ 1,019	**$ —**	$ 203	**$ —**	$ 16	**$ —**	$ 1,238
Net earnings *(b)*	**$ 494**	$ 432	**$ 540**	$ 1,410	**$ 435**	$ 531	**$ 939**	$ 825	**$ 2,408**	$ 3,198
Basic earnings per share *(c)*										
Continuing operations	**$ .56**	$ .43	**$ .61**	$ .40	**$ .49**	$ .36	**$ 1.07**	$ .91	**$ 2.73**	$ 2.09
Discontinued operations	**$ —**	$ .04	**$ —**	$ .03	**$ —**	$ —	**$ —**	$ —	**$ —**	$ .08
Gain from discontinued operations	**$ —**	$ —	**$ —**	$ 1.12	**$ —**	$ .23	**$ —**	$ .01	**$ —**	$ 1.37
Basic earnings per share *(b)*	**$ .56**	$ .47	**$ .61**	$ 1.55	**$ .49**	$ .59	**$ 1.07**	$ .92	**$ 2.73**	$ 3.54
Diluted earnings per share *(c)*										
Continuing operations	**$ .55**	$ .43	**$ .61**	$ .39	**$ .49**	$ .36	**$ 1.06**	$ .90	**$ 2.71**	$ 2.07
Discontinued operations	**$ —**	$ .04	**$ —**	$ .03	**$ —**	$ —	**$ —**	$ —	**$ —**	$ .08
Gain from discontinued operations	**$ —**	$ —	**$ —**	$ 1.11	**$ —**	$ .23	**$ —**	$ .01	**$ —**	$ 1.36
Diluted earnings per share *(b)*	**$ .55**	$ .47	**$ .61**	$ 1.53	**$ .49**	$ .59	**$ 1.06**	$ .91	**$ 2.71**	$ 3.51
Dividends declared per share *(c)*	**$ .08**	$ .07	**$ .10**	$ .08	**$ .10**	$ .08	**$ .10**	$ .08	**$ .38**	$ .31
Closing common stock price										
High	**$ 52.50**	$ 45.63	**$ 59.98**	$ 46.43	**$ 57.80**	$ 50.02	**$ 58.85**	$ 52.43	**$ 59.98**	$ 52.43
Low	**$ 46.41**	$ 38.59	**$ 46.28**	$ 40.80	**$ 50.84**	$ 40.42	**$ 52.61**	$ 48.50	**$ 46.28**	$ 38.59

(a)Minor tax adjustments related to the dispositions of Marshall Field's and Mervyn's were recorded in fourth quarter 2004.

(b)Target adjusted its method of accounting for leases related to a specific category of owned store locations on leased land, which resulted in a non-cash adjustment, primarily attributable to an increase in the straight-line rent accrual, of $65million ($.04 per share) in the fourth quarter of 2004.

(c)Per share amounts are computed independently for each of the quarters presented. The sum of the quarters may not equal the total year amount due to the impact of changes in average quarterly shares outstanding.

Report of Independent Registered Public Accounting Firm on Consolidated Financial Statements
The Board of Directors and Shareholders Target Corporation

We have audited the accompanying consolidated statements of financial position of Target Corporation and subsidiaries as of January 28, 2006 and January 29, 2005, and the related consolidated statements of operations, cash flows, and shareholders' investment for each of the three years in the period ended January 28, 2006. These financial statements are the responsibility of the Corporation's management. Our responsibility is to express an opinion on these financial statements based on our audits.

We conducted our audits in accordance with the standards of the Public Company Accounting Oversight Board (United States). Those standards require that we plan and perform the audit to obtain reasonable assurance about whether the financial statements are free of material misstatement. An audit includes examining, on a test basis, evidence supporting the amounts and disclosures in the financial statements. An audit also includes assessing the accounting principles used and significant estimates made by management, as well as evaluating the overall financial statement presentation. We believe that our audits provide a reasonable basis for our opinion.

In our opinion, the financial statements referred to above present fairly, in all material respects, the consolidated financial position of Target Corporation and subsidiaries at January 28, 2006 and January 29, 2005, and the consolidated results of their operations and their cash flows for each of the three years in the period ended January 28, 2006, in conformity with U.S. generally accepted accounting principles.

We also have audited, in accordance with the standards of the Public Company Accounting Oversight Board (United States), the effectiveness of the Corporation's internal control over financial reporting as of January 28, 2006, based on criteria established in *Internal Control – Integrated Framework*, issued by the Committee of Sponsoring Organizations of the Treadway Commission and our report dated March 29, 2006, expressed an unqualified opinion thereon.

Minneapolis, Minnesota
March 29, 2006

Ernst + Young LLP

Report of Management on Internal Control

Our management is responsible for establishing and maintaining adequate internal control over financial reporting, as such term is defined in Exchange Act Rules 13a-15(f). Under the supervision and with the participation of our management, including our chief executive officer and chief financial officer, we assessed the effectiveness of our internal control over financial reporting as of January 28, 2006, based on the framework in Internal Control – Integrated Framework, issued by the Committee of Sponsoring Organizations of the Treadway Commission. Based on our assessment, we conclude that the Corporation's internal control over financial reporting is effective based on those criteria.

Our management's assessment of the effectiveness of our internal control over financial reporting as of January 28, 2006, has been audited by Ernst & Young LLP, independent registered public accounting firm, whose report also appears on this page.

Robert J. Ulrich
Chairman of the Board and
Chief Executive Officer
March 29, 2006

Douglas A. Scovanner
Executive Vice President and
Chief Financial Officer

Report of Independent Registered Public Accounting Firm on Internal Control over Financial Reporting
The Board of Directors and Shareholders Target Corporation

We have audited management's assessment, included in the accompanying Report of Management on Internal Control, that Target Corporation and subsidiaries maintained effective internal control over financial reporting as of January 28, 2006, based on criteria established in *Internal Control – Integrated Framework*, issued by the Committee of Sponsoring Organizations of the Treadway Commission (the COSO criteria). The Corporation's management is responsible for maintaining effective internal control over financial reporting and for its assessment of the effectiveness of internal control over financial reporting. Our responsibility is to express an opinion on management's assessment and an opinion on the effectiveness of the Corporation's internal control over financial reporting based on our audit.

We conducted our audit in accordance with the standards of the Public Company Accounting Oversight Board (United States). Those standards require that we plan and perform the audit to obtain reasonable assurance about whether effective internal control over financial reporting was maintained in all material respects. Our audit included obtaining an understanding of internal control over financial reporting, evaluating management's assessment, testing and evaluating the design and operating effectiveness of internal control, and performing such other procedures as we considered necessary in the circumstances. We believe that our audit provides a reasonable basis for our opinion.

A company's internal control over financial reporting is a process designed to provide reasonable assurance regarding the reliability of financial reporting and the preparation of financial statements for external purposes in accordance with generally accepted accounting principles. A company's internal control over financial reporting includes those policies and procedures that (1) pertain to the maintenance of records that, in reasonable detail, accurately and fairly reflect the transactions and dispositions of the assets of the company, (2) provide reasonable assurance that transactions are recorded as necessary to permit preparation of financial statements in accordance with generally accepted accounting principles and that receipts and expenditures of the company are being made only in accordance with authorizations of management and directors of the company, and (3) provide reasonable assurance regarding prevention or timely detection of unauthorized acquisition, use, or disposition of the company's assets that could have a material effect on the financial statements.

Because of its inherent limitations, internal control over financial reporting may not prevent or detect misstatements. Also, projections of any evaluation of effectiveness to future periods are subject to the risk that controls may become nadequate because of changes in conditions or that the degree of compliance with the policies or procedures may deteriorate.

In our opinion, management's assessment that Target Corporation and subsidiaries maintained effective internal control over financial reporting as of January 28, 2006, is fairly stated, in all material respects, based on the COSO criteria. Also, in our opinion, the Corporation maintained, in all material respects, effective internal control over financial reporting as of January 28, 2006, based on the COSO criteria.

We also have audited, in accordance with the standards of the Public Company Accounting Oversight Board (United States), the consolidated statements of financial position of Target Corporation and subsidiaries as of January 28, 2006 and January 29, 2005, and the related consolidated statements of operations, cash flows and shareholders' investment for each of the three years in the period ended January 28, 2006, of Target Corporation and subsidiaries and our report dated March 29, 2006, expressed an unqualified opinion thereon.

Minneapolis, Minnesota
March 29, 2006

Ernst + Young LLP

GLOSSARY

A

accelerated depreciation A depreciation method that recognizes greater depreciation in an asset's earlier years and results in less income and less federal tax in those years.

account A category created in order to group similar transactions for the purpose of recording activity and providing information.

accounting The systematic process of measuring the economic activity of an entity to provide useful information to those who make business and economic decisions.

accounting changes Includes a change in accounting principle, a change in estimate, and a change in reporting entity.

accounting information system The processes and procedures required to generate accounting information.

Accounting Principles Board (APB) Predecessor to the FASB.

accounts payable Unwritten obligations usually arising from purchases of inventory, supplies, and services.

accounts receivable Credit sales that have not yet been collected. The relevant amount is the estimated cash to be generated from collections of the accounts. See *allowance for uncollectible accounts* and *net realizable value* for related terms.

accounts receivable as a percent of sales A liquidity ratio used to assess a company's collection procedures and working capital management. Calculated as gross accounts receivable divided by sales.

accrual basis of accounting Records revenues when goods or services have been earned, regardless of when cash is received. Records expenses when incurred, regardless of when cash is distributed.

accrued compensation and benefits Compensation and benefit expenses incurred, but not yet paid by the balance sheet date.

accrued costs of exit and disposal activities The costs of restructuring or terminating a business unit. Such costs are incurred and expensed in the current reporting period.

accrued expenses (liabilities) A current liability that represents services already consumed, but not yet paid.

accrued income taxes Income tax expenses incurred, but not yet paid by the balance sheet date.

accrued restructuring charges See *accrued costs of exit and disposal activities.*

accrued wages and salaries Wage and salary expenses that have been incurred but not yet paid.

accumulated benefit obligation The amount of pension benefits, calculated under actuarial and present value assumptions, already earned by employees (based on current salaries).

accumulated depreciation The total amount of depreciation that has been recognized to date on long-lived assets. It is shown as a "contra-asset" account balance subtracted from the asset's cost to determine its net book value.

acid-test ratio See *quick ratio.*

acquisition A business combination in which a buyer firm acquires more than 50% of the voting stock of an investee firm, and thereby controls the investee.

actuarial assumptions Assumed future events based on historic data such as employee turnover, service lives, and longevity that are used to estimate future costs such as pension benefits.

additional paid-in capital Capital funds invested by shareholders in excess of par value. See *paid-in capital.*

adequacy of the allowance for uncollectible accounts Ratio used to assess the uncollectible accounts receivables; calculated by dividing the allowance for uncollectible accounts by the gross accounts receivable.

adjusting entries Journal entries entered in the accounting records typically before financial statements are prepared. Adjusting entries are needed to ensure that the account balances are correct and accruals are up to date.

adjustment A change in the accounting equation to record accruals, deferrals, and other estimates so that the equation reflects changes in assets, liabilities, and equities. Could also refer to an *adjusting entry.*

administrative expenses Costs incurred to manage the organization. See *general and administrative expenses.*

advance customer payments Amounts paid by customers prior to receiving goods or services. See *unearned revenue.*

affiliated companies Refers to a parent company and related firms that it influences or controls.

aging method Refers to classifying accounts receivable by the number of days they are past due; for example, zero to 30 days, 31 to 60 days, 61 to 90 days, more than 90 days, and so on.

allowance for uncollectible accounts An estimate of accounts receivable amounts that may not be collected. Presented as a contra-asset account that is subtracted from accounts receivable.

American Institute of Certified Public Accountants (AICPA) An organization serving CPAs who are in private practice, or work for public accounting firms, or other organizations (e.g., corporations, government, or non-profits).

amortization The periodic recognition of the cost of using or consuming (expense) an intangible asset.

annual report The annual report includes financial statements, notes, management discussion, and the independent auditor's report.

annuity Equal cash flows over uniform time intervals.

anti-dilutive Common shares outstanding during a year that are omitted from the *Earnings Per Share (EPS)* calculation, because they potentially yield an upward bias in the results.

APB See *Accounting Principles Board.*

arms-length transaction Transactions that are conducted by independent parties, each acting in their own self-interest.

asset management ratios Show the percentage composition of the firm's assets, as well as changes in the composition over time.

assets Valuable resources owned or controlled by the firm. They represent probable future economic benefits and arise as a result of past transactions or events.

associating cause and effect Used to reflect a clear and direct relationship between an expense and its associated revenue. Reflects the matching principle where a clear and direct relationship or link exists between the use of an asset (expense) and its associated revenue. See *matching principle.*

audit An evaluation of the credibility of a firm's financial statements by independent CPAs. The audit opinion is the product of the audit and reflects the auditor's professional judgment regarding whether the financial statements are presented in accordance with GAAP and are free from material misstatement.

audit opinion An auditor's report expressing an opinion as to whether the financial statements were prepared according to GAAP and are free from material misstatement. See *audit.*

auditor's report Element of an annual report containing the independent accountant's report, usually presented as an unqualified opinion or some type of a qualified opinion regarding the financial statements contained in the annual report.

authorized shares Capital stock that the firm is permitted to issue according to its corporate (state) charter.

available-for-sale securities Investments held for the long-term where unrealized gains and losses are *not included* in net income.

average cost method A method for determining the cost per unit of inventories by summing the beginning inventory cost plus all purchases and dividing by the number of units available for sale.

average exchange rate Refers to converting one country's currency into a different monetary unit. The average exchange rate over a month or year can be used to make the foreign currency translation, as compared to using the *current exchange rate.*

B

balanced Used to indicate the status of an account balance at the end of an accounting period. Accounts are balanced by totaling the debits and credits in each account and seeing that they are equal.

balance sheet A financial statement that shows, at a specified time, a firm's financial condition, including its assets, liabilities, and owners' equity. Also referred to as *statement of financial position.*

bank reconciliation An accounting procedure that explains any differences between a firm's cash balance as determined by the firm and the firm's cash balance as determined by the bank.

basic accounting equation A simple three-element equation that corresponds to the balance sheet. The equation is Assets = Liabilities + Owners' Equity, where Owners' Equity is synonymous with Shareholders' Equity.

basic EPS Simple earnings per share calculated by dividing net income by the number of shares outstanding; does not include dilutive or convertible shares. See *earning per share (EPS).*

basis of comparison Assessing a firm's economic condition by establishing a reference or benchmark.

big bath Occurs when a firm reports large accounting losses or expenses in a single year that do not truly reflect the performance or profitability of the firm. Losses or expenses are lumped into a single year such that more favorable results will be shown in later years, perhaps to motivate larger bonuses for managers in subsequent years.

bond or bonds payable Liability in the form of a note, issued to lenders.

bond discount See *discount on bonds.*

bond premium See *premium on bonds.*

book value Asset cost less its accumulated depreciation. See *net book value.*

book value per share The ratio of a firm's total shareholders' equity to the number of outstanding common shares.

bottom line Revenues and gains minus expenses and losses on the income statement. See *net income.*

budgets Used to communicate quantitative expressions of corporate plans and expectations of future results.

budgeting Management accountants create many different budgets or budget scenarios reflecting financial plans for future periods.

buildings Structures shown as fixed assets. See *plant.*

business combination The general term for how one firm takes over or assumes control over another firm. May include *mergers, consolidations, and acquisitions.*

C

calendar year-end Annual reporting period that ends each year on December 31.

capital Investors' interests in a firm. Usually refers to sole proprietorships to show owners' interest in the firm's *net assets.*

capital gains (or losses) Result from increases (or decreases) in the market price of stocks over the period they are held by investors.

capital intensive Firms or industries that require relatively large amounts of property, plant, and equipment to produce their products (or services).

capital lease A lease agreement that is treated like an installment purchase (sale) of an asset. Capital leases increase the amounts of reported long-term assets and long-term debt for the lessee. The lessor records a receivable and eliminates the leased asset from its accounting records

capital structure An analysis of the firm's strategy for financing its assets with debt and equity.

capitalize Record expenditures related to an asset's acquisition, installation, or refurbishment as an asset. The carrying (book) value of the asset is increased by these capitalized costs.

carrying value The historical cost of an asset less its accumulated depreciation. See *book value.*

cash and cash equivalents Includes currency, bank deposits, and marketable securities that have maturities of three months or less (from the date of purchase) and can be turned into cash on short notice. These amounts are available to meet the firm's cash payment requirements.

cash basis of accounting Records revenue when cash is received and records expenses when cash is paid.

cash flow per share cash ratio calculated by dividing operating cash flows by the number of shares outstanding.

cash flows from financing activities Cash flows used to obtain or repay owners' investments, bonds, and long-term loans. Reported on the *statement of cash flows.*

cash flows from investing activities Cash flow transactions for acquiring or disposing of long-term assets and long-term investments. Reported on the *statement of cash flows.*

cash flows from operating activities (CFOA) Reflects the net cash increase (decrease) resulting from the firm's operating activities. Reported on the *statement of cash flows.*

cash interest coverage ratio Shows the relationship between all cash available to pay interest and the interest actually paid. Calculated as CFOA plus interest and taxes paid divided by interest paid.

"Cash is King" An important consideration in any financial analysis.

cash return on assets ratio A ratio used to analyze cash flow relative to assets employed. Calculated as cash flow from operating activities (CFOA) divided by (average) total assets.

cash to current liabilities ratio Ratio used to determine a firm's ability to pay its obligations in a timely manner.

categories Groupings of similar accounting transactions or events, such as purchases or investments, inventory sales, or wages paid.

Certified Fraud Examiner (CFE) Professional certification program administered by the Association for Certified Fraud Examiners.

Certified Internal Auditor (CIA) Professional certification administered by the Institute of Internal Auditors.

Certified Management Accountant (CMA) Professional certification program administered by The Institute of Management Accountants.

Certified Public Accountant (CPA) A certified public accountant licensed by a state board. The American Institute of Certified Public Accountants nationally administers the CPA exam.

change funds Cash funds used to make change for customers. Included in cash on the balance sheet. See *petty cash.*

change in accounting estimate Refers to a change in an estimate that underlies financial statement amounts. Includes changes in useful lives and salvage values.

change in accounting principle Occurs when a firm changes from one GAAP method to another in accounting for items on its financial statements.

change in reporting entity Change in the subsidiaries comprising a consolidated firm.

chart of accounts Lists account titles and account numbers that serve as an index to accounts in the general ledger.

charter Formal registration document filed with the state of incorporation that includes the corporation's business purpose and authorizes the firm to issue one or more types of ownership shares. Referred to as a "corporate charter."

closing entries Transfer the amounts in the revenue and expense (nominal) accounts to retained earnings.

codes of ethics Rules or guidelines identifying the professional conduct appropriate for CPA's serving the public interest.

collateral Specific assets pledged for security as part of a loan agreement. The creditor may have rights to seize the collateral if the borrower defaults on the loan.

collectibility Possibility that an account receivable will actually be collected.

collection period The average length of time it takes to collect a receivable. Calculated by dividing accounts receivable by average sales per day.

commitments Agreements with suppliers, customers, employers, or other entities that relate to "not yet completed" transactions and consequently have not been recognized in the accounts. When significant, they should be disclosed in the notes.

commitments and contingencies A footnote to financial statements that alerts financial statement users to a variety of actual and potential future claims that do not meet the FASB's criteria for recognition as liabilities at the balance sheet date.

common-size balance sheet Report that shows the percentage composition of each major item on the balance sheet. Calculated as percentage of the balance sheet totals.

common-size income statements A vertical analysis that measures and reports all the components on the income statement as a percentage of net sales. This enhances comparability across periods and firms.

common stock The basic type of stock ownership that typically entitles the stockholder to vote on corporate matters and share in profits. Common shareholders are the residual owners of the corporation.

common stock equivalent Securities and stock options that can be converted to common stock.

compensating balances Deposits or funds that a firm agrees to keep in accounts with a lender that pay little or no interest. The lender usually earns interest on such funds and keeps it.

compensation expense An expense incurred by a firm for employee services.

compensation plans An agreement between a firm and select employees, specifying salaries, bonus, options, etc.

complex capital structure Includes common stock and other securities or agreements that represent future sources of equity capital.

composition analysis The starting point for any analysis of capital structure. It provides a description of the relative amounts of capital obtained from each major source of financing. See *asset management ratios or capital structure.*

compound interest Interest this year calculated on principal plus interest from the prior year, "interest on interest".

compound journal entry Journal entry in which more than one account is debited or credited.

compounded semiannually When bonds pay interest each six months, the interest rate is a semiannual rate.

comprehensive income Includes all changes in owners' equity except for investments by owners and distributions to owners.

conflict of interest A firm's management is responsible for preparing its financial statements, which are used to evaluate management's performance, creating a conflict of interest.

conglomerate Companies operating in many diverse industries.

conservatism principle Where two alternative accounting treatments exist for a given transaction, the conservative alternative that reports lower asset values and lower net income is selected.

consolidated adjustments Changes made to the consolidated balance sheet of a parent company after acquiring a subsidiary company, which reflect the combined balance sheet accounts of both companies.

consolidated financial statements Reports that combine financial position, cash flows, and operating results for all firms under the parent company's control.

consolidation A business combination in which a new corporation is created to acquire the stock or the net assets of two or more existing companies. The original companies then cease to exist as separate corporations.

contingencies Conditions which may result in gains and losses and that will be resolved by the occurrence of future events.

contra account An account that is used to record and accumulate reductions in the balance of its related account. A contra account balance is subtracted from the balance of the related account.

contra-asset account A negative asset account that is used to record and accumulate reductions in the balance of its related asset account.

contra-equity account A negative equity account or a deduction from another shareholders' equity account. For example, *treasury stock is* always shown as a deduction from shareholders' equity. See *contra account.*

contributed capital The portion of shareholders' equity that arises from direct contributions (investments) from the owners. See *invested capital.*

convertible bonds Debt securities that may be exchanged for a specified number of shares of stock at a specified future time.

convertible preferred stock Preferred shares that may be exchanged for common shares at a specified future time.

copyright Granted by the Federal government to convey exclusive rights to use artistic or literary works for a period of 70 years beyond the author's death.

corporation A separate accounting and legal entity, apart from its owners (shareholders), with rights to exist under its charter granted by individual states.

cost accounting Determines product costs and other relevant information useful for managerial decision making.

cost flow assumption Assumption about how costs flow from inventory accounts to cost of goods sold. Costs flow differently under each inventory accounting method.

cost method of accounting The parent company recognizes income on its financial statements from the subsidiary only when the subsidiary declares a dividend.

cost of goods available for sale Income statement calculation of beginning inventory plus the cost of all purchases during a period. It reflects the total cost of goods that were held during the period.

cost of goods sold (COGS) The direct cost of acquiring or manufacturing a product that has been sold. Calculated as cost of goods available for sale, less ending inventory.

cost of goods sold percentage Cost of goods sold divided by net sales.

cost of sales See *cost of goods sold.*

coupon rate The stated interest rate in a bond contract. Also referred to as the *nominal, stated, or face rate.*

CPA firms Provide public accounting services including auditing, tax preparation, and management consulting.

creative accounting When assets or liabilities change for no obvious reasons, a firm may be engaging in creative accounting, where assets and revenues are created out of "thin air" with no underlying economic substance.

credit (Cr) The right-hand side of an entry in the double-entry accounting system.

credit ratings Scores provided by various credit bureaus to describe a firm's credit-worthiness, or its potential ability and willingness to pay for its purchases or debts.

cumulative effect The usual approach for recording a change in accounting principle. The cumulative effect from prior years is included in the current year's net income.

cumulative estimate In the year of a change in accounting principle, account balances are restated to show the amounts that would have appeared if the new method had been used in prior years.

cumulative preferred stock Shares that accumulate dividends during periods when the firm does not declare dividends. Accumulated dividends must be paid before any dividends can be paid to common shareholders.

currency forward market Market in which foreign currencies are bought and sold for future delivery.

current assets Cash and other assets that will typically be converted to cash or be consumed in one year or one operating cycle (if greater than one year).

current exchange rate Refers to converting financial amounts expressed in terms of one country's currency into a different monetary unit. The current exchange rate at the end of a month or a year can be used to make the foreign currency translation, as compared to using the average exchange rate.

current liabilities These include trade accounts payable and other short-term obligations that will be due in one year or one operating cycle, if greater than one year. Also includes the *current maturities of long-term debt.*

current maturities of long-term debt The portion of long-term debt due within the upcoming year.

current ratio The most popular liquidity ratio, calculated by dividing current assets by current liabilities.

D

date of declaration Date the firm specifies its intent to make a dividend payment. On that date, owners' equity (retained earnings) is decreased and liabilities (dividends payable) are increased.

date of payment The date the firm actually pays the dividend. Cash and dividends payable (liability) are reduced.

date of record The date that determines who will receive the dividend. Investors that own shares on that day will be paid the dividend.

declining-balance methods (DB) Accelerated depreciation method where depreciation expense is calculated by multiplying an asset's book value at the beginning of the year by a percentage equal to a multiple of the straight-line method rate.

debit (Dr) The left-hand side of an entry in the double-entry accounting system.

debt contracts Legal agreements between borrowers and lenders that impose constraints on the borrower and limit the lender's risk.

debt financing Debt or borrowed funds, used by a firm as a source of capital.

debt management ratios Analysis of the balance sheet that includes all sources of a firm's debt including long-term notes, bonds, and current liabilities.

debt ratio Represents the ratio of debt (debt and debt equivalents) to total capitalization, including all liabilities, deferred income taxes, and shareholders' investment. See *debt-to-assets ratio.*

debt securities Investments in debt instruments such as commercial paper or bonds or mortgages. These instruments provide evidence of indebtedness and can be negotiated (sold).

debt-to-assets ratio A primary indicator of a firm's debt management and leverage position based on percentage composition analysis. Calculated as total debt divided by total assets.

deferred income tax liability A liability for income taxes due in future periods.

deficit Negative figure indicating that the firm incurred overall net losses or negative retained earnings since the firm's inception.

defined benefit plan A pension plan specifying benefits those employees will receive at retirement.

defined contribution plan A pension plan that specifies the periodic payments to a pension fund on behalf of retirees. Current expenses are usually a percentage of an employee's current salary paid monthly to a pension fund.

denominated Refers to the conversion of financial amounts expressed in one country's currency into a different monetary unit. For example, yen might be denominated in U.S. dollars.

depletion The allocation of the cost (using up) of natural resources, which is systematically expensed over time.

deposits-in-transit Bank deposits delayed by processing. These cash receipts have been recorded in the firm's accounting records.

depreciable basis Cost of an asset less its estimated salvage value.

depreciated historical cost The cost of plant, property and equipment assets reported on the balance sheet. Calculated by subtracting accumulated depreciation from the historical cost of the asset.

depreciation Indicates decline, over time, of the service potential of long-lived tangible assets, such as plant and equipment. As the asset's service potential is consumed, a periodic expense is recorded. Depreciation is a method of allocating an asset's cost over its useful life.

depreciation expense An expense that is reported periodically and systematically over the asset's useful life or until its disposal. Depreciating an asset is an allocation of the asset's original cost as an expense to the periods that benefit from the asset's use.

diluted EPS Considers the effects on EPS of all the potential common shares that were outstanding during the year.

dilutive Earnings per share (EPS) may be reduced when common stock equivalents are included in the EPS calculation.

direct approach A method for preparing and displaying the cash flow statement where cash from operating activities is calculated on the basis of all cash flows with customers, suppliers, employees, and other operating activities. Contrast with *indirect approach.*

direct rates Used to indicate the rate at which U.S. dollars are translated into foreign currencies. Direct rates specify the number of units of U.S. dollars that are equivalent to one unit of the foreign currency. See *indirect rates.*

discontinued operations A component of a company that has been sold, abandoned, or disposed that represents a distinct unit of a business. Discontinued operations have both operations and financial information that can be distinguished from the remainder of the company.

discount Reduction in the amount owed to a firm for a credit sale, generally offered if the credit sale is repaid within a specified amount of time from the sale date.

discount on bonds A bond is issued below its face amount, indicating that the coupon rate is lower than the market rate for similar bonds (such as risk, maturity). See *par value and premium on bonds.*

discount rate An interest rate used in calculating the present value of future cash flows. This rate is often not explicit and is derived by taking the risk of the investment and prevailing market rates into account.

discounted note A noninterest-bearing note where the interest charge has been deducted from the principal in advance.

discounts taken Savings in the form of a percentage deducted from the purchase price of goods and services offered by the seller to induce early payment.

disposal Firms may sell fixed assets when needs change or when assets age or become obsolete.

distinguishable operating component A segment of a firm's business that has operations and cash flows that are clearly distinguishable from the rest of the firm.

divestiture Occurs when a parent company decreases its investment in a subsidiary by selling the subsidiary's shares.

diversification A strategy a firm uses for external growth by acquiring another company operating in a completely unrelated field.

dividends Distributions of assets, usually cash, that the corporation elects to make periodically to its stockholders.

double-declining-balance method An accelerated depreciation method using a multiple of 200% of the straight-line rate.

double-entry accounting An accounting method in which transactions are recorded by entering equal amounts in the left-hand (debit) side and right-hand (credit) side of a journal or ledger entry.

double taxation A form of taxation in which income taxes are paid by corporations on their earnings, which are taxed a second time when shareholders pay taxes on the dividends that they received from corporations.

downsizing Restructuring of a corporation that often entails the retraining, layoff, or termination of many employees.

due process Procedure conducted by FASB prior to issuing an accounting standard that provides corporate managers the opportunity to lobby in response to the proposed new standard.

E

earnings See *net income.*

earnings before interest and taxes (EBIT) A firm's earnings minus all costs and expenses occurring during normal operations and before interest expense and taxes have been deducted. See *Operating income.*

earnings management Involves accounting measurement and policy decisions that yield favorable consequences to firms and their managers.

earnings management tools Specific techniques used to manage (adjust) earnings to meet desired target earnings.

earnings per share (EPS) Indicates the net income earned by each share of outstanding common stock. Calculated by dividing net income by the (weighted average) number of outstanding shares.

earnings quality The sustainability of currently reported earnings in future periods. Also relates to *conservatism.*

economic assumptions Under pension accounting, these assumptions include the assumed interest rate used to discount future pension benefits, and the anticipated rate of return on pension plan assets.

economic life The length of time a firm expects to use an asset.

economic value The market value of a company's stock.

effective income tax rate The effective tax rate is the reported income tax expense as a percentage of reported income before tax.

efficient market hypothesis (EMH) Suggests that all publicly available information is reflected in security prices.

Enron-accounting Sarcastic term used to indicate any kind of "funny-business" in accounting or the firm's financial statements

entity assumption A requirement to keep the firm's accounting records separate and distinct from the owners' records. Thus, the firm can be assessed on a standalone basis.

entry See *journal entry.*

equipment Resources include office desks, chairs, tools, drill presses, robots, software, computers, copiers, scanners, artwork, and so on. Equipment and plant are major assets in many organizations.

equity capital Represents ownership interests in a firm in the form of stock bought by investors. Owners' investments are not liabilities to be repaid at a future date.

equity financing Resources obtained by a corporation from its owners and investors. Also called *equity capital.*

equity method of accounting A method in which the parent company recognizes its share of the subsidiary's reported income (or loss) on its financial statements and adjusts annually the basis of its investment (asset) in the subsidiary.

equity securities Represent ownership interests in the form of stocks issued by other corporations. This investment is reported on the balance sheet as an asset.

estimated residual value The amount the firm expects to receive from selling the asset at the end of its useful economic life.

ethics Belief that internal accountants, external auditors, and managers have a responsibility to perform their tasks with integrity and due care.

ex dividend stock A stock that is sold without dividend rights such that subsequent purchasers will not be entitled to receive the previously declared dividend. Owners on the date of record will receive the dividend.

excess capacity Indicates the plant and equipment of a firm are underutilized.

executory contracts Agreements formed by an exchange of promises. No substantive exchange of cash or services has occurred to meet the "past transaction" criterion so the contract is not recognized for financial accounting purposes.

expected return An anticipated increase in the investor's wealth, in the form of increased market value of the investment and dividends.

expenses The consumption of resources as a result of conducting business for the purpose of generating revenues and profits.

explicit interest payments Actual interest paid, usually semiannual interest payments.

external expansion Occurs as firms take over, or merge with, other existing firms.

externally acquired goodwill The amount that a firm pays in excess of the net assets of another business that the firm acquires. The excess is recorded as *goodwill*, an asset on the balance sheet.

extraordinary items Events and transactions that are unusual in nature (not typical of the firm's normal operations) and infrequent in occurrence (not expected to recur in the foreseeable future). These items are reported (net of tax) below income from continuing operations on the income statement.

F

factor Selling accounts receivable for cash.

factor receivables Obtaining funds from a factor or lender by pledging or transferring accounts receivable to the *factor*.

fair value Indicates market values of assets. Also pertaining to employee stock options where compensation expense is measured at the grant date based on the estimated fair market value of the award.

fairly presented in accordance with GAAP Phrase used in audit reports by auditors as they express their professional judgment whether the financial statements were prepared under current accounting standards.

FASB See *Financial Accounting Standards Board.*

FIFO (first in, first out) A method for valuing inventory that assumes the goods bought "first" are those sold "first" as they are sold, or used in manufacturing.

financial accounting Provides financial statements, prepared according to GAAP.

Financial Accounting Standards Board (FASB) A private organization that issues Statements of Financial Accounting Standards (SFAS) that currently are the most authoritative source of *GAAP*. The FASB is empowered by the *SEC* to set GAAP.

financial leverage ratio See *debt-to-assets ratio.*

financing activities Describes a firm's sources of cash through borrowing or equity transactions. It is a category shown on the cash flow statement.

finished goods Completed inventory items awaiting sale.

fiscal year A financial reporting period that may be different from the calendar year. A firm uses a fiscal year because it is conventional in their industry and more convenient to their production or sales cycle.

fixed asset turnover A ratio that shows how effectively a firm is utilizing its productive capacity (fixed assets). Calculated by dividing net sales by the (average) book value of property, plant, and equipment.

fixed assets Tangible, long-lived assets, primarily property, plant, and equipment, used to produce goods or services.

foreign currency transactions Accounts that are paid using a non-domestic currency.

foreign exchange rate Specifies the number of U.S. dollars (from a U.S. perspective) that are needed to obtain one unit of a specific foreign currency.

forward rate The rate of exchange for future delivery of foreign currencies.

franchise Rights to market a particular product or service, typically within a geographic area. These rights have economic value.

free cash flow Generic term to show cash flow from operating activities less cash needed to replace productive resources.

full cost method Capitalizes, as an asset, the exploration costs of both successful and unsuccessful natural resource sites. Used in accounting for mining and other natural resources such as oil and gas wells.

functional currency The currency used to conduct normal business activities.

future value The concept that money earns interest over time and the value of a given sum will be greater in the future as interest accumulates.

future value factor Used to multiply a given sum by a factor from future value tables to convert an initial amount to its future value.

G

GAAP See *generally accepted accounting principles.*

GAAS See *generally accepted auditing standards.*

gains Profits realized from activities that are peripheral to a firm's primary operating activities.

general expenses See *general and administrative expenses.*

general and administrative expenses Support and functional expenses consisting of senior managers' salaries, accounting and auditing costs, insurance, depreciation on administrative assets. See *overhead.*

general journal Formal accounting record for journal entries, adjusting entries and closing entries that cannot be recorded in other more specialized journals.

general ledgers Accounting records used to classify transactions into asset, liability, and equity accounts.

general purpose Used to describe financial statements intended to meet the shared information needs of many users.

generally accepted accounting principles (GAAP) Approved accounting standards used by public companies for financial reporting. The *FASB,* with *SEC* support, sets GAAP.

generally accepted auditing standards (GAAS) Developed by the accounting profession to guide auditors in conducting an audit.

going concern concept The assumption underlying accounting and auditing that a firm will continue doing business in the future.

goodwill The amount paid in excess of the fair market value of an acquired firm's identifiable net assets. Goodwill should not be confused with *internally generated goodwill* that results from reputation, location, customer loyalty, and client lists.

gross margin Revenues less cost of goods sold; indicates primary source of operating profit for retailers or manufacturers. See *gross profit (margin) percentage.*

gross margin percentage See *gross profit (margin) percentage.*

gross profit See *gross margin.*

gross profit (margin) percentage A profitability measure calculated as gross profit (margin) divided by net sales.

growth Term used to describe a firm's success in expanding its market.

guarantees See *warranties.*

H

hedge Entering into a contract to buy or sell foreign currencies in the forward market to protect against the risks of foreign exchange rate fluctuations.

hedging contract A contract to buy or sell foreign currencies in the forward market to protect against the risks of foreign exchange rate fluctuations. Also referred to as a *hedge.*

historical cost The exchange price on the date when an asset was acquired, usually indicated by the amount of cash that changed hands.

historical exchange rates Exchange rates used under foreign currency translations to convert the balances of shareholders' equity, including invested capital, beginning retained earnings, and dividends.

horizontal analysis A trend analysis where components of the current year's financial statements are compared to components of a prior year's statements.

horizontal integration Occurs when a company expands its operations geographically by acquiring a similar business in another market.

hybrid securities A security that is neither clearly debt nor clearly equity. Instead, it combines certain features of both types of securities. See *convertible bonds.*

I

immediate recognition An expenditure is expensed immediately because it has no discernible future benefit and no matching revenue.

impaired An operational asset, such as *property, plant, and equipment,* is impaired if its book value exceeds the value of its expected future cash flows. Goodwill is impaired if its carrying value exceeds its implied fair value.

impairment charge Occurs when a company writes down the value of *goodwill* or operational assets that are overstated.

impairment test Companies with *goodwill* on their balance sheets must perform this test annually to determine whether the goodwill is impaired.

implicit interest payments Reflects imputed interest under *discounted notes.* There are no cash outflows associated with implicit interest.

income statement A financial statement that summarizes the firm's earnings during a specified time period. It contains at least two major sections: revenues and expenses. Also referred to as *statement of earnings* or *statement of operations.*

income taxes Expenses based on the firm's earnings imposed by federal, state, and local governments, and by foreign jurisdictions.

indentures Provisions and restrictions attached to a bond issue that reduces investors' risks and constrains future decisions by the issuer.

indirect approach A method for preparing and displaying the cash flow statement where the cash from operating activities is calculated indirectly by adding or subtracting various non-cash adjustments to the reported net income. Contrast this method with *direct approach.*

indirect rates Used to indicate the rate at which foreign currencies are translated into U.S. dollars. Indirect rates specify the number of foreign currency units that are equivalent to one U.S. dollar. See *direct rates.*

informational role The role of accounting principles in providing useful information to those who make economic decisions.

intangible asset Noncurrent assets with no physical substance, often consisting of legal rights including patents and copyrights. Intangibles are important resources controlled by the organization; could be critical to a firm's success.

intangibles Long-term asset representing legal rights or contractual privileges, such as patents, copyrights, and so on.

intercompany receivables and payables Receivables and payables of a parent company to/from its subsidiary(s). They are eliminated in consolidation reporting.

intercompany sales Sales of a parent company to/from its subsidiary(s). They are eliminated in consolidation reporting.

inter-period comparability Occurs when firms consistently use the same accounting methods over several reporting periods.

interest-bearing note A debt instrument (note) that requires interest payments at a stated rate at a stated due date.

interest cost In pension accounting, this is the interest on the projected benefit obligation. In accounting for postretirement benefit obligations other than pensions, it is the beginning of the year accumulated benefit obligation multiplied by the discount rate.

interest coverage Ratio of pre-tax earnings before unusual items and fixed charges to fixed charges (interest expense excluding loss on debt repurchase, interest equivalent and the interest portion of rent expense).

interest expense The firm's cost of borrowing money from creditors. Often simply referred to as *interest.*

interest payments Payments by a borrower to a lender for using money over time.

interim reporting (interim reports) Reporting financial results more frequently than once a year, usually quarterly.

internal audit Performed within the firm to ensure reliability of financial statements. Internal audits also assess the effectiveness and efficiency of the firm's operations.

internal expansion Occurs as firms invest in new plant and equipment, research, and other productive endeavors to serve growing markets or to extend the scope of their operations into new products and markets.

Internal Revenue Service (IRS) A federal agency that regulates tax laws used to determine individual or corporate income tax liability.

internally generated goodwill The unrecognized costs incurred to enhance the value of an organization. Examples include good reputation and customer base, successful suppliers relationships, skilled labor force, talented managers, and so on. Not reported under GAAP.

Internet A mode of technological communication and information sharing that permits global communication links that were previously unrelated or infeasible.

intrinsic value One way of reporting the cost of employee stock options which measures the compensation cost of stock options as the excess of the stock's market price over the option price at the date of the grant.

inventory Items that have been purchased or manufactured for resale to customers.

invested capital Amounts received by a corporation upon sale of its stock to investors. Includes *par value* and *paid-in capital.*

investee The object of an investment or purchase transaction.

investing activities Describes a firm's uses of cash to acquire other assets. This category is shown on the cash flow statement.

investor ratios Indicates a firm's performance with regard to market value of its shares. Primary focus is on market indicators affecting owners or investors.

issued shares Capital shares (stock) that have been issued (sold) to investors.

J

joint venture An informal business relationship formed for a specific purpose through investments from two or more otherwise unrelated companies.

journal entry An entry that appears in a general or specialized journal consisting of the date, the account(s) to be debited and credited, the amounts, and an explanation.

L

lease An agreement where the lessor conveys to the lessee the right to use property, plant, and equipment for a designated future period.

leased assets Assets controlled by one firm that are owned by some other firm.

legal rights Rights conveyed by contract or other written agreement or federal law.

lessee The user or renter of property under a lease agreement.

lessor The owner of leased property.

leverage Financing a large proportion of asset acquisitions with long-term debt, as opposed to equity, that results in higher returns (profits) to the common equity shareholders.

liabilities Obligations of the entity to convey something of value in the future. They represent probable future sacrifices of economic benefits that arise as a result of past transactions or events.

license The right to engage in a particular activity.

LIFO (last in, first out) A method for valuing inventory that assumes the most recent ("last in") purchases of inventory are those first sold or first used in the production process.

LIFO layers Subsets of inventory costs acquired during earlier time periods; if the LIFO layers are sold or used, higher than normal profits would occur.

LIFO liquidation A practice used by companies to manage earnings by selling or using inventory quantities that are older and have lower costs, resulting in lower COGS and higher profits because these older, lower costs are matched with current, higher revenues.

LIFO reserves Represent low cost inventory acquired when prices were low; when these assets are sold abnormally high profits will be reported. Used under *earnings management* schemes.

liquidate Refers to the firm's sale of inventory and other assets in order to raise cash, usually in crisis circumstances.

liquidity Refers to how quickly the firm's current assets are converted to cash, usually during the normal operating cycle.

liquidity ratios Ratios used to evaluate the firm's short-term solvency and how effectively it manages its *working capital.*

long-lived assets Noncurrent assets that will not be fully used by a firm within a year.

losses Losses realized from a variety of business activities including normal operations and those that are peripheral to a firm's primary operating activities.

lower of cost or market (LCM) Required method of valuing inventory under GAAP. Sets inventory value at the lesser of cost or market (defined as current replacement cost).

M

major customers A customer from whom an organization generates 10% or more of its revenue.

management discussion and analysis (MDA) A narrative report included in the annual report that provides a qualitative description of the year's highlights.

managerial accounting Provides information that is custom-tailored, detailed, and proprietary used internally by a firm's managers to make operating decisions.

manufacturer A firm that buys raw materials and component parts and reshapes them into a finished product.

market rate The "cost of money" (interest), as determined by the monetary market forces (supply and demand).

market-to-book value ratio Indicates the relationship between the market's valuation of the firm and the book values shown in the firm's financial statements. Calculated as the quoted price per share on a stock exchange divided by the firm's net asset value per share.

market value The replacement cost of an asset in the open market. Also, the market price of a debt or equity security that is readily marketable on a securities exchange registered with the SEC, some foreign exchanges, or if its price is available through the National Association of Securities Dealers Automated Quotations Systems (NASDAQ) or the National Quotation Bureau.

marketable A security is marketable if it is traded on a securities exchange registered with the Securities and Exchange Commission (SEC) or if its price is available through the National Association of Securities Dealers Automated Quotations Systems or the National Quotation Bureau. Securities traded on foreign exchanges may also qualify.

marketable securities Short-term investments that typically produce higher earnings than those available from bank accounts. Firms invest excess cash in marketable securities, enabling them to increase their earnings.

matching principle A principle underlying expense recognition indicating that all resources consumed in generating revenue should be recorded in the same time period as the revenue. The matching principle is central to the *accrual basis of accounting* because it provides a more objective indicator of a firm's performance as reflected on the income statement.

materiality principle States that separate disclosure is not required if an item were so small that knowledge of it would not affect the decision of a reasonable financial statement reader. A reporting guideline used by auditors and accountants to determine whether a particular item or cost will have a potential significant effect on a decision.

maturity date Date on which the principal of a note becomes due.

merchandiser A firm that buys and resells goods without changing their shape or form.

merger A business combination in which the buyer firm acquires either the stock, or the net asssets, of an investee firm. The investee is then dissolved, and no longer exists as a separate corporation.

mergers and acquisitions (M&A) A common business activity in which one business acquires another firm. Each entity acquired will file financial statements, but the parent company will also consolidate the subsidiary's results with its own.

minority interest in consolidated subsidiaries The book value of a subsidiary's outstanding shares of stock that are not under the control of the parent.

modified accelerated cost recovery system (MACRS) Modified version of the Accelerated Cost Recovery System (ACRS), which is an *IRS* regulation that allows firms to use an *accelerated depreciation* method to calculate annual depreciation expense.

mortgage payable A loan agreement where the title to real property is secured by the lender to reduce the risk of borrower defaulting on the loan. The mortgage is a liability for the borrower.

multiple-step income statement Calculates certain subtotals on the income statement, such as gross profit and operating income.

N

natural resources Assets such as mines containing gold, silver, copper, or other minerals, wells containing oil or gas, and timberlands. Natural resources are also called "wasting assets".

natural year-end Annual reporting period that ends each year at a pre-determined date, usually after a firm's busy season.

negative (deficit) balance Negative retained earnings balance indicating that the firm's dividends and losses, incurred since inception of the firm, have exceeded its income.

net Implies that certain items have been deducted from the gross (or full) sales price. Also used to denote *net book value* of assets where accumulated depreciation is deducted from an asset's historical cost.

net accounts receivable The net difference between the amounts owed by customers and the allowance for uncollectible accounts.

net assets The excess (residual) amount of assets over liabilities shown on the balance sheet. Net assets are equivalent to owners' equity as shown by rearranging the basic accounting equation: Owners' Equity = Assets − Liabilities. Also referred to as net worth.

net book value The initial (recorded) cost of an asset less its accumulated depreciation. Also referred to as the *carrying value* of an asset.

net income Amount by which total revenues and gains exceed total expenses and losses on the income statement. It is the last line item on the income statement *(bottom line)*.

net income percentage A profitability ratio that indicates the proportion of net income earned on every sales dollar. Calculated as net income divided by net sales revenue.

net loss Occurs when expenses and losses exceed revenues and gains.

net of tax Indicates that expected tax effects have already been included as part of a particular calculation or reported result. Indicates that taxes have been deducted from a particular financial item on a statement.

net profit See *net income.*

net realizable value The estimated cash to be collected by selling an asset.

net sales Gross sales revenue less any allowances or discounts.

net worth See **net assets.**

nominal account Income statement accounts that are initialized to zero at the end of the reporting period. Account balances in nominal accounts are transferred to retained earnings at year-end. Also referred to as a *temporary* account.

nominal rate Stated interest rate on a bond, also called *coupon rate.*

nonbusiness organizations Any organization that does not have a profit objective or investors who require an expected return. May refer to a *nonprofit or not-for-profit organization.*

noncash investing and financing activities A category of investing and financing activities that does not involve cash flows.

noncurrent assets Long-term assets that are used in the conduct of the business. The replacement cycle for a noncurrent asset is greater than one year.

noncurrent liabilities Liabilities that represent obligations, typically from long-term borrowing that generally require payment over periods longer than a year.

nonhomogeneous subsidiaries Subsidiaries whose major operating activities take place in industries that differ from those of the parent company.

noninterest-bearing note A debt instrument (note) that does not explicitly pay interest but is usually bought at a discount.

note A written promise to pay signed by the debtor. The obligation to pay is documented in a legal agreement.

note payable A formal written agreement with stated interest and repayment dates that the debtor signs in order to borrow funds from banks or other lenders. Notes payable may be either interest bearing or noninterest bearing and can usually be renegotiated with the lender.

notes to the financial statements Information that clarifies and extends the material presented in the financial statements with narrative and detail.

number of days' sales in accounts receivable A liquidity ratio that indicates how quickly the firm is "turning" or "cycling" its accounts receivable. A high number indicates poor management of accounts receivable. It's calculated as ending accounts receivable divided by sales per day.

number of days' sales in ending inventory (NDS) A liquidity ratio used to evaluate inventory management. Calculated as ending inventory divided by cost of goods sold per day.

O

obligations for warranties Liabilities resulting from offering assurances of repairs, replacements, and/or refunds in the event of product failures or customer dissatisfaction.

off-balance sheet Financing transactions or risk management strategies that are not reported on the balance sheet.

off-balance sheet financing Term used to describe a firm's financing activities, often through leases that may not be shown on the balance sheet.

on account Purchases or sales on credit.

operating activities Activities involved with completing the ordinary day-to-day transactions needed to conduct business.

operating capacity The ability of a firm to produce goods or services; often requires analysis of the firm's tangible and intangible noncurrent assets.

operating cycle The time needed to purchase raw materials, manufacture finished goods, sell the inventory, and collect cash from the customer.

operating income Gross margin or gross profit less all other operating expenses.

operating income percentage ratio A profitability ratio calculated by dividing operating income by net sales revenues. Also known as operating income ratio.

operating lease A lease agreement treated as an ordinary rental, where the asset is merely used by the lessee and rental payments are reported as expense. Does not require that the lessee report the leased property as an asset.

operating segment A component of a firm (a) that engages in business activities from which it may earn revenues and incur expenses, (b) whose operating results are regularly reviewed by the firm's chief operating decision maker, and (c) for which distinct financial information is available.

opportunity cost A cost that exists as a result of lost profits due to more profitable alternative investments being precluded by less profitable investments currently undertaken.

other items (net) A component of pension expense that includes amortization of the transition amount, prior service cost, and gains and losses.

outstanding checks Checks that are included in the accounting records but not yet shown on the bank statement.

outstanding shares Issued shares that are not held in treasury by the issuing firm. These are the only outstanding shares eligible for dividends.

overhead Manufacturing costs other than direct labor and materials.

owners Investors in a business.

owners' equity Represents the owners' interest in the net assets of the business. It is the residual amount remaining by subtracting liabilities from assets. See *basic accounting equation.*

P

paid-in capital Describes a component of shareholders' equity. Represents the excess amounts invested by shareholders above the par value of their investment. Also called paid-in-excess of par value.

par value (bonds) The face amount on bonds, due at maturity.

par value (stock) Stated amount per share for legal purposes. Usually the amount is small (e.g., $1) and represents a fraction of the market value, or amounts invested by shareholders.

parent company Term applied to the buyer company in a business combination.

partnership An unincorporated business owned by more than one owner and generally operated under a legal contract (partnership agreement) among the partners. Partnerships are not separate legal entities apart from their owners, but they are considered as separate economic entities.

patents Granted by the federal government to convey the exclusive right to use a product or process for a period of 20 years.

pay-as-you-go The method used prior to 1993 for accounting for non-pension postretirement benefits, where expenses were reported on the cash basis, and no obligations were recognized for future payments.

pension plan Compensation benefits provided by firms to their retired employees.

percentage composition (analysis) Refers to a ratio analysis of financial statement data based on the relative proportions of column totals. See *vertical analysis.* Contrast with *horizontal analysis.*

percentage-of-completion Recognizes a portion of the revenue, cost, and profit each year according to the percentage of the job completed. Usually applies to multi-year construction contracts.

percentage of PPE depreciated (age) Ratio used to show approximate age of long-term assets; equals accumulated depreciation divided by PPE (gross).

petty cash (fund) Small quantity of funds kept on hand for incidental expenditures requiring quick cash. These funds are included in the cash amount on the balance sheet, similar to *change funds.*

piecemeal acquisition Occurs when a parent company increases its investment in a subsidiary over time by buying more and more shares in the subsidiary.

plant Includes office, retail or factory buildings, warehouses or supply depots, or hospitals and health clinics. Along with equipment, plant is a primary productive resource of any organization.

political costs Costs imposed on firms in the political process, just by being part of society. Examples include taxes and costs to implement regulations.

pooling of interests The accounting treatment used in a business combination when firms combine by an exchange of voting stock. These combinations represent a "uniting of ownership interests" rather than a purchase of one firm by another. No longer acceptable under *GAAP.*

post-acquisition expenditures Expenditures made by a firm for routine repairs and maintenance of fixed assets during their useful lives, or as capitalized costs that provide future economic benefits.

posting Transferring amounts from journals into ledgers, e.g., into the general ledger.

postretirement benefit obligation (PBO) The actuarial present value of the future postretirement benefits that employees and retirees have earned to date.

pre-acquisition balance sheet Balance sheet of company that is acquired by another firm, dated prior to the acquisition.

preferred stock Equity capital shares that have priority (preferential treatment) over common shares with regard to dividends and distributions of assets in the event of firm liquidation.

premium on bonds The amount by which a bond is bought and sold above its face amount. See *par value* and *discount on bonds.*

prepaid expenses Unexpired current assets that have been paid for in advance of their use; represent the rights to future benefits, e.g., prepaid expenses for rent or insurance.

prepaid rent A prepaid expense representing the right to use property.

present value The value today of an amount to be received or paid in the future.

present value factor Factors from present value table to convert (multiply) a future value to its present value.

price-to-earnings (P/E) ratio Widely used *investor ratio* that indicates the relationship between market prices and earnings. Calculated as the stock's market price per share divided by its earnings per share.

principal The original or base amount of a loan or investment.

privatization Selling government-owned or-controlled enterprises to private investors.

pro forma amount Hypothetical or projected amount. Synonymous with "what if" analyses. Pro forma statements indicate what might happen under specified conditions.

productive capacity Indicates the remaining net book value of buildings and equipment. Calculate by dividing net book value by the asset's initial cost (gross book value). Used by analysts to determine how regularly firms invest in new plant and equipment.

profit See *net income.*

profitability ratios Ratios that analyze the returns on owners' investments; includes ROA, ROE, gross profit percentage, and net profit margins.

projected benefit obligation The amount of pension benefits that employees have earned to date, based on the expected future salary levels.

property Usually represents land on which the firm's offices, factories, and other facilities are located. May also be used generically to refer to factories, warehouses, etc., e.g., *property, plant, and equipment.* Does not include real estate investments.

property, plant, and equipment (PPE) Typical noncurrent assets in many firms; often referred to as *fixed assets.*

proportional revenue recognition Policy of recognizing revenue proportionally over the time period when it is earned.

prospective changes The method of accounting for changes in estimates whereby past financial statements are not affected. Prospective changes only apply to future periods.

prospectively See *prospective changes.*

publicly held Corporations that are quite large and have ownership interests widely dispersed among the public. Regulated by *SEC.*

Q

qualified opinion Audit report issued by an auditor that signals the auditor's concerns about some aspects of the firm's financial statements.

quality of income ratio A cash ratio calculated by dividing cash from operating activities by net income.

quality of sales ratio A liquidity ratio that indicates the proportion of sales revenue that generated cash in the current year. Cash sales are considered high-quality sales while credit sales are lower quality. Calculated as cash received from customers divided by sales.

quick ratio A liquidity ratio that only considers those current assets that may soon be available (month or quarter). Calculated as cash plus cash equivalents plus net receivables divided by current liabilities. Also referred to as the *acid-test ratio.*

R

ratios Calculations made by dividing one amount by another calculated among selected financial statement amounts; used to examine relationships and trends.

raw materials Components or ingredients in the manufacturing process, shown as an inventory account on the balance sheet.

realize Recognizing a gain or loss in the financial statements.

recognition Recognizing revenues or expenses, associated with the *revenue recognition principle* and the *matching principle,* and recording transactions in the accounting records.

relevant Information that can make a difference in the decision making process.

reliable Information that is free from error and bias.

research and development costs Resources used to generate new knowledge or to translate knowledge into a new product or process. According to *GAAP,* these costs should be expensed immediately.

residual interest See *net assets.*

residual owners Refers to constituents who have a secondary or "final" ownership interest in an organization. Often refers to shareholders who take a secondary position relative to bondholders or preferred shareholders.

residual value See *salvage value.*

restrictive covenants Limitations imposed by a creditor on a debtor's actions. Covenants are often based on accounting measurements of assets, liabilities, and/or income.

restructure Term used to describe corporate downsizing and refocusing operations. The total estimated costs of restructuring should be expensed in the current year.

retained earnings Portion of shareholders' equity that reflects the shareholders' residual interests in the firm.

retroactive changes The method of accounting for accounting principle changes whereby past years' financial statements are restated to reflect use of the new method.

retroactively See *retroactive changes.*

return on assets (ROA) ratio A profitability ratio that indicates the rate of return on the firm's assets. It is used to compare the firm's rate of return with alternative investments that could be undertaken. Basic ratio calculated by dividing net income by total assets. Tax-adjusted ratio calculated as net income plus interest expense times one minus the tax rate, all divided by (average) total assets.

return on equity (ROE) ratio A profitability ratio used to relate net income to shareholders' equity. Calculated by dividing net income by (average) shareholders' equity.

return on plan assets As related to pension accounting, it reduces pension expense by the returns expected on the plan's assets. The reduction is based on anticipated, not actual, returns.

return on shareholders' equity ratio See *return on equity (ROE) ratio.*

revenue Inflows of assets (or reductions in liabilities) in exchange for providing goods and services to customers (sales, for example) or from collecting interest, rent, royalties, and so on.

revenue recognition principle States that revenue should be recognized in the accounting period when the earnings process is substantially complete and the amount to be collected is reasonably determinable.

risk The uncertainty surrounding estimates of future cash flows.

S

sale Delivery of goods or services to customers in exchange for cash or other consideration.

sales return Items, usually defective or unacceptable merchandise, returned by customers for credit or other adjustment.

salvage value The estimated amount a firm expects to receive when an asset is sold at the end of its useful life. Also referred to as *residual value.*

Sarbanes-Oxley Act of 2002 Act that imposes strict disclosure and corporate governance mandates for all U.S. and non-U.S. public companies filing periodic reports with the *Securities and Exchange Commission (SEC).*

Securities Exchange Act of 1934 An act that created and empowered the *Securities and Exchange Commission (SEC)* to set accounting principles and financial disclosure requirements for the corporations that it regulates.

Securities Exchange Commission (SEC) Created by the Securities Exchange Act of 1934, the SEC has the power to set accounting principles and financial disclosure requirements for firms with securities traded on public exchanges. SEC has delegated responsibility to the *FASB.*

security As related to debt, it is synonymous with *collateral.* As related to investments, it is synonymous with publicly traded stocks and bonds (securities).

segment reporting Firm provides separate financial reports for each of its various business activities in order to provide more detailed information to investors regarding risk and expected return.

selling expenses A category of expenses shown on the income statement related to marketing and other selling activities.

service cost As related to pension accounting, service cost (normal cost) is the present value of future pension benefits that employees earned during the current year. As related to accounting for postretirement benefit obligations other than pensions, it is the amount of the accumulated benefit obligation earned by employees during the current year.

service lives The working years of employees prior to retirement, as used in accounting for postretirement benefit obligations.

SFAS See *Statements of Financial Accounting Standards* and *FASB.*

shareholders' equity Represents the shareholders' residual interest in the firm's assets. It is the residual amount that equals assets minus liabilities. See *basic accounting equation.*

simple capital structure Includes no "potential" or hybrid common equity securities other than common stock.

single-step format Refers to an income statement format where most revenues are shown in one category, and most expenses are shown in another category, without calculating intermediate subtotals. Contrast with *multiple-step income statement.*

single-step income statement Summarizes most revenues in one section and most expenses in another.

sinking fund Resources designated for a special purpose, such as the retirement of outstanding debt or the replacement of operating assets.

sole proprietorship A business owned and usually operated by the same individual. The owner and business are not separate legal entities but are separate economic entities.

sources of financing The sources where a firm has obtained its capital resources.

special journals Journals constructed to achieve efficiencies in recording transactions. Examples of special journals include sales journals, cash receipts journals, and cash payments journals.

special purpose entities (SPEs) A separate independent company, whose purpose is for firms to obtain funds through "off-balance sheet financing".

specific identification method A method for determining the cost of inventory by maintaining the identity and cost of each item, usually by serial number or other code, such that each item or unit can be tracked throughout the holding and selling process.

spontaneous or operating liabilities The current liabilities of a firm that are closely related to its operations. Examples include trade accounts payable, accrued expenses, and taxes payable.

spot rate The exchange rate for immediate delivery of foreign currencies.

statement of cash flows A financial statement that reports the sources and uses of cash by a firm during a specified period. Three major activities of the firm are reported: operating, investing, and financing. This statement is intended to provide information about a firm's ability to generate cash.

statement of comprehensive income Statement that starts with net income and the other items of comprehensive income are then added to (or subtracted from) net income, with the final figure being the firm's comprehensive income.

statement of earnings A financial statement that summarizes the firm's revenues, expenses, and earnings during a specified time period. It contains at least two major sections: revenues and expenses. Also referred to as the *income statement.*

statement of financial position A financial statement that shows, at a specified time, a firm's financial condition, which is determined by its assets, liabilities, and owners' equity. Also referred to as the *balance sheet.*

statement of owners' equity A financial statement that summarizes the changes in owners' equity over a time period.

statement of shareholders' equity A financial statement that summarizes the changes in shareholders' equity over a time period. See *statement of owners' equity.*

Statements of Financial Accounting Standards (SFAS) The primary sources of *GAAP.* The statements provide explicit accounting treatment for many financial transactions. Currently, they are created by the *FASB.*

statutory rate Rate at which the Federal Government taxes a firm's income.

stock dividend Firms distribute additional shares of stock to investors as a non-cash dividend. Retained earnings are reduced and invested capital is increased.

stock option Rights to purchase a firm's stock at a specific price over some designated future period.

stock split An exchange of shares of a firm's stock for existing outstanding shares that usually results in more shares issued.

straight-line depreciation expense Calculated by first subtracting the residual value from the cost. This difference is the depreciable basis. Next divide the depreciable basis by the number of years in the asset's estimated useful life.

straight-line method (SL) A depreciation method that allocates an equal amount of expense to each year in an asset's life.

subsidiary The term applied to the investee firm in a business combination when the firm continues to exist.

subsidiary ledger Provides detailed information regarding a particular general ledger account.

successful efforts method Immediately expenses the cost of unsuccessful oil and gas sites. Only the costs directly associated with locating and developing successful sites are capitalized.

sum-of-the-years'-digits method (SYD) An accelerated depreciation method where the numerator is the number of useful remaining years and the denominator is the sum of the years' digits in the asset's useful life. The denominator is calculated as $[N \times (N + 1)]/2$, where N is the number of years in the asset's life.

sustainability Describes the ability of an organization to continue its operations and achieve its objectives. Can relate to the *going concern concept.*

sustainable earnings A firm's earnings that will persist in the future.

systematic and rational allocation Method used to implement the matching principle where costs that cannot be directly linked to specific revenue transactions are recognized as an expense in the years it helps generate revenue.

T

T-account Account form in a ledger used to record (or illustrate) the entry of debits and credits into ledger accounts.

tax accounting Encompasses the two functions of tax compliance and tax planning. Tax compliance involves the process of completing tax forms and the calculation of a firm's tax liability. Tax planning entails providing advice about the effects those business transactions will have on the firm's tax liability.

tax basis The basis for which a firm's assets are represented for tax purposes. This may differ from the assets' carrying value due to the accelerated method for depreciating assets for income tax purposes.

tax benefit A reduction in taxes, or a tax credit or refund, due to a particular action or expense incurred by a taxable entity.

tax compliance Entails completing tax returns at period end or year-end.

tax expense An expense that reflects the payments that a corporation must make to the Internal Revenue Service and other taxing authorities.

tax planning Involves structuring transactions so as to minimize their tax effects.

taxable entities Business corporations that must file tax returns with Federal and State Governments.

taxes payable Represents unpaid taxes that are owed to a governmental unit and will be paid within a year.

temporary differences Occurs whenever book accounting and tax accounting measurements differ and will be offset by opposite deviations in later periods.

third party guarantee Type of lease agreement where an insurance company or investment firm acts as a third party guarantor for a lessee in certain lease contracts. This may transform a capital lease into an operating lease because all of the four capital lease criteria are now violated.

time value of money The concept that funds (money) earn interest over time. This is based on the principle that a dollar received a year from now is worth less than a dollar received today.

times interest earned ratio A ratio that indicates the relative risk of bankruptcy or other default. "Times interest earned" indicates the "cushion" or margin of safety that the firm enjoys in meeting its interest expenses. It is calculated as earnings before interest and taxes divided by interest expense.

trade accounts See *trade accounts payable.*

trade accounts payable Current liabilities that occur in the normal course of any trade or business.

trade receivables See *accounts receivable.*

trademarks Words, symbols, or other distinctive elements used to identify a particular firm's products; federal law protects these rights.

trading securities Marketable securities held by firms for brief periods of time that are intended to generate profits from short-term price increases.

transactions The exchange of resources between the firm and other parties.

translation adjustment The process of converting monetary units stated in terms of one country's currency into a different monetary unit. See *foreign currency transactions* and *foreign exchange rate.*

treasury stock Shares of a firm's own stock repurchased by the firm.

trend analysis Comparing financial numbers across time periods.

trial balance A listing of all general ledger account balances for the purpose of verifying that total debits equal total credits.

turnover Describes the efficiency of how the firm's assets are used in generating revenues.

10K report The SEC requires publicly traded companies to file this report annually.

10Q report The SEC requires publicly traded companies to file this report quarterly.

U

uncollectible The portion of accounts receivable, or amounts billed to customers, that management estimates will not be paid.

unearned revenue Advance payments from customers for the right to receive goods or services in the future. The advance payment is recorded as a liability until the goods are delivered or the services are provided to the customer.

unqualified opinion Audit report issued by an auditor that indicates the financial statements are fairly presented under GAAP and free from material misstatement.

unrealized gain (loss) on marketable securities The difference between a security's historical cost and its market value. The term unrealized indicates that the gain or loss has not been confirmed by an actual sale.

unrealized inventory profits Inventory that has been transferred between a parent company and its subsidiary(s). Profits related to these inventories that have not been sold to outside entities are removed from the consolidated financial statements.

useful economic lives See *economic life.*

users of financial statements Interested parties who have an economic interest in the firm need appropriate financial information. Typical users include the firm's owners, creditors, managers, employees, customers, and suppliers. Some users obtain information directly from the firm; others rely on quarterly and annual reports.

uses of resources The resources (assets) obtained by a firm through various sources of financing.

utilization The measure of the effective use of a firm's plant, property and equipment. Determined by calculating the firm's *fixed asset turnover.*

V

vertical analysis Based on the percentage composition of elements on the income statement (or balance sheet) as a percentage of net revenues (or total assets).

vertical integration Occurs when a company acquires another firm involved in its supply or delivery chain.

vertical percentage analysis Refers to a ratio analysis of financial statement data. This is based on relationships between a target figure (like total revenues or total assets) and other figures shown on the same report. It is often used to examine capital structure or other financing relationships. See *percentage composition analysis.*

vested benefit obligation Indicates the amounts to which employees have irrevocable rights, even if they leave the firm prior to retirement.

W

warranties See *warranty obligations.*

warranty obligations Represent the firm's estimated future costs to fulfill its obligations for repair or refund guarantees of products sold or services provided prior to the balance sheet date.

wasting assets Assets such as mines containing gold, silver, copper, or other minerals, wells containing oil or gas, and timberlands. Wasting assets are also called *"natural resources".*

weighted average Each level of outstanding shares of common stock is weighted by the fraction of a year that it stayed constant.

"Where's the Cash?" Financial statement readers should always try to find and follow cash flows, along with accrual-based earnings.

working capital Current assets minus current liabilities; also, called net working capital.

work-in-process Consists of manufactured or assembled items that are partially completed at the balance sheet date

worksheet An extended form of the trial balance. It also indicates a financial analysis model in Excel.

write-down Asset values are reduced when an asset's market value falls below its book value. Assets are written-down to avoid overstating asset values.

write-offs When a firm ascertains that a particular customer will not pay, this is recorded by reducing the customer's accounts receivable balance along with a corresponding reduction in the allowance for uncollectible accounts.

written-off The status of a customer's account that has been reduced because the firm determined that the amount owed by the customer is uncollectible.

Y

Year-end adjustments Adjusting entries needed to ensure tht account balances are correct and accruals are properly recorded.

52-week year Annual reporting period that enhances comparisons across quarterly reports because each quarter will have 13 weeks, and each year has the same number of days and weeks.

INDEX

A

B

E

G

H

M

O

P

S

T

X

Y